Information Ethics

Information Ethics
Privacy, Property, and Power

Edited by Adam D. Moore

University of Washington Press
Seattle and London

University of Washington Press
P.O. Box 50096, Seattle, WA 98145
www.washington.edu/uwpress

Library of Congress Cataloging-in-Publication Data

Information ethics : privacy, property, and power / edited by
Adam D. Moore.—1st ed.
        p. cm.
Includes bibliographical references and index.
ISBN 0-295-98489-9 (pbk. : alk. paper)
1. Freedom of information. 2. Information society. 3. Intellectual
property. 4. Privacy, Right of. 5. Communication—Moral and ethical
aspects. 6. Information technology—Social aspects. I. Moore, Adam
D., 1965–
JC585.I59 2005

323.44'5—dc22   2005000373

The paper used in this publication is acid-free and 90 percent recycled
from at least 50 percent post-consumer waste. It meets the minimum
requirements of the American National Standard for Information
Sciences—Permanence of Paper for Printed Library Materials, ANSI
Z39.48-1984.

CONTENTS

ACKNOWLEDGMENTS

I would like to thank Kristene Unsworth for working on the original manuscript, as well as the Information School at the University of Washington for providing summer RA support. Scott Fields deserves thanks for helping with the index. I would also like to thank Michael Duckworth, Marilyn Trueblood, Charlotte Kuo-Benitez, and the other editors at the University of Washington Press for all of their help in preparing and editing the manuscript.

Special thanks goes to my family and loved ones—Kimberly Moore, Alan Moore, and Amy Moore—for putting up with all of the time I have spent staring at computer screens during this project.

The reprinted articles in this anthology appear in full, unless indicated.

"Introduction to Moral Reasoning" by Tom Regan originally appeared as the introduction to *Matters of Life and Death*, edited by Tom Regan (McGraw-Hill Pub., 1992). Copyright © 1992 McGraw-Hill Pub. This article does not appear in full.

"Feminist Transformations of Moral Theory" by Virginia Held originally appeared in *Philosophy and Phenomenological Research* (Fall 1990). Copyright © *Philosophy and Phenomenological Research*. Reprinted by permission of *Philosophy and Phenomenological Research*.

"Intellectual Property is Still Property" by Frank Easterbrook originally appeared in the *Harvard Journal of Law and Public Policy* 13 (1990). Copyright © *Harvard Journal of Law and Public Policy*. Reprinted by permission of *Harvard Journal of Law and Public Policy*.

"Are Patents and Copyrights Morally Justified? The Philosophy of Property Rights and Ideal Objects" by Tom Palmer originally appeared in the *Harvard Journal of Law and Public Policy* (Summer 1990). Copyright © Tom Palmer. Reprinted by permission of Tom Palmer.

"Intangible Property: Privacy, Power, and Information Control" by Adam D. Moore originally appeared in *American Philosophical Quarterly* (October 1998). Copyright © *American Philosophical Quarterly*. Reprinted by permission of *American Philosophical Quarterly*.

"The Right to Privacy" by Samuel D. Warren and Louis D. Brandeis originally appeared in the *Harvard Law Review* 4 (1890). Endnotes omitted.

Introduction

ADAM D. MOORE and KRISTENE UNSWORTH

Information ethics is a relatively new area of study comprised of several distinct yet interrelated disciplines including applied ethics, intellectual property, privacy, free speech, and societal control of information. The various issues addressed within these disciplines, along with the rise of technology-based information control, have lead many to understand these domains as interconnected. For example, when a photographer captures the image of a nude girl running from a napalm attack, questions arise that are related to each of these areas. Does the photographer own the picture in question? Does the girl have a privacy right that overrides the photographer's ownership claims? Given that important information might be contained in the photograph, do free speech concerns play a role in deciding the moral issues surrounding the publication of the picture? Finally, if there were some reason to suppress the publication of the photograph independent of privacy—perhaps publication would turn public sentiment against some governmental interest, for example—would such interests provide a compelling justification for suppression? Obviously, the justifications and answers we give in one area of study will impact the arguments and policy decisions in other areas.

Needless to say, developing answers to these questions is philosophically challenging. This anthology was put together so that a number of important articles centering on the normative issues surrounding information control—in the broadest sense—could be found in one work. As we move further into the information age, which is marked by the shift from an industrial economy to an information-based economy, clarity is needed at the philosophical level so that morally justified policies and institutions can be adopted.

Information ethics is related to, but not the same as, computer ethics or ethics and information technology. Computer ethics includes topics such as value sensitive design and computers as social actors. The former considers the ethical dimensions of values imposed on users via the user interface while the latter examines the ways in which computers play social roles. Neither of these issues is directly related to information ethics. Moreover, there are areas of information ethics that don't properly fall into the domain of computer ethics or ethics and information technology. For example, when government agents search an apartment, computers and information technology may play no role in the search or the ethical issues surrounding the event.

Before providing a summary of the articles included in this volume, we would like to give a brief overview of the different domains of inquiry that make up information ethics: applied ethics, intellectual property, privacy, free speech, and societal control of information. Each of these specialized areas of study has its own historical context. We will take them up in turn.

Moral Theory and Applied Ethics

Although the readings in Part I provide a general overview of ethical theory and a framework for analysis, we would like to address the relationship between religion and ethical claims—an issue that is only briefly considered in our readings. Ethics as an area of philosophical inquiry has been around for more than two thousand years. Even so, non-religious based ethics is still relatively new and applied ethics—for example medical ethics, business ethics, and environmental ethics—has only gained prominence in the last two decades or so.

The Euthyphro Objection to Theological Ethics

Despite the fact that the Euthyphro objection to theological ethics was formulated by Socrates at the time of his trial and execution in 399 BC, we have only in the last two hundred years started disentangling ethical claims from religious ones. The modern version of the Euthyphro objection to theological ethics goes as follows: First, consider the view which holds that actions are morally correct if and only if they are commanded by God and wrong if and only if they are forbidden by God; there is nothing beyond God's commandments that makes an action morally right or wrong. "Well," paraphrasing Socrates, "is an action right because God commands it or does God command an action because it is right?" More formally, Is X right because God commands X or does God command X because X is right? Suppose we grasp the first part of the dilemma and claim that X is right because God commands X. We may then ask a seemingly innocent question: Does God have reasons for commanding what he does? If He does, then it is these reasons that make an action right or wrong and not His *mere* commandments and we find ourselves grasping the second part of the dilemma. If He has no reasons, then morality is arbitrary and whimsical.

To put the point another way, if X is right simply and for no other reason than God commanded X and if God were to command that we each cause as much suffering to other human beings as possible, then we ought morally to get on with the business of causing suffering. It does no good to say that God would never command such a thing if we are grasping the first horn of the dilemma—if X is right simply and for no other reason than God commanded X. What we want to say is that God would not command such a thing because causing as much suffering to other human beings as possible would be morally wrong. And this is just to grasp the second horn of the dilemma—God commands X because X is right, God forbids Y because Y is wrong. If so, then morality exists independently from God and is perhaps knowable via reason and argumentation. Notice as well, that we do not have to determine which God exists or what He commands, wills, or forbids to engage in moral reasoning.

Professional philosophers have generally accepted the reasoning that surrounds the Euthyphro dilemma, understanding that moral rightness and wrongness, if they exist, are a matter of reason and argument. Sadly, the Euthyphro dilemma is not widely understood. Thus, while the study of ethical principles is quite old, inquiry into non-religious based normative ethical theory is relatively new.

Normative Ethical Theory

Normative ethical theory has been traditionally broken into two domains—theories of the good value or theories of the good, and theories of obligation or theories of right. A theory of the good concerns the moral evaluation of agents, states of affairs, intentions, and the like as good, bad, valuable, and disvaluable. A theory of right concerns the moral rightness or wrongness of actions and policies. In general, theories of the good try to answer the question "What is valuable?" while theories of the right try to answer the question "What makes an action right or wrong?" How these two domains connect or interact determines the type of moral theory in question.

Axiologists claim that the good is prior to, more fundamental than, and determines the right. That is, we know what we ought to do by appealing to value and nothing else. The most prominent example of an axiological theory is consequentialism, which holds that moral rightness and wrongness depends on the value or disvalue of consequences. John Stuart Mill (Chapter 3) is a notable example of a consequentialist. Deontological theories, on the other hand, hold that there is more to moral rightness and wrongness than considerations of value. Immanuel Kant (Chapter 4), probably the most famous deontologist, argued that considerations of value were irrelevant to determining rightness. Rightness, for the deontologist, is prior to, more fundamental than, and determines the good.

Without establishing the "correct" moral theory and the reasons and arguments that generate moral *oughts*, applied ethicists have made progress by asking questions about what would be the case if this or that normative ethical theory turned out to be correct. Moreover, although there are numerous competing normative ethical theories, there may also be broad areas of agreement—and within these areas advances may be made.

Intellectual Property[1]

Although one of the first known references to intellectual property protection dates from 500 BC when chefs in the Greek colony of Sybaris were granted year long monopolies over particular culinary delights, our modern analysis of the normative, political, and legal questions related to intellectual property is tied to the English system that began with the Statute of Monopolies (1624) and the Statute of Anne (1709).[2] The Statute of Monopolies, considered the basis of modern British and American patent systems, granted fourteen-year monopolies to authors and inventors and ended the practice of granting rights to "non-original/new" ideas or works already in the public domain.

Literary works remained largely unprotected until the arrival of Gutenberg's printing press in the fifteenth century. Even then there were few true copyrights issued—most were grants, privileges, and monopolies.[3] The Statute of Anne (1710) established the first modern system of copyright protection. The statute began, "Whereas printers, booksellers, and other persons have lately frequently taken the liberty of printing, reprinting, and publishing books without the consent of the authors and proprietors . . . to their very great detriment, and too often to the ruin of them and their families: for preventing therefore such practices for the future, and for the encouragement of learned men to compose and write use books, be it enacted . . ." The law gave protection to the author by granting fourteen-year copyrights, with a second fourteen-year renewal possible if the author was still alive. In the landmark case *Miller v. Taylor* (1769) the inherent rights of authors to control what they produce, independent of statute or law, was affirmed. While this case was later overruled in *Donaldson v. Becket* (1774) the practice of recognizing the rights of authors had begun.[4]

Anglo-American systems of intellectual property are typically justified on utilitarian grounds. Limited rights are granted to authors and inventors of intellectual property "to promote the progress of science and the useful arts."[5] Thomas Jefferson, a central figure in the formation of American systems of intellectual property, expressly rejected any natural rights foundation for granting control to authors and inventors over their intellectual works. "The patent monopoly was not designed to secure the inventor his natural right in his discoveries. Rather, it was a reward, and inducement, to bring forth new knowledge."[6] Society seeks to maximize utility in the form of scientific and cultural progress by granting rights to authors and inventors as an incentive toward such progress.

In the last few years, however, intellectual property rights have been viewed as state-created entities used by the privileged and economically advantaged to control information access and consumption. Recent legislative and legal decisions dealing with peer-to-peer file sharing and extensions of copyrights have solidified this position. Needless to say, the normative, political, and social issues related to this area of information ethics remain hotly contested.

Privacy: Greece, China, and John Locke

Social recognition of privacy interests, unlike institutions of intellectual property, is older and more widespread. Examining the normative, political, legal, and historical contexts surrounding privacy is difficult because of an overabundance of subject matter—rituals of association and disassociation are cultural universals. To limit the discussion, we will focus on two cultures—ancient Greece and China—and one political and moral theorist—John Locke.

In Greek society the distinction between public and private activity was entrenched by the time of Socrates (470-399 BC), Plato

(427-347 BC), and Aristotle (384-322 BC). Typically the distinction was cast in terms of political activity compared to isolated intellectual pursuits.[7] As an early social critic, Socrates played two roles. He did not hold public office and sought his own personal ends, yet at the same time Socrates challenged many of the customs, institutions, and well-established philosophical theories of his day. In a very public way Socrates voiced the opinion that "the unexamined life is not worth living," calling upon individuals to examine their own personal views and beliefs. Socrates then publicly challenged, and in many cases humiliated, those who had not examined their own beliefs.

Plato was openly hostile to privacy, deeming it unnecessary and counterproductive in relation to the ideal state. In *The Laws* Plato advocates the elimination of private spheres of activity.

> The first and highest form of the state and of the government and of the law is that in which there prevails most widely the ancient saying, that "Friends have all things in common." Whether there is anywhere now, or will ever be, this communion of women and children and of property, in which the private and individual is altogether banished from life, and things which are by nature private, such as eyes and ears and hands, have become common, and in some way see and hear and act in common, and all men express praise and blame and feel joy and sorrow on the same occasions, and whatever laws there are unite the city to the utmost-whether all this is possible or not, I say that no man, acting upon any other principle, will ever constitute a state which will be truer or better or more exalted in virtue.[8]

Plato views privacy as something that is inherently disvaluable in relation to the perfect state. Moreover he recognizes no psychological, sociological, or political needs for individuals to be able to control patterns of association and disassociation with their fellows.

Aristotle, on the other hand, makes use of a public/private distinction in at least two ways. First, he recognizes a boundary between affairs of the state and household affairs. Jürgen Habermas noted, "In the fully developed Greek city-state the sphere of the *polis*, which was common to the free citizens, was strictly separated from the sphere of the *oikos*; in the sphere of the *oikos*, each individual is in his own realm."[9] Second, contemplative activity, which is necessary for human flourishing, requires distance, space, and solitude from public life.

In China, the public/private distinction was well understood by the Warring States period 403—221 BC.[10] Like Aristotle, Confucius (551-479 BC) distinguished between the public activity of government and the private affairs of family life. Confucius also contends that "a private obligation of a son to care for his father overrides the public obligation to obey the law against theft"[11] and that "a timid man who is pretending to be fierce is like a man who is so 'dishonest as to sneak into places where one has no right to be, by boring a hole or climbing through a gap.'"[12] Han Fei Tzu (280-233 BC) writes,

> When T s'ang Chieh [a mythic cultural hero] created the system of writing, he used the character for "private" to express the idea of self-centeredness, and combined the elements for "private" and "opposed to" to form the character for "public." The fact that public and private are mutually opposed was already well understood at the time of T s'ang Chieh. To regard the two as being identical in interest is a disaster which comes from lack of consideration.[13]

While not sophisticated and clearly contentious, the public/private distinction arose and was a matter of philosophical debate in two distinct cultural traditions. In both ancient Greece and China privacy was a commodity purchased with power, money, and privilege. Barriers such as walls, fences, and even servants secured areas of isolation and seclusion for the upper class. To a lesser degree, privacy was also secured by those with more modest means.

For John Locke (1632-1704) the public/private distinction stems from his conception of the state of nature, the legitimate function of government, and property rights. The state of nature was a pregovernmental state in which individuals had perfect freedom bounded by the law of nature.[14] As sovereign and moral equals, individuals in the state of nature had rights to life, liberty, and property. Unlike Thomas Hobbes, who viewed the state of nature as hypothetical rather than actual and conceived of it as a place where life was "solitary, poor, nasty, brutish, and short,"[15] Locke thought of it as a peaceful place governed by morality. Where Hobbes envisioned a "war of all against all" Locke saw mere inconveniencies related to individual prejudices and competing interpretations of the law of nature.[16] The sole reason for uniting into a commonwealth, for Locke, was to remedy these inconveniencies. The function of government was to secure the rights of life, liberty, and property.

As has often been noted, property rights were central to Locke's conception of just government. In the state of nature, individuals could unilaterally take part of the commons—what was available for public consumption—and obtain private property rights.[17] These property rights allowed individuals the moral space to order their lives as they saw fit. On estates and behind fences, walls, and doors Lockean individuals secured a domain of private action free from public pressures. Public incursions into private domains required weighty justification.

It is these traditions that inform our modern conception of privacy which has only recently—in the last one hundred years—been codified in the law. Legal protections for privacy have been justified by appeal to one of three sources. First, in *Griswold v. Connecticut*,[18] Justice Douglas, writing the majority opinion, claimed that a legal right to privacy could be found in the shadows or penumbras of the First, Third, Fourth, and Fifth amendments to the U.S. Constitution. Second, in the same case Justice Goldberg invoked the Ninth and Fourteenth amendments in support of privacy. Goldberg claimed that privacy was one of the rights retained by the people and that the "due process" clause of the Fourteenth Amendment protects privacy as a value "implicit in the concept of ordered liberty."[19] Finally, a privacy interest was said to exist in the common law. In 1890, Samuel D. Warren and Louis D. Brandeis issued a call to arms in their celebrated paper "The Right to Privacy,"[20] the first selection in Part III of this anthology. The remedy for privacy invasions was to create a new tort. Torts are, in general, a negligent or intentional civil wrong that injures someone and for which the injured person may sue for damages.

In spite of these protections Ken Gormley, in "One Hundred Years of Privacy"[21] notes, "the court had found no reasonable expectation of privacy in an individual's bank records; in voice or writing exemplars; in phone numbers recorded by pen registers; in conversations recorded by wired informants; and a growing list of cases involving automobiles, trunks, glove compartments and closed containers therein."[22] The USA Patriot Act, adopted in response to the terrorist attacks of September 11, 2001, further erodes privacy protections.

Privacy interests have also not fared well in relation to free speech and expression. The view that in entering the public domain individuals voluntarily relinquish privacy claims was solidified as a principle of law in a series of cases.[23] As noted by Patrick McNulty, "The public's right to receive news is nearly all encompassing. It extends to publicity about public figures who invite public attention by their activities, those who are involuntarily placed in the public eye such as crime victims, information as hard news, and information as entertainment."[24]

The advancement of information technology, along with recent threats to national security, have highlighted the ethical issues surrounding the use and control of sensitive personal information. The tensions between individual privacy, free speech, and national security continue to generate profound moral, legal, and political disagreements.

Free Speech and Societal Control of Information
One of the most famous defenses of free speech and expression is offered by John Stuart Mill in *On Liberty*. As an act-utilitarian, Mill believed that we should act to maximize overall net utility for everyone affected. In general, utilitarianism centers on the following three components:

i) the consequent component—the rightness of actions is determined by the consequences;

ii) the value component—the goodness or badness of consequences is to be evaluated by means of some standard of intrinsic value;

iii) the range component—it is the consequences of an act (or class of actions) as affecting everyone, and not just the agent himself, that are to be considered in determining rightness.

Act-utilitarianism is a theory which holds that an individual act is morally right if, and only if, it produces at least as much utility as any alternative action when the utility of all is counted equally. For example, classical act-utilitarianism is the view that individual acts are right or wrong solely in virtue of the goodness or badness of their consequences. The value component is identified in terms of pleasure and pain, and the range or scope of the theory touches everyone affected by an act.

Mill viewed rules that govern behavior as mere rules of thumb or strategic rules that serve as helpful guides when there is no time to calculate the probable consequences of our actions or when personal biases cloud judgment.[25] The rightness or wrongness of following some rule on a particular occasion depends only on the goodness or badness of the consequences of keeping or breaking the rule on that particular occasion. If the goodness of the consequences of breaking the rule is greater than the goodness of the consequences of keeping it, then we must abandon the rule. On this account, rules may serve as useful guides but when it is clear that following them leads to bad consequences, we must break the rules. Strategic rules or rules of thumb of this sort may be thought of as rights.

Mill offered three arguments in defense of free speech rights: the benefits of liberty, thought, and expression argument; the argument from intrinsic value; and the best policy argument. In brief, the benefit of liberty argument holds that liberty introduces new ideas which may be correct, partially correct, or lead to truth; prevents received ideas from being held as mere prejudice; and keeps the meaning of received opinions alive. Thus even though Nazi ideology is false, evil, and hateful, Mill would defend such expression on the grounds that having such views presented to us from time to time forces us to think about such matters. Some of us may even try to figure out why we are right and they are wrong. In general, this process leads to good consequences—and for the utilitarian, only consequences matter.

The often-cited criticism of this argument is that it at most shows that liberty generally has some good consequences—this is not sufficient to show that free speech and expression are justified on utilitarian grounds. As Sir James Fitzjames Stephen puts it, "If . . . the object aimed at is good, if the compulsion employed such as to attain it, and if the good obtained overbalances the inconveniences of the compulsion itself, I do not understand how, upon utilitarian principles, the compulsion can be bad."[26] In short, other values or strategic rules—such as privacy or security—may trump expression in certain cases.

The argument from intrinsic value holds that having a sense of dignity, obtaining security, developing one's abilities to a consistent and harmonious whole, and liberty are each intrinsically valuable.

Thus, liberty is not related to flourishing as a cause to an effect but as a part to a whole. On this account any interference with liberty of thought and expression is necessarily a lessening of human flourishing or well-being.

As with the first argument, the argument from intrinsic value doesn't show that, on balance, the best consequences cannot be obtained by interfering with free speech and expression. When liberty conflicts with other elements of well-being, it may still be that interference with liberty is justified on utilitarian grounds.

Mill's final argument, the best policy argument, seeks to show that even if interference with liberty may, in principle, be justified in specific cases, we ought on utilitarian grounds to adopt the sort of absolute principle he endorses. Mill says, "[T]he strongest of all the arguments against the interference of the public with purely personal conduct is that when it does interfere, the odds are that it interferes wrongly and in the wrong place."[27] When government interferes with speech and expression, it will likely mess things up horribly. Thus, the best policy is to severely restrict the government's role in this area.

Nevertheless, in spite of Mill, there have been numerous restrictions placed on speech and expression: obscene pornography, hate speech, sexual harassment, yelling "fire" in a theater, are more prominent examples. Privacy rights and intellectual property rights also restrict speech and expression. In addition, after September 11, 2001, access to vast amounts of information held by government agencies, libraries, and other information storehouses has been restricted in the name of national security.

Overview of Articles

The articles contained in this volume center on the ethical, legal, and applied issues surrounding information control. Part I, An Ethical Framework for Analysis, begins with Tom Regan's "Introduction to Moral Reasoning." Regan provides a thoughtful analysis of several pitfalls related to answering moral questions. We do not answer moral questions by appealing to our feelings, desires, preferences, and beliefs. Moreover, there is no strength in numbers: the rightness or wrongness of an action or policy cannot be determined by appealing to what everyone thinks, feels, or prefers. Moral claims, Regan argues, are fundamentally different from claims about one's feelings, desires, or preferences. After discussing how not to answer moral questions, Regan moves on to how we might obtain ideal moral judgments.

John Stuart Mill in "Utilitarianism" presents and defends utilitarian moral theory. As a consequentialist, Mill argues that moral rightness and wrongness are determined by good and bad consequences. This view is codified in the principle of utility: of the actions or policies available, one should do that act or adopt that policy which maximizes, or is expected to maximize, overall net utility for everyone affected. Mill clarifies and attempts to justify the principle of utility as the sole standard of rightness and wrongness.

Immanuel Kant in "The Metaphysics of Morals" defends a deontological theory which holds that consequences are irrelevant when determining moral oughts. For Kant, moral rightness and wrongness are grounded in a conception of rational agency and have nothing to do with good or bad consequences. Crudely put, you must do the right thing for the right reason—independent of the consequences—in order for your action to have genuine moral worth. Thus the shopkeeper who gives correct change because of a fear of being caught is doing the right thing for the wrong reason. Giving the correct change is morally right. But if the *reason* why someone performs a morally correct action is to *avoid some bad consequence*, then the action has no genuine moral worth.

In the final reading of Part I, is Virginia Held's "Feminist Transformations of Moral Theory." Held points out that the history of philosophy and the history of ethics have been constructed from a male point of view. The assumptions made and the concepts put forth are, however, not gender-neutral. Feminist philosophers reconceptualize ethics and philosophy by consciously examining history differently from non-feminist scholars. Emotion and conceptions of the self and society are taken as critical aspects of moral theory and must be included in a reconstruction of theory to include the experiences of women.

Part II, Intellectual Property: Moral and Legal Concerns, begins with Frank Easterbrook's "Intellectual Property Is Still Property." Easterbrook, a United States Court of Appeal Judge for the Seventh Circuit and a Senior Lecturer in Law at the University of Chicago School of Law, argues that the non-rivalrous nature of intellectual property does not undermine its status as property and that intellectual property should hold the same rights as physical property.

Tom Palmer weighs both sides of the argument in his article, "Are Patents and Copyrights Morally Justified?" He invokes the nineteenth century American abolitionist Lysander Spooner and the Jacksonian editorialist William Leggett to situate the debate in a historical context. While both men were staunch supporters of liberty, private property, and freedom of trade, they held opposing opinions on the status of intellectual property: Spooner advocated intellectual property rights while Leggett supported the unrestricted free exchange of ideas. Palmer uses this example to illustrate the difficult nature of intellectual property debates. Issues which may be clear when considering physical property become murky when applied to intellectual property. In order to examine the issues fully, Palmer looks at four possible theories of intellectual property: labor-desert, personality, utility, and "piggybacking" on the rights of tangible property.

Richard Stallman's essay "Biopiracy or Bioprivateering?" considers the ethics of patent monopolies on biological species. Stallman explains the concept of "biopiracy," in which biotechnology companies pay royalties to indigenous peoples or developing countries for use of human genes or natural varieties found only in given parts of the world. This concept presupposes, according to Stallman, that these things have an owner and can be privatized. Stallman asserts that natural genetic resources are public.

Adam Moore, in "Intangible Property: Privacy, Power, and Information Control," explains and defends a Lockean model of intangible property. The first part consists of a brief introduction to the domain or subject matter of intangible property along with an argument that justifies intangible property rights—including information ownership. Moore argues that if the acquisition of an intangible work satisfies a Pareto-based proviso, then the acquisition and exclusion are justified. Some acts of intangible property creation and possession satisfy a Pareto-based proviso. It follows that some rights to intangible property are justified. In the second part of his essay Moore makes a case for limiting what can be done with intangible property based on a harm restriction and privacy rights. Moore argues that while others may indeed own information about each of us, there are fairly severe restrictions on what can be done with this information, especially when we are considering sensitive personal information.

Part III, Privacy and Information Control, begins with the foundational article "The Right to Privacy" published in 1890 by Samuel

D. Warren and Louis D. Brandeis in the *Harvard Law Review*. The article, which was prompted by intrusions from the press into the private life of the Warren family, considers the tensions between privacy rights and other values like free speech and a free press. This article called for the creation of the tort, "invasion of privacy," which would allow individuals to sue for damages when the realm of private space or the "right to be left alone" was violated. The article was a response, not only to actual events, but also to the advancements of information technology at the time. Technologies such as photography, newspapers, and film presented a real danger to the once more secure realm of private space.

"Do you own your genes?" is the question with which Margaret Everett opened an earlier version of the paper included in this anthology. In this version of "The Social Life of Genes: Privacy, Property, and the New Genetics" she changes the focus of the question slightly and asks: "How did genes become commodities?" The body and its parts, including DNA and genes, have become a potential source of wealth. Licenses to certain DNA sequences are worth billions of dollars to the biotech companies that secure them. Yet are they truly available for sale? Do individuals have property rights over their own DNA? Everett addresses these questions while also examining the broader issue of privacy in relation to genetic information. For example, the results from DNA testing help predict future health and offer an array of other genetic information which can be interesting to employers, insurance companies, researchers, and pharmaceutical concerns.

Adam Moore, in "Employee Monitoring & Computer Technology: Evaluative Surveillance v. Privacy," addresses the tension between evaluative surveillance and privacy against the backdrop of the current explosion of information technology. More specifically, and after a brief analysis and justification of privacy rights, it is argued that information about the different kinds of surveillance used at any given company should be made explicit to the employees. Moreover, there are certain kinds of evaluative monitoring that violate privacy rights and should not be used in most cases.

James Stacey Taylor, in "Personal Autonomy, Privacy, and Caller ID" discusses the privacy-related advantages and disadvantages of Caller ID. Caller ID clearly offers a level of privacy to persons being called because it allows them to monitor and select who they want to speak to on the telephone. However, a disadvantage of Caller ID is that callers, who may legitimately not want to be identified, no longer have the same degree of anonymity they had in the past. Taylor focuses on the issue of personal autonomy and whether services such as Caller ID enhance or diminish the user's ability to exercise autonomy as they wish. It has been argued that the option of subscribing to a Caller ID service provides the user with more options, thereby increasing their autonomy. Taylor questions this view and argues that making more options available may actually diminish the degree of autonomy that an individual is able to exercise. Nevertheless, he claims that respect for autonomy requires persons be allowed to subscribe to such services if they so choose

Part IV, Freedom of Speech and Information Control, focuses on issues of privacy, freedom of speech, and control of information. The section begins with Kent Greenawalt's essay, "Rationales for Freedom of Speech." Greenawalt considers several arguments in favor of free speech in relation to privacy and censorship. Greenawalt goes beyond considerations of a "minimal principle of liberty," which when applied to speech, would establish that "the government should not interfere with communication that has no potential for harm" and argues in favor of a principle of free speech. He considers the justifications for a principle of free speech from consequentialist and nonconsequentialist points of view.

Jack M. Balkin's "Digital Speech and Democratic Culture: A Theory of Freedom of Expression for the Information Society" addresses the tensions between free speech and intellectual property against the backdrop of ever-expanding digital technologies. He argues "to protect freedom of speech in the digital age, we will have to reinterpret and refashion both telecommunications policy and intellectual property law to serve the values of freedom of speech." Freedom of speech depends on the design of technological infrastructures that support expression and secure widespread democratic participation.

The final paper in this section, "Privacy, Photography, and the Press" takes up issues first addressed by Samuel Warren and Louis Brandeis in "The Right to Privacy." Although legitimate expectations of privacy in public space may weigh in favor of additional restrictions on unwanted photography, this essay argues that the important policies underlying the First Amendment's guarantees of freedom of speech and press counsel against the expansion of the right to privacy at the expense of photographic expression.

Part V, Governmental and Societal Control of Information opens with Griffin S. Dunham's "Carnivore, the FBI's E-mail Surveillance System: Devouring Criminals, Not Privacy." Carnivore is an Internet monitoring system. It has been likened to a phone tap and is used to monitor e-mail conversations. The device is portable and can be placed on any server that, according to the FBI and the Department of Justice, is suspected of hosting accounts which are a threat to national security or other types of crimes: terrorism, information warfare, child pornography, fraud, and virus writing and distribution. Concerns that the system could target any innocent person who sends email across a server under surveillance have caused a great deal of debate about the legitimacy of using Carnivore. Dunham argues for the necessity of Carnivore in enabling law enforcement to keep up with criminals who utilize cyberspace to communicate criminal plans. He also attempts to dispel privacy concerns associated with the system by allaying misconceptions and fears related to its implementation and usage.

The second paper in this section looks at the relationship between privacy and accountability. Anita Allen's "Privacy Isn't Everything: Accountability as a Personal and Social Good" examines the concept of accountability in light of John Stuart Mill's essay *On Liberty*, in which he wrote, "the individual is not accountable to society for his actions, insofar as these concern the interests of no person but himself." Accountability is now required far beyond the bounds of actions that appear to "concern the interests of no person" but the actor. Allen defines the term "the New Accountability," which she claims is a product of social, economic and personal freedoms, as well as an ambivalence towards forms of privacy that could be useful to others if uncovered.

The final paper in this anthology is Jacob Lilly's "National Security at What Price? A Look into Civil Liberty Concerns in the Information Age under the USA Patriot Act." Lilly examines the balancing act necessary to ensure that the democratic rights upon which the United States was founded are maintained while measures to protect national security are developed and enforced. He compares the USA Patriot Act with other measures instituted in the name of national security: the declaration of a state of emergency by Lincoln at the outbreak of the Civil War, along with the suspension of all rights in border-states; the internment of Japanese-Americans during World War II; and McCarthyism during the Cold War, just to name a few. Lilly proposes what he refers to as the "One Step

Lower" test which would provide another layer of review before legislation could be implemented. Drastic changes proposed by the government could not be hastily made in times of national crisis.

Conclusion

This anthology offers the reader a wide selection of papers that address issues of information ethics. Many of these articles are foundational and the collection as a whole represents the normative issues surrounding informational control. Though information ethics as such is a relatively new area of study, we have sought in this anthology to unite traditional ethics and philosophical inquiry with contemporary intellectual exploration and debate. The papers collected here represent the different domains of information ethics, and we have attempted to provide a context, based in philosophical thought, from which the entire anthology can be read.

Notes

1. Part of this section is taken from material published in *Intellectual Property and Information Control* (New Brunswick, NJ: Transaction Pub., 2001, 2004), Chapter 2.

2. See Bruce Bugbee, *Genesis of American Patent and Copyright Law* (Washington, D.C.: Public Affairs Press, 1967).

3. For example in 1469 John of Speyer was granted the right to conduct all printing in Venice for a term of five years.

4. *Miller v. Taylor* (1769), 4 Burr. 2303; *Donaldson v. Becket* (1774), 4 Burr. 2408.

5. U.S. Constitution, § 8, para. 8.

6. See W. Francis and R. Collins, *Cases and Materials on Patent Law: Including Trade Secrets - Copyrights - Trademarks*, fourth edition (St. Paul, Minn.: West Publishing Company, 1987), 92-93. Prior to the enactment of the US Constitution a number of states adopted copyright laws that had both a utilitarian component and a natural rights component. A major turning point away from a natural rights framework for American institutions of intellectual property came with the 1834 decision of *Wheaton v. Peters* 33 US (8 Pet.) 591, 660-1 (1834).

7. For a rigorous analysis of the historical, sociological, and cultural aspects of privacy see Barrington Moore, Jr., *Privacy: Studies in Social and Cultural History* (New York: M.E. Sharpe Inc. Pub., 1984).

8. Plato, *The Laws*, translated by Benjamin Jowett (Amherst, N.Y.: Prometheus Books, 2000), Chapter 5, 738d-e.

9. Jürgen Habermas, *The Structural Transformation of the Public Sphere*, translated by Thomas Burger and Frederick Lawrence (Cambridge: MIT Press, 1962) reprinted in part in Richard C. Turkington, George B. Trubow, and Anita L. Allen, eds., *Privacy: Cases and Materials* (Houston, Texas: John Marshall, 1992), p. 3, cited in Judith Wagner DeCew, *In Pursuit of Privacy: Law, Ethics, and the Rise of Technology* (Ithaca NY: Cornell University Press, Ithica, 1997), p. 10.

10. See Barrington Moore, Jr., *Privacy: Studies in Social and Cultural History*, p. 223.

11. Ibid.

12. Ibid.

13. Ibid., p. 221.

14. John Locke, *Second Treatise of Government*, edited by C.B. Macpherson (Indianapolis: Hackett Pub. Co, 1980) Chapter II "Of the State of Nature," p. 8.

15. Thomas Hobbes, *Leviathan*, edited by Michael Oakeshott (New York: Collier Books, 1962), Chapter 13, p. 100. John Locke, *Second Treatise of Government*, Chapters II-IV p. 8-18.

16. Hobbes, *Leviathan*, Chapter 13, p. 101.

17. John Locke, *Second Treatise of Government*, Chapter V. For an account of how a Lockean could argue for intellectual property rights see Adam D. Moore, *Intellectual Property and Information Control: Philosophic Foundations and Contemporary Issues* (New Brunswick: Transaction Publishing/Rutgers University, 2001, 2004).

18. *Griswold v. Connecticut*, 381 U.S. 479 (1965).

19. Ibid.

20. Samuel D. Warren and Louis D. Brandeis, "The Right to Privacy," *Harvard Law Review* 4 (December 15, 1890): 193-220.

21. Ken Gormley, "One Hundred Years of Privacy," *Wisconsin Law Review* (1992): 1369.

22. *Berger v. New York*, 388 U.S. 41 (1967); *United States v. United States Dist. Court*, 407 U.S. 297 (1972); *Camara v. Municipal Court*, 387 U.S. 523 (1967); *G.M. Leasing Corp. v. United States*, 429 U.S. 338 (1977); *Mancusi v. De Forte*, 392 U.S. 364 (1968); *United States v. Chadwick*, 433 U.S. 1 (1977); *Arkansas v. Sanders*, 442 U.S. 753 (1979); *Walter v. United States*, 447 U.S. 649 (1980); *Delaware v. Prouse*, 440 U.S. 648 (1979); *United States v. Miller*, 425 U.S. 435 (1976); *United States v. Dionisio*, 410 U.S. 1 (1973); *Smith v. Maryland*, 442 U.S. 735 (1979); *United States v. White*, 401 U.S. 745 (1971); *Chambers v. Maroney*, 399 U.S. 42 (1970); *South Dakota v. Opperman*, 428 U.S. 364 (1976); *Rakas v. Illinois*, 439 U.S. 128 (1978); *California v. Carney*, 471 U.S. 386 (1985); *United States v. Ross*, 456 U.S. 798 (1982); *New York v. Belton*, 453 U.S. 454 (1981). Cited in Gormley, "One Hundred Years of Privacy" n172-183.

23. See for example *Melvin v. Reid*, 112 Cal.App. 285, 290 (1931) and *Gill v. Hearst Publishing Co.* 40 Cal. 2d 224 (1953).

24. Patrick J. McNulty, "The Public Disclosure of Private Facts: There is Life after Florida Star," *Drake Law Review* 50 (2001): 108.

25. For similar views see J. J. C. Smart, "Extreme and Restricted Utilitarianism," in *Theories of Ethics*, edited by Philippa Foot (Oxford: Oxford University Press, 1967), and David Lyons, *Forms and Limits of Utilitarianism* (Oxford: The Clarendon Press, 1965).

26. Sir James Fitzjames Stephen, *Liberty, Equality, Fraternity: And Three Brief Essays* (Chicago: University of Chicago Press, 1991).

27. Mill, *On Liberty* (London: Longman, Roberts, & Green Co., 1869), Chapter IV.

PART I

An Ethical Framework for Analysis

Introduction to Moral Reasoning

TOM REGAN

1. Some Ways Not to Answer Moral Questions

Moral Judgments and Personal Preferences: Some people like classical music; others do not. Some people think bourbon is just great; others detest its taste. Some people will go to a lot of trouble to spend an afternoon in the hot sun at the beach; others can think of nothing worse. In all these cases disagreement in preference exists. Someone likes something; someone else does not. Are moral disagreements, disagreements over whether something is morally right or wrong, the same as disagreements in preference?

It does not appear so. For one thing, when a person (say, John) says he likes something, he is not denying what another person (Jane) says, if she says she does not like it. Suppose John says "I [John] like bourbon," and Jane says "I [Jane] do not like bourbon." Then clearly Jane does not deny what John says. To deny what John says, Jane would have to say "You [John] do not like bourbon," which is not what she says. So, in general, when two persons express conflicting personal preferences, the one does not deny what the other affirms. It is perfectly possible for two conflicting expressions of personal preference to be true at the same time.

When two people express conflicting judgments about the morality of something, however, the disagreement is importantly different. Suppose John says "Abortion is always wrong," while Jane says "Abortion is never wrong." Then Jane *is* denying what John affirms; she is *denying* that abortion is always wrong, so that, if what she said were true, what John said would have to be false. Some philosophers have denied this. They have maintained that moral judgments should be understood as expressions of personal preferences. Though this view deserves to be mentioned with respect, it is doubtful that it is correct. When people say that something is morally right or wrong, it is always appropriate to ask them to give reasons to support their judgment, reasons for accepting their judgment as correct. In the case of personal preferences, however, such requests are inappropriate. If John says he likes to go to the beach, it hardly seems apt to press him to give reasons to support his judgment; indeed, it hardly seems that he has made a *judgment* at all. If he says abortion is always wrong, however, a judgment has been expressed, and it is highly relevant to press John for his reasons for thinking what he does. If he were to reply that he had no reasons, that he just did not like abortions, it would not be out of place to complain that he speaks in a misleading way. By saying that abortion is wrong, John leads his listeners to believe that he is making a judgment about abortion, not merely expressing some fact about himself. If all that he means is that he personally does not like abortions, that is what he should say, not that abortion is wrong.

This difference between conflicting expressions of personal preference and conflicting moral judgments points to one way not to answer moral questions. Given that moral judgments are not just expressions of personal preference, it follows that moral right and wrong cannot be determined by finding out about the personal preferences of some particular person—say, John. This is true even in the case of our own preferences. Our personal preferences are important certainly, but we do not answer moral questions by saying what we like or dislike.

Moral Judgments and Feelings: Closely connected with personal preferences are a person's feelings, and some philosophers have maintained that words like 'right' and 'wrong' are devices we use to express how we feel about something. On this view, when Jane says that abortion is never wrong, what she conveys is that she has certain positive feelings (or at least that she does not have any feelings of disapproval) toward abortion, whereas when John says abortion is always wrong, what he conveys is that he does have feelings of disapproval. This position encounters problems of the same kind as those raised in the previous section. It is always appropriate to ask that support be given for a moral judgment. It is not appropriate to ask for support in the case of mere expressions of feeling. True, if John is sincere, one can infer that he has strong negative feelings about abortion. But his saying that abortion is always wrong does not appear to be simply a way of venting his feelings. As in the case of a person's preferences, so also in the case of a person's feelings: neither by itself provides answers to moral questions.

Why Thinking It Is So Does Not Make It So: The same is true about what someone thinks. Quite aside from his feelings, John, if he is sincere, does think that abortion is always wrong. Nevertheless, if his judgment ("Abortion is always wrong") is a moral judgment about the wrongness of abortion, what he means cannot be "I [John] think that abortion is wrong." If it were, then he would not be affirming something that Jane denies, when she says "Abortion is never wrong." Each would merely be stating that each thinks something, and it is certainly possible for it *both* to be true that *John* thinks that abortion is always wrong *and*, at the same time, that *Jane* thinks that abortion is never wrong. So if John is denying what Jane affirms, then he cannot merely be stating that he thinks that abortion is always wrong. Thus, the fact that John thinks abortion is wrong is just as irrelevant to establishing its wrongness as the fact that he feels a certain way about it. And the same is true concerning the fact that we think what we think. Our thinking something right or wrong does not make it so.

The Irrelevance of Statistics: Someone might think that though what one person thinks or feels about moral issues does not settle matters, what all or most people think or feel does. A single individual is only one voice; what most or all people think or feel is a great deal more. There is strength in numbers. Thus, the correct method for answering questions about right and wrong is to find out what most or all people think or feel; opinion polls should be conducted, statistics compiled. That will reveal the truth.

This approach to moral questions is deficient. All that opinion polls can reveal is what all or most people think or feel about some moral question—for example, "Is capital punishment morally right or wrong?" What such polls cannot determine is whether what all or most people think about such an issue is true or that what all or most people feel is appropriate. There may be strength in numbers, but not truth, at least not necessarily. . . . *Merely* to establish that all (or most) people think that, say, capital punishment is morally justified is not to establish that it *is* morally justified. In times past, most (possibly even all) people thought the world is flat. And possibly most (or all) people felt pleased or relieved to think of the world as having this shape. But what they thought and felt did not make it true that the world is flat. The question of its shape had to be answered without relying on what most people think or feel. There is no reason to believe moral questions differ in this respect. Questions of right and wrong cannot be answered just by counting heads.

The Appeal to a Moral Authority: Suppose it is conceded that we cannot answer moral questions by finding out what someone (say,

John) thinks or feels; or by finding out what all or most people think or feel. After all, a single individual like John, or most or all people like him, might think or feel one way when he or they should think or feel differently. But suppose there is a being who never is mistaken when it comes to moral questions: if this being judges that something is morally right, it *is* morally right; if it is judged wrong, it *is* wrong. No mistakes are made. Let us call such a being a "moral authority." Might appealing to a moral authority be a satisfactory way to answer moral questions?

Most people who think there is a moral authority think that this being is not an ordinary person but a god. This causes problems immediately. Whether there is a god (or gods) is a very controversial question, and to rest questions of right and wrong on what a god says (or the gods say) is already to base morality on an intellectually unsettled foundation. The difficulties go deeper than this, however, since even if there is a god who is a moral authority, very serious questions must arise concerning whether people have understood (or can understand) what this authority says about right and wrong. The difficulties that exist when Jews and Christians consult the Bible ("God's revelation to man") can be taken as illustrative. Problems of interpretation abound. Some who think that drinking is wrong think they find evidence in the Bible that God thinks so too; others think they find evidence that He does not. Some who think that homosexuality is declared wrong by God cite what they think are supporting chapters and verses; others cite other chapters and verses that they think show God does not think homosexuality is wrong, or they cite the same passages and argue that they should be interpreted differently. The gravity of these and kindred problems of interpretation should not be underestimated. Even if there is a moral authority, and even if the god whom Jews and Christians worship should happen to be this authority, that would not make it a simple matter to find out what is right and wrong. The problem of finding out what God thinks on these matters would still remain. In view of the fundamental and long-standing disagreements concerning the correct interpretation of the Bible, this would be no easy matter.

Problems of interpretation aside, it is clear that the correct method for answering moral questions does not consist in discovering what a moral authority says. Even if there is a moral authority, those who are not moral authorities can have no reason for thinking that there is one unless the judgments of this supposed authority can be checked for their truth or reasonableness, and it is not possible to check for this unless what is true or reasonable can be known independently of any reliance on what the supposed authority says. If, however, there must be some independent way of knowing what moral judgments are true or reasonable, the introduction of a moral authority will not succeed in providing a method for answering moral questions. That method will have to illuminate how what is morally right and wrong can be known independently of the supposed moral authority, not how this can be known by relying on such an authority.

2. The Ideal Moral Judgment . . .
What now needs to be described is an approach to moral questions that is not open to the objections raised against the methods considered so far. The approach described in what follows turns on how the following question is answered: "What requirements would someone have to meet to make an ideal moral judgment?" Considered ideally, that is, what are the conditions that anyone would have to satisfy to reach a moral judgment as free from fault and error as possible? Now, by its very nature, an *ideal* moral judgment is just that—an ideal. Perhaps no one ever has or ever will completely meet all the requirements set forth in the ideal. But that does not make it irrational to strive to come as close as possible to fulfilling it. If we can never quite get to the finish, we can still move some distance from the starting line.

There are at least six different ideas that must find a place in our description of the ideal moral judgment. A brief discussion of each follows.

a. Conceptual Clarity: . . . If someone tells us that euthanasia is always wrong, we cannot determine whether that statement is true before we understand what euthanasia is. Similar remarks apply to other controversies. In the case of abortion, for example, many think the question turns on whether the fetus is a person; and that will depend on what a person is—that is, on how the concept 'person' should be analyzed. Clarity by itself may not be enough, but thought cannot get far without it.

b. Information: We cannot answer moral questions in our closets. Moral questions come up in the real world, and a knowledge of the real-world setting in which they arise is essential if we are seriously to seek rational answers to them. For example, in the debate over the morality of capital punishment, some people argue that convicted murderers ought to be executed because, if they are not, they may be (and often are) paroled; and if they are paroled, they are more likely to kill again than are other released prisoners. Is this true? Is this a fact? We have to come out of our closets to answer this (or to find the answer others have reached on the basis of their research); and answer it we must if we are to reach an informed judgment about the morality of capital punishment. . . . The importance of getting the facts, of being informed, is not restricted just to the case of capital punishment by any means. It applies all across the broad sweep of moral inquiry.

c. Rationality: Rationality is a difficult concept to analyze. Fundamentally, however, it involves the ability to recognize the connection between different ideas, to understand that if some statements are true, then some other statements must be true while others must be false. Now, it is in logic that rules are set forth that tell us when statements do follow from others, and it is because of this that a person who is rational often is said to be logical. When we speak of the need to be rational, then, we are saying that we need to observe the rules of logic. To reach an ideal moral judgment, therefore, we must not only strive to make our judgment against a background of information and conceptual clarity; we must also take care to explore how our beliefs are logically related to other things that we do or do not believe. . . . To fall short of the ideal moral judgment by committing oneself to a contradiction is to fall as far short as one possibly can.

d. Impartiality: Partiality involves favoring someone or something above others. For example, if a father is partial to one of his children, then he will be inclined to give the favored child more than he gives his other children. In some cases, perhaps, partiality is a fine thing; but a partiality that excludes even thinking about or taking notice of the needs, interests, and desires of others seems far from what is needed in an ideal moral judgment. The fact that someone has been harmed, for example, always seems to be a relevant consideration, whether this someone is favored by us or not. In striving to reach the correct answer to moral questions, therefore, we must strive to guard against extreme, unquestioned partiality; otherwise we shall run the risk of having our judgment clouded by bigotry and prejudice.

e. Coolness: All of us know what it is like to do something in the heat of anger that we later regret. No doubt we have also had the experience of getting so excited that we do something that later on we wish we had not done. Emotions are powerful forces, and though life would be a dull wasteland without them, we need to appreciate that the more volatile among them can mislead us; strong emotion is not a reliable guide to doing (or judging) what is best. This brings us to the need to be "cool." 'Being cool' here means "not being in an emotionally excited state, being in an emotionally calm state of mind." The idea is that the hotter (the more emotionally charged) we are, the more likely we are to reach a mistaken moral conclusion, while the cooler (the calmer) we are, the greater the chances that we will avoid . . . making mistakes.

The position is borne out by common experience. People who are in a terribly excited state may not be able to retain their rationality. Because of their deep emotional involvement, they may not be able to attain impartiality; and because they are in an excited emotional state, they may not even care about learning what happened or why. Like the proverb about shooting first and asking questions later, a lack of coolness can easily lead people to judge first and ask about the facts afterwards. The need to be "cool," then, seems to merit a place on our list.

f. Correct Moral Principles: The concept of a moral principle has been analyzed in different ways. At least this much seems clear, however: For a principle to be a *moral* principle (as distinct from, say, a scientific or legal principle), it must declare how all rational, free beings ought to act. The explanation of why a moral principle can apply only to free beings (those having free will) is as follows. Beings who lack free will cannot control how they behave; the only way they *can* behave is as they *do* behave, which makes it pointless to say how they *ought* to behave. Beings who have free will, however, *can* control how they behave; it is up to them whether they choose to act in one way rather than another; and thus it is meaningful to say that they ought or ought not to act in certain ways.

The explanation of why moral principles are restricted to rational beings is similar. The whole point of a moral principle is to provide rational guidance to beings faced with choices among various alternatives. It would therefore be senseless to think that moral principles apply to things (for example, sticks and stones) incapable of being guided by what is rational. Only rational beings can be guided by rational principles. Thus, it is only to rational beings that moral principles can apply.

Now, it is commonly thought that human beings have free will and are rational beings. At least this is commonly thought to be true of most humans. Small babies and severely mentally deficient humans, for example, are unable to make free choices based on reason. Thus, they cannot be guided by moral principles, and moral principles cannot apply to their conduct. Most humans, however, do have the capacity to reason. Whether they also have free will is far less certain. The existence of free will is one of the oldest and most controversial of philosophy's problems, one that is well beyond the scope of this anthology. For present purposes, it is enough to realize that moral principles can apply only to rational, free beings *and* that the contributors all assume that their readers are likely to be amongst those beings to whom these principles do apply.

How does the idea of a correct moral principle relate to the concept of an ideal moral judgment? In an ideal moral judgment, it is not enough that the judgment be based on complete information, complete impartiality, complete conceptual clarity, etc. It is also essential that the judgment be based on *the correct* or *the most reasonable* moral principle(s). Ideally, one wants not only to make the correct judgment, but to make it for the correct reasons. . . .

3. Normative Ethics

Philosophers engaged in normative ethics attempt to go beyond the questions concerning method that arise in meta-ethics; the goal they set themselves is nothing short of determining what are the correct moral principles—those principles, that is, by which all free, rational beings ought morally to be guided. Thus, there is an important connection between the goal of normative ethics and the concept of an ideal moral judgment. An ideal moral judgment, we have said, must be based on correct moral principles, and it is just the question 'What principles are the correct ones?' that is at the heart of normative ethics. Unless the normative ethical philosopher succeeds in stating what are the correct moral principles, there can be no hope of even approaching the ideal moral judgment.

What then are the correct moral principles? Not surprisingly, a variety of answers has been offered. Not all of them can be considered here, and no one can be considered in much detail. But enough can be said to make some important ideas intelligible.

Consequentialist Theories: One way to begin the search for the correct moral principle(s) is to think about cases where we all believe that something wrong has been done. However, it is important to understand that the class of persons referred to by the expression 'we all believe' is not necessarily as universal as it might at first appear. For suppose that Henry's belief or judgment is based on very sketchy information, or was formed in the heat of anger, or is a product of unquestioned prejudice. Then Henry's belief does not compute, so to speak; that is, because Henry's judgment falls so far short of the ideal moral judgment, we are justified in (that is, we have good reasons for) excluding it. Thus, the persons referred to by 'we all believe' are not just anybody and everybody; they are only those persons who most fully satisfy the first five conditions of the ideal moral judgment explained previously—those who are conceptually clear, informed, rational, impartial, and cool. It is the beliefs of these persons, not the beliefs of those who are prejudiced, say, that provide us with a place to begin the search for the final element in the ideal moral judgment—namely, the correct moral principle(s). So, by saying that a place to begin this search is with "what we all believe," we do not contradict what was said earlier about the irrelevance of statistics. What was said there *still* remains true: *Merely* to establish what all (or most) people think or believe about moral questions is not to establish what is right or wrong, let alone why it is.

So let us begin with a case where those who most fully approach the requirements of impartiality, conceptual clarity, etc. would all agree that something wrong has been done. For example, imagine that Beth has a favorite record. She enjoys listening to it and likes to share it with her friends. Sue likes the record too, and could afford to buy it, only then she could not afford to buy something else she wants but does not need. So, Sue steals the record. As a result, Beth experiences some unhappiness. When she thinks about the missing record, she is distraught and frustrated, and the enjoyment she would have had, if Sue had not stolen the record, is canceled. Beth, then, is worse off, both in terms of the unhappiness she experiences and in terms of lost enjoyment. Thinking along these lines has led some philosophers to theorize that what makes stealing wrong is that it is the cause of bad results—for example, it causes such experiences as the frustration and disappointment Beth feels.

Next imagine this case. Suppose there is a certain country that forbids black people from being in public after six o'clock. Bill, who is black, could get a job and support his family if the law did not prevent his free movement. As it is, he is chronically unemployed, and he and his family suffer accordingly. Thus, like the case of stealing, here we again have something that is the cause of bad results, and some philosophers have theorized that it is this fact that makes the law in question unjust.

Many philosophers have not stopped with the cases of stealing and injustice. Roughly speaking, the one common and peculiar characteristic of every wrong action, they have theorized, is that it leads to bad results, whereas the one common and peculiar characteristic of every right action, again roughly speaking, is that it leads to good results. Philosophers who accept this type of view commonly are referred to as *consequentialists,* an appropriate name, given their strong emphasis on the results or consequences of actions. Theories of this type are also called *teleological theories,* from the Greek *telos,* meaning "end" or "purpose," another fitting name, since, according to these thinkers, actions are not right or wrong in themselves; they are right or wrong, according to these theories, if they promote or frustrate the purpose of morality—namely, to bring about the greatest possible balance of good over evil.

Now, in normative ethics, when someone advances a principle that states what makes all right actions right and all wrong actions wrong, they do so in the course of advancing a *normative ethical theory.* Theoretically, there are at least three different types of teleological, normative ethical theories.

1. *Ethical egoism:* According to this theory, roughly speaking, whether any person (A) has done what is morally right or wrong depends solely on how good or bad the consequences of A's action are *for A.* How *others* are affected is irrelevant, unless how they are affected in turn alters the consequences for A.

2. *Ethical altruism:* According to this theory, roughly speaking, whether any person (B) has done what is morally right or wrong depends solely on how good or bad the

consequences of B's action are for *everyone except B*. How B is affected is irrelevant, unless how B is affected in turn alters the consequences for anyone else.

3. *Utilitarianism:* According to this theory, roughly speaking, whether any person (C) has done what is morally right or wrong depends solely on how good or bad the consequences of C's action are *for everyone affected*. Thus, how C is affected is relevant; but so is how *others* are affected. How *everyone* concerned is affected by the good or bad consequences is relevant.

These are not very exact statements of these three types of teleological, normative ethical theories, but enough has been said about two of them—namely, ethical egoism and ethical altruism—to enable us to understand why most philosophers find them unsatisfactory. Both seem to fall far short of the ideal of impartiality, ethical egoism because it seems to place arbitrary and exclusive importance on the good or welfare of the individual agent, and ethical altruism because it seems to place arbitrary and exclusive importance on the good or welfare of everyone else. Moreover, both theories arguably lead to consequences that clash with undoubted cases of wrong action. This is perhaps clearest in the case of ethical egoism. Provided only that, all things considered, stealing the record did not lead to less than the best results *for Sue,* what she did was not morally wrong, according to ethical egoism. But that is something we would most likely deny. Faced with the choice between accepting ethical egoism or giving up that what Sue did was wrong, most philosophers choose to reject the theory and retain the conviction.

It is utilitarianism, then, that seems to represent the strongest possible type of teleological theory. Certainly it is the one that has attracted the most adherents; not unexpectedly, therefore, it is the one that figures most prominently in the essays in this volume. It will be worth our while, therefore, to examine it at slightly greater length.

Utilitarianism: 'The Principle of Utility' is the name given to the fundamental principal advocated by those who are called utilitarians. This principle has been formulated in different ways. Here is a common formulation:

Everyone ought to act so as to bring about the greatest possible balance of intrinsic good over intrinsic evil for everyone concerned.

Already it must be emphasized that utilitarians do not agree on
everything. In particular, they do not all agree on what is intrinsically good and evil. Some philosophers (called *ethical hedonists)*
think that pleasure and pleasure alone is intrinsically good (or good
in itself), whereas pain, or the absence of pleasure, and this alone, is
intrinsically evil (or evil in itself). Other philosophers have different
theories of intrinsic good and evil. These troubled waters can be
bypassed, however, since the ideas of special importance for our
purposes can be discussed independently of whether ethical
hedonism, for example, is true.

Act- and *Rule-Utilitarianism:* One idea of special importance is
the difference between act-utilitarianism and rule-utilitarianism.
Act-utilitarianism is the view that the Principle of Utility should be
applied to individual actions; *rule-utilitarianism* states that the
Principle of Utility should be applied mainly to rules of action. The
act-utilitarian says that whenever people have to decide what to do,
they ought to perform that act which will bring about the greatest
possible balance of intrinsic good over intrinsic evil. The rule-
utilitarian says something different: People ought to do what is
required by justified moral rules. These are rules that would lead to
the best possible consequences, all considered, if everyone were to
abide by them. If a justified rule unambiguously applies to a
situation, and if no other justified moral rule applies, then the
person in that situation ought to choose to do what the rule requires, even if, in that particular situation, performing this act will
not lead to the best consequences. Thus, act-utilitarians and rule-
utilitarians, despite the fact that both profess to be utilitarians, can
reach opposing moral judgments. An act that is wrong according to
the rule-utilitarian, because it is contrary to a justified moral rule,
might not be wrong according to the act-utilitarian's position.

Some Problems for Act-Utilitarianism: Is act-utilitarianism correct?
Many philosophers answer no. Among the reasons given against
this theory is that act-utilitarianism appears to imply that some acts
that are most certainly wrong might be right. Recall the example of
Sue's stealing. According to act-utilitarianism, whether Sue's theft
was morally right or not depends on this and this alone: Were the
net consequences of her act at least as good as the consequences that

would have resulted if she had done anything else? Suppose they were. Then act-utilitarianism would imply that what she did was right. Yet her theft seems clearly wrong. Thus, we again seem to be faced with a choice between either (a) retaining the conviction that Sue's theft was wrong, or (b) accepting the theory of act-utilitarianism. We cannot choose to have both. In the face of such a choice, reason seems to be on the side of retaining the conviction and rejecting the theory.

Act-utilitarians actively defend their position against this line of criticism. The debate is among the liveliest and most important in normative ethics. The point that bears emphasis here is that *rule*-utilitarians do not believe that *their* version of utilitarianism can be refuted by the preceding argument. This is because they maintain that Sue's theft is wrong because it violates a justified moral rule—the rule against stealing. Thus, the rule-utilitarian holds that his position not only does not lead to a conclusion that clashes with the conviction that Sue's theft is wrong; this position actually illuminates *why* the theft is wrong—namely, because it violates a rule whose adoption by everyone can be defended by an appeal to the Principle of Utility.

Some Problems for Rule-Utilitarianism: One success does not guarantee that all goes well, and many philosophers think that rule-utilitarianism, too, is inadequate. The most important objection turns on considerations about justice. The point of the objection is that rule-utilitarianism apparently could justify rules that would be grossly unjust. To make this clearer suppose there were a rule that discriminated against persons because of the color of their skin. Imagine this rule *(R):* "No one with black skin will be permitted in public after six o'clock." If we think about *R*, its unfairness jumps out at us. It is unjust to discriminate against people simply on the basis of skin color. However, although it is clear that *R* would be unjust; might not *R* conceivably be justified by appealing to the Principle of Utility? Certainly it seems possible that everyone's acting according to *R* might bring about the greatest possible balance of intrinsic good over intrinsic evil. True, black people are not likely to benefit from everyone's acting according to *R*. Nevertheless, on balance, their loss might be more than outweighed by non-black' gains, especially if blacks are a small minority. Thus, if rule-utilitarianism could be used to justify flagrantly unjust rules, it is not a satisfactory theory.

Can the rule-utilitarian meet this challenge? Philosophers are not unanimous in their answer. As was the case with the debate over the correctness of act-utilitarianism, this debate is too extensive to be examined further here. . . .

Nonconsequentialism: 'Nonconsequentialism' is a name frequently given to normative ethical theories that are not forms of consequentialism. In other words, any theory that states that moral right and wrong are *not* determined solely by the relative balance of intrinsic good over intrinsic evil commonly is called a nonconsequentialist theory. Theories of this type are also called *deontological* theories, from the Greek *deon*, meaning given "duty." Such theories might be either (a) extreme or (b) moderate. An extreme deontological theory holds that the intrinsic good and evil of consequences are totally irrelevant to determining what is morally right or wrong. A moderate nonconsequentialist theory holds that the intrinsic good and evil of consequences are relevant to determining what is morally right and wrong but that they are not the only things that are relevant and may not be of greatest importance in some cases. A great variety of nonconsequentialist theories, both extreme and moderate, have been advanced. Why have some philosophers been attracted to such theories?

The Problem of Injustice: A central argument advanced against all forms of consequentialism by many nonconsequentialists is that no consequentialist theory (no form of ethical egoism, ethical altruism, or utilitarianism) can account for basic convictions about justice and injustice—for example, that it is unjust to deny Bill his liberty just because he is black. The point these deontologists make is that to treat Bill unjustly not only is wrong; to treat him unjustly is to wrong or harm *him*. Fundamentally, according to these thinkers, it is because people are wronged or harmed when treated unjustly, quite apart from the value of the consequences this may have for everyone else involved, that all consequentialist theories ultimately prove to be deficient.

Suppose these deontologists are correct. Some deontological theory would then be called for. A number of such theories have been advanced. Some theorists, following the lead of the German philosopher Immanuel Kant (1724—1804), have argued that injustice is wrong because it fails to show proper respect for free, rational beings; in particular, it involves treating such beings as mere means to someone else's end. Precisely what it means to treat someone without "proper respect" or as a "mere means" is not transparent. . . . To understand this position requires understanding the idea of basic moral rights.

Basic Moral Rights versus *Correlative Moral Rights: Basic* moral rights are rights that *do not follow from* any more basic moral principle. In particular, these rights do not follow from the Principle of Utility. It is difficult to overemphasize this point. A utilitarian might be able to consistently maintain that people have moral rights in a certain sense; possibly he or she could allow that moral rights are *correlated* with duties—for example, correlated with Sue's duty not to steal Beth's record is Beth's moral right not to have Sue (or anyone else) steal from her. However, for a utilitarian, moral rights cannot be *basic;* at the very most they can be correlated with those duties that, given the Principle of Utility, we are supposed to have. Those who believe in basic moral rights are of another mind. For example, if the right to life is a basic moral right, then this *right, not* the Principle of Utility or any other moral principle, is the ground or basis of the duty not to take the life of another person. In a word, basic moral rights, if there are any, are themselves the grounds of moral duties, not *vice versa.*

Both those who believe in basic moral rights and those who believe that moral rights are correlated with moral duties can agree on certain points about moral rights. In particular, both can agree that the concept of a moral right differs from the concept of a legal right. An explanation of some principal differences follows.

4. *Legal Rights and Moral Rights*

First, moral rights, if there are any, are *universal*, while legal rights need not be. Legal rights depend upon the law of this or that country and what is a matter of legal right in one country may not be so in another. For example, in the United States any citizen eighteen years old or older has the legal right to vote in federal elections; but not everyone in every nation has this same legal right. If, however, persons living in the United States have a moral right to, say, life, then *every* person in every nation has this same moral right, whether or not it is also recognized as a legal right.

Second, moral rights are *equal* rights. If all persons have a moral right to life, then all have this right equally; it is not a right that some (for example, males) can possess to a greater extent than others (for example, females). Neither, then, could this moral right be possessed to a greater extent by the inhabitants of one country (for example, one's own) than by the inhabitants of some other country (for example, a country with which one's own country is waging war). . . .

Third, moral rights are *inalienable,* meaning they cannot be transferred to another—for example, they cannot be lent or sold. If Bill has a moral right to life, then it is his and it cannot become anyone else's. Bill may give his life for his country, sacrifice it in the name of science, or destroy it himself in a fit of rage or despair. But he cannot give, sacrifice, or destroy his right to life. Whether he can do anything that, so to speak, cancels his right (the more common terminology is 'forfeit his right') is an important and difficult question. . . .

5. *Legal Justice and Moral Justice*

Moral and legal rights are connected in important ways with moral and legal justice. Legal justice requires that one respect the legal rights of everyone, while moral justice demands that everyone's moral rights be honored. The two—legal justice and moral justice— do not necessarily coincide. Laws themselves may be morally unjust. For example, a country might have a law that unfairly discriminates against some of its inhabitants because of their sex; imagine that it denies that women have a legal right to life but guarantees this legal right to all males. Then legal justice is done in this country if this law is enforced. But it does not follow that moral justice is done. That depends not on whether there is a law in this country, but on whether the law recognizes and protects the moral rights of the country's inhabitants. If it does, then the law is both legally and morally just; if it does not, then, though the law may be legally just, it lacks moral justice. . . .

6. *What are Rights?*

Whether rights are moral or legal, basic or correlative, the question remains: What are rights? How is the concept of a right to be analyzed? Various answers have been given, ranging from the view that rights are an individual's entitlements to be treated in certain ways to the view that they are valid claims that an individual can make, or have made on his or her behalf, to have one's interests or welfare taken into account. What is common to these answers is that a right involves the idea of a *justified constraint upon how others may act.* If Beth has a right to *x,* then others are constrained not to interfere with her pursuit or possession of *x,* at least so long as her pursuit or possession of *x* does not come into conflict with the rights of others. If it does, Beth may be exceeding her rights, and a serious moral question would arise. But aside from cases of exceeding one's rights and, as may sometimes be the case, of forfeiting them, the possession of a right by one individual places a justified limit on how other individuals may treat the person possessing the right. Whether rights are entitlements or valid claims, and whether they are basic or correlative, rights involve a justified constraint or limitation on how others may act. . . .

One Role of the Principle of Utility: All but the most extreme non-consequentialist can allow that an appeal to the Principle of Utility is always relevant even if not always decisive. Possibly utility has a role to play when the rights of innocent persons conflict. To illustrate this possibility, suppose a hijacker has attached to an innocent hostage a time bomb that, if it goes off, will kill ten other innocent persons; and suppose that the only possible way to prevent the bomb from going off is to kill the hostage. What ought to be done? If we kill the hostage, we kill an innocent person; but if we do not kill the hostage, ten innocent persons will be killed. The innocence of the persons involved may not be enough to give us moral direction. Possibly an appeal to the Principle of Utility would. The point is, even if there are *basic* moral rights, and even if the utilitarian cannot account for them, one could *both* believe in basic moral rights *and* allow that the Principle of Utility should play some role in our thinking about what is right and wrong—for example, in cases where the basic moral rights of innocent people conflict. . . .

Utilitarianism

JOHN STUART MILL

What Utilitarianism Is

The creed which accepts as the foundation of morals, Utility, or the Greatest Happiness Principle, holds that actions are right in proportion as they tend to promote happiness, wrong as they tend to produce the reverse of happiness. By happiness is intended pleasure, and the absence of pain; by unhappiness, pain, and the privation of pleasure. To give a clear view of the moral standard set up by the theory, much more requires to be said; in particular, what things it includes in the ideas of pain and pleasure; and to what extent this is left an open question. But these supplementary explanations do not affect the theory of life on which this theory of morality is grounded—namely, that pleasure, and freedom from pain, are the only things desirable as ends; and that all desirable things (which are as numerous in the utilitarian as in any other scheme) are desirable either for the pleasure inherent in themselves, or as means to the promotion of pleasure and the prevention of pain.

Now, such a theory of life excites in many minds, and among them in some of the most estimable in feeling and purpose, inveterate dislike. To suppose that life has (as they express it) no higher end than pleasure—no better and nobler object of desire and pursuit—they designate as utterly mean and grovelling; as a doctrine worthy only of swine, to whom the followers of Epicurus were, at a very early period, contemptuously likened; and modern holders of the doctrine are occasionally made the subject of equally polite comparisons by its German, French, and English assailants.

When thus attacked, the Epicureans have always answered, that it is not they, but their accusers, who represent human nature in a degrading light; since the accusation supposes human beings to be capable of no pleasures except those of which swine are capable. If this supposition were true, the charge could not be gainsaid, but would then be no longer an imputation; for if the sources of pleasure were precisely the same to human beings and to swine, the rule of life which is good enough for the one would be good enough for the other. The comparison of the Epicurean life to that of beasts is felt as degrading, precisely because a beast's pleasures do not satisfy a human being's conceptions of happiness. Human beings have faculties more elevated than the animal appetites, and when once made conscious of them, do not regard anything as happiness which does not include their gratification. I do not, indeed, consider the Epicureans to have been by any means faultless in drawing out their scheme of consequences from the utilitarian principle. To do this in any sufficient manner, many Stoic, as well as Christian elements require to be included. But there is no known Epicurean theory of life which does not assign to the pleasures of the intellect, of the feelings and imagination, and of the moral sentiments, a much higher value as pleasures than to those of mere sensation. It must be admitted, however, that utilitarian writers in general have placed the superiority of mental over bodily pleasures chiefly in the greater permanency, safety, uncostliness, etc., of the former—that is, in their circumstantial advantages rather than in their intrinsic nature. And on all these points utilitarians have fully proved their case; but they might have taken the other, and, as it may be called, higher ground, with entire consistency. It is quite compatible with the principle of utility to recognise the fact, that some kinds of pleasure are more desirable and more valuable than others. It would be absurd that while, in estimating all other things, quality is considered as well as quantity, the estimation of pleasures should be supposed to depend on quantity alone.

If I am asked, what I mean by difference of quality in pleasures, or what makes one pleasure more valuable than another, merely as a pleasure, except its being greater in amount, there is but one possible answer. Of two pleasures, if there be one to which all or almost all who have experience of both give a decided preference, irrespective of any feeling of moral obligation to prefer it, that is the more desirable pleasure. If one of the two is, by those who are competently acquainted with both, placed so far above the other that they prefer it, even though knowing it to be attended with a greater amount of discontent, and would not resign it for any quantity of the other pleasure which their nature is capable of, we are justified in ascribing to the preferred enjoyment a superiority in quality, so far outweighing quantity as to render it, in comparison, of small account.

Now it is an unquestionable fact that those who are equally acquainted with, and equally capable of appreciating and enjoying, both, do give a most marked preference to the manner of existence which employs their higher faculties. Few human creatures would consent to be changed into any of the lower animals, for a promise of the fullest allowance of a beast's pleasures; no intelligent human being would consent to be a fool, no instructed person would be an ignoramus, no person of feeling and conscience would be selfish and base, even though they should be persuaded that the fool, the dunce, or the rascal is better satisfied with his lot than they are with theirs. They would not resign what they possess more than he for the most complete satisfaction of all the desires which they have in common with him. If they ever fancy they would, it is only in cases of unhappiness so extreme, that to escape from it they would exchange their lot for almost any other, however undesirable in their own eyes. A being of higher faculties requires more to make him happy, is capable probably of more acute suffering, and certainly accessible to it at more points, than one of an inferior type; but in spite of these liabilities, he can never really wish to sink into what he feels to be a lower grade of existence. We may give what explanation we please of this unwillingness; we may attribute it to pride, a name which is given indiscriminately to some of the most and to some of the least estimable feelings of which mankind are capable: we may refer it to the love of liberty and personal inde- pendence, an appeal to which was with the Stoics one of the most effective means for the inculcation of it; to the love of power, or to the love of excitement, both of which do really enter into and contribute to it: but its most appropriate appellation is a sense of dignity, which all human beings possess in one form or other, and in some, though by no means in exact, proportion to their higher faculties, and which is so essential a part of the happiness of those in whom it is strong, that nothing which conflicts with it could be, otherwise than momentarily, an object of desire to them.

Whoever supposes that this preference takes place at a sacrifice of happiness—that the superior being, in anything like equal circumstances, is not happier than the inferior—confounds the two very different ideas, of happiness, and content. It is indisputable that the being whose capacities of enjoyment are low, has the greatest chance of having them fully satisfied; and a highly en- dowed being will always feel that any happiness which he can look for, as the world is constituted, is imperfect. But he can learn to bear its imperfections, if they are at all bearable; and they will not make him envy the being who is indeed unconscious of the imperfections, but only because he feels not at all the good which those imperfections qualify. It is better to be a human being dissatisfied than a pig satisfied; better to be Socrates dissatisfied than a fool satisfied. And if the fool, or the pig, are a different opinion, it is because they only know their own side of the question. The other party to the comparison knows both sides.

It may be objected, that many who are capable of the higher pleasures, occasionally, under the influence of temptation, postpone them to the lower. But this is quite compatible with a full appreciation of the intrinsic superiority of the higher. Men often, from infirmity of character, make their election for the nearer good, though they know it to be the less valuable; and this no less when the choice is between two bodily pleasures, than when it is between bodily and mental. They pursue sensual indulgences to the injury of health, though perfectly aware that health is the greater good.

It may be further objected, that many who begin with youthful enthusiasm for everything noble, as they advance in years sink into indolence and selfishness. But I do not believe that those who undergo this very common change, voluntarily choose the lower description of pleasures in preference to the higher. I believe that before they devote themselves exclusively to the one, they have already become incapable of the other. Capacity for the nobler feelings is in most natures a very tender plant, easily killed, not only by hostile influences, but by mere want of sustenance; and in the majority of young persons it speedily dies away if the occupations to which their position in life has devoted them, and the society into which it has thrown them, are not favourable to keeping that higher capacity in exercise. Men lose their high aspirations as they lose their intellectual tastes, because they have not time or opportunity for indulging them; and they addict themselves to inferior pleasures, not because they deliberately prefer them, but because they are either the only ones to which they have access, or the only ones which they are any longer capable of enjoying. It may be questioned whether any one who has remained equally susceptible to both classes of pleasures, ever knowingly and calmly preferred the lower; though many, in all ages, have broken down in an ineffectual attempt to combine both.

From this verdict of the only competent judges, I apprehend there can be no appeal. On a question which is the best worth having of two pleasures, or which of two modes of existence is the most grateful to the feelings, apart from its moral attributes and from its consequences, the judgment of those who are qualified by knowledge of both, or, if they differ, that of the majority among them, must be admitted as final. And there needs be the less hesitation to accept this judgment respecting the quality of pleasures, since there is no other tribunal to be referred to even on the question of quantity. What means are there of determining which is the acutest of two pains, or the intensest of two pleasurable sensations, except the general suffrage of those who are familiar with both? Neither pains nor pleasures are homogeneous, and pain is always heterogeneous with pleasure. What is there to decide whether a particular pleasure is worth purchasing at the cost of a particular pain, except the feelings and judgment of the experienced? When, therefore, those feelings and judgment declare the pleasures derived from the higher faculties to be preferable in kind, apart from the question of intensity, to those of which the animal nature, disjoined from the higher faculties, is suspectible, they are entitled on this subject to the same regard.

I have dwelt on this point, as being a necessary part of a perfectly just conception of Utility or Happiness, considered as the directive rule of human conduct. But it is by no means an indispensable condition to the acceptance of the utilitarian standard; for that standard is not the agent's own greatest happiness, but the greatest amount of happiness altogether; and if it may possibly be doubted whether a noble character is always the happier for its nobleness, there can be no doubt that it makes other people happier, and that the world in general is immensely a gainer by it. Utilitarianism, therefore, could only attain its end by the general cultivation of nobleness of character, even if each individual were only benefited by the nobleness of others, and his own, so far as happiness is concerned, were a sheer deduction from the benefit. But the bare enunciation of such an absurdity as this last, renders refutation superfluous.

According to the Greatest Happiness Principle, as above explained, the ultimate end, with reference to and for the sake of which all other things are desirable (whether we are considering our own good or that of other people), is an existence exempt as far as possible from pain, and as rich as possible in enjoyments, both in point of quantity and quality; the test of quality, and the rule for measuring it against quantity, being the preference felt by those who in their opportunities of experience, to which must be added their habits of self-consciousness and self-observation, are best furnished with the means of comparison. This, being, according to the utilitarian opinion, the end of human action, is necessarily also the standard of morality; which may accordingly be defined, the rules and precepts for human conduct, by the observance of which an existence such as has been described might be, to the greatest extent possible, secured to all mankind; and not to them only, but, so far as the nature of things admits, to the whole sentient creation.

Against this doctrine, however, arises another class of objectors, who say that happiness, in any form, cannot be the rational purpose of human life and action; because, in the first place, it is unattainable: and they contemptuously ask, What right hast thou to be happy? a question which Mr. Carlyle clenches by the addition, What right, a short time ago, hadst thou even to be? Next, they say, that men can do without happiness; that all noble human beings have felt this, and could not have become noble but by learning the lesson of Entsagen, or renunciation; which lesson, thoroughly learnt and submitted to, they affirm to be the beginning and necessary condition of all virtue.

The first of these objections would go to the root of the matter were it well founded; for if no happiness is to be had at all by human beings, the attainment of it cannot be the end of morality, or of any rational conduct. Though, even in that case, something might still be said for the utilitarian theory; since utility includes not solely the pursuit of happiness, but the prevention or mitigation of unhappiness; and if the former aim be chimerical, there will be all the greater scope and more imperative need for the latter, so long at least as mankind think fit to live, and do not take refuge in the simultaneous act of suicide recommended under certain conditions by Novalis. When, however, it is thus positively asserted to be impossible that human life should be happy, the assertion, if not something like a verbal quibble, is at least an exaggeration. If by happiness be meant a continuity of highly pleasurable excitement, it is evident enough that this is impossible. A state of exalted pleasure lasts only moments, or in some cases, and with some intermissions, hours or days, and is the occasional brilliant flash of enjoyment, not its permanent and steady flame. Of this the philosophers who have taught that happiness is the end of life were as fully aware as those who taunt them. The happiness which they meant was not a life of rapture; but moments of such, in an existence made up of few and transitory pains, many and various pleasures, with a decided predominance of the active over the passive, and having as the foundation of the whole, not to expect more from life than it is capable of bestowing. A life thus composed, to those who have been fortunate enough to obtain it, has always appeared worthy of the name of happiness. And such an existence is even now the lot of many, during some considerable portion of their lives. The present wretched education, and wretched social arrangements, are the only real hindrance to its being attainable by almost all.

The objectors perhaps may doubt whether human beings, if taught to consider happiness as the end of life, would be satisfied with such a moderate share of it. But great numbers of mankind have been satisfied with much less. The main constituents of a satisfied life appear to be two, either of which by itself is often found sufficient for the purpose: tranquillity, and excitement. With much tranquillity, many find that they can be content with very little pleasure: with much excitement, many can reconcile themselves to a considerable quantity of pain. There is assuredly no inherent impossibility in enabling even the mass of mankind to unite both; since the two are so far from being incompatible that they are in natural alliance, the prolongation of either being a preparation for, and exciting a wish for, the other. It is only those in whom indolence amounts to a vice, that do not desire excitement after an interval of repose: it is only those in whom the need of excitement is a disease, that feel the tranquillity which follows excitement dull and insipid, instead of pleasurable in direct proportion to the excitement which preceded it. When people who are tolerably fortunate in their outward lot do not find in life sufficient enjoyment to make it valuable to them, the cause generally is, caring for nobody but themselves. To those who have neither public nor private affections, the excitements of life are much curtailed, and in any case dwindle in value as the time approaches when all selfish interests must be terminated by death: while those who leave after them objects of personal affection, and especially those who have also cultivated a fellow-feeling with the collective interests of mankind, retain as lively an interest in life on the eve of death as in the vigour of youth and health. Next to selfishness, the principal cause which makes life unsatisfactory is want of mental cultivation. A cultivated mind—I do not mean that of a philosopher, but any mind to which the fountains of knowledge have been opened, and which has been taught, in any tolerable degree, to exercise its faculties—finds sources of inexhaustible interest in all that surrounds it; in the objects of nature, the achievements of art, the imaginations of poetry, the incidents of history, the ways of man-kind, past and present, and their prospects in the future. It is possible, indeed, to become indifferent to all this, and that too without having exhausted a thousandth part of it; but only when one has had from the beginning no moral or human interest in these things, and has sought in them only the gratification of curiosity.

Now there is absolutely no reason in the nature of things why an amount of mental culture sufficient to give an intelligent interest in these objects of contemplation, should not be the inheritance of every one born in a civilised country. As little is there an inherent necessity that any human being should be a selfish egotist, devoid of every feeling or care but those which centre in his own miserable individuality. Something far superior to this is sufficiently common even now, to give ample earnest of what the human species may be made. Genuine private affections and a sincere interest in the public good, are possible, though in unequal degrees, to every rightly brought up human being. In a world in which there is so much to interest, so much to enjoy, and so much also to correct and improve, every one who has this moderate amount of moral and intellectual requisites is capable of an existence which may be called enviable; and unless such a person, through bad laws, or subjection to the will of others, is denied the liberty to use the sources of happiness within his reach, he will not fail to find this enviable existence, if he escape the positive evils of life, the great sources of physical and mental suffering—such as indigence, disease, and the unkindness, worthlessness, or premature loss of objects of affection. The main stress of the problem lies, therefore, in the contest with these calamities, from which it is a rare good fortune entirely to escape; which, as things now are, cannot be obviated, and often cannot be in any material degree mitigated. Yet no one whose opinion deserves a moment's consideration can doubt that most of the great positive evils of the world are in themselves removable, and will, if human affairs continue to improve, be in the end reduced within narrow limits. Poverty, in any sense implying suffering, may be completely extinguished by the wisdom of society, combined with the good sense and providence of individuals. Even that most intractable of enemies, disease, may be indefinitely reduced in dimensions by good physical and moral education, and proper control of noxious influences; while the progress of science holds out a promise for the future of still more direct conquests over this detestable foe. And every advance in that direction relieves us from some, not only of the chances which cut short our own lives, but, what concerns us still more, which deprive us of those in whom our happiness is wrapt up. As for vicissitudes of fortune, and other disappointments connected with worldly circumstances, these are principally the effect either of gross imprudence, of ill-regulated desires, or of bad or imperfect social institutions. . . .

And this leads to the true estimation of what is said by the objectors concerning the possibility, and the obligation, of learning to do without happiness. Unquestionably it is possible to do without happiness; it is done involuntarily by nineteen-twentieths of mankind, even in those parts of our present world which are least deep in barbarism; and it often has to be done voluntarily by the hero or the martyr, for the sake of something which he prizes more than his individual happiness. But this something, what is it, unless the happiness of others or some of the requisites of happiness? It is noble to be capable of resigning entirely one's own portion of happiness, or chances of it: but, after all, this self-sacrifice must be for some end; it is not its own end; and if we are told that its end is not happiness, but virtue, which is better than happiness, I ask, would the sacrifice be made if the hero or martyr did not believe that it would earn for others immunity from similar sacrifices? Would it be made if he thought that his renunciation of happiness for himself would produce no fruit for any of his fellow creatures, but to make their lot like his, and place them also in the condition of persons who have renounced happiness? All honour to those who can abnegate for themselves the personal enjoyment of life, when by such renunciation they contribute worthily to increase the amount of happiness in the world; but he who does it, or professes to do it, for any other purpose, is no more deserving of admiration than the ascetic mounted on his pillar. He may be an inspiriting proof of what men can do, but assuredly not an example of what they should. . . .

Meanwhile, let utilitarians never cease to claim the morality of self devotion as a possession which belongs by as good a right to them, as either to the Stoic or to the Transcendentalist. The utilitarian morality does recognise in human beings the power of sacrificing their own greatest good for the good of others. It only refuses to admit that the sacrifice is itself a good. A sacrifice which does not increase, or tend to increase, the sum total of happiness, it considers as wasted. The only self-renunciation which it applauds, is devotion to the happiness, or to some of the means of happiness, of others;

either of mankind collectively, or of individuals within the limits imposed by the collective interests of mankind.

I must again repeat, what the assailants of utilitarianism seldom have the justice to acknowledge, that the happiness which forms the utilitarian standard of what is right in conduct, is not the agent's own happiness, but that of all concerned. As between his own happiness and that of others, utilitarianism requires him to be as strictly impartial as a disinterested and benevolent spectator. In the golden rule of Jesus of Nazareth, we read the complete spirit of the ethics of utility. To do as you would be done by, and to love your neighbour as yourself, constitute the ideal perfection of utilitarian morality. As the means of making the nearest approach to this ideal, utility would enjoin, first, that laws and social arrangements should place the happiness, or (as speaking practically it may be called) the interest, of every individual, as nearly as possible in harmony with the interest of the whole; and secondly, that education and opinion, which have so vast a power over human character, should so use that power as to establish in the mind of every individual an indissoluble association between his own happiness and the good of the whole; especially between his own happiness and the practice of such modes of conduct, negative and positive, as regard for the universal happiness prescribes; so that not only he may be unable to conceive the possibility of happiness to himself, consistently with conduct opposed to the general good, but also that a direct impulse to promote the general good may be in every individual one of the habitual motives of action, and the sentiments connected therewith may fill a large and prominent place in every human being's sentient existence. If the, impugners of the utilitarian morality represented it to their own minds in this its, true character, I know not what recommendation possessed by any other morality they could possibly affirm to be wanting to it; what more beautiful or more exalted developments of human nature any other ethical system can be supposed to foster, or what springs of action, not accessible to the utilitarian, such systems rely on for giving effect to their mandates.

The objectors to utilitarianism cannot always be charged with representing it in a discreditable light. On the contrary, those among them who entertain anything like a just idea of its disinterested character, sometimes find fault with its standard as being too high for humanity. They say it is exacting too much to require that people shall always act from the inducement of promoting the general interests of society. But this is to mistake the very meaning of a standard of morals, and confound the rule of action with the motive of it. It is the business of ethics to tell us what are our duties, or by what test we may know them; but no system of ethics requires that the sole motive of all we do shall be a feeling of duty; on the contrary, ninety-nine hundredths of all our actions are done from other motives, and rightly so done, if the rule of duty does not condemn them. It is the more unjust to utilitarianism that this particular misapprehension should be made a ground of objection to it, inasmuch as utilitarian moralists have gone beyond almost all others in affirming that the motive has nothing to do with the morality of the action, though much with the worth of the agent. He who saves a fellow creature from drowning does what is morally right, whether his motive be duty, or the hope of being paid for his trouble; he who betrays the friend that trusts him, is guilty of a crime, even if his object be to serve another friend to whom he is under greater obligations.

But to speak only of actions done from the motive of duty, and in direct obedience to principle: it is a misapprehension of the utilitarian mode of thought, to conceive it as implying that people should fix their minds upon so wide a generality as the world, or society at large. The great majority of good actions are intended not for the benefit of the world, but for that of individuals, of which the good of the world is made up; and the thoughts of the most virtuous man need not on these occasions travel beyond the particular persons concerned, except so far as is necessary to assure himself that in benefiting them he is not violating the rights, that is, the legitimate and authorised expectations, of any one else. The multiplication of happiness is, according to the utilitarian ethics, the object of virtue: the occasions on which any person (except one in a thousand) has it in his power to do this on an extended scale, in other words to be a public benefactor, are but exceptional; and on these occasions alone is he called on to consider public utility; in every other case, private utility, the interest or happiness of some few persons, is all he has to attend to. Those alone the influence of whose actions extends to society in general, need concern themselves habitually about large an object. In the case of abstinences indeed—of things which people forbear to do from moral considerations, though the consequences in the particular case might be beneficial—it would be unworthy of an intelligent agent not to be consciously aware that the action is of a class which, if practised generally, would be generally injurious, and that this is the ground of the obligation to abstain from it. The amount of regard for the public interest implied in this recognition, is no greater than is demanded by every system of morals, for they all enjoin to abstain from whatever is manifestly pernicious to society. . . .

Again, defenders of utility often find themselves called upon to reply to such objections as this—that there is not time, previous to action, for calculating and weighing the effects of any line of conduct on the general happiness. This is exactly as if any one were to say that it is impossible to guide our conduct by Christianity, because there is not time, on every occasion on which anything has to be done, to read through the Old and New Testaments. The answer to the objection is, that there has been ample time, namely, the whole past duration of the human species. During all that time, mankind have been learning by experience the tendencies of actions; on which experience all the prudence, as well as all the morality of life, are dependent. People talk as if the commencement of this course of experience had hitherto been put off, and as if, at the moment when some man feels tempted to meddle with the property or life of another, he had to begin considering for the first time whether murder and theft are injurious to human happiness. Even then I do not think that he would find the question very puzzling; but, at all events, the matter is now done to his hand.

Of What Sort of Proof the Principle of Utility Is Susceptible.

It has already been remarked, that questions of ultimate ends do not admit of proof, in the ordinary acceptation of the term. To be incapable of proof by reasoning is common to all first principles; to the first premises of our knowledge, as well as to those of our conduct. But the former, being matters of fact, may be the subject of a direct appeal to the faculties which judge of fact—namely, our senses, and our internal consciousness. Can an appeal be made to the same faculties on questions of practical ends? Or by what other faculty is cognisance taken of them?

Questions about ends are, in other words, questions about what things are desirable. The utilitarian doctrine is, that happiness is desirable, and the only thing desirable, as an end; all other things being only desirable as means to that end. What ought to be required of this doctrine—what conditions is it requisite that the doctrine should fulfil—to make good its claim to be believed?

The only proof capable of being given that an object is visible, is that people actually see it. The only proof that a sound is audible, is that people hear it: and so of the other sources of our experience. In like manner, I apprehend, the sole evidence it is possible to produce that anything is desirable, is that people do actually desire it. If the end which the utilitarian doctrine proposes to itself were not, in theory and in practice, acknowledged to be an end, nothing could ever convince any person that it was so. No reason can be given why the general happiness is desirable, except that each person, so far as he believes it to be attainable, desires his own happiness. This, however, being a fact, we have not only all the proof which the case admits of, but all which it is possible to require, that happiness is a good: that each person's happiness is a good to that person, and the general happiness, therefore, a good to the aggregate of all persons. Happiness has made out its title as one of the ends of conduct, and consequently one of the criteria of morality.

But it has not, by this alone, proved itself to be the sole criterion. To do that, it would seem, by the same rule, necessary to show, not only that people desire happiness, but that they never desire anything else. Now it is palpable that they do desire things which, in common language, are decidedly distinguished from happiness. They desire, for example, virtue, and the absence of vice, no less really than pleasure and the absence of pain. The desire of virtue is not as universal, but it is as authentic a fact, as the desire of happiness. And hence the opponents of the utilitarian standard deem that they have a right to infer that there are other ends of human action besides happiness, and that happiness is not the standard of approbation and disapprobation. . . .

It results from the preceding considerations, that there is in reality nothing desired except happiness. Whatever is desired otherwise than as a means to some end beyond itself, and ultimately to happiness, is desired as itself a part of happiness, and is not desired for itself until it has become so. Those who desire virtue for its own sake, desire it either because the consciousness of it is a pleasure, or because the consciousness of being without it is a pain, or for both reasons united; as in truth the pleasure and pain seldom exist separately, but almost always together, the same person feeling pleasure in the degree of virtue attained, and pain in not having attained more. If one of these gave him no pleasure, and the other no pain, he would not love or desire virtue, or would desire it only for the other benefits which it might produce to himself or to persons whom he cared for. We have now, then, an answer to the question, of what sort of proof the principle of utility is susceptible. If the opinion which I have now stated is psychologically true—if human nature is so constituted as to desire nothing which is not either a part of happiness or a means of happiness, we can have no other proof, and we require no other, that these are the only things desirable. If so, happiness is the sole end of human action, and the promotion of it the test by which to judge of all human conduct; from whence it necessarily follows that it must be the criterion of morality, since a part is included in the whole.

On the Connection between Justice and Utility.

In all ages of speculation, one of the strongest obstacles to the reception of the doctrine that Utility or Happiness is the criterion of right and wrong, has been drawn from the idea of justice. The powerful sentiment, and apparently clear perception, which that word recalls with a rapidity and certainty resembling an instinct, have seemed to the majority of thinkers to point to an inherent quality in things; to show that the just must have an existence in Nature as something absolute, generically distinct from every variety of the Expedient, and, in idea, opposed to it, though (as is commonly acknowledged) never, in the long run, disjoined from it in fact. . . .

To find the common attributes of a variety of objects, it is necessary to begin by surveying the objects themselves in the concrete. Let us therefore advert successively to the various modes of action, and arrangements of human affairs, which are classed, by universal or widely spread opinion, as Just or as Unjust. The things well known to excite the sentiments associated with those names are of a very multifarious character. I shall pass them rapidly in review, without studying any particular arrangement.

In the first place, it is mostly considered unjust to deprive any one of his personal liberty, his property, or any other thing which belongs to him by law. Here, therefore, is one instance of the application of the terms just and unjust in a perfectly definite sense, namely, that it is just to respect, unjust to violate, the legal rights of any one. But this judgment admits of several exceptions, arising from the other forms in which the notions of justice and injustice present themselves. . . .

Secondly; the legal rights of which he is deprived, may be rights which ought not to have belonged to him; in other words, the law which confers on him these rights, may be a bad law. When it is so, or when (which is the same thing for our purpose) it is supposed to be so, opinions will differ as to the justice or injustice of infringing it. Some maintain that no law, however bad, ought to be disobeyed by an individual citizen; that his opposition to it, if shown at all, should only be shown in endeavouring to get it altered by competent authority. This opinion (which condemns many of the most illustrious benefactors of mankind, and would often protect pernicious institutions against the only weapons which, in the state of things existing at the time, have any chance of succeeding against them) is defended, by those who hold it, on grounds of expediency; principally on that of the importance, to the common interest of mankind, of maintaining inviolate the sentiment of submission to law. Other persons, again, hold the directly contrary opinion, that any law, judged to be bad, may blamelessly be disobeyed, even though it be not judged to be unjust, but only inexpedient; while others would confine the licence of disobedience to the case of unjust laws: but again, some say, that all laws which are inexpedient are unjust; since every law imposes some restriction on the natural liberty of mankind, which restriction is an injustice, unless legitimated by tending to their good. Among these diversities of opinion, it seems to be universally admitted that there may be unjust laws, and that law, consequently, is not the ultimate criterion of justice, but may give to one person a benefit, or impose on another an evil, which justice condemns. When, however, a law is thought to be unjust, it seems always to be regarded as being so in the same way in which a breach of law is unjust, namely, by infringing somebody's right; which, as it cannot in this case be a legal right, receives a different appellation, and is called a moral right. We may say, therefore, that a second case of injustice consists in taking or withholding from any person that to which he has a moral right.

Thirdly, it is universally considered just that each person should obtain that (whether good or evil) which he deserves; and unjust that he should obtain a good, or be made to undergo an evil, which he does not deserve. This is, perhaps, the clearest and most emphatic form in which the idea of justice is conceived by the general mind. As it involves the notion of desert, the question arises, what constitutes desert? Speaking in a general way, a person is understood to deserve good if he does right, evil if he does wrong; and in a more particular sense, to deserve good from those to whom he does or has done good, and evil from those to whom he does or has done evil. The precept of returning good for evil has never been regarded as a case of the fulfilment of justice, but as one in which the claims of justice are waived. . . .

Fourthly, it is confessedly unjust to break faith with any one: to violate an engagement, either express or implied, or disappoint expectations raised by our conduct, at least if we have raised those expectations knowingly and voluntarily. Like the other obligations of justice already spoken of, this one is not regarded as absolute, but as capable of being overruled by a stronger obligation of justice on the other side; or by such conduct on the part of the person concerned as is deemed to absolve us from our obligation to him, and to constitute a forfeiture of the benefit which he has been led to expect.

Fifthly, it is, by universal admission, inconsistent with justice to be partial; to show favour or preference to one person over another, in matters to which favour and preference do not properly apply. Impartiality, however, does not seem to be regarded as a duty in itself, but rather as instrumental to some other duty; for it is admitted that favour and preference are not always censurable, and indeed the cases in which they are condemned are rather the exception than the rule. A person would be more likely to be blamed than applauded for giving his family or friends no superiority in good offices over strangers, when he could do so without violating any other duty; and no one thinks it unjust to seek one person in preference to another as a friend, connection, or companion. Impartiality where rights are concerned is of course obligatory, but this is involved in the more general obligation of giving to every one his right. A tribunal, for example, must be impartial, because it is bound to award, without regard to any other consideration, a disputed object to the one of two parties who has the right to it. There are other cases in which impartiality means, being solely influenced by desert; as with those who, in the capacity of judges, preceptors, or parents, administer reward and punishment as such. There are cases, again, in which it means, being solely influenced by consideration for the public interest; as in making a selection among candidates for a government employment. Impartiality, in short, as an obligation of justice, may be said to mean, being exclusively influenced by the considerations which it is supposed ought to influence the particular case in hand; and resisting the solicitation of any motives which prompt to conduct different from what those considerations would dictate. . . .

To recapitulate: the idea of justice supposes two things; a rule of conduct, and a sentiment which sanctions the rule. The first must be supposed common to all mankind, and intended for their good. The other (the sentiment) is a desire that punishment may be suffered by those who infringe the rule. There is involved, in addition, the conception of some definite person who suffers by the infringement; whose rights (to use the expression appropriated to the case) are violated by it. And the sentiment of justice appears to me to be, the animal desire to repel or retaliate a hurt or damage to oneself, or to those with whom one sympathises, widened so as to include all persons, by the human capacity of enlarged sympathy, and the human conception of intelligent self-interest. From the latter elements, the feeling derives its morality; from the former, its peculiar impressiveness, and energy of self-assertion.

I have, throughout, treated the idea of a right residing in the injured person, and violated by the injury, not as a separate element in the composition of the idea and sentiment, but as one of the forms in which the other two elements clothe themselves. These elements are, a hurt to some assignable person or persons on the one hand, and a demand for punishment on the other. An examination of our own minds, I think, will show, that these two things include all that we mean when we speak of violation of a right. When we call anything a person's right, we mean that he has a valid claim on society to protect him in the possession of it, either by the force of law, or by that of education and opinion. If he has what we consider a sufficient claim, on whatever account, to have something guaranteed to him by society, we say that he has a right to it. If we desire to prove that anything does not belong to him by right, we think this done as soon as it is admitted that society ought not to take measures for securing it to him, but should leave him to chance, or to his own exertions. Thus, a person is said to have a right to what he can earn in fair professional competition; because society ought not to allow any other person to hinder him from endeavouring to earn in that manner as much as he can. But he has not a right to three hundred a-year, though he may happen to be earning it; because society is not called on to provide that he shall earn that sum. On the contrary, if he owns ten thousand pounds three per cent stock, he has a right to three hundred a-year; because society has come under an obligation to provide him with an income of that amount.

To have a right, then, is, I conceive, to have something which society ought to defend me in the possession of. If the objector goes on to ask, why it ought? I can give him no other reason than general utility. If that expression does not seem to convey a sufficient feeling of the strength of the obligation, nor to account for the peculiar energy of the feeling, it is because there goes to the composition of the sentiment, not a rational only, but also an animal element, the thirst for retaliation; and this thirst derives its intensity, as well as its moral justification, from the extraordinarily important and impressive kind of utility which is concerned. The interest involved is that of security, to every one's feelings the most vital of all interests. All other earthly benefits are needed by one person, not needed by another; and many of them can, if necessary, be cheerfully foregone, or replaced by something else; but security no human being can possibly do without—on it we depend for all our immunity from evil, and for the whole value of all and every good, beyond the passing moment; since nothing but the gratification of the instant could be of any worth to us, if we could be deprived of anything the next instant by whoever was momentarily stronger than ourselves. Now this most indispensable of all necessaries, after physical nutriment, cannot be had, unless the machinery for providing it is kept unintermittedly in active play. Our notion, therefore, of the claim we have on our fellow-creatures to join in making safe for us the very groundwork of our existence, gathers feelings around it so much more intense than those concerned in any of the more common cases of utility, that the difference in degree (as is often the case in psychology) becomes a real difference in kind. The claim assumes that character of absoluteness, that apparent infinity, and incommensurability with all other considerations, which constitute the distinction between the feeling of right and wrong and that of ordinary expediency and inexpediency. The feelings concerned are so powerful, and we count so positively on finding a responsive feeling in others (all being alike interested), that ought and should grow into must, and recognised indispensability becomes a moral necessity, analogous to physical, and often not inferior to it in binding force exhorted.

It appears from what has been said, that justice is a name for certain moral requirements, which, regarded collectively, stand higher in the scale of social utility, and are therefore of more paramount obligation, than any others; though particular cases may occur in which some other social duty is so important, as to overrule any one of the general maxims of justice. Thus, to save a life, it may not only be allowable, but a duty, to steal, or take by force, the necessary food or medicine, or to kidnap, and compel to officiate, the only qualified medical practitioner. In such cases, as we do not call anything justice which is not a virtue, we usually say, not that justice must give way to some other moral principle, but that what is just in ordinary cases is, by reason of that other principle, not just in the particular case. By this useful accommodation of language, the character of indefeasibility attributed to justice is kept up, and we are saved from the necessity of maintaining that there can be laudable injustice. . . .

Justice remains the appropriate name for certain social utilities which are vastly more important, and therefore more absolute and imperative, than any others are as a class (though not more so than others may be in particular cases); and which, therefore, ought to be, as well as naturally are, guarded by a sentiment not only different in degree, but also in kind; distinguished from the milder feeling which attaches to the mere idea of promoting human pleasure or convenience, at once by the more definite nature of its commands, and by the sterner character of its sanctions.

The Metaphysics of Morals

IMMANUEL KANT
translated by Thomas Kingsmill Abbott

Transition from the Common Rational Knowledge of Morality to the Philosophical

Nothing can possibly be conceived in the world, or even out of it, which can be called good, without qualification, except a good will. Intelligence, wit, judgment, and the other talents of the mind, however they may be named, or courage, resolution, perseverance, as qualities of temperament, are undoubtedly good and desirable in many respects; but these gifts of nature may also become extremely bad and mischievous if the will which is to make use of them, and which, therefore, constitutes what is called character, is not good. It is the same with the gifts of fortune. Power, riches, honour, even health, and the general well-being and contentment with one's condition which is called happiness, inspire pride, and often presumption, if there is not a good will to correct the influence of these on the mind, and with this also to rectify the whole principle of acting and adapt it to its end. The sight of a being who is not adorned with a single feature of a pure and good will, enjoying unbroken prosperity, can never give pleasure to an impartial rational spectator. Thus a good will appears to constitute the indispensable condition even of being worthy of happiness.

There are even some qualities which are of service to this good will itself and may facilitate its action, yet which have no intrinsic unconditional value, but always presuppose a good will, and this qualifies the esteem that we justly have for them and does not permit us to regard them as absolutely good. Moderation in the affections and passions, self-control, and calm deliberation are not only good in many respects, but even seem to constitute part of the intrinsic worth of the person; but they are far from deserving to be called good without qualification, although they have been so unconditionally praised by the ancients. For without the principles of a good will, they may become extremely bad, and the coolness of a villain not only makes him far more dangerous, but also directly makes him more abominable in our eyes than he would have been without it.

A good will is good not because of what it performs or effects, not by its aptness for the attainment of some proposed end, but simply by virtue of the volition; that is, it is good in itself, and considered by itself is to be esteemed much higher than all that can be brought about by it in favour of any inclination, nay even of the sum total of all inclinations. Even if it should happen that, owing to special disfavour of fortune, or the niggardly provision of a step-motherly nature, this will should wholly lack power to accomplish its purpose, if with its greatest efforts it should yet achieve nothing, and there should remain only the good will (not, to be sure, a mere wish, but the summoning of all means in our power), then, like a jewel, it would still shine by its own light, as a thing which has its whole value in itself. Its usefulness or fruitfulness can neither add nor take away anything from this value. . . .

And, in fact, we find that the more a cultivated reason applies itself with deliberate purpose to the enjoyment of life and happiness, so much the more does the man fail of true satisfaction. And from this circumstance there arises in many, if they are candid enough to confess it, a certain degree of misology, that is, hatred of reason, especially in the case of those who are most experienced in the use of it, because after calculating all the advantages they derive, I do not say from the invention of all the arts of common luxury, but even from the sciences (which seem to them to be after all only a luxury of the understanding), they find that they have, in fact, only brought more trouble on their shoulders rather than gained in happiness; and they end by envying, rather than despising, the more common stamp of men who keep closer to the guidance of mere instinct and do not allow their reason much influence on their conduct. And this we must admit, that the judgement of those who would very much lower the lofty eulogies of the advantages which reason gives us in regard to the happiness and satisfaction of life, or who would even reduce them below zero, is by no means morose or ungrateful to the goodness with which the world is governed, but that there lies at the root of these judgements the idea that our existence has a different and far nobler end, for which, and not for happiness, reason is properly intended, and which must, therefore, be regarded as the supreme condition to which the private ends of man must, for the most part, be postponed.

For as reason is not competent to guide the will with certainty in regard to its objects and the satisfaction of all our wants (which it to some extent even multiplies), this being an end to which an implanted instinct would have led with much greater certainty; and since, nevertheless, reason is imparted to us as a practical faculty, i.e., as one which is to have influence on the will, therefore, admitting that nature generally in the distribution of her capacities has adapted the means to the end, its true destination must be to produce a will, not merely good as a means to something else, but good in itself, for which reason was absolutely necessary. This will then, though not indeed the sole and complete good, must be the supreme good and the condition of every other, even of the desire of happiness. Under these circumstances, there is nothing inconsistent with the wisdom of nature in the fact that the cultivation of the reason, which is requisite for the first and unconditional purpose, does in many ways interfere, at least in this life, with the attainment of the second, which is always conditional, namely, happiness. Nay, it may even reduce it to nothing, without nature thereby failing of her purpose. For reason recognizes the establishment of a good will as its highest practical destination, and in attaining this purpose is capable only of a satisfaction of its own proper kind, namely that from the attainment of an end, which end again is determined by reason only, notwithstanding that this may involve many a disappointment to the ends of inclination.

We have then to develop the notion of a will which deserves to be highly esteemed for itself and is good without a view to anything further, a notion which exists already in the sound natural understanding, requiring rather to be cleared up than to be taught, and which in estimating the value of our actions always takes the first place and constitutes the condition of all the rest. In order to do this, we will take the notion of duty, which includes that of a good will, although implying certain subjective restrictions and hindrances. These, however, far from concealing it, or rendering it unrecognizable, rather bring it out by contrast and make it shine forth so much the brighter.

I omit here all actions which are already recognized as inconsistent with duty, although they may be useful for this or that purpose, for with these the question whether they are done from duty cannot arise at all, since they even conflict with it. I also set aside those actions which really conform to duty, but to which men have no direct inclination, performing them because they are impelled thereto by some other inclination. For in this case we can readily distinguish whether the action which agrees with duty is done from duty, or from a selfish view. It is much harder to make this distinction when the action accords with duty and the subject has besides a direct inclination to it. For example, it is always a matter of duty that a dealer should not over charge an inexperienced purchaser; and wherever there is much commerce the prudent tradesman does not overcharge, but keeps a fixed price for everyone, so that a child buys of him as well as any other. Men are thus honestly served; but this is not enough to make us believe that the tradesman has so acted from duty and from principles of honesty: his own advantage required it; it is out of the question in this case to suppose that he might besides have a direct inclination in favour of the buyers, so that, as it were, from love he should give no advantage to one over another. Accordingly the action was done neither from duty nor from direct inclination, but merely with a selfish view.

On the other hand, it is a duty to maintain one's life; and, in addition, everyone has also a direct inclination to do so. But on this account the anxious care which most men take for it has no intrinsic worth, and their maxim has no moral import. They preserve their life as duty requires, no doubt, but not because duty requires. On the other hand, if adversity and hopeless sorrow have completely taken away the relish for life; if the unfortunate one, strong in mind, indignant at his fate rather than desponding or dejected, wishes for death, and yet preserves his life without loving it—not from inclination or fear, but from duty—then his maxim has a moral worth.

To be beneficent when we can is a duty; and besides this, there are many minds so sympathetically constituted that, without any other motive of vanity or self-interest, they find a pleasure in spreading joy around them and can take delight in the satisfaction of others so far as it is their own work. But I maintain that in such a case an action of this kind, however proper, however amiable it may be, has nevertheless no true moral worth, but is on a level with other inclinations, e.g., the inclination to honour, which, if it is happily directed to that which is in fact of public utility and accordant with duty and consequently honourable, deserves praise and encouragement, but not esteem. For the maxim lacks the moral import, namely, that such actions be done from duty, not from inclination. Put the case that the mind of that philanthropist were clouded by sorrow of his own, extinguishing all sympathy with the lot of others, and that, while he still has the power to benefit others in distress, he is not touched by their trouble because he is absorbed with his own; and now suppose that he tears himself out of this dead insensibility, and performs the action without any inclination to it, but simply from duty, then first has his action its genuine moral worth. Further still; if nature has put little sympathy in the heart of this or that man; if he, supposed to be an upright man, is by temperament cold and indifferent to the sufferings of others, perhaps because in respect of his own he is provided with the special gift of patience and fortitude and supposes, or even requires, that others should have the same—and such a man would certainly not be the meanest product of nature—but if nature had not specially framed him for a philanthropist, would he not still find in himself a source from whence to give himself a far higher worth than that of a good-natured temperament could be? Unquestionably. It is just in this that the moral worth of the character is brought out which is incomparably the highest of all, namely, that he is beneficent, not from inclination, but from duty.

To secure one's own happiness is a duty, at least indirectly; for discontent with one's condition, under a pressure of many anxieties and amidst unsatisfied wants, might easily become a great temptation to transgression of duty. But here again, without looking to duty, all men have already the strongest and most intimate inclination to happiness, because it is just in this idea that all inclinations are combined in one total. But the precept of happiness is often of such a sort that it greatly interferes with some inclinations, and yet a man cannot form any definite and certain conception of the sum of satisfaction of all of them which is called happiness. It is not then to be wondered at that a single inclination, definite both as to what it promises and as to the time within which it can be gratified, is often able to overcome such a fluctuating idea, and that a gouty patient, for instance, can choose to enjoy what he likes, and to suffer what he may, since, according to his calculation, on this occasion at least, he has not sacrificed the enjoyment of the present moment to a possibly mistaken expectation of a happiness which is supposed to be found in health. But even in this case, if the general desire for happiness did not influence his will, and supposing that in his particular case health was not a necessary element in this calculation, there yet remains in this, as in all other cases, this law, namely, that he should promote his happiness not from inclination but from duty, and by this would his conduct first acquire true moral worth.

It is in this manner, undoubtedly, that we are to understand those passages of Scripture also in which we are commanded to love our neighbour, even our enemy. For love, as an affection, cannot be commanded, but beneficence for duty's sake may; even though we are not impelled to it by any inclination—nay, are even repelled by a natural and unconquerable aversion. This is practical love and not pathological—a love which is seated in the will, and not in the propensions of sense—in principles of action and not of tender sympathy; and it is this love alone which can be commanded.

The second proposition is: That an action done from duty derives its moral worth, not from the purpose which is to be attained by it, but from the maxim by which it is determined, and therefore does not depend on the realization of the object of the action, but merely on the principle of volition by which the action has taken place, without regard to any object of desire. It is clear from what precedes that the purposes which we may have in view in our actions, or their effects regarded as ends and springs of the will, cannot give to actions any unconditional or moral worth. In what, then, can their worth lie, if it is not to consist in the will and in reference to its expected effect? It cannot lie anywhere but in the principle of the will without regard to the ends which can be attained by the action. For the will stands between its a priori principle, which is formal, and its a posteriori spring, which is material, as between two roads, and as it must be determined by something, is that it must be determined by the formal principle of volition when an action is done from duty, in which case every material principle has been withdrawn from it.

The third proposition, which is a consequence of the two preceding, I would express thus: Duty is the necessity of acting from respect for the law. I may have inclination for an object as the effect of my proposed action, but I cannot have respect for it, just for this reason, that it is an effect and not an energy of will. Similarly I cannot have respect for inclination, whether my own or another's; I can at most, if my own, approve it; if another's, sometimes even love it; i.e., look on it as favourable to my own interest. It is only what is connected with my will as a principle, by no means as an effect—what does not subserve my inclination, but overpowers it, or at least in case of choice excludes it from its calculation—in other words, simply the law of itself, which can be an object of respect, and hence a command. Now an action done from duty must wholly exclude the influence of inclination and with it every object of the will, so that nothing remains which can determine the will except objectively the law, and subjectively pure respect for this practical law, and consequently the maxim that I should follow this law even to the thwarting of all my inclinations.

Thus the moral worth of an action does not lie in the effect expected from it, nor in any principle of action which requires to borrow its motive from this expected effect. For all these effects—agreeableness of one's condition and even the promotion of the happiness of others—could have been also brought about by other causes, so that for this there would have been no need of the will of a rational being; whereas it is in this alone that the supreme and unconditional good can be found. The pre-eminent good which we call moral can therefore consist in nothing else than the conception of law in itself, which certainly is only possible in a rational being, in so far as this conception, and not the expected effect, determines the will. This is a good which is already present in the person who acts accordingly, and we have not to wait for it to appear first in the result.

But what sort of law can that be, the conception of which must determine the will, even without paying any regard to the effect expected from it, in order that this will may be called good absolutely and without qualification? As I have deprived the will of every impulse which could arise to it from obedience to any law, there remains nothing but the universal conformity of its actions to law in general, which alone is to serve the will as a principle, i.e., I am never to act otherwise than so that I could also will that my maxim should become a universal law. Here, now, it is the simple conformity to law in general, without assuming any particular law applicable to certain actions, that serves the will as its principle and must so serve it, if duty is not to be a vain delusion and a chimerical notion. The common reason of men in its practical judgements perfectly coincides with this and always has in view the principle here suggested. Let the question be, for example: May I when in distress make a promise with the intention not to keep it? I readily distinguish here between the two significations which the question may have: Whether it is prudent, or whether it is right, to make a false promise? The former may undoubtedly be the case. I see clearly indeed that it is not enough to extricate myself from a present difficulty by means of this subterfuge, but it must be well considered whether there may not hereafter spring from this lie much greater inconvenience than that from which I now free myself, and as, with all my supposed cunning, the consequences cannot be so easily foreseen but that credit once lost may be much more injurious to me than any mischief which I seek to avoid at present, it should be considered whether it would not be more prudent to act herein according to a universal maxim and to make it a habit to promise nothing except with the intention of keeping it. But it is soon clear to me that such a maxim will still only be based on the fear of consequences. Now it is a wholly different thing to be truthful from duty and to be so from apprehension of injurious consequences. In the first case, the very notion of the action already implies a law for me; in the second case, I must first look about elsewhere to see what results may be combined with it which would affect myself. For to deviate from the principle of duty is beyond all doubt wicked; but to be unfaithful to my maxim of prudence may often be very advantageous to me, although to abide by it is certainly safer. The shortest way, however, and an unerring one, to discover the answer to this question whether a lying promise is consistent with duty, is to ask myself, "Should I be content that my maxim (to extricate myself from difficulty by a false promise) should hold good as a universal law, for myself as well as for others?" And should I be able to say to myself, "Every one may make a deceitful promise when he finds himself in a difficulty from which he cannot otherwise extricate himself?" Then I presently become aware that while I can will the lie, I can by no means will that lying should be a universal law. For with such a law there would be no promises at all, since it would be in vain to allege my intention in regard to my future actions to those who would not believe this allegation, or if they over hastily did so would pay me back in my own coin. Hence my maxim, as soon as it should be made a universal law, would necessarily destroy itself.

I do not, therefore, need any far-reaching penetration to discern what I have to do in order that my will may be morally good. Inexperienced in the course of the world, incapable of being prepared for all its contingencies, I only ask myself: Canst thou also will that thy maxim should be a universal law? If not, then it must be rejected, and that not because of a disadvantage accruing from it to myself or even to others, but because it cannot enter as a principle into a possible universal legislation, and reason extorts from me immediate respect for such legislation. I do not indeed as yet discern on what this respect is based (this the philosopher may inquire), but at least I understand this, that it is an estimation of the worth which far outweighs all worth of what is recommended by inclination, and that the necessity of acting from pure respect for the practical law is what constitutes duty, to which every other motive must give place, because it is the condition of a will being good in itself, and the worth of such a will is above everything.

Thus, then, without quitting the moral knowledge of common human reason, we have arrived at its principle. And although, no doubt, common men do not conceive it in such an abstract and universal form, yet they always have it really before their eyes and use it as the standard of their decision. Here it would be easy to show how, with this compass in hand, men are well able to distinguish, in every case that occurs, what is good, what bad, conformably to duty or inconsistent with it, if, without in the least teaching them anything new, we only, like Socrates, direct their attention to the principle they themselves employ; and that, therefore, we do not need science and philosophy to know what we should do to be honest and good, yea, even wise and virtuous. Indeed we might well have conjectured beforehand that the knowledge of what every man is bound to do, and therefore also to know, would be within the reach of every man, even the commonest. Here we cannot forbear admiration when we see how great an advantage the practical judgement has over the theoretical in the common understanding of men. In the latter, if common reason ventures to depart from the laws of experience and from the perceptions of the senses, it falls into mere inconceivabilities and self-contradictions, at least into a chaos of uncertainty, obscurity, and instability. But in the practical sphere it is just when the common understanding excludes all sensible springs from practical laws that its power of judgement begins to show itself to advantage. It then becomes even subtle, whether it be that it chicanes with its own conscience or with other claims respecting what is to be called right, or whether it desires for its own instruction to determine honestly the worth of actions; and, in the latter case, it may even have as good a hope of hitting the mark as any philosopher whatever can promise himself. Nay, it is almost more sure of doing so, because the philosopher cannot have any other principle, while he may easily perplex his judgement by a multitude of considerations foreign to the matter, and so turn aside from the right way. Would it not therefore be wiser in moral concerns to acquiesce in the judgement of common reason, or at most only to call in philosophy for the purpose of rendering the system of morals more complete and intelligible, and its rules more convenient for use (especially for disputation), but not so as to draw off the common understanding from its happy simplicity, or to bring it by means of philosophy into a new path of inquiry and instruction? . . .

Everything in nature works according to laws. Rational beings alone have the faculty of acting according to the conception of laws, that is according to principles, i.e., have a will. Since the deduction of actions from principles requires reason, the will is nothing but practical reason. If reason infallibly determines the will, then the actions of such a being which are recognised as objectively necessary are subjectively necessary also, i.e., the will is a faculty to choose that only which reason independent of inclination recognises as practically necessary, i.e., as good. But if reason of itself does not sufficiently determine the will, if the latter is subject also to subjective conditions (particular impulses) which do not always coincide with the objective conditions; in a word, if the will does not in itself completely accord with reason (which is actually the case with men), then the actions which objectively are recognised as necessary are subjectively contingent, and the determination of such a will according to objective laws is obligation, that is to say, the relation of the objective laws to a will that is not thoroughly good is conceived as the determination of the will of a rational being by principles of reason, but which the will from its nature does not of necessity follow.

The conception of an objective principle, in so far as it is obligatory for a will, is called a command (of reason), and the formula of the command is called an imperative. All imperatives are expressed by the word ought [or shall], and thereby indicate the relation of an objective law of reason to a will, which from its subjective constitution is not necessarily determined by it (an obligation). They say that something would be good to do or to forbear, but they say it to a will which does not always do a thing because it is conceived to be good to do it. That is practically good, however, which determines the will by means of the conceptions of reason, and consequently not from subjective causes, but objectively, that is on principles which are valid for every rational being as such. It is distinguished from the pleasant, as that which influences the will only by means of sensation from merely subjective causes, valid only for the sense of this or that one, and not as a principle of reason, which holds for every one. . . .

The dependence of the desires on sensations is called inclination, and this accordingly always indicates a want. The dependence of a contingently determinable will on principles of reason is called an interest. This therefore, is found only in the case of a dependent will which does not always of itself conform to reason; in the Divine will we cannot conceive any interest. But the human will can also take an interest in a thing without therefore acting from interest. The former signifies the practical interest in the action, the latter the pathological in the object of the action. The former indicates only dependence of the will on principles of reason in themselves; the second, dependence on principles of reason for the sake of inclination, reason supplying only the practical rules how the requirement of the inclination may be satisfied. In the first case the action interests me; in the second the object of the action (because it is pleasant to me). We have seen in the first section that in an action done from duty we must look not to the interest in the object, but only to that in the action itself, and in its rational principle (viz., the law).

A perfectly good will would therefore be equally subject to objective laws (viz., laws of good), but could not be conceived as obliged thereby to act lawfully, because of itself from its subjective constitution it can only be determined by the conception of good. Therefore no imperatives hold for the Divine will, or in general for a holy will; ought is here out of place, because the volition is already of itself necessarily in unison with the law. Therefore imperatives are only formulae to express the relation of objective laws of all volition to the subjective imperfection of the will of this or that rational being, e.g., the human will.

Now all imperatives command either hypothetically or categorically. The former represent the practical necessity of a possible action as means to something else that is willed (or at least which one might possibly will). The categorical imperative would be that which represented an action as necessary of itself without reference to another end, i.e., as objectively necessary.

Since every practical law represents a possible action as good and, on this account, for a subject who is practically determinable by reason, necessary, all imperatives are formulae determining an action which is necessary according to the principle of a will good in some respects. If now the action is good only as a means to something else, then the imperative is hypothetical; if it is conceived as good in itself and consequently as being necessarily the principle of a will which of itself conforms to reason, then it is categorical.

Thus the imperative declares what action possible by me would be good and presents the practical rule in relation to a will which does not forthwith perform an action simply because it is good, whether because the subject does not always know that it is good, or because, even if it know this, yet its maxims might be opposed to the objective principles of practical reason. Accordingly the hypothetical imperative only says that the action is good for some purpose, possible or actual. In the first case it is a problematical, in the second an assertorial practical principle. The categorical imperative which declares an action to be objectively necessary in itself without reference to any purpose, i.e., without any other end, is valid as an apodeictic (practical) principle.

Whatever is possible only by the power of some rational being may also be conceived as a possible purpose of some will; and therefore the principles of action as regards the means necessary to attain some possible purpose are in fact infinitely numerous. All sciences have a practical part, consisting of problems expressing that some end is possible for us and of imperatives directing how it may be attained. These may, therefore, be called in general imperatives of skill. Here there is no question whether the end is rational and good, but only what one must do in order to attain it. The precepts for the physician to make his patient thoroughly healthy, and for a poisoner to ensure certain death, are of equal value in this respect, that each serves to effect its purpose perfectly. Since in early youth it cannot be known what ends are likely to occur to us in the course of life, parents seek to have their children taught a great many things, and provide for their skill in the use of means for all sorts of arbitrary ends, of none of which can they determine whether it may not perhaps hereafter be an object to their pupil, but which it is at all events possible that he might aim at; and this anxiety is so great that they commonly neglect to form and correct their judgement on the value of the things which may be chosen as ends.

There is one end, however, which may be assumed to be actually such to all rational beings (so far as imperatives apply to them, viz., as dependent beings), and, therefore, one purpose which they not merely may have, but which we may with certainty assume that they all actually have by a natural necessity, and this is happiness. The hypothetical imperative which expresses the practical necessity of an action as means to the advancement of happiness is assertorial. We are not to present it as necessary for an uncertain and merely possible purpose, but for a purpose which we may presuppose with certainty and a priori in every man, because it belongs to his being. Now skill in the choice of means to his own greatest well-being may be called prudence, in the narrowest sense. And thus the imperative which refers to the choice of means to one's own happiness, i.e., the precept of prudence, is still always hypothetical; the action is not commanded absolutely, but only as means to another purpose.

Finally, there is an imperative which commands a certain conduct immediately, without having as its condition any other purpose to be attained by it. This imperative is categorical. It concerns not the matter of the action, or its intended result, but its form and the principle of which it is itself a result; and what is essentially good in it consists in the mental disposition, let the consequence be what it may. This imperative may be called that of morality.

There is a marked distinction also between the volitions on these three sorts of principles in the dissimilarity of the obligation of the will. In order to mark this difference more clearly, I think they would be most suitably named in their order if we said they are either rules of skill, or counsels of prudence, or commands (laws) of morality. For it is law only that involves the conception of an unconditional and objective necessity, which is consequently universally valid; and commands are laws which must be obeyed, that is, must be followed, even in opposition to inclination. Counsels, indeed, involve necessity, but one which can only hold under a contingent subjective condition, viz., they depend on whether this or that man reckons this or that as part of his happiness; the categorical imperative, on the contrary, is not limited by any condition, and as being absolutely, although practically, necessary, may be quite properly called a command. We might also call the first kind of imperatives technical (belonging to art), the second pragmatic (to welfare), the third moral (belonging to free conduct generally, that is, to morals). . . .

Since the universality of the law according to which effects are produced constitutes what is properly called nature in the most general sense (as to form), that is the existence of things so far as it is determined by general laws, the imperative of duty may be expressed thus: Act as if the maxim of thy action were to become by thy will a universal law of nature.

We will now enumerate a few duties, adopting the usual division of them into duties to ourselves and ourselves and to others, and into perfect and imperfect duties.

A man reduced to despair by a series of misfortunes feels wearied of life, but is still so far in possession of his reason that he can ask himself whether it would not be contrary to his duty to himself to take his own life. Now he inquires whether the maxim of his action could become a universal law of nature. His maxim is: "From self-love I adopt it as a principle to shorten my life when its longer duration is likely to bring more evil than satisfaction." It is asked then simply whether this principle founded on self-love can become a universal law of nature. Now we see at once that a system of nature of which it should be a law to destroy life by means of the very feeling whose special nature it is to impel to the improvement of life would contradict itself and, therefore, could not exist as a system of nature; hence that maxim cannot possibly exist as a universal law of nature and, consequently, would be wholly inconsistent with the supreme principle of all duty.

Another finds himself forced by necessity to borrow money. He knows that he will not be able to repay it, but sees also that nothing will be lent to him unless he promises stoutly to repay it in a definite time. He desires to make this promise, but he has still so much conscience as to ask himself: "Is it not unlawful and inconsistent with duty to get out of a difficulty in this way?" Suppose however that he resolves to do so: then the maxim of his action would be expressed thus: "When I think myself in want of money, I will borrow money and promise to repay it, although I know that I never can do so." Now this principle of self-love or of one's own advantage may perhaps be consistent with my whole future welfare; but the question now is, "Is it right?" I change then the suggestion of self-love into a universal law, and state the question thus: "How would it be if my maxim were a universal law?" Then I see at once that it could never hold as a universal law of nature, but would necessarily contradict itself. For supposing it to be a universal law that everyone when he thinks himself in a difficulty should be able to promise whatever he pleases, with the purpose of not keeping his promise, the promise itself would become impossible, as well as the end that one might have in view in it, since no one would consider that anything was promised to him, but would ridicule all such statements as vain pretences.

A third finds in himself a talent which with the help of some culture might make him a useful man in many respects. But he finds himself in comfortable circumstances and prefers to indulge in pleasure rather than to take pains in enlarging and improving his happy natural capacities. He asks, however, whether his maxim of neglect of his natural gifts, besides agreeing with his inclination to indulgence, agrees also with what is called duty. He sees then that a system of nature could indeed subsist with such a universal law although men (like the South Sea islanders) should let their talents rest and resolve to devote their lives merely to idleness, amusement, and propagation of their species—in a word, to enjoyment; but he cannot possibly will that this should be a universal law of nature, or be implanted in us as such by a natural instinct. For, as a rational being, he necessarily wills that his faculties be developed, since they serve him and have been given him, for all sorts of possible purposes.

A fourth, who is in prosperity, while he sees that others have to contend with great wretchedness and that he could help them, thinks: "What concern is it of mine? Let everyone be as happy as Heaven pleases, or as he can make himself; I will take nothing from him nor even envy him, only I do not wish to contribute anything to his welfare or to his assistance in distress!" Now no doubt if such a mode of thinking were a universal law, the human race might very well subsist and doubtless even better than in a state in which everyone talks of sympathy and good-will, or even takes care occasionally to put it into practice, but, on the other side, also cheats when he can, betrays the rights of men, or otherwise violates them. But although it is possible that a universal law of nature might exist in accordance with that maxim, it is impossible to will that such a principle should have the universal validity of a law of nature. For a will which resolved this would contradict itself, inasmuch as many cases might occur in which one would have need of the love and sympathy of others, and in which, by such a law of nature, sprung from his own will, he would deprive himself of all hope of the aid he desires.

These are a few of the many actual duties, or at least what we regard as such, which obviously fall into two classes on the one principle that we have laid down. We must be able to will that a maxim of our action should be a universal law. This is the canon of the moral appreciation of the action generally. Some actions are of such a character that their maxim cannot without contradiction be even conceived as a universal law of nature, far from it being possible that we should will that it should be so. In others this intrinsic impossibility is not found, but still it is impossible to will that their maxim should be raised to the universality of a law of nature, since such a will would contradict itself. It is easily seen that the former violate strict or rigorous (inflexible) duty; the latter only laxer (meritorious) duty. Thus it has been completely shown how all duties depend as regards the nature of the obligation (not the object of the action) on the same principle.

If now we attend to ourselves on occasion of any transgression of duty, we shall find that we in fact do not will that our maxim should be a universal law, for that is impossible for us; on the contrary, we will that the opposite should remain a universal law, only we assume the liberty of making an exception in our own favour or (just for this time only) in favour of our inclination. Consequently if we considered all cases from one and the same point of view, namely, that of reason, we should find a contradiction in our own will, namely, that a certain principle should be objectively necessary as a universal law, and yet subjectively should not be universal, but admit of exceptions. As however we at one moment regard our action from the point of view of a will wholly conformed to reason, and then again look at the same action from the point of view of a will affected by inclination, there is not really any contradiction, but an antagonism of inclination to the precept of reason, whereby the universality of the principle is changed into a mere generality, so that the practical principle of reason shall meet the maxim half way. Now, although this cannot be justified in our own impartial judgement, yet it proves that we do really recognise the validity of the categorical imperative and (with all respect for it) only allow ourselves a few exceptions, which we think unimportant and forced from us. . . .

Now I say: man and generally any rational being exists as an end in himself, not merely as a means to be arbitrarily used by this or that will, but in all his actions, whether they concern himself or other rational beings, must be always regarded at the same time as an end. All objects of the inclinations have only a conditional worth, for if the inclinations and the wants founded on them did not exist, then their object would be without value. But the inclinations, themselves being sources of want, are so far from having an absolute worth for which they should be desired that on the contrary it must be the universal wish of every rational being to be wholly free from them. Thus the worth of any object which is to be acquired by our action is always conditional. Beings whose existence depends not on our will but on nature's, have nevertheless, if they are irrational beings, only a relative value as means, and are therefore called things; rational beings, on the contrary, are called persons, because their very nature points them out as ends in themselves, that is as something which must not be used merely as means, and so far therefore restricts freedom of action (and is an object of respect). These, therefore, are not merely subjective ends whose existence has a worth for us as an effect of our action, but objective ends, that is, things whose existence is an end in itself; an end moreover for which no other can be substituted, which they should subserve merely as means, for otherwise nothing whatever would possess absolute worth; but if all worth were conditioned and therefore contingent, then there would be no supreme practical principle of reason whatever.

If then there is a supreme practical principle or, in respect of the human will, a categorical imperative, it must be one which, being drawn from the conception of that which is necessarily an end for everyone because it is an end in itself, constitutes an objective principle of will, and can therefore serve as a universal practical law. The foundation of this principle is: rational nature exists as an end in itself. Man necessarily conceives his own existence as being so; so far then this is a subjective principle of human actions. But every other rational being regards its existence similarly, just on the same rational principle that holds for me: so that it is at the same time an objective principle, from which as a supreme practical law all laws of the will must be capable of being deduced. Accordingly the practical imperative will be as follows: So act as to treat humanity, whether in thine own person or in that of any other, in every case as an end withal, never as means only. We will now inquire whether this can be practically carried out.

To abide by the previous examples: Firstly, under the head of necessary duty to oneself: He who contemplates suicide should ask himself whether his action can be consistent with the idea of humanity as an end in itself. If he destroys himself in order to escape from painful circumstances, he uses a person merely as a mean to maintain a tolerable condition up to the end of life. But a man is not a thing, that is to say, something which can be used merely as means, but must in all his actions be always considered as an end in himself. I cannot, therefore, dispose in any way of a man in my own person so as to mutilate him, to damage or kill him. (It belongs to ethics proper to define this principle more precisely, so as to avoid all misunderstanding, e. g., as to the amputation of the limbs in order to preserve myself, as to exposing my life to danger with a view to preserve it, etc. This question is therefore omitted here.)

Secondly, as regards necessary duties, or those of strict obligation, towards others: He who is thinking of making a lying promise to others will see at once that he would be using another man merely as a mean, without the latter containing at the same time the end in himself. For he whom I propose by such a promise to use for my own purposes cannot possibly assent to my mode of acting towards him and, therefore, cannot himself contain the end of this action. This violation of the principle of humanity in other men is more obvious if we take in examples of attacks on the freedom and property of others. For then it is clear that he who transgresses the rights of men intends to use the person of others merely as a means, without considering that as rational beings they ought always to be esteemed also as ends, that is, as beings who must be capable of containing in themselves the end of the very same action.

Thirdly, as regards contingent (meritorious) duties to oneself: It is not enough that the action does not violate humanity in our own person as an end in itself, it must also harmonize with it. Now there are in humanity capacities of greater perfection, which belong to the end that nature has in view in regard to humanity in ourselves as the subject: to neglect these might perhaps be consistent with the maintenance of humanity as an end in itself, but not with the advancement of this end.

Fourthly, as regards meritorious duties towards others: The natural end which all men have is their own happiness. Now humanity might indeed subsist, although no one should contribute anything to the happiness of others, provided he did not intentionally withdraw anything from it; but after all this would only harmonize negatively not positively with humanity as an end in itself, if every one does not also endeavour, as far as in him lies, to forward the ends of others. For the ends of any subject which is an end in himself ought as far as possible to be my ends also, if that conception is to have its full effect with me.

This principle, that humanity and generally every rational nature is an end in itself (which is the supreme limiting condition of every man's freedom of action), is not borrowed from experience, firstly, because it is universal, applying as it does to all rational beings whatever, and experience is not capable of determining anything about them; secondly, because it does not present humanity as an end to men (subjectively), that is as an object which men do of themselves actually adopt as an end; but as an objective end, which must as a law constitute the supreme limiting condition of all our subjective ends, let them be what we will; it must therefore spring from pure reason. In fact the objective principle of all practical legislation lies (according to the first principle) in the rule and its form of universality which makes it capable of being a law (say, e. g., a law of nature); but the subjective principle is in the end; now by the second principle the subject of all ends is each rational being, inasmuch as it is an end in itself. Hence follows the third practical principle of the will, which is the ultimate condition of its harmony with universal practical reason, viz.: the idea of the will of every rational being as a universally legislative will.

On this principle all maxims are rejected which are inconsistent with the will being itself universal legislator. Thus the will is not subject simply to the law, but so subject that it must be regarded as itself giving the law and, on this ground only, subject to the law (of which it can regard itself as the author).

Feminist Transformations of Moral Theory

VIRGINIA HELD

The history of philosophy, including the history of ethics, has been constructed from male points of view, and has been built on assumptions and concepts that are by no means gender-neutral.[1] Feminists characteristically begin with different concerns and give different emphases to the issues we consider than do non-feminist approaches. And, as Lorraine Code expresses it, "starting points and focal points shape the impact of theoretical discussion."[2] Within philosophy, feminists often start with, and focus on, quite different issues than those found in standard philosophy and ethics, however "standard" is understood. Far from providing mere additional insights which can be incorporated into traditional theory, feminist explorations often require radical transformations of existing fields of inquiry and theory.[3] From a feminist point of view, moral theory along with almost all theory will have to be transformed to take adequate account of the experience of women.

I shall in this paper begin with a brief examination of how various fundamental aspects of the history of ethics have not been gender-neutral. And I shall discuss three issues where feminist rethinking is transforming moral concepts and theories.

The History of Ethics

Consider the ideals embodied in the phrase "the man of reason." As Genevieve Lloyd has told the story, what has been taken to characterize the man of reason may have changed from historical period to historical period, but in each, the character ideal of the man of reason has been constructed in conjunction with a rejection of whatever has been taken to be characteristic of the feminine. "Rationality," Lloyd writes, "has been conceived as transcendence of the 'feminine,' and the 'feminine' itself has been partly constituted by its occurrence within this structure."[4]

This has of course fundamentally affected the history of philosophy and of ethics. The split between reason and emotion is one of the most familiar of philosophical conceptions. And the advocacy of reason "controlling" unruly emotion, of rationality guiding responsible human action against the blindness of passion, has a long and highly influential history, almost as familiar to non-philosophers as to philosophers. We should certainly now be alert to the ways in which reason has been associated with male endeavor, emotion with female weakness, and the ways in which this is of course not an accidental association. As Lloyd writes, "From the beginnings of philosophical thought, femaleness was symbolically associated with what Reason supposedly left behind—the dark powers of the earth goddesses, immersion in unknown forces associated with mysterious female powers. The early Greeks saw women's capacity to conceive as connecting them with the fertility of Nature. As Plato later expressed the thought, women imitate the earth."[5]

Reason, in asserting its claims and winning its status in human history, was thought to have to conquer the female forces of Unreason. Reason and clarity of thought were early associated with maleness, and as Lloyd notes, "what had to be shed in developing culturally prized rationality was, from the start, symbolically associated with femaleness."[6] In later Greek philosophical thought, the form/matter distinction was articulated, and with a similar hierarchical and gendered association. Maleness was aligned with active, determinate, and defining form; femaleness with mere passive, indeterminate, and inferior matter. Plato, in the Timaeus, compared the defining aspect of form with the father, and indefinite matter with the mother; Aristotle also compared the form/matter distinction with the male/female distinction. To quote Lloyd again, "This comparison . . . meant that the very nature of knowledge was implicitly associated with the extrusion of what was symbolically associated with the feminine."[7]

The associations, between Reason, form, knowledge, and maleness, have persisted in various guises, and have permeated what has been thought to be moral knowledge as well as what has been thought to be scientific knowledge, and what has been thought to be the practice of morality. The associations between the philosophical concepts and gender cannot be merely dropped, and the concepts retained regardless of gender, because gender has been built into them in such a way that without it, they will have to be different concepts. As feminists repeatedly show, if the concept of "human" were built on what we think about "woman" rather than what we think about "man," it would be a very different concept. Ethics, thus, has not been a search for universal, or truly human guidance, but a gender-biased enterprise.

Other distinctions and associations have supplemented and re-inforced the identification of reason with maleness, and of the irrational with the female; on this and other grounds "man" has been associated with the human, "woman" with the natural. Prominent among distinctions reinforcing the latter view has been that between the public and the private, because of the way they have been interpreted. Again, these provide as familiar and en-trenched a framework as do reason and emotion, and they have been as influential for non-philosophers as for philosophers. It has been supposed that in the public realm, man transcends his animal nature and creates human history. As citizen, he creates govern-ment and law; as warrior, he protects society by his willingness to risk death; and as artist or philosopher, he overcomes his human mortality. Here, in the public realm, morality should guide human decision. In the household, in contrast, it has been supposed that women merely "reproduce" life as natural, biological matter. Within the household, the "natural" needs of man for food and shelter are served, and new instances of the biological creature that man is are brought into being. But what is distinctively human, and what transcends any given level of development to create human progress, are thought to occur elsewhere.

This contrast was made highly explicit in Aristotle's concep-tions of polis and household; it has continued to affect the basic assumptions of a remarkably broad swath of thought ever since. In ancient Athens, women were confined to the household; the public sphere was literally a male domain. In more recent history, though women have been permitted to venture into public space, the associations of the public, historically male sphere with the distinc-tively human, and of the household, historically a female sphere, with the merely natural and repetitious, have persisted. These associations have deeply affected moral theory, which has often supposed the transcendent, public domain to be relevant to the foundations of morality in ways that the natural behavior of women in the household could not be. To take some recent and representa-tive examples, David Heyd, in his discussion of supererogation, dismisses a mother's sacrifice for her child as an example of the supererogatory because it belongs, in his view, to "the sphere of natural relationships and instinctive feelings (which lie outside morality)."[8] J. Urmson had earlier taken a similar position. In his discussion of supererogation, Urmson said, "Let us be clear that we are not now considering cases of natural affection, such as the sacrifice made by a mother for her child; such cases may be said with some justice not to fall under the concept of morality. . . ."[9] And in a recent article called "Distrusting Economics," Alan Ryan argues persuasively about the questionableness of economics and other branches of the social sciences built on the assumption that human beings are rational, self-interested calculators; he discusses various examples of non self-interested behavior, such as of men in wartime, which show the assumption to be false, but nowhere in the article is there any mention of the activity of mothering, which would seem to be a fertile locus for doubts about the usual picture of rational man.[10] Although Ryan does not provide the kind of explicit reason offered by Heyd and Urmson for omitting the context of mothering from consideration as relevant to his discussion, it is difficult to understand the omission without a comparable assumption being implicit here, as it so often is elsewhere. Without feminist insistence on the relevance for morality of the experience in mothering, this context is largely ignored by moral theorists. And yet, from a gender-neutral point of view, how can this vast and fundamental domain of human experience possibly be imagined to lie "outside morality"?

The result of the public/private distinction, as usually formulated, has been to privilege the points of view of men in the public domains of state and law, and later in the marketplace, and to discount the experience of women. Mothering has been conceptualized as a primarily biological activity, even when performed by humans, and virtually no moral theory in the history of ethics has taken mothering, as experienced by women, seriously as a source of moral insight, until feminists in recent years have begun to.[11] Women have been seen as emotional rather than as rational beings, and thus as incapable of full moral personhood. Women's behavior has been interpreted as either "natural" and driven by instinct, and thus as irrelevant to morality and to the construction of moral principles, or it has been interpreted as, at best, in need of instruction and supervision by males better able to know what morality requires and better able to live up to its demands.

The Hobbesian conception of reason is very different from the Platonic or Aristotelian conceptions before it, and from the conceptions of Rousseau or Kant or Hegel later; all have in common that they ignore and disparage the experience and reality of women. Consider Hobbes' account of man in the state of nature contracting with other men to establish society. These men hypothetically come into existence fully formed and independent of one another, and decide on entering or staying outside of civil society. As Christine Di Stefano writes, "What we find in Hobbes's account of human nature and political order is a vital concern with the survival of a self conceived in masculine terms. . . . This masculine dimension of Hobbes's atomistic egoism is powerfully underscored in his state of nature, which is effectively built on the foundation of denied maternity."[12] In *The Citizen,* where Hobbes gave his first systematic exposition of the state of nature, he asks us to "consider men as if but even now sprung out of the earth, and suddenly, like mushrooms, come to full maturity, without all kind of engagement with each other."[13] As Di Stefano says, it is a most incredible and problematic feature of Hobbes's state of nature that the men in it "are not born of, much less nurtured by, women, or anyone else."[14] To abstract from the complex web of human reality an abstract man for rational perusal, Hobbes has, Di Stefano continues, "expunged human reproduction and early nurturance, two of the most basic and typically female-identified features of distinctively human life, from his account of basic human nature. Such a strategy ensures that he can present a thoroughly atomistic subject. . . ."[15] From the point of view of women's experience, such a subject or self is unbelievable and misleading, even as a theoretical construct. The Leviathan, Di Stefano writes, "is effectively comprised of a body politic of orphans who have reared themselves, whose desires are situated within and reflect nothing but independently generated movement. . . . These essential elements are natural human beings conceived along masculine lines."[16]

Rousseau, and Kant, and Hegel, paid homage to the emotional power, the aesthetic sensibility, and the familial concerns, respectively, of women. But since in their views morality must be based on rational principle, and women were incapable of full rationality, or a degree or kind of rationality comparable to that of men, women were deemed, in the view of these moralists, to be inherently wanting in morality. For Rousseau, women must be trained from childhood to submit to the will of men lest their sexual power lead both men and women to disaster. For Kant, women were thought incapable of achieving full moral personhood, and women lose all charm if they try to behave like men by engaging in rational pursuits. For Hegel, women's moral concern for their families could be admirable in its proper place, but is a threat to the more universal aims to which men, as members of the state, should aspire.[17]

These images, of the feminine as what must be overcome if knowledge and morality are to be achieved, of female experience as naturally irrelevant to morality, and of women as inherently deficient moral creatures, are built into the history of ethics. Feminists examine these images, and see that they are not the incidental or merely idiosyncratic suppositions of a few philosophers whose views on many topics depart far from the ordinary anyway. Such views are the nearly uniform reflection in philosophical and ethical theory of patriarchal attitudes pervasive throughout human history. Or they are exaggerations even of ordinary male experience, which exaggerations then reinforce rather than temper other patriarchal conceptions and institutions. They distort the actual experience and aspirations of many men as well as of women. Annette Baier recently speculated about why it is that moral philosophy has so seriously overlooked the trust between human beings that in her view is an utterly central aspect of moral life. She noted that "the great moral theorists in our tradition not only are all men, they are mostly men who had minimal adult dealings with (and so were then minimally influenced by) women."[18] They were for the most part "clerics, misogynists, and puritan bachelors," and thus it is not surprising that they focus their philosophical attention "so single-mindedly on cool, distanced relations between more or less free and equal adult strangers. . . ."[19]

As feminists, we deplore the patriarchal attitudes that so much of philosophy and moral theory reflect. But we recognize that the problem is more serious even than changing those attitudes. For moral theory as so far developed is incapable of correcting itself without an almost total transformation. It cannot simply absorb the gender that has been "left behind," even if both genders would want it to. To continue to build morality on rational principles opposed to the emotions and to include women among the rational will leave no one to reflect the promptings of the heart, which promptings can be moral rather than merely instinctive. To simply bring women into the public and male domain of the polis will leave no one to speak for the household. Its values have been hitherto unrecognized, but they are often moral values. Or to continue to seek contractual restraints on the pursuits of self-interest by atomistic individuals, and to have women join men in devotion to these pursuits, will leave no one involved in the nurturance of children and cultivation of social relations, which nurturance and cultivation can be of greatest moral import.

There are very good reasons for women not to want simply to be accorded entry as equals into the enterprise of morality as so far developed. In a recent survey of types of feminist moral theory, Kathryn Morgan notes that "many women who engage in philosophical reflection are acutely aware of the masculine nature of the profession and tradition, and feel their own moral concerns as women silenced or trivialized in virtually all the official settings that define the practice."[20] Women should clearly not agree, as the price of admission to the masculine realm of traditional morality, to abandon our own moral concerns as women.

And so we are groping to shape new moral theory. Understandably, we do not yet have fully worked out feminist moral theories to offer. But we can suggest some directions our project of developing such theories is taking. As Kathryn Morgan points out, there is not likely to be a "star" feminist moral theorist on the order of a Rawls or Nozick: "There will be no individual singled out for two reasons. One reason is that vital moral and theoretical conversations are taking place on a large dialectical scale as the feminist community struggles to develop a feminist ethic. The second reason is that this community of feminist theoreticians is calling into question the very model of the individualized autonomous self presupposed by a star-centered male-dominated tradition. . . . We experience it as a common labour, a common task."[21]

The dialogues that are enabling feminist approaches to moral theory to develop are proceeding. As Alison Jaggar makes clear in her useful overview of them, there is no unitary view of ethics that can be identified as "feminist ethics." Feminist approaches to ethics share a commitment to "rethinking ethics with a view to correcting whatever forms of male bias it may contain."[22] While those who develop these approaches are "united by a shared project, they diverge widely in their views as to how this project is to be accomplished."[23]

Not all feminists, by any means, agree that there are distinctive feminist virtues or values. Some are especially skeptical of the attempt to give positive value to such traditional "feminine virtues" as a willingness to nurture, or an affinity with caring, or reluctance to seek independence. They see this approach as playing into the hands of those who would confine women to traditional roles.[24] Other feminists are skeptical of all claims about women as such, emphasizing that women are divided by class and race and sexual orientation in ways that make any conclusions drawn from "women's experience" dubious.[25]

Still, it is possible, I think, to discern various important focal points evident in current feminist attempts to transform ethics into a theoretical and practical activity that could be acceptable from a feminist point of view. In the glimpse I have presented of bias in the history of ethics, I focused on what, from a feminist point of view, are three of its most questionable aspects: 1) the split between reason and emotion and the devaluation of emotion; 2) the public/private distinction and the relegation of the private to the natural; and 3) the concept of the self as constructed from a male point of view. In the remainder of this article, I shall consider further how some feminists are exploring these topics. We are showing how their previous treatment has been distorted, and we are trying to re-envision the realities and recommendations with which these aspects of moral theorizing do and should try to deal.

I. Reason and Emotion

In the area of moral theory in the modern era, the priority accorded to reason has taken two major forms. A) On the one hand has been the Kantian, or Kantian-inspired search for very general, abstract, deontological, universal moral principles by which rational beings should be guided. Kant's Categorical Imperative is a foremost example: it suggests that all moral problems can be handled by applying an impartial, pure, rational principle to particular cases. It requires that we try to see what the general features of the problem before us are, and that we apply an abstract principle, or rules derivable from it, to this problem. On this view, this procedure should be adequate for all moral decisions. We should thus be able to act as reason recommends, and resist yielding to emotional inclinations and desires in conflict with our rational wills.

B) On the other hand, the priority accorded to reason in the modern era has taken a Utilitarian form. The Utilitarian approach, reflected in rational choice theory, recognizes that persons have desires and interests, and suggests rules of rational choice for maximizing the satisfaction of these. While some philosophers in this tradition espouse egoism, especially of an intelligent and long-term kind, many do not. They begin, however, with assumptions that what are morally relevant are gains and losses of utility to theoretically isolatable individuals, and that the outcome at which morality should aim is the maximization of the utility of individuals. Rational calculation about such an outcome will, in this view, provide moral recommendations to guide all our choices. As with the Kantian approach, the Utilitarian approach relies on abstract general principles or rules to be applied to particular cases. And it holds that although emotion is, in fact, the source of our desires for certain objectives, the task of morality should be to instruct us on how to pursue those objectives most rationally. Emotional attitudes toward moral issues themselves interfere with rationality and should be disregarded. Among the questions Utilitarians can ask can be questions about which emotions to cultivate, and which desires to try to change, but these questions are to be handled in the terms of rational calculation, not of what our feelings suggest.

Although the conceptions of what the judgments of morality should be based on, and of how reason should guide moral decision, are different in Kantian and in Utilitarian approaches, both share a reliance on a highly abstract, universal principle as the appropriate source of moral guidance, and both share the view that moral problems are to be solved by the application of such an abstract principle to particular cases. Both share an admiration for the rules of reason to be appealed to in moral contexts, and both denigrate emotional responses to moral issues.

Many feminist philosophers have questioned whether the reliance on abstract rules, rather than the adoption of more context-respectful approaches, can possibly be adequate for dealing with moral problems, especially as women experience them.[26] Though Kantians may hold that complex rules can be elaborated for specific contexts, there is nevertheless an assumption in this approach that the more abstract the reasoning applied to a moral problem, the more satisfactory. And Utilitarians suppose that one highly abstract principle, The Principle of Utility, can be applied to every moral problem no matter what the context.

A genuinely universal or gender-neutral moral theory would be one which would take account of the experience and concerns of women as fully as it would take account of the experience and concerns of men. When we focus on the experience of women, however, we seem to be able to see a set of moral concerns becoming salient that differs from those of traditional or standard moral theory. Women's experience of moral problems seems to lead us to be especially concerned with actual relationships between embodied persons, and with what these relationships seem to require. Women are often inclined to attend to rather than to dismiss the particularities of the context in which a moral problem arises. And we often pay attention to feelings of empathy and caring to suggest what we ought to do rather than relying as fully as possible on abstract rules of reason.

Margaret Walker, for instance, contrasts feminist moral "understanding" with traditional moral "knowledge." She sees the components of the former as involving "attention, contextual and narrative appreciation, and communication in the event of moral deliberation."[27] This alternative moral epistemology holds that "the adequacy of moral understanding decreases as its form approaches generality through abstraction.[28]

The work of psychologists such as Carol Gilligan and others has led to a clarification of what may be thought of as tendencies among women to approach moral issues differently. Rather than interpreting moral problems in terms of what could be handled by applying abstract rules of justice to particular cases, many of the women studied by Gilligan tended to be more concerned with preserving actual human relationships, and with expressing care for those for whom they felt responsible. Their moral reasoning was typically more embedded in a context of particular others than was the reasoning of a comparable group of men.[29] One should not equate tendencies women in fact display with feminist views, since the former may well be the result of the sexist, oppressive conditions in which women's lives have been lived. But many feminists see our own consciously considered experience as lending confirmation to the view that what has come to be called "an ethic of care" needs to be developed. Some think it should supercede "the ethic of justice" of traditional or standard moral theory. Others think it should be integrated with the ethic of justice and rules.

In any case, feminist philosophers are in the process of reevaluating the place of emotion in morality in at least two respects. First, many think morality requires the development of the moral emotions, in contrast to moral theories emphasizing the primacy of reason. As Annette Baier notes, the rationalism typical of traditional moral theory will be challenged when we pay attention to the role of parent. "It might be important," she writes, "for father figures to have rational control over their violent urges to beat to death the children whose screams enrage them, but more than control of such nasty passions seems needed in the mother or primary parent, or parent-substitute, by most psychological theories. They need to love their children, not just to control their irritation,"[30] So the emphasis in many traditional theories on rational control over the emotions, "rather than on cultivating desirable forms of emotion,"[31] is challenged by feminist approaches to ethics.

Secondly, emotion will be respected rather than dismissed by many feminist moral philosophers in the process of gaining moral understanding. The experience and practice out of which feminist moral theory can be expected to be developed will include embodied feeling as well as thought. In a recent overview of a vast amount of writing, Kathryn Morgan states that "feminist theorists begin ethical theorizing with embodied, gendered subjects who have particular histories, particular communities, particular allegiances, and particular visions of human flourishing. The starting point involves valorizing what has frequently been most mistrusted and despised in the western philosophical tradition. . . ."[32] Among the elements being reevaluated are feminine emotions. The "care" of the alternative feminist approach to morality appreciates rather than rejects emotion. The caring relationships important to feminist morality cannot be understood in terms of abstract rules or moral reasoning. And the "weighing" so often needed between the conflicting claims of some relationships and others cannot be settled by deduction or rational calculation. A feminist ethic will not just acknowledge emotion, as do Utilitarians, as giving us the objectives toward which moral rationality can direct us. It will embrace emotion as providing at least a partial basis for morality itself, and for moral understanding.

Annette Baier stresses the centrality of trust for an adequate morality.[33] Achieving and maintaining trusting, caring relationships is quite different from acting in accord with rational principles, or satisfying the individual desires of either self or other. Caring, empathy, feeling with others, being sensitive to each other's feelings, all may be better guides to what morality requires in actual contexts than may abstract rules of reason, or rational calculation, or at least they may be necessary components of an adequate morality.

The fear that a feminist ethic will be a relativistic "situation ethic" is misplaced. Some feelings can be as widely shared as are rational beliefs, and feminists do not see their views as reducible to "just another attitude."[34] In her discussion of the differences between feminist medical ethics and non-feminist medical ethics, Susan Sherwin gives an example of how feminists reject the mere case by case approach that has come to predominate in nonfeminist medical ethics. The latter also rejects the excessive reliance on abstract rules characteristic of standard ethics, and in this way resembles feminist ethics. But the very focus on cases in isolation from one another deprives this approach from attending to general features in the institutions and practices of medicine that, among other faults, systematically contribute to the oppression of women.[35] The difference of approach can be seen in the treatment of issues in the new reproductive technologies, where feminists consider how the new technologies may further decrease the control of women over reproduction.

This difference might be thought to be one of substance rather than of method, but Sherwin shows the implications for method also. With respect to reproductive technologies one can see especially clearly the deficiencies of the case by case approach: what needs to be considered is not only choice in the purely individualistic interpretation of the case by case approach, but control at a more general level and how it affects the structure of gender in society. Thus, a feminist perspective does not always counsel attention to specific case versus appeal to general considerations, as some sort of methodological rule. But the general considerations are often not the purely abstract ones of traditional and standard moral theory, they are the general features and judgments to be made about cases in actual (which means, so far, patriarchal) societies. A feminist evaluation of a moral problem should never omit the political elements involved; and it is likely to recognize that political issues cannot be dealt with adequately in purely abstract terms any more than can moral issues.

The liberal tradition in social and moral philosophy argues that in pluralistic society and even more clearly in a pluralistic world, we cannot agree on our visions of the good life, on what is the best kind of life for humans, but we can hope to agree on the minimal conditions for justice, for coexistence within a framework allowing us to pursue our visions of the good life.[36] Many feminists contend that the commitment to justice needed for agreement in actual conditions on even minimal requirements of justice is as likely to demand relational feelings as a rational recognition of abstract principles. Human beings can and do care, and are capable of caring far more than at present, about the sufferings of children quite distant from them, about the prospects for future generations, and about the well-being of the globe. The liberal tradition's mutually disinterested rational individualists would seem unlikely to care enough to take the actions needed to achieve moral decency at a global level, or environmental sanity for decades hence, as they would seem unable to represent caring relationships within the family and among friends. As Annette Baier puts it, "A moral theory, it can plausibly be claimed, cannot regard concern for new and future persons as an optional charity left for those with a taste for it. If the morality the theory endorses is to sustain itself, it must provide for its own continuers, not just take out a loan on a carefully encouraged maternal instinct or on the enthusiasm of a self-selected group of environmentalists, who make it their business or hobby to be concerned with what we are doing to mother earth."[37]

The possibilities as well as the problems (and we are well aware of some of them) in a feminist re-envisioning of emotion and reason need to be further developed, but we can already see that the views of nonfeminist moral theory are unsatisfactory.

II. The Public and the Private

The second questionable aspect of the history of ethics on which I focused was its conception of the distinction between the public and the private. As with the split between reason and emotion, feminists are showing how gender-bias has distorted previous conceptions of these spheres, and we are trying to offer more appropriate understandings of "private" morality and "public" life.

Part of what feminists have criticized has been the way the distinction has been accompanied by a supposition that what occurs in the household occurs as if on an island beyond politics, whereas the personal is highly affected by the political power beyond, from legislation about abortion to the greater earning power of men, to the interconnected division of labor by gender both within and beyond the household, to the lack of adequate social protection for women against domestic violence.[38] Of course we recognize that the family is not identical to the state, and we need concepts for thinking about the private or personal, and the public or political. But they will have to be very different from the traditional concepts.

Feminists have also criticized deeper assumptions about what is distinctively human and what is "natural" in the public and private aspects of human life, and what is meant by "natural" in connection with women.[39] Consider the associations that have traditionally been built up: the public realm is seen as the distinctively human realm in which man transcends his animal nature, while the private realm of the household is seen as the natural region in which women merely reproduce the species.[40] These associations are extraordinarily pervasive in standard concepts and theories, in art and thought and cultural ideals, and especially in politics.

Dominant patterns of thought have seen women as primarily mothers, and mothering as the performance of a primarily biological function. Then it has been supposed that while engaging in political life is a specifically human activity, women are engaged in an activity which is not specifically human. Women accordingly have been thought to be closer to nature than men,[41] to be enmeshed in a biological function involving processes more like those in which other animals are involved than like the rational discussion of the citizen in the polis, or the glorious battles of noble soldiers, or the trading and rational contracting of "economic man." The total or relative exclusion of women from the domain of public life has then been seen as either inevitable or appropriate.

The view that women are more determined by biology than are men is still extraordinarily prevalent. It is as questionable from a feminist perspective as many other traditional misinterpretations of women's experience. Human mothering is an extremely different activity from the mothering engaged in by other animals. The work and speech of men is recognized as very different from what might be thought of as the "work" and "speech" of other animals. Human mothering is fully as different from animal mothering. Of course all human beings are animal as well as human. But to whatever extent it is appropriate to recognize a difference between "man" and other animals, so would it be appropriate to recognize a comparable difference between "woman" and other animals, and between the activities—including mothering—engaged in by women and the behavior of other animals.

Human mothering shapes language and culture, it forms human social personhood, it develops morality. Animal behavior can be highly impressive and complex, but it does not have built into it any of the consciously chosen aims of morality. In creating human social persons, human mothering is different in kind from merely propagating a species. And human mothering can be fully as creative an activity as those activities traditionally thought of as distinctively human, because to create new persons, and new types of persons, can surely be as creative as to make new objects, products, or institutions. Human mothering is no more "natural" or "primarily biological" than is any other human activity.

Consider nursing an infant, often thought of as the epitome of a biological process with which mothering is associated and women are identified. There is no reason to think of human nursing as any more simply biological than there is to think of, say, a businessmen's lunch this way. Eating is a biological process, but what and how and with whom we eat are thoroughly cultural. Whether and how long and with whom a woman nurses an infant, are also human, cultural matters. If men transcend the natural by conquering new territory and trading with their neighbors and making deals over lunch to do so, women can transcend the natural by choosing not to nurse their children when they could, or choosing to nurse them when their culture tells them not to, or singing songs to their infants as they nurse, or nursing in restaurants to overcome the prejudices against doing so, or thinking human thoughts as they nurse, and so forth. Human culture surrounds and characterizes the activity of nursing as it does the activities of eating, or governing, or writing, or thinking.

We are continually being presented with images of the humanly new and creative as occurring in the public realm of the polis, or the realms of marketplace or of art and science outside the household. The very term 'reproduction' suggests mere repetition, the "natural" bringing into existence of repeated instances of the same human animal. But human reproduction is not repetition.[42] This is not to suggest that bringing up children in the interstices of patriarchal society, in society structured by institutions supporting male dominance, can achieve the potential of transformation latent in the activity of human mothering. But the activity of creating new social persons and new kinds of persons is potentially the most transformative human activity of all. And it suggests that morality should concern itself first of all with this activity, with what its norms and practices ought to be, and with how the institutions and arrangements throughout society and the world ought to be structured to facilitate the right kinds of development of the best kinds of new persons. The flourishing of children ought to be at the very center of moral and social and political and economic and legal thought, rather than, as at present, at the periphery, if attended to at all.

Revised conceptions of public and private have significant implications for our conceptions of human beings and relationships between them. Some feminists suggest that instead of seeing human relationships in terms of the impersonal ones of the "public" sphere, as standard political and moral theory has so often done, we might consider seeing human relationships in terms of those experienced in the sphere of the "private," or of what these relationships could be imagined to be like in post-patriarchal society.[43] The traditional approach is illustrated by those who generalize, to other regions of human life than the economic, assumptions about "economic man" in contractual relations with other men. It sees such impersonal, contractual relations as paradigmatic, even, on some views, for moral theory. Many feminists, in contrast, consider the realm of what has been misconstrued as the "private" as offering guidance to what human beings and their relationships should be like even in regions beyond those of family and friendship. Sara Ruddick looks at the implications of the practice of mothering for the conduct of peace politics.[44] Marilyn Friedman and Lorraine Code consider friendship, especially as women understand it, as a possible model for human relationships.[45] Others see society as non-contractual rather than as contractual.

Clearly, a reconceptualization is needed of the ways in which every human life is entwined with personal and with social components. Feminist theorists are contributing imaginative work to this project.

III. The Concept of Self

Let me turn now to the third aspect of the history of ethics which I discussed and which feminists are re-envisioning: the concept of self. One of the most important emphases in a feminist approach to morality is the recognition that more attention must be paid to the domain between, on the one hand, the self as ego, as self-interested individual, and, on the other hand, the universal, everyone, others in general.[46] Traditionally, ethics has dealt with these poles of individual self and universal all. Usually, it has called for impartiality against the partiality of the egoistic self; sometimes it has defended egoism against claims for a universal perspective. But most standard moral theory has hardly noticed as morally significant the intermediate realm of family relations and relations of friendship, of group ties and neighborhood concerns, especially from the point of view of women. When it has noticed this intermediate realm it has often seen its attachments as threatening to the aspirations of the Man of Reason, or as subversive of "true" morality. In seeing the problems of ethics as problems of reconciling the interests of the self with what would be right or best for "everyone," standard ethics has neglected the moral aspects of the concern and sympathy which people actually feel for particular others, and what moral experience in this intermediate realm suggests for an adequate morality.

The region of "particular others" is a distinct domain, where what can be seen to be artificial and problematic are the very egoistic "self" and the universal "all others" of standard moral theory. In the domain of particular others, the self is already constituted to an important degree by relations with others, and these relations may be much more salient and significant than the interests of any individual self in isolation.[47] The "others" in the picture, however, are not the "all others," or "everyone," of traditional moral theory; they are not what a universal point of view or a view from nowhere could provide.[48] They are, characteristically, actual flesh and blood other human beings for whom we have actual feelings and with whom we have real ties.

From the point of view of much feminist theory, the individualistic assumptions of liberal theory and of most standard moral theory are suspect. Even if we would be freed from the debilitating aspects of dominating male power to "be ourselves" and to pursue our own interests, we would, as persons, still have ties to other persons, and we would at least in part be constituted by such ties. Such ties would be part of what we inherently are. We are, for instance, the daughter or son of given parents, or the mother or father of given children, and we carry with us at least some ties to the racial or ethnic or national group within which we developed into the persons we are.

If we look, for instance, at the realities of the relation between mothering person (who can be female or male) and child, we can see that what we value in the relation cannot be broken down into individual gains and losses for the individual members in the relation. Nor can it be understood in universalistic terms. Self-development apart from the relation may be much less important than the satisfactory development of the relation. What matters may often be the health and growth of and the development of the relation-and-its-members in ways that cannot be understood in the individualistic terms of standard moral theories designed to maximize the satisfaction of self-interest. The universalistic terms of moral theories grounded in what would be right for "all rational beings" or "everyone" cannot handle, either, what has moral value in the relation between mothering person and child.

Feminism is of course not the only locus of criticism of the individualistic and abstractly universalistic features of liberalism and of standard moral theory. Marxists and communitarians also see the self as constituted by its social relations. But in their usual form, Marxist and communitarian criticisms pay no more attention than liberalism and standard moral theory to the experience of women, to the context of mothering, or to friendship as women experience it.[49] Some recent nonfeminist criticisms, such as offered by Bernard Williams, of the impartiality required by standard moral theory, stress how a person's identity may be formed by personal projects in ways that do not satisfy universal norms, yet ought to be admired. Such views still interpret morality from the point of view of an individual and his project, not a social relationship such as that between mothering person and child. And recent nonfeminist criticisms in terms of traditional communities and their moral practices, as seen for instance in the work of Stuart Hampshire and Alasdair MacIntyre, often take traditional gender roles as given, or provide no basis for a radical critique of them.[50] There is no substitute, then, for feminist exploration of the area between ego and universal, as women experience this area, or for the development of a refocused concept of relational self that could be acceptable from a feminist point of view.

Relationships can be evaluated as trusting or mistrustful, mutually considerate or selfish, harmonious or stressful, and so forth. Where trust and consideration are appropriate, which is not always, we can find ways to foster them. But understanding and evaluating relationships, and encouraging them to be what they can be at their best, require us to look at relationships between actual persons, and to see what both standard moral theories and their nonfeminist critics often miss. To be adequate, moral theories must pay attention to the neglected realm of particular others in the actual relationships and actual contexts of women's experience. In doing so, problems of individual self-interest versus universal rules may recede to a region more like background, out-of-focus insolubility or relative unimportance. The salient problems may then be seen to be how we ought best to guide or to maintain or to reshape the relationships, both close and more distant, that we have, or might have, with actual other human beings. Particular others can be actual children in need in distant continents, or the anticipated children of generations not yet even close to being born. But they are not "all rational beings" or "the greatest number," and the self that is in relationships with particular others and is composed to a significant degree by such relations is not a self whose ego must be pitted against abstract, universal claims. Developing the needed guidance for maintaining and reshaping relationships presents enormous problems, but a first step is to recognize how traditional and nonfeminist moral theory of both an individualistic and communitarian kind falls short in providing it.

The concept of the relational self which is evolving within feminist thought is leading to interesting inquiry in many fields. An example is the work being done at the Stone Center at Wellesley College.[51] Psychologists there have posited a self-in-relation theory and are conducting empirical inquiries to try to establish how the female self develops. They are working with a theory that a female relational self develops through a mutually empathetic mother-daughter bond.

The work has been influenced by Jean Baker Miller's re-evaluation of women's psychological qualities as strengths rather than weaknesses. In her book *Toward a New Psychology of Women*, published in 1976, Miller identified women's "great desire for affiliation" as one such strength.[52] Nancy Chodorow's *The Reproduction of Mothering*, published in 1978, has also had a significant influence on the work done at the Stone Center, as it has on much feminist inquiry.[53] Chodorow argued that a female affiliative self is reproduced by a structure of parenting in which mothers are the primary caretakers, and sons and daughters develop differently in relation to a parent of the same sex, or a parent of different sex, as primary caretaker. Daughters develop a sense of self by identifying themselves with the mother; they come to define themselves as connected to or in relation with others. Sons, in contrast, develop a sense of self by differentiating themselves from the mother; they come to define themselves as separate from or unconnected to others. An implication often drawn from Chodorow's work is that parenting should be shared equally by fathers and mothers so that children of either sex can develop with caretakers of both same and different sex.

In 1982, Carol Gilligan, building on both Miller and Chodorow, offered her view of the "different voice" with which girls and women express their understanding of moral problems.[54] Like Miller and Chodorow, Gilligan valued tendencies found especially in women to affiliate with others and to interpret their moral responsibilities in terms of their relationships with others. In all, the valuing of autonomy and individual independence over care and concern for relationships, was seen as an expression of male bias.

The Stone Center has tried to elaborate and to study a feminist conception of the relational self. In a series of Working Papers, researchers and clinicians have explored the implications of this conception for various issues in women's psychology (e.g. power, anger, work inhibitions, violence, eating patterns) and for therapy.

The self as conceptualized in these studies is seen as having both a need for recognition and a need to understand the other, and these needs are seen as compatible. They are created in the context of mother-child interaction, and are satisfied in a mutually empathetic relationship. This does not require a loss of self, but a relationship of mutuality in which self and other both express intersubjectivity. Both give and take in a way that not only contributes to the satisfaction of their needs as individuals, but also affirms the "larger relational unit" they compose.[55] Maintaining this larger relational unit then becomes a goal, and maturity is seen not in terms of individual autonomy but in terms of competence in creating and sustaining relations of empathy and mutual intersubjectivity.

The Stone Center psychologists contend that the goal of mutuality is rarely achieved in adult male-female relationships because of the traditional gender system. The gender system leads men to seek autonomy and power over others, and to undervalue the caring and relational connectedness that is expected of women. Women rarely receive the nurturing and empathetic support they provide. Accordingly, these psychologists look to the interaction that occurs in mother-daughter relationships as the best source of insight into the promotion of the healthy, relational self. This research provides an example of exploration into a refocused, feminist conception of the self, and into empirical questions about its development and implications.

In a quite different field, that of legal theory, a refocused concept of self is leading to reexaminations of such concepts as property and autonomy and the role these have played in political theory and in constitutional law. For instance, the legal theorist Jennifer Nedelsky questions the imagery that is dominant in constitutional law and in our conceptions of property: the imagery of a bounded self, a self contained within boundaries and having rights to property within a wall allowing it to exclude others and to exclude government. The boundary metaphor, she argues, obscures and distorts our thinking about human relationships and what is valuable in them. "The boundedness of selves," Nedelsky writes, "may seem to be a self-evident truth, but I think it is a wrongheaded and destructive way of conceiving of the human creatures law and government are created for."[56] In the domain of the self's relation to the state, the central problem, she argues, is not "maintaining a sphere into which the state cannot penetrate, but fostering autonomy when people are already within the sphere of state control or responsibility."[57] What we can from a feminist perspective think of as the male "separative self" seems on an endless quest for security behind such walls of protection as those of property. Property focuses the quest for security "in ways that are paradigmatic of the efforts of separative selves to protect themselves through boundaries"[58] But of course property is a social construction, not a thing; it requires the involvement of the state to define what it is and to defend it. What will provide what it seeks to offer will not be boundaries and exclusions, but constructive relationships.

In an article on autonomy, Nedelsky examines the deficiencies in the concept of self with which so much of our political and legal thinking about autonomy has been developed. She well recognizes that of course feminists are centrally concerned with freedom and autonomy, with enabling women to live our own lives. But we need a language with which to express these concerns which will also reflect "the equally important feminist precept that any good theorizing will start with people in their social contexts. And the notion of social context must take seriously its constitutive quality; social context cannot simply mean that individuals will, of course, encounter one another."[59] The problem, then, is how to combine the claim of the constitutiveness of social relations with the value of self-determination. Liberalism has been the source of our language of freedom and self-determination, but it lacks the ability to express comprehension of "the reality we know: the centrality of relationships in constituting the self."[60]

In developing a new conception of autonomy that avoids positing self-sufficient and thus highly artificial individuals, Nedelsky point out first that "the capacity to find one's own law can develop only in the context of relations with others (both intimate and more broadly social) that nurture this capacity, and second, that the 'content' of one's own law is comprehensible only with reference to shared social norms, values, and concepts."[61] She sees the traditional liberal view of the self as implying that the most perfectly autonomous man is the most perfectly isolated, and finds this pathological.

Instead of developing autonomy through images of walls around one's property, as does the Western liberal tradition and as does U.S. constitutional law, Nedelsky suggests that "the most promising model, symbol, or metaphor for autonomy is not property, but childrearing. There we have encapsulated the emergence of autonomy through relationship with others. . . . Interdependence [is] a constant component of autonomy."[62] And she goes on to examine how law and bureaucracies can foster autonomy within relationships between citizen and government. This does not entail extrapolating from intimate relations to large-scale ones; rather, the insights gained from experience with the context of childrearing allow us to recognize the relational aspects of autonomy. In work such as Nedelsky's we can see how feminist reconceptualizations of the self can lead to the rethinking of fundamental concepts even in terrains such as law, thought by many to be quite distant from such disturbances.

To argue for a view of the self as relational does not mean that women need to remain enmeshed in the ties by which they are constituted. In recent decades, especially, women have been breaking free of relationships with parents, with the communities in which they grew up, and with men, relationships in which they defined themselves through the traditional and often stifling expectations of others.[63] These quests for self have often involved wrenching instability and painful insecurity. But the quest has been for a new and more satisfactory relational self, not for the self-sufficient individual of liberal theory. Many might share the concerns expressed by Alison Jaggar that disconnecting ourselves from particular others, as ideals of individual autonomy seem to presuppose we should, might make us incapable of morality, rather than capable of it, if, as so many feminists think, "an ineliminable part of morality consists in responding emotionally to particular others."[64]

I have examined three topics on which feminist philosophers and feminists in other fields are thinking anew about where we should start and how we should focus our attention in ethics. Feminist reconceptualizations and recommendations concerning the relation between reason and emotion, the distinction between public and private, and the concept of the self, are providing insights deeply challenging to standard moral theory. The implications of this work are that we need an almost total reconstruction of social and political and economic and legal theory in all their traditional forms as well as a reconstruction of moral theory and practice at more comprehensive, or fundamental, levels.

Notes

1. See e.g. Cheshire Calhoun, "Justice, Care, Gender Bias," *The Journal of Philosophy* 85 (September, 1988): 451-63.

2. Lorraine Code, "Second Persons," in *Science, Morality and Feminist Theory*, ed. Marsha Hanen and Kai Nielsen (Calgary: University of Calgary Press, 1987), p. 360.

3. See e.g. *Revolutions in Knowledge: Feminism in the Social Sciences*, ed. Sue Rosenberg Zalk and Janice Gordon-Kelter (Boulder: Westview Press, forthcoming).

4. Genevieve Lloyd, *The Man of Reason: 'Male' and 'Female' in Western Philosophy* (Minneapolis: University of Minnesota Press, 1984), p. 104.

5. Ibid., p. 2.

6. Ibid., p. 3.

7. Ibid., p. 4. For a feminist view of how reason and emotion in the search for knowledge might be reevaluated, see Alison M. Jaggar, "Love and Knowledge: Emotion in Feminist Epistemology," *Inquiry* 32 (June, 1989): 151-76.

8. David Heyd, *Supererogation: Its Status in Ethical Theory* (New York: Cambridge University Press, 1982), p.134.

9. J. Urmson, "Saints and Heroes," in *Essays in Moral Philosophy*, ed. A. I. Melden (Seattle: University of Washington Press, 1958), p. 202. I am indebted to Marcia Baron for pointing out this and the previous example in her "Kantian Ethics and Supererogation," *The Journal of Philosophy* 84 (May, 1987): 237-62.

10. Alan Ryan, "Distrusting Economics," *New York Review of Books* (May 18, 1989): 25-27. For a different treatment, see *Beyond Self-Interest*, ed. Jane Mansbridge (Chicago: University of Chicago Press, 1990).

11. See especially *Mothering: Essays in Feminist Theory*, ed. Joyce Trebilcot (Totowa, New Jersey: Rowman and Allanheld, 1984); and Sara Ruddick, *Maternal Thinking: Toward a Politics of Peace* (Boston: Beacon Press, 1989).

12. Christine Di Stefano, "Masculinity as Ideology in Political Theory: Hobbesian Man Considered," Women's Studies International Forum (Special Issue: *Hypatia*), Vol. 6, No. 6 (1983): 633-44, p. 637.

13. Thomas Hobbes, *The Citizen: Philosophical Rudiments Concerning Government and Society*, ed. B. Gert (Garden City, New York: Doubleday, 1972 (1651)), p. 20.

14. Di Stefano, op. cit., p. 638.

15. Ibid.

16. Ibid., p. 639.

17. For examples of relevant passages, see *Philosophy of Woman: Classical to Current Concepts*, ed. Mary Mahowald (Indianapolis: Hackett, 1978); and *Visions of Women*, ed. Linda Bell (Clifton, New Jersey: Humana, 1985). For discussion, see Susan Moller Okin, *Women in Western Political Thought* (Princeton, New Jersey: Princeton University Press, 1979); and Lorenne Clark and Lynda Lange, eds., *The Sexism of Social and Political Theory* (Toronto: University of Toronto Press, 1979).

18. Annette Baier, "Trust and Anti-Trust," *Ethics* 96 (1986): 231-60, esp. 247-48.

19. Ibid.

20. Kathryn Pauly Morgan, "Strangers in a Strange Land: Feminists Visit Relativists" in *Perspectives on Relativism*, ed. D. Odegaard and Carole Stewart (Toronto: Agathon Press, 1990).

21. Kathryn Morgan, "Women and Moral Madness," in *Science, Morality and Feminist Theory*, ed. Hanen and Nielsen, p. 223.

22. Alison M. Jaggar, "Feminist Ethics: Some Issues For The Nineties," *Journal of Social Philosophy* 20 (Spring/Fall 1989), p. 91.

23. Ibid.

24. One well-argued statement of this position is Barbara Houston, "Rescuing Womanly Virtues: Some Dangers of Moral Reclamation," in *Science, Morality and Feminist Theory*, ed. Hanen and Nielsen.

25. See e.g. Elizabeth V. Spelman, *Inessential Woman: Problems of Exclusion in Feminist Thought* (Boston: Beacon Press, 1988). See also Sarah Lucia Hoagland, *Lesbian Ethics: Toward New Value* (Palo Alto, California: Institute of Lesbian Studies, 1989); and Katie Geneva Cannon, *Black Womanist Ethics* (Atlanta, Georgia: Scholars Press, 1988).

26. For an approach to social and political as well as moral issues that attempts to be context-respectful, see Virginia Held, *Rights and Goods: Justifying Social Action* (Chicago: University of Chicago Press, 1989).

27. Margaret Urban Walker, "Moral Understandings: Alternative 'Epistemology' for a Feminist Ethics," *Hypatia* 4 (Summer, 1989): 15-19.

28. Ibid., p. 20. See also Iris Marion Young, "Impartiality and the Civic Public. Some Implications of Feminist Critiques of Moral and Political Theory," in Seyla Benhabib and Drucilla Cornell, *Feminism as Critique* (Minneapolis: University of Minnesota Press, 1987).

29. See especially Carol Gilligan, *In a Different Voice: Psychological Theory and Women's Development* (Cambridge, Massachusetts: Harvard University Press, 1988); and Eva Feder Kittay and Diana T. Meyers, eds., *Women and Moral Theory* (Totowa, New Jersey: Rowman and Allanheld, 1987).

30. Annette Baier, "The Need for More Than Justice," in *Science, Morality and Feminist Theory*, ed. Hanen and Nielsen, p. 55.

31. Ibid.

32. Kathryn Pauly Morgan, "Strangers in a Strange Land . . . ," p. 2.

33. Annette Baier, "Trust and Anti-Trust."

34. See especially Kathryn Pauly Morgan, "Strangers in a Strange Land . . ."

35. Susan Sherwin, "Feminist and Medical Ethics: Two Different Approaches to Contextual Ethics," *Hypatia* 4 (Summer, 1989): 57-71.

36. See especially the work of John Rawls and Ronald Dworkin; see also Charles Larmore, *Patterns of Moral Complexity* (Cambridge: Cambridge University Press, 1987).

37. Annette Baier, "The Need for More Than Justice," pp. 53-54.

38. See e.g. Linda Nicholson, *Gender and History: The Limits of Social Theory in the Age of the Family* (New York: Columbia University Press, 1986); and Jean Bethke Elshtain, *Public Man, Private Woman* (Princeton, New Jersey: Princeton University Press, 1981). See also Carole Pateman, *The Sexual Contract* (Stanford, California: Stanford University Press, 1988).

39. See e.g. Susan Moller Okin, *Women in Western Political Thought*. See also Alison M. Jaggar, *Feminist Politics and Human Nature* (Totowa, New Jersey: Rowman and Allanheld, 1983).

40. So entrenched is this way of thinking that it was even reflected in Simone de Beauvoir's pathbreaking feminist text *The Second Sex*, published in 1949. Here, as elsewhere, feminists have had to transcend our own early searches for our own perspectives.

41. See e.g. Sherry B. Ortner, "Is Female to Male as Nature is to Culture?" in *Woman, Culture, and Society*, ed. Michelle Z. Rosaldo and Louise Lamphere (Stanford: Stanford University Press, 1974).

42. For further discussion and an examination of surrounding associations, see Virginia Held, "Birth and Death," in *Ethics* (January 1989): 361-88.

43. See e.g., Virginia Held, "Non-contractual Society: A Feminist View," in *Science, Morality and Feminist Theory*, ed. Hanen and Nielsen.

44. Sara Ruddick, *Maternal Thinking*.

45. See Marilyn Friedman, "Feminism and Modern Friendship: Dislocating the Community," *Ethics* (January 1989): 175-90; and Lorraine Code, "Second Persons."

46. See Virginia Held, "Feminism and Moral Theory," in *Women and Moral Theory*, ed. Kittay and Meyers.

47. See Seyla Benhabib, "The Generalized and the Concrete Other: The Kohlberg-Gilligan Controversy and Moral Theory," in *Women and Moral Theory*, ed. Kittay and Meyers. See also Caroline Whitbeck, "Feminist Ontology: A Different Reality," in *Beyond Domination*, ed. Carol Gould (Totowa, New Jersey: Rowman and Allanheld, 1983).

48. See Thomas Nagel, *The View from Nowhere* (New York: Oxford University Press, 1986). For a feminist critique, see Susan Bordo, "Feminism, Postmodernism, and Gender-Skepticism," in *Feminism/Postmodernism*, ed. Linda Nicholson (New York: Routledge, 1989).

49. On Marxist theory, see e.g. *Women and Revolution,* ed. Lydia Sargent (Boston: South End Press, 1981); Alison Jaggar, *Feminist Politics and Human Nature*; and Ann Ferguson, *Blood at the Roo:. Motherhood, Sexuality and Male Dominance* (London: Pandora, 1989). On communitarian theory, see Marilyn Friedman, "Feminism and Modern Friendship . . . ," and also her paper "The Social Self and the Partiality Debates," presented at the Society for Women in Philosophy meeting in New Orleans, April 1990.

50. Bernard Williams, *Moral Luck* (Cambridge: Cambridge University Press, 1981); Public and Private Morality, ed. Stuart Hampshire (Cambridge: Cambridge University Press, 1978); Alasdair MacIntyre, *After Virtue: A Study in Moral Theory* (Notre Dame, Indiana: University of Notre Dame Press, 1981). For discussion see Susan Moller Okin, *Justice, Gender, and the Family* (New York: Basic Books, 1989).

51. On the Stone Center concept of the self see especially Jean Baker Miller, "The Development of Women's Sense of Self" (Wellesley, Massachusetts: Stone Center Working Paper No. 11); Janet Surrey, "The 'Self-in-Relation': A Theory of Women's Development" (Wellesley, Massachusetts: Stone Center Working Paper No. 13); and Judith Jordan, "The Meaning of Mutuality" (Wellesley, Massachusetts: Stone Center Working Paper No. 23). For a feminist but critical view of this work, see Marcia Westkott, "Female Relationality and the Idealized Self," *American Journal of Psychoanalysis* 49 (September, 1989): 239-50.

52. Jean Baker Miller, *Toward a New Psychology of Women* (Boston: Beacon Press, 1976).

53. Nancy Chodorow, *The Reproduction of Mothering: Psychoanalysis and the Sociology of Gender* (Berkeley: University of California Press, 1978).

54. Carol Gilligan, *In a Different Voice.*

55. J. V. Jordan, "The Meaning of Mutuality," p. 2.

56. Jennifer Nedelsky, "Law, Boundaries, and the Bounded Self," *Representations* 30 (Spring, 1990): 161-89, p. 167.

57. Ibid., p. 169.

58. Ibid., p. 181.

59. Jennifer Nedelsky, "Reconceiving Autonomy: Sources, Thoughts and Possibilities," *Yale Journal of Law and Feminism* 1 (Spring, 1989): 7-36, p. 9. See also Diana T. Meyers, *Self, Society, and Personal Choice* (New York: Columbia University Press, 1989).

60. Ibid.

61. Ibid., p. 11.

62. Ibid., p. 12. See also Man J. Matsuda, "Liberal Jurisprudence and Abstracted Visions of Human Nature," *New Mexico Law Review* 6 (Fall, 1986): 613-30.

63. See e.g. *Women's Ways of Knowing. The Development of Self, Voice, and Mind,* by Mary Field Belenky, Blyth McVicker Clinchy, Nancy Rule Goldberger, and Jill Mattuck Tarule (New York: Basic Books, 1986).

64. Alison Jaggar, "Feminist Ethics: Some Issues for the Nineties," p. 11.

* This paper is based in part on my Truax Lectures on "The Prospect of Feminist Morality" at Hamilton College on November 8 and 9, 1989. Early versions were also presented at Colgate University; at Queens University in Kingston, Ontario; at the University of Kentucky; and at the New School for Social Research. I am grateful to all who made possible these occasions and commented on the paper at these times, and to Alison Jaggar, Laura Purdy, and Sara Ruddick for additional discussion.

Part I: Discussion Cases

Case #1: Trapped in an Underwater Sea-Cave

In an effort to alleviate end-of-the-term stress related to exams and term papers your professor has invited you to join her on a trip to an underwater sea-cave. You, along with your classmates (31 in all), agree to go and are happy to be told that no scuba gear will be necessary—the sea-cave is only underwater at high tide which won't occur for several hours. After exploring the sea-cave for over an hour you notice a slight tremor and that the only opening to the cave has become narrower. With high tide approaching you and your classmates decide to exit the cave and one of them—through no fault of her own—Ginger, gets stuck. In fact, so stuck that she cannot be pulled back or pushed out. Moreover, it just so happens that her head is above high tide. It looks pretty bad for you and the rest of your classmates who are stuck down in the cave with the water rising. Except, one of you brought a stick of dynamite and a match—and there is only one place it can be used. You could, shove the dynamite next to Ginger, blow her up, and at the same time widen the opening so that no one else gets stuck. What, morally, should you do?

Case #2: The Case of Reluctant Donation

After your first complete medical exam the doctor informs you that you are a universal donor—your blood, heart, lungs, kidneys, etc. could be taken from you and used to save others no matter what their blood type or genetic makeup. The doctor then takes you to the waiting-for-donors floor of the hospital and begins telling you about all the people that you could save by being re-distributed. In fact, he reminds you how pathetic and miserable your life is compared to the extremely happy lives that would result from your donation. As you look up in horror the doctor says "This is a no-brainer isn't it?—killing one to save thirty is the right thing to do." You try to voice a concern but can't. The doctor has given you a sedative and . . . . Do any of the moral theories covered in Part I give adequate guidance in this case? Which one and why?

Case #3: Killing One to Save Nine

There are ten individuals dying of a rare viral infection at a hospital near your house—they are all quarantined in one room and can only be medically treated as a group. If nothing is done, the doctors claim that nine of the patients will die and one will live. Moreover, the doctors are fairly sure who will die and who will live—it seems that left-handed people have a natural ability to fight off the illness (there is only one left-handed person in the quarantine group). There is an antidote to the illness. But there is a catch—the antidote that you have found is fatal to left-handers and must be administered in gaseous form to all the quarantined patients. Explain how Mill, Kant, Aristotle, and Held would approach this problem.

Case #4: Torturing for Good Consequences

You are in charge of an investigation related to terrorist activities and have a known terrorist leader in custody. Moreover, there are terrorist cells in operation in the area and evidence that an attack is being planned sometime soon. All traditional police procedures have failed to uncover the details of the attack. A fellow investigator suggests torturing the terrorist leader in order to obtain the relevant information and stop the attack. Is torture morally permissible in this case? Why or why not? Would any of the theories that we have covered sanction torture?

PART II

Intellectual Property:
Moral and Legal Concerns

Intellectual Property Is Still Property

FRANK H. EASTERBROOK*

I agreed to discuss intellectual property at this symposium to fulfill the duty of every judge of an inferior federal court: to praise my superiors. It also offered a chance to explore a corner of federal law closed to judges such as me by the Federal Circuit's exclusive jurisdiction of patent questions.

Judges long took a Manichaean view of intellectual property. There is the good side: invention, equating to progress. New and better products and methods of making them are the principal source of economic betterment. The gains they produce swamp all other forms of wealth—even one percent per year compounded over a long period yields fabulous returns. Then there is the dark side of the Force: monopoly. To give someone a patent is to give him the right to control output, with the associated overcharge. This means not only a transfer of wealth but also a short-term loss in allocative efficiency. Whether the long-run gains outweigh the short-run losses is a difficult question, on which the patent laws struck a rough balance.

Economists also spoke of intellectual property in the same way. Joseph Schumpeter proposed that monopoly is a spur to innovation because the monopolist could amass the full gains from invention. He thought that the long-run gains from innovation outweigh the allocative loss and was satisfied with this trade.[1] Most economists disagreed, thinking monopoly unambiguously evil. Judges were skeptical, resolving conflicts in favor of competition—and defining anything other than Adam Smith's atomistic pin-makers as monopoly. Thus the antitrust laws had a strict rule against tying patented articles to unpatented ones. Lest the monopoly be "extended"[2] the patent laws were read as implicitly prohibiting any other way to protect intellectual property. The Sears[3] and Compco[4] cases of 1964, which held state anti-copying laws inconsistent with the balance struck by the patent laws, are the starkest expressions of this perspective.[5] Judges found this convivial because they understood patent laws as a swap of protection for "disclosure"; an inventor who disclosed his product to the public with protection obviously didn't "need" the inducement provided by monopoly. In addition, because the deal was seventeen years, protection of a defined product in exchange for disclosure there could be no extension of the domain in time or product. This left out of the equation any consideration of incentives to invent in the first place. It was a classic ex post view of the world, assuming that the invention had been made and asking only whether we would have benign competition or wicked monopoly.[6]

Problem: Patents are not monopolies, and the tradeoff is not protection for disclosure. Patents give a right to exclude, just as the law of trespass does with real property. Intellectual property is intangible, but the right to exclude is no different in principle from General Motors' right to exclude Ford from using its assembly line, or an apple grower's right to its own crop. A patent may create a monopoly—just as an auto manufacturer may own all of the auto production facilities—but property and monopoly usually differ. That a patent covers an "entire" idea or product no more implies monopoly than the fact that USX Corporation owns the "entire" South Works in Chicago. Frequently, indeed almost always, different patented goods and processes compete with each other and with unpatented goods and processes. Before crying "monopoly" in either case, we must determine what substitutes a customer could obtain and whether the seller could raise prices by curtailing output.

The idea that a patent represents an exchange of protection for disclosure makes no sense, except perhaps with respect to process patents. The product itself, not the patent papers, usually discloses things. Inventors want and need patents only when disclosure is inevitable in the absence of protection. When the product can be sold without disclosure, the manufacturer can use trade secret law to protect its contribution, getting even better protection—not only perpetual, but also guarding by secrecy against infringement. Infringement is difficult to detect and penalize; why disclose anything in exchange for what is at best a limit on the duration of your returns? Lawyers use the utmost skill to draft patent applications so that they do not disclose enough to practice the invention, and the omitted details frequently are vital. Patents thus are valuable when the product itself, not the papers filed in the Patent Office, discloses the invention.

The tradeoff is not monopoly versus competition, or protection in exchange for disclosure. It is dynamic gains in exchange for allocative losses. The lure of extra return induces extra invention—valuable invention, too, because unless an idea is better than the next-best way of doing things, there won't be a reward. After the creation, though, compensating the inventor reduces the use that can be made of the idea. If General Motors uses its plant twenty-four hours a day, nothing is left for Ford to use. Ordinary property is occupied and wears out to boot. Intellectual property can be used by many at once, without being used up. The marginal cost of its use is zero; intellectual property rights allow the inventor to set price in excess of marginal cost and therefore create an allocative loss—although usually a small one, limited by the second-best technology in the market. Allocative loss accompanies the reward for invention.

This is not necessarily a "monopoly" reward, though. Price exceeding marginal cost of use, given the existence of the asset, is common in competition. Any time a business creates a specialized asset, one that cannot be turned to other uses after its creation, we could say that the asset should be "free" for all—because to charge a price for use is to discourage that use and give the owner "more" than necessary to hold the asset in the business. Think of a large printing press, which cannot be moved or devoted to some other use (the metal in it could have been used to produce cars, but the die was cast with construction). If the owner of the printing press were forbidden to charge a price in excess of the maintenance and electricity needed to get it to work, the press wouldn't be turned to some other use. So it looks like any payment covering the cost of constructing the press is "too much," just as any compensation for the use of a patented idea is excessive. Nonetheless the owner must be paid; else there would be too few presses tomorrow. Payment is compensation for the value of the asset, not for monopoly. Economists call such payments quasi-rents, and they are common in every industry with specialized assets.[7]

The patent system has effects other than compensating inventors. As Edmund Kitch stressed, many patents are useless in themselves yet convey rights to coordinate development and standardize products, and therefore they may promote social welfare by cutting down the time between invention and commercial production, while yielding uniform standards.[8] This proposition is something any admirer of Japanese processes concedes, although the initial reaction to Kitch's idea was hostile.[9] Patents also create the opportunity to engage in price discrimination, which reduces the allocative loss of intellectual property. The price-discriminating patent holder extracts a return on invention (encouraging new ideas), while pricing less than the second-best technology where the holder encounters competition (ensuring that the customer does not substitute away from the patented, but costly, item)—the best of both worlds.[10]

I started by saying that I came in praise of my superiors. What I meant is that in recent years the Justices have seen the real tradeoff and dropped the cant. In Kewanee[11] they allowed trade secret law to exist—and a brief from Kitch may have helped.[12] In Aronson[13] they allowed private contracts for intellectual property to be enforced even though an application for a patent had been denied. Old rhetoric about intellectual property equating to monopoly seemed to have vanished, replaced by a recognition that a right to exclude in intellectual property is no different in principle from the right to exclude in physical property. In the Betamax case[14] the Justices recognized the tradeoff between optimal use (at marginal cost of zero) and optimal creation, looking at things in advance and on the margin rather than inquiring what would be a "fair" return given yesterday's successful intellectual endeavors.

This recognition of the real nature of the problem had reverberations in antitrust law as well. Old cases holding that copyrights and patents are monopolies, so that tie-ins and bundling are illegal per se, were condemned to benign neglect. In 1979, the BMJ case[15] upheld the blanket license issued by copyright owners, recognizing that this apparently tied package was just a low-cost method of selling, and in particular was terrific price discrimination: the network could use songs at no marginal cost while still rewarding authors.[16] The tying doctrine was linked to market power in Hyde,[17] and although some lower courts missed the message and continued to hold that copyrights and patents are monopolies, most got on board.[18]

Congress is moving in the same direction. In February 1989 the Senate Judiciary Committee reported out the Intellectual Property Antitrust Protection Act of 1989, providing that patents, trademarks, and copyrights do not support a presumption of market power.[19] Bye-bye any special treatment of tying and other practices just because intellectual property is in the picture. The bill assimilates intellectual property to other property, recognizing that the right to exclude others from using your idea is no more a monopoly than is the right to exclude others from using your barn. All depends on what the market share of each may be.

Treating intellectual property as property should appeal not only to utilitarians but also to libertarians. Intellectual property is no less the fruit of one's labor than is physical property True, you need the government to enforce your property right by preventing strangers from using your ideas to make their own products, but you ordinarily need the government to enforce your rights in physical property against predators. Libertarians should be especially pleased that you can create most of the interesting features of intellectual property by contract. For example, a manufacturer may refuse to sell its widget but lease it on terms that prevent its duplication or sale. Common-law rules about "restraints on alienation" don't apply to leased products—and anyway are limitations on contract rather than limits on what could be done by contract in principle. An author may do the same as an inventor (contractual limitations of this kind have become common in the area of computer software). The one important feature of patent law that cannot be created by contract between seller and customer is the rule that only the first among independent inventors obtains the right to exploit the idea, and even this could, in principle, be created by agreement in advance among those working in the same fields. We see a few such agreements, called "patent pools," and although some of these doubtless violate the antitrust laws (they are equivalent to horizontal mergers), they are still private arrangements.[20]

Contracts limiting the use of intellectual property are hard to enforce because violations are so hard to detect--one reason why patent holders so often sue contributory infringers that furnish unpatented, but essential, articles to the true infringers. A federal law of intellectual property may promote enforcement while duplicating the terms that would (presumptively) be set by contract. If Congress misunderstands the optimal terms, any of the entitlements pre-set in the law may be eliminated by contract. Authors and inventors may put their work in the public domain. If they obtain copyrights or patents, they may sell on terms that curtail their rights. Customers could refuse to buy except on terms that limit the sellers' statutory rights, or demand compensation (in the form of a lower price) if the sellers insist on maintaining these rights. So in the end intellectual property may be understood as the result of voluntary undertakings, which the government simply enforces. Many contemporary cases treat it this way.

Yet for all this, my plan to ingratiate myself with my superiors by lavishing praise on their astuteness, their wisdom, and their all-around goodness has come unglued. For less than a month ago, the Court took a step in the wrong direction--and took it unanimously. The case is *Bonito Boats, Inc. v. Thunder Craft Boats, Inc.*[21] The problem is the copying of unpatented articles, here a boat hull. Florida passed a law forbidding the copying of hulls by using an existing product to form a mold, then using the mold to reproduce the hull.

Such a law forces the copier to bear the same costs to a part as the originator. The originator must design the product, make a wooden model, and then use the model as the basis of a mold. This is difficult and costly. Under the Florida law, the costs of production for all firms making an item in the public domain should be similar. Even so, the copier retains vantage for two reasons. First, the copier does not bear the costs of design. Second, there is a selection bias. You can think of innovation (or design in general) as a process of prospecting. There will be hits and misses. The original designer bears the costs of both; the copier duplicates only the hits. These differential costs make it worthwhile to be a copier rather innovator even under the Florida law. Much of the law of intellectual property, like Florida's statute, is designed to prevent such cherry-picking. In economic terms, the first producer faces a "barrier to entry" because its costs will exceed those of the copier. Removing barriers to entry often is thought to be an important objective of economic policy.[22]

Now from my affecting tale—of never-ending progress legal thought, Excelsior!—one would have supposed that the Court would examine this law by asking whether requiring the imitator to bear the same costs as the originator contradicts any rule of patent law—which it doesn't. Patent law addresses whether you can make something at all, not whether there is to be a "level playing field" in the costs of manufacture. A legislature might believe that the innovator's advantage from its product on sale first is large enough to attract creative efforts, or it might believe that selection bias is so serious that the first mover needs a rule equalizing production costs. But as these questions of manufacturing processes are outside the main of patent law, we should expect the Supreme Court to put the case aside. Florida's law, after all, offered much less protection than trade secrets, which allow the designer of a process to keep the rewards until rivals "reverse engineer" the product—a process often more costly than developing it in the first place.

Patent law differs from Florida's statute in other ways. To have a patent is to be able to block anyone from making and selling your item, even if the second producer designed it independently. Florida didn't offer that boon; its law governed manufacturing within its borders and did not ban independent design. The statute inevitably was limited to copying; a truly independent designer would have started from wooden models much like the original manufacturer. Any adverse effects, therefore, would be felt within Florida. Federal law presumptively leaves states free to follow their own destinies.[23] Perhaps price of boat hulls would rise in Florida, but manufacturers could use injection molding in Mississippi to sell to Louisiana boaters. No one doubts that Florida could set minimum prices for boat hulls, as New York does for milk; that Florida could impose a ten-percent tax on injection molding, just as Minnesota used to tax margarine to encourage the use of butter; or that Florida could favor one method of production over others by a myriad of devices, just as states commonly favor ophthalmologists over opticians by limiting who can write prescriptions for eyeglasses. States often establish monopolies, as in the liquor and electricity businesses. Any of these may be wasteful—I suspect most of them are—but the gains and losses are felt locally. When the voters pay the piper, they may call the tune.

Federal law does not preempt all bad state laws, and the existence of a "balance" in federal law does not mean the states must adopt the same policy. Thus state trade secret laws are permissible, even though they do not duplicate federal rules. In securities law, the Williams Act reflects one balance for regulating tender offers, but the Court has held that States may protect managers more than federal law does.[24] Indeed, every federal law reflects a balance of some sort: We know that the political forces in Congress went "x far" but no further, because they believed it would be a political or prudential mistake to do so. If the conclusion "x far is right for us" preempted state laws, there could be no state laws.

This is what I had expected the Court to say. It didn't. Instead it told us that patents are monopolies, that by controlling injection molding Florida had bestowed a monopoly on the innovator just as a patent would do, and that the monopoly was unnecessary because the designer had already disclosed boat hull to the public without the lure of patent royalties.

Madisonian questions of federalism went unmentioned. The fact that every federal law reflects a decision about the "right" amount of regulation, yet without preempting, went unaddressed. No Justice questioned the equation of patent to monopoly. Selection bias did not come up. Only in passing did the Court discuss the link between innovation and compensation for intellectual effort; it seemed fixated instead on some supposed deal by which patents are exchanged for disclosure. The Justices attributed this view to Thomas Jefferson, but his position was subtly different; he opposed the grant of patents for ideas already in the public domain but did not suppose that disclosure and protection are an invariable quid pro quo.[25] Anyway, why should a link between disclosure and protection that might have influenced federal policy mold development in the States? We know from Kewanee and other cases that a product need not be patentable to receive protection under state law.[26]

The proposition that one state's law concerning injection molding gave anyone a monopoly profit is hilarious. There are hundreds of boat manufacturers and thousands of boat designs. Even if fifty percent of these are free from copying in Florida as a result of the state law, there is no monopoly profit to be had. There is a short-run allocative loss if a piece of intellectual property fetches more than the cost of use (that is, if the holder receives any compensation at all for the marginal output), but as I've mentioned, this compensation is a quasi-rent, a reward to the initial investment now sunk into a specialized resource—not a monopoly profit. Under Florida's scheme, the designer never receives more than the difference in the costs of production of the two methods and is unlikely to get even that, being constrained by other boats (including used ones) with other designs The decision seems to have been based on an economic misconception.

As one who sees interesting cases slaughtered every day by lawyers who parrot the language of older cases rather than figuring out the functional considerations I'm willing to chalk up this opinion to poor input. That's my fallback position when someone criticizes one of my opinions. One case is just an argument, a nudge to the legal culture. Isolated cases are not influential. It takes a pattern, a web of decisions, to have even a small effect on the economic, political, or legal climate.

So, lest the climate turn cloudy, I return to my theme. Rights to exclude are not monopolies just because the property involved is an intangible rather than something you can walk across or hold in your hand. The hard questions concern the right tradeoff between quasi-rents that create short-run allocative losses and incentives to invent that lead to dynamic gains over the longer course. Patents may promote coordination, price discrimination, and innovation. Except in the rarest case, we should treat intellectual and physical property identically in the law—which is where the broader currents are taking us, in a sweep no hull protection case will stop.

Notes

* Judge, United States Court of Appeals for the Seventh Circuit; Senior Lecturer, The Law School, The University of Chicago.

1.. See, J. Schumpeter, *Capitalism, Socialism and Democracy* (New York: Harper & Row, 1948).

2. See, e.g., *International Salt Co. v. United States*, 332 U.S. 392, 395-96 (1947).

3. *Sears, Roebuck & Co. v. Stiffel Co.*, 376 U.S. 225 (1964).

4. *Compco Corp. v. Day-Brite Lighting, Inc.*, 376 U.S. 234 (1964).

5. See also *Fashion Originators' Guild of America v. FTC*, 312 U.S. 457 (1941).

6. See W. Bowman, *Patent and Antitrust Law* (1973)pp. 140-99. Ward Bowman describes and trenchantly criticizes the cases embodying this perspective. The many cases provide ample support for Ronald Coase's observation that judges, like economists, attributed every poorly understood arrangement to monopoly: "And as we are very ignorant in this field, the number of ununderstandable practices tends to be rather large, and the reliance on a monopoly explanation is frequent." Coase, "Industrial Organization: A Proposal for Research," in *Policy Issues and Research Opportunities in Industrial Organization* 67 (V. Fuchs ed. 1972), reprinted in R.H. Coase, *The Firm, the Market and the Law* (University of Chicago Press, 1988) p. 67.

7. Economists hotly debate the optimal length of the patent period in a way they do not debate the length of the payment stream for printing presses. Three things underlie this difference: Printing presses wear out in a way that ideas don't; an invention has the potential to dominate an entire market (to monopolize) in a way that physical assets rarely do; and new ideas incorporate old ideas, creating difficult problems of tracing and compensating the contributions. Much of the time, however, we can put differences aside. Ideas do "wear out"; they are superseded by newer and better approaches. Most patents are unsuccessful, and the returns to even the inventions taper down before the end of the seventeen-year period. We grant perpetual life to trademarks and trade secrets, and life exceeding one hundred years to copyrights (technically, the life of the author plus fifty years), precisely because the force of competition from other marks and writings is evident. See Landes & Posner, "An Economic Analysis of Copyright Law," *Journal of Legal Studies* 18 (1989): 325, 361-63.

Copyright and trademark law cover expression but not ideas; copyright and trade secret law do not interfere with independent creations. Patents' potential to monopolize is more serious because now and again an idea proves to be the cornerstone of a flourishing technology. One essential patent might entitle the inventor to control gasoline cracking, plain-paper copying, and so on, with later inventions improving the original idea but not dispensing with it. Yet patents grant the first inventor to exploit the idea even though many other persons might have come up with it soon thereafter, so that the patent holder's contribution to social welfare—the value of the idea during the time before someone else would have devised it—is dramatically less than the allocative loss from an enduring monopoly. It is important to understand, however, that the monopoly return comes from horizontal control of the entire market, something that should be set aside for separate analysis.

The tracing problem arises because new ideas stand on the shoulders of old ideas, and as time passes it becomes difficult to determine how much of the latest idea is attributable to some older one (more likely, to thousands of older ones). If patent holders never behaved strategically, we could disregard the problem because after a time they could not collect royalties covering the costs of tracing; ideas then would be in the public domain in fact if not in law. Rent-seeking behavior is possible, however; patent owners could threaten costly litigation, and the large number of sources of a contemporary product would expose the producer to demands from many sources. Patent pools (analogous to the "blanket license" used in the music industry) would alleviate much but not all of this and would encounter antitrust problems of their own. So the costs of tracing supply a strong argument for an arbitrary cutoff in intellectual property rights. Daily treatment of intellectual property, however, cannot be held in thrall to complex arguments about monopoly and tracing.

8. See Kitch, "The Nature and Function of the Patent System," *Journal of Law and Economics* 20 (1977): 265, 275-80.

9. See, e.g., F. Scherer, *Industrial Market Structure and Economic Performance,* 2d ed. (Chicago: Rand McNally College Pub. Co., 1980) p. 447 (Kitch's article is "little influenced by any concern for reality"; after delivering the unsupported insult, Scherer never mentions Kitch again).

10. See Hausman & MacKie-Mason, "Price Discrimination and Patent Policy," *Rand Journal of Economics* 19 (1988): 253; cf. Baxter, "Legal Restrictions on Exploitation of the Patent Monopoly: An Economic Analysis," *Yale Law Journal* 76 (1966): 267.

11. *Kewanee Oil Co. v. Bicron Corp.,* 416 U.S. 470 (1974).

12. The Court has also held that states may offer some protection to written and recorded works that are not covered by federal copyright law. See *Goldstein v. California,* 412 U.S. 546 (1973).

13. *Aronson v. Quick Point Pencil Corp.,* 440 U.S. 257 (1979).

14. *Sony Corp. of America. v. Universal City Studios, Inc.,* 464 U.S. 417 (1984).

15. *Broadcast Music, Inc. v. CBS Inc.* 441 U.S. 1 (1979).

16. See ibid.; see also R. Posner & F. Easterbrook, *Antitrust: Cases, Economic Notes and other Materials.* (2d ed. 1981), pp. 144-46.

17. *Jefferson Parish Hosp. Dist. No. 2 v. Hyde,* 466 US. 2 (1984).

18. The Ninth Circuit held in *Digidine Corp. v. Data General Corp.,* 734 F.2d 1336 (9th Cir. 1984), that the software of a computer representing less than one percent of any market represented economic power sufficient to bar a tie-in between hardware and software. Almost everyone else, including the Seventh Circuit, in *Will v. Comprehensive Accounting Corp.,* 776 F.2d 665 (7th Cir. 1985), rejected that view and held that intellectual property is now just like other property.

19. S. 270, 10 1st Cong., 1st. Sess. (1989).

20. See Priest, "Cartels and Patent License Arrangements," *Journal of Law and Economics* 20 (1977): 309; Kaplow, "The Patent-Antitrust Intersection: A Reappraisal," *Harvard Law Review* 97 (1984): 1813, 1867-73. But see W. Bowman, supra note 6; Bittlingmayer, "Property Rights, Progress, and the Aircraft Patent Agreement," *Journal of Law and Economics* 31 (1988): 227.

21. 109 S. Ct. 971 (1989).

22. See G. Stigler, *The Organization of Industry* (University of Chicago Press, 1968) p. 67-72; cf. Demsetz, "Barriers to Entry," *American Economics Review* 72 (1982): 42.

23. A point the Court emphasized when holding in *California v. ARC America Corp.,* 109 S. Ct. 1661 (1989) (decided shortly after this symposium), that the antitrust laws do not forbid states from authorizing "indirect purchasers" of overpriced goods to obtain damages, even though *Illinois Brick Co. v. Illinois,* 431 U.S. 720 (1977), had held such awards antithetical to federal antitrust policy. *ARC America* did not cite *Bonito Boats;* the approaches of the two cases are antithetical, but each was unanimous. See generally Easterbrook, "Antitrust and the Economics of Federalism," *Journal of Law and Economics* 26 (1983): 23.

24. See *CTS Corp. v. Dynamics Corp. of Am.,* 481 U.S. 69 (1987); *Amanda Acquisition Corp. v. Universal Foods Corp.,* 877 F.2d 496 (7th Cir. 1989), cert. denied, 110 Ct. 367 (1989).

25. See *Writings of Thomas Jefferson* 13 (Library ed. 1903) p. 326-27.

26. *Kewanee* and *Goldstein* also show that *Bonito Boats* cannot be understood as a simple application of *stare decisis.* Undoubtedly judges should be chary about departing from established meanings of statutes. See Easterbrook, "Stability and Reliability in Judicial Decisions," *Cornell Law Review* 73 (1988):422. But a court could follow *Sears* and *Compco* faithfully without extending them; the central premises on which extensions could rest were demolished by *Kewanee, Goldstein,* and *Aronson.* I therefore agree with Professor Wiley, who concludes that *Bonito Boats* must stand or fall on its own reasoning, without the shelter of precedent. See Wiley, "The Bonito Boats Decision: Uninformed But Mandatory Federal Innovation Policy," *Supreme Court Review* (1989).

Are Patents and Copyrights Morally Justified? The Philosophy of Property Rights and Ideal Objects

TOM G. PALMER*

Introduction

Arguments for the right of property ownership are manifold. It is quite common for a single author to invoke a wide range of these arguments to support private property rights, as in John Locke's famous chapter on property in his *Second Treatise of Government.* Indeed, the convergence of varying and noncontradicting arguments on the same conclusion tends to make us more confident of that conclusion. It serves as a kind of "fail-safe" device in intellectual discourse: If five different but all plausible arguments lead to the same conclusion, we are generally more justified in accepting that conclusion than if only one of those arguments supported it.[1] Intellectual property, however, is a different matter. Interestingly, the various leading arguments that normally buttress each other and converge in support of private property diverge widely when applied to intellectual property. For example, a theory wherein property is viewed as the just reward for labor (a "desert theory") might very well support intellectual property rights, while at the same time a theory in which property is defined as the concretion of liberty might not.

Most of the arguments discussed in this article, both for and against intellectual property rights, emanate from staunch defenders of a private property, free market system. That is not surprising, because those who strongly favor liberty and property are apt to see the concepts as intimately connected and are thus more likely to be very concerned with the theory and application of property rights. With respect to intellectual property, however, one should not be surprised if they come to differing conclusions. That happens because liberty and property in this context may be irreconcilable; copyrights and patents seem to be property, but they also seem to restrict liberty. One would be hard-pressed, for example, to find two stronger defenders of liberty and property in 19th-century America than the abolitionist Lysander Spooner, and the Jacksonian editorialist William Leggett. Yet on the subject of intellectual property rights, each came to opposite conclusions: Spooner steadfastly championed intellectual property rights while Leggett advocated with equal force the unrestricted exchange of ideas. Although they came to opposite conclusions, each argued that his beliefs were consistent with his overall stance in favor of liberty, private property, and freedom of trade.[2]

Sometimes the best developed arguments in support of intellectual property rights are advanced by relatively marginal authors, like Spooner for example. This is because the great pioneers of the philosophy of property rights wrote before property rights for authors or inventors had become a popular issue; it remained for later figures to mold the arguments for intellectual property based on the property theories that had been developed earlier by more prominent thinkers. Consequently, while Locke, Hume, Kant, Hegel, and other philosophers will figure significantly in this article, attention will also be devoted to later interpreters, who applied the ideas of those and other great philosophers in new ways.

Intellectual property rights are rights in ideal objects, which are distinguished from the material substrata in which they are instantiated.[3] Much of this article will therefore be concerned with the ontology of ideal objects. That is because the subject of intellectual property, indeed, the very idea of exercising property rights over ideas, processes, poems, and the like, leads directly to speculation about how such objects are similar to or different from other objects of property rights, such as trees, land, or water flows. One cannot address how (or whether) such things ought to be made the objects of ownership without addressing their fundamental nature. To those who criticized the notion that ideas could be made into exclusive property, the political economist Michel Chevalier properly rejoined: After having fired off at patents this shot, so difficult to escape, the *Expose' des motifs* concludes by saying that all this is metaphysics on which it will not enter. An unhappy way of refuting itself; it is to fly from a discussion which the reporters had opened of their own accord. Should the legislator be ashamed of metaphysics? On the contrary, he ought to be a metaphysician, for what would laws be in the absence of what they call metaphysics; that is to say, recourse to first principles. If the legislator does not consent to be a metaphysician in this sense, he is likely to do his work badly.[4] Thus, discussions in this article about the legal foundations of intellectual property cannot proceed without our taking up the ontological foundations of intellectual property.

Many defenses of intellectual property rights are grounded in the natural law right to the fruit of one's labor.[5] Just as one has a right to the crops one plants, so one has a right to the ideas one generates and the art one produces.

Another tradition of property rights argument bases itself on the necessity of property for the development of personality. Personality develops itself in its interaction with the world; without a sphere of property over which we exercise control, for example, moral responsibility is unlikely to develop. Property rights, in this tradition, may incorporate an "economic" aspect, but this approach is fundamentally distinguished from other conceptions of property rights. Rather than looking to moral desert, or to maximization of utility, or to the omnipresence of scarcity, personality-based rights theories begin with a theory of the person. Often harkening back to Kant's discussions of the nature of authorship and publication and to Hegel's theory of cultural evolution, personality-based rights theory forms the foundation of German and French copyright law. Several personality-based arguments will be considered in this article. As we shall see, some of these approaches provide a foundation for a more expansive form of intellectual property rights than do moral desert or utilitarian theories, extending, for example, to artists' inalienable "personal rights"[6] over their products.

Utilitarian arguments of various sorts can either support or undercut claims for intellectual property rights. Contingent matters of fact form an especially important part of the utilitarian structure. As I have written elsewhere on the utilitarian arguments for and against intellectual property rights,[7] I will limit myself in this article to a few brief remarks on that subject.

Attempts have also been made to derive intellectual property rights from the retention of certain tangible property rights. Thus, ownership rights to tangible objects are constituted by a bundle of rights that may be alienated or rearranged to suit contracting parties. In selling or otherwise transferring a piece of property, like a copy of a book for example, some of those rights may be reserved, such as the right to make additional copies. The owner of the material substratum in which an ideal object is instantiated may reserve the right to use the material substratum for the purpose of copying the ideal object. This argument might be labeled the "piggyback" theory: the intellectual property right obtains its moral force from its dependence on a more conventional right of property.

I will take the opportunity in this article to present as clearly and fairly as possible each of those four kinds of property arguments. In turn, I will offer criticisms of each of those arguments' internal structures and then attempt to apply them to ideal objects. I will first take up the labor theory of property then the personality theory. I will address utilitarian concerns, but, as I have stated, only briefly. Also, I will discuss the attempt to derive intellectual property rights indirectly, that is, by "piggybacking" on rights to tangible property, and then conclude by presenting my own system that does not recognize copyrights and patents.[8]

I make no claims to an exhaustive taxonomy of property rights theories. Other important theories of property and other theoretical concerns are not dealt with here, because I have chosen to concentrate on those most relevant to the problem of intellectual property. Further, I will have little to say about the actual historical genesis of intellectual property; while intellectual property originated in grants of monopoly from the state and received its legitimacy from that source, the public debate over its legitimacy shifted radically in the late 18th century. As Fritz Machlup and Edith Penrose note, "those who started using the word property in connection with inventions had a very definite purpose in mind: they wanted to substitute a word with a respectable connotation, 'property,' for a word that had an unpleasant ring, 'privilege.' "[9] Given this shift in the popular conception of patents and copyrights, I intend to question whether they are *legitimate* forms of property.

Labor and the Natural Right to Property

Lysander Spooner was surely one of the most remarkable American men of letters of the 19th century. He was a constitutional scholar, a fervent crusader for the abolition of slavery, an entrepreneur who succeeded through competition in forcing the American postal service to lower its rates, a philosopher, a writer on economic matters, and more.

Spooner begins his book, *The Law of Intellectual Property: or An Essay on the Right of Authors and Inventors to a Perpetual Property in Their Ideas,*[10] by establishing the status of immaterial objects as wealth. "Everything—whether intellectual, moral, or material, however gross, or however subtle; whether tangible or intangible, perceptible or imperceptible, by our physical organs—of which the human mind can take cognizance, and which, either as a means, occasion, or end, can either contribute to, or of itself constitute, the well-being of man, is wealth."[11] That obviously includes ideas, which are often the objects of economic transactions. Property, as Spooner defines it, is "simply wealth, that is possessed—that has an owner."[12] The right of property is the "right of dominion," the right "which one man has, as against all other men, to the exclusive control, dominion, use, and enjoyment of any particular thing."[13]

Thus, according to Spooner's definitions, the ideas we have, as well as our feelings and our emotions, are our property. "If the ideas, which a man has produced, were not rightfully his own, but belonged equally to other men, they would have the right imperatively to require him to give his ideas to them, without compensation; and it would be just and right for them to punish him as a criminal, if he refused."[14]

The foundations of property, according to Spooner, are the acts of possession and of creation. Property is necessary to secure the "natural right of each man to provide for his own subsistence; and, secondly, . . . his right to provide for his general happiness and wellbeing, in addition to a mere subsistence."[15] Thus, while Spooner's account of the natural right to property, and especially of intellectual property, falls among the moral-desert arguments for property, it contains a consequentialist element: property is justified because it is a necessary means to the attainment of man's natural end. Having established that ideas are wealth and that all wealth is the product of intellect,[16] Spooner argues analogically that ideas are just as much property as tangible objects. If ideas pre-exist in nature and are merely discovered (as, for example, scientific principles or naturally occurring substances),[17] then "he who does discover, or first takes possession of, an idea, thereby becomes its lawful and rightful proprietor; on the same principle that he, who first takes possession of any material production of nature, thereby makes himself its rightful owner."[18] On the other hand, if ideas are not pre-existing in nature, but are the products of an active intellect, then "the right of property in them belongs to him, whose labor created them."[19]

Spooner spends the rest of the book defending his argument against objections. Against the objection that ideas are incorporeal, he argues that other incorporeal entities can also be objects of property rights, such as labor, a ride, one's reputation and credit; even the right to property is itself inalienable property. To the objection that property rights in ideas cease on publication or communication of an idea to another (*"because that other person thereby acquires as complete possession of the idea, as the original proprietor"*[20]), Spooner responds that it falsely assumes that "if a man once intrust his property in another man's keeping, he thereby loses his own right of property in it."[21] Possession is not equivalent to the right of use, for "where one man intrusts his property in another man's possession, the latter has no right whatever to use it, otherwise than as the owner consents that he may use it."[22]

Against the objection that some ideas are social in nature, Spooner argues that the role of society in the production of ideas is nil. Ideas are created by individuals, and only individuals have rights to them. As Spooner counters, "Nothing is, by its own essence and nature, more perfectly susceptible of exclusive appropriation, than a thought. It originates in the mind of a single individual. It can leave his mind only in obedience to his will. It dies with him, if he so elect."[23] Even granting the truth of the objection, he asks, do we deny private ownership of tangible objects because their creators availed themselves of pre-existing knowledge, or cooperated with others in their production?[24]

Spooner also rebuts the objection that ideas are nonrivalrous in consumption; that is, that the use by one person of an idea does not diminish anyone else's use, and that ideas are therefore unsuitable candidates for the status of property, by showing its consequences if applied to tangible property, for: if it be a true principle, that labor and production give no exclusive right of property, and that every commodity, by whomsoever produced, should, without the consent of the producer, be made to serve as many persons as it can, without bringing them in collision with each other, that principle as clearly requires that a hammer should be free to different persons at different times, and that a road, or canal should be free to as many persons at once, as can use it without collision, as it does that an idea should be free to as many persons at once as choose to use it.[25]

The key to Spooner's approach is to deny those defenses of property that rest on the joint operation of scarcity, the law of the excluded middle, and the desirability of avoiding violent conflict. He writes, "The right of property, or dominion, does not depend, as the objection supposes, upon either the political or moral necessity of men's avoiding collision with each other, in the possession and use of commodities. . . ."[26] Rather, "the right of property, or dominion, depends upon the necessity and right of each man's providing for his own subsistence and happiness; and upon the consequent necessity and right of every man's exercising exclusive and absolute dominion over the fruits of his labor."[27] Similarly, the argument that the propagation of an idea is like the lighting of one candle by another, illuminating the former without darkening the latter, would "apply as well to a surplus of food, clothing, or any other commodity, as to a surplus of ideas, or—what is the same thing—to the surplus capacity of a single idea, beyond the personal use of the producer—by which I mean the capacity of a single idea to be used by other persons simultaneously with the producer, without collision with him."[28]

A similar argument, but one that stops short of property rights in perpetuity, is offered by Ayn Rand. Rand states, "patents and copyrights are the legal implementation of the base of all property rights: a man's right to the product of his mind."[29] Patents and copyrights are moral rights, and not merely legal rights: "The government does not 'grant' a patent or copyright, in the sense of a gift, privilege, or favor; the government merely secures it—i.e., the government certifies the origination of an idea and protects its owner's exclusive right of use and disposal."[30] Like many other advocates of intellectual property rights, Rand sees patents as the highest form of property: "the heart and core of property rights."[31]

In stopping short of granting to scientists and mathematicians rights to the facts or theories they discover, Rand relies on the same general moral principles as Spooner in her defense of the right to intellectual property, but adds a twist. Because of her focus on the role of "productive work" in human happiness, she advocates limits on the temporal duration of intellectual property: "[I]ntellectual property cannot be consumed. If it were held in perpetuity, it would lead to the opposite of the very principle on which it is based: it would lead, not to the earned reward of achievement, but to the unearned support of parasitism. It would become a cumulative lien on the production of unborn generations, which would immediately paralyze them. . . . The inheritance of material property represents a dynamic claim on a static amount of wealth; the inheritance of intellectual property represents a static claim on a dynamic process of production."[32]

Herbert Spencer, who testified on behalf of copyright before the Royal Commission of 1878, presented an argument for patents and copyrights based on moral desert.[33] "[J]ustice under its positive aspect," he argued, "consists in the reception by each individual of the benefits and evils of his own nature and consequent conduct"; therefore, "it is manifest that if any individual by mental labor achieves some result, he ought to have whatever benefit naturally flows from this result."[34] To the objection that the use of another's idea does not take property away from the originator of the idea but only allows its use, he responded, first, that "the use by others may be the contemplated source of profit," second, that a "tacit understanding" limits the rights transferred to "the printed paper, the right of reading and of lending to read, but not the right of reproduction," and, third, that patents and copyrights are not monopolies because monopoly is the use of force to constrain others in the use of what would "in the absence of such law . . . be open to all," while inventions and the like could not be said to exist before their creation.[35]

Lord Coke had defined monopoly as "an institution, or allowance by the king by his grant, commission, or otherwise to any person or persons . . . whereby any person or persons . . . are sought to be restrained of any freedom, or liberty that they had before, or hindered in their lawful trade."[36] Thus, reasoned proponents of patents and copyrights, an exclusive right over an innovation could not be a monopoly, because prior to its invention it was not a "liberty that they had before."[37]

Another labor-based moral desert argument has been advanced by Israel Kirzner.[38] Kirzner begins with the assumption that one is entitled to "what one has produced." His primary concern is to provide a justification for entrepreneurial profits. He asks whether that entitlement derives from the contribution to the production process of factors of production or from entrepreneurial activity. Following what he calls the "finders-keepers" rule, he argues that "a producer is entitled to what he has produced not because he has contributed anything to its physical fabrication, but because he perceived and grasped the opportunity for its fabrication by utilizing the resources available in the market."[39] He contrasts "ownership-by-creation" with "ownership-by-just-acquisition-from-nature" and argues that the former better justifies entrepreneurial profit because "until a resource has been discovered, it has not, in the sense relevant to the rights of access and common use, existed at all. By this view it seems plausible to consider the discoverer of the hitherto 'nonexistent' resource as, in the relevant sense, the creator of what he has found."[40] Clearly, if one were to substitute such an "ownership by creation" theory (or "finders-keepers") for "ownership-by-just-acquisition-from-nature," then the case for intellectual property rights would become much more plausible.

All of these lines of argument strongly emphasize the *moral* desert of the creator, inventor, or author.[41] They are consistent with the argument of John Locke in his *Second Treatise* that no one, so long as there was "as good left for his Improvement," should "meddle with what was already improved by another's Labour; If he did, 'tis plain he desired the benefit of another's Pains, which he had no right to."[42] When one has improved what was before unimproved (or created what before did not exist), one is entitled to the result of one's labor. One deserves it.

Objections to Labor-Based Moral Desert Theories

Arguments such as Spooner's and Rand's encounter a fundamental problem. While they pay homage to the right of self-ownership, they restrict others' uses of their own bodies in conjunction with resources to which they have full moral and legal rights. Enforcement of a property right in a dance, for example, means that force can be used against another to stop him from taking certain steps with his body; enforcement of a property right in an invention means that force can be used against another to stop him from using his hands in certain ways. In each case, an intellectual property right is a claim of a right over how another person uses her body.

As the pro-liberty journalist William Leggett, a leader of the Jacksonian Loco-Foco party and editor of the *New York Evening Post*, wrote, "We do not wish to deny to British authors a right; but we do desire that a legal privilege, which we contend has no foundation in natural right, and is prejudicial to "the greatest good of the greatest number," should be wholly annulled, in relation to all authors, of every name and country. Our position is, that authors have no natural right of property in their published works, and that laws to create and guard such a right are adverse to the true interests of society."[43]

Leggett opposed copyright and patent rights for two reasons: First, he argued that intellectual property rights stifled the free spread of ideas and damaged the public interest.[44] Second, he argued that such rights were in reality statutory monopolies that infringed upon the rights of others to the ownership of their own bodies: Our position that an author has an exclusive natural right of property in his manuscript, was meant to be understood only in the same sense that a mechanic has an exclusive natural right of property in the results of his labour. The mental process by which he contrived those results are not, and cannot properly be rendered, exclusive property; since the right of a free exercise of our thinking faculties is given by nature to all mankind, and the mere fact that a given mode of doing a thing has been thought of by one, does not prevent the same ideas presenting themselves to the mind of another and should not prevent him from a perfect liberty of acting upon them.[45]

Leggett's argument, while containing strong consequentialist elements, rests on the intimate relationship between liberty and property: "The rights of corporeal property may be asserted, without the possibility of infringing any other individual's rights. Those of incorporeal property may obviously give rise to conflicting claims, all equally well founded. . . . If you assert an exclusive right to a particular idea, you cannot be sure that the very same idea did not at the same moment enter some other mind."[46]

Israel Kirzner's attempt to substitute "ownership by creation" for "ownership by just acquisition from nature" encounters difficulty because it leaves us with a mere assumption, that "a man deserves what he has produced," as a justification for property. However, entrepreneurial profits can be justified in other ways consistent with the theory of ownership by just acquisition.[47] "Profits" are justified if they arise by means of Nozickian "justice-preserving transformations."[48] A rearrangement of property titles that emerged through a series of voluntary transfers, each of which was just, and which began on a foundation of just property titles, is itself just. If in the process profits or losses are generated, then those are just as well. The Kirznerian substitute, in contrast, suffers from a lack of grounding. "Because we produced it" is an inadequate answer to the question of why we deserve what we have produced.

These authors do not effectively deal with the important problem of simultaneous invention or discovery, which is often raised as an objection to positions such as those taken by Spooner and Rand. According to Rand:

> As an objection to the patent laws, some people cite the fact that two inventors may work independently for years on the same invention, but one will beat the other to the patent office by an hour or a day and will acquire an exclusive monopoly, while the loser's work will be totally wasted. . . . Since the issue is one of commercial rights, the loser in a

case of that kind has to accept the fact that in seeking to trade with others he must face the possibility of a competitor winning the race. . . .[49]

That response does not comport well with her earlier claim that intellectual property rights are natural rights that are merely recognized—not granted—by government; in this case a full monopoly is awarded by government to one inventor, while another with a claim equally valid in every respect except for a 10-minute lead time at the patent office is denied any right to exploit the invention.

Spooner offers a very different response to the problem:

[T]he fact that two men produce the same invention, is a very good reason why the invention should belong to both; but it is no reason at all why both should be deprived of it. If two men produce the same invention, each has an equal right to it; because each has an equal right to the fruits of his labor. Neither can deny the right of the other, without denying his own.[50]

What if, however, one of the inventors were to give this right to the rest of mankind? As Leggett argued, in the case of authorship: Two authors, without concert or intercommunion, may describe the same incidents, in language so nearly identical that the two books, for all purposes of sale, shall be the same. Yet one writer may make a free gift of his production to the public, may throw it open in common; and then what becomes of the other's right of property?[51]

The same argument can be extended, of course, to inventions. Liberty and intellectual property seem to be at odds, for while property in tangible objects limits actions only with respect to particular goods, property in ideal objects restricts an entire range of actions unlimited by place or time, involving legitimately owned property (VCRs, tape recorders, typewriters, the human voice, and more) by all but those privileged to receive monopoly grants from the state. To those who might argue that any form of property limits liberty in some way, Jan Narveson responds: "This is to talk as though the "restrictions" involved in ownership were nothing but that. But that's absurd! The essence of my having an Apple Macintosh is that I *have* one, at my disposal when and as I wish, which latter of course requires that you not be able simply to use it any time you like; it's *not that you can't have one unless I say so.*"⁵²

My ownership claim over my computer restricts your access to that computer, but it is not a blanket restriction on your liberty to acquire a similar computer, or an abacus, or to count on your fingers or use pencil and paper. In contrast, to claim a property right over a process is to claim a blanket right to control the actions of others. For example, if a property right to the use of the abacus were to be granted to someone, it would mean precisely that others could not make an abacus unless they had the permission of the owner of that right. It would be a restriction on the liberty of everyone who wanted to make an abacus with their own labor out of wood that they legitimately owned. That is a restriction on action qualitatively different from the restriction implied in my ownership of a particular abacus.

The previous paragraph illustrates that intellectual property rights are not equivalent to other property rights in "restricting liberty." Property rights in tangible objects do not restrict liberty at all—they simply restrain action. Intellectual property rights, on the other hand, do restrict liberty.

Arguments from self-ownership, including Spooner's (but perhaps not Rand's), hinge upon the idea of liberty. As I argued above, there is no reason that a number of different arguments might not be marshaled in favor of property. Locke's argument for labor as the foundation of property has three principal pillars: First, having established the right to property in oneself, how can we determine when something has become "so his, *i.e.*, a part of him, that another can no longer have any right to it?"⁵³ The annexation of labor is the relevant point at which a thing becomes owned by becoming assimilated to one's body, the violation of which constitutes an infringement of liberty. Second, [God] gave [the earth] to the Industrious and Rational, (and *Labour* was to be *his Title* to it;) not to the Fancy or Covetousness of the Quarrelsom and Contentious. He that had as good left for his Improvement, as was already taken up, needed not complain, ought not to meddle with what was already improved by another's Labour: If he did, 'tis plain he desired the benefit of another's Pains, which he had no right to. . . .⁵⁴ Third, "'tis *Labour* indeed that *puts the difference of value* on every thing . . . . [T]he improvement of *labour makes* the far greater part of *the value.*" Indeed, "in most of them 99/100 are wholly to be put on the account of *labor.*"⁵⁵

These three arguments all lend support, each in a different way, to private property rights in land—Locke's primary interest in the chapter on property. They diverge when it comes to ideal objects, however. Although the second and third arguments lend support to intellectual property rights claims, the first emphatically does not.

For Locke, self-ownership serves several important functions. First, it is the foundation of liberty; indeed, it is synonymous with liberty. Second, it allows Locke to respond effectively to Filmer's criticism of the consent theories of property set forth by Hugo Grotius and Samuel Pufendorf. If appropriation of common property rests on unanimous consent, Filmer knows of at least one person who would refuse his consent, thus knocking the struts out from under the entire edifice. Locke seeks to show "how Men might come to have a *property* in several parts of that which God gave to Mankind in common, and that without any express Compact of all the Commoners,"[56] that is, in a way that will avoid Filmer's other-wise fatal objection. By beginning with one tangible thing that is so clearly one's own that no one else can claim it—one's own body— Locke shows how property rights can legitimately emerge without requiring universal consent, thus sidestepping Filmer's objection.[57]

Locke sees this right of self-ownership as necessary for liberty. He explicitly rules out "voluntary slavery" (or absolutism along Hobbesian lines) and takes care to argue that our self-ownership is inalienable.[58] Indeed, the preface of the *Two Treatises,* in which he states that he hopes that his words *"are sufficient to establish the Throne of our Great Restorer, Our present King William; to make good his Title, in the Consent of the People, which being the only one of all lawful Governments, he has more fully and clearly than any Prince in* Christendom,"[59] indicates that the arguments are intended to overthrow Stuart despotism and usher in an era of liberty. (Re-markably, one of the principal popular complaints against the Stuarts was their patent policy.)[60] Ownership in ourselves is the foundation for ownership of alienable objects because they become assimilated to our bodies.[61] At a highly strategic point in his argument, Locke raises the following problem: "He that is nour-ished by the Acorns he pickt up under an Oak, or the Apples he gathered from the Trees in the Wood, has certainly appropriated them to himself. No Body can deny but the nourishment is his. I ask then, When did they begin to be his? When he digested? Or when he eat? Or when he boiled? Or when he brought them home? Or when he pickt them up?"[62]

Clearly, to force a man to disgorge his meal after he has eaten it would be to infringe his rights to his own body. But at what point does it become so intimately related to him, "so his, *i.e.* a part of him, that another can no longer have any right to it,"[63] that to take it from him would be an injustice? Locke settles on the transformation of the object through labor as the demarcation point: "And 'tis plain, if the first gathering made them not his, nothing else could. That *labour* put a distinction between them and common. That added something to them more than Nature, the common Mother of all, had done; and so they became his private right."[64]

If the hinge to a Lockean labor theory of property, then, is ownership in ourselves (as I believe it is), the fact that Locke's two additional supplementary arguments point toward a form of "property" that would infringe on our ownership in ourselves (as copyrights and patents do) indicates that they should be detached from the argument from self-ownership as contradictory to it, in the case of patents and copyrights, at least. If one wished to insist on the justice of intellectual property claims, ownership rights in ourselves would have to be rejected as a foundation for property and independent arguments offered for rewarding moral desert based on labor. That is a difficult task, and one that has not been adequately undertaken, for reasons that Hume, Kant, and others have pointed out: desert has no principle, that is, no readily available and intersubjectively ascertainable measure.[65] Such an inherently subjective standard provides a poor foundation for the abstract and general rules that guide conduct in a great society.[66] In a great society, not all labor is rewarded;[67] and not all of the rewards to labor are in the form of property rights.[68]

Our ownership rights in ourselves are based on our natural freedom, and are indeed synonymous with it; they cannot rest on labor-based moral desert, as we are not the products of our own labor. But that is the subject of the next section of this article.

Personality and Intellectual Property Rights

The development of personality has been linked to property rights by a number of pro-property writers, notably the German classical liberal Wilhelm von Humboldt. In his seminal work, *The Limits of State Action*, von Humboldt declared that "[t]he true end of Man . . . is the highest and most harmonious development of his powers to a complete and consistent whole."[69] Further, he wrote: "[R]eason cannot desire for man any other condition than that in which each individual not only enjoys the most absolute freedom of developing himself by his own energies, in his perfect individuality, but in which each external nature itself is left unfashioned by any human agency, but only receives the impress given to it by each individual by himself and of his own free will, to the measure of his wants and instincts, and restricted only by the limits of his powers and his rights."[70] "Every citizen," wrote von Humboldt, "must be in a position to act without hindrance and just as he pleases, so long as he does not transgress the law. . . . If he is deprived of this liberty, then his right is violated, and the cultivation of his faculties—the development of his individuality—suffers."[71]

Respect for property is intimately related to this self-development. "[T]he idea of property grows only in company with the idea of freedom, and it is to the sense of property that we owe the most vigorous activity."[72] Provision of security from external force is the proper end of government: "I call the citizens of a State secure, when, living together in the full enjoyment of their due rights of person and property, they are out of the reach of any external disturbance from the encroachments of others."[73]

This line of argument—deriving property from the requirements of personal development—seems in some ways a restatement of Locke's basic argument,[74] but with a different twist. Rather than emphasize the satisfaction of man's material wants and, through that, fulfillment of God's injunction to man in the Garden of Eden to prosper and multiply, von Humboldt emphasizes the development of human potential.[75] The key to both the Lockean and the Humboldtean arguments is ownership in ourselves, with state power severely constrained and limited to the protection of liberty. As J. W. Burrow notes, "[Humboldt's] view of the State's functions may not differ in practice from a natural rights theory of the traditional Lockean kind."[76]

In practice, the Lockean and Humboldtean liberty-based arguments for property are fundamentally the same, although the emphasis differs. At base, each is intimately concerned with freedom. Indeed, von Humboldt's argument against the validity of testamentary dispositions that go beyond mere transference of property titles to one's heirs shows the primacy of freedom in his theory:

[A]s long as he lives, man is free to dispose of his things as he pleases, to alienate them in part or altogether—their sub-

> stance, use, or possession; . . . But he is in no way entitled to
> define, in any way binding on others, what shall be done
> with his property after his decease, or to determine how its
> future possessor is to act. . . . [This] restricts that freedom
> which is essential to human development, and so runs
> counter to every principle we have put forward.[77]

That argument from personality offers little support for patents and
copyrights, and, like other arguments from ownership rights in
ourselves, would be more likely to undercut claims for intellectual
property rights.

A superficially similar, but in reality very different, argument
based on personality is offered by Hegel in his *Philosophy of Right*.[78]
Unlike von Humboldt's appeal to the development of personality,
the Hegelian argument sees property not only as a necessary
condition for this development but as the manifestation of this
development itself. In the *Phenomenology of Spirit*, Hegel emphasized
that it is through work that spirit comes to know itself.[79] In the
Philosophy of Right, a treatise on law, property fills the role of work.
Notably, the discussion of property culminates in patents and
copyrights. For Hegel, personality forms the foundation of any
system of rights: "Personality essentially involves the capacity for
rights and constitutes the concept and the basis (itself abstract) of
the system of abstract and therefore formal right. Hence the imperative of rights: 'Be a person and respect others as persons.' "[80]
Personality must be translated from mere potentiality into actuality,
or, in Hegelian terms, from Concept (*Begriff*) to Idea (*Idee*).

A person must translate his freedom into an external sphere in
order to exist as Idea. Personality is the first, still wholly abstract,
determination of the absolute and infinite will, and therefore this
sphere distinct from the person, the sphere capable of embodying
his freedom, is likewise determined as what is immediately different and separable from him.[81] Hegel specifically eschews utilitarian
justifications for property, for "[i]f emphasis is placed on my needs,
then the possession of property appears as a means to their satisfaction, but the true position is that, from the standpoint of freedom,
property is the first embodiment of freedom and so is in itself a
substantive end."[82] The metaphysical grounding of this theory of
private property is straightforward: "Since my will, as the will of a
person, and so as a single will, becomes objective to me in property,
property acquires the character of private property. . . ."[83] Personal-

ity does not simply require external objects for its development. Its development *is* its objectification through externalization of its will.

Occupancy, not labor, is the act by which external things become property: "The principle that a thing belongs to the person who happens to be the first in time to take it into his possession is immediately self-explanatory and superfluous, because a second person cannot take into his possession what is already the property of another."[84] This occupancy, or taking possession, can take three forms: (1) by directly grasping it physically, (2) by forming it, and (3) by merely marking it as ours.[85] It is the second of these forms of possession that is most interesting for our purposes. As Hegel remarks, "When I impose a form on something, the thing's determinate character as mine acquires an independent externality and ceases to be restricted to my presence here and now and to the direct presence of my awareness and will."[86]

Unlike Locke, Hegel does not see man as naturally free, and therefore as having natural or pre-political ownership rights in himself. It is only through the historical process of objectification and hence self-confrontation that one comes to be free: "It is only through the development of his own body and mind, essentially through his self-consciousness's apprehension of itself as free, that he takes possession of himself and becomes his own property and no one else's."[87]

When it comes to intellectual property, Hegel does not go nearly as far as his epigoni, such as Otto Von Gierke and Josef Kohler. Like Kant, Hegel offers great protection to literary works, but very little to the plastic arts. Kant argued for the protection of literary works in his essay, "On the Injustice of the Pirating of Books."[88] A brief digression on Kant's theory of copyright is appropriate here, after which we shall return to Hegel's treatment and to its reformulation and extraordinary extension in more recent years.

In a chapter of his *Metaphysics of Morals* titled "What Is a Book," Kant identified the equivocal use of the term "book" as the source of the dispute over copyrights.

The basic cause of an appearance of legality in something that is nevertheless, at the first inspection, such an injustice—as book piracy is—lies in this: that the book is, on the one hand, a corporeal product of art (*opus mechanicum*), which can be copied (by him, who finds himself in legal possession of an exemplar of this product)—consequently has a real right therein; on the other hand, however, a book is also merely an address of the publisher to the public, which this publisher, without having the authorization thereto of the author, may not publicly repeat (*praestatio operae*)—a personal right; and now the error consists in this, that the two are confused with each other.[89]

Thus, a "book" is both the corporeal thing I hold when I read ("my book"), and also the address by one person to another (the "author's book"). Kant argued that a book or other literary product is not simply "a kind of merchandise," but an *"exercise of his* [the author's] *powers (opera),* which he can grant to others (*concedere*), but can never alienate."[90] A copier, or infringer, offers to the public the thoughts of another, the author. That is, he speaks in the author's name, which he can properly do only with permission. The author has given permission, however, only to his authorized publisher, who is wronged when a book edition is pirated.

The extension of such a personal right beyond a real right is shown in the case of the death of an author prior to publication of his work:

> That the publisher does not conduct his business in his own name, but in that of another, is confirmed by certain obligations which are universally acknowledged. Were the author to die after he had confided his [manuscript] to the publisher for printing and the publisher had agreed to the conditions, still the publisher is not free. In default of heirs, the public has a right to compel him to publish it, or to give over the [manuscript] to another who may offer himself as publisher. For it had been a business which the author, through him, wished to carry on with the public, and for which he offered himself as agent. [H]e [the publisher] possesses the [manuscript] only on condition that he shall use it with the public in the interest of the author. If the publisher should mutilate or falsify the work after the death of the author, or if he should fail in producing a number of copies equal to the demand, then the public would have the right to require him to enlarge the edition and to exact greater accuracy, and, if he refused to meet these demands, to go elsewhere to get them complied with.[91]

Importantly, Kant limits those rights against copiers or mutilators to literary products and denies them to the plastic and representational arts.[92] Kant wrote:

> Works of art, as things, can, on the contrary, from a copy of them which has been lawfully procured, be imitated, modeled, and the copies openly sold, without the consent of the creator of their original, or of those whom he has employed to carry out his ideas. A drawing which some one has designed, or through another caused to be copied in copper or stone, metal or plaster of Paris, can by those who buy the production be printed or cast, and so openly made traffic of. So with all which anyone executes with his own things and in his own name, the consent of another is not necessary. For it is a work—an *opus*, not an *opera alterius*—which each who possesses, without even knowing the name of the artist, can dispose of, consequently can imitate, and in his own name expose for sale as his own. But the writing of another is the speech of a person—*opera*—and he who publishes it can only speak to the public in the name of the author. He himself has nothing further to say than that the author, through him, makes the following speech to the public.[93]

Thus, the key to Kantian copyright is speech; when no speech is present, no copyright accrues to the creator. Accordingly, Kant claimed consistently that translations or derivative works cannot be restricted by copyright: "He [an editor] represents himself, not as that author as if he were speaking through him, but as another. Translation into another language is also not infringement, for it is not the very speech of the author although the thoughts may be the same."[94]

Like Kant, Hegel argues that artistic reproductions are "so peculiarly the property of the individual artist that a copy of a work of art is essentially a product of the copyist's own mental and technical ability," while the reproduction of literary works or of inventions "is of a mechanical kind."[95] Hegel declared further that "this power to reproduce has a special character, viz. it is that in virtue of which the thing is not merely a possession but a capital asset."[96] The right of reproduction of inventions or literary works derives from their nature as capital assets, and not mere possessions. They yield an income stream, the diminution of which substantially diminishes the value of the capital.

The theories of personal rights and of personality set forth by Kant and Hegel have been extended in the last hundred years or so to embrace a range of rights to artistic productions far wider than they envisioned. Indeed, those alleged rights are not, like Anglo-American copyrights, fully alienable, but are, as the French 1957 Law on Artistic and Literary Property[97] declares, "perpetual, inalienable, and imprescriptible."[98] Substantial efforts have been made to import that notion into American law, much of them occasioned by the introduction of the technique of "colorizing" films originally produced in black-and-white.[99]

As developed under French law, four such personal rights are retained by artists: the right of disclosure, the right of attribution, the right of integrity, and the right of retraction.[100] Rather than offering a survey of some of the more *outre'* results of this law, I will present instead a brief statement of its theoretical grounding.

Such rights entered the law (in France, at least, the place where they have received the greatest legal recognition) in court decisions governing the division of artistic property. In a 1902 case before the Court of Cassation, the court had to consider whether the ex-wife of an artist had the right to share in the commercial exploits of her husband's work.[101] The court ruled that she had a right to a share of the economic proceeds, but that this decision would not "detract from the right of the author, inherent in his personality, of later modifying his creation, or even suppressing it."[102]

Josef Kohler, author of an influential treatise on law, argued: "Personality must be permitted to be active, that is to say, to bring its will to bear and reveal its significance to the world; for culture can thrive only if persons are able to express themselves, and are in a position to place all their inherent capacities at the command of their will."[103] So far, this sounds familiar. But Kohler argued further:

> [T]he writer can not only demand that no strange work be presented as his, but that his own work not be presented in a changed form. The author can make this demand even when he has given up his copyright. This demand is not so much an exercise of dominion over my own work, as it is of dominion over my being, over my personality which thus gives me the right to demand that no one shall share

in my personality and have me say things which I have not said.[104]

Damage to a work of art, even after ownership rights to it have been transferred to another party, constitutes damage to the personality of the creator; the work of art is an extension of the personality of the creator. Thus, according to Kohler, issuing an unauthorized, or *bowdlerized*, edition of an author's work, hanging red ribbons on a sculpture, or tearing down a piece of sculpture even so offensively ugly as Richard Serra's "Tilted Arc" (as was recently done in New York) all constitute damage to the personality of the creator. In fact, the relationship between creator and creation is so intimate that when the personality of the former changes, so too can the treatment of the latter. Under article 32 of the French 1957 law, for example: "Notwithstanding the transfer of his right of exploitation, the author, even after the publication of his work, enjoys a right of modification or withdrawal vis-a-vis his transferee."[105] The concept of personal rights has also been extended to encompass the so-called *droit de suite*, or inalienable resale royalty rights. According to this idea, a part of French law[106] and relatively recently adopted into law by several American states, a percentage of the resale profits beyond a certain level must be given to the original creator.

Objections to Personality-Based Intellectual Property Theories

At their foundation, personality-based theories of intellectual property suffer from a confusion about the ontological status of ideal objects and their relationship to their creators. If, as Hegel insists, "[a] person must translate his freedom into an external sphere in order to exist as Idea,"[107] this does not mean that that "translation" is constitutive of the person himself, nor that the artifacts resulting from that translation become inextricably bound up with the person.

This is especially obvious in the case of such artifacts as a puff of smoke, a tracing in the sand, or a knot in a piece of rope. The smoke may dissipate; the tracing may be washed away by the tide; the knot may come undone; but in none of these cases is the personality of the creator diminished. Most claims on behalf of personality-based rights are confined to "artistic" creations. Thus, Rep. Edward J. Markey (D-Mass.) argues that: "A work of art is not a utilitarian object, like a toaster; it is a creative work, like a song, a poem, or a novel. We should not pretend that all connection between the artist and the creation is severed the first time the work is sold."[108]

Representative Markey, like the philosophers who have influenced him, has misunderstood the ontology of the work of art. The connection between "the artist and the creation" is indeed severed, not the first time the work is sold, but the moment that it is finished.[109] Referents of discourse can enjoy various kinds of dependent being. They may, for example, be dependent upon another thing, as the brightness of a surface is "dependent" on the surface, or they may be dependent in another way, as a hand is dependent for its being on the body to which it is attached, although the hand and the body may become separated, unlike the surface and the brightness.[110]

Two senses of dependence are confused by advocates of personality-based intellectual property theories: the dependence of the art work on a human agent or agents for its *creation,* and the dependence of that same work of art on a human agent or agents for its continued existence. While a work of art obviously depends on its creator(s) for its creation, and is therefore a "translation of his freedom into an external sphere," once it is created it enjoys its own objectivity. The sign that an art work exists as an objectivity is that we can always return to it and find the same work. We do not experience a different work every time we see or read Shakespeare's *Othello.*[111] Once created, works of art are independent of their creators, as should be evident by the fact that works of art do not "die" when their creators do. While no longer dependent on their creators, they nevertheless remain dependent on some human agency for their continued existence. The agents they depend on, however, are not artists but audiences.[112]

Romantic notions of creativity, which stress subjective experience and its expression, emphasize the sublime experience of the artist. The reproduction of this experience is what constitutes the artistic attitude. The artist recreates her own experience in the audience by means of artistic works or performances. But the concrete experience of the artist cannot be identical with the concrete experience of the audience—the readers, listeners, or viewers. In opposition to the romantic notions of art taken up in personality theories of intellectual property, with their emphasis on the subjective, Roman Ingarden argues that the identification of the work of art with its creator's subjective experiences would mean that "it would be impossible either to have a direct intercourse with the work or to know it."[113] The reason is that everything that would be directly accessible to us—except for the perceived characters—would be only our ideas, thoughts, or, possibly, emotional states. No one would want to identify the concrete psychic contents experienced by us during the reading with the already long gone experiences of the author. Thus, the work is either not directly comprehensible, or else it is identical with our experiences. Whatever the case, the attempt to identify the literary work with a manifold of the author's psychic experiences is quite absurd. The author's experiences cease to exist the moment the work created by him comes into existence.[114] In addition, as Ingarden points out, we would have to ask how we could exclude from an author's experiences "a toothache he might have had in the course of writing," while simultaneously including in his work "the desires of a character . . . which the author himself certainly did not, and could not, experience."[115]

The fact that two of us can appreciate the "same" work (say, for example, a sonata), although we each undergo different perceptual experiences (you are in the front of the hall, I am at the back, etc.), indicates that the work enjoys at least an inter-subjective availability. We do not say that we went to two different performances, nor that we heard two different sonatas, simply because our perceptions (or impressions) were not entirely the same. The objectivity of Shakespeare's *Othello* consists in precisely this: that there is one *Othello* for all of us, rather than one *Othello* for each of us, or even one for each of our separate readings or viewings of the play.[116]

Each separate performance of *Othello* is a real event and as such is governed by property rights (the rights of self-ownership of the actors, the property rights of the theater owners, etc.), while *Othello* itself is neither a real event nor a real object. While the work of art does indeed originate in a definite time, as Ingarden notes: not everything which originates in a definite time must therefore be something real. . . . Every real object and every real event is, above all, something which exists or takes place *hic et nunc*. But . . . the categories of *here* and *now* cannot be applied to the musical work and its content. . . . What is it supposed to mean, for example, that Beethoven's sonata, *Opus* 13, is "here"? Where is "here"?[117]

The sameness, intersubjectivity, and objectivity of the work are intimately related. Without a manifold of appearances—like presentations and interpretations—the work cannot appear to us as "the same"; without appearing to us as the same, it cannot be intersubjective; and without intersubjectivity, it cannot be objective. In the dialectic of same and other, we cannot have the former without the latter; we cannot have "same" without "other." Thus, we cannot have the sameness of a work of art without a manifold of otherness in which its sameness can appear as an immanent pole of unity.[118]

Thus, a work of art enjoys its peculiar kind of objectivity only through a multitude of presentations and interpretations that provide the manifold within which it can appear as the same, not only to one interpreter but to many.[119] The special kind of objectivity enjoyed by art is called "heteronomy" by Roman Ingarden.[120] The art work is objective but "other ruled."

This situation of being "other ruled" arises from the dependence of the art work not only on the creative activity of the artist but—even more—on the activity of its audience. In order to exist as an art work, an object must have an audience that can appreciate it, that is, an audience with the appropriate capacities.[121] An audience of the tone deaf would be incapable of appreciating certain kinds of music; a group of Kalahari bushmen would be unlikely to appreciate a play by Molière; and an audience of modern Americans would probably not grasp the subtleties of Japanese "No" theater. A special competence is presupposed on the part of an audience for a work of art to be distinguished from a mere thing or event.

Thus, if special personal rights governing works of art are to be recognized anywhere, they should be in the audience, and not in the artist, for it is on the audience that the art work depends for its continued existence and not the artist. The concept of the *droit moral* for artists is completely misguided. It reveals a faulty appreciation of the relationship between artist, art work, and audience.[122]

If rights do exist to enjoy works unaltered from their original state, they inhere, as Kant noted, not in the artist (or author) but in the audience. A publisher who passed off as Shakespeare's *Hamlet* a work that was missing the soliloquy would be defrauding the audience; he would not be doing any harm to the personality of the late Mr. Shakespeare. If, however, the work were published as "Shakespeare's Hamlet, Minus Various Indecisive Parts," then the purchasers of the work would have no grounds for legal complaint. Personality-based intellectual property rights attaching to manufacturing processes or algorithms lack any of the special ontological claims of personal rights for artists; the scientist may realize his freedom in his discoveries, the inventor in his inventions, but the personality of neither is harmed when their results are put to new uses.[123] Those claims to property rights as necessary to the realization of freedom reduce, then, to the argument of Wilhelm von Humboldt, which, as noted above,[124] is another version of the principal argument of John Locke. And that liberty-based argument, in its primary implications, is hostile rather than friendly to intellectual property claims, for such claims represent liberty restrictions on others in ways that tangible property rights do not.

As to the *droite de suite*, or inalienable resale royalty right, the economic consequences of that notion have been explored elsewhere.[125] It should suffice to point out that this resale royalty right benefits some established artists by awarding to them unearned windfall profits, while others suffer by having their freedom to negotiate over the schedule of payments coercively abridged. The prospect of having to part with a share of the appreciation of a work is capitalized into the sale price, meaning that the money received at the point of sale by the artist will be less.[126] In addition, like inalienable personal rights over art works, such "rights" reduce the moral agency of artists by restricting their rights to make contracts with others. The terms of the contract are fixed by others, and the contracting parties are constrained from freely transferring their property by contract.

The Basic Structure of Utilitarian Arguments and Intellectual Property Rights

As noted earlier, utilitarian arguments of a certain class can cut for or against intellectual property rights claims. As dealt with in much of the economics literature, for example, the utility gains from increased incentives for innovation must be weighed against the utility losses incurred from monopolization of innovations and their diminished diffusion. Some have argued that the first part of the comparison may be either negative or positive; patents or copyrights may actually decrease innovation rather than increase it.[127]

Thus, the specific situation matters a great deal in such arguments. But that kind of utilitarian argument does not exhaust the range of possible utilitarian approaches. Here, I will simply contrast arguments of that sort, which I will call "X-maximization arguments" (with "X" standing in for utility, wealth, or some other welfare-related maximand), with another sort of broad utilitarian concern: justice-as-order.[128] The former seeks to arrange property rights in such a way that some quantity is maximized; the latter seeks to create an overarching order within which human beings can realize their various ends without suffering from uncertainty arising from scarce resources, social conflict, and violent predation.[129]

X-maximization arguments over intellectual property rights hinge on contingent matters of fact. The relevant facts may change; technology, social practices, and other factors cannot be held constant in the real world.[130] Scarcity plays a vital role within such approaches. Innovations and research are scarce in the sense that they "use up" resources, and the allocation of those resources involves opportunity costs, that is, alternative uses of the resources that are foregone. The problem, then, is to allocate property rights— including intellectual property rights—in such a way that the greatest net "X" (utility, wealth, and so on) is produced.

The role of scarcity within the justice-as-order approach is equally important, but leads us in an entirely different direction. Rights to property are allocated precisely because the scarcity of resources means human beings would come into violent conflict over these resources. That relationship between justice-as-order and property rights is what Hume is getting at when he argues that without property there is no justice:

> [T]ho' I assert, that in the *state of nature,* or that imaginary state, which preceded society, there be neither justice nor injustice, yet I assert not, that it was allowable, in such a state, to violate the property of others. I only maintain that there was no such thing as property; and consequently cou'd be no such thing as justice or injustice.[131]

Scarcity in X-maximization arguments is the relevant factor in deciding whether intellectual property rights should be recognized, and if so, what form they should take. Scarcity in justice-as-order arguments is the relevant factor in determining when rights can or should be granted to resources over which humans may come into violent conflict. Intellectual property, however, does not have the "static" scarcity that tangible property has, and therefore does not qualify as a *locus* of property rights within justice-as-order arguments.[132] Two of us can think the same thought, sing the same song, or use the same method of making fishhooks without coming into violent conflict over the thought, song, or method. Justice-as-order is incompatible with intellectual property rights.[133]

Piggybacking on the Rights to Tangible Property

One final argument for intellectual property rights, or at least for copyright, deserves consideration before turning to the foundation of a property-rights system consistent with liberty. That is the argument that intellectual property rights can be justified as "piggyback" rights, logical extensions of the right to own and control tangible objects. Thus, Murray Rothbard justifies what he incorrectly[134] calls "common-law copyright" as amounting to "the author or publisher selling all rights to his property *except* the right to resell it."[135]

Rothbard's argument implicitly rests on the distinction drawn by Kant between a "book" (or other object) as a material thing, and a "book" as the work that is instantiated in a material object but is capable of being instantiated in other such substrata ad infinitum.[136] He extends his argument beyond the realm of literature to include any artifact that incorporates or instantiates an ideal object— whether a mousetrap (its design or the process by which it was made), a map, or a dance step—which is always materially instantiated in some way, whether in a performance on some piece of property, or through a description in a book, film, or other device. That would extend a copyright-type of protection to the subject matter of patents as well. Thus, argues Rothbard, Suppose that Brown builds a better mousetrap and sells it widely, but stamps each mousetrap 'copyright Mr. Brown.' What he is then doing is selling not the entire property right in each mousetrap, but the right to do anything with the mousetrap except to sell it or an identical copy to someone else. The right to sell the Brown mousetrap is retained in perpetuity by Brown.[137]

The fact that a property right can be conceived as a bundle of rights to a thing indicates that one right among the many may be retained by the original producer, in this case, the right to reproduce the item. Just as a piece of land may be sold and certain rights retained (easements, building restrictions, etc.), so all the rights to a mousetrap could be sold except one, the right to copy it. That argument is not novel, and was in fact criticized by Kant and Hegel.[138]

The separation and retention of the right to copy from the bundle of rights that we call property is problematic. Could one reserve the right, for example, to remember something? Suppose that I wrote a book and offered it to you to read but I had retained one right: the right to remember it. Would I be justified in taking you to court if I could prove that you had remembered the name of the lead character in the novel? Could the retention of the right to copy include the right to remember? Suppose that I had memorized the book and then spoke the words aloud to another. Would I be violating a retained right to the tangible object?[139] What if I had heard another person recite the work and then wrote it down and published it? Would I be guilty of a violation of the creator's property rights by publishing a work that I had heard another recite? What if I recorded a broadcast on my VCR? Does the broadcaster own my television set and reserve the right to determine its use in recording signals that come over the airwaves? [140] If the answer is yes, then advocates of a "piggyback" copyright cannot base their argument simply on a retained right to tangible property, for this amounts to asserting a direct claim to the ideal object itself.[141]

Rothbard would have been far better off looking to the law of trade secrets rather than to the law of copyright as a foundation for a retained right, or for quasi-contractual legal exclusivity in the results of the creator's efforts. Under the law of trade secrecy, "trade secrets are not given protection against all the world, but only against one who has learned the secret by improper means or by virtue of a confidential relation."[142] Thus, if a secret, such as a manufacturing process, a design, or the internal operation of a device, is revealed to others who are not bound by contract or by a fiduciary relationship to keep the secret confidential, then the original proprietor of the secret has no grounds for legal action against others who would duplicate his product or otherwise use what was previously secret.

If a chemist for the Coca-Cola Company were to reproduce the formula for Coca-Cola (a trade secret, unprotected by patent) on leaflets and drop them over New York City, the Coca-Cola Company would have uncontestable grounds for (drastic) legal action against the violator of their secret and any of his conspirators, but not against all those on whom the leaflets fell who proceeded to duplicate the firm's production efforts. Similarly, independent inventors would be immune from legal action. If the proprietor of the trade secret were unable to show that another user had improper access to his product, his production process, or some other relevant aspect of his business, then he has no legal claim against the independent inventor. Thus, an ideal object can be constrained within a contractual nexus by property rights, but once that ideal object has somehow escaped the nexus, it can no longer be restrained by force of law. Such an approach is fully consistent with the property rights regime set forth in the remainder of this article.

Justice and the Right to Property

Having offered criticisms of various property rights claims, it is incumbent upon me to offer an alternative argument that will establish property rights in tangible objects while denying them in ideal objects.

As noted above, liberty-based arguments for property rights are fundamentally hostile to intellectual property claims, for patent and copyright monopolies interfere with the freedom of others to use their own bodies or their own justly acquired property in certain ways. Establishing a liberty-based right to self-ownership would create the foundation for property in tangible objects while excluding property in ideal objects, for the latter amounts simply to controls placed on the use of our own bodies and on the use of our legitimately acquired property.[143]

The arguments of Locke and von Humboldt on the importance of ownership rights in ourselves and in tangible objects have already been discussed, so there is no need to review them further. What I do propose, however, is 1) that such rights have their foundation in nature and can without confusion be called natural rights, even though they emerge through a historical process and necessarily contain an element of the conventional and contingent (nature revealing itself through history); and 2) that self-ownership rights are consistent with justice-as-order (as discussed in the section on the structure of utilitarian arguments above).

The role played by scarcity in self-ownership theories is central, for the most obviously scarce of all physical resources is one's own body. If justice has any meaning at all, it refers at least to the allocation of various rights to control physical resources. Such a system of justice can emerge from a flow of historical events by an "invisible hand" process, without diminishing its "naturalness." As Hume remarks, "Tho' the rules of justice be artificial, they are not arbitrary. Nor is the expression improper to call them Laws of Nature; if by natural we understand what is common to any species, or even if we confine it to mean what is inseparable from the species."[144] To say that a law is natural is not, however, to affirm that it is self evident, or even that a sufficiently powerful deductive mind could arrive at it. As Hume remarks, "Nor is the rule concerning the stability of possessions the less deriv'd from human conventions, that it arises gradually, and acquires force by a slow progression, and by our repeated experience of the inconveniences of transgressing it."[145] Practice, in social experience as well as personal, plays a significant factor in the formation of ethics. ("Ethics" is, after all, but a transliteration of the Greek word perhaps best translated as "habit," that is, what is formed through practice.)

The fundamental question of who should have the right to control one's body and, by implication, the products of one's labor, is, in many respects, a problem of coordination. It is a problem of arriving at a stable equilibrium solution in a "game" that has no *unique* stable solution. Our bodies could be considered the property of the king; some class of people could be owned by another; each of us could be common property, in the sense that a social decision would be made to determine every use of our bodies (participatory collectivism); or we could each be the owners of ourselves. Each of those possible solutions has been tried at one time or another. Modern society has tended to converge on the last, on self-ownership.[146] What is it that might lead "players" in coordination "games" to converge on self-ownership? In coordination problems there is a natural tendency for players to converge on "obvious" solutions. The pioneering work of Thomas Schelling has shown that players in games with monetary payoffs for successful coordination tend to converge on certain solutions.[147] As Schelling remarks, "A prime characteristic of these 'solutions' to the problems, that is, of the clues or coordinators or focal points, is some kind of prominence or conspicuousness."[148] These conspicuous "clues" have come to be known as "Schelling points."

We can find Schelling points in "property games" as well. In the case of ownership of our bodies, what can be more natural— more prominent—than the allocation of personal ownership rights to each person?[149] As Dectutt de Tracy affirms, [I]f it be certain that the idea of property can arise only in a being endowed with will, it is equally certain that in such a being it arises necessarily and inevitably in all its plenitude; for, as soon as this individual knows accurately itself, or its moral person, and its capacity to enjoy and to suffer, and to act necessarily, it sees clearly also that this self is the exclusive proprietor of the body which it animates, of the organs which it moves, of all their passions and their actions; for all this finishes and commences with this self, exists but by it, is not moved but by its acts, and no other moral person can employ the same instruments nor be affected in the same manner by their effects.[150]

Such an allocation may not make the best sense from a "social" perspective, that is, in terms of increasing the total utility of a group. But human beings typically are unable to make (and do not have to make) such God-like choices; our real choices are inevitably constrained by our own horizons. "Society" is not a single choosing entity, nor can it be considered as such.[151] The prominence of individuality and of our control of our own bodies naturally lends itself to a process whereby agreement is secured (it need not be explicit agreement) to respect rights to self-ownership and to the products of our labor. As Hume notes, "it must immediately occur, as the most natural expedient, that every one continue to enjoy what he is at present master of, and that property or constant possession be conjoin'd to the immediate possession."[152]

Let us make a distinction between goods that are simply given (if there are such goods) and goods that must be produced; one rule for allocating goods (such as equal division) might have a greater degree of "obviousness" when the goods are simply given than when they are produced; in the latter case the association of self to labor to product is more prominent.

Hume proposes a thought experiment: "Suppose a German, a Frenchman, and a Spaniard to come into a room, where there are plac'd upon the table three bottles of wine, Rhenish, Burgundy and Port; and suppose they shou'd fall a quarrelling about the division of them; a person, who was chosen for umpire, wou'd naturally, to shew his impartiality, give every one the product of his own country. . . . [T]here is first a natural union betwixt the idea of the person and that of the object, and afterwards a new and moral union produc'd by that right or property, which we ascribe to the person."[153] That seems to be a sensible solution that the three drinkers might also arrive at themselves.

Now suppose that the things to be divided must be produced by the three persons and are not merely found at hand. Is it not more reasonable to suppose that they will insist on a division of the product that recognizes the separate contributions of each, rather than, say, equal division or, as in the case of the wine, division by national origin? Further, let us suppose that the problem is faced, not by three laborers who know each other immediately and are engaged in a joint enterprise, but by members of an extended order who, while necessarily dependent upon each other for sustenance, have no knowledge whatsoever of each other.[154] Is it not even more reasonable to suppose that they will converge, not on some principle of even distribution, or of distribution to the most deserving (desert having, as noted earlier, no principle), but that each be awarded his "own" product, that is, what he produces? (In a market system, this need not bear any close relationship to the "amount of labor" that might have been expended, but to what can be claimed on the basis of self-ownership rights and mutually satisfactory agreements among contracting parties.)

Such a system of self-ownership and derived ownership of tangible objects provides the foundation for a society and economy based on contract,[155] as well as for justice-as-order. Property rights in ourselves and in alienable, material objects allow us to cooperate peacefully. They create an order within which people can pursue their separate or common ends.

By allocating resources through a property system we allow agents to negotiate (for example, through the price system) without resort to force in order to decide among potentially conflicting resources.[156] If a river can be used for boating, fishing, or swimming, but not for any combination of these three, then property rights and the market system that emerges from such rights allow parties that are potentially in conflict to use reason, rather than brute force, to decide how the river will be used.[157] As Adam Smith noted of the market exchange system, "If we should enquire into the principle in the human mind on which this disposition of trucking [exchange] is founded, it is clearly the natural inclination every one has to persuade. The offering of a shilling, which to us appears to have so plain and simple a meaning, is in reality offering an argument to persuade one to do so and so as it is for his interest. Men always endeavour to persuade others to be of their opinion even when the matter is of no consequence to them."[158] The function of property rights in such a liberal order, then, is not to maximize some maximand, but to allow human beings to cooperate in the allocation of scarce resources. Intellectual property rights, on the other hand, do not arise from scarcity but are its cause. As Arnold Plant observes, "It is a peculiarity of property rights in patents (and copyrights) that they do not arise out of the scarcity of the objects which become appropriated. They are not a consequence of scarcity. They are the deliberate creation of statute law; and, whereas in general the institution of private property makes for the preservation of scarce goods, tending (as we might somewhat loosely say) to lead us 'to make the most of them,' property rights in patents and copyright make possible the creation of a scarcity of the products appropriated which could not otherwise be maintained."[159] Scarcity of that sort being central to the legitimation of property rights, intellectual property rights have no legitimate moral grounding.

Conclusion

Four possible theories of intellectual property rights have been examined: labor-desert, personality, utility, and "piggybacking" on rights to tangible property. In each case I have argued either that the particular arguments cannot be applied to ideal objects or that the arguments themselves are weak. That is not to deny that each contains some grain of truth, nor does that mean that they contribute nothing to our understanding of the moral foundations of property.

The idea of desert has an important place among our moral intuitions, although such moral intuitions may have their proper role in the moral order of the small group such as the family, and not in the extended order, where abstract rules prevail.[160] If the foundation of the natural right to ownership is ownership in one's self, however, then claims to own ideas or other ideal objects conflict with this right to self-ownership, for such a claim is no less than a claim to the right to control how another uses his or her body. When one claims to own a dance step, for example, one claims that no one else can so move his or her body so as to perform this dance, and therefore that one has a right of dominion over the bodies of everyone else. Similarly, a copyright over a musical composition means that others cannot use their mouths to blow air in certain sequences and in certain ways into musical instruments they own without obtaining the permission of the copyright holder. Thus the real objects the copyright holder controls are the bodies and instruments of the other musicians. The same holds true of a patent governing the combination of a group of chemicals or the arrangement of the parts of a fishhook.

The theory of property that emphasizes personality also has something to add to our understanding of property. The development of personality and moral agency is certainly a good thing, and for full development it requires at least a minimal sphere of property. Aristotle recognized, for example, that liberality is impossible without property and liberty, the necessary conditions for the expression of that virtue.[161] But the more elaborate attempts to use this as a foundation for property, such as those of Hegel and his epigoni, suffer from serious philosophical difficulties. That is most notable when a theory of an inalienable *droit moral* for artists is built upon it. The relationship between artist, art work, and audience is a complex one, but it does not lend support to the idea that the work of the artist is an extension of the artist's personality, capable of being damaged in a way analogous to the bodily damage that could be inflicted on the artist. Personality and property are indeed related, as expressed by Richard Overton's statement: "To every individual in nature, is given an individual property by nature, not to be invaded or usurped by any: for every one as he is himself, so he hath a self propriety, else could he not be himself."[162] But such necessity of property for one to "be oneself" means preeminently self-ownership, which is a principle in conflict with intellectual property rights.

Utilitarian arguments also have a role to play in understanding the moral grounds of property rights. That people will be more productive and will generate wealth that can be enjoyed by all only when they can reap the rewards of their efforts is certainly true and has been recognized at least from the time of Aristotle's criticism of communism.[163] That is certainly an important consideration in judging whether private property is superior or inferior to state ownership. But to tailor legislatively the abstract rules of the extended order in an effort to reach predetermined results reveals a serious misunderstanding of the rule of (abstract) law, which aims at no definite result but which provides the framework within which just results can emerge. In contrast, the kind of utilitarian[164] account of law that has been characterized as "justice-as-order" does not seek to maximize some particular maximand, but to create an overarching order within which human beings can realize their various ends without coming into violent conflict over resources. As an empirical matter, we have good reason to believe that when individuals know what their property rights are, they will be more productive and prosperous than if such rights are uncertain. The key, therefore, in such a legal system is to avoid conflicts between rights.[165] Intellectual property rights, however, do create conflicts between rights to self and to tangible goods. Moreover, it is far from clear that intellectual property rights increase incentives for innovation rather than hamper them. (That last consideration is a matter for empirical investigation and cannot be decided on a priori grounds.)

The case for "piggyback" rights is also built around a hard kernel of truth. Various rights that resemble in some respects intellectual property rights, such as trade secrets, can indeed be built on the foundation of rights to tangible objects. But a trade secret is not a right against the whole world, as a patent is, but a right against those who interfere with rights to tangible goods or who violate legally binding contracts. A monopoly right restricting others, for example, from independently inventing and building a new contraption cannot rest on a foundation of contract, for contract presupposes consent and the point of intellectual property rights is that they bind non-consenting parties.

Finally, property has been examined as a means of realizing freedom and achieving social coordination, "justice-as-order." The foundation of such a system of social coordination is self-ownership, the "node" around which the conventions of property are constructed. Self-ownership is an "obvious" solution to coordination games and plays an important role in the historical development of natural law. Such "games" in real life are played because of the scarcity of resources. If goods were truly superabundant, there would be no need for property, for conflicts could not arise. The very nature of an economic good involves choice, however, and choice implies scarcity. That is most obviously true of our own bodies, which can be used as food for others, as objects to gratify the sexual lusts of others, or in any number of other ways. The problem for which self-ownership provides the answer is how to allocate rights over the most scarce of scarce resources, one's own body. The principle of self-ownership then, by analogy, provides the basis for ownership of objects that are not parts of our body.[166]

The key to all of this is scarcity. Without scarcity, an argument based either on the realization of freedom or on finding a solution to coordination games cannot generate a property right. Tangible goods are clearly scarce in that there are conflicting uses. It is that scarcity that gives rise to property rights. Intellectual property rights, however, do not rest on a natural scarcity of goods, but on an "artificial, self-created scarcity." That is to say, legislation or legal fiat limits the use of ideal objects in such a way as to create an artificial scarcity that, it is hoped, will generate greater revenues for innovators. Property rights in tangible goods channel them into their most highly valued uses. The possibility for exchanging transferable property titles means that holders of property will constantly rearrange the titles in search of profit. Without scarcity this process would be unnecessary. But the attempt to generate profit opportunities by legislatively limiting access to certain ideal goods, and therefore to mimic the market processes governing the allocation of tangible goods, contains a fatal contradiction: It violates the rights to tangible goods, the very rights that provide the legal foundations with which markets begin.

Notes

* This essay was written in the late 1980s and appeared in the *Harvard Journal of Law and Public Policy* 13, no. 3 (Summer 1990). Although in the intervening years I've improved my writing and my views on some important matters have evolved, I've made only a few cosmetic changes for this book. I've corrected some typographical errors in the original edition, modified for style a few exceptionally ugly sentences, and changed a few citations to direct readers to newer and more readily accessible editions of books. Other than those small changes, the essay is unchanged.

1. Randy Barnett, "Foreword: Of Chickens and Eggs—The Compatibility of Moral Rights and Consequentialist Analyses," *Harvard Journal of Law and Public Policy* 12 (1989).

2. See, for example, Lysander Spooner, "A Letter to Scientists and Inventors, on the Science of Justice, and Their Right of Perpetual Property in Their Discoveries and Inventions," in *The Collected Works of Lysander Spooner*, ed. Charles Shively (Weston, Mass.: M&S Press, 1971), and William Leggett, *Democratick Editorials: Essays in Jacksonian Political Economy*, ed. Lawrence H. White (Indianapolis: Liberty Press, 1984).

3. This catch-all category covers the subject matter of patents and copyrights, including those for algorithms, computer programs, manufacturing processes, inventions, musical or literary works, pictorial or other kinds of representations, sculptures, designs, and more. The relevant difference between such goods and tangible goods is that the former can be instantiated an indefinite number of times, that is, they are not scarce in a static sense, while tangible goods are spatially circumscribed and are scarce in both the static and dynamic senses of the term.

4. Michel Chevalier, "Patents for Inventions Examined in Their Relations to the Principle of Freedom of Industry, and That of Equality among Citizens," in *Copyright and Patents for Inventions*, ed. R.A. Macfie (New York: Scribner and Welford, 1883).

5. Natural rights arguments and utilitarian arguments (very broadly conceived) are close cousins. Utilitarian theories are explicitly consequentialist (and welfarist), while natural rights theories usually contain what Alan Ryan calls "a buried utilitarian assumption." (Alan Ryan, *Property* [University of Minnesota Press, 1987], p. 63). Such "buried assumptions" concern human flourishing or the attainment of a man's natural end. Those consequences are usually attained indirectly, through respect for general rights, or rules of conduct, rather than directly, as in most utilitarian theories. The sharp separation between natural rights and utility, or the common good, is, however, an artificial one and would certainly be foreign to any of the great natural law theorists.

6. Or *droit moral*, sometimes confusingly translated simply as "moral rights."

7. See Tom G. Palmer, "Intellectual Property Rights: A Non-Posnerian Law and Economics Approach," *Hamline Law Review* 12 (1989): reprinted in Adam D. Moore, ed., *Intellectual Property: Moral, Legal, and International Dilemmas* (New York: Rowman & Littlefield, 1997), pp. 179–224. That essay also reviews the history of intellectual property, considers the problem of whether common-law copyright extends after the act of publication, reevaluates the economics of public goods and property rights, and examines how markets for ideal objects without intellectual property rights function. For criticisms of my position, see Wendy Gordon, "An Inquiry into the Merits of Copyright: The Challenges of Consistency, Consent, and Encouragement," *Stanford Law Review* 41 (1989).

8. As will be shown, however, the approach I set forth would include trademarks and trade secrets as legitimate. Trademarks and trade secrets have roots in the common law and enjoy a contractual or quasi-contractual moral grounding.

9. Fritz Machlup and Edith Penrose, "The Patent Controversy in the Nineteenth Century," *The Journal of Economic History* 10, no. 1 (May 1950): 16.

10. Lysander Spooner, "The Law of Intellectual Property: or an Essay on the Right of Authors and Inventors to a Perpetual Property in Their Ideas," in *The Collected Works of Lysander Spooner*, Vol. III, ed. Charles Shively (Weston, Mass.: M&S Press, 1971).

11. Ibid., p. 13.

12. Ibid., p. 15.

13. Ibid., p. 15.

14. Ibid., p. 19. That assumes that a common right would necessarily entail a common right to access.

15. Ibid., p. 28.

16. See ibid., p. 27: "All that labor, which we are in the habit of calling physical labor, is in reality performed wholly by the mind, will, or spirit, which uses the bones and muscles merely as tools . . . There is, therefore, no such thing as the physical labor of men, independently of their intellectual labor."

17. See Spooner, "A Letter to Scientists and Inventors," p. 10.

18. Ibid, p. 26. Note that this would go far beyond the traditional scope of the patent laws of the United States, which explicitly exclude discoveries of scientific or mathematical laws or of naturally occurring substances from patent protection. Recently, however, the U.S. Patent Office has been awarding patents to discoverers of useful mathematical algorithms, a trend that would surely have pleased Spooner.

19. Ibid., p. 27.

20. Ibid., p. 42 (emphasis in original).

21. Ibid., p. 42.

22. Ibid., p. 52.

23. Ibid., p. 58.

24. Ibid., pp. 61–64.

25. Ibid., p. 79.

26. Ibid., p. 81.

27. Ibid., pp. 81–82.

28. Ibid., p. 94.

29. Ayn Rand, "Patents and Copyrights," in *Capitalism: The Unknown Ideal* (New York: New American Library, 1966), p. 125.

30. Ibid., p. 126.

31. Ibid., p. 128.

32. Ibid., p. 127.

33. See Herbert Spencer, *The Principles of Ethics* (1893; Indianapolis: Liberty Classics, 1978), Vol. II, p. 121.

34. Ibid., p.121. Spencer specifically disavows reliance on utilitarian concerns. "Even were an invention of no benefit to society unless thrown open to unbought use, there would still be no just ground for disregarding the inventor's claim; any more than for disregarding the claim of one who labors on his farm for his own benefit and not for public benefit." Ibid., pp. 127–28.

35. Ibid., pp. 122–24.

36. Edward Coke, "The Third Part of the Institutes of the Laws of England: Concerning High Treason, and Other Pleas of Common, and Criminal Causes," quoted in Stephen D. White, *Sir Edward Coke and "The Grievances of the Commonwealth,"* 1612–1628 (Chapel Hill: University of North Carolina Press, 1979), p. 119.

37. Robert Nozick argues on this basis that patents and copyrights do not run afoul of the "Lockean Proviso": "An inventor's patent does not deprive others of an object which would not exist if not for the inventor." Robert Nozick, *Anarchy, State, and Utopia* (New York: Basic Books, 1974), p. 182.

38. See Israel Kirzner, "Producer, Entrepreneur, and the Right to Property," in *Perception, Opportunity, and Profit* (Chicago: University of Chicago Press, 1979), pp. 185–99, and Israel Kirzner, "Entrepreneurship, Entitlement, and Economic Justice," in ibid., pp. 200–24. Kirzner

does not apply the theory he advances directly to intellectual property, but the implication of his argument would plausibly lead one to support patents and copyrights.

39. Ibid., p. 196.

40. Ibid., pp. 212–13.

41. Moral desert plays a powerful role in many theories of property. According to Lawrence C. Becker, "the concept of desert is constitutive of the concept of morality per se." Lawrence C. Becker, *Property Rights: Philosophic Foundations* (London: Routledge and Kegan Paul, 1977), p. 51.

42. John Locke, *Two Treatises of Government*, ed. Peter Laslett (Cambridge: Cambridge University Press, 1988), 2nd Treatise, Chapter V, §34, p. 291.

43. William Leggett, *Democratick Editorials: Essays in Jacksonian Political Economy*, ed. Lawrence H. White, pp. 397–98. Interestingly, Leggett and Spooner not only agreed on the abolition of slavery, but also agreed that, if intellectual property rights are indeed natural rights, then they should be limited in duration. According to Leggett, "An author either has a natural and just right of property in his production, or he has not. If he has, it is one not to be bounded by space, or limited in duration, but, like that of the Indian to the bow and arrow he has shaped from the sapling and reeds of the unappropriated wilderness, his own exclusively and forever" (p. 398).

44. Ibid., p. 394: "If the principle of copyright were wholly done away, the business of authorship, we are inclined to think, would readily accommodate itself to the change of circumstances, and would be more extensively pursued, and with more advantage to all concerned than is the case at present."

45. Ibid., p. 399.

46. Ibid., pp. 399–400.

47. See Randy Barnett, "A Consent Theory of Contract," *Columbia Law Review* 86 (1986). The arrangements of property that result from transference of justly acquired property titles are themselves just, and if some arrangements mean profits for some and losses for others, the justice of the profits or losses is ancillary to the justice of the resulting arrangements of property titles.

48. Nozick, *Anarchy, State, and Utopia*, p. 151.

49. Rand, "Patents and Copyrights," p. 133.

50. Spooner, "A Letter to Scientists and Inventors," p. 68; see also Nozick, *Anarchy, State, and Utopia*, p. 182.

51. Leggett, *Democratick Editorials*, p. 402.

52. Jan Narveson, *The Libertarian Idea* (Philadelphia: Temple University Press, 1988), p. 77. For a liberty-based argument for property, see pp. 62–93. For another view, see David Kelly, "Life, Liberty, and Property," in *Human Rights*, ed. Ellen Frankel Paul, Fred D. Miller, Jr., and Jeffrey Paul (Oxford: Basil Blackwell, 1984), pp. 108–18.

53. Locke, *Two Treatises of Government*, 2nd Treatise, Chapter V, §26, p. 287

54. Ibid., §34, p. 291.

55. Ibid., §40, p. 296.

56. Ibid., §25, p. 286.

57. "Though the Earth, and all inferior Creatures be common to all Men, yet every Man has a *Property* in his own *Person*. This no Body has any Right to but himself. The *Labour* of his Body, and the *Work* of his Hands, we may say, are properly his." Ibid., §27, pp. 287–88.

58. Ibid., 2nd Treatise, Chapter IV, §23, p. 284. "This *Freedom* from Absolute, Arbitrary Power, is so necessary to, and closely joyned with a Man's Preservation, that he cannot part with it, but by what forfeits his Preservation and Life together. For a Man, not having the Power of his own Life, *cannot*, by Compact, or his own Consent, *enslave himself* to any one, nor part himself under the Absolute, Arbitrary Power of another, to take away his Life, when he pleases."

59. Ibid., p. 137.

60. See Christine MacLeod, *Inventing the Industrial Revolution: The English Patent System, 1660-1800* (Cambridge: Cambridge University Press, 1989).

61. See Samuel C. Wheeler, III, "Natural Property Rights as Body Rights," in *Noûs* 14, no. 2 (May 1980).

62. Locke, 2nd Treatise, Chapter V, §28, p. 288.

63. Ibid., §26, p. 287.

64. Ibid., §28, p. 288.

65. As David Hume notes, "'T'were better, no doubt, that every one were possess'd of what is most suitable to him, and proper for his use: But besides, that this relation of fitness may be common to several at once, 'tis liable to so many controversies and men are so partial and passionate in judging of these controversies, that such a loose and uncertain rule wou'd be absolutely incompatible with the peace of human society." David Hume, *A Treatise of Human Nature*, ed. P. H. Nidditch (New York: Oxford University Press, 1978), p. 502; see also F. A. Hayek, *The Fatal Conceit: The Errors of Socialism* (Chicago: University of Chicago Press, 1989), pp. 73–75.

66. Frank Knight has characterized the patent system as "an exceedingly crude way for rewarding invention," for "as the thing works out, it is undoubtedly a very rare and exceptional case where the really deserving inventor gets anything like a fair reward. If any one gains, it is some purchaser of the invention or at best an inventor who adds a detail or finishing touch that makes an idea practicable where the real work of pioneering and exploration has been done by others." Frank Knight, *Risk, Uncertainty, and Profit* (Boston: Houghton Mifflin Company, 1921), p. 372.

67. Indeed, often the greatest rewards go to those who have—in the usual sense of the word—labored the least. We may owe more to the laziest among us: to the person who was too lazy to carry loads by hand and came upon the idea of using a wheelbarrow, for example. Attempts to reduce such differentials in productivity to a substrata of undifferentiated labor are inherently doomed, as the failed attempt of Marxism indicates.

68. The reward to labor for inventiveness in marketing, for example, is greater sales or market share, not property rights in marketing techniques or (even less plausibly) in market share.

69. Wilhelm von Humboldt, *The Limits of State Action*, trans. J. Coulthard, ed. J. W. Burrow (Cambridge: Cambridge University Press, 1969), p. 16.

70. Ibid., pp. 20–21.

71. Ibid., p. 116.

72. Ibid., p. 39.

73. Ibid., p. 83.

74. See notes 53–67 and accompanying text.

75. As the English Leveller leader Richard Overton similarly argued, "To every individual in nature is given an individual property by nature, not to be invaded or usurped by any. For every one, as he is himself, so he hath a self-propriety, else could he not be himself; and of this no second may presume to deprive any of without manifest violation and affront to the very principles of nature and of the rules of equity and justice between man and man. Mine and thine cannot be, except this be. No man hath power over my rights and liberties, and I over no man's. I may be but an individual, enjoy my self and my self propriety, and may right my self no more then my self, or presume any further; if I do, I am an encroacher and an invader upon another man's right—to which I have no right." Richard Overton, "An Arrow against All Tyrants," in Andrew Sharp, ed., *The English Levellers* (Cambridge: Cambridge University Press, 1998), p. 55.

76. J. W. Burrow, Editor's Introduction to von Humboldt, *The Limits of State Action*, p. xxxix.

77. Von Humboldt, *The Limits of State Action*, pp. 96–97.

78. See G. W. F. Hegel, *The Philosophy of Right*, trans. T. M. Knox (Oxford: Clarendon Press, 1952).

79. See G. W. F. Hegel, *The Phenomenology of Spirit*, trans. A. V. Miller (Oxford: Oxford University Press, 1977).

80. Hegel, *The Philosophy of Right*, p. 37. Knox (p. 315, n. 58) points to a similarity in the treatment of *Bildung* (loosely translatable as "education" or "spiritual development") in both Humboldt and Hegel. The difference is that whereas Humboldt saw the role of the state in the process of *Bildung* as "negative," that is, protecting citizens from violence but otherwise keeping out of the way, Hegel sees a positive role for the state in this process.

81. Ibid., p. 40.

82. Ibid., p. 42.

83. Ibid., p. 42.

84. Ibid., p. 45. Further, "[s]ince property is the *embodiment* of personality, my inward idea and will that something is to be mine is not enough to make it my property; to secure this end occupancy is requisite" (emphasis in original).

85. Ibid., p. 46.

86. Ibid., p. 47. This is the "mode of taking possession most in conformity with the Idea to this extent, that it implies a union of subject and object."

87. Ibid., p. 47. This process, as Hegel remarks in his notes, is the same as the dialectic of lord and bondsman described in the *Phenomenology of Spirit*. Remarkably, self-ownership emerges only at the end of a historical process of self-confrontation through possession of and transformation of the external world. The anti-liberal character of Hegel's approach is made most clear in his identification of the "Idea" of freedom (its concretion and synthesis with the content of its concept) with the state:

"But that objective mind, the content of the right, should no longer be apprehended in its subjective concept alone, and consequently that man's absolute unfitness for slavery should no longer be apprehended as a mere 'ought to be', is something which does not come home to our minds until we recognize that the Idea of freedom is genuinely actual only as the state" (p. 48).

88. See Immanuel Kant, "Von der Unrechtmässigkeit des Büchernachdrucks," in *Copyrights and Patents for Inventions*, ed. R. A. Macfie (1883), p. 580.

89. Immanuel Kant, "Was ist ein Buch?" (trans. Tom G. Palmer) in Wilhelm Weischedel, ed. *Die Metaphysik der Sitten* (Frankfurt amMain: Suhrkamp, 1977), p. 405.

90. Kant, "Von der Unrechtmässigkeit des Büchernachdrucks," p. 582.

91. Ibid., p. 584.

92. This may reflect the fact that Kant was a writer and not a sculptor.

93. Ibid., p. 585.

94. Ibid., p. 585.

95. Hegel, *The Philosophy of Right*, p. 54.

96. Ibid., p. 55.

97. C. civ. art. 543, Code pe´nal [C.pe´n.] arts. 425–429 ("Law of March 11, 1957 on literary and artistic property"); see also "Loi du 11 mars 1957 sur la proprie´te´ litte´raire et artistique," 1957 *Journal Officiel de la Re´publique Franc͵aise* [J.O.] 2723, 1957 *Recueil Dalloz Le´gislation [D.L.]*102 (for amendments and cases interpreting the statute).

98. Ibid.

99. For an overview of the proposed legislation, as well as a discussion of the pros and cons of those proposals, see Donnelly, "Artist's Rights and Copyrights," 1 *Congressional Quarterly's 1 Res. Rep. 245* (1988); see also *Washington Post*, May 22, 1988, F1, col. 1.

100. See Edward Damich, "The Right of Personality: A Common Law Basis for the Protection of the Moral Rights of Authors," *Georgia Law Review* 23, no.1 (1988): pp. 6–25.

101. *Cinquin v. Lecocq*, Req. Sirey, 1900.2.121. note Saleilles (1902) (cited in S. Stromholm, *Le Droit Moral de l'Auteur* [1966], p. 29).

102. Ibid., p. 285.

103. Josef Kohler, *Philosophy of Law*, trans. Adalbert Albrecht (New York: A. M. Kelley, 1969), p. 80

104. J. Kohler, *Urheberrecht an Schriftwerken und Verlagsrecht 15* (1907) (quoted in Edward Damich, "The Right of Personality," p. 29); see also Arther S. Katz, "The Doctrine of Moral Right and American Copyright Law — AProposal," *Southern California Law Review* 24, no. 402 (1951).

105. C. civ. art. 543, Code pe´nal [C.pe´n] arts. 425–429, art. 34. Damich, however, argues that, due to difficulties presented by practical application and conflict with other rights, the right of retraction is "a 'dead letter' even in French Law." Damich, "The Right of Personality," p. 25.

106. C. civ. art. 543, Code pe´nal [C.pe´n.] arts. 425–429 ("The authors of graphic or plastic works of art have, notwithstanding any transfer of the original work, an inalienable right to participate in the product of all sales of this work made at auction or through the intermediation of dealers.")

107. Hegel, *The Philosophy of Right*, p. 40.

108. Edward J. Markey, "Let Artists Have a Fair Share of Their Profits," *New York Times*, Dec 20, 1987.

109. That of course raises the question of when the work is finished. Who would know when it was finished? Would anyone else undertake to finish Schubert's "Unfinished Symphony"? The artist may indeed be in the privileged position of determining when a work is finished, but that does not privilege the subjective experience of theartist in the constitution of the art work as such.

110. The strategic differentiation between various kinds of dependence is elaborated in Edmund Husserl, "Investigation III: On the Theory of Wholes and Parts," in Husserl, *Logical Investigations*, trans. J. Findlay (London: Routledge & Kegan Paul, 1970), pp. 435–89; see also *Parts and Moments: Studies in Logic and Formal Ontology*, ed. Barry Smith (Mu¨nchen and Wien: Philosophia Verlag, 1982).

111. I used the possessive—"Shakespeare's"—in describing that play to highlight the relationship of dependence that the work does have on its author. Shakespeare has been dead for centuries, while *Othello* lives on. One might say, however, that Shakespeare's mind remains active or still "lives" in *Othello*.

112. Of course, an artist may also be her own audience, but we are here speaking of ideal roles; one and the same person may fulfill various roles. When the term "artist" is used, it will be understood that artist qua artist is meant, and similarly of other roles, such as "audience."

113. Roman Ingarden, The Literary Work of Art: An Investigation on the Borderlines of Ontology, Logic and Theory of Literature, trans. George G. Grabowicz (Evanston, Ill.: Northwestern University Press, 1973), p. 13.

114. Ibid., p. 13.

115. Ibid., p. 14.

116. That is what accounts for the nonrivalrous nature of the consumption of works of art and other ideal objects; their enjoyment by one person need not diminish their enjoyment by another. This also shows the difference between the concretion of a work, such as a performance, and the work itself. My enjoyment of a performance may diminish your ability to enjoy the same performance, perhaps because I block your view, but it does not exhaust or in any way diminish the work itself. It is for this reason that Thomas Jefferson denied any natural property right in ideal objects:

"If nature has made any one thing less susceptible than all others of exclusive property, it is the action of the thinking power called an idea, which an individual may exclusively possess as long as he keeps it to himself; but the moment it is divulged, it forces itself into the possession of every one, and the receiver cannot dispossess himself of it. Its peculiar character, too, is that no one possesses the less, because every other possesses the whole of it. He who receives an idea from me, receives instruction himself without lessening mine; as he who lights his taper at mine, receives light without darkening me."

Thomas Jefferson, "Letter to Isaac McPherson, Monticello, August 13, 1813," in Joyce Appleby and Terenu Ball, eds., *Thomas Jefferson, Political Writings* (Cambridge: Cambridge University Press, 1999), p. 580.

117. R. Ingarden, *Ontology of the Work of Art: The Musical Work, the Picture, the Architectural Work, the Film*, trans. Raymond Meyer with John T. Goldthwait (Athens, Ohio: Ohio University Press, 1989), pp. 35–36.

118. See Robert Sokolowski, *Husserlian Meditations: How Words Present Things* (Evanston, Ill.: Northwestern University Press, 1974), p. 99. ("Every 'cultural object' which requires a performance to be actualized—a musical composition, a play, dance, or poem—appears through a manifold of interpretations. All of them present the object itself, and the object is the identity within the interpretation."); see also Ingarden, *The Ontology of the Work of Art*, p. 36: "[H]ow does a literary work appear during reading, and what is the immediate correlate of this reading?. . . [A] distinction should be drawn between the work and its concretions, which differ from it in various respects. These concretions are precisely what is constituted during the reading and what, in a manner of speaking, forms the mode of appearance of a work, the concrete form in which the work itself is apprehended." Hans-Georg Gadamer, *Truth and Method*, ed. Joel C. Weinsheimer and Donald G. Marshall (New York: Continuum, 1982), p. 274: "Interpretation is not an occasional additional act subsequent to understanding, but rather understanding is always an interpretation, and hence interpretation is the explicit form of understanding." Rather than simply reproducing the experience of the artist, each member of the audience contributes a different interpretation —the way in which the work "speaks to us" and allows us to learn from it, rather than simply reproducing "in us" someone else's experience. That manifold of interpretations is what makes possible the special kind of intersubjectivity and objectivity that works of art enjoy. The manifold of interpretations provide the "other" that is the necessary condition for the appearance of the "same."

119. For the general approach to objectivity outlined here, see Edmund Husserl, *Formal and Transcendental Logic* (Hingham, Mass.: Kluwer Academic Publishers, 1978), pp. 232–66.

120. Ingarden, *The Literary Work of Art*, pp. 340, 349; for a discussion of the kinds of dependence and independence set forth by Ingarden, see Peter Simons, "The Formalization of Husserl's Theory of Holes and Parts," in Barry Smith, ed., *Parts and Moments: Studies in Logic and Formal Ontology*, pp. 135–42. Note that, while I have earlier used the term "ideal object" to cover all of the subject matter of copyrights and patents, Ingarden would limit that term to scientific discoveries, mathematical theorems, and the like (that is, typically to the subject matter of patents), and would consider works of art in a different category, since they come into being during a definite period of time and are not, unlike what he terms ideal objects, atemporal.

121. See Ingarden, *The Literary Work of Art*, pp. 336–55; see also Barry Smith, "Practices of Art," in *Practical Knowledge: Outlines of a Theory of Traditions and Skills*, ed. J. Nyiri and Barry Smith (London and New York: Croom Helm, 1988), p. 174:

"Art works are dependent, now, not only upon the activities of their creators, but also upon certain correlated activities of an appropriately receptive audience. A shell, a leaf, or a relic of some lost civilization, existing in a world lacking every tendency toward appreciative evaluation, would be simply a shell, a leaf, or a lump of stone."

Compare Nelson Goodman, *Languages of Art: An Approach to a Theory of Symbols* (Indianapolis: Hackett, 1976), p. 20:

"The distant or colossal sculpture has also to be shaped very differently from what it depicts in order to be realistic, in order to 'look right.' And the ways of making it 'look right' are not reducible to fixed and universal rules, for how an object looks depends not only upon its orientation, distance, and lighting, but upon all we know of it and upon our training, habits, and concerns."

122. As a practical matter, one also faces the problem of identifying just who the artist is in any collaborative work. Testifying on the behalf of moral rights legislation, film director and producer George Lucas referred to film colorizers and others who alter art works as "barbarians." His colleague Stephen Spielberg insisted that "without the agreement and permission of the two artistic authors (the principal director and principal screen writer), no material alterations [should] be made in a film following its first, paid, public exhibition." See Tom G. Palmer, "Artists Don't Deserve Special Rights," *Wall Street Journal*, March 8, 1988 (quoting testimony that Spielberg and Lucas gave to a Senate subcommittee). But, by his own theory, is not Mr. Lucas (not to mention Mr. Spielberg) a barbarian? What of the art of the actors? Why should they submit to having their work distorted or left on the cutting room floor? And what of the lighting crew, and so on? Are not those other collaborators also artists? Why should only directors and screen writers enjoy such moral rights?

123. Whether they are harmed in the economic sense, by losing revenue, is another matter; as I have noted elsewhere, however, purely utilitarian claims on behalf of intellectual property rights are shaky, at best. See Tom G. Palmer, "Intellectual Property: A Non-Posnerian Law and Economics Approach."

124. See notes 69–77 above and accompanying text.

125. See, for example, Simon Rottenberg, "The Remuneration of Artists," in *Frontiers of Economics*, ed. Kenneth J. Arrow and Seppo Honkapohja (Oxford: Basil Blackwell, 1985), pp. 47–51; and Ben W. Bolch, William Damon, and C. Elton Hinshaw, "An Economic Analysis of the California Art Royalty Statute," *Connecticut Law Review* 10 (1978).

126. Those who prefer payment now to payment later, such as the many artists who sell their work "on the street," are harmed by such a requirement. As Ben W. Bolch remarks: "Many artists, 'starving' or not, want their money now, not tomorrow. Otherwise, they would 'invest' in the art by keeping it for themselves." Ben W. Bolch, "There Is No Just Price for Art," *New York Times*, Nov. 28, 1987.

127. By diminishing pre-patent cooperation among researchers, for example, or through diminishing opportunities for playwrights to emulate William Shakespeare, who rewrote Thomas Kyd's now forgotten play "The Spanish Tragedy" and gave us "Hamlet." See also Georg Bittlingmayer, "Property Rights, Progress, and the Aircraft Patent Agreement," *Journal of Law and Economics* 30 (1988).

128. See Henry Sidgwick, *The Methods of Ethics* (Indianapolis: Hackett, June 1981), p. 440: "What Hume . . . means by Justice is rather what I should call Order."

129. Aristotle seems to have used both arguments in his dispute with Plato over the community of possessions. In his *Politics* he argued: "What belongs in common to the most people is accorded the least care: they take thought for their own things above all, and less about the

things in common, or only so much as falls to each individually." Aristotle, *The Politics*, ed. Carnes Lord (Amherst: Prometheus Books, 1984), p. 57. That corresponds, more or less, to justice as "X-maximization." He addresses justice-as-order later. "In general, to live together and be partners in any human matter is difficult, and particularly things of this sort [owning common property]. This is clear in partnerships of fellow travelers, most of whom are always quarreling as a result of friction with one another over everyday and small matters. Again, friction particularly arises with the servants we use most frequently for regular tasks." Ibid., p. 60.

130. For a discussion of the impact of the printing press on a variety of matters, including intellectual property, see Elizabeth Eisenstein, *The Printing Press as an Agent of Change: Communications and Cultural Transformations in Early-Modern Europe* (Cambridge: Cambridge University Press, 1979).

131. Hume, *A Treatise of Human Nature*, p. 501 (emphasis in original).

132. Such objects, however, must be produced. In this sense they do share the kind of scarcity relevant to the X-maximization arguments.

133. As I shall argue at the conclusion of this article, justice-as-order is *consistent* with—indeed it is the genus for—the self-ownership, liberty-based argument for property that, as I have argued above, is *inconsistent* with patent and copyright.

134. Compare Howard Abrams, "The Historic Foundation of American Copyright Law: Exploding the Myth of Common Law Copyright, "*Wayne Law Review* 29 (1983).

135. Murray Rothbard, *The Ethics of Liberty* (Atlantic Highlands: Humanities Press, 1982), p. 144. (Rothbard seems to have made a slip here; he does not mean the right to "resell" the property but the right to copy it.)

136. See Kant, "Was ist ein Buch?"

137. Rothbard, *The Ethics of Liberty*, p. 123. Rothbard seems to have confused what is being made the subject of a property right. Clearly he cannot mean the right to *sell* the object, for then nothing that was copyrighted could be resold, and the market system would either grind to a halt or copyright would become a dead letter. He must mean the right to *reproduce*, rather than to resell. Note that the argument Rothbard presents in *The Ethics of Liberty* represents a shift from the argument presented in his early treatise on economics, *Man, Economy, and State: A Treatise on Economic Principles* (Los Angeles: Nash Publishing, 1970), in which he attacked patents as monopolies, but justified copyrights as a form implicit of contractual agreement not to copy. (See especially pp. 654–55) Such an implicit agreement differs from the right *reserved* by the creator. "[T]he inventor could mark his machine *copyright*, and then anyone who buys the machine buys it *on the condition* that he will not reproduce and sell such a machine for profit. Any violation of this contract would constitute implicit theft. . . . " (p. 654; emphasis in original). Rothbard's more recent proposal at least avoids the most obvious problem with his earlier position: what right would the originator have against a copier who did not buy the item, but simply saw it, heard of it, or found it. There would be no agreement, implicit or explicit, on the part of such a copier, and hence no obligation to refrain from copying. The later "reserved right" position allows the right to be reserved regardless of who comes into possession of the object, although it might face difficulties in enforcing the claim against someone, who, say, recorded an illegally broadcast song or movie.

138. Kant's remarks deserve repeating: "Those who regard the publication of a book as the exercise of the rights of property in respect of a single copy—it may have come to the possessor as a [manuscript] of the author, or as a work printed by some prior publisher—and who yet would, by the reservation of certain rights (whether as having their origin in the author or in the publisher in whose favour he has denuded himself of them), go on to restrict the exercise of property rights, maintaining the illegality of reproduction—will never attain their end. For the rights of the author regarding his own thoughts remain to him notwithstanding the reprint; and as there cannot be a distinct permission given to the purchaser of a book for, and a limitation of, its use as property, how much less is a mere presumption sufficient for a weight of obligation?" Kant, "Von der Unrechtmässigkeit des Büchernachdrucks," p. 58. Hegel argues; "The substance of an author's or an inventor's right cannot in the first instance be found in the supposition that when he disposes of a single copy of his work, he arbitrarily makes it a condition that the power to produce facsimiles as things, a power which thereupon passes into another's possession, should not become the property of another but should remain his own. The first question is whether such a separation between ownership of the things and the power to produce facsimiles which is given with the thing is compatible with the concept of property, or whether it does not

cancel the complete and free ownership on which there originally depends the option of the single producer of intellectual work to reserve to himself the power to reproduce, or to part with this power as a thing of value, or to attach no value to it at all and surrender it together with the single exemplar of his work." Hegel, *The Philosophy of Right*, p. 55.

139. It is important to remember that the retained right involved is a right to control a tangible object. No claim is made to a direct right to own the ideal object embedded in the tangible object. The control over this ideal object is an indirect consequence of a property right over a tangible object.

140. If an advocate of "piggyback rights" were to respond that the airwaves can and should be the objects of ownership, as some have argued, he would reveal a misunderstanding of the status of "the airwaves." One cannot own the broadcast spectrum, although one can have the right to use one's broadcasting or receiving equipment without interference from others. Thus, the first broadcaster over a frequency in a given spectrum area can have a legally recognized right to broadcast over a part of the electro-magnetic spectrum without interfering with another broadcaster. But if another broadcaster can send out a narrow beam signal within that spectrum that does not interfere with the first broadcaster's signal (and hence with his use of his tangible property), then the first should have no right to stop the second. As Ronald Coase argues, assigning direct property rights over the broadcast spectrum is as sensible as assigning direct property rights over "the notes of the musical scale or the colors of the rainbow." Ronald Coase, "The Federal Communications Commission," *Journal of Law and Economics* 2, no.1 (1959): 33. In a private property system "if there were a market, what would be sold, is the right to use a piece of equipment to transmit signals in a particular way. The right in question would be a right over a tangible object, not over the immaterial broadcast spectrum." See also Milton Mueller, "Reforming Telecommunications Regulation," in Edwin Diamond, Norman Sandler, and Milton Mueller, eds., *Telecommunications in Crisis: The First Amendment, Technology, and Deregulation* (Washington: Cato Institute, 1983).

141. The general thrust of Rothbard's overall argument for property seems to be consistent with the "justice-as-order" notion, although he sometimes does not make the distinctions necessary in order to address intellectual property issues. Thus, Rothbard defends the property right in a sculptor's creation without distinguishing between the different ways in which the sculptor might own his "product," like ownership of the material artifact, or ownership of the form embedded in it: "[T]he sculptor has in fact 'created' this work of art—not of course in the sense that he has created matter—but that he has produced it by transforming nature-given matter (the clay) into another form in accordance with his own ideas and his own labor and energy. Surely, if every man has the right to own his own body, and if he must use and transform material natural objects in order to survive, then he has the right to own the product that he has made, by his energy and effort, into a veritable extension of his own personality." Rothbard, *The Ethics of Liberty*, p. 48.

142. Earl Kintner and Jack Lahr, *An Intellectual Property Law Primer* (New York: Clark Boardman Company, 1982), p. 168 (quoting *Carver v. Harr*, 132 N.J. Eq. 207, 209. 27 A.2d 895, 897 [1942]).

143. But see Wendy Gordon, "An Inquiry into the Merits of Copyright: The Challenge of Consistency, Consent, and Encouragement Theory," *Stanford Law Review* 41 (1989). Arguing against my earlier essay, which was critical of patents and copyrights (Tom G. Palmer, "Intellectual Property: A Non-Posnerian Law and Economics Approach"). Gordon agrees that intellectual property claims are restraints on other property rights but responds, in Hohfeldian and positivist fashion, that "all entitlements limit each other." (p. 1423).

144. Hume, *A Treatise of Human Nature*, p. 484.

145. Ibid., p. 490.

146. For a contrast in this respect between the ancient world and modernity, see Benjamin Constant, "The Liberty of the Ancients Contrasted with That of the Moderns," in *Political Writings*, ed. Biancarmaria Fontana (Cambridge: Cambridge University Press, 1988), pp. 308–28.

147. See Thomas Schelling, *The Strategy of Conflict* (Cambridge, Mass: Harvard University Press, 1960) pp. 53–58.

148. Ibid., p. 57.

149. See Thomas Hodgskin, *The Natural and Artificial Right of Property Contrasted*, (London: B. Steil, 1832; reprinted Clifton, N.J.: Augustus Kelley, 1973), pp. 28–29: "Mr. Locke says, that every man has a property in his own person; in fact individuality—which is signified by the

word own—cannot be disjoined from the person. Each individual learns his own shape and form, and even the existence of his limbs and body, from seeing and feeling them. These constitute his notion of personal identity, both for himself and others; and it is impossible to conceive—it is in fact a contradiction to say—that a man's limbs and his body do not belong to himself: for the words him, self, and his body, signify the same material thing. As we learn the existence of our own bodies from seeing and feeling them, and as we see and feel the bodies of others, we have precisely similar grounds for believing in the individuality or identity of other persons, as for behaving in our own identity. The ideas expressed by the words mine and thine, as applied to the produce of labour, are simply then an extended form of the ideas of personal identity and individuality." On the appreciation of the individuality and special status of other humans, see Edmund Husserl, *Cartesian Meditations*, trans. Dorion Cairns (The Hague, Netherlands: Martinus Nijhoff, 1960), p. 129. Husserl argues that the reason we do not simply consider others as things or as meat is that we apprehend that we exist in a community, with an *"[o]bjectivating equalization of existence with that of all others."*

150. Destutt De Tracy, *A Treatise of Political Economy*, trans. by Thomas Jefferson (1817; New York: August Kelly, 1970), p. 47.

151. James Mirrlees, "The Economic Uses of Utilitarianism," in *Utilitarianism and Beyond*, ed. Amertya Sen and Bernard Williams (Cambridge: Cambridge University Press, 1982), p. 71: "Roughly speaking, [in a society of identical individuals] the totality of all individuals can be regarded as a single individual. Therefore total social utility, the sum of the total utilities of the separate individuals, is the right way to evaluate alternative patterns of outcomes for the whole society. That should be the view of any individual within society, and therefore of any outside observer." This approach is subjected to withering criticism in Robert Sugden, "Labour, Property and the Morality of Markets," in *The Market in History*, ed. B. L. Anderson and A. J. H. Latham (London: Croom Helm, 1986) pp. 9–28. See also Robert Sugden, *The Economics of Rights, Co-Operation, and Welfare* (Oxford: Basil Blackwell, 1986), pp. 6–8, for a criticism of the "U.S. Cavalry Model" of moral philosophy and a presentation of an alternative based on the viewpoint of the individual decision maker. Sugden presents an extended argument about how property rights and other conventions can emerge spontaneously, without any centralized agency or guiding hand, and how they can gain in the process the moral approbation of the participants in the process, even though they may be "suboptimal" from some external perspective. I am deeply indebted to Professor Sugden's work for my own views on morality and property.

152. Hume, *A Treatise of Human Nature*, p. 503.

153. Ibid., pp. 509–10.

154. By "extended order" I mean what Adam Smith referred to as a "Great Society." That is a sort of order that extends beyond the small group to include individuals who, while part of the same economic or legal order, will never have any face-to-face relationships.

155. For further elaboration of this approach, see Randy Barnett, "A Consent Theory of Contract," and Randy Barnett, "Contract Remedies and Inalienable Rights," *Social Philosophy and Policy* 4, no. 179 (1986). As Barnett argues, a natural-rights self-ownership model leads not to absolutism and slavery (as Richard Tuck has argued in *Natural Rights Theories: Their Origin and Development* [Cambridge: Cambridge University Press, 1981]) but to inalienable liberty. Although Tuck has argued that self-ownership must imply that one could alienate all rights over oneself to a sovereign, Barnett argues that that rests on an ontological impossibility, the alienation of one's self from oneself. On the consent theory of contract and inalienable rights, see also von Humboldt, *The Limits of State Action*, pp. 94–95.

156. See Harold Demsetz, "Towards a Theory of Property Rights," *American Economic Review* 57, no. 2 (1967). Note that in Demsetz's model, scarcity—in the static sense—is central to the origin of property rights.

157. Lysander Spooner objects that the argument from avoiding "collision" would as clearly require "that a hammer should be free to different persons at different times, and that a road, or canal should be free to as many persons at once, as can use it without collision, as it does that an idea should be free to as many persons at once as choose to use it." Spooner, *The Law of Intellectual Property*, Vol. III, p. 79. That response ignores the fact that use of tangible objects can come into collision, even if at any particular moment they are not in collision. In addition, it ignores the fact that "nonuse," such as speculative withholding from the market, is as legitimate a use of one's property as is its active exploitation. Further, the "externalities-

based" approach explains how property rights can emerge and change over time, as expanding populations, changing market conditions, and new technologies make possible forms of "collision" that were previously unknown. See Mueller, "Reforming Telecommunications Regulation," and Demsetz, "Towards a Theory of Property Rights."

158. Adam Smith, *Lectures on Jurisprudence* (Oxford: Oxford University Press, 1978), p. 352.

159. Arnold Plant, "The Economic Theory Concerning Patents for Inventions," in *Selected Economic Essays and Addresses* (London: Routledge & Kegan Paul, 1974), p. 56; see also F. A. Hayek, *The Fatal Conceit: The Errors of Socialism* (Chicago: University of Chicago Press, 1989), p. 6: "The difference between these [copyrights and patents] and other kinds of property rights is this: while ownership of material goods guides the use of scarce means to their most important uses, in the case of immaterial goods such as literary productions and technological inventions the ability to produce them is also limited, yet once they have come into existence, they can be indefinitely multiplied and can be made scarce only by law in order to create an inducement to produce such ideas. Yet it is not obvious that such forced scarcity is the most effective way to stimulate the human creative process."

160. See Hayek, *The Fatal Conceit*, pp. 11–21. We learn our mortality, Hayek argues, within the small group, notably the family, in which face-to-face interaction prevails. But we must also live in a world of strangers, in which "concrete, commonly perceived aims" cannot be assumed, nor can knowledge of the needs or abilities of others. "Part of our present difficulty is that we must constantly adjust our lives, our thoughts and our emotions, in order to live simultaneously within different kinds of orders according to different rules. If we were to apply the unmodified, uncurbed, rules of the microcosmos (i.e., of the small band or troop, or of, say, families) to the macrocosmos (our wider civilization), as our instincts and sentimental yearnings often make us do, we would destroy it. Yet if we were always to apply the rules of the extended order to our more intimate groupings, we would crush them. So we must learn to live in two sorts of worlds at once" (p. 18).

161. See Aristotle, *The Politics*, p. 61.

162. Overton, "An Arrow against All Tyrants," p. 55.

163. See Aristotle, *The Politics*, pp. 55–61.

164. I use the term here in a broad enough sense to include David Hume.

165. Of course, people of good faith sometimes do come into conflict, which is why we have courts of law to adjudicate disputes. To admit the possibility of such conflicts, however, is a far cry from seeing conflict as a built-in feature of social life.

166. Recall the discussion by John Locke regarding the question of when acorns that a person has eaten become his own: "so his, *i.e.*, a part of him, that another can no longer have any right to it." Locke, *Two Treatises of Government*, 2nd Treatise, Chapter V, §26, p. 287.

Biopiracy or Bioprivateering?

RICHARD STALLMAN

For decades, new drugs have been found in exotic animals and plants. Genes from rare species and subspecies are also useful in producing new breeds, whether by genetic engineering or ordinary cross-breeding. The drugs, and nowadays the new breeds as well, are typically patented. This causes trouble for developing countries that could use them.

Patent monopolies on plant and animal varieties, on genes, and on new medicines, threaten to harm developing countries in three ways. First, by raising prices so far that most citizens have no access to these new developments; second, by blocking local production when the patent owner so chooses; third, for agricultural varieties, by forbidding farmers to continue breeding them as has been done for thousands of years.

Just as the United States, a developing country in the 1800s, refused to recognize patents from advanced Britain, today's developing countries need to protect their citizens' interest by shielding them from such patents. To prevent the problems of monopolies, don't establish monopolies. What could be simpler?

But developing countries need support from world opinion in order to do this. It means going against a view that companies strongly advocate: that biotech company investors are entitled to monopolies, regardless of how they affect anyone else. It means going against treaties that these companies have prevailed on the US to force through threats of economic warfare on most of the world.

To challenge an idea which is backed by so much money is not easy. So some have proposed the concept of "biopiracy" as an alternative approach. Instead of opposing the existence of biological monopolies, this approach aims to give the rest of the world a share in the profits from them. The claim is that biotechnology companies are committing "biopiracy" when they base their work on natural varieties, or human genes, found in developing countries or among indigenous peoples--and therefore they ought to be required to pay "royalties" for this. "Biopiracy" is appealing at first glance, because it takes advantage of the current trend towards more and bigger monopoly powers. It goes with the flow, not against. But it will not solve the problem, because the problem stems from the trend that this concept legitimizes and fails to criticize.

Useful varieties and genes are not found everywhere or with even distribution. Some developing countries and indigenous peoples will be lucky, and receive substantial funds from such a system, at least for the twenty years that a patent lasts; a few may become so rich as to cause cultural dislocation, with a second episode to follow when the riches run out. Meanwhile, most of these countries and peoples will get little or nothing from this system. "Biopiracy" royalties, like the patent system itself, will amount to a kind of lottery.

The "biopiracy" concept presupposes that natural plant and animal varieties, and human genes, have an owner as a matter of natural right. Once that assumption is granted, it is hard to question the idea that an artificial variety, gene, or drug is property of the biotechnology company by natural right, and thus hard to deny the investors' demand for total and worldwide power over the use of it.

The idea of "biopiracy" offers the multinationals, and the governments that work for them, an easy way to cement forever their regime of monopolies. With a show of magnanimity, they can concede a small part of their income to a few lucky indigenous peoples; from then on, when anyone questions whether biological patents are a good idea, they can cite these indigenous peoples along with the fabled "starving genius inventor" to paint such questioning as plundering the downtrodden. (This behavior pattern is widespread among business today. For instance, the "music industry" lobbies for increased copyright powers in the name of musicians, who they like to call the "creators," while paying musicians only 4% of the companies' total income.)

What people outside the developed world really need, for their agriculture and medicine, is to be exempt from all such monopolies. They need to be free to manufacture medicine without paying royalties to multinationals. They need to be free to grow and breed all sorts of plants and animals for agriculture; and if they decide to use genetic engineering, they should be free to commission the genetic modifications that suit their needs. A lottery ticket for a share of royalties from a few varieties and genes is no compensation for losing these freedoms.

It is indeed wrong for biotech companies to convert the world's natural genetic resources into private monopolies--but the wrong is not a matter of taking someone else's rightful property, it is a matter of privatizing what ought to be public. These companies are not biopirates. They are bioprivateers.

Intangible Property:
Privacy, Power, and Information Control[*]

ADAM D. MOORE

Introduction

It is an obvious truism that the proliferation of computer networks and the digitization of everything not obstinately physical[1] is radically changing the human experience. As more individuals obtain access to computer networks such as the Internet or the World Wide Web—the official word for this is to become "wired"— digital based environments and information have come to play a central role in our everyday lives. Our money is stored and transmitted digitally, we listen to CDs where the music is recorded and played digitally, there are now digital cell-phones, cable television, and musical instruments. And all of this lies outside of the bit streams of 1's and 0's that make up computer networks, software programs, and operating systems. Many claim that the future holds information that cascades, not just through a PC, but across all forms of communication devices—headlines that flash across your watch, or a traffic map popping up on a cellular phone. It means content that will not hesitate to find you—whether you have clicked on something or not.[2] The integration, by digital technology, of what used to be disparate forms of communication is radically changing how we work and play.

At the center of this communication revolution is the control of information—who has it, how can it be gathered, can databases be owned, should information be "pulled" by users as a request or "pushed" to users who have shown interest? These concerns have obvious import into the areas of privacy and power. We each leave "digital footprints" that can be tracked by data mining companies and used to create purchasing profiles, medical summaries, political agendas, and the like. Moreover, this information is then sold to direct marketing companies—who will then call, write, or in the future, e-mail us—government agencies, private investigators, or to anyone for any reason. There used to be domains of a person's life that were totally inaccessible. A person's home and bedroom, notebook and hard drive, were all sanctuaries against the prying eyes and ears of others. It is alarming that digital technology is sweeping these domains away. Deborah Johnson accurately captures this sentiment.

> We have the technological capacity for the kind of massive, continuous surveillance of individuals that was envisioned in such frightening early twentieth-century science fiction works as George Orwell's *1984* and Zamyatin's *We*. The only difference between what is now possible and what was envisioned then are that much of the surveillance of individuals that is now done is by private institutions (marketing firms, insurance companies, credit agencies), and much of the surveillance now is via electronic records instead of by direct human observation. . . .[3]

The power of having such information should be obvious. Companies will be able to (and are able to) directly contact individuals who have shown interest in their products, or similar products, or their rival's products. And there are even more insidious uses for such information. Imagine a child custody case where one of the parents claims that the other is an unfit custodian for the children because the accused parent frequently views pornographic videos. Think of how governments could use such information to control populations or political opponents, or how insurance companies could use such information. In controlling information, especially sensitive personal information, the stakes could not be higher.

What follows is an explication and defense of a Lockean model of intangible property.[4] My goal is not to defend this model against all comers—rather, I will begin with weak, and hopefully, widely shared assumptions, sketch a theory based on these assumptions, and then proceed to the more meaningful task of analyzing a number of issues related to information control. Simply put, I will argue that individuals can own information about themselves and others. Moreover, I will make a case for limiting what can be done with intangible property based, in part, on privacy rights.

Before continuing, I would like to note a few important differences between intangible and property and tangible or physical property. The domain of intangible property includes that of intellectual property—the subject matter of copyrights and patents (books, movies, computer programs, processes of manufacture,

etc.)—as well as personal information, reputation, lists of facts, and
the like. Intangible property is generally characterized as non-
physical property where owner's rights surround control of physical manifestations or tokens of some abstract idea or type. Ideas or
collections of ideas are readily understood in terms of non-physical
types, while the physical manifestations of ideas can be modeled in
terms of tokens. Intangible property rights surround control of
physical tokens, and this control protects rights to types or abstract
ideas.[5]

Intangible works, unlike tangible goods, are non-rivalrous.
Computer programs, books, movies, and lists of customers can all
be used and consumed by many individuals concurrently.[6] This is
not the case for cars, computers, VCRs, and most other tangible
goods. Intangible property, unlike physical property, is also non-
zero-sum. In the clearest case, when I eat an apple there is one less
apple for everyone else—my plus one and everyone else's minus
one sum to zero. With intangible property it is not as if my acquisition leaves one less for everyone else.

Another difference between physical and intangible property
concerns what is available for acquisition. While matter, owned or
unowned, already exists, the same is not true of all intangible
works. What is available for acquisition in terms of intangible
property can be split into three domains. There is the domain of
ideas yet to be discovered (new scientific laws, mapping the human
genome, etc.), the domain of ideas yet to be created (the next *Lord of
the Rings*, *Star Wars*, etc.), and the domain of intangible works that
are privately owned. Since it is possible for individuals to independently invent or create the same intangible work and obtain
rights, we must include currently owned intangible works as
available for acquisition.[7] Only the set of ideas that are in the public
domain or those ideas that are a part of the common culture are not
available for acquisition and exclusion. I take this latter set to be
akin to a public park.

A Lockean Model of Intangible Property

We may begin by asking how property rights to unowned objects
are generated. This is known as the problem of original acquisition
and a common response is given by John Locke. "For this labor
being the unquestionable property of the laborer, no man but he can
have a right to what that is once joined to, at least where there is
enough and as good left for others."[8] As long as the proviso that

"enough and as good" is satisfied, an acquisition is of prejudice to no one. Locke argues that "Nobody could think himself injured by the drinking of another man, though he took a good draught, who had a whole river of the same left him to quench his thirst. . . ."[9] While the proviso is generally interpreted as a necessary condition for legitimate acquisition, I would like to examine it as a sufficient condition.[10] If the appropriation of an unowned object leaves enough and as good for others, then the acquisition is justified.

Suppose that mixing one's labor with an unowned object creates a prima facie claim against others not to interfere that can only be overridden by a comparable claim. The role of the proviso is to provide one possible set of conditions where the prima facie claim remains undefeated.[11] Another way of stating this position is that the proviso in addition to X, where X is labor or first occupancy or some other weak claim generating activity, provides a sufficient condition for original appropriation.

Justification for the view that labor or possession may generate prima facie claims against others could proceed along several lines. First, labor, intellectual effort, and creation are generally voluntary activities that can be unpleasant, exhilarating, and everything in-between. That we voluntarily do these things as sovereign moral agents may be enough to warrant non-interference claims against others.[12] A second, and possibly related justification, is based on desert. Sometimes individuals who voluntarily do or fail to do certain things deserve some outcome or other. Thus, students may deserve high honor grades and criminals may deserve punishment. When notions of desert are evoked claims and obligations are made against others—these non-absolute claims and obligations are generated by what individuals do or fail to do. Thus in fairly uncontroversial cases of desert, we are willing to acknowledge that weak claims are generated and if desert can properly attach to labor or creation, then claims may be generated in these cases as well.

Finally, a justification for the view that labor or possession may generate prima facie claims against others could be grounded in respect for individual autonomy and sovereignty. As sovereign and autonomous agents, especially within the liberal tradition, we are afforded the moral and legal space to order our lives as we see fit. As long as respect for others is maintained we are each free to set the course and direction of our own lives, to choose between various lifelong goals and projects, and to develop our capacities and talents accordingly. Simple respect for individuals would prohibit wresting from their hands an unowned object that they acquired or produced. I hasten to add that at this point we are trying to justify weak non-interference claims, not full blown property rights. Other things being equal, when an individual labors to create an intangible work, then weak presumptive claims of non-interference have been generated on grounds of labor, desert, or autonomy.

As noted before, the role of the proviso is to stipulate one possible set of conditions where the prima facie claim remains undefeated. Suppose Fred appropriates a grain of sand from an endless beach and paints a lovely, albeit small, picture on the surface. Ginger, who has excellent eyesight, likes Fred's grain of sand and snatches it away from him. On this interpretation of Locke's theory, Ginger has violated Fred's weak presumptive claim to the grain of sand. We may ask, what legitimate reason could Ginger have for taking Fred's grain of sand rather than picking up her own grain of sand? If Ginger has no comparable claim, then Fred's prima facie claim remains undefeated. An undefeated prima facie claim can be understood as a right.[13]

A Pareto-Based Proviso

The underlying rationale of Locke's proviso is that if no one's situation is worsened, then no one can complain about another individual appropriating part of the commons. Put another way, an objection to appropriation, which is a unilateral changing of the moral landscape, would focus on the impact of the appropriation on others. But if this unilateral changing of the moral landscape makes no one worse off, there is no room for rational criticism. The proviso permits individuals to better themselves so long as no one is worsened (weak Pareto superiority). The base level intuition of a Pareto improvement is what lies behind the notion of the proviso.[14] If no one is harmed by an acquisition and one person is bettered, then the acquisition ought to be permitted. In fact, it is precisely because no one is harmed that it seems unreasonable to object to a Pareto-superior move. Thus, the proviso can be understood as a version of a "no harm, no foul" principle.[15]

Before continuing, I will briefly consider the plausibility of a Pareto-based proviso as a moral principle. First, to adopt a less-than-weak Pareto principle would permit individuals, in bettering themselves, to worsen others. Such provisos on acquisition are troubling because at worst they may open the door to predatory activity and at best they give anti-property theorists the ammunition to combat the weak presumptive claims that labor and possession may generate. Part of the intuitive force of a Pareto-based proviso is that it provides little or no grounds for rational complaint. Moreover, if we can justify intangible property rights with a more stringent principle, a principle that is harder to satisfy, then we have done something more robust, and perhaps more difficult to attack, when we reach the desired result.

To require individuals, in bettering themselves, to better others is to require them to give others free rides. In the absence of social interaction, what reason can be given for forcing one person, if she is to benefit herself, to benefit others?[16] If, absent social interaction, no benefit is required then why is such benefit required within society? The crucial distinction that underlies this position is between worsening someone's situation and failing to better it[17] and I take this intuition to be central to a kind of deep moral individualism.[18] Moreover, the intuition that grounds a Pareto-based proviso fits well with the view that labor and possibly the mere possession of unowned objects creates a prima facie claim to those objects. Individuals are worthy of a deep moral respect and this grounds a liberty to use and possess unowned objects.

Bettering, Worsening, and the Baseline Problem

Assuming a just initial position[19] and that Pareto-superior moves are legitimate, there are two questions to consider when examining a Pareto-based proviso. First, what are the terms of being worsened? This is a question of scale, measurement, or value. An individual could be worsened in terms of subjective preference satisfaction, wealth, happiness, freedoms, opportunities, et cetera. Which of these count in determining bettering and worsening? Second, once the terms of being worsened have been resolved, which two situations are we going to compare to determine if someone has been worsened? Is the question one of how others are now, after my appropriation, compared to how they would have been were I absent, or if I had not appropriated, or some other state? Here we are trying to answer the question, "Worsened relevant to what?" This is known as the baseline problem.

In principle, the Lockean theory of intangible property being developed is consistent with a wide range of value theories.[20] So long as the preferred value theory has the resources to determine bettering and worsening with reference to acquisitions, then Pareto-superior moves can be made and acquisitions justified on Lockean grounds. For now, assume an Aristotelian eudaimonist account of value exhibited by the following theses is correct.

1. Human well-being or flourishing is the sole standard of intrinsic value.

2. Human persons are rational project pursuers, and well-being or flourishing is attained through the setting, pursuing, and completion of life goals and projects.[21]

3. The control of physical and intangible objects is valuable. At a specific time each individual has a certain set of things she can freely use and other things she owns, but she also has certain opportunities to use and appropriate things. This complex set of opportunities along with what she can now freely use or has rights over constitutes her position materially—this set constitutes her level of material well-being.

While it is certainly the case that there is more to bettering and worsening than an individual's level of material well-being including opportunity costs, I will not pursue this matter further at present. Needless to say, a full-blown account of value will explicate all the ways in which individuals can be bettered and worsened with reference to acquisition. Moreover as noted before, it is not crucial to the Lockean model being presented to defend some preferred theory of value against all comers. Whatever value theory that is ultimately correct, if it has the ability to determine bettering and worsening with reference to acquisitions, then Pareto-superior moves can be made and acquisitions justified on Lockean grounds.

The Baseline of Comparison
Lockeans as well as others who seek to ground rights to property in the proviso generally set the baseline of comparison as the state of nature. The commons or the state of nature is characterized as that state where the moral landscape has yet to be changed by formal property relations. Indeed, it would be odd to assume that individuals come into the world with complex property relations already intact with the universe. Prima facie, the assumption that the world is initially devoid of such property relations seems much

more plausible.[22] The moral landscape is barren of such relations until some process occurs—and it is not assumed that the process for changing the moral landscape the Lockean would advocate is the only justified means to this end.[23]

For now, assume a state of nature situation where no injustice has occurred and where there are no property relations in terms of use, possession, or rights. All anyone has in this initial state are opportunities to increase her material standing. Suppose Fred creates an intangible work and does not worsen his fellows—alas, all they had were contingent opportunities and Fred's creation and exclusion adequately benefits them in other ways. After the acquisition, Fred's level of material well-being has changed. Now he has a possession that he holds legitimately, as well as all of his previous opportunities. Along comes Ginger who creates her own intangible work and considers whether her exclusion of it will worsen Fred. But what two situations should Ginger compare? Should the acquisitive case (Ginger's acquisition) be compared to Fred's initial state, where he had not yet legitimately acquired anything, or to his situation immediately before Ginger's taking? If bettering and worsening are to be cashed out in terms of an individual's level of well-being with opportunity costs and this measure changes over time, then the baseline of comparison must also change. In the current case we compare Fred's level of material well-being when Ginger possesses and excludes an intangible work to his level of well-being immediately before Ginger's acquisition.

The result of this discussion of bettering, worsening, and the baseline problem is the following proviso on original acquisition:[24]

> If the acquisition of an intangible work makes no one worse-off in terms of her level of well-being (including opportunity costs) compared to how she was immediately before the acquisition, then the taking is permitted.

If correct, this account justifies rights to control intangible property. When an individual creates or compiles an intangible work and fixes it in some fashion, then labor and possession create a prima facie claim to the work. Moreover, if the proviso is satisfied the prima facie claim remains undefeated and rights are generated.

Suppose Ginger, who is living off of the commons, creates a new gathering technique that allows her to live better with less work. The set of ideas that she has created can be understood as an intangible work. Given that Ginger has labored to create this new gathering technique, it has been argued that she has a weak presumptive claim to the work. Moreover, it looks as if the proviso has been satisfied given that her fellows are left, all things considered, unaffected by her acquisition. This is to say that they are free to create, through their own intellectual efforts, a more efficient gathering system, or even one that is exactly the same as Ginger's.

Overall, the structure of the argument that I have given is:

1. If the acquisition of an intangible work satisfies a Pareto-based proviso, then the acquisition and exclusion are justified.
2. Some acts of intangible property creation and possession satisfy a Pareto-based proviso.
3. So, some intangible property rights are justified.

Support for the first premise can be summarized in three related points: 1(a) *The Paretian Intuition*—if no one is harmed by an acquisition and one person is bettered, then the acquisition ought to be permitted. This "no harm no foul" principle leaves little room for rational complaint; 1(b) A less-weak-Pareto principle would allow predation and a stronger-than-weak Pareto principle would allow parasitism; and 1(c) A Pareto-based proviso is consistent with the view that individuals are worthy of a deep moral respect, that their lives and lifelong goals and projects are not justifiably sacrificed for incremental gains in social utility.

Support for the second premise can be summarized as follows: 2(a) Intangible property is non-rivalrous—it is capable of being used and possessed by many individuals concurrently; 2(b) The "same" intangible work may be created and owned by many different individuals concurrently (zero-sum); 2(c) The number of ideas, collections of ideas, or intangible works available for appropriation is practically infinite (this makes the acquisition of intangible goods similar to Locke's water drinker example); 2(d) Institutions or systems of intangible property may provide compensation for apparent worsening that occur at the level of acts;[25] and 2(e) Many creations and inventions are strongly Pareto-superior, meaning that everyone is bettered and no one is worsened.

Property, Privacy, and Information Control

Although I have made a case for granting intangible property rights to individuals who satisfy the Paretian test this does not mean that owners can do anything they want with their property. To take a simple example, my property right in a Louisville slugger does not allow me swing it at your knees, nor can I throw it at your car. Property rights are generally limited by the rights of others. More specifically, there is a prohibition of harm with respect to property rights.[26] This means that you can do what you want with your property short of unjustly harming others. Furthermore, this restriction—call it the harm restriction—fits well with the Lockean model under consideration. The proviso, a no harm no foul rule, allows individuals to acquire unowned goods. The harm restriction limits harmful uses of those goods.

A second constraint has to do with privacy and information control. Privacy may be understood as that state where others do not have access to you or to information about you. I hasten to note that there are degrees of privacy. There are our own private thoughts that are never disclosed to anyone, as well as information we share with loved ones. Furthermore, there is information that we share with mere acquaintances and the general public. These privacy relations with others can be pictured "in terms of a series of 'zones' or 'regions' . . . leading to a 'core self.'"[27] Thus, secrets shared with a loved one can still be considered private, even though they have been disclosed.

In an important article dealing with privacy, morality, and the law, William Parent offers the following definition for privacy.

> *Privacy is the condition of not having undocumented personal knowledge about one possessed by others.* A person's privacy is diminished exactly to the degree that others possess this kind of knowledge about him. Documented information is information that is found in the public record or is publicly available (e.g. information found in newspapers, court proceedings, and other official documents open to public inspection).[28]

The problem with this definition is that it leaves the notion of privacy dependent upon what a society or culture takes as documentation and what information is available via the public record. Parent acts as if undocumented information is private while documented information is not, and this is the end of the matter. But surely the secret shared between lovers is private in one sense and not in another. To take another case, consider someone walking in a public park. There is almost no limit to the kinds of information that can be acquired from this public display. One's image, height, weight, eye color, approximate age, and general physical abilities are all readily available. Moreover, biological matter will also be left in the public domain—strands of hair and the like may be left behind. Since this matter, and the information contained within, is publicly available it would seem that all of one's genetic profile is not private information.

Furthermore, what is publicly available information is dependent upon technology. Telescopes, listening devices, heat imaging sensors, and the like, open up what most would consider private domains for public consumption. What we are worried about is what should be considered a "private affair"—something that is no one else's business. Parent's conception of privacy is not sensitive to these concerns.

A right to privacy can be understood as a right to maintain a certain level of control over the inner spheres of personal information. It is a right to limit public access to the "core self"—personal information that one never discloses—and to information that one discloses only to family and friends. For example, suppose that I wear a glove because I am ashamed of a scar on my hand. If you were to snatch the glove away you would not only be violating my right to property—alas the glove is mine to control—you would also violate my right to privacy; a right to restrict access to information about the scar on my hand. Similarly, if you were to focus your x-ray camera on my hand, take a picture of the scar through the glove, and then publish the photograph widely, you would violate a right to privacy.

Legal scholar William Prosser separated privacy cases into four distinct but related torts.[29]

> *Intrusion*: Intruding (physically or otherwise) upon the solitude of another in a highly offensive manner. For example, a woman sick in the hospital with a rare disease refuses a reporter's request for a photograph and interview. The reporter photographs her anyway, over her objection.

Private facts: Publicizing highly offensive private information about someone which is not of legitimate concern to the public. For example, photographs of an undistinguished and wholly private hardware merchant carrying on an adulterous affair in a hotel room are published in a magazine.

False light: Publicizing a highly offensive and false impression of another. For example, a taxi driver's photograph is used to illustrate a newspaper article on cabdrivers who cheat the public when the driver in the photo is not, in fact, a cheat.

Appropriation: Using another's name or likeness for some advantage without the other's consent. For example, a photograph of a famous actress is used without her consent to advertise a product.

What binds these seemingly disparate cases under the heading "privacy invasions" is that they each concern personal information control. And while there may be other morally objectionable facets to these cases, for example the taxi driver case may also be objectionable on grounds of defamation, there is arguably privacy interests at stake as well.

Having said something about what a right to privacy is we may ask how such rights are justified. A promising line of argument combines notions of autonomy and respect for persons. A central and guiding principle of western liberal democracies is that individuals, within certain limits, may set and pursue their own life goals and projects. Rights to privacy erect a moral boundary that allows individuals the moral space to order their lives as they see fit. Clinton Rossiter puts the point succinctly.

Privacy is a special kind of independence, which can be understood as an attempt to secure autonomy in at least a few personal and spiritual concerns, if necessary in defiance of all the pressures of the modern society. . . . It seeks to erect an unbreachable wall of dignity and reserve against the entire world. The free man is the private man, the man who still keeps some of his thoughts and judgments entirely to himself, who feels no over-riding compulsion to share everything of value with others, not even those he loves and trusts.[30]

Privacy protects us from the prying eyes and ears of governments, corporations, and neighbors. Within the walls of privacy we may experiment with new ways of living that may not be accepted by the majority. Privacy, autonomy, and sovereignty, it would seem come bundled together.

A second but related line of argument rests on the claim that privacy rights stand as a bulwark against governmental oppression and totalitarian regimes. If individuals have rights to control personal information and to limit access to themselves, within certain constraints, then the kinds of oppression that we have witnesses in the twentieth century would be near impossible. Put another way, if oppressive regimes are to consolidate and maintain power, then privacy rights (broadly defined) must be eliminated or severely restricted. If correct, privacy rights would be a core value that limited the forces of oppression.[31]

Arguably any plausible account of human well being or flourishing will have as a component a strong right to privacy. Controlling who has access to ourselves is an essential part of being a happy and free person. This may be why "peeping Toms" and rapists are held up as moral monsters—they cross a boundary that should never be crossed without consent.

Surely each of us has the right to control our own thoughts, hopes, feelings, and plans, as well as a right to restrict access to information about our lives, family, and friends. I would argue that what grounds these sentiments is a right to privacy—a right to maintain a certain level of control over personal information.[32] While complete control of all our personal information is a pipe dream for many of us, simply because the information is already out there and most likely cannot or will not be destroyed, this does not detract from the view of personal information ownership. Through our daily activities we each create and leave digital footprints that others may follow and exploit—and that we do these things does not obviously sanction the gathering and subsequent disclosure of such information by others.

Whatever kind of information we are considering there is a gathering point that individuals have control over. For example, in purchasing a new car and filling out the car loan application, no one would deny we each have the right to demand that such information not be sold to other companies. I would argue that this is true for any disclosed personal information whether it be patient questionnaire information, video rental records, voting information, or credit applications. In agreeing with this view, one first has to agree that individuals have the right to control their own personal information—i.e., binding agreements about controlling information presuppose that one of the parties has the right to control this information.

Having said all of this, I would like to test the Lockean model of intangible property with a very tricky case dealing with personal information control.

> A woman is kidnapped, taken to an apartment, stripped, and terrorized. The police—and the media—surround the apartment. The police eventually overcome the kidnapper and rush the woman, who clutches a dish towel in a futile attempt to conceal her nudity, to safety. A photograph of her escape is published in the next day's newspaper. She sued for invasion of privacy and eventually lost the case. (*Cape Publications, Inc. v. Bridges*, Florida 1982).[33]

According to the theory that I have sketched, the photographer may indeed have a property right to the photograph he took—if his mere acquisition does not worsen—but this does not mean that he can do anything with the photograph. His rights to control the picture are limited by the harm and privacy restrictions. So even if publishing the photograph did not harm the woman involved, it would still be an illicit violation of privacy.

Now, it is clear that my view runs counter to prevailing attitudes about the First Amendment. I would place more restrictions on speech or expression than is currently found in the law. Not only can we not yell "fire" in a crowded theater—this would violate the harm restriction—we cannot publish sensitive personal information without permission. This is not to say that the harm restriction and the privacy restriction are exceptionless—those who live their lives in the public realm may have to endure a more limited sphere of privacy. Moreover, certain harms may be permitted in order to protect a community from criminals and the like—for example, consider laws that require public notification when a child predator is relocated to a new community. Politicians and entertainers, in a sense, sanction a more limited sphere of privacy by choosing a certain career path and a similar point can be made with respect to criminals. While the sphere of privacy protection may be more limited in these cases there are still boundaries that cannot be crossed. Becoming a "public figure" does not sanction continual harassment for autographs, pictures, and interviews. Access, in many ways, is still left to the individual—and this is how it should be.

In my view, an important part of a right to privacy is the right to control personal information; "control" in the sense of deciding who has access and to what uses the information can be put; "personal" in the sense of being about some individual as opposed to being about inanimate objects, corporations, institutions, and the like. These are not intended to be precise definitions—rather I am trying to capture the common everyday notion of a privacy interest. The appropriateness of who knows particular facts about an individual is, in an important sense, dependent on certain relationships. The kind of information access between doctor and patient, husband and wife, mother and child, and total strangers, are all appropriately different.[34]

Against this backdrop what sense can be made of the public's "right to know?" A newspaper may publish information about a kidnapping and rescue, but this does not sanction publishing sensitive personal information about the victim. Right-to-know arguments may carry some weight in cases where public funds are being spent or when a politician reverses his stand on a particular issue, but they seem to be suspect when used to justify intrusions. Sissela Bok echoes these concerns when she writes,

> Taken by itself, the notion that the public has a "right to know" is as quixotic from an epistemological as from a moral point of view, and the idea of the public's "right to know the truth" even more so. It would be hard to find a more fitting analogue to Jeremy Bentham's characterization of talk about natural and imprescriptible rights as "rhetorical nonsense—nonsense upon stilts." How can one lay claim to a right to know the truth when even partial knowledge is out of reach concerning most human affairs, and when bias and rationalization and denial skew and limit knowledge still further?
>
> So patently inadequate is the rationale of the public's right to know as a justification for reporters to probe and

expose, that although some still intone it ritualistically at the slightest provocation, most now refer to it with a tired irony.[35]

The social and cultural benefits of free speech and free information is generally cited as justification for a free press and the public's right to know. This is why news-services can publish photographs and stories that contain sensitive personal information about almost anyone. But computer technology has changed the playing field and such arguments seem to lose force when compared to the overwhelming loss of privacy that we now face. The kinds of continual and systematic invasions by news-services, corporations, data mining companies, and other individuals that will be possible in a few short years is quite alarming.

Conclusion

While there is still much to be worked out, I think that important steps have been taken toward a Lockean theory of intangible property. If no one is worsened by an acquisition, then there seems to be little room for rational complaint. The individual who takes a good long drink from a river does as much as to take nothing at all and the same may be said of those who acquire intangible property. Given allowances for independent creation and that the frontier of intangible property is practically infinite, the case for Locke's water-drinker and the author or inventor are quite alike.

Even so, such rights are not without limitations. I cannot justifiably slash your tires with my knife nor may I publish your medical records on my web site. The proliferation of the Internet and the World Wide Web into everyday life is forcing us to rethink our views about information access and control. The claim is not that controlling information used to be unimportant and now it is important—alas, censorship in various forms has always been with us. What I think true, however, is that computer networks coupled with digitally stored information is significantly changing the way we interact and communicate. We will have to be much more careful about what we do and say in the future both publicly and privately. Any information or ideas that we disclose, including inventions, recipes, or sensitive personal information, might soon be bouncing around cyberspace for anyone to access. Many net anarchists claim that "information wants to be free" and advocate a model of unrestricted access to all kinds of information. In this article I have argued otherwise—information, especially sensitive personal information, can be owned and restricted on grounds of property or privacy. And if we are to err on the side of too much access or too much privacy, better—far better—the latter.

Notes

*Copyright *American Philosophical Quarterly*, Vol. 35 (October, 1998): 365-375. Portions of this paper were presented at the 1997 Central Division Meeting of the APA and at the 1998 Ohio Philosophical Association conference. I would like to thank David Wasserman, Jim Swindler, Earl Spurgin, Don Hubin, and Ken Itzkowitz for their suggestions and comments.

1. This phrase comes from John Perry Barlow, "The Economy of Ideas: Everything You Know About Intellectual Property is Wrong" in *Intellectual Property: Moral, Legal, and International Dilemmas*, edited by A. Moore (Lanham, MD.: Rowman & Littlefield, 1997), Chapter 15.

2. Kevin Kelly and Gary Wolf, "Push," *Wired Magazine* (March 1997), 14.

3. Deborah Johnson, *Computer Ethics* (Upper Saddle River, N.J.: Prentice Hall, 1994), 84.

4. For a lengthy defense of the following Lockean model see *Intellectual Property and Information Control* (New Brunswick: Transaction Pub., 2001, 2004). See also, "A Lockean Theory of Intellectual Property," *Hamline Law Review* 21 (1997): 65-108 and "Toward a Lockean Theory of Intellectual Property," in *Intellectual Property: Moral, Legal, and International Dilemmas*, edited by A. Moore.

5. American copyright law prohibits the ownership of abstract ideas—copyright protects new and original expressions, not the ideas that stand behind the expressions. Nevertheless there is still a type/token model here because copyrights protect expressions of a certain type.

6. It may be objected that some intangible works are rivalrous, for example the Mona Lisa or Michelangelo's David. What is rivalrous about these works is not the ideas that are embodied in the canvas or stone, it is the physical works themselves. We can all hang a copy of the Mona Lisa in our living rooms—we just can't have the original embodiment.

7. Unlike copyrights and trade secrets, patents exclude other independent inventors from obtaining rights to a work already patented. The Lockean model of intangible property that I will sketch does not include such a rule.

8. John Locke, *The Second Treatise of Government,*§ 27 (italics mine).

9. Locke, *Second Treatise,* § 33.

10. Both Jeremy Waldron, "Enough and as Good Left for Others," *Philosophical Quarterly* (1979): 319-328, and Clark Wolf, "Contemporary Property Rights, Lockean Provisos, and the Interests of Future Generation," *Ethics* (July, 1995): 791-818, maintain that Locke thought of the proviso as a sufficient condition and not a necessary condition for legitimate acquisition.

11. This view is summed up nicely by Wolf, "Contemporary Property Rights," 791-818.

12. Even Marx never explicitly denies that laborers are entitled to the fruits of their labor— "Indeed, it is natural to think that his condemnation of capitalist exploitation depends on a conviction that laborers are entitled to the whole fruits of their labor." Lawrence Becker, *Property Rights: Philosophic Foundations*, (London: Routledge & Kegan Paul, 1977), n2, p. 121. See also, Karl Marx, *Capital* (New York: International Publishers, 1967), vol. 1, part VIII, chapter xxvi.

13. For a defense of this view of rights see G. Rainbolt, "Rights as Normative Constraints," *Philosophy and Phenomenological Research* (1993): 93-111, and Joel Feinberg, *Freedom and Fulfillment: Philosophical Essays* (Princeton University Press, 1986).

14. One state of the world, S1, is Pareto-superior to another, S2, if and only if no one is worse-off in S1 than in S2, and at least one person is better-off in S1 than in S2. S1 is *strongly* Pareto-superior to S2 if everyone is better-off in S1 than in S2, and *weakly* Pareto-superior if at least one person is better-off and no one is worse-off. State S1 is Pareto optimal if no state is Pareto superior to S1: it is *strongly* Pareto-optimal if no state is *weakly* Pareto-superior to it, and *weakly* Pareto-optimal if no state is *strongly* Pareto-superior to it. Throughout this essay I will use Pareto-superiority to stand for *weak* Pareto-superiority. Adapted from G. A. Cohen's "The Pareto Argument For Inequality" in *Social Philosophy & Policy* 12 (Winter 1995): 160.

15. It is important to note that compensation is typically built into the proviso and the overall account of bettering and worsening. David Gauthier echoes this point in the following case. "In acquiring a plot of land, even the best land on the island, Eve may initiate the possibility of more diversified activities in the community as a whole, and more specialized activities for particular individuals with ever-increasing benefits to all." Gauthier, *Morals By Agreement* (Oxford: Clarendon Press, 1986), 204. Eve's appropriation may actually benefit her fellows and the benefit may serve to cancel the worsening that occurs from restricted use. Moreover, compensation can occur at both the level of the act and at the level of the institution. This is to say that Eve herself may compensate or that the system in which specific property relations are determined may compensate.

16. I have in mind Nozick's Robinson Crusoe case in *Anarchy, State, And Utopia* (New York: Basic Books, 1974), 185.

17. The distinction between worsening someone's position and failing to better it is a hotly contested moral issue. See Gauthier, *Morals By Agreement*, 204; Shelly Kagan, *The Limits of Morality* (Oxford University Press, 1989), chap. 3; John Harris, "The Marxist Conception of Violence," *Philosophy & Public Affairs* 3 (1973-74): 192-220; John Kleinig, "Good Samaritanism," *Philosophy & Public Affairs* 5 (1975-76): 382-407; and Eric Mack's two articles, "Bad Samaritanism and the Causation of Harm," *Philosophy & Public Affairs* 9 (1979-80): 230-259, and "Causing and Failing To Prevent Harm," *Southwestern Journal of Philosophy* 7 (1976): 83-90. This distinction is even further blurred by my account of opportunities. See Moore "Toward A Lockean Theory" 88-89.

18. This view is summed up nicely by A. Fressola. "Yet, what is distinctive about persons is not merely that they are agents, but more that they are rational planners—that they are capable of engaging in complex projects of long duration, acting in the present to secure consequences in the future, or ordering their diverse actions into programs of activity, and ultimately, into plans of life." Anthony Fressola, "Liberty and Property," *American Philosophical Quarterly* (Oct. 1981): 320.

19. One problem with a Pareto condition is that it says nothing about the initial position from which deviations may occur. If the initial position is unfair then our Pareto condition allows that those who are unjustly better off to remain better off. This is why the problem of original acquisition is traditionally set in the state of nature or the commons. The state of nature supposedly captures a fair initial starting point for Pareto improvements.

20. It has been argued that subjective preference satisfaction theories fail to give an adequate account of bettering and worsening. See D. Hubin and M. Lambeth's "Providing For Rights" *Dialogue* 27 (1989).

21. For similar views see: Rawls, *A Theory of Justice* (Cambridge: Harvard University Press, 1971), cha. VII.; Aristotle, *Nicomachean Ethics*, bks. I and X; Kant, *The Fundamental Principles of The Metaphysics of Morals*, Academy Edition; Sidgwick, *Methods of Ethics*, 7th ed. (London: Macmillian, 1907); R. B. Perry, *General Theory of Value* (New York: Longmans, Green, 1926); and Loren Lomasky, *Persons, Rights, and the Moral Community* (New York: Oxford University Press, 1987).

22. One plausible exception is body rights which are similar to, if not the same as, many of the rights that surround property.

23. There may be many others such as, consent theories, consequentialist theories, social contract theories, theories of convention, and so on.

24. The proviso permits the use, exclusion, and augmentation of an object. Although this does not give us a complete theory of property relations it begins the process. I would argue that the proviso, whatever other forms of property relations it might allow, permits private property relations.

25. Suppose that one way to achieve Pareto-superior results is by adopting an institution that promotes and maintains restricted access, or fencing, of intellectual works. This is to say that, given our best estimates, everyone is better-off living within an institution where fencing is permitted and protected as opposed to alternative institutions where fencing is prohibited. If such a case can be made, then the Paretian may have a way to justify specific acts of appropriation by appealing to the level of institutions.

26. The "harm" that I have in mind here is in terms of an individual's level of well being. Obviously alternative accounts of bettering and worsening will defend a different standard of harm.

27. Alan Westin, "Privacy in the Modern Democratic State" in D. Johnson and J. Snapper, *Ethical Issues in the Use of Computers* (Belmont, CA: Wadsworth Pub.: 1985): 187.

28. W. A. Parent, "Privacy, Morality, and the Law" *Philosophy & Public Affairs* 12 (Fall 1983): 269-288, reprinted in D. Johnson and J. Snapper, *Ethical Issues in the Use of Computers,* 203 (all page citations refer to the reprint).

29. Dean William Prosser, "Privacy," *California Law Review* 48 (1960): 383, 389, quoted in E. Alderman and C. Kennedy, *The Right to Privacy* (New York: Alfred A. Knopf, 1995), 155-56.

30. C. Rossiter, *Aspects of Liberty* (Ithaca, NY: Cornell University Press, 1958) quoted in Westin, "Privacy in the Modern Democratic State," 188.

31. For more about privacy rights see, Charles Fried, "Privacy," *Yale Law Journal* 77 (1968): 477; A. Westin and M. Baker, *Databanks in a Free Society* (New York: Quadrangle Press, 1972); and J. Rachels, "Why Privacy is Important," *Philosophy and Public Affairs* 4 (Summer 1975): 323-33.

32. Would I be doing something morally illicit if I put on my new anti-monitoring suit that afforded me complete protection from every surveillance devise except the human eye?

33. This case is cited in E. Alderman and C. Kennedy's *The Right to Privacy,* 171.

34. Rachels in "Why Privacy is Important" argues that privacy is valuable because it is necessary for creating and maintaining different kinds of relationships with people.

35. Sissela Bok, *Secrets* (New York: Pantheon, 1982), 254.

Why Collaborative Free Works Should Be Protected by the Law

LAWRENCE M. SANGER

The Internet has, famously, made possible a radically new sort of collaboration among software and content developers from around the world. The results of many of these collaborations are distributed free of charge and under licenses that permit further development and free release. Until only recently, such productions—the Linux operating system, many thousands of free software packages, and free content like the Wikipedia encyclopedia—have been received, for the most part, as idealistic, innocuous efforts to bring free stuff to the world. In coming years, the world will be lucky to escape considerable corporate, political, and legal turmoil over this free stuff. So this paper will defend a modest thesis, on utilitarian grounds: the law should be written in such a way as to make it possible for free collaborative works to survive because society will greatly benefit from them.

"Open source software" and "open content" might sound like tech-head buzzwords today, but as free works become increasingly user-friendly, they could pose a threat to the profits of some commercial software developers, as well as publishers. Linux has developed from something that only the geekiest of geeks could love to an actually usable operating system—usable if only by "power users"—and with further development, it could become a serious competitor of Windows and Macintosh operating systems. Linux is already running many Internet servers. Moreover, there are, for all platforms, free word processors, spreadsheets, graphics programs, media players, and many more kinds of software. The best of these are usable, but occasionally "clunky," and although opinions vary, usually decidedly inferior to the best of the popular commercial products. But this could change, and there is some reason to think that it will change.

The situation is similar with regard to content and publishing. In under four years, the free encyclopedia Wikipedia (found at Wikipedia.org) developed nearly one million articles in dozens of languages including over 300,000 in English. It is perhaps surprising that such an uncontrolled collaboration can produce work as useful as it is; but, admittedly, as in the case of free software, this "free content" still lacks the reliability of the commercially-available versions. Yet this could change as well, and probably will: if and when such a more reliable review process is added to the current, remarkably robust one, it is hard to see what advantages *Encyclopaedia Britannica,* Microsoft's *Encarta,* and other proprietary encyclopedias might have over Wikipedia.

A need and motivation similar to what led to the creation of Wikipedia is bound to lead to many free textbooks. Already, virtually all of the major (public domain) classics are available online, and these free copies are starting to be used in coursework. Many free textbooks are available online, although admittedly few have actually been adopted by instructors. But again, this could change, and probably will: there are enough scholars and teachers in the world, motivated not by money but simply by a desire to teach, who will probably together create, co-edit, and maintain up-to-date textbooks in most fields. It seems to be merely a matter of time before this happens on a large scale.

In short, *whatever* people can work on together over the Internet and release under a free license, the results of that collaborative work may very well, in coming years, be developed to the point where it will pose a threat to the profits of entities that develop similar work under the old proprietary model. Publishers and software manufacturers clearly have something to worry about from the "free stuff" movement, I and many others think. This paper cannot take the space to support this claim rigorously; the above will have to suffice to make the claim worth considering, at least.

This paper will be focused on the more philosophical aspects of the situation, and in general, on this question: given that copyright violations, libel, and other abuses of free speech will take place when software and content—*work* for short—is developed and released under open source/open content licenses, what relief is reasonable and just? This is actually a broader question than I want to address. For one thing, in many cases, despite the unorthodox licensing, no significantly different circumstances present themselves in the case of free works.

What I want to address is a more obviously difficult, and interesting, sort of case. I mean the sort of case in which free works are developed in a *strongly* collaborative way—i.e., there is no single copyright holder, the project lacks a central, controlling authority, and there is no "endpoint" at which the project is considered complete. I will call such work *shopwork* (a neologism I will discuss more carefully below).

The purpose of this paper is to clarify, argue for, and defend the claim that shopwork *per se* deserves protection by the law, which is to say that the law should see to it that it is *possible* to pursue shopwork. The claim is similar in some ways to the claim that private property *per se* deserves protection by the law: the *institution* of shopwork, like that of private property, deserves to be protected, even while the law provides relief against the inevitable abuses of the institution. So I will first clarify what "shopwork" is, then offer a utilitarian argument for the claim, and finally address some objections to the argument.

I. What Is Shopwork?

Shopwork, briefly, stands for any strongly collaborative, open source/open content work. The word is a portmanteau constructed from "*sh*ared *op*en *work*," and it arguably has the advantages of suggesting collaboration in both the original meaning of "shop-work" (which implies something constructed or fixed in a shop, perhaps by several workers together) and, with its parts reversed, "workshop" (which implies participatory learning).

A shopwork has at least two essential features: (1) it is free, or open source/open content; (2) it is "strongly" collaborative. In this section of the paper, I will elaborate on each point.

Shopwork is free. First, there is much jargon and many buzz-words describing a family of related, overlapping concepts, all having to do with guaranteeing that software and content of various sorts remains "free," in various ways: *open source, open content, free software, copyleft, open access, freeware,* and *Creative Commons,* as well as good old *public domain.* Part of the reason for the proliferation of jargon is that different groups have promoted different licenses and projects using their own specific jargon.

To say that a work is *free,* in the special sense in which I will use it,[1] is to say that it is released to the world (1) free of charge and (2) under a license that permits others to view, copy, and distribute the work, as well as develop and release their own altered versions of the work—as long as their versions are also released under the same open content license. In the case of software, this requires that programmers be able to view the source code of the program. Not only works but also licenses are said to be free (or open source, etc.); the license that makes the work free in the above-defined sense can be called a "free" license.

There are other permissive licenses that are nonetheless not free licenses. For example, if the license were to require that no one *sell* derivative versions of the work, then that would not be a free license. Or if the license permitted viewing, copying, and distributing exact or verbatim copies of the work, but not developing new versions thereof, that, again, would not be a free license. Or one might declare the work to be in the public domain, available for any legal use whatsoever; but this would permit others to make proprietary versions of the work, and hence this too is different from free work. There are other variants, of course; the variety of kinds of unusual permissions an author or creator might want to grant others is large.[2] But the sort of license that shopwork uses is a free one. In short, such a license guarantees that a work not only is, but will remain, free.

Shopwork is "strongly" collaborative. Secondly, works can be "collaborative" in various ways. At a minimum, shopwork has multiple authors; if a work has a single creator; it is not, or not yet, shopwork. Moreover, these authors do not contribute bits and pieces which are then stitched together, as with patchwork quilts, anthologies, or many reports written by committee; instead, every aspect of any work contributed is open to revision by the other contributors. These two features, multiple authorship and joint editorship, make shopwork collaborative. A third feature makes shopwork *strongly* collaborative: it is developed not just by multiple authors, but a constantly changing battery of authors, including even (perhaps) some anonymous authors.

I do not want to claim that the arguments below do not apply to work that is collaborative in any less robust sense than this. But the strongest version of the argument can be developed with respect to work that is collaborative in all three ways listed.

The free encyclopedia Wikipedia provides perhaps the best example of a work that is strongly collaborative in this sense. At present—and this seems unlikely to change—virtually anyone with an Internet connection can visit a Wikipedia article, click an "edit" button, and proceed to make changes to the article. Changes are logged on a "recent changes" page, and often (surely not always) duly checked over by members of the Wikipedia "community." This community—not anyone who has special editorial control—is the ultimate arbiter of what is and is not included in Wikipedia. Hence it is easy to see that Wikipedia has multiple authors who act as each other's editors, and that the battery of authors/editors is constantly changing.

Radical collaboration is one of the key values of the open source and free software movements. Open source software, it is widely held, is best developed by a body of programmers who develop and edit each other's work, rather than follow edicts issued from on high.[3]

But open source software and free works generally, need not be created by collaboration. If a programmer does not succeed in attracting other coders to his project, it will remain uncollaborative. Moreover, there is of course nothing stopping a small group of experts in a field from jointly writing a textbook on a subject and then releasing it under a free license. Such a textbook might feature multiple authorship and joint editorship, but not a constantly changing battery of authors.

This being admitted, any very successful free software project will now probably attract a changeable body of developers. This is in part because programmers are used to working together, creating different modules of one whole software project. The situation is currently different for written (prose) works, with one notable exception in Wikipedia. This has a perhaps obvious explanation. A researcher who releases a text, paper, etc., under an open content or open access license (and there is a growing number who have done so) cannot expect to see it developed further by others unless they are mostly in agreement with the first author. Even then, the desire (or professional need) for personal credit suggests the obvious response is another paper—not editing and releasing of someone else's paper.

The situation could turn out to be different with textbooks. The novel concept and collaborative ethos behind free works developed in the context of software, however, and so it is not surprising that the idea should not yet have caught on among academics. But the future success of a more carefully edited Wikipedia might demonstrate the power of a new, strongly collaborative, model of content development. The next section will suggest further support of this prediction.

II. Why Shopwork *Per Se* Should Be Protected by the Law

I will now argue that at least some shopworks are, precisely in virtue of their being both free and collaborative, potentially of considerable benefit to society. Hence, it is in society's interest to protect shopwork as a new sort of institution, for, without it, some such benefits could not, or not as easily, be obtained.

First, note that in general, free software and content is useful and becoming more so, as I was concerned to point out in this paper's introductory paragraphs. To be sure, this is a benefit of shopwork, but it is not *unique* to or due to any *special features* of shopwork. If one wishes to argue on utilitarian grounds, as I do, that shopwork *per se* deserves the protection of the law, it will have to be on grounds of some benefit of shopwork *per se*.

To this end, I want to make two observations, that shopworks are *autonomous* in a certain sense, and that they are or can be *perpetual*, from which I will conclude that the projects that develop shopworks are or can be natural *institutions*.

Shopwork, because it is free, is released to a public that may use and develop it with minimal restrictions. Consequently, any person or group who develops a shopwork knows that other persons or groups are free to take the shopwork and develop it in different, and perhaps better, ways. This, in the open source software community, is known as *forking* a project. In fact, forking is a relatively rare occurrence (for reasons we need not explore), but it is certainly not unheard-of. Hence we may say that shopworks are, in a certain sense, *legally* autonomous: versions of them exist, or *may* (legally) exist, independently of any entities that initially develop them. (That, anyway, is the ideal behind their licenses.) The program I work on now and freely release to the world may look very different in ten years, and this is out of my control; the free license is my renunciation of such control.

It seems likely that some projects, such as Wikipedia if it survives until 2050 (and it is hard to see why it would not), could develop into very many different versions over the years. The local control and histories of some versions might be difficult to trace, obscured by anonymous developers, fading memories, and/or poor record-keeping.[4] Such a project is what we might call *untethered*, in a robust sense—that is, entirely lacking an entity that bears any clear *causal* responsibility for it. This is not to deny, however, that as long as a work lives on the Internet, there will always be someone *legally* responsible (a "designated agent," in the United States under the Digital Millennium Copyright Act) for the website contents.

The other point mentioned above is that, because a shopwork has, potentially at least, a changeable body of collaborators, many shopworks, especially autonomous ones, are perpetual; they have no set endpoint. Unlike most textbooks, for example, the editions do not necessarily end when the author dies. When a constantly-changing collaborative body develops a work, new editions can appear for as long as there are willing personnel. The situation is more similar to that with *Encyclopaedia Britannica,* a venerable institution, the rights to which have passed from owner to willing owner for many years. But unlike the case of the *Britannica,* if the particular organization controlling a free work were simply to cease to exist, or to lose interest in developing the project, that would not mean that all project development would also, necessarily, have to end as well. As long as *other* people can be found to make useful developments to a shopwork, it can live on long past the lifetimes of its founders. This is what I mean when I say that shopworks are perpetual.

Being potentially, at least, autonomous and perpetual, it follows, I think, that successful shopworks are natural *institutions,* in two senses.

First, we may anticipate that, probably, some of the *projects that develop* shopworks will become institutions. Perhaps the Free Software Foundation and the Wikimedia Foundation will develop into institutions in this sense.

But second, one will also be able to speak of the results, the shopworks themselves, as institutions. A shopwork that develops in enough depth to inspire many forks, or versions, is probably going to stick around for a while. Moreover, a shopwork's autonomy—the fact that it lacks essential ties to a particular organization ensures that it can last as long as we want it to, and the fact that it is developed by a strong collaboration ensures that it can outlast any particular person or set of people. So shopworks will probably become institutions in roughly the same sense that law, scientific practice, and marriage are institutions, independent of court systems, research institutions, and particular marriages. It is possible that, in one hundred years, books will be written about the rich, free operating system tradition, the institution of free encyclopedias and collaborative science textbooks, and perhaps of strongly collaborative *research* itself.

Let us review the highlights of this section so far: shopworks can and already do have considerable usefulness to society; moreover, both shopworks and their development projects may well become autonomous, perpetual institutions. Now observe that it is one thing to say that a word processing program helps its particular users to write papers, etc. It is another, much more significant thing to say that an *institution* of free word processing programs can serve a significant, salutary purpose to millions of people around the world over a long span of time. The difference is one of scale. Shopworks, particularly when viewed as institutions, could benefit humanity tremendously.

There is a third sense in which shopwork could be considered an institution. We can identify a general institution of shopwork that groups all individual shopwork projects together over time, in roughly the same way that the general institution of education involves taking, among other things, all individual educational institutions (schools and universities) together over time. What I want to urge is that society respect and, through its laws, support the existence of the presently-nascent general institution of shopwork.

I will make this thesis a bit more precise later, but more can be said in defense of the thesis as stated in this general form. Being both free and collaborative, shopworks potentially have two significant advantages over proprietary works: low cost and collaboration of unusually large numbers of well-qualified people.

First, perhaps most obviously, shopworks are *free of charge.* Most people involved in shopwork development are volunteers. This saves a lot of money. For example, it has been estimated that well over one billion dollars in development costs have been saved in the development of Linux and the software bundled with it in Red Hat Linux 7.1; that is, it would have cost a corporation over a billion dollars to develop Red Hat's operating system, user interface, and accompanying software.[5] That cost would have been passed on to users, had the bundle been proprietary. So the users can save that money. Collectively, this will provide *many* billions of dollars in savings over the long term.

In fairness, it must be admitted that this advantage is still theoretical in large part. As long as, at present, there are difficult-to-quantify costs such as the time spent learning Linux, the inconvenience of using "clunky" amateurish programs, and having little in the way of product support—and other such hidden costs—we can dismiss a simplistic analysis which compares a zero price tag to the price tag of Windows and comparable software. Similarly, at this writing few would suggest that the *Britannica* cannot compete with Wikipedia since Wikipedia is available free of cost: the *Britannica* obviously has the advantage of reliability that Wikipedia currently lacks. All this, however, with regard to both free software and free content, might well change. It seems to be only a matter of time; remember that free projects have the considerable advantage of perpetuity. Indeed, it could turn out that open source products (and the argument is the same for open content) would end up being on the cutting edge, so that, to keep up, corporations might have to become shopwork developers.[6]

Second, shopworks have been and will continue to be developed by collaboration among *unusually large* numbers of intelligent, able people. Many programmers and intellectuals have a strong urge to create and to teach, and to a great extent, this desire is independent of a desire for personal financial gain—particularly when such people believe their work will reach many others and not go to profit any one person or corporation in particular. Moreover, many people enjoy working and learning together, collaboratively. Shopwork combines the latter with the aforementioned desire to create and teach for the general benefit of humanity and is, thus, *inherently* attractive to many people.

Presently, the firms that are behind the most successful proprietary operating systems, software, textbooks, and encyclopedias have the advantage of having many well-paid employees. What remains to be seen is whether corporations will be able to compete with the depth and breadth of personnel that shopwork projects can front, and not just at any one moment, but institutionally, over time. This is a difficult question. Admittedly, it *could* turn out that proprietary products will *always* turn out to be developed by better staff and—hence?—be better products. That suggestion will certainly appeal to some.

The proprietary model does currently appear to enjoy an advantage in this regard, but this could easily change. Consider, for example, the case of Wikipedia. In its first few years it has become clear that, on many (not all) topics, the ordinary educated public of the Internet can write encyclopedia articles that are equal to or better than those written by experts for proprietary encyclopedias. Already, many of Wikipedia's participants have been very highly credentialed. Over time, as new editorial systems that appeal more to the academic/research turn of mind are tried out, more of the most highly qualified people will be attracted to the project, or to its offshoots or imitators. Just for example, a university might sponsor a vetting process for Wikipedia; some famous scholar might sign on and become a spokesperson for the project; then, suitably "academicized," many more academics might want to get on board. If this happens, it seems likely that no traditional proprietary encyclopedias would be able to compete, because shopworks are perpetual and autonomous, and natural institutions. When a high-quality, enormously comprehensive encyclopedia is available free of charge, no business that must pay its employees will be able to compete.

Similar flights of fancy suggest new possibilities for textbooks and—though this raises other issues—the news media, and even research itself. Bear in mind that much research work is intended to be free of the constraints of profit, and a kind of collaborative work (via academic and professional journals) is essentially how the world of research has been organized. So open content research might appeal to academics when they come to understand it and its potential; though not much more collaborative than traditional research (and hence not shopwork), the success of "open access" research publishing indicates the appeal and actual growing popularity of the general idea of free work among researchers.[7]

But to return to the philosophical argument, suppose that the above suggestions are roughly correct. That is, suppose that successful, useful shopworks will very probably develop into institutions. As such, what benefits they offer are magnified. Moreover, such institutions might well become competitive vis-à-vis proprietary products in terms of both cost and personnel (and hence, quality). Finally, recall that their institutional nature is a function of their being both free and collaborative—which is to say, of their being shopworks. Considering these potential benefits, and that they stem from the very nature of shopwork, we may conclude on utilitarian grounds that society, and particularly the law, should see to it that shopwork is made possible and that shopwork institutions are protected. We may advance a Shopwork Protection Rule:

Laws should be written so as to be consistent with the existence of works that are free as well as strongly collaborative in the above-defined senses.

Given the benefit to society, some may be tempted to conclude a bit more than this: the law should actually *support* such works, either through funding or other special legislative support. I do not want to urge this stronger conclusion, however. To the contrary, the difficulty is that shopworks are, after all, *free*. When government gets involved in giving positive support to socially useful projects, whether through funding or through other support, conditions are always imposed; and conditions generally mean restrictions on freedom. Shopwork as an institution is threatened to the extent to which government or any single entity is given authority over it.

The Shopwork Protection Rule has important legal consequences. In particular, the law should treat matters of copyright violation, libel, and other abuses of free speech in the context of shopwork development in a way that is consistent with the *autonomous* nature of shopworks. That is, whatever remedies are chosen must be consistent with a robust respect for the free, uncontrolled nature of the shopworks. For example, to provide for control over a shopwork, as relief for an abuse, would essentially be to eliminate it as a shopwork. Granted, this might be warranted if, for example, large portions of code were stolen from a proprietary program. This should, however, be the rare exception, not the rule. For similar reasons, the law should jealously enforce contracts and laws that preserve the openness of shopworks. Some might disagree with this, however, which is what I want to address next.

III. Objections and Replies

One might maintain on various grounds that shopwork does not deserve any specific protection, and hence we should not endorse the Shopwork Protection Rule. In the following I will lay out and reply to three objections.

First objection: shopwork is too open to abuse. One might object that, precisely because shopwork is *both* free and strongly collaborative, it is open to various kinds of abuse; and the only adequate relief is to reduce the degree of freedom or the strength of the collaboration.

Consider an illustration of an abuse. Imagine a wiki—a website in which any visitor can edit any page, like Wikipedia—the contents of which are released under a free license. Suppose the full text of (copyrighted) news articles frequently appears on the wiki, together with many clear examples of libel. The website has repeatedly refused to remove the offending text. Suppose also that the website is for whatever reason popular and influential. The victims of copyright infringement and libel have clear cases against the website and/or its collaborators, and they could have the website shut down.

This fits the definition of 'shopwork' offered above. On first glance, it appears to be precisely the *free* nature of the website that lends itself to the abuse. But this first impression is mistaken. The fact that the contents of the website can be freely distributed played no role in explaining the copyright infringement or libel. Neither free works nor collaboration *inherently* or *necessarily* invite abuse any more than does an individual's privately owned website.

There are, however, related problems associated more closely with strong collaboration and with free works. If it is correct to say that successful shopworks invite large numbers of contributors, the sheer numbers of those involved increases the likelihood that copyright and free speech abuses will occur. But—again—this in itself should not pose a threat to shopwork, any more than it would to any large web content host, as long as there are statutes in place that permit the entity legally responsible for the website (in the U.S., the "designated agent") to avoid a copyright lawsuit by removing copyright violations from the website when given notice to do so.[8] Surely any organization managing a large, successful shopwork will not put its version of the project at risk by tolerating abuses.

What could be a more serious problem with regard to some shopworks, for example Wikipedia, is that *wholly anonymous* contribution opens the project up to serious liability. A hostile anonymous contributor could threaten the entire project by changing IP numbers and "handles" and deliberately upload copyrighted and libelous material. But even Wikipedia, a very large and popular website, has been able to manage potential copyright and other free speech problems (so far) that bad-faith anonymous contributors might set up. Generally speaking, the vast majority of the contributors of shopworks are, naturally, people of good will; they far outnumber the bad eggs, such that the potentially dangerous contributions of the latter can be prevented and managed without much difficulty.

In this case, the strongest remedy the law might reasonably require is the removal of the option of anonymous contribution. The possibility of anonymous contribution is regarded by some as an essential part of strongly collaborative projects; but it is not, I think, absolutely essential. That is, if a shopwork project were to decide to remove the option of anonymous contribution, it would not be any less of a *shopwork*. Admittedly, the degree of collaboration would be reduced, since those who would refuse to contribute under their own real identities would not participate. Hence, if out of concern over copyright and free speech abuses, the law were to make wholly anonymous contribution impossible, that would not in itself constitute a ban on shopworks.

But what if some small, previously undetected, and particularly damaging instance of libel or copyright violation comes to light, which has been smuggled into some "untethered" shopworks, existing in multiple copies of indeterminate provenance? Surely the law has some reason to take control of the situation, precisely because there is no central authority or other means of relief. Hence we can easily imagine the plaintiff or the government advocating either seizing control of the projects or shutting them all down. And in this case, it is *precisely* the fact that the offense occurs within the context of a *shopwork* that is the cause of the problem.[9] The remedy can only be—one might suggest—to undermine the shopwork project in one way or another.

I suspect this is not as serious a problem as it might sound. Anyone familiar with shopworks knows that unedited copies of shopworks are somewhat like bathroom walls—short of being caught in the act, no one can be held responsible for the mere existence of an obscenity, though the owner of the bathroom might be responsible for painting it over. What, precisely, is the difference between this case and more ordinary cases of copyright and free speech abuse? Only the number of copies in existence, it seems. What difference does it make, as far as the appropriate remedy is concerned, whether or not a shopwork project can trace the origin of a given contribution? In cases of copyright and libel, at the very least, all that the "designated agent" of a website should have to do is remove the offending content. If the "designated agent" is not willing to do so, then perhaps the copy of the shopwork should be shut down.

Yet the problem might not exist online only, one might argue, and so removing the offending content from websites will not necessarily solve the problem: copies might exist on individual hard drives, CDs, in print, and in other media. The only way to be sure that such abuses are not distributed into posterity, as far as more permanent media is concerned, is not to permit free distribution of collaborative efforts in the first place.

Of course, many libelous materials and copyright violations are even now gathering dust in libraries. The remedies offered for these offenses, against newspapers and publishers for example, have not generally shut down their businesses, much less rendered impossible the very institution of publishing. Similarly, there *will* be lawsuits against shopwork projects and those who make use of shopworks (and already have been[10]), and eventually, rich shopwork organizations will very likely be forced to pay large sums of money. Particularly negligent organizations might be forced to shut down. This is as it should be. But it will never be necessary or warranted to shut down the institution of shopwork generally.

Second objection: shopwork is hostile to private enterprise. A second objection can be explained and dealt with more briefly. The institution of shopwork might tend to undermine certain kinds of private enterprise, namely, software, encyclopedia and textbook publishing, and perhaps others; that is part of my own argument, above. But private enterprise is very efficient at and very important for producing goods at low prices. So it should be protected. Therefore— someone might argue—threats to the very existence of parts of it should be prohibited, so shopwork should be prohibited.

This argument, while it might appeal to some corporate executives, will not wash for anyone else, even for defenders of capitalism. If private enterprise is to be protected because it produces cheap goods efficiently, then shopwork should be protected for the same reason. If shopwork does a better job of producing cheap (indeed, free) goods than private enterprise, then so much the worse for the latter in the affected sector.

Third objection: there are no "institutions" yet. An objection aimed specifically at the argument of section II above states that if a given free collaborative work is not useful or does not constitute an institution *yet*, one cannot argue that it should be protected, at least not on grounds of my argument. After all, a significant aspect of my argument was precisely that the *institutional* nature of shopwork magnifies the societal benefit of shopwork projects. If my predictions of shopwork institutions do not come to fruition, then, it seems, my argument would turn out not to be nearly as strong as I want it to be. I admit that this is at least *possible,* though I do not think it is very likely. It is possible that, every five or ten years, software, textbooks, reference materials, and other shopwork projects simply go belly-up and no one is interested in carrying them on. As the best going concern loses its luster for whatever reason, totally independent replacement shopwork projects start up, or, perhaps, no comparable project ever starts up again. In any case, there is no continuous *tradition* of project development that can be called an institution. In other words, it might turn out that the vaunted hopes of Linux, free software, open content encyclopedias, collaborative textbooks, and the like will have been either a fad of the '90s and '00s, or (puzzlingly) constantly reinventing the wheel, or (most likely) always lagging behind proprietary works.

I should first acknowledge that mine is not the only possible argument for the Shopwork Protection Rule. One could defend the rule on the basis of rights to private property, contract, and free association. I do not wish to elaborate such an argument here; but such an argument would not be open to this particular objection.

Perhaps it is most judicious not to venture a reply to this objection. It is probably most reasonable to want to wait and see whether the grand hopes of shopwork and shopwork "institutionalization" ever come to fruition. But if, in the meantime, there are court decisions and legislative efforts that have the general effect of making shopwork impossible (or more difficult), I hope it will *not* be as a result of corporate lawsuits and lobbying that guard their turf. Then the failure of shopwork to achieve institutionalization would be actually *created* by law, while the very lawsuits and lobbying in question would *themselves* point to worries, on the part of corporations or other vested interests, that increasingly powerful shopwork institutions would soon be ruining their operations.

Notes

1. This is similar to (but not exactly the same as) the usage employed by Richard Stallman and the Free Software Foundation (see http://www.fsf.org). I use the term merely because it is brief, and neither to endorse Stallman's theory about free software, nor to reject the use of "open source" and "open content"; these latter terms are favored by some of those not fully in agreement with Stallman's theories. Stallman and his followers are careful to point out that there is an important distinction between "free" in the *gratis* sense (free of charge) and "free" in the *libre* sense (free of most constraints). I think that the argument I make does not work so well if free works are not necessarily understood to be free of charge; hence I include this in the definition. This is not a point I need insist upon strongly, however.

2. For more information, a useful resource is Creative Commons' page describing its various licenses. See "licenses explained," *Creative Commons,* http://creativecommons.org/learn/licenses/ (accessed August 3, 2004).

3. This is one of the main themes of what has become a key manifesto of the open source movement; see Eric Raymond's essay "The Cathedral and the Bazaar," http://www.catb.org/~esr/writings/cathedral-bazaar/cathedral-bazaar/ (accessed August 2, 2004).

4. Wikipedia might, perhaps, be a poor example of this, since Wikipedia's "Copyrights" project information page, found at http://en.wikipedia.org/wiki/Wikipedia:Copyrights (retrieved August 1, 2004) presently requires links back to the original article. Hence it is unclear whether a third-generation encyclopedia, i.e., one based on a project that was itself based on Wikipedia, would require links back to Wikipedia; but so it appears. More generally, there are many difficult legal questions that this introductory sort of discussion cannot adequately address.

5. David A. Wheeler, "More Than a Gigabuck: Estimating GNU/Linux's Size" vers. 1.07, http://www.dwheeler.com/sloc/redhat71-v1/redhat71sloc.html (accessed August 1, 2004).

6. This point is made by Petr Hrebejk and Tim Boudreau, "The coming 'open monopoly' in software," *c|net news.com*, October 24, 2001, http://news.com.com/2010-1071-281588.html?legacy=cnet (accessed August 2, 2004).

7. See, for example, the *Open Access Now* website: http://www.biomedcentral.com/openaccess/ (accessed August 1, 2004).

8. In the U.S., this is the function of the Online Copyright Infringement Liability Limitation Act, part of the Digital Millennium Copyright Act (1998).

9. The most famous case of this is *SCO v. IBM*. See "SCO v. IBM Linux lawsuit," Wikipedia, retrieved August 1, 2004, from http://en.wikipedia.org/wiki/SCO_v._IBM_Linux_lawsuit

10. Most famously, *SCO v. IBM*. See "SCO v. IBM Linux lawsuit," Wikipedia, http://en.wikipedia.org/wiki/SCO_v._IBM_Linux_lawsuit (accessed August 1, 2004).

Part II: Discussion Cases

Case #1: Libraries and Fair Use

After visiting the library and checking out several books you notice that someone had taken your car and returned it. When caught the "thief" claims that he was just borrowing the vehicle while you weren't using it. Should libraries be able to lend copyrighted works to non-buyers? Why is fair use without compensation legitimate when intellectual property is the issue but not for physical property? You can't loan my car without consent, why can you loan my poem or movie? Suppose everything goes on-line and when a hard copy is desired you just download a copy to your cool book-making printer. Should individuals be able to browse an on-line library or a program library? How would you maintain the free use zone of fair use in such environments?

Case #2: No Harm, No Foul—Right?

Suppose a fiendishly clever mad-scientist discovered a way to use and exploit the bodies of unsuspecting victims while they sleep. In the morning, after a night of work, the mad-scientist rejuvenates the bodies of his victims with a special pill. Has the mad-scientist done anything morally wrong? Couldn't he justify his actions via a no harm, no foul principle? If this principle justifies the copying of intellectual works, why wouldn't it justify the use of your body by the mad-scientist?

Case #3: Making an Extra Back-up Copy

With two youngsters running about the house it is difficult for you to keep track of all legitimately purchased CDs and DVDs in your possession. In fact, before you can make a legally sanctioned back-up copy of your CDs and DVDs your kids have scratched them beyond repair. In an effort to obtain undamaged copies you go online and download replacements via your favorite file sharing program. Shortly thereafter, new trouble comes your way—the RIAA is suing you for copyright infringement. Have you done anything illegal or immoral?

PART III

Privacy and Information Control

The Right to Privacy

SAMUEL D. WARREN and **LOUIS D. BRANDEIS**

The Right to Privacy

That the individual shall have full protection in person and in property is a principle as old as the common law; but it has been found necessary from time to time to define anew the exact nature and extent of such protection. Political, social, and economic changes entail the recognition of new rights, and the common law, in its eternal youth, grows to meet the new demands of society. Thus, in very early times, the law gave a remedy only for physical interference with life and property, for trespasses *vi et armis*. Then the "right to life" served only to protect the subject from battery in its various forms; liberty meant freedom from actual restraint; and the right to property secured to the individual his lands and his cattle. Later, there came a recognition of man's spiritual nature, of his feelings and his intellect. Gradually the scope of these legal rights broadened; and now the right to life has come to mean the right to enjoy life—the right to be let alone; the right to liberty secures the exercise of extensive civil privileges; and the term "property" has grown to comprise every form of possession— intangible, as well as tangible.

Thus, with the recognition of the legal value of sensations, the protection against actual bodily injury was extended to prohibit mere attempts to do such injury; that is, the putting another in fear of such injury. From the action of battery grew that of assault. Much later there came a qualified protection of the individual against offensive noises and odors, against dust and smoke, and excessive vibration. The law of nuisance was developed. So regard for human emotions soon extended the scope of personal immunity beyond the body of the individual. His reputation, the standing among his fellow-men, was considered, and the law of slander and libel arose. Man's family relations became a part of the legal conception of his life, and the alienation of a wife's affections was held remediable. Occasionally the law halted, as in its refusal to recognize the intrusion by seduction upon the honor of the family. But even here the demands of society were met. A mean fiction, the action per *quod servitium amisit*, was resorted to, and by allowing damages for injury to the parents' feelings, an adequate remedy was ordinarily afforded. Similar to the expansion of the right to life was the growth of the legal conception of property. From corporeal property arose the incorporeal rights issuing out of it; and then there opened the wide realm of intangible property, in the products and processes of the mind, as works of literature and art, goodwill, trade secrets, and trademarks.

This development of the law was inevitable. The intense intellectual and emotional life, and the heightening of sensations which came with the advance of civilization, made it clear to men that only a part of the pain, pleasure, and profit of life lay in physical things. Thoughts, emotions, and sensations demanded legal recognition, and the beautiful capacity for growth which characterizes the common law enabled the judges to afford the requisite protection, without the interposition of the legislature.

Recent inventions and business methods call attention to the next step which must be taken for the protection of the person, and for securing to the individual what Judge Cooley calls the right "to be let alone." Instantaneous photographs and newspaper enterprise have invaded the sacred precincts of private and domestic life; and numerous mechanical devices threaten to make good the prediction that "what is whispered in the closet shall be proclaimed from the house-tops." For years there has been a feeling that the law must afford some remedy for the unauthorized circulation of portraits of private persons; and the evil of invasion of privacy by the newspapers, long keenly felt, has been but recently discussed by an able writer. The alleged facts of a somewhat notorious case brought before an inferior tribunal in New York a few months ago, directly involved the consideration of the right of circulating portraits; and the question whether our law will recognize and protect the right to privacy in this and in other respects must soon come before our courts for consideration.

Of the desirability—indeed of the necessity—of some such protection, there can, it is believed, be no doubt. The press is overstepping in every direction the obvious bounds of propriety and of decency. Gossip is no longer the resource of the idle and of the vicious, but has become a trade, which is pursued with industry as well as effrontery. To satisfy a prurient taste the details of sexual relations are spread broadcast in the columns of the daily papers. To occupy the indolent, column upon column is filled with idle gossip, which can only be procured by intrusion upon the domestic circle. The intensity and complexity of life, attendant upon advancing civilization, have rendered necessary some retreat from the world, and man, under the refining influence of culture, has become more sensitive to publicity, so that solitude and privacy have become more essential to the individual; but modern enterprise and invention have, through invasions upon his privacy, subjected him to mental pain and distress, far greater than could be inflicted by mere bodily injury. Nor is the harm wrought by such invasions confined to the suffering of those who may be the subjects of journalistic or other enterprise. In this, as in other branches of commerce, the supply creates the demand. Each crop of unseemly gossip, thus harvested, becomes the seed of more, and, in direct proportion to its circulation, results in the lowering of social standards and of morality. Even gossip apparently harmless, when widely and persistently circulated, is potent for evil. It both belittles and perverts. It belittles by inverting the relative importance of things, thus dwarfing the thoughts and aspirations of a people. When personal gossip attains the dignity of print, and crowds the space available for matters of real interest to the community, what wonder that the ignorant and thoughtless mistake its relative importance. Easy of comprehension, appealing to that weak side of human nature which is never wholly cast down by the misfortunes and frailties of our neighbors, no one can be surprised that it usurps the place of interest in brains capable of other things. Triviality destroys at once robustness of thought and delicacy of feeling. No enthusiasm can flourish; no generous impulse can survive under its blighting influence.

It is our purpose to consider whether the existing law affords a principle which can properly be invoked to protect the privacy of the individual; and, if it does, what the nature and extent of such protection is.

Owing to the nature of the instruments by which privacy is invaded, the injury inflicted bears a superficial resemblance to the wrongs dealt with by the law of slander and of libel, while a legal remedy for such injury seems to involve the treatment of mere wounded feelings, as a substantive cause of action. The principle on which the law of defamation rests, covers, however, a radically different class of effects from those for which attention is now asked. It deals only with damage to reputation, with the injury done to the individual in his external relations to the community, by lowering him in the estimation of his fellows. The matter published of him, however widely circulated, and however unsuited to publicity, must, in order to be actionable, have a direct tendency to injure him in his intercourse with others, and even if in writing or in print, must subject him to the hatred, ridicule, or contempt of his fellowmen--the effect of the publication upon his estimate of himself and upon his own feelings not forming an essential element in the cause of action. In short, the wrongs and correlative rights recognized by the law of slander and libel are in their nature material rather than spiritual. That branch of the law simply extends the protection surrounding physical property to certain of the conditions necessary or helpful to worldly prosperity. On the other hand, our law recognizes no principle upon which compensation can be granted for mere injury to the feelings. However painful the mental effects upon another of an act, though purely wanton or even malicious, yet if the act itself is otherwise lawful, the suffering inflicted is *dannum absque injuria*. Injury of feelings may indeed be taken account of in ascertaining the amount of damages when attending what is recognized as a legal injury; but our system, unlike the Roman law, does not afford a remedy even for mental suffering which results from mere contumely and insult, but from an intentional and unwarranted violation of the "honor" of another.

It is not however necessary, in order to sustain the view that the common law recognizes and upholds a principle applicable to cases of invasion of privacy, to invoke the analogy, which is but superficial, to injuries sustained, either by an attack upon reputation or by what the civilians called a violation of honor; for the legal doctrines relating to infractions of what is ordinarily termed the common-law right to intellectual and artistic property are, it is believed, but instances and applications of a general right to privacy, which properly understood afford a remedy for the evils under consideration.

The common law secures to each individual the right of determining, ordinarily, to what extent his thoughts, sentiments, and emotions shall be communicated to others. Under our system of government, he can never be compelled to express them (except when upon the witness stand); and even if he has chosen to give them expression, he generally retains the power to fix the limits of the publicity which shall be given them. The existence of this right does not depend upon the particular method of expression adopted. It is immaterial whether it be by word or by signs, in painting, by sculpture, or in music. Neither does the existence of the right depend upon the nature or value of the thought or emotions, nor upon the excellence of the means of expression. The same protection is accorded to a casual letter or an entry in a diary and to the most valuable poem or essay, to a botch or daub and to a masterpiece. In every such case the individual is entitled to decide whether that which is his shall be given to the public. No other has the right to publish his productions in any form, without his consent. This right is wholly independent of the material on which the thought, sentiment, or emotions is expressed. It may exist independently of any corporeal being, as in words spoken, a song sung, a drama acted. Or if expressed on any material, as in a poem in writing, the author may have parted with the paper, without forfeiting any proprietary right in the composition itself. The right is lost only when the author himself communicates his production to the public—in other words, publishes it. It is entirely independent of the copyright laws, and their extension into the domain of art. The aim of those statutes is to secure to the author, composer, or artist the entire profits arising from publication; but the common-law protection enables him to control absolutely the act of publication, and in the exercise of his own discretion, to decide whether there shall be any publication at all. The statutory right is of no value, unless there is a publication; the common-law right is lost as soon as there is a publication.

What is the nature, the basis, of this right to prevent the publication of manuscripts or works of art? It is stated to be the enforcement of a right of property; and no difficulty arises in accepting this view, so long as we have only to deal with the reproduction of literary and artistic compositions. They certainly possess many of the attributes of ordinary property; they are transferable; they have a value; and publication or reproduction is a use by which that value is realized. But where the value of the production is found not in the right to take the profits arising from publication, but in the peace of mind or the relief afforded by the ability to prevent any publication at all, it is difficult to regard the right as one of property, in the common acceptation of that term. A man records in a letter to his son, or in his diary, that he did not dine with his wife on a certain day. No one into whose hands those papers fall could publish them to the world, even if possession of the documents had been obtained rightfully, and the prohibition would not be confined to the publication of a copy of the letter itself, or of the diary entry;

the restraint extends also to a publication of the contents. What is the thing which is protected? Surely, not the intellectual act of recording the fact that the husband did not dine with his wife, but that fact itself. It is not the intellectual product, but the domestic occurrence. A man writes a dozen letters to different people. No person would be permitted to publish a list of the letters written. If the letters or the contents of the diary were protected as literary compositions, the scope of the protection afforded should be the same secured to a published writing under the copyright law. But the copyright law would not prevent an enumeration of the letters, or the publication of some of the facts contained therein. The copyright of a series of paintings or etchings would prevent a reproduction of the paintings as pictures; but it would not prevent a publication of a list or even a description of them. Yet in the famous case of *Prince Albert v. Strange*, the court held that the common-law rule prohibited not merely the reproduction of the etchings which the plaintiff and Queen Victoria had made for their own pleasure, but also "the publishing (at least by printing or writing), though not by copy or resemblance, a description of them, whether more or less limited or summary, whether in the form of a catalogue or other-wise." Likewise, an unpublished collection of news possessing no element of a literary nature is protected from privacy.

That this protection cannot rest upon the right to literary or ar-tistic property in any exact sense, appears the more clearly, when the subject-matter for which protection is invoked is not even in the form of intellectual property, but has the attributes of ordinary tangible property. Suppose a man has a collection of gems or curiosities which he keeps private: it would hardly be contended that any person could publish a catalogue of them, and yet the articles enumerated are certainly not intellectual property in the legal sense, any more than a collection of stoves or of chairs.

The belief that the idea of property in its narrow sense was the basis of the protection of unpublished manuscripts led an able court to refuse, in several cases, injunctions against the publication of private letters, on the ground that "letters not possessing the attributes of literary compositions are not property entitled to protection;" and that it was "evident the plaintiff could not have considered the letters as of any value whatever as literary produc-tions, for a letter cannot be considered of value to the author which he never would consent to have published." But those decisions have not been followed, and it may not be considered settled that the protection afforded by the common law to the author of any writing is entirely independent of its pecuniary value, its intrinsic merits, or of any intention to publish the same and, of course, also, wholly independent of the material, if any, upon which, or the mode in which, the thought or sentiment was expressed.

Although the courts have asserted that they rested their decisions on the narrow grounds of protection to property, yet there are recognitions of a more liberal doctrine. Thus in the case of *Prince Albert v. Strange*, already referred to, the opinions of both the Vice-Chancellor and of the Lord Chancellor, on appeal, show a more or less clearly defined perception of a principle broader than those which were mainly discussed, and on which they both place their chief reliance. Vice-Chancellor Knight Bruce referred to publishing of a man that he had "written to particular persons or on particular subjects" as an instance of possibly injurious disclosures as to private matters, that the courts would in a proper case prevent; yet it is difficult to perceive how, in such a case, any right of privacy, in the narrow sense, would be drawn in question, or why, if such a publication would be restrained when it threatened to expose the victim not merely to sarcasm, but to ruin, it should not equally be enjoined, if it threatened to embitter his life. To deprive a man of the potential profits to be realized by publishing a catalogue of his gems cannot per se be a wrong to him. The possibility of future profits is not a right of property which the law ordinarily recognizes; it must, therefore, be an infraction of other rights which constitutes the wrongful act, and that infraction is equally wrongful, whether its results are to forestall the profits that the individual himself might secure by giving the matter a publicity obnoxious to him, or to gain an advantage at the expense of his mental pain and suffering. If the fiction of property in a narrow sense must be preserved, it is still true that the end accomplished by the gossip-monger is attained by the use of that which is another's, the facts relating to his private life, which he has seen fit to keep private. Lord Cottenham stated that a man "is that which is exclusively his," and cited with approval the opinion of Lord Eldon, as reported in a manuscript note of the case of *Wyatt v. Wilson*, in 1820, respecting an engraving of George the Third during his illness, to the effect that "if one of the late king's physicians had kept a diary of what he heard and saw, the court would not, in the king's lifetime, have permitted him to print and publish it;" and Lord Cottenham declared, in respect to the acts of the defendants in the case before him, that "privacy is the right invaded." But if privacy is once recognized as a right entitled to legal protection, the interposition of the courts cannot depend on the particular nature of the injuries resulting.

These considerations lead to the conclusion that the protection afforded to thoughts, sentiments, and emotions, expressed through the medium of writing or of the arts, so far as it consists in preventing publication, is merely an instance of the enforcement of the more general right of the individual to be let alone. It is like the right not be assaulted or beaten, the right not be imprisoned, the right not to be maliciously prosecuted, the right not to be defamed. In each of these rights, as indeed in all other rights recognized by the law, there inheres the quality of being owned or possessed--and (as that is the distinguishing attribute of property) there may some propriety in speaking of those rights as property. But, obviously, they bear little resemblance to what is ordinarily comprehended under that term. The principle which protects personal writings and all other personal productions, not against theft and physical appropriation, but against publication in any form, is in reality not the principle of private property, but that of an inviolate personality.

If we are correct in this conclusion, the existing law affords a principle from which may be invoked to protect the privacy of the individual from invasion either by the too enterprising press, the photographer, or the possessor of any other modern device for rewording or reproducing scenes or sounds. For the protection afforded is not confined by the authorities to those cases where any particular medium or form of expression has been adopted, not to products of the intellect. The same protection is afforded to emotions and sensations expressed in a musical composition or other work of art as to a literary composition; and words spoken, a pantomime acted, a sonata performed, is no less entitled to protection than if each had been reduced to writing. The circumstance that a thought or emotion has been recorded in a permanent form renders its identification easier, and hence may be important from the point of view of evidence, but it has no significance as a matter of substantive right. If, then, the decisions indicate a general right to privacy for thoughts, emotions, and sensations, these should receive the same protection, whether expressed in writing, or in conduct, in conversation, in attitudes, or in facial expression.

It may be urged that a distinction should be taken between the deliberate expression of thoughts and emotions in literary or artistic compositions and the casual and often involuntary expression given to them in the ordinary conduct of life. In other words, it may be contended that the protection afforded is granted to the conscious products of labor, perhaps as an encouragement to effort. This contention, however plausible, has, in fact, little to recommend it. If the amount of labor involved be adopted as the test, we might well find that the effort to conduct one's self properly in business and in domestic relations had been far greater than that involved in painting a picture or writing a book; one would find that it was far easier to express lofty sentiments in a diary than in the conduct of a noble life. If the test of deliberateness of the act be adopted, much casual correspondence which is now accorded full protection would be excluded from the beneficent operation of existing rules. After the decisions denying the distinction attempted to be made between those literary productions which it was intended to publish and those which it was not, all considerations of the amount of labor involved, the degree of deliberation, the value of the product, and the intention of publishing must be abandoned, and no basis is discerned upon which the right to restrain publication and reproduction of such so-called literary and artistic works can be rested, except the right to privacy, as a part of the more general right to the immunity of the person—the right to one's personality.

It should be stated that, in some instances where protection has been afforded against wrongful publication, the jurisdiction has been asserted, not on the ground of property, or at least not wholly on that ground, but upon the ground of an alleged breach of an implied contract or of a trust or confidence.

Thus, in *Abernethy v. Hutchinson*, 3 L. J. Ch. 209 (1825), where the plaintiff, a distinguished surgeon, sought to restrain the publication in the "Lancet" of unpublished lectures which he had delivered as St. Bartholomew's Hospital in London, Lord Eldon doubted whether there could be property in lectures which had not been reduced to writing, but granted the injunction on the ground of breach of confidence, holding "that when persons were admitted as pupils or otherwise, to hear these lectures, although they were orally delivered, and although the parties might go to the extent, if they were able to do so, of putting down the whole by means of short-hand, yet they could do that only for the purposes of their own information, and could not publish, for profit, that which they had not obtained the right of selling."

In *Prince Albert v. Strange*, I McN. & G. 25 (1849), Lord Cotten-ham, on appeal, while recognizing a right of property in the etchings which of itself would justify the issuance of the injunction, stated, after discussing the evidence, that he was bound to assume that the possession of the etching by the defendant had "its founda-tion in a breach of trust, confidence, or contract," and that upon such ground also the plaintiff's title to the injunction was fully sustained.

In *Tuck v. Priester*, 19 Q.B.D. 639 (1887), the plaintiffs were own-ers of a picture, and employed the defendant to make a certain number of copies. He did so, and made also a number of other copies for himself, and offered them for sale in England at a lower price. Subsequently, the plaintiffs registered their copyright in the picture, and then brought suit for an injunction and damages. The Lords Justices differed as to the application of the copyright acts to the case, but held unanimously that independently of those acts, the plaintiffs were entitled to an injunction and damages for breach of contract.

In *Pollard v. Photographic Co.*, 40 Ch. Div. 345 (1888), a photogra-pher who had taken a lady's photograph under ordinary circum-stances was restrained from exhibiting it, and also from selling copies of it, on the ground that it was a breach of an implied term in the contract, and also that it was a breach of confidence. Mr. Justice North interjected in the argument of the plaintiff's counsel the inquiry: "Do you dispute that if the negative likeness were taken on the sly, the person who took it might exhibit copies?" and counsel for the plaintiff answered: "In that case there would be no trust or consideration to support a contract." Later, the defendant's counsel argued that "a person has no property in his own features; short of doing what is libelous or otherwise illegal, there is no restriction on the photographer's using his negative." But the court, while expressly finding a breach of contract and of trust sufficient to justify its interposition, still seems to have felt the necessity of resting the decision also upon a right of property, in order to bring it within the line of those cases which were relied upon as prece-dents.

This process of implying a term in a contract, or of implying a trust (particularly where a contract is written, and where these is no established usage or custom), is nothing more nor less than a judicial declaration that public morality, private justice, and general convenience demand the recognition of such a rule, and that the publication under similar circumstances would be considered an intolerable abuse. So long as these circumstances happen to present a contract upon which such a term can be engrafted by the judicial mind, or to supply relations upon which a trust or confidence can be erected, there may be no objection to working out the desired protection though the doctrines of contract or of trust. But the court can hardly stop there. The narrower doctrine may have satisfied the demands of society at a time when the abuse to be guarded against could rarely have arisen without violating a contract or a special confidence; but now that modern devices afford abundant opportunities for the perpetration of such wrongs without any participation by the injured party, the protection granted by the law must be placed upon a broader foundation. While, for instance, the state of the photographic art was such that one's picture could seldom be taken without his consciously "sitting" for the purpose, the law of contract or of trust might afford the prudent man sufficient safeguards against the improper circulation of his portrait; but since the latest advances in photographic art have rendered it possible to take pictures surreptitiously, the doctrines of contract and of trust are inadequate to support the required protection, and the law of tort must be resorted to. The right of property in its widest sense, including all possession, including all rights and privileges, and hence embracing the right to an inviolate personality, affords alone that broad basis upon which the protection which the individual demands can be rested.

Thus, the courts, in searching for some principle upon which the publication of private letters could be enjoined, naturally came upon the ideas of a breach of confidence, and of an implied contract; but it required little consideration to discern that this doctrine could not afford all the protection required, since it would not support the court in granting a remedy against a stranger; and so the theory of property in the contents of letters was adopted. Indeed, it is difficult to conceive on what theory of the law the casual recipient of a letter, who proceeds to publish it, is guilty of a breach of contract, express or implied, or of any breach of trust, in the ordinary acceptation of that term. Suppose a letter has been addressed to him without his solicitation. He opens it, and reads. Surely, he has not made any contract; he has not accepted any trust. He cannot, by opening and reading the letter, have come under any obligation save what the law declares; and, however expressed, that obligation is simply to observe the legal right of the sender, whatever it may be, and whether it be called his right or property in the contents of the letter, or his right to privacy.

A similar groping for the principle upon which a wrongful publication can be enjoined is found in the law of trade secrets. There, injunctions have generally been granted on the theory of a breach of contract, or of an abuse of confidence. It would, of course, rarely happen that any one would be in possession of a secret unless confidence had been reposed in him. But can it be supposed that the court would hesitate to grant relief against one who had obtained his knowledge by an ordinary trespass--for instance, by wrongfully looking into a book in which the secret was recorded, or by eavesdropping? Indeed, in *Yovatt v. Winyard,* I J.&W. 394 (1820), where an injunction was granted against making any use or of communicating certain recipes for veterinary medicine, it appeared that the defendant while in the plaintiff's employ, had surreptitiously got access to his book of recipes, and copied them. Lord Eldon "granted the injunction, upon the ground of there having been a breach of trust and confidence;" but it would seem difficult to draw any sound legal distinction between such a case and one where a mere stranger wrongfully obtained access to the book.

We must therefore conclude that the rights, so protected, whatever their exact nature, are not rights arising from contract or from special trust, but are rights as against the world; and, as above stated, the principle which has been applied to protect these rights is in reality not the principle of private property, unless that word be used in an extended and unusual sense. The principle which protects personal writings and any other productions of the intellect or the emotions, is the right to privacy, and the law has no new principle to formulate when it extends this protection to the personal appearance, sayings, acts, and to personal relation, domestic or otherwise.

If the invasion of privacy constitutes a legal injuria, the elements for demanding redress exist, since already the value of mental suffering, caused by an act wrongful in itself, is recognized as a basis for compensation.

The right of one who has remained a private individual, to prevent his public portraiture, presents the simplest case for such extension; the right to protect one's self from pen portraiture, from a discussion by the press of one's private affairs, would be a more important and far-reaching one. If casual and unimportant statements in a letter, if handiwork, however inartistic and valueless, if possessions of all sorts are protected not only against reproduction, but also against description and enumeration, how much more should the acts and sayings of a man in his social and domestic relations be guarded from ruthless publicity. If you may not reproduce a woman's face photographically without her consent, how much less should be tolerated the reproduction of her face, her form, and her actions, by graphic descriptions colored to suit a gross and depraved imagination.

The right to privacy, limited as such right must necessarily be, has already found expression in the law of France.

It remains to consider what are the limitations of this right to privacy, and what remedies may be granted for the enforcement of the right. To determine in advance of experience the exact line at which the dignity and convenience of the individual must yield to the demands of the public welfare or of private justice would be a difficult task; but the more general rules are furnished by the legal analogies already developed in the law of slander and libel, and in the law of literary and artistic property.

1. The right to privacy does not prohibit any publication of matter which is of public or general interest. In determining the scope of this rule, aid would be afforded by the analogy, in the law of libel and slander, of cases which deal with the qualified privilege of comment and criticism on matters of public and general interest. There are of course difficulties in applying such a rule; but they are inherent in the subject-matter, and are certainly no greater than those which exist in many other branches of the law—for instance, in that large class of cases in which the reasonableness or unreasonableness of an act is made the test of liability. The design of the law must be to protect those persons with whose affairs the community has no legitimate concern, from being dragged into an undesirable and undesired publicity and to protect all persons, whatsoever their position or station, from having matters which they may properly prefer to keep private, made public against their will. It is the unwarranted invasion of individual privacy which is reprehended, and to be, so far as possible, prevented. The distinction, however, noted in the above statement is obvious and fundamental. There are persons who may reasonably claim as a right, protection from the notoriety entailed by being made the victims of journalistic enterprise. There are others who, in varying degrees, have renounced the right to live their lives screened from public observation. Matters which men of the first class may justly con-

tend, concern themselves alone, may in those of the second be the subject of legitimate interest to their fellow-citizens. Peculiarities of manner and person, which in the ordinary individual should be free from comment, may acquire a public importance, if found in a candidate for public office. Some further discrimination is necessary, therefore, than to class facts or deeds as public or private according to a standard to be applied to the fact or deed per se. To publish of a modest and retiring individual that he suffers from an impediment in his speech or that he cannot spell correctly, is an unwarranted, if not an unexampled, infringement of his rights, while to state and comment on the same characteristics found in a would-be congressman could not be regarded as beyond the pale of propriety.

The general object in view is to protect the privacy of private life, and to whatever degree and in whatever connection a man's life has ceased to be private, before the publication under consideration has been made, to that extent the protection is likely to be withdrawn. Since, then, the propriety of publishing the very same facts may depend wholly upon the person concerning whom they are published, no fixed formula can be used to prohibit obnoxious publications. Any rule of liability adopted must have in it an elasticity which shall take account of the varying circumstances of each case—a necessity which unfortunately renders such a doctrine not only more difficult of application, but also to a certain extent uncertain in its operation and easily rendered abortive. Besides, it is only the more flagrant breaches of decency and propriety that could in practice be reached, and it is not perhaps desirable even to attempt to repress everything which the nicest taste and keenest sense of the respect due to private life would condemn.

In general, then, the matters of which the publication should be repressed may be described as those which concern the private life, habits, acts, and relations of an individual, and have no legitimate connection with his fitness for a public office which he seeks or for which he is suggested, or for any public or quasi public position which he seeks or for which he is suggested, and have no legitimate relation to or bearing upon any act done by him in a public or quasi public capacity. The foregoing is not designed as a wholly accurate or exhaustive definition, since that which must ultimately in a vast number of cases become a question of individual judgment and opinion is incapable of such definition; but it is an attempt to indicate broadly the class of matters referred to. Some things all men alike are entitled to keep from popular curiosity, whether in public life or not, while others are only private because the persons concerned have not assumed a position which makes their doings legitimate matters of public investigation.

2. The right to privacy does not prohibit the communication of any matter, though in its nature private, when the publication is made under circumstances which would render it a privileged communication according to the law of slander and libel. Under this rule, the right to privacy is not invaded by any publication made in a court of justice, in legislative bodies, or the committees of those bodies; in municipal assemblies, or the committees of such assemblies, or practically by any communication in any other public body, municipal or parochial, or in any body quasi public, like the large voluntary associations formed for almost every purpose of benevolence, business, or other general interest; and (at least in many jurisdictions) reports of any such proceedings would in some measure be accorded a like privilege. Nor would the rule prohibit any publication made by one in the discharge of some public or private duty, whether legal or moral, or in conduct of one's own affairs, in matters where his own interest is concerned.

3. The law would probably not grant any redress for the invasion of privacy by oral publication in the absence of special damage. The same reasons exist for distinguishing between oral and written publications of private matters, as is afforded in the law of defamation by the restricted liability for slander as compared with the liability for libel. The injury resulting from such oral communications would ordinarily be so trifling that the law might well, in the interest of free speech, disregard it altogether.

4. The right to privacy ceases upon the publication of the facts by the individual, or with his consent.

This is but another application of the rule which has become familiar in the law of literary and artistic property. The cases there decided establish also what should be deemed a publication;—the important principle in this connection being that a private communication of circulation for a restricted purpose is not a publication within the meaning of the law.

5. The truth of the matter published does not afford a defence. Obviously this branch of the law should have no concern with the truth or falsehood of the matters published. It is not for injury to the individual's character that redress or prevention is sought, but for injury to the right of privacy. For the former, the law of slander and

libel provides perhaps a sufficient safeguard. The latter implies the right not merely to prevent inaccurate portrayal of private life, but to prevent its being depicted at all.

6. The absence of "malice" in the publisher does not afford a defence. Personal ill-will is not an ingredient of the offence, any more than in an ordinary case of trespass to person or to property. Such malice is never necessary to be shown in an action for libel or slander at common law, except in rebuttal of some defence, e.g., that the occasion rendered the communication privileged, or, under the statutes in this State and elsewhere, that the statement complained of was true. The invasion of the privacy that is to be protected is equally complete and equally injurious, whether the motives by which the speaker or writer was actuated are taken by themselves, culpable or not; just as the damage to character, and to some extent the tendency to provoke a breach of the peace, is equally the result of defamation without regard to motives leading to its publication. Viewed as a wrong to the individual, this rule is the same pervading the whole law of torts, by which one is held responsible for his intentional acts, even thought they care committed with no sinister intent; and viewed as a wrong to society, it is the same principle adopted in a large category of statutory offences.

The remedies for an invasion of the right of privacy are also suggested by those administered in the law of defamation, and in the law of literary and artistic property, namely:

1. An action of tort for damages in all cases. Even in the absence of special damages, substantial compensation could be allowed for injury to feelings as in the action of slander and libel.
2. An injunction, in perhaps a very limited class of cases.

It would doubtless be desirable that the privacy of the individual should receive the added protection of the criminal law, but for this, legislation would be required. Perhaps it would be deemed proper to bring the criminal liability for such publication within narrower limits; but that the community has an interest in preventing such invasions of privacy, sufficiently strong to justify the introduction of such a remedy, cannot be doubted. Still, the protection of society must come mainly through a recognition of the rights of the individual. Each man is responsible for his own acts and omissions only. If he condones what he reprobates, with a weapon at hand equal to his defence, he is responsible for the results. If he resists, public opinion will rally to his support. Has he then such a weapon? It is believed that the common law provides him with one, forged in the slow fire of the centuries, and today fitly tempered to his hand. The common law has always recognized a man's house as his castle, impregnable, often, even to his own officers engaged in the execution of its command. Shall the courts thus close the front entrance to constituted authority, and open wide the back door to idle or prurient curiosity?

The Social Life of Genes:
Privacy, Property and the New Genetics

MARGARET EVERETT

Introduction

In an earlier version of this paper, I began with the question, "Do you own your DNA?" Yet, the more I consider the complexities of gene patenting and genetic privacy, the more I think the question to start with must be: How did genes become commodities? Scientific and legal changes are of course central to this development. Condit identifies the transformation of the biosciences into biotechnology in the 1980s as critical to the commodification of genes (Condit, 1999, p. 159). Others cite changes in U.S. patent laws and the development of recombinant DNA technology (Andrews and Nelkin, 2001, p. 43). Rifkin (1998) points to the U.S. Supreme Court case of *Diamond v Chakrabarty* in 1971 as an especially important turning point. Equally important, however, is the social process by which the body and its parts, even its most microscopic parts, have come to be thought of as a source of wealth. With the discovery of the structure of DNA in 1953 and the initiation of the Human Genome Project (HGP) in 1986, the gene has become a cultural icon *and* a valuable commodity. Despite the growing commercialization of genes, it is equally clear that there is significant cultural resistance to such commodification. Public opinion polls suggest widespread suspicion about the use of human subjects for DNA research along with deep concerns about ethics and privacy. Social critics worry that commercial interests negate or ignore the social meanings of the body.

Exclusive licenses to DNA sequences through patent protection could bring biotech companies billions of dollars in the development of new drugs, gene-based therapies, and diagnostic tests. Others have sought to confer property rights on individuals to their DNA, thus protecting them from potential employment and insurance discrimination and unwanted participation in research. We need to ask what gets left out when property dominates the debate over DNA? This essay considers the debate over genetic privacy and property in the context of the commodification of the body and its parts. The controversy surrounding Oregon's Genetic

Privacy Act (Senate Bill 276/95) offers a useful case for exploring the application of property metaphors to human DNA.

Do Genes Have Social Lives?

The contributors to the edited volume *The Social Life of Things* (Appadurai, ed., 1986) begin with the intriguing premise that commodities have social lives. As Igor Kopytoff explains, for example, "From a cultural perspective, the production of commodities is also a cultural and cognitive process: commodities must be not only produced materially as things, but also culturally marked as being certain kinds of things" (1986, p. 64). Things may be marked for exchange in one social or historical context and not another. A thing might be said to have a biography, or life history, moving in and out of the commodity state (Appadurai, 1986, p. 18). Moreover, there is in any exchange system a tension between "the tendency of all economies to expand the jurisdiction of commoditization and of all cultures to restrict it" (Appadurai 1986, p. 17; see also Kopytoff, 1986, pp. 72-73). In the West, people have proven particularly resistant to commodification.[1] Kopytoff suggests, however, that the human sphere may become increasingly vulnerable to commodification "especially in a secularized society that finds it increasingly difficult to appeal to any transcendental sanctions for cultural discrimination and classification" (1986, p. 84). These insights on the nature of commodities and commodification are particularly useful as a starting point for discussing how human genes have become commodities, and how their commodification has been resisted.

Demand, Appadurai explains, is not only a mechanical response to supply, but rather is "a complex social mechanism" (1986, p. 41). Demand for genetic research may seem self-evident—the promise of longer life, better health care, higher quality of life; but just as we learn to think of ourselves as a product of our DNA, we learn (through media representations and scientific discourses) that we need genetic medicine. The desire for full hair, thin bodies, even longevity, is socially constructed: we are taught to want these things, just as we are taught that the secret is in our genes (Consider the recent book title that implores one to *Turn off the Fat Genes*). Are we developing a fetish for DNA, and if so, how does this shape ethics debates about the management and use of genetic information?

Yours, Mine and Ours: Contested DNA

Why has the New Genetics stirred such concerns over privacy? Several characteristics of genetic information make it unique from other kinds of medical records. First, genetic tests can be predictive of future health. DNA testing can be used, for example, to identify carriers of the mutations that are believed to cause breast cancer and Huntington's disease. It is even possible to learn about someone's likely future that even the individual does not know, which led some observers to consider our DNA a "coded probabilistic future diary" (Annas, 1995, p. 20). Another term used to describe DNA is that of the genetic "blueprint," a metaphor that points to the deterministic assumptions embedded in contemporary understandings of genetics. As James Watson, former director of the Human Genome Project, once declared, "We used to think our fate is in the stars. Now we know, in large measure, our fate is in our genes" (quoted in Weiner, 1994, p. 31). Many observers worry that such determinism tends to ignore the social, economic, and environmental factors involved in disease, as well as the value judgements inherent in definitions of "normal" and "abnormal" (see Lloyd, 1994). Genetic information is also unique because it implicates families and groups. As the authors of the GPA explain, "Decoding DNA also divulges information about a person's parents, siblings, and children, and can therefore affect how family members perceive and relate to one another" (Annas et al., 1995, p. 3).[2]

Given these unique characteristics, genetic information is potentially valuable to employers and insurance companies, and to researchers and pharmaceutical concerns. The growing demands for privacy and the protection of genetic information, then, emerge directly from this growing commercialization.

A number of commentators argue that in light of the accessibility of medical records generally, especially with increasing computerization of records and the growth of the Internet, genetic information will require special protection (Annas, 1993; Lebacqz, 1994).[3] According to George Annas, a leading voice in the genetic privacy movement, "Genetic information is both potentially embarrassing and uniquely personal. The existence of such decodable information could either impel us to take privacy much more seriously in the genetic realm than we have in the medical and criminal realms, or lead us to give up on maintaining personal privacy altogether" (Annas, 1993, p. 106) A few recent surveys suggest that the public does have strong concerns about their privacy and the effects of genetic research. A CNN-Time Magazine poll in June 2000, for example, found that 46 percent of respondents thought that obtaining the genetic code would have harmful consequences (*LA Times*, 28 June 2000). A Gallup survey in September 2000 asked Americans about their concerns over medical privacy. An overwhelming majority (93 percent) responded that medical and government researchers should not be allowed to study an individual's genetic information unless they first obtain his or her consent (Institute for Health Freedom, 2000).

Efforts to pass genetic privacy legislation often focus on the threat of employment and insurance discrimination. While evidence of actual discrimination has been largely anecdotal, the media have reported on a number of cases of interest. In one recent case, the federal government sued Burlington Northern Santa Fe Railroad for requiring genetic testing of employees filing claims for work-related injuries. The company asserted that some workers were genetically predisposed to carpal tunnel syndrome, thus making them ineligible for work-related claims (*Oregonian*, 10 February 2001, p.10a). The best known example of widespread abuse is the employment and insurance discrimination that resulted from sickle-cell anemia screening programs in the 1970s (see Murray, 2001). The Air Force Academy also used the results of such screenings to exclude carriers (see Hubbard and Wald, 1999, p. 34). More recent accounts cite the use of genetic information to deny medical benefits to retirees (Fuller et al., 1999, p. 1359). A recent survey of 1500 genetic counselors and physicians reported 785 cases where patients had lost jobs or insurance because of a genetic condition or test.[4] A survey by the American Management Association found that 30 percent of large and mid-size companies sought some form of genetic information about employees and 7 percent used that information in hiring and promotion decisions (Martindale, 2001, pp. 19-20). Citing other examples of genetic discrimination, Andrews and Nelkins conclude, "the body in the biotechnology age betrays" (2001, 98). In order to prevent such discrimination, 33 states have enacted legislation dealing with health insurance discrimination based on genetic testing, and 19 states have laws regarding employment discrimination and genetic testing (National Cancer Institute, 1999; see also National Conference of State Legislatures, 1999).

Privacy, particularly in relation to genetic testing, does not only imply the right to keep others from accessing and using one's genetic information. "Genetic privacy" advocates also include the right not to share information with others, but also the right not to know one's own genetic fate, as well as the right to use information in accordance with one's own values (see Lebacqz, 1994, p. 40). Observers worry, for example, about the psychological effects of learning one's predisposition to a deadly disease, particularly in the absence of any effective treatments (Johnson et al., 1999). Not only could this lead to detrimental psychological effects for individuals and their families, but it could also lead to a kind of stigmatization and societal discrimination that goes well beyond the economic concerns of most legislation to date. As Annas puts it, "Genetic information can be toxic" (1996, p. 19).

Some argue that the prospect of labeling healthy people as patients may discourage many from genetic testing, or at the very least encourage people to want to protect their genetic information (see Martindale, 2001, p. 20). Medical information, particularly genetic information, would seem to have the power to both liberate and constrain individual choice. Nowhere is this more apparent than in the alarmist references to the 'new eugenics.' One observer calls worries of a 'new eugenics,' in other words the idea that genetic "defects" can and should be eliminated from the population, "the approved [Human Genome] project anxiety" (Paul, 1994, p. 143). Media reports are full of warnings about the dangers of coercive policies that would seek to weed out genetic mutations. The solution, according to many, is individual choice and autonomy in genetic counseling and screening programs. Still, a number of ethicists argue that privacy and individual choice are problematic. Even in the absence of coercive policies, they argue, there will be social pressures to screen for certain disorders, and pressure to use information in certain ways. Rifkin (1998) foresees a "eugenic civilization" in which we will be able to reengineer our species to suit our own whims and desires. Ridley, on the other hand, argues that the key distinction between current genetic technologies and the eugenics movement is coercion: "genetic screening is about giving private individuals private choices on private criteria. Eugenics was about nationalizing that decision to make people breed not for themselves but for the state" (1999, 299). Rapp predicts that contemporary eugenics dilemmas will have more to do with the market economy rather than coercive policies: "Threats of eugenic exclusions now involve insurance coverage or its lack, employer discrimination, and struggles around extending coverage of disability legislation to those with genetic susceptibilities" (2000, p. 37).

Others worry that the New Genetics may help turn social problems into personal problems, placing blame and responsibility for social ills on individuals. Moreover, the more genetics becomes a legitimate tool for explanation of normal and abnormal, disease and health, the more we may turn away from other forms of explanation—social, physical and environmental (see Finkler, 2000, p. 49).[5] This could be particularly detrimental to women, the poor, and minorities. As Lebacqz argues, for example, "Privacy does not change [the discourse of discrimination] but only reinforces it: social problems become privatized and turned back onto oppressed people" (Lebacqz, 1994, p. 48).[6]

The Commerce of Genes

Like demands for privacy, informed consent has become a major issue in genetic research precisely because of the growing potential for commercialization. Researchers may want to avoid obtaining informed consent for the use of human tissues, worrying that the process will slow down or threaten potentially lucrative discoveries. At the same time, the perception that genes are a source of wealth fuels public suspicions about the ethics of DNA research. We might ask not only who owns our genes, but also to what extent we are able to give or withhold consent to researchers who want to use our DNA.

Gene patenting is of course at the center of this debate and intimately tied to privacy concerns. The efforts of Decode Genetics, an Icelandic subsidiary of a U.S. company, to identify the genetic causes of diseases such as cancer by using the medical records, genealogies, and genetic information of the entire country, has brought the issues of informed consent, privacy, and property together. In Iceland, an individual is assumed to have consented to have their DNA and medical records used for research unless they opt out by notifying his or her physician. Annas (2000) is critical of this "presumed consent" and argues that individual consent should be required. He also questions whether real benefits will be delivered to the Icelandic people that outweigh the risks. Any research that could result in stigmatization or discrimination of the Icelandic people should require the consultation of the population, he argues. Informed consent requires an adequate assessment of risks and benefits psychological, physical, and social (see Johnson, et al.,

1999). The project certainly begs the question, how does an entire country give informed consent? Despite assurances that records will be encrypted and individual identities protected, critics worry about loss of privacy and potential discrimination. While proponents say it will be good for the Icelandic economy, others say it is unfair for one company to benefit from such a potentially valuable resource (see Rose, 2003; Pálsson and Harðardóttir, 2002).

In the United States, researchers frequently request waivers of informed consent requirements, not only when samples are used anonymously, but when samples are linked to clinical information through encryption. Researchers argue that these projects pose little or no risk to the people from whom samples were originally taken. But promises of confidentiality may not always be realistic, even in studies involving large populations such as Iceland. For example, it would be difficult if not impossible to guarantee the confidentiality of persons with rare disorders (Clayton, 1998, p. 129).

The Icelandic case exemplifies the battle over the commercial use of human tissue, and of genetic information in particular. Biotech companies have flooded the federal patent office with applications to patent newly-discovered genes. The standard for patentability is that an invention must be new, useful, and nonobvious, yet genes are naturally-occurring substances. This contradiction has caused outrage, even within the medical community. The American College of Medical Genetics, for example, has taken the position that genes should not be patented, and cites the growing evidence that patents limit access to genetic screening, negatively impacting patient care. Organizations representing those affected by genetic conditions have taken a similar position (Wexler, 2000; Meyers, 2000; Nader, 2000). While the US Patent and Trade Office issued stricter guidelines for patents on genes in 2000, these organizations remain opposed to gene patenting under any conditions.

Companies are also trying to own patents to random DNA sequences, even without knowing their function or where they occur on chromosomes (Hubbard and Wald, 1999, pp. 124-25).[7] The patenting of such random sequences has been particularly controversial. As one bioethicist told *USA Today*, "It's like patenting the alphabet and charging people every time they speak" (*USA Today Online*, 25 September 2000). Others argue that unfettered gene patenting reflects the market-driven approach to research that can have negative effects on the advancement of science, and ultimately on patient care (Knoppers et al., 1999). While the biotech industry argues that it is the profit motive that drives new research, that competition may also hinder collaboration when information is not shared freely by researchers around the world. Heller and Eisenberg describe an emerging scenario they call the "tragedy of the anticommons" in which "too many owners hold rights in previous discoveries that constitute obstacles to future research" (1998, p. 698). Bill Clinton and Tony Blair expressed those concerns in March 2000, when they issued a joint statement urging scientists to release the raw data from the HGP. The statement came days after negotiations to merge the public and private efforts to map the genome broke down. When the US and Britain agreed to share data from the publicly-funded project, the Nasdaq stock exchange fell on the news. Biotech companies that had been banking on selling genetic data to pharmaceuticals and researchers fell sharply, indicating that the open exchange of information is not good for business (*LA Times*, 14 March 2000).

While some analysts argue that DNA should be the property of individuals, and others argue that those who 'discover' genes should earn the right to patent them, case law on whether or not human tissue can be considered property at all is contradictory. According to Markett, "The common law has a long tradition of denying persons property rights in their bodies" (1996, p. 216). With the exception of blood and semen, humans do not have commercial rights in their body parts. Markett argues that because body parts have increased in value, the courts should recognize commercial rights. The often cited California Supreme Court case of *Moore v. Regents of the University of California* illustrates the difficulty in recognizing property rights of donors of human tissue.

When John Moore sought treatment at the UCLA Medical Center for hairy-cell leukemia, he was apparently unaware that his removed spleen and other samples were being retained by his doctor for research purposes. When Moore eventually learned that his tissue enabled the creation of a cell-line potentially worth billions of dollars, he sued his doctor and the University of California, arguing that his samples had effectively been stolen from him, and claiming a share of the profits. The court, fearing a chilling effect on research, found that Moore had forfeited any rights he had to his tissue because he did not retain possession or assert ownership of his spleen once it had been removed. Proponents of gene patenting often refer to the Moore case as a clear precedent denying donors a share in the profits from discoveries made using their tissues. Other cases, however, do seem to recognize DNA as property.[8] Critics of the Moore decision argue that without recognizing a donor's property interest in their tissue, most states offer little legal recourse to those who feel their DNA has been used without their consent (Markett, 1996). Rao offers a different critique of the Moore decision. She finds the court's ruling contradictory in that it rejected Moore's property claim to his spleen while upholding the researchers' property rights to the resulting cell lines. "The case does not stand for the proposition that spleens can never become property . . . it simply holds that Moore's spleen was not his property" (2000, p. 374). Some even argue that the rising value of human tissue merits the creation of a royalty system, much like that used in the music industry, that would compensate donors for each use of their tissue (Lin, 1996, p. 121).

Another battle over the commercialization of a specific gene highlights the conflicting interests of researchers and their subjects. When several families affected by Canavan's disease, a fatal and rare recessive disorder, allowed their children's tissue samples to be used for research, they hoped that a prenatal diagnostic test for the disorder and new treatments would be developed. Many of the same families were outraged when Miami Children's Hospital, where researchers identified the mutation which causes the disorder, patented the gene and began charging a royalty fee on each test for the disorder.[9] In some cases, the very families that had helped make the research possible were later being charged a fee when testing for the disorder in other family members. The hospital argued that the royalty would help them recover some of the millions of dollars they put into finding the gene. They also reasoned that a laboratory with an exclusive license would be more likely to market the test to at-risk families (see *Miami Herald*, 15 December 1999, p. 8b; see also Andrews and Nelkin, 2001, pp. 51-52). In a letter to the editor of the Miami Herald, one parent of a child who died of Canavan disease explained that the hospital had failed in its obligation to obtain informed consent from the families:

"While we did give samples voluntarily to help eliminate a disease that was killing our children, we did not give consent to the research in writing as required by federal law, and we were not informed that our mutations would be patented. We also were not informed that Miami Children's would charge a royalty to any laboratory testing for one of our Canavan-disease mutations and then limit the facilities that can perform the test. Miami Children's

Hospital's claim that its profit-driven approach to licensing will encourage at-risk families to be tested is self-serving fantasy." (*Miami Herald*, 2 December 1999, p. 8b)

The controversy over the patenting of this particular mutation is especially significant, because it indicates that while the subjects of DNA research are quite often not interested in getting a share of the profits, they are concerned about retaining some control over the use of their DNA through informed consent procedures.

In fact, what this and other similar conflicts between researchers and subjects may show is that what many research subjects want is not privacy, not even profits, but assurances that their body parts will not be turned into marketable products. At present, informed consent is required for federally funded research through the Common Rule and with oversight by Institutional Review Boards.[10] While much of the focus of legislation to date has been on protecting privacy, researchers continue to be able to use DNA that is "anonymous" or linked to a subject through encryption without informed consent. Whether their privacy is violated or not, many people are uncomfortable with the idea of the commercialization of their DNA or tissue.

Commodified Bodies, Commodified DNA

The commodification of the body is not a new phenomenon; slavery, prostitution, and the sale of corpses, for example, attest to this fact. However, new biotechnologies do challenge and expand the ways in which we value the body. As Gold explains, "The products of biotechnology from gene therapies, to hormones, to pharmaceuticals are things that we buy and sell, and trade. The body itself, when understood as the mine from which we extract these products, is similarly valuable as a commodity" (1996, p. 2).

The commodification of the body is closely associated with "medicalization," the dehumanizing process by which "even living bodies are quickly fragmented and transformed into scientific work objects" (Sharp, 2000, p. 298). Objectification is necessary for transforming persons and their bodies into objects of economic desire. Some even argue that new biotechnologies, especially genetic engineering and cloning, encourage "self-objectification," in which we may see ourselves as both "subject and object, transformable and literally creatable through biological engineering" (Morgan, 1991, p. 30, cited in Sharp, 2000, p. 297).[11] Andrews and Nelkin point to the increasingly commercial language of science as a reflection of this objectification: "Body parts are *extracted* like a mineral, *harvested* like a crop, or *mined* like a resource" (2001, p. 5, emphasis in original). Not surprisingly, the metaphors of scientific language conflict increasingly with the social meanings of the body.

Anthropologists, in particular, have criticized this separation of body and self that allows for the commodification of the body and its parts. "Embodiment" refers to the notion of the body-as-self and to the rejection of the separation of body and self in medical practice (see Sharp, 2000, p. 290). One of the most fruitful areas of medical anthropology has been the reconceptualization of the body and the rejection of the Cartesian separation of mind and body. Medical anthropologists blame Descartes for the "mechanistic-materialistic background to biomedicine" (Strathern, 1996, p. 5). A refinement of the "mindful body" concept advanced by Lock and Scheper-Hughes (1987), embodiment "collapses the duality of mind and body . . . essentially by infusing body with mind" (Stathern, 1996, p. 181).

De Witte and Ten Have, in examining body commodification in the context of genetic material, argue "The distinction between person and body is contrary to the existential identity with our bodies and the self-experience of ourselves as embodied selves" (1997, p. 52). Despite such reservations, court decisions tend to favor valuing the body, like other "goods," in economic ways. The famous Moore decision, discussed above, exemplifies this tendency: the court rejected Moore's attempt to claim his spleen as his property, but did not challenge the doctor's patent claim on Moore's cell-line. Gold, a critic of the Moore decision, argues more generally that "courts allocate right of control to those individuals who present themselves to the court as valuing the contested good in terms of economic modes of valuation" (1996, p. 17). A similar pattern has emerged in public policy and legal decisions around the ownership of DNA. While the United States has one of the most liberal policies regarding the patenting of DNA sequences, courts, as well as state and federal legislators, have largely rejected the notion that an individual could claim ownership of his/her DNA either for the purposes of protecting their privacy or for claiming a share of profits derived from their genome.[12]

Not surprisingly, there has been considerable resistance to the commodification of the body, and gene patenting is no exception. Before turning to the objections to gene patenting, however, it might be useful to look at the debate over organ donation, which offers certain similarities. Due to a perceived shortage of organs for transplant, some suggest a market approach, in which individuals would be allowed to sell their own organs. Andrews, for example, argues that individuals should have the right to sell their organs, while claiming that this would not contribute to the commodification of the body: "I am not advocating that people be treated as property, but only that they have the autonomy to treat their own parts as property, particularly their regenerative parts" (1992, p. 2151). As with the debate over genetic ownership, as will be discussed below, it seems difficult to believe that one could have it both ways. Childress rejects the sale of organs, primarily because he does not believe it would increase supply and might have the opposite effect (1992, p. 2145).

According to Joralemon the controversy over procurement strategies "signal[s] an ongoing cultural dispute over the meaning of the body as its parts acquire utility beyond their natural anatomical function" (1995, p. 336). Joralemon argues that there is considerable cultural resistance to transplantation as it promotes the notion of the body as a collection of replaceable parts rather than integral to the self. An example of such resistance occurred in Brazil with the passage in 1997 of a "presumed consent" law for organ donation. The law made every citizen a potential organ donor, unless an individual went to the considerable trouble of having himself or herself declared a "non-donor," something particularly difficult for poor and illiterate individuals to accomplish. In a country where urban legends about organ stealing for profit abound, the Presumed Organ Donor Law prompted widespread fear and anger (McDaniels, 1998). The law was repealed only one year later with pressure from the medical community.

This debate relates very well to the drive to commodify genes and the cultural resistance to that commodification. In terms of the implications of new biotechnologies for the conceptualization of the body, the focus on property and autonomy is problematic (see Sharp, 2000, p. 299). Most do not question whether or not DNA can be claimed as property, but rather by whom—the researchers who discover "new" sequences and mutations, or the individuals from whom such discoveries are mined. By countering biotech efforts to patent the genome with assertions of individual ownership rights to the body and to one's DNA, opponents of patenting fail to address the fundamental issue of body fragmentation and commodification. By rejecting individual property claims to DNA, patenting advocates contradict themselves when defending the notion of DNA as an invention of the laboratory. This contradiction will be illustrated with the Oregon example below.

According to Sharp, the era of the New Genetics makes possible "bodily fragmentation par excellence" as well as the notion that the essence of our humanity is located in our DNA (2000, p. 309). Such genetic determinism, according to Rabinow, represents the ultimate displacement of the soul in Western discourse (1992, cited in Sharp, 2000, p. 309). Some have argued that the denial of individual property rights to the body constitutes a loss of our identities to the biotechnology industry, an argument I myself made (see Everett, 1999). However, it may be more accurate to say that we lost our identities when they became reduced to our DNA. Finkler (2000) aptly describes this determinism as the "hegemony of the gene" and illustrates the disquieting ways in which the new genetics affects family relationships, our identities and our bodies.[13] According to Finkler, the new genetics promotes the "medicalization of kinship," whereby family and kin are increasingly conceived in biomedical terms. No wonder so many are fighting to own their DNA, having been encouraged by the media and scientists alike to believe they *are* their DNA. As one proponent of individual property rights to DNA argued, "DNA is you, it's the coding for the most important part of you—your own body. . . . The ability to own yourself is a basic right" (Onion, 2001, p. 2).

Genetic Privacy: The Debate in Oregon

Critics of the *Moore v. Regents* decision argue that passage of the GPA would resolve the legal uncertainty over commercial rights in human tissue, thus adequately protecting individuals (Lin, 1996; Markett, 1996). Others argue that giving individuals the power to prevent research on their tissue in an anonymous form is socially harmful, and that the provisions of the GPA related to informed consent would be too costly to enforce (Reilly, 1995, pp. 379-80). Another critic reasoned that because DNA is only a "blueprint," and cannot predict with certainty a person's medical future, additional protections were not necessary; genetic information could be protected like other medical information (Troy, 1997). Others have even argued that special protection for genetic information will do more social harm than good by reinforcing genetic determinism (Wilcox, et al., 1999).

The issues outlined above prompted a number of leading bio-ethicists to craft the GPA in 1995 (Annas, Glantz, and Roche, 1995).

The proposal for national legislation intended to protect privacy and guarantee informed consent for subjects of DNA testing. The act's provisions included the requirement of informed consent for the collection, analysis, and disclosure of DNA information, a statement that DNA is the property of the individual, and a requirement that DNA samples must be destroyed when analysis has been completed. To date, the federal government has failed to enact comprehensive legislation governing genetic privacy.[14] In the absence of such federal legislation, many states have acted to protect privacy and discourage discrimination, including Oregon, which in 1995 became the first state to declare DNA to be the property of the individual. Since 1995, academic researchers and the pharmaceutical lobby have challenged the law, arguing that it inhibits important research and damages the biotech industry in the state by clouding intellectual property rights. In 1999, an effort to eliminate Oregon's property clause ended with the creation of a government committee charged with reporting to the legislature on how best to protect genetic privacy. After the death of my son from a rare genetic disorder, I wrote in the newspaper about my own concerns over genetic privacy and the treatment of research subjects, and was asked to serve on the committee as a "consumer" representative.

Though the GPA has sparked much debate and discussion nationally, Oregon and Louisiana are the only states to enact its property provision. Efforts to pass similar legislation failed in Maryland, where a bill modeled on the GPA was opposed by the medical society, insurance industry, and chamber of commerce, the latter arguing that it would discourage the development of a biotech industry in the state (Holtzman, 1995). After the New Jersey legislature passed genetic privacy legislation, Governor Christie Todd Whitman replaced the property clause with privacy protections, citing the potentially negative effect the former would have on research (Stepanuk, 1998). Michigan similarly rejected the property approach with more cautious privacy protections (Calvo, 2000). Public and private leaders of the human genome project, as well as biotechnology spokesmen, typically support these measures. By reassuring a nervous public about privacy, while excluding individuals from making property claims, they create a predictable environment in which to do business. As of January 1999, 44 states had enacted legislation of varying scope concerning genetic privacy or discrimination (Mulholland and Jaeger, 1999).[15]

The Oregon Genetic Privacy Act of 1995 (SB 276/95) was the state's first attempt to regulate the collection, retention, and disclosure of genetic information. Previously, genetic privacy concerns had been only partially covered by civil rights law and specific mandates about research. A group of geneticists, lawyers, and bioethicists concerned about genetic privacy formed the Oregon Genetic Privacy Advisory Committee (OGPAC) in 1994 and proposed the law. Their primary concern was to prevent insurance and employment discrimination based on the results of genetic tests. The law identifies the circumstances under which genetic tests may be conducted, and when insurance companies can use an individual's genetic information. The most controversial aspect of the bill by far is the "property clause," which simply states that "An individual's genetic information is the property of the individual" (SB 276, Section 4). During the 1997 legislative session, the statute was subsequently revised to exempt samples used for anonymous and encoded research, another point of controversy (ORS 659.715, par. 1). OGPAC believed that the property clause would give courts clear guidance on the nature of an individual's rights in genetic information. In other words, a person whose genetic information had been retained or disclosed without informed consent could effectively argue that their DNA had been stolen and pursue damages. OGPAC reasoned that this was an easy concept for laypersons and the courts alike to understand. They also argued that the clause would allow blood relatives to assert ownership of genetic information that could be damaging to their own privacy through existing inheritance laws (GRAC minutes, December 1, 1999).

Changes to the Oregon GPA in 1997 and 1999 provided protections for anonymous and encoded research, exempting such testing from the informed consent requirements. Also during the 1999 session, the Pharmaceuticals Researchers and Manufacturers of America (PhRMA) and Oregon Health Sciences University (OHSU), where most biotech research in the state is done, led an effort to eliminate the property clause, replacing it with a broadly worded mandate to protect patient privacy and confidentiality. The Oregon Senate approved the bill, but the House rejected it, and instead appointed a committee to study the question and make recommendations for the 2001 session (SB 937/99). Composed of representatives from government, industry, the medical profession, and health care consumers, the Genetic Research Advisory Committee (GRAC) met from October 1999 to November 2000.

As a member of the committee, my own thoughts on genetic privacy were admittedly guided as much by emotions as by theory. My son, Jack, died in 1998 as a result of a rare genetic disorder, the mutation for which had not yet been discovered. While the disorder affects no more than a few hundred individuals in the world, researchers believe it may reveal valuable information about the genetic basis of more widespread diseases, particularly skin cancers. My husband and I agonized over the decision to allow researchers to use Jack's tissue samples after his death. In an opinion column in the newspaper, I wrote, "Is it appropriate to consider DNA 'private property?' I cannot answer that in the abstract, but I do know that I feel very 'proprietary' about my son's cells" (Everett, 1999). I joined the GRAC probably with the notion that I was there to defend the property clause, which I felt underscored individual and family rights to retain control over the use of one's own DNA. By the time the GRAC completed its work, however, I was less certain of the benefits of declaring DNA to be the property of individuals. I was troubled by some suggestions that individuals should share the profits of discoveries made using their DNA, or even that individuals might be allowed to accept payment in exchange for consent to use their DNA. How could such benefits be distributed when family members share even rare mutations? How could informed consent be protected with the coercive effects of payments? I began to feel that the proponents of individual property rights were encouraging, perhaps unwittingly, the very commodification and objectification that I had found so troubling in my own experience. In the end, I lent my support to the elimination of the property clause.

The voices against the property clause typically focused on the threat it posed to the development of a biotech industry in Oregon. In criticizing the property clause, James Gardner, lobbyist for PhRMA, told the Oregon Senate that "the business climate in Oregon is inhospitable to the fledgling Oregon biotech industry" (Gardner, 1999, p. 1). By considering DNA the property of the individual, a company's intellectual property rights to research discoveries would be clouded. He further argued that the property clause could create a situation in which an individual could sell his or her DNA, effectively selling one's privacy rights. Gardner repeated these concerns to the GRAC, where he represented PhRMA (December 1, 1999 minutes) and in media interviews (see

Onion, 2001). Other lobbyists warned the committee that Oregon was losing out on biotech dollars because of its unique statute. A representative of Smith Kline Beecham told the committee that her employer had decided not to fund research in Oregon until the property issue was resolved (GRAC minutes, 1 December 1999). Lawyer William Noonan argued that the property clause conflicted with federal patenting laws, and also warned that risk-averse corporations would do business in other states rather than fund research and development in Oregon (GRAC minutes, 5 January 2000). Representatives of OHSU claimed that the medical school had been unable to participate in certain national studies because of the Oregon law.

Several members of the committee challenged the assertion that the growth of the biotech industry had been hampered by Oregon's unique statute (GRAC minutes, 3 May 2000). Representatives from OGPAC further argued that deleting the property clause would seriously compromise the protection of privacy rights. In his testimony to the Oregon Senate in 1999, Bradley Popovich, chair of OGPAC, argued for an alternative that would keep the property clause while allowing tissue banks to use archived specimens under the regulations of the federal "Common Rule" (Popovich, 1999).

While property was the most controversial issue, the committee also considered other matters related to genetic privacy, such as issues of informed consent. OGPAC representatives, following the lead of the National Bioethics Advisory Commission (NBAC), expressed concerns about the use of clinical specimens for research (GRAC minutes, June 7, 2000). With regard to informed consent, the NBAC report recommends that "when informed consent to the research use of human biological materials is required, it should be obtained separately from informed consent to clinical procedures" (1999, p. iv). NBAC also recommends that consent forms offer subjects a variety of options, such as the refusal of their biological materials for research, the use of their materials for anonymous research only, or the use of the biological materials for en-coded/encrypted research. While geneticists on the GRAC tended to stress the fact that most people willingly participated in research projects in the hope of positive benefits for their families or society in general, one geneticist acknowledged that her patients were often concerned about what happened to their samples after testing (GRAC minutes, November 3, 1999). A series of focus group discussions around Oregon, commissioned by a non-profit educational organization, identified similar concerns (Davis and Hibbitts, 2000). The GRAC final report does recommend that when informed consent is required under the federal "Common Rule," that consent should be specifically for genetic research and not simply a blanket consent that covers testing for clinical and research purposes (GRAC, 2000).

A few members of the committee also attempted to raise the issue of federal gene patenting in relation to the property clause. These members raised their opposition to gene patenting as a reason to retain the property clause. Though Oregon law obviously has no authority over federal patenting policies, some members reasoned that if DNA were treated essentially as property at the federal level, individuals could only truly be protected from misuse of their DNA by declaring it their property. The opposition to patenting and support of the property clause as a temporary solution (in the absence of federal legislation) matches the arguments of George Annas and the proposal for national privacy legislation. In a recent interview, Annas commented on the efforts to remove the property clause in Oregon, referring to the practice of patenting:

"That property notion was developed on the basis of the common-sense notion that no one should have greater authority over your own body and DNA than you. . . . The idea that anyone else can own your DNA—like the biotech companies or the researchers—while you can't strikes me as nonsense. It can't possibly be that everyone else in the world can own my DNA, but I can't. So when researchers at biotech companies complain about the property notion potentially interfering with what they're doing, what they're really balking at is having to go to the trouble of getting explicit authorization from individuals before using their DNA for commercial or research purposes (Compton, 2000, p. 1)."

Despite the efforts of OGPAC members to introduce patenting into the debate, the only person who testified before the committee on patenting was a lawyer who supported gene patenting (GRAC minutes, January 5, 2000). Representatives from both OHSU and PhRMA rejected taking up the issue of patenting in the committee, stating that it was a federal issue and was unrelated to the issue of privacy (GRAC minutes, April 5, 2000).

The Oregon Compromise

While the GRAC's final report did recommend eliminating the property clause, it also proposed changes to Oregon's GPA that would make the law more explicit with regard to penalties, discrimination, and obtaining informed consent. The GRAC presented its bill, Senate Bill 114, to the Oregon Senate in January of 2001, and the bill was passed into law in May of 2001 with widespread support from health care and biotechnology interests as well as the consensus opinion of the GRAC. Oregon will still have one of the most comprehensive genetic privacy laws in the country. Important questions, however, are still unresolved. The law protects only those who have a genetic test, not those who seek genetic counseling. The law also does not prevent insurance companies from using family history, or the test results of blood relatives, in determining coverage. The GRAC's called for the creation of another advisory committee to study these questions as well as the issue of gene patenting. The consumer representatives were successful in getting an agreement that the new committee, if created by the legislature, would include public involvement and education in its activities. However, representatives from the health-care, insurance, and biotechnology industries would still dominate the new committee.

The committee also avoided some deeper questions about informed consent, such as the way barriers of language, culture or class might affect the context in which consent is obtained. The committee also agreed that while a health crisis might be a difficult time for a person to carefully consider risks and benefits, such concerns were beyond the scope of the GRAC (GRAC minutes, 1 December 1999).

Opposition to the bill surfaced from consumer groups, including Oregonians for Genetic Integrity (OGI), an organization that formed specifically to fight the bill. OGI supports individual ownership rights to DNA and opposes patents. They argue that property rights are the best way for individuals to avoid being used in unethical or immoral experiments, such as human cloning (OGI, 2001). In his testimony before the judiciary, founder Steve Chase also reasoned that individuals should be allowed to seek profits from research using their DNA. Another member of OGI wrote to a newspaper, "without ownership of our genetic information we will have no way to prevent uses we find unethical once it has been extracted from us. Technology now allows mind-boggling opportunities to violate our sensibilities of right and wrong" (Howard, 2001).

Just as the GRAC finished its report on genetic privacy in Oregon, OHSU announced plans to raise $500 million to pursue biotech research made possible by the HGP (*Oregonian*, 26 October 2000, p. D1). The university plans to build a large new facility and hire 300 new scientists. This latest venture suggests why changes to Oregon's genetic privacy legislation are so important to the medical school at this time. It also suggests that the dispute over the ownership of DNA is far from over in Oregon.

Conclusions: What to Do with DNA?

With the development of the biotechnology industry, genes have taken on a (social) life of their own. The commodification of DNA has also met with resistance on the part of research subjects as well as the general public, all potential DNA donors. The construction of DNA as property with commercial value, the identification of the self with DNA, and the objectification of body parts are all necessary to this process of commodification. As the contributors to *The Social Life of Things*, introduced at the beginning of this essay, might have predicted, however, the process of transforming the social meanings of the body, including its most microscopic parts, is uneven and highly contested.

The passionate claims and counter-claims over DNA ownership themselves are noteworthy for several reasons. Proponents of individual property rights in DNA themselves acknowledge the lack of widespread employment and insurance discrimination thus far. Likewise, the fears expressed by biotechnology companies about research subjects scrambling for a share of the profits have thus far not been confirmed. The heated nature of the debate, then, seems to indicate not only the enormous amount of money at stake, but also deep cultural ambivalence about the commodification of the body and its parts. I have argued that those who assert claims of ownership in their own bodies have failed to challenge the inexorable commodification and objectification of the body made possible by the HGP. In fact, the most vocal critics of gene patenting have sometimes played their own role in making genes commodities—by supporting property laws in the body, by sometimes suggesting that we should be able to sell our own DNA, and by emphasizing deterministic assumptions about the DNA as the locus of our identities. Legal scholars argue for or against property rights to the body, for or against gene patenting, but rarely argue against *ever* treating the body or its parts as property. Medical ethicists tend to privilege individual autonomy, many suggesting that individuals should have the autonomy to sell their parts, including their DNA, while arguing rather disingenuously that this would not encourage the commodification of the body. Given the way in which genetics refigures kin and family relations, individual autonomy seems an inappropriate principle to apply here at any rate. Even rare mutations are shared by family members, raising complicated questions about to whom ownership and use rights would apply (see Finkler, 2000, p. 4). Trapped in a debate over ownership claims, neither side questioned, in a meaningful way, assumptions about genetic determinism, or the way in which property claims negate other social meanings of the body.

The debate in Oregon exemplifies this dilemma. PhRMA's representative repeatedly asserted that individuals should not be allowed a property right to their genetic information, since one's privacy should be considered an inalienable right. Yet this contradicts the pharmaceutical industry's patent claims on human DNA. Those who challenge gene patenting claims have found it difficult to do so outside of the property framework, as exemplified by Oregon's "property clause" proponents. If the reaction to genetic privacy legislation in Oregon is any indication, however, the public's ambivalence over the promises of the new genetics, and resistance to the commodification of DNA will continue.

Notes

1. Kopytoff acknowledges that slavery clearly belied the conceptual separation between "the universe of people and the universe of objects" but noted that slavery was a moral problem in the West and not elsewhere (1986, p. 84).

2. Critics have recently argued that DNA should not be treated as significantly different from other types of medical information. For the debate over "genetic exceptionalism" see Green and Botkin, 2003; Murray, 1999; and Everett, 2004.

3. For background on legislation regarding medical records and the handling of genetic information specifically, see *Congressional Digest*, 2000a and 2000b.

4. Another study of genetics counselors argued that while fears of discrimination are high, the actual risk of insurance or employment discrimination was quite low (Hall and Rich, 2000).

5. The mapping of the human genome, as Rothman explains, requires choices about what constitutes "normal": "Certain political and ethical issues make themselves immediately apparent: which do you think will be the standard, the allele that is believed to 'cause' homosexuality, or that which is believed to 'cause' heterosexuality?" (1998, p. 96).

6. The debate over prenatal screening is beyond the scope of this paper, but see Parsons (1997, p. 253) who similarly argues that screening programs have the risk of placing blame and

responsibility on individual parents and poses a narrowly medical solution to disability rather than challenging societal assumptions about normal/abnormal.

On the effect of the HGP on minorities, see also the Zilinskas and Balint (2001) volume, which emphasizes the possible benefits of the HGP for minority communities, who are at higher risk for many health problems. Murray (same volume) argues that past abuses, such as the sickle-cell screening program, can be avoided with privacy protections.

7. Louisiana has defined genetic information as the property of the individual. Like Oregon, the law exempts anonymous research and makes other exceptions. Louisiana Administrative Code, June 1999, Chapter 45, Regulation 63, p. 255.

8. Markett and others cite *United States v. Arora, York v. Jones,* and *Davis v. Davis* as recognizing a property right in human tissue. The latter established a property interest in frozen sperm. According to Markett, these cases establish that "A court must recognize property rights in a donor's body parts where, through enforcement of a contract or through a tort action, the donor seeks return of, or damages for, misuse of his or her body parts" (1996, p. 225).

9. See Merz, 2002 for a detailed account of the controversy.

10. See Office of Science and Technology Policy 1991 for the "Common Rule."

11. For example, see the recent revelation about genetically altered babies in the UK (*BBC News Online,* 4 May 2001).

12. For a comparison of patent policies in different countries, see UNESCO 2001.

13. See Lippman (1993) and Hubbard and Wald (1997) for similar discussions of "geneticization."

14. A few federal laws may provide limited protections for genetic privacy. The Health Insurance Portability and Accountability Act of 1996 (HIPPA) prevents insurance companies from treating a predictive genetic test as a pre-existing condition. The Americans with Disability Act (ADA), while not mentioning genetic conditions specifically, may provide some limited protections against discrimination. See Jones, 1996. Weiner (1994) documents the history of congressional failure to prevent or control the negative effects of biomedical research. Though a number of genetic privacy and anti-discrimination laws have been put forward in the past 10 years, none has become law. See also Draper, 1999.

15. It is important to note that there is little evidence to date to support the notion that the public finds such laws reassuring. For example, a recent study of genetics counselors found that while privacy concerns were widespread among those who sought genetic counseling, testing decisions were based more on the urgency of the information sought or the psychological effects of testing on individuals and families rather than on privacy concerns (Hall and Rich, 2000).

References

Andrews, L. B. 1992. "The Body as Property: Some Philosophical Reflections—A Response to J.F. Childress." Transplantation Proceedings 24:5(October):2149-2151.

Andrews, L. B., and D. Nelkin. 2001. *Body Bazaar.* New York: Crown Publishers.

Annas, G. 1993. "Privacy Rules for DNA Databanks." *Journal of the American Medical Association* 270(17): 2346-50. Reprinted in *Genetics and Society,* Penelope Barker, ed., 100-112. New York: H.W. Wilson Company, 1995.

Annas, G. 1996. "Genetic Prophecy and Genetic Privacy." *Trial* 32(1): 18-25.

Annas, G. 2000. "Rules for Research on Human Genetic Variation—Lessons from Iceland." *New England Journal of Medicine* 342(24): 1830-1833.

Annas, G, L. Glantz, and P. Roche. 1995. *The Genetic Privacy Act and Commentary.* Boston University School of Public Health.

Appadurai, A. 1986. "Introduction: Commodities and the Politics of Value." In *The Social Life of Things: Commodities in Cultural Perspective,* A. Appadurai, ed., 3-63. Cambridge: Cambridge University Press.

Calvo, C. 2000. "Engineering Genetics Policy." *State Legislatures* 26:8(September): 28-31.

Childress, J. F. 1992. "The Body as Property: Some Philosophical Reflections." *Transplant Proceedings* 24:5(October): 2143-2148.

Clayton, E. W. 1998. "Informed Consent and Genetic Research." In *Genetic Secrets: Protecting Privacy and Confidentiality in the Genetic Era,* M.A. Rothstein, ed., New Haven: Yale University Press, 127-136.

Compton, M. 2000. "Genetic Turf Wars: Whose DNA is it Anyway? An Interview with George Annas." *DNA Dispatch* 1:2(September).

Condit, C. M. 1999. *The Meanings of the Gene.* Madison: The University of Wisconsin Press.

Congressional Digest. 2000a. "Medical Records Privacy" *Congressional Digest* 79:8/9(August/September): 193.

Congressional Digest. 2000b. "Legislative Background" *Congressional Digest* 79:8/9 (August/September): 201.

Davis and Hibbitts, Inc. 2000. "Geneforum Genetic Privacy Project Focus Group Report: A Qualitative Research Project for geneforum.org." (March), Davis and Hibbitts, Inc., Portland, OR.

De Witte, J. I., and H. Ten Have. 1997. "Ownership of Genetic Material and Information." *Social Science and Medicine* 45:1(1997):51-60.

Draper, E. 1999. "The Screening of America: The Social and Legal Framework of Employers' Use of Genetic Information." *Berkeley Journal of Employment and Labor Law* 20(2): 286-324.

Enserink, M. 1998. "Physicians Wary of Scheme to Pool Icelanders' Genetic Data." *Science* 281:5379(August 14):890-891.

Everett, M. 1999. "In My Opinion: Cells are not my son, but still deserve dignity." *Oregonian* (June 2).

Everett, M. 2004. "Can You Keep a (Genetic) Secret? The Genetic Privacy Movement." *Journal of Genetic Counseling* 13:4.

Finkler, K. 2000. *Experiencing the New Genetics: Family and Kinship on the Medical Frontier.* Philadelphia: University of Pennsylvania Press.

Fuller, B.P., et al. 1999. "Privacy in Genetic Research." *Science* 285 (27 August): 1359.

Gardner, J. 1999. "Outline of Testimony of James N. Gardner on Behalf of PhRMA in Support of Senate Bill 937." Oregon SB 937, Exhibit H, Senate Judiciary Committee.

Genetic Research Advisory Committee (GRAC). 2000. "Assuring Genetic Privacy in Oregon: The Report of the Genetic Research Advisory Committee." Oregon Health Plan Policy and Research.

Gold, E. R. 1996. *Body Parts: Property Rights and the Ownership of Human Biological Materials.* Washington, D.C.: Georgetown University Press.

Green, M., and J. Botkin. 2003. "'Genetic Exceptionalism' in Medicine: Clarifying the Differences between Genetic and Nongenetic Tests." *Annals of Internal Medicine* 138: 571-575.

Hall, M., and S. Rich. 2000. "Genetic Privacy Laws and Patients' Fear of Discrimination by Health Insurers: The View from Genetic Counselors." *Journal of Law, Medicine & Ethics* 28:3(Fall):245-258.

Heller, M., and R. Eisenberg. 1998. "Can Patents Deter Innovation? The Anticommons in Biomedical Research." *Science* 280(May 1): 698-701.

Holtzman, N. 1995. "The Attempt to Pass the Genetic Privacy Act in Maryland." *Journal of Law, Medicine and Ethics* 23: 367-70.

Howard, P. 2001. "With DNA protections, people own who they are." *Portland Tribune* (17 April).

Hubbard, R., and E. Wald. 1999. *Exploding the Gene Myth: How Genetic Information is Produced and Manipulated by Scientists, Physicians, Employers, Insurance Companies, Educators, and Law Enforcers.* Boston: Beacon Press.

Institute for Health Freedom. 2000. "Gallup Survey Finds Americans' Concerns About Medical Privacy Run Deep." September 26 (www.forhealthfreedom.com)

Johnson, A. M., D. S. Wilkinson, S. Taylor-Brown. 1999. "Genetic Testing: Policy Implications for Individuals and Their Families." *Families, Systems and Health* 17(1): 49-61.

Jones, N. 1996. "Genetic Information, Discrimination and Privacy Issues." Washington, D.C.: Congressional Research Service, Library of Congress.

Joralemon, D. 1995. "Organ Wars: The Battle for Body Parts." *Medical Anthropology Quarterly* 9(3):335-356.

Knoppers, B., M. Hirtie, and K. C. Glass. 1999. "Commercialization of Genetic Research and Public Policy." *Science* 286(17 December): 2277-2278.

Kopytoff, I. 1986. "The Cultural Biography of Things: Commoditization as Process." In *The Social Life of Things: Commodities in Cultural Perspective*, A. Appadurai, ed., 64-91. Cambridge: Cambridge University Press.

Lebacqz, K. 1994. "Genetic Privacy: No Deal for the Poor." *Dialog* 33(1): 39-48.

Lin, M. 1996. "Conferring a Federal Property Right in Genetic Material: Stepping into the Future with the Genetic Privacy Act." *American Journal of Law and Medicine* 22(1): 109-134.

Lippman, A. 1993. "Prenatal Genetic Testing and Geneticization: Mother Matters for All." *Fetal Diagnosis and Therapy* 8(Supp.1): 175-188.

Lloyd, E. 1994. "Normality and Variation: The Human Genome Project and the Ideal Human Type." In *Are Genes Us? The Social Consequences of the New Genetics*, Carl Cranor, ed. New Brunswick, NJ: Rutgers University Press, 99-112.

Lock, M., and N. Scheper-Hughes. 1987. "The Mindful Body." *Medical Anthropology Quarterly* 1(1): 6-41.

Lohr, F. 1999. "On Losing Your Molecular Privacy." *British Medical Journal* 7225(December 18): 1651-1652.

Longman, P. 2000. "The Genetic Surprise." *Wilson Quarterly* 24:4(Autumn): 40-50.

Markett, M. 1996. "Genetic Diaries: An Analysis of Privacy Protection in DNA Data Banks." *Suffolk University Law Review* 30(1): 185-226.

Martindale, D. 2001. "Pink Slip in Your Genes" *Scientific American* 284:1(January): 19-20.

McDaniels, A. 1998. "Brazil Mandates Organ 'Donation' for Transplants." *Christian Science Monitor* 90:36 (January 6): 1.

Merz, Jon. 2002. "Discoveries: Are There Limits on What May be Patented?" In *Who Owns Life*, David Magnus, Arthur Caplan, and Glenn McGee, eds. New York: Prometheus Books, 99-116.

Meyers, A. 2000. Letter from the President of the National Organization for Rare Disorders to Mark Nagumo, Commissioner of the USPTO regarding comments on the Revised Utility Examination and Written Description Guidelines (January 10).

Mulholland, W., and A. Jaeger. 1999. "Genetic Privacy and Discrimination: A Survey of State Legislation." *Jurimetrics* 39(Spring): 317-326.

Muller, J. 1994. "Anthropology, Bioethics, and Medicine: A Provocative Trilogy." *Medical Anthropology Quarterly* 8(4): 448-467.

Murray, T. 1999. "Genetic Exceptionalism and 'Future Diaries': Is Genetic Information Different from Other Medical Information?" In *Genetic Secrets*, Mark Rothstein, ed. 60-73. New Haven: Yale University Press.

Murray, R. F. 2001. "Social and Medical Implications of New Genetic Techniques." In *The Human Genome Project and Minority Communities*, R. Zilinskas and P. Balint, eds. Westport, CT: Praeger, 67-82.

Nader, C. 2000. Letter from the Chair of the Board of the Council for Responsible Genetics to Mark Nagumo, Commissioner of the USPTO regarding comments on the Revised Interim Guidelines for Examination of Patent Applications (March 20).

National Bioethics Advisory Commission (NBAC). 1999. "Research Involving Human Biological Materials: Ethical Issues and Policy Guidance." Rockville, MD: NBAC.

National Cancer Institute. 1999. State Cancer Legislative Database Program. Bethesda, MD.

National Conference of State Legislatures. 1999. "Genetic Testing Issues Statutory Chart." (June).

Office of Science and Technology Policy. 1991. "Federal Policy for the Protection of Human Subjects; Notices and Rules." Federal Register 56:117(June 18): 28002-28032.

Oregonians for Genetic Privacy. 2001. "Save Your Genetic Rights—Stop Oregon Senate Bill 114." http://www.angelfire.com/or2/genetics/OGI.html (5/9/01).

Onion, A. 2001. "Should You Own Your Genes?" abcNews.com (May 8) http://abcnews.go.com/sections/scitech/DailyNews/oregonlaw010507.html

Pálsson, G., and K. Harðardóttir. 2002. "For Whom the Cell Tolls: Debates about Biomedicine." *Current Anthropology* 43(2):271-301.

Parsons, E. 1997. "Culture and Genetics: Is Genetics in Society or Society in Genetics?" In *Culture, Kinship and Genes: Towards Cross-Cultural Genetics*, Angus Clarke and Evelyn Parsons, eds. New York: St. Martins Press, 245-260.

Paul, D. 1994. "Eugenic Anxieties, Social Realities, and Political Choices." In *Are Genes Us? The Social Consequences of the New Genetics*, Carl Cranor, ed. New Brunswick, NJ: Rutgers University Press, 142-154.

Popovich, B. 1999. "Testimony of Brad Popovich, Oregon Senate Judiciary Committee, March 30, 1999." Oregon SB 1008, Exhibit F, Senate Judiciary Committee.

Rabinow, P. 1999. *French DNA*. Chicago: University of Chicago Press.

Rao, R. 2000. "Property, Privacy, and the Human Body." *Boston University Law Review* 80 (341): 359-460.

Reilly, P. 1991. "Rights, Privacy, and Genetic Screening." *The Yale Journal of Biology and Medicine* 64(1): 43-45.

Reilly, P. 1995. "The Impact of the Genetic Privacy Act on Medicine." *Journal of Law, Medicine and Ethics* 23(4): 378-381.

Ridley, M. 1999. *Genome: The Autobiography of a Species in 23 Chapters*. New York: Harper Collins.

Rose, Hilary. 2003. "The Commodification of Virtual Reality: The Icelandic Health Sector Database." In *Genetic Nature/Culture*, Alan Goodman, Deborah Heath, and M. Susan Lindee, eds. Berkeley: University of California Press, 77-95.

Rothman, B. K. 1999. *The Book of Life: A Personal and Ethical Guide to Race, Normality, and the Implications of the Human Genome Project*. Boston: Beacon Press.

Sharp, L. 2000. "The Commodification of the Body and its Parts." *Annual Review of Anthropology* 29: 287-328.

Strathern. A. 1996. *Body Thoughts*. Ann Arbor: University of Michigan Press.

Stepanuk, N. 1998. "Genetic Information and Third Party Access to Information: New Jersey's Pioneering Legislation as a Model for Federal Privacy Protection of Genetic Information." *Catholic University Law Review* 47:3(Spring): 1105-45.

Suzuki, D., and P. Knudtson. 1989. *Genethics: The Clash Between the New Genetics and Human Values*. Cambridge, MA: Harvard University Press.

Troy, E. 1997. "The Genetic Privacy Act: An Analysis of Privacy and Research Concerns." *Journal of Law, Medicine and Ethics* 25(4): 256-72.

UNESCO. 2001. "Intellectual Property in the Field of the Human Genome." International Symposium: Ethics, Intellectual Property and Genomics. Paris.

Visco, F. 2000. Letter from the President of the National Breast Cancer Coalition to Mark Nagumo, Commissioner of the USPTO, regarding comments on the Revised Utility Examination and Written Description Guidelines (March 22).

Weiner, C. 1994. "Anticipating the Consequences of Genetic Engineering: Past, Present, and Future." In *Are Genes Us? The Social Consequences of the New Genetics*, Carl Cranor, ed. New Brunswick, NJ: Rutgers University Press, 31-51.

Whitehouse, D. 2001. "Genetically Altered Babies Born." *BBC News Online* (May 4): http://news.bbc.co.uk/hi/english/sci/tech/newsid_1312000/1312708.stm

Wilcox, A., et al. 1999. "Genetic Determinism and the Overprotection of Human Subjects." *Nature Genetics* 21(April):362.

Zilinskas, R., and P. Balint. 2001. *The Human Genome Project and Minority Communities: Ethical, Social and Political Dilemmas*. Westport, CT: Praeger.

Employee Monitoring:
Evaluative Surveillance v. Privacy*

ADAM D. MOORE

Introduction

Few would deny the profound impact, both positive and negative, that computers and digital technology are having in the modern workplace. Some of the benefits include safer working conditions, increased productivity, and better communication between employees, clients, and companies. The downside of this revolution can be tedious working conditions and the loss of privacy and autonomy. In the workplace there is a basic tension between surveillance technology and privacy. Companies want to monitor employees and reward effort, intelligence, productivity, and success while eliminating laziness, stupidity, theft, and failure. The market demands no less of most businesses. But against this pressure stands the individual within the walls of privacy—walls that protect against invasions into private domains.

Jeremy Bentham once envisioned a prison workhouse that placed overseers in a central tower with glass walled cells and mirrors placed so that inmates could never know if they were being watched.[1] The idea was that "universal transparency" would keep the prisoners on their best behavior. Recent developments in surveillance technology are promising to turn the workplace into the modern equivalent of Bentham's workhouse. There are now computer programs that allow employers to monitor and record the number of keystrokes per minute an employee completes. Employee badges may allow the recording of movements and time spent at different locations while working. There is now the possibility of monitoring voice mail, e-mail, and phone logs—and all without the knowledge or consent of those being watched. There are even global positioning systems that allow companies to track employee movements cross-country. While employers have always sought to monitor employees it is arguably the case that digital technology has changed the game, so to speak. For example, there are now computer programs that can search massive e-mail and voice data files for particular words and expressions. We may wonder, in a networked world, when this kind of surveillance technology will be used to monitor all of us? And not by just governments, although this Orwellian nightmare will be possible, but by our employers.

In this article I will address the tension between evaluative surveillance and privacy against the backdrop of the current explosion of information technology. More specifically, I will argue that knowledge of the different kinds of surveillance used at any given company should be made explicit to the employees. Moreover, there will be certain kinds of evaluative monitoring that violate privacy rights and should not be used in most cases. As we shall see, certain jobs may warrant a smaller domain of privacy. We should not conclude, however, that the arguments used in these cases are easily generalized.

Privacy[2]

I favor what has been called a "control" based definition of privacy (see pp. 181-85). That is, privacy has to do with control over access to oneself and to information about oneself.[3] William Parent has attacked "control" definitions of privacy arguing,

> All of these definitions should be jettisoned. To see why, consider the example of a person who voluntarily divulges all sorts of intimate, personal, and undocumented information about herself to a friend. She is doubtless exercising control . . . But we would not and should not say that in doing so she is preserving or protecting her privacy. On the contrary, she is voluntarily relinquishing much of her privacy. People can and do choose to give up privacy for many reasons. An adequate conception of privacy must allow for this fact. Control definitions do not.[4]

Parent is quick to add in a footnote that those who defend a control definition of privacy might be worried about a *right* to privacy rather than the *condition* of privacy.[5] He charged that, if so, they should have made this explicit and, in any case, are confusing a liberty right with a privacy right.

Parent's argument, however, is anemic. On these grounds we could complain that control definitions of property rights or life rights are similarly confused with liberty rights. Following Hohfeld and others, the root idea of a "right" can be expressed as follows:

> To say someone has a right is to say that there exists a state
> of affairs in which one person (the right-holder) has a claim
> on act or forbearance from another person (the duty-
> bearer) in the sense that, should the claim be exercised or in
> force, and the act or forbearance not be done, it would be
> justifiable, other things being equal, to use coercive meas-
> ures to extract either the performance required or compen-
> sation in lieu of that performance.[6]

This broad characterization holds of both moral rights and legal
rights.

Given this it should be clear that Parent's attack on control definitions is based on an overly simplistic account of rights. Ginger's
property right to a Louisville Slugger yields her a particular sort of
control over the baseball bat in question. It also justifiably limits the
liberty of everyone else—they cannot interfere with Ginger's control
of the bat without her consent. A liberty right is not a freedom to do
whatever one likes—it is not a license. Liberty rights, like property
rights, are limited by the rights of others. In the most basic terms,
rights, liberty, and control, come bundled together. When one gives
up control and yields access in an intimate relationship for example,
one is giving up privacy within a limited domain. Parent's attack
thus misses the mark.

Privacy may be understood as a right to control both tokens and
types. In terms of tokens, privacy yields control over access to one's
body, capacities, and powers. A privacy right in this sense is a right
to control access to a specific token or object. But we may also
control access to sensitive personal information about ourselves. In
this sense a privacy right affords control over types or ideas. For
example when a rape victim suppresses the dissemination of
sensitive personal information about herself, she is exercising a
right to control a set of ideas no matter what form they take. It does
not matter if the information in question is written, recorded,
spoken, or fixed in some other fashion.

In the most general terms, privacy is a culturally and species
relative right to a level of control over access to bodies and information. Normative claims surrounding control over access are relative
to culture and species. Judith Wagner DeCew argues that this sort
of definition fails because "if a police officer pushes one out of the
way of an ambulance, one has lost control of what is done to one,
but we would not say that privacy has been invaded. Not just any

touching is a privacy intrusion."[7] I think that this sort of attack is too quick. First, whether or not a privacy invasion will have occurred in a case of "touching" will depend on the privacy norms found within the culture in question. A right to control access may take many forms. Thus, one cannot refute this account by finding a single example where a loss of control over bodily access does not include a loss of privacy. Second, the case that DeCew presents may be an example of a slight privacy invasion being overridden by other more weighty considerations.

Given that I have already covered several arguments in favor of privacy rights (see pp. 183-85), I will briefly consider the claim that privacy is valuable. While privacy rights may entail obligations and claims against others—obligations and claims that are beyond the capacities of most non-human animals—a case can still be offered in support of the claim that separation is valuable for animals. Although privacy may be linked to freewill, the need for separation provides an evolutionary first step. It is this capacity of freewill that changes mere separation into privacy. Alan Westin in *Privacy and Freedom* notes,

> One basic finding of animal studies is that virtually all animals seek periods of individual seclusion of small-group intimacy. This is usually described as the tendency toward territoriality, in which an organism lays private claim to an area of land, water, or air and defends it against intrusion by members of its own species.[8]

More important for our purposes are the ecological studies demonstrating that a lack of private space, due to overpopulation and the like, will threaten survival. In such conditions animals may kill each other or engage in suicidal reductions of the population. Lemmings may march into the sea or there may be what is called a "biochemical die-off."

If it is plausible to maintain that humans evolved from non-human animals, then it is also plausible that we may retain many of the same traits. For example Lewis Mumford notes similarities between rat overcrowding and human overcrowding. "No small part of this ugly urban barbarization has been due to sheer physical congestion: a diagnosis now partly confirmed by scientific experiments with rats—for when they are placed in equally congested quarters, they exhibit the same symptoms of stress, alienation, hostility, sexual perversion, parental incompetence, and rabid violence that we now find in Megapolis."[9] If so, like other basic requirements for living, we may plausibly conclude that privacy is valuable.

If I am correct about all of this, then there is a fairly strong presumption in favor of individual privacy rights—even in the workplace. What justifies a photographer taking pictures of me about the house is my consent. Most would agree that absent such consent a serious violation of privacy would have occurred. Consent is also necessary, I will argue, for employee monitoring. But therein lies the problem. Under what conditions does consent or agreement yield the appropriate sort of permission? Alas the initial bargaining situation must be fair if we are to be morally bound by the outcome.

Privacy in the Workplace

We are now in a position to consider an individual's right to privacy in the context of a working environment where evaluative surveillance is both necessary and desirable. If pay increases, promotion, profit sharing awards, and incentive pay are to be based on effort, desert, and success, there must be acceptable methods of monitoring employees.

Consider the following case. In January 1990, Alana Shoars, an administrator for the electronic mail system at Epson America, Inc., discovered that the company was monitoring the e-mail messages of its employees. She was shown a batch of printouts of employee e-mail messages—messages that she thought were protected through the use of passwords. "I glanced over at some of the printouts, and a lot of warning bells went off in my head. As far as I'd known, as e-mail coordinator, it wasn't possible to do such a thing."[10] Upon criticizing this breach of employee privacy, Ms. Shoars was dismissed from the company for insubordination.[11]

This case represents only the tip of the iceberg with respect to employee monitoring. A survey of companies in *Macworld* concerning electronic monitoring "reported that 21.6 percent of the 301 participating companies admitted searching employee files, including electronic work files (73.8 percent), e-mail (41.5 percent), network messages (27.7 percent) and voice mail (15.4 percent)."[12] And even more alarming, only 30.8 percent of the companies surveyed gave advance warning of the monitoring activities.

In the most general terms, the case of Alana Shoars and e-mail monitoring highlights the tension between rights to control information and individual privacy in the workplace. What was objectionable with Epson America's monitoring was not their wish to control the information that was found on the company's computer network. The objection is that their employees were not notified of the monitoring nor were they notified of the strict company policy forbidding personal use of the network.

Epson argued that the system was company-owned and therefore any information found in e-mail accounts, private or otherwise, was justifiably available for inspection. Moreover, it could be argued that notification of surveillance was both unnecessary and unwise from a corporate perspective. If each instance of monitoring was known to an employee, then the data collected would be almost worthless. It would be like telling the fakes to start faking.

Thin Consent

Justifying employee monitoring in light of privacy rights begins with what I call thin consent. A first step in justifying a kind of monitoring is employee notification. The consent takes the following form: if your employment is to continue then you must agree to such-and-so kinds of surveillance. This is appropriately called "thin consent" because it is assumed that jobs are hard to find, the employee in question needs the job, etc. Nevertheless, quitting is a viable option. The force of such agreements or contracts is echoed by Ronald Dworkin.

If a group contracted in advance that disputes amongst them would be settled in a particular way, the fact of that contract would be a powerful argument that such disputes should be settled in that way when they do arise. The contract would be an argument in itself, independent of the force of the reasons that might have led different people to enter the contract. Ordinarily, for example, each of the parties supposes that a contract he signs is in his own interest; but if someone has made a mistake in calculating his self-interest, the fact that he did contract is a strong reason for the fairness of holding him nevertheless to the bargain.[13]

An employee cannot consent, even thinly, to a type of monitoring if it is unknown to her. Given a fairly strong presumption in favor of privacy, thin consent would seem obligatory. Here the employee would be notified of each different type of monitoring. Individual acts of surveillance, however, would not require notification — thus slackers would not be notified to stop slacking.

Moreover, a thin consent policy for each different type of surveillance allows companies and businesses to seize the moral high ground in one important respect. There is no sneaking around riffling through office files, midnight program installations, or hidden backdoor keys into e-mail accounts. All of this up front and in the open. Part of what makes this kind of employee monitoring distasteful is the deceit involved. Locked voice-mail accounts, e-mail files, and desk drawers present the air of privacy when these domains are anything but private.

In any case it should be clear that thin consent is not enough to justify the array of monitoring systems that are now possible or will soon be possible—not in every case. When jobs are scarce, unemployment high, and government assistance programs swamped, thin consent becomes thin indeed. In these conditions employees will be virtually forced to relinquish privacy because of the severe consequences if they don't. But notice what happens when we slide to the other extreme. Assume a condition of negative unemployment where there are many more jobs than employees and where changing jobs is relatively easy. In circumstances such as these, thin consent has become quite thick. And if employees were to agree to a certain type of monitoring in these favorable conditions most would think it justified.

As we slide from one extreme to the other—from a pro-business environment (lots of workers and few jobs yields low wage overhead) to a pro-employee environment (lots of jobs and few workers yields high employee compensation)—this method of justification becomes more plausible. What begins looking like a necessary condition ends up looking like a sufficient condition. To determine the exact point where thin consent becomes thick enough to bear the justificatory burden required is a difficult matter. The promise of actual consent depends on the circumstances. Minimally, if the conditions favor the employee then it is plausible to maintain that actual consent would be enough to override a presumption in favor of privacy.

Hypothetical Thick Consent

As noted above, thick consent is possible when employment conditions minimize the costs of finding a comparable job for an employee. Put another way, an employee who doesn't have to work, but agrees to anyway, has given the right kind of consent—assuming of course they have been notified of the different types of monitoring that will occur. What justifies a certain type of surveillance is that it would be agreeable to a worker in a pro-employee environment. If thin consent is obtained and the test of hypothetical thick consent is met, then we have reason to think that a strong presumption in favor of privacy has been justifiably surpassed.

We will also have to assume that the hypothetical worker making the choice is modestly interested in maintaining control over private information. If this constructed individual has nothing to hide and a general attitude of openness, then any type of surveillance will pass the test. And if I am correct about the importance of privacy with respect to sovereignty and autonomy, anyone would be interested in retaining such control. Rawls' notion of placing individuals behind a veil of ignorance may be of some service here.[14] If the individual agreeing did not know whether she was a worker, manager, or owner and if we assume that anyone would be interested in retaining control over private domains, then the correct vantage point for determining binding agreements will have been attained.

The force of hypothetical contracts has been called into question by Dworkin and others—"A hypothetical contract is not simply a pale form of an actual contract; it is no contract at all."[15] Here I agree with Dworkin. The moral bindingness of hypothetical contracts has to do with the reasons for why we would choose to do this or that. Viewing it this way, hypothetical contracts are simply devices that enable us to more clearly understand the reasons, moral or otherwise, for adopting a particular institution or process. Dworkin notes,

> There must be reasons, of course, why I would have agreed if asked in advance, and these may also be reasons why it is fair to enforce these rules against me even if I have not agreed. But my hypothetical consent does not count as a reason, independent of these other reasons, for enforcing the rules against me, as my actual agreement would have.[16]

Thus the test of hypothetical thick consent can be understood as a way of clarifying, and allowing us to arrive at, a position that is fair and sensible. Hereafter, when I talk of hypothetical consent and the moral force of such agreements, be aware that this is simply a tool or device that is notifying us when privacy rights may be justifiably relaxed.

Taking up the Epson case again, we may ask if a policy of e-mail monitoring would satisfy the test of hypothetical thick consent. Here we are to imagine a world where there were numerous jobs like the ones found at Epson and that moving to these other jobs would be relatively easy. Moreover, given that there is no industry-wide interest in monitoring e-mail activity, many of these other positions would not include e-mail monitoring. If an employee would not agree under these conditions, then this type of surveillance would fail the test. Had Epson notified its employees of a company e-mail monitoring policy, then those employees who stayed on at Epson would have given thin consent. But we should not rush to judge that such a policy would be automatically justified unless the test hypothetical thick consent is also met. Meeting this latter test in the Epson case seems unlikely.

I take a virtue of hypothetical thick consent to be that satisfaction is determined by imagining a pro-employee situation and then asking what an employee would do in the face of some kind of surveillance. Some may charge that I am stacking the deck however. Why not imagine a pro-business situation and then ask what an employee would do. We wouldn't have to do much imagining though, and employee consent in such conditions wouldn't justify anything. Moreover, if I am correct in positing privacy rights for each of us, then the deck is already stacked. There is a presumption in favor of individuals having control over personal information—we have privacy rights. Since employee surveillance may cross into private domains, we must consider under what conditions a privacy right may be given up or relaxed. In relatively few cases is thin consent thick enough to handle the justificatory burden. Hence, the use of hypothetical thick consent. We are imagining a case where the bargaining situation favors the employee—and if agreement is offered in these conditions, then we may have binding consent.

Note that even in a pro-employee environment there would be certain kinds of employee monitoring that would be necessary for any business. Punching a time clock or measuring time spent working, for example, would occur in almost any business or company. Even in a pro-employee market theft would have to be minimized. It is not as if McDonalds would become so desperate for workers that they would leave the register drawers open, allow employees to come and go as they please, and continue to pay wages. The market demands that businesses make a profit or at least break even. Given this, there will be certain kinds of employee monitoring that every business will use.

Moreover, there will be employment specific monitoring as well. For example trucking companies will have to monitor driving records and ensure that drivers maintain the appropriate skills needed to operate the big rigs. This kind of surveillance may be required by the market or by legislation of one kind or another. There may be laws that require certain licenses that make businesses liable for noncompliance. Absent laws or other government regulation, market efficiency may require certain kinds of monitoring. An example of the latter may be employee time monitoring. The hypothetical or constructed truck driver, no matter where he goes, will be subject to certain kinds of monitoring. So, even in a pro-employee environment certain kinds of surveillance will be justified—those kinds that are necessary for doing business.

So far I have been pursuing a kind of top-down strategy in presenting certain principles and considering arguments that may be marshaled to support these principles. If I am correct, thin consent will justify certain kinds of monitoring when employment conditions favor the employee. Absent such conditions actually occurring, we can imagine what an employee would choose if she were in a pro-employee environment. If she would agree to a type of monitoring from this vantage point—either because, every business in her field will monitor in the way she is considering or she just simply agrees (maybe because the new monitoring policy will benefit her in some way)—then the monitoring is permitted. In the next section I will pursue a bottom-up strategy by presenting certain cases and then examining how the proposed model fits with these cases and our intuitions about them.

Test Cases and Illustrations

Let us begin with an easy one first. Suppose that one day an employee is approached by his boss and is informed that the company will be moving to a new building. Excited about the new digs the employee tours the recently constructed office and is quite dismayed. It seems that management has been reading Bentham's *Panopticon* and the site has been built so that employee cubicles can be monitored by an overseer who can't himself be seen. The video cameras found in the new office have been placed so that computer screens can be watched as well as facial expressions, body motions, and the like. The employee complains and asks what conceivable purpose such a system could have at an insurance company. Management replies that only someone with something to hide would object and this system of monitoring will allow hard workers to be recognized and fairly compensated.

We may now ask if such a monitoring system is justified in relation to hypothetical thick consent. I think it is clear that an individual who is modestly interested in protecting privacy and in a pro-employee environment would leave, other things being equal, and find similar employment elsewhere. The "other things being equal" exception is important because if management were to double employee salaries then maybe a deal could be made—no privacy at work for lots of cash.[17] Outside of such offers the presumption in favor of privacy rights would not have been surpassed for this type of surveillance.

Before moving on, I would like to briefly address the kinds of replies that were offered for why employees shouldn't oppose this kind of monitoring. First, that an employee should have nothing to hide is irrelevant. It is her private life that is being monitored and so it is up to her to deny access. Whether or not she has something to hide is nobody's business. We all may have perfectly normal bedroom lives and have nothing to hide in this area. Nevertheless, mounting a company video camera and wake-up siren on the bedroom wall cannot in the least bit be supported by such reasons. Employee benefit is equally, and for the same reasons, dubious.

Consider a different case. Suppose in an effort to eliminate "time theft" a company begins using "active badges" that monitor employee movements while at work. These badges are sophisticated enough to monitor time spent in a specific area. So, employees who linger in the break-room, arrive late, leave early, and stroll the halls, will be discovered and treated accordingly.

Few would deny that time monitoring is a necessary part of any business. Nevertheless, there will be more and less invasive ways to monitor time. Bentham's Panopticon with a time overseer is one of the more invasive methods. Given that there are various less invasive ways to obtain this information about employees, it would seem that a constructed individual interested in maintaining private domains would not agree to this type of surveillance. Thus for most companies such a policy would be unjustified. There may be exceptions however. For example the U.S. Pentagon, Arms R&D departments, and the like, may have to maintain this level of monitoring to ensure secrecy. Monitoring college professors in this way is clearly unjustifiable.

A final case, that I would like to discuss, deals with remote computer monitoring. The case is provided by John Whalen.

> A recent ad for Norton-Lambert's Close-Up/LAN software package tempted managers to "look in on Sue's computer screen. . . . Sue doesn't even know you're there!". . . these "remote monitoring" capabilities, . . . allow network administrators to peek at an employee's screen in real time, scan data files and e-mail at will, tabulate keystroke speed and accuracy, overwrite passwords, and even seize control of a remote workstation. Products like Dynamics Corp.'s Peak and Spy; Microcom Inc.'s LANlord; Novell Inc.'s Net Ware; and Neon Software's NetMinder not only improve communications and productivity, they turn employees' cubicles into covert listening stations.[18]

While this kind of employee monitoring may yield some benefits the preponderance of the evidence would suggest otherwise. Some studies have shown that these monitoring systems produce fear, resentment, and elevate stress levels.[19] Another study concluded that "the introduction of computerized performance monitoring may result in a workplace that is less satisfying to many employees . . . [and] creates a more competitive environment which may decrease the quality of social relationships."[20]

Putting aside the unsavory consequences we may ask if such monitoring passes either test under consideration. First the test of thin consent would not be passed if the employees being monitored were not notified of such practices. Given the absence of a clear pro-employee environment in most industries that would use such surveillance, even if employees were notified the consent would seem too thin. Moreover, remote computer monitoring would fail the test of hypothetical thick consent for most companies. Individuals who did not know if they were the owner, manager, or employee would not agree to such privacy invasions. The presumption in favor of privacy would thus remain intact.

Conclusion

As noted in the opening, high tech surveillance is promising to turn the modern workplace into an Orwellian nightmare achieving

Bentham's ideal workhouse for prisoners—"universal transparency." And even if such monitoring somehow produced an overall net increase in utility, it would still be unjustifiable. Sometimes the consequences be damned. Not that I think generally good consequences could be had from such surveillance. Arguably, human beings are the most productive and creative in conditions completely opposite than those found in Bentham's *Panopticon*.

In this article I have argued that individuals have rights to privacy that shield us from the prying eyes and ears of neighbors, governments, and corporations—electronic eyes and ears are no more welcome. If we begin with a fairly strong presumption in favor of privacy and test different types of employee monitoring with thin and hypothetical thick consent, many currently used kinds of surveillance will be unjustified. Arguably this consent is necessary and sufficient for overriding or relaxing privacy rights with respect to employee monitoring.[21] We will each spend at least a quarter of our lives and a large part of our most productive years at work. This environment should be constructed to promote creative and productive activity while maintaining the zones of privacy that we all cherish. Although privacy rights are not absolute, it would seem that in a networked world filled with devices that may be used to capture information about each of us we should take privacy invasions—whether at home, on a public street, or in the workplace—much more seriously.

Notes

*Copyright, *Business Ethics Quarterly* Vol. 10 (July 2000): 697. I would like to thank Kimberly Moore, Scott Rothwell, and an anonymous reviewer at *Business Ethics Quarterly* for their suggestions and comments.

1. J. Bentham, *Panopticon* (The Inspection House), originally published in 1791.

2. Part of this section on privacy was originally published in "Privacy: Its Meaning and Value," *American Philosophical Quarterly* 40 (2003): 215-227.

3. See also, Anita Allen, *Why Privacy Isn't Everything: Feminist Reflections on Personal Accountability* (Lanham, MD: Rowman & Littlefield 2003) and Ruth Gavison, "Information Control: Availability and Control" *Public and Private in Social Life*, Benn, Stanley and G. Gaus eds. (New York: St. Martin's Press, 1983), p. 113-134; Charles Fried, *An Anatomy of Values* (Cambridge, MA: Harvard University Press, 1970) Cha. 9; Richard Wasserstrom, "Privacy: Some Assumptions and Arguments," *Philosophical Law*, R. Bronaugh ed. (Westport, CT: Greenwood Press, 1979), p. 148; Hyman Gross, "Privacy and Autonomy," *Privacy: Nomos XIII* (1971), p. 170; Ernest Van Den Haag, "On Privacy," *Privacy: Nomos XIII* (1971), p. 147; and Richard Parker, "A Definition of Privacy," *Rutgers Law Review* 27 (1974): 280.

4. Parent, "Privacy, Morality, and the Law," *Philosophy and Public Affairs* 12 (1983): 273.

5. Ibid., 273 n11.

6. Lawrence Becker, *Property Rights, Philosophic Foundations* (London: Routledge & Kegan Paul 1977). Hohfeld distinguishes four types of rights, claim-rights, liberty-rights, power-rights, and immunity-rights. See W. N. Hohfeld, "Fundamental Legal Conceptions," *Yale Law Journal* (New Haven, Yale University Press, 1919).

7. See DeCew *In Pursuit of Privacy: Law, Ethics, and the Rise of Technology* (Ithaca and London: Cornell University Press, 1997), p. 53.

8. Westin, *Privacy and Freedom* (New York: Atheneum, 1968), p. 8.

9. Lewis Mumbord, *The City in History* (New York: Harcourt Brace, 1961), p. 210 cited in Theodore D. Fuller, et al. "Chronic Stress and Psychological Well-being: Evidence from Thailand on Household Crowding," *Social Science Medicine*, 42 (1996): 267. This view is echoed by Desmond Morris who writes, "Each kind of animal has evolved to exist in a certain amount of living space. In both the animal zoo and the human zoo [when] this space is severely curtailed . the consequences can be serious." D. Morris, *The Human Zoo* (New York: McGraw Hill, 1969), p. 39.

10. IDG Communications, Inc., *Infoworld* (October 22, 1990), quoted in Anne Wells Branscomb in *Who Owns Information?* (New York: Basic Books, 1994), 92.

11. Alana Shoars filed a wrongful termination suit. "The lower court agreed with Epson's lawyer that neither state privacy statutes nor federal statutes address confidentiality of E-mail in the workplace and dismissed the case." Branscomb, *Who Owns Information?*, 93. See *Alana Shoars v. Epson America, Inc.*, No. SWC112749 (L.A. Super. Ct. 1990).

12. Branscomb, *Who Owns Information?*, 93.

13. Ronald Dworkin, *Taking Rights Seriously* (Cambridge: Harvard University Press, 1977) reprinted in James Sterba, *Justice: Alternative Political Perspectives*, 3rd edition (Belmont Wadsworth Publishing, 1999), 126 (all page references refer to the reprint).

14. J. Rawls, *A Theory of Justice* (Cambridge: Harvard University Press, 1971), 136-142.

15. Dworkin, *Taking Rights Seriously*, 126-27.

16. Ibid., 127.

17. Employment agreements grant rights, powers, liberties, and duties to both parties. Thus an employee may trade privacy for some kind of compensation like time off or the opportunity to learn. When trade offs such as these have occurred we may take the obligations, generated by the agreement, as prima facie—alas, the agreement may have been brokered in unfair conditions. If I am correct, fairness of conditions and binding agreements that justifiably relax rights are guaranteed when the tests of thin and hypothetical thick consent are passed.

18. J. Whalen, "You're Not Paranoid: They Really Are Watching You," *Wired Magazine* (March 1995).

19. Richard Spinello's *Ethical Aspects of Information Technology* (Englewood Cliffs, NJ: Prentice Hall, 1995), 128.

20. R. H. Irving, C. A. Higgins, and F. R. Safayeni, "Computerized Performance Monitoring Systems: Use and Abuse," *Communications of the ACM* (August, 1986): 800.

21. I take consequentialist concerns to be factored into laws or market demands. That is, hypothetical thick consent includes utility maximization arguments for requiring licenses, safety regulations, and the like.

Personal Autonomy and Caller ID

JAMES STACEY TAYLOR

In July 1987 the New Jersey Bell Telephone Company introduced the Caller Identification service to the United States.[1] This service allowed its subscribers to identify who was calling them on the telephone before answering it, thus enabling them to avoid answering the telephone when called by persons they did not wish to speak to, such as telephone marketers or creditors. The opportunity to monitor and select who one talked to on the telephone in this way was so attractive to telephone subscribers that within a decade the "Caller ID" service was offered by many different companies, with almost half of the telephone subscribers in the United States and Canada using it.[2] In addition to being a commercial success, the various Caller ID services on offer were also held by their proponents to be an *ethical* success, insofar as they were enhancing the privacy of their subscribers, providing them with "the hope of blocking . . . [a] route through which even the most rank stranger can electronically invade the privacy of a home."[3]

The privacy-related ethical advantages that are claimed for Caller ID services are important—and not only because privacy is a central value in contemporary Western life. Like other new information technologies (such as databases, new surveillance devices, and genetic screening techniques), Caller ID services are subject to a great deal of moral condemnation. Those who are opposed to Caller ID services claim that their use would decrease, rather than increase, the overall amount of privacy that is enjoyed by persons within the society in which they are used, by rendering it impossible to make anonymous telephone calls.[4] This concern is especially pertinent for persons who might have very good reasons for placing anonymous calls, such as those who wish to provide tips to hotlines dealing with criminal cases, or those who might wish to call a telephone-based counseling service, such as the Samaritans. Concerns about the privacy of persons making telephone calls are also expressed by some who worry that businesses might refuse to answer telephone calls from persons calling from an area code associated with a geographical area that is inhabited by the poor or by ethnic minorities.[5] The official bodies responsible for regulating the telecommunications industry take these concerns very seriously. For example, in Australia these concerns led to long delays in the implementation of Caller ID services, and telecommunications companies were required to address these issues by subsidizing public education campaigns about the ethical issues raised by the use of Caller ID.[6]

The question of whether Caller ID services enhance or diminish personal privacy has been thoroughly covered in the literature that addresses the ethical implications of such services.[7] What has not been so widely addressed, however, is the question of whether Caller ID services would enhance or diminish the ability of persons to exercise their autonomy. Given that personal autonomy is, like privacy, one of the primary moral values in contemporary Western society, this oversight is surprising, for if it can be shown that Caller ID services would enhance the ability of persons to exercise their autonomy, this would be a significant point in the services' favor. On the other hand, if it can be shown that Caller ID services diminish the ability of persons to exercise their autonomy, this would be an equally significant strike against them. In this paper, I will address the issue of whether Caller ID services enhance or diminish the ability of individuals to exercise their autonomy, arguing that respect for personal autonomy should favor the provision of such services. I will not, however, argue that Caller ID services will enhance a persons' ability to exercise their autonomy by providing them with more options from which to choose. Despite the elegance and simplicity of such an autonomy-based argument for Caller ID, I argue that this approach to defending this service is seriously flawed. This is because it is based on a misunderstanding of the relationship between one's autonomy and the expansion of one's option set. Insofar as the arguments in this paper address the broader issue of the relationship between autonomy and options, they will be of interest not only to persons concerned with the ethical implications of Caller ID, but to all who are concerned with the concept of autonomy as it applies within the field of information ethics.

An Autonomy-Based Argument for Caller ID

It is easy to see why persons who hold Caller ID to be morally permissible could defend it on the grounds that it enhances one's ability to exercise autonomy. The term "autonomy" stems from the Greek words "autos" (self) and "nomos" (rule). Taking etymology seriously, then, a person enjoys autonomy with respect to his actions when he performs them as a result of "ruling himself." That is, he enjoys autonomy with respect to his actions when he acts under his own direction, rather than that of another. In the West, personal autonomy, or individual self-rule, is held to be of great moral importance—indeed, some writers claim that autonomy is a "super value" that is prior to all others.[8] Since this is so, anything that enhances a person's ability to exercise his autonomy has a prima facie claim to be not only morally permissible, but morally laudable. And since to provide a person with more options would be to provide him with more ways to exercise his autonomy, then it seems that increasing a person's set of options would be morally praiseworthy from the point of view of one who holds autonomy to be of great moral value. Thus, insofar as the introduction of optional Caller ID services will provide persons with an increased range of options (they can now choose to subscribe to this service, or not; they can now choose to answer the telephone when they know who is calling, or not), it seems that respect for their autonomy should support the view that Caller ID services are morally permissible—and even morally laudable.

Autonomy and Options

Yet despite its intuitive appeal, this autonomy-based argument for the ethical value of Caller ID services is deeply flawed. It is simply not true that providing a person with more options will enhance their ability to exercise autonomy. The mere fact that the introduction of the option to subscribe to a Caller ID service would expand a person's range of options does not show that one's ability to exercise autonomy is thereby enhanced. There are two reasons why the expansion of options does not correlate with the enhancement of a person's ability to exercise autonomy.

First, the degree to which a person enjoys the exercise of autonomy is in no way correlated to the range of options available. This can be readily shown. A person's choice set might, for example, be provided with many additional options, but these may be options that he or she has no interest in acting upon. Since such options would not affect this person's actions or decisions in any positive way (that is, these options will not enable one to better direct one's actions in pursuit of a desired outcome), they would not enable their recipient to exercise autonomy to a greater degree than before.[9]

The second reason why the mere expansion of a person's options does not necessarily enhance their ability to exercise autonomy is more troubling. Providing a person with more options might, in some cases, neither enhance their ability to exercise autonomy nor be neutral with respect to it, but instead actually serve to *diminish* it. An option that produces such a deleterious effect on the ability to exercise autonomy is termed a "constraining option."

Such constraining options are of two types. The first type, which I shall term "exclusionary constraining options," are those whose existence in a choice set excludes a person from pursuing other options that might otherwise have been pursued. If the presence of this type of constraining option excludes people from directing their actions as they would have preferred, such a constraining option would compromise, rather than enhance, the ability to exercise autonomy. Richard Titmuss, for example, argues that the addition of the option to sell blood into a society where previously blood had only been procured through altruistic donation was an exclusionary constraining option of this sort.[10] This is because, Titmuss argues, the introduction of the option of *selling* blood necessarily excluded the option of altruistically *donating* blood in a situation in which it could not be bought. As such, argues Titmuss, the introduction of the option of selling blood would compromise the autonomy of those persons who wanted to donate "priceless" blood—that is, those who wanted to donate blood in a situation in which it could not be bought. The second sort of constraining option, which I shall term "potentially compromising constraining options," are those which are likely to lead to a future compromising of the autonomy of the person who chooses them. Paul Hughes argues that the option to refrain from pressing charges against one's assailant in a domestic violence case is an example of this sort of option.[11] This is because, Hughes argues, a person who is subjected to domestic violence is in an autonomy-compromising situation. If one pursues the option not to press charges, it is likely that this would result in one's continuing to be in the autonomy-undermining abusive situation. Thus, according to Hughes, the option not to press charges is an option that, if pursued, is likely to lead to a failure to escape from the situation in which autonomy was compromised.

Caller ID as an Exclusionary Constraining Option

Given that increasing options would not necessarily enhance a person's ability to exercise autonomy (indeed, such an expansion might even decrease a person's ability to exercise autonomy), the mere fact that the existence of Caller ID increases the number of options available to potential subscribers does not in itself show that the offer of this service is likely to enhance their autonomy. To show that the option of subscribing to a Caller ID service does enhance a person's ability to exercise autonomy, the proponent of the above autonomy-based argument in favor of Caller ID must show that the option of subscribing to Caller ID is both desirable and also not a constraining option.

It is easy to show that the option of having Caller ID satisfies the first of these conditions: That over half of the telephone subscribers in Canada and the United States chose to subscribe to Caller ID within a decade of its introduction clearly shows that this is an option that a significant number of persons wish to pursue. It is also easy to show that the option to subscribe to Caller ID is not a potentially compromising constraining option: the choice to subscribe to Caller ID in no way limits a person's future ability to exercise autonomy. Alas, even though the option to subscribe to Caller ID is not a potentially compromising constraining option, it *is* an exclusionary constraining option.

Recall that an exclusionary constraining option is one that, if offered, would necessarily exclude some other option from the choice set of the persons to whom it is offered. When Caller ID is offered to a population, this necessarily excludes from its option set the possibility of making a telephone call in a situation where all calls are made anonymously. This is not to claim that the option to subscribe to Caller ID excludes the possibility of persons making anonymous telephone calls. This is not true, for persons can still make anonymous calls—even to persons who subscribe to Caller ID—by using, for example, pre-paid cell phones, public call boxes, or telephone technology that hides the caller's number from the call's recipient.[12] Rather, claiming that Caller ID precludes persons from making telephone calls in a situation where all calls are made anonymously is to claim that, in a situation where Caller ID is available, the *nature* of one's telephone call would be changed from the situation in which Caller ID was not available. This would be so even if one took steps to preserve one's anonymity: one would no longer be making a telephone call that was, with respect to its anonymity, on par with all other telephone calls. Instead, in a situation where persons had the option of using Caller ID, one's anonymous telephone call would be in a *special* class of telephone calls that did not exist prior to the introduction of Caller ID— namely, telephone calls whose callers might have deliberately decided to hide their identity from the person they are calling.

The introduction of Caller ID is thus an exclusionary constraining option, for its introduction into the option set of a population automatically eliminates another option that the population previously had. Since this is so, the original autonomy-based pro-Caller ID argument outlined above does *not* show that allowing persons to have the option to subscribe to a Caller ID service is required out of respect for their autonomy. Since the option to subscribe to a Caller ID service is an exclusionary constraining option, it might be the case that its introduction into the option set of a population would overall *diminish* rather than *enhance* the population members' ability to exercise their autonomy.

Some Clarifications

To show that respect for autonomy still requires that persons be afforded the opportunity to subscribe to a Caller ID service if they wish, the concept of an exclusionary constraining option must be clarified. Unlike a potentially compromising constraining option, an exclusionary constraining option is not likely to lead to a diminution in the autonomy of the person who chooses it. Instead, an exclusionary constraining option is an option that, if available to the members of a group, would compromise the autonomy of some who, as a result of its introduction, would be unable to exercise their autonomy by pursuing the option that the exclusionary constraining option eliminated. This would be the case irrespective of whether or not any member of the group actually chose to pursue the exclusionary constraining option in question. Furthermore, an exclusionary constraining option is not likely to compromise the autonomy of those who chose it. Instead, such an option serves to compromise the autonomy of those who are *not* likely to choose it, for it is these persons whose preferred option would have been eliminated by the introduction of the exclusionary constraining option.

With these clarifications in hand, two further (and interrelated) points must be made prior to considering what conclusions can be drawn from the fact that the option to subscribe to Caller ID is an exclusionary constraining option. First, a distinction must be made between a person who suffers from *compromised autonomy* and a person for whom the *instrumental value of autonomy* has been compromised. The former suffers from a diminution in self-direction, self-rule. A person who is, for example, coerced into performing an action that, absent the coercion, she would not perform suffers from a diminution in autonomy to the extent that it is not she, but her coercer, who is directing the performance. By contrast, people who suffer from a *diminution in the value of their autonomy* need not suffer from any loss of self-direction or self-rule. Instead, they are simply unable to exercise their autonomy as they would prefer to exercise it. For example, a person who wished to be a champion jockey but weighed four hundred pounds would be unable to exercise their autonomy as they wished, since they would be unable to pursue their chosen career. As such, their being an autonomous person, a person capable of directing their own life free from the direction of others, would have diminished instrumental value to the extent that they would be unable to use their autonomy to achieve desired goals.

Having clearly distinguished between a person suffering from compromised autonomy per se and a person suffering from a diminution in the instrumental value of autonomy, one can move to make the second point. A person who holds autonomy to be of great moral value would be more concerned with a person suffering from compromised autonomy per se than with a person who suffers from a diminution in the *value* of autonomy. This is because in the former case autonomy itself is lost, whereas in the latter no autonomy need be lost (i.e., the person need not suffer from any compromise of autonomy per se); there is only a diminution in the instrumental value of the autonomy of the person in question.

The Effects on Autonomy of Allowing or Banning Caller ID

With this clarification of the nature of exclusionary constraining options and the above two points in hand, it is now possible to show that the mere fact that the option of subscribing to Caller ID is an exclusionary constraining option does *not* show that respect for autonomy militates against allowing persons to have this option.

Recall that if the option to subscribe to Caller ID services is allowed, it would be an exclusionary constraining option because some members of the group to whom this option will be offered would, as a result of its offering, be unable to exercise their autonomy (that is, they would be unable to place telephone calls in a situation where all such calls were anonymous). With the above distinctions in place, it is clear that this inability would not *compromise* their autonomy, for it would not make them any less able to direct their acts than they were prior to the introduction of this service. Instead, it would make their autonomy *less valuable* for them, for they would now be unable to direct themselves in the way that they wanted to. However, although the instrumental value of the autonomy of this subgroup of persons would be diminished, the instrumental value of the autonomy of the subgroup of persons who wishes to subscribe to such a Caller ID service would be enhanced. If, on the other hand, the option to subscribe to a Caller ID service were prohibited, the persons who wished to place telephone calls in a situation where all calls were anonymous would be able to exercise their autonomy as they wished (at least in this sphere of their lives). They would thus suffer no diminution in the value of their autonomy. On the other hand, those who would have wanted to subscribe would not be able to exercise their autonomy as they wished, and so the value of their autonomy would be diminished. (Similarly, those who wished to offer such a service would also have the value of their autonomy diminished as a result of its prohibition.)

Banning Caller ID, Coercion, and Compromised Autonomy

One might be led by this brief discussion to think that the issue of whether respect for autonomy requires that persons be allowed access to such a service simply hinges on the number of persons who wanted this and the number of persons who didn't, with the aim of the decision of whether or not to prohibit such services being to maximize the instrumental value of the autonomy possessed by the persons that this decision affects. If this were so, then it seems that respect for autonomy would require that persons be allowed to subscribe to Caller ID services, at least in the United States and Canada, since over half of the telephone users in those countries have subscribed. Moreover, of those persons who did not subscribe, it is likely that only a minority wish to place telephone calls in a situation where calls are anonymous; the rest of the non-subscribers are likely to have little interest in whether or not their telephone calls are placed anonymously.

The situation is, however, more complicated—although in a way that further shows that respect for autonomy militates in favor of allowing persons the option to subscribe to Caller ID. If Caller ID services were to be prohibited, then in addition to having the instrumental value of their autonomy diminished, the persons who would be prevented from subscribing to such a service would also suffer from having their autonomy compromised. This is because those who prohibit Caller ID services would impose penalties (such as fines or prison time) on persons who offer them or subscribe to them. These are coercive measures. As such, if these threatened penalties are effective in preventing persons from offering or subscribing to Caller ID services, they will have caused persons who would have otherwise offered or subscribed to these services to direct their actions so that they are in accord with the desires of those persons who wanted such services prohibited. That is, the threatened penalties would be severe enough to lead those persons who would have otherwise offered or purchased Caller ID services to cede a degree of control over their actions in this sphere of their lives to the persons who enact the prohibitions.[13] To the extent that persons who would have otherwise offered or subscribed to a Caller ID service do this, they are no longer behaving in a self-directed and autonomous way, but rather heteronomously. Their autonomy with respect to Caller ID-related actions would thus be compromised. Since this is so, the issue of whether or not to allow persons to offer or subscribe to Caller ID services cannot be settled merely by deciding on the degree to which the *instrumental value* of the autonomy of the persons in the affected group is raised or lowered overall. Instead, a person who respects autonomy, and who, as was outlined above, believes that the diminution in a person's autonomy per se is *qualitatively* worse than a diminution in the instrumental value of that autonomy would have to take into account the fact that the prohibition of Caller ID services would compromise the autonomy of persons adversely affected, as well as reduce the instrumental value of their autonomy. One who respects autonomy would thus have to hold that a situation in which Caller ID was prohibited would be *worse* than a situation in which it was allowed. This is because in the former situation persons would suffer from compromised autonomy *as well as* a diminution in its instrumental value, whereas in the latter situation persons (i.e., those who want to place telephone calls where all calls are anonymous) would only suffer from diminution in the instrumental value of their autonomy. Thus, even though the option of subscribing to a Caller ID service might be, for some, an exclusionary constraining option that would adversely affect the value of their autonomy, the prohibitory alternative would, from the point of view of one who respects autonomy, be much worse.

Conclusion

It is now time to take stock. Like other new information technologies, the introduction of Caller ID services raises new ethical questions. Much of the discussion has, in the past, focused on whether or not the introduction of Caller ID would enhance or diminish the privacy that was enjoyed by the persons affected by it. The purpose of this paper is to highlight the fact that the introduction of the option of subscribing to a Caller ID service would affect (either positively or negatively) the degree to which the persons would be able to exercise their autonomy. Since personal autonomy is a core ethical value in the West, the issue of how Caller ID would affect it is an important one. With the debate over the ethical implications of Caller ID thus refocused, I argue that even though the option to subscribe to a Caller ID service is an exclusionary constraining option, respect for autonomy requires that persons be allowed to subscribe to such services if they so choose.

Notes

1. G. Smith, "We've Got Your Number (Is It Constitutional To Give It Out?): Caller Information Technology and the Right to Informational Privacy," *UCLA Law Review* 37 (1989): 145.

2. Figure cited in Kenneth G. Ferguson, "Caller ID—Whose Privacy Is It, Anyway?" *Journal of Business Ethics* 29 (2001), 227.

3. Ibid., 227.

4. Ibid., 227-228.

5. D. Stover, "Look Who's Calling," *Popular Science* (July 1990): 77-78.

6. See R. Whittle, "Calling Number Display: AUSTEL's PAC Report," *Australasian Privacy Law and Privacy Reporter* 3 (1996): 8-11.

7. See, for example, Smith, "We've Got Your Number;" Ferguson, "Caller ID;" R. Crook, "Sorry, Wrong Number: The Effect of Telephone Technology on Privacy Rights," *Wake Forest Law Review* 26 (1991): 669-710; P. Henroid, "Caller Intellidata: Privacy in the Developing Communications Industry," *Washington University Law Quarterly* 78 (1998): 351-376; and H. Nissenbaum, "Toward an Approach to Privacy in Public: Challenges of Information Technology," *Ethics and Behavior* 7 (1997): 207-219.

8. Thomas May, *Autonomy, Authority, and Moral Responsibility* (Dordrecht: Kluwer Academic Publishers, 1997).

9. This and related points are discussed at length in Gerald Dworkin, *The Theory and Practice of Autonomy* (Cambridge: Cambridge University Press, 1988), 62-81.

10. See Richard Titmuss, *The Gift Relationship: From human blood to social policy*, eds. Ann Oakley and John Ashton (New York: The New Press, 1997), 307. I argue against Titmuss's argument in James Stacey Taylor, *Stakes and Kidneys: Why markets in human body parts are morally imperative* (Aldershot, UK: Ashgate Press, 2005), Chapter 8.

11. Paul M. Hughes, "Paternalism, Battered Women and the Law," *Journal of Social Philosophy* 30 (1999): 18-28.

12. Ferguson, "Caller ID," 235-236.

13. For a more detailed discussion of how subjecting a person to coercion would compromise their autonomy, see James Stacey Taylor, "Autonomy, Duress, and Coercion," *Social Philosophy & Policy* 20 (2003): 127-155.

Part III: Discussion Cases

Case #1: Video Voyeurs and Privacy

Suppose that you are working as a security guard at a local mall and notice an individual engaging in suspicious behavior. The suspect is following women up escalators and placing a shopping bag directly behind them. You also notice that the suspect is only following women who are wearing skirts. When confronted, the suspect shows you what it is in the bag—it is a video camera along with several video tapes—and announces how he is going to upload the material to the web. When you move to seize the voyeuristic tapes, the suspect notes that 1) there are no legal or moral privacy rights in public places, 2) even if privacy rights hold in public places there are no privacy interests at stake in this case—the women will never be linked to the footage, and 3) he has intellectual property rights in the footage found on the tapes. Are these considerations legally or morally compelling? Why/Why not?

Case #2: Menos Greece and Sickle-cell Anemia

In Menos Greece, there are many individuals who have a gene that causes sickle-shaped red blood cells. The problem is that when two parents both carry the gene their offspring may develop sickle-cell anemia. In an effort to prevent this disease researchers tested everyone in the village so that marriages between gene carriers could be avoided. After the testing was complete and published, the carriers became further stigmatized. Did the researchers do the right thing? Is this a case where public health concerns should override individual privacy rights?

Case #3: *Shahar v. Bowers*

In September 1990, Attorney General of the State of Georgia, Michael Bowers, offered Shahar a position of Staff Attorney after she graduated from law school. Shahar accepted the offer and was scheduled to begin work in September 1991. Upon hearing that Shahar was going to be married to a same sex partner, Bowers withdrew the job offer claiming that Shahar's same sex marriage would likely conflict with Georgia's anti-sodomy laws. Should Georgia or any State prohibit peaceful behavior between consenting adults in private places? Why/Why not?

PART IV

Freedom of Speech and Information Control

Rationales for Freedom of Speech

KENT GREENAWALT

This article explores the justifications for freedom of speech. If sound political philosophy supports something properly called a principle of free speech, there will be reasons why a government should be hesitant to punish verbal or written expression even when it has made a judgment that the expression is potentially harmful. The discussion in this article underlies the development of standards for determining which communications raise free speech problems and which may appropriately be suppressed, and it is also critical for the subsequent examination of constitutional issues.

A principle of freedom of speech asserts some range of protection for speech. Given the uneven application of various reasons for free speech to different sorts of communications, there is some question whether one should speak of "a principle" or "principles" of free speech. For simplicity's sake, I adopt the singular form, but that form should not obscure the complexities of the subject.

Beyond A Minimal Principle of Liberty
A political principle of free speech is warranted only if reasons to protect speech go beyond the reasons for what I shall call a *minimal principle of liberty*. According to a minimal principle of liberty, the government should not prohibit people from acting as they wish unless it has a positive reason to do so. The ordinary reason for prohibiting action is that the action is deemed harmful or potentially harmful in some respect; driving a car 100 miles per hour is forbidden because people are likely to get hurt. Although sometimes the government may compel behavior in order to generate benefits rather than prevent harms,[1] I shall disregard that subtlety and concentrate on harm. What legitimately counts as "harm" is an important and controversial aspect of political theory[2] but here I mean the term in an inclusive, nonrestrictive sense, including indirect harms, psychological harms, harms to the actor, and even harms to the natural order. Thus, as far as anything I say here is concerned, sexual intercourse between human beings and animals might be prohibited on the ground that it has deleterious indirect

effects on family life, is psychologically bad for the people involved, or is intrinsically "unnatural."

As far as speech is concerned, the minimal principle of liberty establishes that the government should not interfere with communication that has no potential for harm. To be significant, a principle of freedom of speech must go beyond this,[3] positing constraints on the regulation of speech which are more robust.

A principle of free speech could establish more stringent constraints than the minimal principle of liberty, either by barring certain possible reasons for prohibition or by establishing a special value for speech. The latter way is the easier to understand. If some human activities have special value, a good government will need stronger reasons to prohibit them than to prohibit other activities. If speech has more positive value than acts of physical aggression, for example, more powerful reasons will be needed to warrant its suppression. A related but more subtle point is that legislatures or other political actors may be prone in particular instances to undervalue certain kinds of acts; if that were true about speech, a principle of free speech might compensate for that tendency. In effect the principle would tell those involved in government that acts of speech should be assumed to have a higher value than they seem to have in the immediate context.

The second way in which a principle might give special protection to speech is by positing that the government is barred from employing certain reasons for prohibiting speech. Such a constraint might derive from a notion that particular reasons for prohibitions are at odds with how human beings should be regarded or with the proper role of government. Thus, it might be claimed that, because an aspect of the autonomy of human beings is that people should discover for themselves what is true, suppressing speech to prevent contamination by false ideas is impermissible. Or it might be said that the government cannot suppress political ideas that pose challenges to it, because one aspect of a legitimate government is that criticism of those presently in power may be entertained. The import of a "disqualifying" principle might be less extreme than total exclusion of a reason for prohibition. A reason might be viewed with great suspicion, but treated as a legitimate basis for prohibition if the case were sufficiently compelling.[4]

Using threads like these, a principle or theory of freedom of speech would claim that expression cannot be regulated on every basis that could surmount the minimal principle of liberty and satisfy ordinary prudential considerations regarding effective legislation.[5]

Some claims about the value of speech or about the inappropriateness of certain reasons for prohibition could be thought to be largely independent of wider assertions of political ideology, but many claims bear a distinctive relation to liberal political theory. A proponent of claims that involve a controverted liberal view of human autonomy and government might assert that the liberal view is fundamentally correct and should be embraced by all peoples or by all peoples at a certain stage of economic and social development; in that event, a complete defense of the claims about free speech would require argument for the superiority of the liberal perspective. Alternatively, one who advances liberal claims might assert that, since a particular society is grounded on liberal ideas, that society should act on their implications, at least in the absence of opposed premises for social life that are clearly preferable and attainable.

Because I aim to elucidate standards that could be endorsed by people who disagree about many fundamental matters, my account does not depend on a single systematic version of liberal political theory. But, doubting whether there is a better form of government for large developed countries and strongly believing that no other form is clearly preferable and attainable, I assume in this study that conclusions about freedom of speech that can be drawn from *basic premises* of liberal democracy are sound, without examining possible competing premises.[6] My reliance on basic premises does not mean that I accept without analysis every "liberal" idea; discrete arguments having to do with freedom of speech are scrutinized carefully.

Consequentialist and Nonconsequentialist Reasons

There is no single correct way of presenting the justifications that matter for a principle of freedom of speech. One can distinguish, for example, between reasons that focus on individuals and those which focus on society at large, between reasons that relate to speakers and those which relate to listeners or a broader public, between reasons that relate to the form of government and those which do not, between reasons that reflect optimism about human capacities and those which reflect pessimism, between reasons that concentrate on the positive value of speech and those which emphasize the untrustworthiness of government. Because the reasons for free speech are based on complex and somewhat overlapping elements, no basic division or multiple categorization can be wholly satisfactory.

I have chosen to distinguish between consequentialist and nonconsequentialist reasons. This approach too has its drawbacks, requiring, among other things, somewhat strained divisions between arguments concerning individual autonomy and between arguments concerning democracy. Nonetheless, this familiar way of distinguishing reasons for action is useful here, because it differentiates claimed reasons that are to be viewed in light of factual evidence and claimed reasons that rest more purely on normative claims.[7]

A practice has value from a *consequentialist* point of view if it contributes to some desirable state of affairs. Thus, to say that free speech contributes to honest government is to advance a consequentialist reason for free speech. The force of a consequentialist reason is dependent on the factual connection between a practice and the supposed results of the practice. A *nonconsequentialist* reason claims that something about a particular practice is right or wrong without regard to the consequences. Notable among reasons of this sort are reasons cast in terms of present rights or claims of justice: "Suppressing Joan's ideas is wrong because it violates rights or is unjust."

Consequentialist Justifications

During most of the twentieth century consequentialist arguments have dominated discussion of freedom of speech, although the last two decades have seen a resurgence of nonconsequentialist arguments cast in terms of basic human rights and dignity.[8] Consequentialist arguments reach public and private life; they reach governmental and nongovernmental matters; they reach speakers, listeners, and others who are indirectly affected.

"Truth" Discovery — The Basic Justification

The most familiar argument for freedom of speech is that speech promotes the discovery of truth. Found in Milton's *Areopagitica*[9] and in eloquent opinions by Oliver Wendell Holmes[10] and by Louis Brandeis,[11] the argument is the core of John Stuart Mill's defense of freedom of speech in *On Liberty*.[12] Mill says that, if the government suppresses communications, it may suppress ideas that are true or partly true. Even if an idea is wholly false, its challenge to received understanding promotes reexamination which vitalizes truth. When Mill asserts that government suppression of ideas rests necessarily on a false assumption of infallibility, he overstates his case: suppression might reflect cynical skepticism about any truth, or a belief that, fallible as it is, the government is likely to judge more accurately than would a dissident minority; or a conviction that, true or not, some ideas are too destructive of a social order to be tolerated. But Mill's basic point that speech contributes greatly to the search for truth does not depend on whether suppression always represents a claim of infallibility. Mill's sense of truth is broad, covering correct judgments about issues of value as well as ordinary empirical facts and embracing knowledge conducive to a satisfactory personal life as well as facts of general social importance.

Although he does not assume that people will grasp the truth whenever it appears, Mill believes that, if voice is given to a wide variety of views over the long run, true views are more likely to emerge than if the government suppresses what it deems false. In this standard form, the truth-discovery justification combines a contained optimism that people have some ability *over time* to sort out true ideas from false ones with a realism that sees that governments, which reflect presently dominant assumptions and have narrow interests of their own to protect, will not exhibit exquisite sensitivity if they get into the business of settling what is true.

Often taken as an axiom in liberal societies, the truth-discovery justification is subject to a number of possible challenges: that objective "truth" does not exist; that, if truth does exist, human beings cannot identify it or cannot identify the conditions under which it is discovered; that, even if human beings can identify truth sometimes, free discussion does not evidently contribute to their capacity to do so; and that the way "free" discussion works in practice contravenes the open market of ideas that the truth-discovery justification assumes.[13] A searching answer to these doubts would require a systematic examination of notions of truth and evidences of truth and of human learning. . . .

Exposure and Deterrence of Abuses of Authority
Closely linked to truth discovery and interest accommodation is a consequentialist justification that warrants separate mention because of its historical significance and central importance: free speech as a check on abuse of authority, especially governmental authority. The idea, powerfully developed by Vincent Blasi in a

well-known article,[14] is that, if those in power are subject to public exposure for their wrongs in the manner exemplified by journalists' accounts of the Watergate scandal, corrective action can be taken. And if public officials know they are subject to such scrutiny, they will be much less likely to yield to the inevitable temptation presented to those with power to act in corrupt and arbitrary ways.

In major part, the justification based on exposure and deterrence of government abuse can be seen as a subcategory of the truth-discovery justification. When truths about abuse of authority are revealed, citizens or other officials can take corrective action. But an extra dimension of truth discovery is important here. In areas of human life involving choice, what people do is partly dependent on what they think will become known. Most particularly, persons are less likely to perform acts which are widely regarded as wrong and which commonly trigger some sanction if they are not confident they can keep the acts secret. Thus the prospect of truth's being discovered influences what happens; public scrutiny deters. Viewed from the perspective of interest accommodation, a free press that exposes wrongs affects the balance of sensitivity in the direction of the interests of ordinary citizens as compared with the interests of the officials themselves and of those to whom they feel especially aligned by mutual advantage or common feeling. Perhaps the benefits of exposure and deterrence reach beyond anything neatly captured by truth discovery or interest accommodation. Apart from truths it actually reveals and even when what it claims turns out to be inaccurate, a critical press affects how officials and citizens regard the exercise of governmental power, subtly supporting the notion that government service is a responsibility, not an opportunity for personal advantage.

It is worth mentioning that the ways in which exposures of abuse contribute to healthy government are not limited to liberal democracies. Even in relatively authoritarian regimes where ordinary citizens have little to say about who makes up the government, the threat of exposure can restrain officials from personal abuses of office. In fact, in some countries, such as Yugoslavia, where selection for office remains largely the responsibility of a single party and proposals for complete change of that social system are beyond bounds, press criticism of official inadequacies can be quite sharp.

Autonomy: Independence of Judgment and Considerate Decision
By affording people an opportunity to hear and digest competing positions and to explore options in conversations with others, freedom of discussion is thought to promote independent judgment and considerate decision, what might be characterized as *autonomy*.[15] This is the consequentialist argument that connects free speech to autonomy.

This claim, as I mean to consider it here, is not true by definition. If freedom of speech failed to bring the range of relevant considerations before people as effectively as would a structure of discourse controlled by government or if, despite opportunities to converse and exposure to various relevant points of view, people in a regime of free speech passively followed the opinions of persons in authority or decided on the basis of irrational passions, then freedom of speech would not promote autonomy in this sense. The factual premises of the claim about autonomous decisions are that, when all ideas can be expressed, people will be less subject in their decisions to the dictates of others, and that they will be encouraged to exercise this independence in a considerate manner that reflects their fullest selves. The supposition is not that freedom of speech will actually produce fully autonomous persons or even that it will produce people who are by some measure more autonomous than not; the claim is only that people will be *more* autonomous under a regime of free speech than under a regime of substantial suppression.

I shall not attempt to establish the claimed factual links. Any attempt to do so convincingly faces severe difficulties. It is very hard to compare degrees of autonomy among citizens of different societies, and whether a country enjoys free speech is only one of many relevant cultural factors. Moreover, it is possible that a certain kind of freedom lulls people into a passive acceptance of things as they are, whereas stark suppression forces them to focus on their values. In support of the dangers of the "repressive tolerance" of freedom, it is sometimes remarked that political discussions at the dinner table in countries tending toward totalitarianism have a liveliness that is lacking in liberal democracies. On the other hand, lively conversation is sometimes an outlet for those incapable of making choices that influence events, and the liveliness of ordinary conversation under the most oppressive regimes, such as Nazi Germany, was certainly not great. Matters of degree are important here, and confidence in generalizations must be modest, but I think we are warranted in believing that government control of communication usually tends to induce unreflective reliance on authority and that, if one regards societies in history, comparative autonomy of individuals is linked to relative freedom of opinion.

If one grants that free speech contributes to autonomy, there is still the question of why independence of judgment and considerate decision are good. It may be believed that those who decide for themselves and in a rational manner are acting in a more distinctly human and intrinsically better way than those who passively submit to authority; these personal qualities will then be valued for their own sakes. The qualities may also be means of achieving other values. For example, despite the burden of anxiety that often accompanies serious personal choice, many people can work out for themselves a style of life that is more fulfilling than what they could achieve by simply conforming to standards set by others. Both the valuation of autonomy for its own sake and the belief that it contributes to other satisfactions are aspects of traditional liberal theory.

Emotional Outlet, Personal Development, and Sense of Dignity

The practice of free speech enhances in various other ways the lives of those who seek to communicate. For the speaker, communication is a crucial way to relate to others; it is also an indispensable outlet for emotion and a vital aspect of the development of one's personality and ideas.[16] The willingness of others to listen to what one has to say generates self-respect. Limits on what people can say curtail all these benefits. If the government declares out of bounds social opinions that a person firmly holds or wishes to explore, he is likely to suffer frustration and affront to his sense of dignity.

Because communication is so closely tied to our thoughts and feelings, suppression of communication is a more serious impingement on our personalities than many other restraints of liberty; but some noncommunicative restraints, for example, those relating to sexual involvements or drug use, may equally impair personal self-expression in a broad sense. An argument based on the value of liberty as an emotional outlet and means of personal development is not restricted to speech alone. Indeed, it may reach widely and strongly enough to some other matters so that alone it would not warrant anything properly identified as a distinctive principle of free speech. But if a principle of free speech is supportable on other grounds, this justification does provide an extra reason why speech should not be prohibited and, may help determine what the boundaries of protected speech should be.

Liberal Democracy

I turn now to arguments from democracy, which have been said in a comparative study to be the "most influential . . . in the development of twentieth-century free speech law."[17] Here, I consider the claim that free speech contributes importantly to the functioning of liberal democracy and to the values it serves.

This claim is largely reducible to reasons I have already discussed as those reasons apply to political discourse and decisions and to the participation of people in the political process. A liberal democracy rests ultimately on the choices of its citizens. Free speech can contribute to the possibility that they and their representatives can grasp truths that are significant for political life, it can enhance identification and accommodation of interests, and it can support wholesome attitudes about the relations between officials and citizens.[18] Government officials are especially to be distrusted in deciding what political messages may be heard, because of their interest in staying in office and in promoting the political ideas in which they believe. And government suppression of political messages is particularly dangerous because it can subvert the review of ordinary political processes which might serve as a check on other unwarranted suppression.[19] I have already mentioned the notion of unrestrained speech as a check on abuse of office; since citizens' votes are essential in a liberal democracy, the importance of their being informed of government misconduct is particularly great under that form of government. It has long been assumed, though it is perhaps hard to prove, that a better-informed citizenry will yield a better government and better political decisions.[20]

Whether participation in the political order is deemed uniquely important for people or one among many opportunities for realizing participatory values, that participation can be more autonomous if relevant information and arguments are available, and a regime of free speech may help develop the kinds of self-reliant, courageous citizens that Justice Brandeis holds up as an ideal in his opinion in *Whitney v. California*.[21] Finally, the healthy sense that one is participating as an equal citizen is enhanced if what one believes about politics can be communicated, and speech about injustice can help relieve frustration about an undesired course of political events.

Because a decent political process and informed decision-making by citizens are such critical aspects of a model of liberal democracy, and because government suppression of political ideas is so likely to be misguided, the application of a principle of freedom of speech to political affairs is centrally important. The sorts underlying consequentialist reasons for freedom are not radically different for political speech from those for speech about nonpolitical facts and values, but these reasons take on extra weight when political matters are involved.

Promoting Tolerance

It has been suggested, in a thoughtful recent book by Lee Bollinger, that the main modern justification for a principle of free speech is its capacity to promote tolerance.[22] The basic idea is that if we are forced to acknowledge the right of detested groups to speak, we are taught the lesson that we should be tolerant of the opinions and behavior of those who are not like us. Almost certainly the core of Bollinger's claim is true; living in a regime of free speech helps teach tolerance of many differences, just as living in a regime of religious liberty helps teach tolerance of religious diversity. But it does not follow either that promoting tolerance is now the primary justification for free speech or that attention to tolerance should play the critical role in decisions whether to restrict speech.

If it is true that people in liberal societies have so internalized a norm of free speech that traditional justifications are no longer extensively argued and if the potential acts of suppression these justifications cover most strongly are not even attempted, that does not mean these justifications have somehow been supplanted by the aim of promoting toleration. And, even if Bollinger is right that the tolerance justification has more force than any other for the extremist destructive speech of the Nazis, it is not the primary justification for many other forms of speech. Given the assumption that broad tolerance of how others live can be encouraged in different ways, it is doubtful that one would introduce and defend a principle of freedom of speech in the absence of other more basic justifications, and it is questionable whether a persuasive argument against particular suppression can be grounded mainly in the tolerance justification.[23]

Nonconsequentialist Justifications

Not all arguments for free expression rest on desirable consequences; some liberal conceptions of the relationship between state and citizen may suggest a liberty of citizens to express opinions which is independent of the likely consequences of prohibition. As the phrase "liberal conceptions" implies, these justifications draw more distinctly on characteristic value premises of liberal theory than do the consequentialist justifications, though embedded in many of the latter are common liberal assumptions about facts and values.

Social Contract Theory: Consent and the Private Domain

The Anglo-American tradition of liberal democracy has historically been linked to a theory of social contract, which grounds the legitimacy of the state in the consent of the governed and establishes significant limits on the authority of government. According to John Locke, whose views greatly influenced the revolutionary generation of Americans, the legitimate authority of government is based on consent and is limited to the protection of rights and interests that individuals could not adequately safeguard.[24] Individuals entering into a social contract consent to government power to secure their lives, liberty, and property, but they do not give the state authority to interfere in other domains. In his *Letter Concerning Toleration*, Locke employs this analysis to put control of religious beliefs and expressions outside the ambit of secular authority, but his conclusions have broader implications, reaching all states of mind and activities that do not threaten interference with the limited aims a government may permissibly have.

Locke apparently supposed that at some early age in history people actually entered into a social contract. That is implausible, but his theory can be interpreted in a hypothetical way, as indicating what form and purposes of government individuals leaving a state of nature would consent to. To be morally legitimate a government needs to take this form and pursue only the prescribed purposes. Even in this hypothetical version, the theory is now highly controversial, because it posits individuals outside of organized society with needs, desires, talents, and property. Such an approach pays insufficient regard to the extent to which human nature and human purposes are themselves determined by organized society, and it underestimates positive contributions society and government can make to human flourishing. Still, the ideas that government should take a form to which people do or would consent and that it should do only those things which people need it to do (or which it is uniquely suited to accomplish) retain a powerful appeal in liberal societies. The implications of these ideas reach far beyond speech, but they have considerable relevance for speech as well.

I shall focus first on the conditions of consent. No doubt, valid consent to something can often be based on less than full information, but a problem arises when the authority that seeks consent also controls the available information. If someone asks my agreement to a course of action, then actively conceals much relevant information that would affect my judgment, my "consent" is of lessened or no effect. Under social contract theory, a government is legitimate only if it receives or warrants consent from the people under it. It may be debated exactly what conditions are required for valid actual consent or for the hypothetical consent of persons whose nature and social condition fit some model.[25] However, a claim of actual consent would certainly be undermined if information highly relevant to evaluation of the government was systematically suppressed; and rational actors in some idealized setting could not be expected to give valid consent in such circumstances and would be unlikely to approve in advance a regime that would conceal such information from actual citizens.[26] Thus, the idea that government should be of a kind that people would consent to and the idea that actual citizens should have the opportunity to consent to the legitimacy of their governments underlie a substantial argument against the suppression of political ideas and facts, even when a present majority approves that suppression.

I turn now to the notion of limited government. That notion most obviously constrains what can count as harms and as proper purposes for a liberal society. Suppressing expressions of belief simply to prevent mistakes about religion or aesthetics would not, for example, constitute a proper purpose. And the propriety of suppressing obscenity because it tends to make those who look at it unhappy would be doubtful, since liberal governments should not often be protecting individuals against themselves. Although I do not develop in this book any full theory about the limits of government, I do identify situations in which arguments about suppression of speech rest on contested claims about those limits.

Most claims in favor of prohibiting speech in modern Western societies do not rest on asserted harms that are controversial in this way, perhaps partly because critical assumptions about the limits of government are deeply entrenched. Usually the harm that is to be avoided by prohibiting speech is a harm that a liberal government undoubtedly can try to prevent. But questions about limits on governmental power may remain. These are more subtle questions about remoteness of cause and about the extent to which the government may interfere in a normally private realm to accomplish concededly valid objectives. To take an extreme case, imagine a proposal that, because the attitude of racial prejudice generates the social harm of racial discrimination,[27] the government should undertake compulsory psychological conditioning to erase that attitude from individuals who have it. Almost everyone would agree that such an interference with the private domain would be unacceptable, and many would say that the connection between private thought and harmful act is too remote or indirect to warrant social control[28] even though the government's ultimate objective is appropriate. Similar concerns would be raised if, instead of trying to control thoughts themselves, the government forbade all expressions of racial prejudice. The communication of attitudes would be regarded as closer to the private domain of having the attitudes than to the public domain of acting upon the attitudes in a socially unacceptable way.

In summary, we can think of the traditional idea of limited government as operating at two levels in respect to free speech: as setting some constraints on appropriate governmental objectives and as requiring that the connection between prohibited speech and social harm be reasonably direct. Although social contract theory cannot plausibly be thought to yield the conclusion that all communication must be left untouched by government prohibition, the theory may illuminate some inhibitions on government interference with private individuals.

Recognition of Autonomy and Rationality

Respect for individual autonomy may curb interference with expression. In my treatment of consequentialist justifications, I have already suggested how speech can contribute to the development of autonomous individuals. Here I focus on two related nonconsequentialist arguments for the view that the government should treat people as it would treat autonomous persons. Of course, every governmental prohibition of action interferes with free choice and, therefore, with the *exercise* of autonomy. If autonomy is to undergird a principle of freedom of speech, a notion of autonomy is required which has some special relation to communication and which helps draw lines between permissible and impermissible regulation.

The most straightforward claim is that the government should always treat people as rational and autonomous by allowing them to have all the information and all the urging to action that might be helpful to a rational, autonomous person making a choice. This claim focuses on the autonomy of the recipient of communication. As Thomas Scanlon has put it, an "autonomous person cannot accept without independent consideration the judgment of others as to what he should believe or what he should do."[29] As we shall see in more detail later, a principle that the government should always treat its citizens as autonomous would not necessarily lead to freedom for every kind of communication—outright lies and subliminal manipulation may not contribute to autonomous choice and might be restricted. But a strong version of a principle that the government must always treat citizens as autonomous by maximizing opportunities for informed choice would be powerfully protective of many kinds of speech.

The difficulty with the principle in this strong form lies in its implausibility. The government must protect citizens from social harms, and many fellow citizens do not act in a rational and autonomous way. If some communications are especially likely to lead irrational people to do harmful things, why must the government permit them access to those communications as if they were rational and autonomous, rather than protect potential victims of their irrational actions? Few suppose that compulsory commitment of insane people who are demonstrably dangerous to others is a violation of liberal government; we cannot rule out in advance the possibility that the government may regulate communications in a manner that takes account of frequent deviations from an ideal of autonomy.

Further, a deep ambiguity lurks in the concept of rationality and autonomy. Does a rational and autonomous person always act with appropriate regard for interests of others, or might such a person pursue his own interests unjustly at the expense of others? I do not want to explore here the complex question of whether rationality and autonomy imply acceptance of all valid moral claims. If it is supposed that the rational autonomous person always acts morally, then such a person can be trusted with as complete information and as much urging to action as is possible. In that event the only worry about treating actual people as rational and autonomous is how far people fall short of being rational and autonomous. Matters are more complicated if it is supposed, to the contrary, that rational, autonomous people may freely choose to pursue their own interests immorally. In that case, if rational, autonomous people were given, for example, full information about how to engage in undetectable cheating on their income taxes, many would take advantage of the information by cheating. A principle ensuring full freedom of speech might thus lead to social harms that could be avoided if some information were suppressed. Of course, one might contend that the government's treating people as autonomous is more important than preventing the social harms that would result from full information, but a defense of that position would then be needed.

In an article[30] whose major thesis he no longer defends,[31] Thomas Scanlon developed a somewhat more complex claim about autonomy and expression. He took as a standard for the limits of legitimate government "the powers of a state . . . that citizens could recognize while still regarding themselves as equal, autonomous, rational agents."[32] In this form the claim in favor of treating people as autonomous is grounded in a version of social contract theory that asks what rational autonomous people would agree to. This extra step actually eliminates assurance that the government should treat people as autonomous and rational on every occasion. For the reasons that have just been rehearsed, rational autonomous people deciding on the general limits of government interference would want to protect themselves from harms wrought by irrational people and by rational, immoral people (Scanlon is quite clear that his notion of autonomy and rationality does not guarantee moral action). To protect themselves from those harms, rational autonomous people *might* agree to constraints that would inhibit to some degree the extent to which all citizens, including themselves, would have available information and advocacy that would maximally serve rational and autonomous choice.

In brief, if one asks what limits on government rational autonomous people would set, they might well conclude that the government should not always allow people everything a rational autonomous person would want to have in making a particular choice. And if one simply asserts a principle that the government should never act to inhibit conditions for rational autonomous choice, it is hard to see how that principle could be supported.

What may remain is a less rigorous standard, namely, a premise of liberal democracy that human beings are largely rational and autonomous and should be treated as such. That a proposed prohibition would not treat people in this manner counts against it, and prohibitions that do not respect autonomy may call for especially careful review of possible justifications.

Dignity and Equality

A justification for free speech which is closely related to the points just made but which focuses on the speaker more than on his or her listeners is the idea that the government should treat people with dignity and equality. As a matter of basic human respect we may owe it to each other to listen to what each of us has to say, or at least not to foreclose the opportunity to speak and to listen. Under this view, suppression represents a kind of contempt for citizens that is objectionable regardless of its consequences, and when suppression favors some points of view over others, it may be regarded as failing to treat citizens equally.

How to take this argument depends on whether any infringement of liberty impairs dignity and on whether any infringement that is significantly selective impairs equality. Many actions that people would like to engage in must be restricted, and some of these restrictions, e.g., denying the right to practice medicine to those not certified in a prescribed way, are bound to be "selective." The concerns about dignity and equality may seem not to be specially related to speech but to be arguments, perhaps rather weak ones, in favor of liberty generally.

There may, however, be a tighter connection between restrictions on communications and affronts to dignity and equality. Expressions of beliefs and feelings lie closer to the core of our persons than do most actions we perform; restrictions of expression may offend dignity to a greater degree than most other restrictions; and selective restrictions based on the content of our ideas may imply a specially significant inequality. So put, the notion of affront to dignity and equality bears a plausible relationship to free speech, though it also reaches other forms of liberty, such as liberty of sexual involvement and liberty of personal appearance, which lie close to how we conceive ourselves.

The Import of the Justifications

The nonconsequentialist justifications, like the consequentialist ones, fall short of setting clear principles that can be confidently applied to decide what practices of suppression are unwarranted. What all these perspectives do provide, however, is a set of considerations, a set of standards for the relation of government to citizens, which help to identify which interferences with expression are most worrisome and which operate as counters, sometimes powerful ones, in favor of freedom.

Notes

1. This subject is complicated in ways that would demand examination were this not just a preface to a discussion of free speech. Parents may be directly compelled to confer benefits on their children. One argument for forbidding adultery is that it threatens families and the benefits children receive. Other acts might be compelled or forbidden in order that people develop regular habits of behavior that will lead overall to benefits for others. How far the last justification for control of adults is acceptable is something that may separate "liberal" societies from many others.

2. See, generally, J. Feinberg, *Harm to Others* (New York, Oxford University Press 1984).

3. See F. Schauer, *Free Speech: A Philosophical Enquiry* 5-12 (Cambridge, Cambridge University Press 1982).

4. One might say, to illustrate with an example not involving speech, that any governmental justification for enforced segregation based on violence that might flow from hostility between members of different racial groups should be viewed with extreme suspicion, but that temporary racial segregation in a prison might be warranted after an extensive race riot in which prisoners have been killed.

5. I add this phrase because the costs of administration and other considerations may make it unwise to forbid much behavior that could be forbidden under a minimal principle of liberty.

6. The discussion that follows suggests what I consider the basic premises of liberal democracy. My views on that subject are developed in *Religious Convictions and Political Choice,* especially at 14-29 (New York, Oxford University Press 1988). I do not think that the basic premises of liberal democracy include extreme rationalism, extreme individualism, neutrality among ideas of the good, or exclusive reliance for political choice on shared premises and publicly accessible grounds for determining truth.

7. It is likely that many nonconsequentialist claims rest on deep factual assumptions about human nature; so in this respect the distinction between consequentialist and nonconsequentialist reasons is less sharp than the text indicates. I address this problem in relation to a "natural duty" to obey the law in *Conflicts of Law and Morality* 159-86 (New York, Oxford University Press 1987).

8. For excellent modern discussions, see T. Emerson, "Towards a General Theory, of the First Amendment," 72 *Yale Law Journal* 877-86 (1963); J. Feinberg, "Limits to the Free Expression of Opinion," in J. Feinberg and H. Gross, eds., *Philosophy of Law* 217-32 (3d ed., Belmont, Calif., Wadsworth Publishing Co. 1986); T. Scanlon, "Freedom of Expression and Categories of Expression," 40 *University of Pittsburgh Law Review* 519 (1979).

9. J. Milton, *Areopagitica* (London, for Hunter & Stevens 1819).

10. *Abrams v. United States,* 250 U.S. 616, 624, 630 (1919) (dissenting opinion).

11. *Whitney v. California* 274 U.S. 357, 372, 377 (1927) (concurring opinion).

12. J. S. Mill, *On Liberty in Three Essays* 22-68 (World Classics ed., Oxford University Press 1912) (1st ed. of *On Liberty* 1859).

13. See B. DuVal, "Free Communication of Ideas and the Quest for Truth: Toward a Teleological Approach to First Amendment Adjudication," 41 *George Washington Law Review* 161, 191-94 (1972).

14. See V. Blasi, "The Checking Value in First Amendment Theory," 1977 *American Bar Foundation Research Journal* 521, providing both an account of this rationale of free speech and an argument about its implications.

15. The role of free speech in protecting those who "speak out against . . . existing institutions, habits, customs, and traditions" is stressed by Steven Shiffrin, *The First Amendment, Democracy, and Romance,* Ch. 2, Cambridge, Mass.: Harvard University Press, 1990.

16. See Emerson, note 8 supra, at 879-80; Redish, note 12 supra, at 20-30. As these writings reflect, consequentialist arguments in respect to personality development and autonomy are not sharply distinct.

17. E. Barendt, *Freedom of Speech* 23 (Oxford, Clarendon Press 1985).

18. See generally A. Meiklejohn, *Political Freedom* (New York, Harper & Brothers 1960).

19. This, it seems to me, is the main reason why the fact of a majority vote to suppress is not sufficient. Even a majority should not be able to undermine the conditions for a fair political process. See, e.g., J. Ely, *Democracy and Distrust* 105-36 (Cambridge, Mass., Harvard University Press 1980).

20. This conclusion does not itself depend on a presumed equality of all citizens. Even if some citizens could not vote, as women in the past could not vote, or if citizens had weighted votes, there would still be strong reasons for each citizen to be as fully informed as possible.

21. See V. Blasi, "The First Amendment and the Ideal of Civic Courage: The Brandeis Opinion in *Whitney* v. *California,*" 29 *William and Mary Law Review* 6 (1988).

22. L. Bollinger, *The Tolerant Society* (New York, Oxford University Press 1986). The book leaves some doubt about how far more traditional justifications that lie in the background still have force and how far the tolerance justification applies to matters other than dissenting and extremist speech. For a thorough and perceptive review of the book, see V. Blasi, 87 *Columbia Law Review* 387 (1987).

23. See P. Schlag, "Freedom of Speech as Therapy," 34 *University of California in Los Angeles Law Review,* 265, 281—82 (1986). One of the great strengths of Bollinger's book is its illuminating analysis of the dimensions of tolerance. Since too much tolerance, as Bollinger recognizes, presents social dangers of its own, the use of tolerance to decide whether to suppress is troublesome.

24. John Locke, [Second] *Treatise of Civil Government* and *A Letter Concerning Toleration,* ed. Charles L. Sherman (New York, D. Appleton-Century Co. 1937) (1st eds., London 1690 and 1689, respectively). Garry Wills, in *Inventing America* (Garden City, N.Y., Doubleday & Co. 1978), suggests that the influence of the less individualist Scottish "common sense" philosophy was greater than has been commonly realized.

25. As in the original-position analysis of John Rawls. See J. Rawls, *A Theory of Justice* (Cambridge, Mass., Harvard University Press 1971).

26. In considering possible hypothetical consent one needs to think of two stages of consent. The first involves the conditions under which the hypothetical actors consent, the second the conditions under which real people consent in an actual political order. For the first stage, it is hard to imagine any model that permits actively misleading hypothetical actors about actual facts (although they may be in *ignorance* of certain facts, especially relating to their own personal talents and position). But it is conceivable that actors deciding in hypothetical "presocial" conditions might knowingly consent to live in a political regime that would then engage in active suppression of important political ideas. They might do so, for example, if their judgment (as hypothetical rational beings) was that actual people are so irrational and destructive that necessary social solidarity can be achieved only by the government's rigidly controlling opinion. The sentence in the text assumes that their factual judgment would not lead the hypothetical actors to confer on the government such unbounded power over ideas.

27. I am assuming here (what not everyone accepts) that a liberal government can properly prevent "private" racial discrimination in housing and employment.

28. To be more precise, one would need to distinguish children from adults and educational from coercive efforts to influence thoughts. The government's latitude in respect to school children is greater in some respects than its latitude in respect to adults. Even for adults, education to influence thoughts may be warranted. What is objectionable is coercive effort to invade the "private domain."

29. T. Scanlon, "A Theory of Freedom of Expression," 1 *Philosophy & Public Affairs* 204, 215-16 (1972).

30. Ibid. The article and its claimed connection between freedom of speech and autonomy are perceptively criticized in R. Admur, "Scanlon on Freedom of Expression," 9 *Philosophy & Public Affairs* 287 (1980).

31. See Scanlon, note 29 supra.

32. Scanlon, note 29 supra, at 215.

Digital Speech and Democratic Culture: A Theory of Freedom of Expression for the Information Society

JACK M. BALKIN

Introduction: Novelty and Salience

What do digital technologies teach us about the nature of freedom of speech? How should our theories of freedom of expression change to take these technologies into account? In this essay, I argue that the Internet and digital technologies help us look at freedom of speech from a different perspective. That is not because digital technologies fundamentally change what freedom of speech is. Rather, it is because digital technologies change the social conditions in which people speak, and by changing the social conditions of speech, they bring to light features of freedom of speech that have always existed in the background but now become foregrounded.

This effect—making more central and visible what was already always present to some degree—is important in any study of the Internet and digital technologies. In studying the Internet, to ask "What is genuinely new here?" is to ask the wrong question. If we assume that a technological development is important to law only if it creates something utterly new, and we can find analogues in the past—as we always can—we are likely to conclude that because the development is not new, it changes nothing important.[1] That is the wrong way to think about technological change and public policy, and in particular, it is the wrong way to think about the Internet and digital technologies.

Instead of focusing on novelty, we should focus on salience. What elements of the social world does a new technology make particularly salient that went relatively unnoticed before? What features of human activity or of the human condition does a technological change foreground, emphasize, or problematize? And what are the consequences for human freedom of making this aspect more important, more pervasive, or more central than it was before?

The digital revolution places freedom of speech in a new light, just as the development of broadcast technologies of radio and television did before it. The digital revolution brings features of the system of free expression to the forefront of our concern, reminding us of things about freedom of expression that were always the case, but now have become more central and thus more relevant to the policy issues we currently face. The digital revolution makes possible widespread cultural participation and interaction that previously could not have existed on the same scale. At the same time, it creates new opportunities for limiting and controlling those forms of cultural participation and interaction. The digital age makes the production and distribution of information a key source of wealth. Therefore it creates a new set of conflicts over capital and property rights that concern who has the right to distribute and gain access to information. Not surprisingly, the free speech principle sits at the center of these conflicts. Freedom of speech is rapidly becoming the key site for struggles over the legal and constitutional protection of capital in the information age, and these conflicts will shape the legal definition of freedom of speech. The digital revolution offers unprecedented opportunities for creating a vibrant system of free expression. But it also presents new dangers for freedom of speech, dangers that will be realized unless we accommodate ourselves properly to the changes the digital age brings in its wake. The emerging conflicts over capital and property are very real. If they are resolved in the wrong way, they will greatly erode the system of free expression and undermine much of the promise of the digital age for the realization of a truly participatory culture.

Digital technologies highlight the cultural and participatory features of freedom of expression. In this essay, I offer a theory of freedom of speech that takes these features into account. The purpose of freedom of speech, I shall argue, is to promote a democratic culture. A democratic culture is more than representative institutions of democracy, and it is more than deliberation about public issues. Rather, a democratic culture is a culture in which individuals have a fair opportunity to participate in the forms of meaning-making that constitute them as individuals.[2] Democratic culture is about individual liberty as well as collective self-governance; it is about each individual's ability to participate in the production and distribution of culture.

Freedom of speech allows ordinary people to participate freely in the spread of ideas and in the creation of meanings that, in turn, help constitute them as persons. A democratic culture is democratic in the sense that everyone—not just political, economic, or cultural elites—has a fair chance to participate in the production of culture, and in the development of the ideas and meanings that constitute them and the communities and subcommunities to which they belong.[3] People have a say in the development of these ideas and meanings because they are able to participate in their creation, growth, and spread.

Like democracy itself, democratic culture exists in different societies in varying degrees; it is also an ideal toward which a society might strive. Freedom of expression protects the ability of individuals to participate in the culture in which they live and promotes the development of a culture that is more democratic and participatory.

Freedom of speech is interactive and appropriative. It is interactive because speech is about speakers and listeners, who in turn become speakers themselves. Speech occurs between people or groups of people; individual speech acts are part of a larger, continuous circulation. People participate in culture by interacting with others and influencing and affecting them through communication. This is obvious in the case of speech directed at persuasion, but is true of all speech. Even when we dislike what someone else is saying, we are often affected and influenced by it. Our exposure to speech, our attempt to understand it, to bring it within our understanding, continually reshapes us. Our continuous participation in cultural communication, our agreement with and reaction to what we experience, our assimilation and rejection of what culture offers us, makes us the sort of people that we are.

Freedom of speech is appropriative because it draws on existing cultural resources; it builds on cultural materials that lay to hand. Dissenters draw on what they dislike in order to criticize it; artists borrow from previous examples and build on artistic conventions; even casual conversation draws on common topics and expressions. People participate in culture through building on what they find in culture and innovating with it, modifying it, and turning it to their purposes. Freedom of speech is the ability to do that. In a democratic culture people are free to appropriate elements of culture that lay to hand, criticize them, build upon them, and create something new that is added to the mix of culture and its resources.

The idea of a democratic culture captures the inherent duality of freedom of speech: Although freedom of speech is deeply individual, it is at the same time deeply collective because it is deeply cultural. Freedom of speech is, in Thomas Emerson's words, a system.[4] It is a cultural system as well as a political system. It is a network of people interacting with each other, agreeing and disagreeing, gossiping and shaming, criticizing and parodying, imitating and innovating, supporting and praising. People exercise their freedom by participating in this system: They participate by interacting with others and by making new meanings and new ideas out of old ones. Even when people repeat what others have said, their reiteration often carries an alteration in meaning or context.[5] As people express themselves, make music, create works of art, sing, gossip, converse, accuse, deny, complain, celebrate, enthuse, boast, and parody, they continually add something to the cultural mixture in which they live. They reshape, however imperceptibly, cultural conventions about what things mean, what is proper and improper, what is important and less important, how things are done and how they are not done. Through communicative interaction, through expression, through exchange, individual people become the architects of their culture, building on what others did before them and shaping the world that will shape them and those who follow them. And through this practice of interaction and appropriation, they exercise their freedom.

Freedom of speech is thus both individual and cultural. It is the ability to participate in an ongoing system of culture creation through the various methods and technologies of expression that exist at any particular point in time. Freedom of speech is valuable because it protects important aspects of our ability to participate in the system of culture creation. Participation in culture is important because we are made of culture; the right to participate in culture is valuable because it lets us have a say in the forces that shape the world we live in and make us who we are.

The digital age provides a technological infrastructure that greatly expands the possibilities for individual participation in the growth and spread of culture and thus greatly expands the possibilities for the realization of a truly democratic culture. But the same technologies can also produce new methods of control that can limit democratic cultural participation. Therefore, free speech values— interactivity, mass participation, and the ability to modify and transform culture—must be protected through technological design and through administrative and legislative regulation of technology, as well as through the more traditional method of judicial creation and recognition of constitutional rights. Increasingly, freedom of speech will depend on the design of the technological infrastructure that supports the system of free expression and secures widespread democratic participation. Institutional limitations of courts will prevent them from reaching the most important questions about how that infrastructure is designed and implemented. Safeguarding freedom of speech will increasingly fall to legislatures, administrative agencies, and technologists. Protecting freedom of speech in the digital age will require a new class of cyberlawyers, who understand the impact of technological design on free speech values and can help shape regulatory solutions that promote technologies that, in turn, will help secure the values of free expression.

I: How the Digital Age Changes the Conditions of Speech

The next Part of this essay describes how the digital revolution alters our perspective on freedom of speech and leads to a series of disputes about what the free speech principle means. By the "digital revolution," I mean the creation and widespread availability of technologies that make it easy to copy, modify, annotate, collate, transmit, and distribute content by storing it in digital form. These technologies also include the development of vast communication networks that connect every part of the world for the purpose of distributing digital content. The digital revolution changes the factual assumptions underlying the social organization and social practices of freedom of speech in four important ways.

First, the digital revolution drastically lowers the costs of copying and distributing information. Large numbers of people can broadcast and publish their views cheaply and widely. Websites, for example, are easy to construct and easy to access. We do not yet know how low the costs of information transfer will become. For example, the development of weblogs (or blogs) allows people to publish content to the Internet with the press of a button, lowering the costs of publication and distribution even further.

Before the Internet, free speech theorists worried about the scarcity of bandwidth for broadcast media. Frequencies were limited, so only a relatively few people could broadcast to a large number of people. The digital revolution made a different kind of scarcity salient. It is not the scarcity of bandwidth but the scarcity of audiences, and, in particular, scarcity of audience attention. My speech has always competed with yours; as the costs of distribution of speech are lowered, and more and more people can reach each other easily and cheaply, the competition for audience attention has grown ever more fervent.[6] An interesting side effect of lowering the costs of distribution and transmission is that it can alter the relative costs of receiving versus sending information. Although receiving information is easier, sending information can become even less costly. The classic example is spam e-mail, which shifts the costs of distribution from speakers to audiences. Because so many people are producing content and sending it everywhere, audiences are pummeled with vast amounts of information which they must collate, sort, filter, and block. Hence, the digital revolution brings to the forefront the importance of organizing, sorting, filtering, and limiting access to information, as well as the cultural power of those who organize, sort, filter, and limit access.[7]

Second, the digital revolution makes it easier for content to cross cultural and geographical borders. Not only can speakers reach more people in the country in which they live, they can also interact with and form new communities of interest with people around the globe. It has long been possible to send information globally, but the cost and effort were comparatively great. The Internet gives people abilities that were previously enjoyed only by large commercial enterprises; it offers them access to an infrastructure for sending information worldwide.[8]

Third, the digital revolution lowers the costs of innovating with existing information, commenting on it, and building upon it. An important feature of the digital revolution is the development of common standards for storing and encoding information digitally. Common standards are absolutely crucial to lowering the costs of transmission and distribution. (We might make a rough analogy to the role of standardization that accompanied the Industrial Revolution.) However, the same features of content that make it possible for people to transmit and distribute information cheaply and easily also make it possible to manipulate, copy, and alter information cheaply and easily. In the past it was always possible to copy a text or a drawing by hand, but such copying was comparatively expensive and time-consuming. Once people have a common metric for storing images, music, and text, they can copy, cut, and paste information and send it to others. Common standards for encoding images, music, and text not only make it easy to copy and distribute content, they also make it easier to appropriate, manipulate, and edit content.

The link between the ability to copy and the ability to modify information is central to understanding the possibilities created by the digital revolution. Consumers of digital media products[9] are not simply empowered to copy digital content; they are also empowered to alter it, annotate it, combine it, and mix it with other content and produce something new. Software allows people to innovate with and comment on other digital media products, including not only text, but also sounds, photographs, and movies. The standard example is the well-known story of The Phantom Edit, in which an individual reedited George Lucas's Star Wars movie *The Phantom Menace* to eliminate as much as possible of the screen time devoted to a particularly obnoxious character, Jar Jar Binks.[10] The Phantom Edit exemplifies what the digital age makes possible. It is not simply piracy; it is also innovation, although certainly not the sort of innovation that LucasFilms was interested in promoting.[11] This innovation goes hand in hand with the possibility of digital piracy; both are forms of appropriation made possible by digital technologies and digital communications networks. Lowering the costs of both distribution and appropriation are central features of the digital age. Digital media, in short, invite not only simple copying but also annotation, innovation, and collage.[12]

Fourth, and most importantly, lowering the costs of transmission, distribution, appropriation, and alteration of information democratizes speech. Speech becomes democratized because technologies of distribution and transmission are put in the hands of an increasing number of people and increasingly diverse segments of society throughout the planet. More and more people can publish content using digital technologies and send it worldwide; conversely, more and more people can receive digital content, and receive it from more and more people. Equally important, speech becomes democratized because technologies of innovation are available to a wider range of people. In the digital age, distribution and innovation go hand in hand.

II: Routing Around and Glomming On

In the early days of the Internet, many people assumed that the Internet would displace the mass media and publishing houses as traditional gatekeepers of content and quality. This has not occurred. Rather, the Internet has provided an additional layer of communication that rests atop the mass media, draws from it, and in turn influences it.

Mass media are asymmetrical and unidirectional. The ability to broadcast widely is held in relatively few hands; what is broadcast is sent out to a large number of people with very little opportunity for people to talk back. Access to mass media is comparatively limited. Mass media create a technological bottleneck, and the people who control mass media are gatekeepers controlling its use. As a result, in a world dominated by mass media, the recurring problem for people who want to speak effectively and reach large numbers of people is how to gain access to an effective podium. People can purchase access if they own a significant amount of property; in the alternative, they can stage media events to draw the mass media's attention. In the latter case, however, speakers cannot easily control their message.

The Internet offers two different strategies for dealing with the mass media: routing around and glomming on. Routing around means reaching audiences directly, without going through a gatekeeper or an intermediary. For example, you can publish content on your own website or distribute copies of your band's music on the Internet. Routing around relieves the bottleneck problem to some extent, but it does not eliminate it. Mass media are still quite important, because they are still comparatively few and individual speakers are many. Mass media provide a focal point for audience attention: Most people still pay much more attention to the relatively small number of traditional mass media speakers than they do to almost any particular website. That should not be surprising, for two reasons. First, traditional mass media have a head start in achieving a sizeable and stable audience because culture has been organized around them for so long. Second, the large number of speakers on the Internet dilutes audience share and fragments audience attention for any single website, depriving the vast majority of Internet speakers of mass audiences of the same size as the traditional mass media have enjoyed.

Therefore, although the Internet allows people to shape public opinion by routing around traditional mass media, the latter still play a crucial role in setting agendas because they still provide the lion's share of news and information to most people. Mass media remain dominant sources of entertainment, and are likely to be so for the foreseeable future. Because of economies of scale in production costs, mass media can also provide much more impressive and entertaining content than most individuals can.

The second strategy for dealing with mass media responds to this fact. It is the strategy of glomming on. To "glom on" means to appropriate and use something as a platform for innovation. "Glomming on" as a strategy means appropriating things from mass media, commenting on them, criticizing them, and above all, producing and constructing things with them: using them as building blocks or raw materials for innovation and commentary.

The word "appropriate" means to make something one's property. It is sometimes defined as making something one's exclusive property, as in appropriating a common benefit. But the glomming on characteristic of the digital age is precisely the opposite—it is nonexclusive appropriation. One appropriates something for one's own use, but others are free to appropriate it as well. This is especially the case with information goods, which are nonrivalrous and can be copied repeatedly at minimal cost.

Glomming on, then, is nonexclusive appropriation of media content for the purpose of commentary, annotation, and innovation. Here are four examples. The first is the use and development of weblogs, or blogs. Blogs grab quotes and information from other sources, including the websites run by mass media like the *New York Times* and the *Washington Post*, and use them as launching pads for commentary. Although a few blogs do original reporting, most of the blogosphere is devoted to commentary.[13] A second example is the website Television Without Pity, run by a group of Canadian and American viewers.[14] The site offers detailed scene-by-scene accounts of popular television shows in North America, laced with humorous and often biting commentary. Television Without Pity has grabbed the attention of television companies, which are eager to know how their shows are being received by their audiences.[15] The strategy of glomming on allows at least some television viewers to talk back to television producers. Fan fiction sites, which are devoted to the creation of stories about particular movies, books, and television shows, are a third example of glomming on.[16] The Phantom Edit, which I mentioned earlier, is a fourth example of glomming on; it uses a traditional mass media product as an artistic platform for innovation.

Glomming onto the work of others has always existed. It is a standard form of cultural transmission and evolution. The digital revolution enhances opportunities for glomming on to the work of traditional mass media and distributing these innovations and commentary worldwide. The point is not that more glomming on is occurring, although that may be the case, but that more people are able to glom on with greater effect. In theory, at least, digital technology allows glomming on to be broadcast as widely as the media product itself. People used to talk about last night's television programs at the water cooler the next morning; now they can publish their thoughts and distribute them to a global and anonymous audience. People have long written stories about their favorite literary characters, created parodies of familiar stories and songs, and gossiped about their favorite artists. These cultural appropriations were commonplace but moved in relatively constricted circles. They existed everywhere but were not distributed everywhere. All this has changed. The very technologies that make transmission and distribution of digital information relatively costless have made glomming on a force to be reckoned with.

What I have called glomming on—the creative and opportunistic use of trademarks, cultural icons, and bits of media products to create, innovate, reedit, alter, and form pastiches and collage—is a standard technique of speech in the digital world. Glomming on is cultural bricolage using cultural materials that lay to hand. Precisely because of the astounding success of mass media in capturing the public imagination during the twentieth century, the products of mass media, now everywhere present, are central features of everyday life and thought. Mass media products—popular movies, popular music, trademarks, commercial slogans, and commercial iconography—have become the common reference points of popular culture. Hence, it is not surprising that they have become the raw materials of the bricolage that characterizes the Internet.

Indeed, as they were originally developed, significant aspects of the Internet and digital technology facilitate glomming on. I have already mentioned the creation of common standards for encoding digital content. HTML and its successors also encourage glomming on, because they facilitate copying of source material and allow documents to point to each other. This, in turn, allows people to move seamlessly between documents and blurs the lines between them. To be sure, these features of the digital revolution need not remain untouched: As I shall now describe, businesses have tried to erect technological and legal barriers to glomming on. My point, however, is that what gives rise to these reactions by businesses are the characteristics of digital media that facilitate the cheap and widespread appropriation, manipulation, distribution, and exchange of digital information. Those very characteristics lead to attempts to undermine, limit, and cabin the facility that digital media provide.

Indeed, routing around and glomming on are not merely specific responses to mass media; they are basic characteristics of Internet speech generally. Unless the Internet's architecture has been specifically modified to prevent it,[17] it is usually possible to route around any existing channel or site of discourse and start a conversation elsewhere. Similarly, unless there are technological devices put in place to avoid it, the Internet lends itself to the nonexclusive appropriation of existing content and its subsequent modification, annotation, and parody.

III: The Social Contradictions of the Digital Revolution

Digital technology lowers the costs of distribution and production of content, both locally and worldwide. It makes it easier for people to innovate using existing information and copy and distribute what they produce to others. It makes it possible for more and more people to participate in the creation and distribution of new forms of public discourse, new forms of art, and new expressions of creativity.

The very same features of the digital age that empower ordinary individuals—low costs of distribution and ease of copying and transformation—empower businesses as well. Because it is easier and cheaper to copy and distribute media products worldwide, the digital age opens new markets for media products in digital formats, like compact discs, DVDs, and streaming media.

The digital revolution, after all, is an economic revolution as well as a technological one. Because more types of media and information products can be sold to more people in more places, media products and, more generally, information itself, become increasingly important sources of wealth. In the same fashion, the infrastructure necessary to communicate and distribute information widely becomes an important source of wealth. As happened in the first age of industrialization, businesses discover economies of scale in the creation and distribution of information and media products. They become larger and more powerful; media and information industries become increasingly concentrated.

So the digital age produces two crucial trends: the democratization of digital content and the increasing importance of digital content as a source of wealth and economic power. These trends quickly come into conflict. That conflict, and its consequences for freedom of speech, is the central problem of the digital age.

The irony is this: The very same features of the digital age that empower ordinary individuals also lead businesses continually to expand markets for intellectual property and digital content. Yet as businesses do so, they must deal with features of the digital age that empower consumers and give them new abilities to copy, distribute, and manipulate digital content. Businesses wish to use the new technologies to deliver more and more content to more and more consumers, providing ever new services, ever new opportunities to purchase, and ever new forms of customization. But the technologies that allow the penetration and expansion of markets also allow consumers to route around existing media and glom on to digital content.[18]

It is obvious that businesses are worried about digital piracy — and, more generally, forms of digital appropriation — made possible by digital technologies. That is why conflicts between freedom of speech and intellectual property have come to the forefront of concern. But businesses are also concerned about the ability of consumers to alter or even refuse the conditions under which digital content is delivered and offered. Businesses would like to offer goods and services under conditions that encourage consumers to buy them. They want to facilitate advertising that supports their ventures. They want consumers to experience digital products in ways that will encourage consumption and increase profits, and they want to structure the digital environment accordingly. But digital technologies allow consumers the ability to route around these conditions. Thus, the conflict produced by the digital age is not simply a conflict about copying and piracy. It is also a conflict about control.

In a sense, this conflict was inevitable: Once intellectual property, information exchange, and media products become important sources of wealth, it is only natural that businesses will seek to maintain their profits through increasingly aggressive forms of legal and technological control. Thus, at the very moment when ordinary people are empowered to use digital technologies to speak, to create, to participate in the creation of culture, and to distribute their ideas and innovations around the world, businesses are working as hard as possible to limit and shut down forms of participation and innovation that are inconsistent with their economic interests.

We face, in other words, what Marx would have called a contradiction in social relations produced by technological innovation.[19] By "contradiction," I don't mean a logical contradiction, but rather an important and pervasive social conflict brought about by technological change, a conflict that gets fought out in culture, in politics, and, perhaps equally importantly, in law. The social contradiction of the digital age is that the new information technologies simultaneously create new forms of freedom and cultural participation on the one hand, and, on the other hand, new opportunities for profits and property accumulation that can only be achieved through shutting down or circumscribing the exercise of that freedom and participation.

The social conflict produced by technological change is both a conflict of interests and a conflict of values. It produces opposed ideas of what freedom of speech means. The social contradictions of the digital age lead to opposing views about the scope and purposes of the free speech principle. This conflict appears in a number of different areas. Here I will mention only two of them: intellectual property and telecommunications policy.

A. Intellectual Property

The first example is the growing tension between intellectual property and freedom of speech. That conflict has always existed, but new digital technologies have made it more salient and important.[20] In hindsight, the conflict between intellectual property and freedom of speech is obvious: The whole point of intellectual property law is to bestow monopoly rights in certain forms of expression, subject to safety valves like fair use and limited times. In fact, in the United States one can even get injunctive relief against prospective copyright infringement, which flies directly in the face of the basic presumption against prior restraints on speech.[21]

In the past, the conflict was often avoided through benign neglect. People engaged in technical violations of intellectual property rights all the time, but their activities were not widespread and distribution was relatively limited. It didn't matter much to IP owners if a few people wrote fan fiction on their typewriters, made jokes about trademarked elements in casual conversation or in limited geographic areas, or made the occasional copy of a record on their cassette tape recorder. However, once digital content could be produced and distributed at relatively low cost and broadcast around the world, owners of intellectual property became much more worried about digital copying and trademark infringement on a massive scale, even as they became increasingly interested in exploiting derivative rights in works they already owned.

Digital content produced by isolated individuals now competes more easily with existing media products, and more easily undermines or tarnishes existing trademarks. Conversely, lower costs of distribution of digital content encourage businesses to promote their rights ever more aggressively because they can expand into new geographical markets and achieve greater market penetration. Technological change exacerbates a tension that was always present but remained dormant until low-cost methods of distribution arrived on the scene. Indeed, the digital revolution is merely the latest episode in a much longer series of technological innovations that have led to the current conflict between freedom of speech and intellectual property rights. Throughout the twentieth century, mass media have become increasingly pervasive in cultural life. Print media spread more widely through technological innovation. The motion picture industry took off in the early part of the twentieth century, followed by radio, television, cable, and satellite broadcasting. All of these technologies changed how widely and cheaply one could distribute content. Each of them, in their own way, lowered distribution costs, even if they also raised the costs of content creation.

As these forms of mass media became increasingly pervasive parts of our life, the industries that create content—Hollywood, the publishing industry, and the advertising industry to name only three examples—began to push for increased protections of intellectual property rights. The reason is simple. Being able to distribute media products to more and more people justifies greater and greater investments in content creation, including, among other things, the assembly of vast teams of people to create movies, television shows, advertising campaigns, and the like. To recoup these costs, producers sought to squeeze as much profit as they could out of their media products, and one way to do that was to make their rights more valuable by pushing aggressively for additional legal protections.

Thus, during the twentieth century intellectual property rights have expanded both horizontally and vertically.[22] Examples of horizontal expansion include increasing the scope of derivative rights that apply to a work at a particular point in time—the right to plot, characters, sequels, design features, orchestration, and so forth.

Other examples are the development of process patents and the creation of trademark dilution law. Intellectual property rights have also expanded vertically, as the length of copyright terms has been repeatedly extended forward, and previous works have been retroactively given extensions to keep them in parity with newer works. A recent example in the United States is the Sonny Bono Copyright Term Extension Act of 1998,[23] named after the former pop singer and Congressman. It extended copyrights in the United States from the life of the author plus 50 years to life plus 70 years; it also extended copyright terms to 95 years after publication for works created by corporate or anonymous authors (or 120 years after creation, whichever is shorter).

Media companies, however, have not limited themselves to legal devices. They have also attempted to use technology to protect their interests in intellectual property. An increasingly important form of intellectual property protection involves digital rights management schemes, technological devices that prevent copying of and control access to digital content. The Digital Millennium Copyright Act of 1998[24] created a new species of legal rights, sometimes called "paracopyright," that make it unlawful to circumvent these technological devices or distribute circumvention devices to others. Although digital rights management is often justified as a means of preventing unauthorized copying, it actually goes much further. It is part of a general strategy of control over access to digital content, including digital content that has been purchased by the end user.[25] Digital rights management schemes, for example, can make digital content unreadable after a certain number of uses; they can control the geographical places where content can be viewed; they can require that content be viewed in a particular order; they can keep viewers from skipping through commercials; and so on. Paracopyright creates legal rights against consumers and others who wish to modify or route around these forms of technological control. Once again we see how technological innovation produces social conflict: Because digital technologies make it easier to manipulate digital content in ever new ways, both businesses and consumers want increased control over how digital content is experienced.

Matters have come to a head as copying and modification of digital content have become widespread, and media companies have sought in increasingly aggressive ways to protect their existing rights and expand them further. The problem is that these legal and technological strategies are seriously curtailing freedom of expression. Not surprisingly, media companies have generally resisted the idea that freedom of speech limits the expansion of intellectual property rights. Nevertheless, at the same time that media corporations have resisted free speech objections to the expansion of intellectual property rights, they have avidly pushed for constitutional limits on telecommunications regulation on the ground that these regulations violate their own First Amendment rights.

B. Telecommunications Policy

This brings us to the second great battleground over freedom of speech: telecommunications policy. Mass media communication delivers content through some medium of transmission, whether it be spectrum, networks, telephone wires, or cables. Technologies of distribution are the "pipes" through which content travels. The key question in the digital age is who will control these "pipes."

Historically, telecommunications policy in the United States has developed through several different models. Telephone companies have been viewed as conduits for the speech of others, exercising no independent editorial function. They are regarded as common carriers required to provide access to all. Broadcasters, cable companies, and satellite companies, by contrast, have been treated as hybrid enterprises. Because they provide programming and exercise editorial judgment, they have been treated as speakers with free speech rights. However, because they control key communications networks that are not freely available to all,[26] they have also been subject to structural public-interest regulation. Broadcasters were at one point required to cover public issues and cover both sides of these issues fairly; they are still required to provide equal time to political candidates and to sell advertising time to federal candidates for office; cable companies have been required to make room for public, educational and government channels, to carry signals from spectrum broadcasters, and to provide cable access to low-income areas; satellite companies have been required to set aside space for educational purposes, and so on.[27]

The digital revolution has undermined one of the traditional justifications for structural regulation of the mass media—scarcity of bandwidth. Cable can accommodate hundreds of channels, as can satellite broadcasting. The number of speakers on the Internet seems limitless. Broadcast media now compete with cable, satellite, and the Internet for viewer attention. In theory, at least, digital technologies offer everyone the potential to become broadcasters.

Telecommunications companies have pointed to these changes as reasons to loosen or eliminate structural regulations of broadcast, cable, satellite, and Internet access. Businesses have argued that must-carry requirements for cable, open access requirements for broadband companies, limitations on how many media outlets a single business entity can own, and other structural and public interest obligations interfere with media companies' rights to convey the content they wish to as large an audience as possible. They have argued that these regulations, and others like them, violate their First Amendment rights as speakers and editors, and courts in the United States have increasingly begun to agree with them.[28]

Implicit in these arguments is a controversial capitalist theory of freedom of speech. The theory is controversial not because it accepts capitalism as a basic economic ordering principle, but because it subordinates freedom of expression to the protection and defense of capital accumulation in the information economy. The capitalist theory identifies the right to free speech with ownership of distribution networks for digital content. Although distribution networks are "public" in the sense that lots of different people use them and rely on them for communication, their hardware and software are privately owned. Hence, businesses argue, regulation of the distribution network is a regulation of the freedom of speech of the network owner, because the network owner "speaks" through its decisions about which content to favor and disfavor. Must-carry rules interfere with the editorial judgment of cable companies; open access requirements interfere with the programming choices of broadband companies; restrictions on the amount and geographical scope of media ownership interfere with the ability of media companies to send their content to as many people as possible.

The capitalist theory is controversial precisely because telecommunication enterprises are hybrids of content providers and conduits for the speech of others. This is especially true for broadband, cable, and satellite transmission. Recent telecommunications mergers have further exacerbated this hybridization by forming a small number of large, vertically integrated media conglomerates with interests in broadcast media, cable, satellite, book publishing, movie production, telephone, and Internet services.

The argument that structural regulation of telecommunications networks restricts the First Amendment rights of telecommunications companies ties the right to speak ever more closely to ownership of capital. Arguing by analogy to print media, the capitalist theory of free speech identifies the right to produce and control digital content with ownership of a communications network. Nevertheless, conflating the right to speak with the right to control a communication network is problematic for two reasons. First, because they are conduits and networks, digital communications networks are designed to provide access to multiple voices. However, under the capitalist theory, these conduits exist primarily to promote the speech of the owner of the conduit, just as newspapers exist to promote the speech of the newspaper's owner. The second problem follows from the first: Content providers who also act as conduits have incentives to favor their content over the content of others. For example, cable companies may be tempted to favor streaming media and digital music coming from the company's content providers and advertising partners, while slowing down or refusing content coming from competitors, or, for that matter, from subscribers who want to be their own broadcasters.[29] Broadband companies may seek to provide "walled gardens" or "managed content areas" which limit consumer access to that of the company's proprietary network and its approved content partners.[30] Broadband companies may attempt to control the end user's Internet experience by creating what Cisco Systems has called "captive portals," which, in the company's own words, give a cable system owner "the ability to advertise services, build its brand, and own the user experience."[31] The purpose of these innovations is to guide the end user into a continuous series of offers to consume goods and services from which the Internet access provider will glean profits. Through skillful control of the distribution network, access providers can determine who gets to see what programming and under what terms. The goal is not simple ideological censorship but diversion of end users into ever new consumption possibilities. Access providers seek to cocoon their customers, offering continuous promotion of brands and shopping possibilities while the end user surfs the Internet.

Here we can see a second aspect of the social conflict brought about by technological innovation. New telecommunications networks allow ordinary people to communicate with vast numbers of fellow human beings, routing around existing media gatekeepers and offering competing content. People are no longer simply consumers of prepackaged content from mass media companies that are controlled by a limited number of speakers. Instead, people can use the new telecommunications networks to become active participants in the production of public culture. But the very same technologies that offer these possibilities also offer media companies ever new ways to advertise, sell products, and push their favored content. Thus, just as in the case of intellectual property, businesses that control telecommunications networks will seek to limit forms of participation and cultural innovation that are inconsistent with their economic interests. Once again, the goal is not necessarily censorship of unpopular ideas but rather diversion and co-optation of audience attention. Businesses want to direct the Internet user toward increased consumption of their own goods and services as well as the products of their advertising partners. Recognizing that there is money to be made in advertising, sales, and delivery of content, telecommunications companies do not want to be pure conduits for the speech of others, and they do not want too much content competition from their customers. Instead, they want to use the architecture of the Internet to nudge their customers into planned communities of consumerist experience, to shelter end users into a world that combines everyday activities of communication seamlessly with consumption and entertainment. In some respects, businesses seek to push consumers back into their pre-Internet roles as relatively passive recipients of mass media content. In other respects, however, they openly encourage interactivity, but interactivity on their terms—the sort of interactivity that facilitates or encourages the purchase of goods and services.

Another way of seeing the social "contradiction" created by the Internet is through the concept of "public" space. Is the Internet a private space or a public space? Digital communications networks are held in private hands, increasingly by large media conglomerates who also hold interests in digital content production and who wish to sell their own goods and services and advertise the goods and services of others. From their perspective, the "publicness" of digital communications networks is merely a side effect of the use of private property by private actors. Because digital communications networks are privately owned, those who own them have the right to structure entry to and use of the network by other private actors. Rather than vindicating free speech values, regulating digital communications networks violates the free speech rights of tele-communications companies.

On the other hand, digital communications networks are "public" in the sense that the public uses them as a space for general interaction. The information superhighway is a public highway used by the public for public communication, debate, gossip, and every possible form of exchange of information. Digital communications networks are also "public" in the sense that their value as networks arises from public participation that produces network effects: Communications networks are valuable to individuals because the public in general uses them, and the larger share of the public that uses the network, the more valuable the network becomes. In other words, a key source of value of the communications network is its publicness, the fact that its inhabitants and its users are the public at large. Because digital communications networks serve a public function and because they gain their value from public participation, the argument goes, digital communications networks should be regulated to serve the public interest and to allow members of the public to use them as public spaces for communication, cultural innovation, and public participation. Without such regulation, powerful private interests will trample on free speech values in the relentless pursuit of profits.

IV: Freedom of Speech in the Second Gilded Age

Let me summarize the argument so far: Technological innovations in the digital age have produced conflicts about the meaning of free expression in two different locations. The first is the scope of intellectual property; the second is the regulation of telecommunications networks. The conflict over freedom of speech looks quite different in these two areas. In intellectual property, media corporations have pushed for ever-greater protection of intellectual property through both legal and technological means. They have rejected complaints that ever-expanding intellectual property rights and digital rights management schemes inhibit freedom of expression because they eliminate fair use and shrink the public domain. In telecommunications regulation, by contrast, media corporations have aggressively pushed for expansion of free speech rights, arguing that the right to free speech includes the right to control communications networks. Invoking a property-based theory of free expression, they have rejected arguments that public regulation is necessary to keep conduits open and freely available to a wide variety of speakers.

Thus, in the digital age, media corporations have interpreted the free speech principle broadly to combat regulation of digital networks and narrowly in order to protect and expand their intellectual property rights. What is more, courts increasingly have begun to agree with these two positions.[32]

These positions seem inconsistent on their face. In fact, they are not. They reflect a more basic agenda: It is not the promotion and protection of freedom of speech per se, but the promotion and protection of the property rights of media corporations. Both intellectual property and freedom of speech have been reconceptualized to defend capital investments by media corporations. Intellectual property rights, paracopyright, and digital rights management are justified as necessary to protect property rights and maintain a fair return on investment. Freedom of speech increasingly is being reinterpreted as the right to be free from economic regulation of digital communications networks. This is part of a larger trend of the past twenty-five years, in which businesses have also used the First Amendment to attack restrictions on advertising and campaign finance.[33] We are just beginning to see the First Amendment invoked to defend the accumulation and sale of consumer data against government regulation.[34] One of the most important developments of the past quarter century is the emergence of the First Amendment and the free speech principle as anti-regulatory tools for corporate counsel.[35] At the same time, intellectual property, paracopyright, and digital rights management are being invoked not only to restrict cultural experimentation and innovation, but to control how ordinary individuals experience the Internet.[36] What these positions have in common is not a libertarian impulse, but a desire for greater control over how individuals will be permitted to use digital networks and digital content; which is to say, it is a desire for control over the very technologies that had created new possibilities for individual freedom and cultural innovation in the digital age.

In a sense, this development was inevitable. In the world in which we live, intellectual property and control of digital communications networks are increasingly important sources of wealth. The defense of those forms of wealth must find a legal manifestation. Intellectual property and freedom of speech serve these functions admirably.

We have been through this before. Jacksonian and abolitionist ideas before the Civil War produced a constitutional vision of free labor and free contract. This constitutional vision celebrated the right of ordinary individuals to own their labor. Laissez-faire was defended as a means of keeping government from giving special benefits to the wealthy. As America industrialized, corporations took up these Jacksonian and abolitionist ideas and reinterpreted them, transforming them into defenses of corporate property rights and constitutional attacks on government regulation of employment conditions. Courts issued labor injunctions against union organizing on the grounds that allowing workers to form unions undermined the value of employer investments in capital.[37] Courts turned the ideology of free labor into a constitutional principle of liberty of contract that prevented governments from regulating wages and working conditions.[38]

In what Clinton Rossiter called the "Great Train Robbery of Intellectual History,"[39] laissez-faire conservatives appropriated the words and symbols of early nineteenth-century liberalism—liberty, opportunity, progress, and individualism—and gave them an economic reinterpretation that served corporate interests.[40] They massaged and refitted the existing rhetoric of free labor and the right of ordinary citizens to pursue a calling into a sophisticated defense of corporate power and privilege that smashed labor unions, protected sweatshops, and eviscerated health and safety laws.[41] By the turn of the twentieth century, the best legal minds that money could buy had reshaped the liberal rights rhetoric of the 1830s into a powerful conservative defense of property that they claimed was the rightful heir to the best American traditions of individualism and personal freedom.

A similar transvaluation of values is overtaking the free speech principle today.[42] The right to speak has been recast as a right to be free from business regulation. Copyright is slowly being converted to property simpliciter with virtually perpetual terms; trademark and patent have steadily grown in scope; and database protection, already extant in the European Union,[43] is on the horizon in the United States.[44] Indeed, in some respects, digital rights management and paracopyright offer copyrighted works even greater protection than ordinary property receives.[45] Intellectual property, which was originally viewed as a limited government monopoly designed to encourage innovation, has been transformed into a bulwark against innovation, facilitating control over digital content and limiting the speech of others.

We are living through a Second Gilded Age, which, like the first Gilded Age, comes complete with its own reconstruction of the meaning of liberty and property.[46] Freedom of speech is becoming a generalized right against economic regulation of the information industries. Property is becoming the right of the information industries to control how ordinary people use digital content. We can no more capitulate to the Second Gilded Age's construction of these ideas than to the constructions offered in the first Gilded Age. We must offer a critical alternative to this construction, much as progressive thinkers did a century ago.

V: The Progressivist Theory and Its Limitations

So far, I have explained how digital technologies have changed the social conditions in which speech is produced, and I have described the way that the information industries have attempted to reinterpret freedom of speech. These reinterpretations reflect the interests of businesses attempting to secure certain privileges in a changing economy. They are by no means necessary or inevitable, and indeed, I think that they are in many respects mistaken.

There is a better way to understand the free speech principle in the digital era. The alternative is a theory of freedom of speech based on the idea of a democratic culture. In order to explain this alternative, I would like to retrace my steps and think about how free speech theory dealt with the last great technological change, the rise of broadcast media.

Probably the most important theoretical approach to freedom of speech in the twentieth century has argued that freedom of speech is valuable because it preserves and promotes democracy and democratic self-government. The notion that there is an important connection between freedom of speech and democracy is hardly new—people have understood the connection for as long as democracies have been around. But the twentieth century produced a special emphasis on that connection, and during the course of the twentieth century, many thinkers claimed that the very purpose of freedom of speech was not so much to promote individual autonomy or personal fulfillment as to promote democratic deliberation about public issues. We can find the beginnings of this idea in Progressive Era thinkers in the first two decades of the twentieth century.[47] The most famous statement is by the philosopher of education Alexander Meiklejohn,[48] and his approach has greatly influenced later theorists.[49]

As a shorthand, I will call the democracy-based approach of Meiklejohn and his followers the "republican" or "progressivist" approach. That is because a focus on democratic deliberation rather than individual autonomy is characteristic of republican political theory, and it is also characteristic of much thinking in the Progressive Era in the United States.[50] Progressivism is a sensibility, an attitude about what democracy is and what wise government can do. The progressive has faith in government's ability to promote the public interest through rational deliberation, works to structure government and public decisionmaking to promote deliberation and consensus about important public policy issues, worships expertise, and views popular attitudes and popular culture with suspicion because they tend to be emotional, parochial, irrational, untutored, and in need of channeling, refinement, and education.[51]

I think it is no accident that the progressivist/republican approach to free speech arose in the twentieth century, for this was also the century of mass media. People who endorse democratic theories of free speech understand that although mass media can greatly benefit democracy, there is also a serious potential conflict between mass media and democratic self-governance. The reason is that mass media are held by a comparatively few people, and their ownership gives this relatively small group enormous power to shape public discourse and public debate. The danger is that they will use their dominant position in three equally worrisome ways.

The first worry is that the people who control mass media will skew coverage of public issues to promote views that they support. In a world where ownership of mass media is concentrated in the hands of a relatively few very wealthy individuals and corporate conglomerates, the agendas and concerns of the wealthy will prevail, constricting discussion of serious issues and serious alternatives to the status quo. As a result, people will get disinformation or a skewed picture of the world around them, and this will be harmful for democracy.

The second worry is that mass media will omit important information, issues, and positions that the public should take into account. As a result, people will be exposed to only a limited set of issues to deliberate about, and to only a limited number of ways of thinking about and dealing with this limited set of issues.

The third worry is that mass media will reduce the quality of public discourse in the drive for higher ratings and the advertising revenues and other profits that come with them. Mass media will oversimplify and dumb down discussions of public issues, substitute sensationalism and amusement for deliberation about public questions, and transform news and politics into forms of entertainment and spectacle. The endless drive for advertising revenues and profits tends to drive out serious discourse and replaces it with mind-numbing entertainment. This demobilizes the public, leaving them less and less interested in focusing on important public issues of the day.

For these three reasons, democracy-based theorists of free speech in the twentieth century have argued that government must regulate the mass media in a number of different ways: (1) by restricting and preventing media concentration; (2) by imposing public-interest obligations that require the broadcast media to include programming that covers public issues and covers them fairly; and (3) by requiring the broadcast media to grant access to a more diverse and wide-ranging group of speakers in order to expand the agenda of public discussion.

The progressivist/republican approach is an important counterweight to a market-oriented approach to freedom of speech that ties speech rights closely to ownership of property. I mentioned this approach in my discussion of telecommunications policy in the digital age, but of course, the argument that people who own telecommunications media should be free of government regulation predates the Internet. Indeed, the new market-based arguments are simply logical continuations of arguments for deregulation of the broadcast media that have been going on for many years.[52] The Internet has simply given media corporations a new justification for using the free speech principle as an anti-regulatory tool: Because people do not need access to the mass media to speak, governments have lost their greatest justification for mass media regulation.

However, we cannot expect that the Internet will adequately compensate for any loss in media diversity that might come from deregulation, elimination of public interest obligations, and increased media concentration. First, market concentration in mass media is not unrelated to market concentration in cable and broadband ownership. Many of the same companies that have gobbled up an increasingly large share of mass media markets also have control over cable companies and broadband companies. As we have seen, these companies have interests in eliminating competition and controlling the Internet experience of end users. So increased media concentration may actually exacerbate or dovetail with loss of end-user autonomy on the Internet. Second, the quality and diversity of information that flows over the Internet is inevitably shaped by the quality and diversity of information available in broadcast media and cable, because that is where a very large number of people still get most of their news and information. If more traditional mass media provide disinformation, constrict agendas of public discussion, displace discussion of public issues, and demobilize audiences, Internet speech can only partially compensate. We cannot view the Internet as a complete substitute for mass media. Instead, Internet speech is layered on top of the forms of public discourse and discussion that cable and broadcast media provide. This follows from my argument that speech on the Internet routes around and gloms onto the products of the mass media. The mass media remain a central substrate on which Internet speech builds.

Nevertheless, the Internet does make a difference to freedom of speech. The digital age exposes weaknesses and limitations in democracy-based theories of free speech, just not the ones with which the capitalist approach is concerned.

Progressivist and republican approaches arose in response to the challenge to democracy posed by mass media. And their limitations arise from the same set of concerns. The progressivist/republican approach is limited in three important respects. First, it emphasizes political questions and deliberation about public issues over other forms of speech. It tends to value other kinds of speech to the extent that they contribute to public discussion of political questions rather than for their own sake. Second, for the same reason, the progressivist/republican approach tends to downplay the importance of popular culture, too often seeing it as ill-informed and a distraction from serious issues. Third, because its paradigmatic concern is broadcast media held by a relatively small number of people, who may misuse their power to control the public agenda or demobilize the citizenry, the progressivist/republican approach tends to downplay the centrality of liberty and personal autonomy to freedom of speech.[53] It focuses instead on equality and on the production of a suitable agenda for public discussion. In Meiklejohn's famous phrase, the point of freedom of speech is not that everyone shall speak, but that "everything worth saying shall be said."[54]

The progressivist/republican argument that we should not tie the right of free speech too closely to the right of private property remains valid, particularly in an age of increasing media concentration. That is because the liberty of speech and the liberties involved in property ownership are two different kinds of freedom. Although property rights often assist free expression—think of the right to use the software and the computer that one own—they can also undermine it, as suggested by the examples of content discrimination in telecommunications networks and the use of digital rights management to control the end user's experience.

Nevertheless, the paradigm case that motivates the progressivist agenda—the case of few speakers broadcasting to a largely inactive mass audience—no longer describes the world we live in. Even if, as I have argued, the new digital technologies do not displace mass media, they exist alongside it and build on top of it. Digital technologies give lots of people, more than ever before, a chance to participate in the creation and development of public culture. Technological changes in how speech is transmitted, and in who gets to participate in that transmission, change the focus of free speech theory.

VI: The Idea of a Democratic Culture

Let me begin by pointing to five characteristics of Internet speech that I believe are exemplary of freedom of speech generally. These characteristics are hardly new to the Internet; rather, my point is that the Internet makes them particularly salient. That salience, I shall argue, reshapes our conception of the free speech principle.

First, speech on the Internet ranges over every possible subject and mode of expression, including the serious, the frivolous, the gossipy, the erotic, the scatological, and the profound. The Internet reflects popular tastes, popular culture, and popular enthusiasms.

Second, the Internet, taken as a whole, is full of innovation. The tremendous growth of the Internet in a relatively short period of time shows how enormously creative ordinary people can be if given the chance to express themselves. And it demonstrates what ordinary people can do when they are allowed to be active producers rather than passive recipients of their cultural world.

Third, much of the source of that creativity is the ability to build on something else. This is particularly true of the World Wide Web.

As originally conceived, the very structure of HTML code encourages copying, imitation, and linking. The continual innovation and transformation we see in digital media stems directly from their ability to use the old to make the new. Digital media allow lots of people to comment, absorb, appropriate, and innovate—to add a wrinkle here, a criticism there. Internet speech continually develops through linkage, collage, annotation, mixture, and through what I have called routing around and glomming on. Internet speech, like all speech, appropriates and transforms. It imitates, copies, builds upon and mixes.

Fourth, Internet speech is participatory and interactive. People don't merely watch (or listen to) the Internet as if it were television or radio. Rather, they surf through it, they program on it, they publish to it, they write comments and continually add things to it. Internet speech is a social activity that involves exchange, give and take. The roles of reader and writer, producer and consumer of information are blurred and often effectively merge.

Fifth, and finally, because Internet speech is a social activity, a matter of interactivity, of give and take, it is not surprising that Internet speech creates new communities, cultures, and subcultures. In this way, it exemplifies an important general feature of freedom of speech: Freedom of speech allows us, each of us, to participate in the growth and development of the cultures and subcultures that, in turn, help constitute us as individuals. Freedom of speech is part of an interactive cycle of social exchange, social participation, and self-formation. We speak and we listen, we send out and we take in. As we do this, we change, we grow, we become something other than we were before, and we make something new out of what existed before.

To sum up, the Internet makes particularly salient five facts about free speech: Speech ranges over a wide variety of subjects, including not only politics but also popular culture. The speech of ordinary people is full of innovation and creativity. That creativity comes from building on what has come before. Speech is participatory and interactive as opposed to mere receipt of information. It merges the activities of reading and writing, of production and consumption. Finally, speech involves cultural participation and self-formation. The Internet reminds us how central and important these features are to speech generally. It reveals to us in a new way what has always been the case.

And this brings me to a central point: The populist nature of freedom of speech, its creativity, its interactivity, its importance for community and self-formation, all suggest that a theory of freedom of speech centered around government and democratic deliberation about public issues is far too limited. The free speech principle has always been about something larger than democracy in the narrow sense of voting and elections, something larger even than democracy in the sense of public deliberation about issues of public concern. If free speech is about democracy, it is about democracy in the widest possible sense, not merely at the level of governance, or at the level of deliberation, but at the level of culture. The Internet teaches us that the free speech principle is about, and always has been about, the promotion and development of a democratic culture.

Democracy is far more than a set of procedures for resolving disputes. It is a feature of social life and a form of social organization. Democratic ideals require a further commitment to democratic forms of social structure and social organization, a commitment to social as well as political equality.[55] And the forces of democratization operate not only through regular elections, but through changes in institutions, practices, customs, mannerisms, speech, and dress. A "democratic" culture, then, means much more than democracy as a form of self-governance. It means democracy as a form of social life in which unjust barriers of rank and privilege are dissolved, and in which ordinary people gain a greater say over the institutions and practices that shape them and their futures.

What makes a culture democratic, then, is not democratic governance but democratic participation. A democratic culture includes the institutions of representative democracy, but it also exists beyond them, and, indeed undergirds them. A democratic culture is the culture of a democratized society; a democratic culture is a participatory culture.

If the purpose of freedom of speech is to realize a democratic culture, why is democratic cultural participation important? First, culture is a source of the self. Human beings are made out of culture. A democratic culture is valuable because it gives ordinary people a fair opportunity to participate in the creation and evolution of the processes of meaning-making that shape them and become part of them; a democratic culture is valuable because it gives ordinary people a say in the progress and development of the cultural forces that in turn produce them.

Second, participation in culture has a constitutive or performative value: When people are creative, when they make new things out of old things, when they become producers of their culture, they exercise and perform their freedom and become the sort of people who are free. That freedom is something more than just choosing which cultural products to purchase and consume; the freedom to create is an active engagement with the world.[56]

By "culture" I mean the collective processes of meaning-making in a society. The realm of culture, however, is much broader than the concern of the First Amendment or the free speech principle. Armaments and shampoo are part of culture; so too are murder and robbery. And all of these things can affect people's lives and shape who they are. The realm of culture for purposes of the free speech principle is a subset of what anthropologists study as forms of culture. It refers to a set of historically contingent and historically produced social practices and media that human beings employ to exchange ideas and share opinions.[57] These are the methods, practices, and technologies through which dialogue occurs and public opinion is formed. For example, today people generally regard art as a social practice for the exchange of ideas, and they regard motion pictures as a medium of expression.[58] These practices and media of social communication construct the realm that we regard as "speech" for purposes of the free speech principle.[59] We cannot give an exhaustive list of these practices and media precisely because the social conventions and technologies that define them are always evolving; even so, it seems clear enough that the Internet and other digital technologies are media for the communication of ideas, and an increasingly important way for people to express their ideas and form their opinions.[60] They are central—and I would say crucial—media for the realization of a democratic culture.

Culture has always been produced through popular participation. Digital technology simply makes this aspect of democratic life more obvious, more salient. Radio and television are technologies of mass cultural reception, where a few speakers can reach audiences of indefinite size. But the Internet is a technology of mass cultural participation in which audiences can give as well as receive, broadcast as well as absorb, create and contribute as well as consume. Digital technology makes the values of a democratic culture salient to us because it offers the technological possibility of widespread cultural participation.

What is the difference between grounding freedom of speech on the promotion of democracy and grounding it on the promotion of a democratic culture? What is at stake in the move to culture?

There are three important differences, I think, and each stems from the weaknesses of the progressivist/republican model: They concern the status of nonpolitical expression, the role of popular culture, and the importance of individual participation and individual liberty.

A. Nonpolitical Expression

A serious difficulty with the progressivist/republican model has always been that a wide variety of activities, of which art and social commentary are only the most salient examples, have always fit poorly into a democratic theory of free expression. Lots of speech is not overtly political. Nevertheless, it gets protected under the progressivist/republican model because it is useful for political discussion, because it may become enmeshed in political controversies (and thus threatened or suppressed for political reasons), or because it is very hard to draw lines separating what is political from what is not.[61] In like fashion, lots of activities cannot easily be classified as deliberation—like singing, shouting, protesting, gossiping, making fun of people, or just annoying them or getting them angry. Nevertheless, these activities are protected because we can think of them as raw materials for further democratic deliberation or because we cannot easily draw lines separating them from the social practice of deliberation.[62] In both cases, then, we have kinds of speech that are at the periphery rather than the core; we protect them in aid of something more central and precious. In short, the progressivist vision sees democratic deliberation about public issues at the core of constitutional concern and other subjects and other forms of expression as peripheral or supplementary.

I have never been satisfied with this approach. I think something is missing here, and the notion of democratic culture helps us understand why. The point of democracy, as its name implies, is to put power in the hands of the people, to give ordinary people some measure of control over the forces that shape their lives and some degree of say about how the world around them develops. But law and governance are only parts of this world. Culture is an even larger part, and in some ways it has an even more capacious role in structuring our lives. The various processes of communication and cultural exchange are the sources of the self and its development over time. Our ideas, our habits, our thoughts, our very selves are produced through constant communication and exchange with others.[63] The influence is reciprocal: Through this continuous communication and exchange, we shape culture and are shaped by it in turn. We absorb it, we inhabit it, we make it new. We send it out into the world, we make it part of us.

Culture is more than governance, more than politics, more than law. And if democracy is giving power to the people, then true democracy means allowing people not only to have a say about who represents them in a legislature, or what laws are passed, but also to have a say about the shape and growth of the culture that they live in and that is inevitably part of them. Power to the people—democracy—in its broadest, thickest sense, must include our relationship not simply to the state but to culture as a whole, to the processes of meaning-making that constitute us as individuals. Those processes of meaning-making include both the ability to distribute those meanings and the ability to receive them.[64]

Culture is an essential ingredient of the self, and so freedom of speech means participation in the forces of culture that shape the self. We participate in the growth and development of culture through interaction, through communicating to others and receiving ideas from others. Cultural democracy is memetic democracy, the continuous distribution, circulation, and exchange of bits of culture from mind to mind.[65] This vision of culture is not democratic because people are voting on what is in their culture. It is democratic because they get to participate in the meaning-making processes that form and reproduce culture. They do this through communicating with and interacting with others. Moreover, democratic culture is not democratic because people are participating in processes of deliberation about governance, or even public issues. Rather it is democratic because it is participation in the creation and shaping of culture, which is, at the same time, participation in the growth and development of the self.

B. Popular Culture

The second basic problem with the work of Meiklejohn and his heirs has been its relative neglect and suspicion of popular culture. Popular culture is often seen as mass culture controlled by corporations, which demobilizes the citizenry; as sensationalism or dumbed-down speech, which adds little of importance to democratic deliberation; or as mere entertainment, which distracts people from serious discussion of public issues.[66] But from the perspective of democratic culture, popular culture and entertainment should not be merely peripheral or a distraction. They should be a central part of what freedom of speech is about.

In an age of unidirectional mass media, popular culture was, to a very large extent, mass culture—a set of commodities manufactured and sent out to be consumed by a mass audience. But the Internet allows mass culture to be appropriated by ordinary citizens and become, more than ever before, a truly popular culture, because it allows what I have called routing around and glomming on.[67]

We can understand the controversies over intellectual property in this light. Media corporations are turning to digital rights management to avoid digital piracy. But much of what traditional mass media most fears and resents is not piracy but cultural appropriation—individual riffs on mass media digital products shared with others—and the ability of consumers to route around a controlled advertising and marketing environment. Shifting our focus from democracy to democratic culture helps us see that the problem in the digital age is not just deliberation about public issues. It is also the importance of letting ordinary people engage in appropriation and innovation rather than mere consumption; it is the value of ordinary people being able to "rip, mix, and burn,"[68] to route around traditional media gatekeepers and glom onto existing media products.

In a democratic culture, we are interested in protecting not only speech about public issues, but also speech that concerns popular expression in art, as well as cultural concerns such as gossip, mores, fashions, and popular music. The progressivist/republican approach has tended to valorize high culture and high quality programming as aids to democratic deliberation (often conflating the two in the process), with "low" culture protected only as a peripheral concern.[69] But if freedom of speech is concerned with the promotion of a truly democratic culture, popular culture is every bit as important as so-called high culture.[70] In fact, in a democratic culture, the distinction between high culture and low culture begins to blur and the difference between them becomes increasingly difficult to maintain. High culture continually borrows from popular culture; moreover, as culture becomes increasingly democratized, the popular culture of today often turns out to be the high culture of tomorrow.

C. Individual Participation

A third problem with the progressivist/republican model has been its tendency to seek to manage discourse and structure public debate.[71] This desire is hardly surprising: In a world dominated by mass media controlled by a relative handful of very wealthy corporations, it seems important to make sure that dissenting views get a word in edgewise, that serious issues are not driven out by the media's never-ending quest for profits, and that audiences are not stultified and demobilized by an endless stream of increasingly vapid entertainment. As a result, the progressivist model has downplayed individual liberty and instead played up the protection of democratic processes, including robust debate on public issues and the creation of an informed citizenry. Earlier, I noted Meiklejohn's famous statement that the point of freedom of speech is not that everyone shall speak, but that everything worth saying shall be said. Meiklejohn even analogized the system of free expression to a town meeting.[72] The purpose of the town meeting was to shape a public agenda for discussion of serious issues; there would be time for only some people to speak. The important point was that the participants in the meeting be informed and stick to the agenda because everyone would decide what to do on the basis of the information presented. Although Meiklejohn's town meeting seems quite distant from the electronic mass media, it had many of the same features: scarcity of time, the need for a public agenda, and the importance of an informed citizenry. Hence the need for regulation was very much the same.

Democratic culture, by contrast, is not solely concerned with people's ability to be informed about a particular agenda. It is concerned with participation, interaction, and the ability of people to create, to innovate, to borrow ideas and make new ones. Meiklejohn remarked that his ideal town meeting was "self-government," not a "dialectical free-for-all."[73] That opposition may hold true for a particular form of democracy. But in a democratic culture, and especially the culture of the Internet, freedom of expression is a dialectical free-for-all, a continuous process of interactivity and innovation, in which culture and discussion move and grow in any number of different directions.

Here again a shift in focus from democracy to democratic culture responds to the sorts of freedoms that digital technologies make possible. Digital technologies and telecommunications networks mean that people are no longer forced into the role of mere spectators and consumers; they can be active participants, creating, commenting, and broadcasting their own ideas to a larger public. And in a world in which active participation in the creation and distribution of culture becomes possible for so many, liberty is an important good to be prized, valued, and nourished.

The progressivist/republican conception of free speech arose in the twentieth century because ordinary people were shut out of the most pervasive and important forms of speech and were reduced to the roles of spectators, consumers, and recipients. In that world, protecting the liberty of a favored few who owned the means of communication from regulation was less important than producing discussion on public issues and promoting a robust agenda of diverse and antagonistic sources so that the citizenry could be well-informed and engaged with the great public issues of the day. But new technologies make it possible for vast numbers of people to participate, innovate, and create, to route around and glom on to the traditional mass media and their products. This has increased enormously the practical liberty of the ordinary citizen to speak, and to reach a vast audience. When technology makes liberty possible, liberty once again must return to the forefront of concern.[74]

The twentieth-century concern with speech as a method of democratic deliberation privileges the delivery of information about issues of public concern to the public, who receive this information through asymmetric and unidirectional mass media. I do not wish to deny the importance of that conception; I merely want to insist that it is only a partial conception, inadequate to deal with the features of speech that the new digital technologies bring to the foreground of our concern. The values behind freedom of speech are about production as much as reception, about creativity as much as deliberation, about the work of ordinary individuals as much as the mass media.

Freedom of speech is more than the freedom of elites and concentrated economic enterprises to funnel media products for passive reception by docile audiences. Freedom of speech is more than the choice of which media products to consume. Freedom of speech means giving everyone—not just a small number of people who own dominant modes of mass communication, but ordinary people, too—the chance to use technology to participate in their culture, to interact, to create, to build, to route around and glom on, to take from the old and produce the new, and to talk about whatever they want to talk about, whether it be politics, public issues, or popular culture.

VII: Digital Liberty

Shifting our focus from democracy to democratic culture helps us better understand the idea of freedom of speech in the digital age. Indeed, I would go even further. Digital technologies change our understanding of what liberty of speech is. They make salient features of freedom of speech that have always been present. Digital technologies offer people the liberty to participate in culture through application of existing cultural materials, the ability to appropriate and innovate using tools freely available to all. Digital technology offers a possibility, not yet fully realized (and conceivably one that will never be fully realized), of what democratic culture might be.

A democratic culture is the culture of widespread "ripping, mixing, and burning,"[75] of nonexclusive appropriation, innovation, and combination. It is the culture of routing around and glomming on, the culture of annotation, innovation, and bricolage. Democratic culture is not the same thing as mass culture. It makes use of the instrumentalities of mass culture, but transforms them, individualizes them, and sends what it produces back into the cultural stream. In democratic culture, individuals are not mere consumers and recipients of mass culture but active appropriators. Culture has always had opportunities for popular participation. The Internet and digital technologies merely increase the number of opportunities for widespread distribution, their scope, and their power; and, in the process, make them more obvious to us. Digital speech places these features of liberty - and the possibility of democratic culture— more clearly and centrally before us.

What is the liberty of expression, viewed from the perspective of the ideal of democratic culture? I would say that it has four important components that have been made more salient by digital technology: (1) the right to publish, distribute to, and reach an audience; (2) the right to interact with others and exchange ideas with them, which includes the right to influence and to be influenced, to transmit culture and absorb it; (3) the right to appropriate from cultural materials that lay at hand, to innovate, annotate, combine, and then share the results with others; and (4) the right to participate in and produce culture, and thus the right to have a say in the development of the cultural and communicative forces that shape the self.

What these facets of liberty have in common is that they are not self-regarding. Communication is interacting, sharing, influencing, and being influenced in turn. Creation is not creation ex nihilo, but building on the work of others; appropriation is not exclusive appropriation but making use of tools that lay to hand that are part of a common pool of resources. Distribution is not isolated but occurs through public pathways and networks that many can travel on. Finally, development of the self is a project that one shares with others.

In short, what the Internet makes salient to us is that freedom of expression, that most individualistic of liberties, that most personal of activities, is at the very same time deeply communal, because it is interactive, because it is participatory, because it builds on the work of what others have done, and because it makes use of public networks and pathways of distribution. I do not mean by this that liberty exists merely for the purposes of the state, or that individual liberty is an illusion. Far from it. I mean precisely the opposite—that the realization of individuality, the expression of one's individual self, the promotion of one's individual dignity, comes out of and through culture, a shared feature of life. Culture is the substrate, the raw materials of individual freedom, from which individual liberty emerges and within which individual liberty operates and innovates.[76]

The concept of a democratic culture restores freedom to its central place in free speech theory, but in the process, offers a particular conception of what that freedom is: Freedom is participation. Freedom is distribution. Freedom is interaction. Freedom is the ability to influence and be influenced in turn. Freedom is the ability to change others and to be changed as well. Freedom is the ability to glom on and route around. Freedom is appropriation, transformation, promulgation, subversion, the creation of the new out of the old. Freedom is mixing, fusing, separating, conflating, and uniting. Freedom is the discovery of synergies, the reshuffling of associations and connections, the combination of influences and materials.

Dissent is central to this conception of free speech, for dissent is cultural as well as political.[77] Just as the progressivist/republican critique has too narrow a focus on why speech is valuable, it has too limited a conception of dissent. People may disagree with what the government is doing, and they may express themselves in politics, in music, or in art. But they can also disagree with the aesthetics and mores of others, and they can dissent by borrowing from and subverting what they borrow. And just as democratic culture undergirds democracy in the narrow sense without being identical to it, cultural dissent is an important source of political dissent without being subsumed by it.

Perhaps equally important, dissent involves all of the features of liberty I have just described: interaction, appropriation, and transformation. Dissent reacts to, borrows from, and builds on what it disagrees with. Dissent, whether in culture or in politics, is not mere negation. Rather, dissent is creative and cumulative. It appropriates elements of what it objects to and uses them in the process of critique, often through subverting or parodying them.[78] The nature and focus of dissent is shaped by what the dissenter disagrees with, and the form of response is shaped by the way the problem appears to the critic. Thus, dissent exists in an interactive and interdependent relationship to the object of its criticism, appropriating elements of what it rebukes in order to make its claims. Dissent makes use of the raw materials that inspire its disagreement and resistance. In this way, dissent, and responses to dissent, are not mere repudiations of what has come before, but have a cumulative effect, building on existing materials and practices, and propelling and transforming culture forward.

I have emphasized that the ability of ordinary individuals to produce their own culture is a central aspect of the liberty of free expression. What justifies this populist focus? Why shouldn't we organize telecommunications and intellectual property law to maximize the ability of large business enterprises to make large investments in cultural products (e.g., blockbuster movies) while allowing consumers to choose which ones they prefer to consume in the marketplace? Why isn't this cultural division of labor an equally good protection of freedom of speech?

One answer is that the ability to participate in culture and produce one's own meanings can offer people greater self-realization and self-fulfillment than perpetually being relegated to the docile consumption of mass media products. But even if we remain agnostic on that point, being an active producer/creator is at least as good a way of living as being a passive consumer/recipient, and it is an equally important part of the liberty of expression.

Market forces are likely to underprotect the right of ordinary individuals to be active cultural producers, because media companies are likely to make more money from consumption of the media products they advertise and sell. From the standpoint of these companies, individual cultural production has no independent value except to the extent that it involves or leads to the consumption of media goods. And to the extent that active cultural participation diverts end users from greater consumption of media products, interferes with the companies' expansive definition of intellectual property rights, or challenges corporate technologies of control, it is less valuable than passive consumption; indeed it is positively harmful and must be cabined in.

One might object that media companies will invest in products and services that facilitate individual cultural appropriation and production if consumers want them badly enough. To some extent this is true: We have already seen the beginnings of this in multi-user online games. But individual cultural production often has high positive externalities; it provides benefits and satisfactions that are not easily captured by markets.[79] So media companies may have insufficient incentives to facilitate individual cultural appropriation and production. Conversely, they will tend to over-invest in products that relegate individuals to a position of relatively passive consumers.

Choosing what products to consume is a kind of liberty, but it does not exhaust the liberty of free expression. The ability to produce, create, and innovate is just as important. These two forms of liberty are not fungible, and markets do not adequately measure the difference between them.[80] To protect freedom of expression, then, we must make a space for individual cultural appropriation and production. We should not choose a form of political economy that gives greater incentives to be a passive recipient than an active creator of culture.

Democratic culture is a regulative ideal. It offers a picture of what the world could look like given the technology we now have. It offers a picture of what freedom of speech could be in a digital world. Nevertheless, digital technology does not guarantee the production of a democratic culture. As I noted previously, businesses are now using the new technologies to attempt to constrain and channel democratic participation. They are doing so both through laws and through technological solutions, including packet discrimination and digital rights management. And they are justifying these innovations through an interpretation of freedom of speech that ties speech to property rights. This capitalist conception is important both for its explanation of what freedom of speech is (freedom from business regulation) and what it is not (an enforceable limit on the expansion of intellectual property rights).

The ideal of democratic culture is important precisely as a critical perspective that allows us to criticize this emerging interpretation of free speech and intellectual property. The developing capitalist conception of freedom of speech (and its accompanying denial of free speech limitations on the growth of intellectual property) is inconsistent with the promotion of a democratic culture. The same technological changes that suggested what a democratic culture might become have produced a very different interpretation of the free speech principle that ties it ever more closely to the ownership of the forms of capital characteristic of the information age—intellectual property and control over distribution networks. The idea of a democratic culture stands as a critique of this emerging property-based conception. That critique is crucial, because the architecture of the digital age and the law that governs distribution networks are up for grabs. They can develop in many different ways, and the point is to ensure that they develop in the right ways.

VIII: The Judicial Model and Its Limitations
To protect freedom of speech in the digital age, we will have to reinterpret and refashion both telecommunications policy and intellectual property law to serve the values of freedom of speech, which is to say, we will have to fashion and interpret them with the goals of a democratic culture in mind.

How is this to be done? I have argued that the digital age subtly alters our understanding of liberty of expression. I believe it also changes how that liberty might be protected.

Throughout the twentieth century, the most familiar method of protecting freedom of speech was through the judicial creation and protection of individual legal rights, and in particular, constitutional rights. Of course, when we look more closely, we will also discover many other features of public policy that promoted free speech values. They include, among other things, free public education, the creation and maintenance of public libraries, a nationwide public mail system, subsidies for postage for books and publications by nonprofit organizations, the use of common carrier models for telephony, and national telecommunications policies that attempted to lower costs and increase access to radio and television. For the most part, however, these policies have been regarded as largely peripheral to the main event—the judicial recognition and creation of doctrines that protect free speech rights from government censorship or other forms of government regulation.

Indeed, the very success of the program of expanding individual free speech rights protected by courts made it an article of faith that this was how freedom of speech should be secured—through the judicial creation and protection of individual rights of free expression enforceable against state actors. This notion has two important and distinct assumptions. First, it assumes that one protects freedom of expression through protecting individual rights of free speech, rather than through creating systems of communication and information-sharing used by lots of people that facilitate free expression. Put differently, it views the system of free expression as no more than the sum of all of the individual rights of free expression. Second, the model assumes that these individual rights will be created and protected primarily by courts, rather than by legislatures or administrative agencies, or, for that matter, by engineers, software designers, and technology companies.

Nevertheless, the examples I mentioned earlier—free public education, free public libraries, common carrier rules in telephony, public interest rules in telecommunications, a public mail system, government subsidies for books and nonprofit publications, and so on—do not match these assumptions. They are policies and institutions that promote a healthy and democratic system of free expression, but they are not composed of individual free speech rights. Rather, they combine lots of different private rights with various government programs and entitlements, and in the case of telecommunications regulations, they may even include requirements for technological design. Second, these features of the system of free expression are not always primarily created or protected by courts. Rather, they are created by a number of parties, including legislatures and administrative agencies.

The model of judicial protection of individual rights remains crucially important in the digital age. But it will not be able to protect freedom of speech fully. The digital age makes increasingly apparent what has always been the case—that the system of free expression relies on something more than the sum of all individual free speech rights. It relies on a technological and regulatory infrastructure. That infrastructure is produced through government regulation, through government subsidies and entitlement programs, and through technological design. Freedom of speech is, and always has been, a cultural phenomenon as well as a legal or political one. A healthy and well-functioning system of free expression depends on technologies of communication and a public ready and able to use those technologies to participate in the growth and development of culture.

In the digital age, the technological and regulatory infrastructure that undergirds the system of free expression has become increasingly important. Elements of the system of free expression that were backgrounded in the twentieth century will become foregrounded in the twenty-first. They will be foregrounded, I argue, because the guarantee of a pure formal liberty to speak will increasingly be less valuable if technologies of communication and information storage are biased against widespread individual participation and toward the protection of property rights of media corporations. If we place too much emphasis on judicial doctrine at the expense of infrastructure, we will be left with formal guarantees of speech embedded in technologies of control that frustrate their practical exercise.

The system of free expression is produced through the synergy of (1) government policies that promote popular participation in technologies of communication, (2) technological designs that facilitate decentralized control and popular participation rather than hinder them, and (3) the traditional recognition and enforcement of judicially created rights against government censorship. The last of these—judicial creation and enforcement of rights of free speech against government abridgement—is the great achievement of the twentieth century. Nevertheless, I believe that in the long run it will be recognized as only one leg of a three-legged stool that supports the system of free expression. The other elements will increasingly move to the foreground of concern as it becomes clear that they are necessary to the promotion of a democratic culture.

IX: The Infrastructure of Free Expression: From Free Speech Rights to Free Speech Values

As the focus shifts from an exclusive concern with judicially protected individual constitutional rights to an additional concern with infrastructure, we must also shift our concern from free speech rights narrowly considered to free speech values. Free speech rights are rights of individuals enforceable by courts. Free speech values are values that we seek to promote through legislative and administrative regulation and through technological design.

Protecting freedom of speech in the digital age means promoting a core set of values in legislation, administrative regulation, and the design of technology. What are those values? They are interactivity, broad popular participation, equality of access to information and communications technology, promotion of democratic control in technological design, and the practical ability of ordinary people to route around, glom on, and transform. Free speech values include those aspects of liberty of expression that the digital age makes most salient: popular participation, interactivity, and the encouragement and protection of cultural creativity and cultural transformation.

Both technological architectures and legal regimes of regulation must be structured to make possible full and robust participation by individuals. Free speech values must enter both into the content of laws and the design of architectures of communication. That is because the key forms of capital in the digital era—intellectual property and telecommunications networks—can serve both as conduits for increased democratic cultural participation or as chokepoints and bottlenecks, centralizing control in the hands of a relatively few persons and organizations. What form informational capital will take, how it will be used, how it will be shared or if it will be shared at all, are the crucial questions of the digital age.

At stake in both intellectual property and telecommunications regulation is the question of democratic participation versus centralized control. This is most obvious in the context of distribution networks: The capitalist theory of free speech asserts the right of the owner of a communications network to control the flow of digital content through the network. But the capitalist theory also seeks to expand intellectual property rights so that rights holders can control the distribution, use, and transformation of media products even after these products are distributed and sold to a mass audience. The theory of free speech as democratic culture, by contrast, argues that both communications networks and intellectual property rights must facilitate broad cultural participation. Communications networks are public in nature even if their technological infrastructure is privately owned. Therefore they must grant fair access to their networks, they must not act as chokepoints or bottlenecks, and they must not unfairly discriminate against content from other sources. Intellectual property rights must also serve democratic ends: They exist to promote the spread of culture and possibilities for cultural innovation and transformation.

To make intellectual property consistent with the idea of free speech as democratic culture, there must be a robust and ever expanding public domain with generous fair use rights. Intellectual property also must not be permitted to create chokepoints or bottlenecks in the spread of knowledge and the distribution of culture.

Judicial creation and protection of individual rights is ill equipped to deal with many of the most important problems of freedom of speech in the digital era. Free speech values are often either promoted or hindered by the ways that technologies are designed and the ways that technological standards are set. Technological designs and standards can let private parties become gatekeepers and bottlenecks controlling the flow of information and the scope of permissible innovation; or, conversely, they can promote widespread participation and innovation.

Law has an important role to play here. Laws affect how technology is designed, the degree of legal protection that a certain technology will enjoy, and whether still other technologies that modify or route around existing technological forms of distribution and control will be limited or forbidden. But increasingly, these sorts of decisions will be made by legislatures and administrative agencies in consultation with private parties. Generally speaking, courts come to free speech controversies after technologies are already in place and deals between stakeholders have already been struck. Courts can construe existing statutes to protect free speech values. But in most cases they cannot easily order that particular new technologies or new standards be implemented. They cannot easily hold, for example, that a certain technological design must be adopted. They cannot insist that private companies refrain from using certain digital rights management technologies in return for a congressional statute that sets up a compulsory licensing scheme. Courts can remand lower court and administrative agency decisions, but they cannot easily remand technologies to their designers and ask them to make the technology more free speech friendly. Nor can they order or oversee the sort of comprehensive bargains that contemporary intellectual property regulation increasingly requires. Those tasks will fall to other actors, with courts enforcing the legal bargains that are produced consistent with free speech values.

The free speech values I have identified—participation, access, interactivity, democratic control, and the ability to route around and glom on—won't necessarily be protected and enforced through judicial creation of constitutional rights. Rather, they will be protected and enforced through the design of technological systems—code—and through legislative and administrative schemes of regulation, for example, through open access requirements or the development of compulsory license schemes in copyright law.

This transforms the study of freedom of speech to the study of the design of architectures and regulatory systems. It is no accident, I think, that many of the people who are at the forefront of the push for freedom in cyberspace are computer scientists, engineers, and software programmers, and it is no accident that lawyers who do cyberlaw spend an increasing amount of time thinking about technological and administrative solutions to civil rights issues. That is because, as I have argued, free speech values are embedded both in administrative regulations and in technological design. To protect free speech in the digital age, lawyers have to become cyberlawyers,[81] not simply lawyers who study cyberlaw, but lawyers who think about how technology can best be structured and how public policies can best be achieved through wise technological design.[82]

Conclusion: Rights Dynamism

I return to the question I posed at the beginning of this essay: How should the theoretical justifications for freedom of speech change given the change in social conditions produced by the digital age?

We can now offer an answer to this question. Technological change presents new possibilities for freedom of expression, shows the value of free speech in a different light, and makes particular features of freedom of speech particularly salient. These features include interactivity, mass participation, nonexclusive appropriation, and creative transformation. This in turn leads us to a new conception of the purposes of freedom of speech, which I have called the promotion of a democratic culture.

However, these same technological changes also create new forms of social conflict, as business interests try to protect new forms of capital investment. This leads, in turn, to attempts to protect and expand rights in intellectual property and in the control of telecommunications networks. These rights claims clash with freedom of speech values in ever new ways; and the attempt to protect property rights in capital investment leads to competing visions of what freedom of speech is and what it is not.

Finally, as technological innovation alters the social conditions of speech, the technological and legal infrastructure that supports the system of free expression becomes foregrounded. As a result, free speech values must be articulated and protected in new ways, in particular, through the design of technology and through legislative and administrative regulation of technology, in addition to the traditional focus on judicial doctrines that protect constitutional rights.

As the world changes around us, as the possibilities and problems of new technologies are revealed, our conception of the free speech principle begins to change with them. Our sense of what freedom of speech is, why we value it, and how best to preserve that which we value, reframes itself in the changing milieu. And as we respond to these changes, retracing our steps and rethinking our goals, we eventually come to understand what the free speech principle is about, and more importantly, what it always was about but only now can be adequately expressed. That experience is not the experience of making something new. It is the experience of finding something old, of recognizing principles and commitments already dimly understood, which suddenly are thrown into sharper focus by the alteration in our circumstances.

The arguments in this essay are an outgrowth of a more general way of thinking about rights and fundamental liberties. Call it a dynamic theory of rights, or rights dynamism. Rights dynamism is the claim that the nature, scope, and boundaries of rights, and in particular fundamental rights like speech, are continually shifting with historical, political, economic, and technological changes in the world.[83] The content and scope of those rights, the interests they protect and the interests they leave unprotected, change as the language of rights and the enforcement of rights are placed in new contexts, and are invoked by different actors and different economic and social interests. Hence it is necessary for those who believe in the language of rights—and in the recognition and protection of basic and fundamental rights such as the liberty of expression—to rethink the premises of rights as the discourse of rights is invoked in emerging social contexts. For only through constant rethinking, in the face of changed circumstances, can we recall and rediscover what our deepest commitments truly are. What appears to be change is actually continuity; what appears to be revision is actually the deepest form of remembrance.

Most people, I suspect, will be wary of such historicism for an obvious reason. If rights are truly fundamental, and therefore worth protecting and fighting for, their content should be relatively fixed over time. We should not alter what is protected and what is not protected every time we come across a result we do not like, for if the content and scope of basic liberties can change, and if they must be retheorized and reconceptualized in each generation, who is to say that they will not be eroded, undermined, or effectively destroyed? Even if we only set out to change our attitudes about these basic rights at the margins, jettisoning some elements and adding others, who is to say that we will not throw out the baby with the bathwater? What security do we have in rights that can change as history changes?

I do not underestimate these worries, or the force of these concerns. They describe a great danger for liberty. They articulate the threat that all historicism (and all relativism) present to principle and to principled argument. But here is the catch. If we do not, from time to time, rethink the scope and extension of our basic liberties, their scope and extension will change anyway, whether we like it or not. For faced as we are with social, technological, and economic change, other people will be busily rewriting rights and turning them to their own advantage. And if we do nothing to contest their work in an altered environment, we will soon find ourselves living with a set of fundamental rights framed and shaped according to their interests and their agendas.

Rights are a form of discourse, a way of thinking about the needs of social order and human liberty in the context of a changing world. Rights are also a source of power—first, because they are a powerful form of rhetorical appeal, and second, because the enforcement of rights recognized by the state is backed up the power of the state. Because of this, rights and rights discourse are continually invoked by people and by groups to further their ideals, interests, and agendas: For the discourse of rights is the discourse of power, the restructuring of rights is the restructuring of power, and the securing of rights is the securing of power.

As people face new problems and altered circumstances, they naturally invoke elements of existing rights discourses, hoping to extend them in preferred directions in order to articulate their moral and political ends and further their favored policies. They call upon the struggles and victories of the past and the legal concepts of the present in order to shape the future. This is as true of groups and interests we like as those we oppose.

Rights are not simply a fixed set of protections that the state affords or fails to afford. Rights are a terrain of struggle in a world of continuous change—a site of ongoing controversies, a battle-ground where the shape and contours of the terrain are remade with each victory. Rights, and particularly fundamental rights, far from being fixed and immovable, are moving targets. They are worth fighting over because the discourse of rights has power and because that discourse can be reshaped and is reshaped through intellectual debate and political struggle.

This feature of rights discourse is a special case of what I have called "ideological drift." The liberty of expression has no special security from such drift. To the contrary, it is subject to the pushing and pulling, the reconceptualizations and transvaluations to which all other rights are heir. The capitalist theory of rights that I have described previously is only the most recent example.

If one loves liberty, and believes that there are basic liberties that every decent society should recognize and protect, one must also recognize that the rhetorical reconstruction of rights will be ongoing whether we or others perform it. What we do not do for ourselves will surely be done to us.

Eternal vigilance, it is often said, is the price of liberty. But that vigilance is of two forms. The first kind of vigilance is the vigilance of the guardian, who attempts to ensure that every feature and aspect of liberty is preserved today just as it was in ages past. But the second and far more important form of vigilance is the vigilance of the guide or explorer, who helps others make the transition from the world they knew to the one that awaits them.

People are continually thrown into new circumstances and they must articulate the meaning of liberty in those new circumstances. The task of such a guide or explorer is to find the meaning of the old in the new, and to prevent the rhetoric of liberty from becoming liberty's prison. Such vigilance is every bit as important as the vigilance of the guardian. And this vigilance, too, is eternal, and its exercise, too, is the ineluctable price of liberty. The world will not stand still and let us enjoy our freedoms. It will continually make itself anew, and as it does, we must consider the ever-changing predicament of liberty, and the ever new methods by which it may be augmented or curtailed.

The digital revolution is a revolution, and like all revolutions, it is a time of confusion, a time of transition, and a time of opportunity for reshaping the structures of the economy and the sources of power. As a time of opportunity it is also a time of opportunism, a period in which the meaning of liberty of expression will be determined for good or for ill, just as the meaning of economic liberty was determined in an earlier age. Make no mistake: The digital age will change the meaning of freedom of expression. The only question is how it will change. If we do not reconsider the basis of liberty in this age, if we do not possess the vigilance of the guide as well as the guard, we shall end up like every person who travels through the wilderness without a compass, or through the forest without the forester. We shall end up lost.

Notes

1. See, e.g., Frank H. Easterbrook, "Cyberspace and the Law of the Horse," *University of Chicago Legal Forum* (1996): 207, 216 (arguing that clear rules, property rights, and facilitating bargains will resolve regulatory problems in cyberspace much as they do in real space); Joseph H. Sommer, "Against Cyberlaw," *Berkeley Technology Law Journal* 15 (2000): 1145, 1148 ("Few of the legal issues posed by the new informatics technologies are novel.").

2. See J.M. Balkin, "Populism and Progressivism as Constitutional Categories," *Yale Law Journal* 104 (1995): 1935, 1948-49 (reviewing Cass R. Sunstein, *Democracy and the Problem of Free Speech* (1993), and defining democratic culture as popular participation in culture).

Media and popular culture theorist John Fiske has coined the term "semiotic democracy" to describe popular participation in the creation of meanings, often by turning existing forms of mass culture to different uses. John Fiske, *Television Culture* (London: Methuen, 1987) pp. 236-39; see also Michael Madow, "Private Ownership of Public Image: Popular Culture and Publicity Rights," *California Law Review* (1993): 125, 146 (defining semiotic democracy as "a society in which all persons are free and able to participate actively, if not equally, in the generation and circulation of meanings and values"). Fiske's idea has become particularly important in the intellectual property literature. See infra article 56.

3. Balkin, supra article 2, at 1948-49.

4. Thomas I. Emerson, *The System of Freedom of Expression* (Vintage Books: New York, 1970) p. 3.

5. Cf. Jacques Derrida, *Limited Inc.: a b c . . .,* in Glyph #2 (Baltimore: Johns Hopkins University Press, 1977) pp. 162, 200. Jed Rubenfeld expresses a similar idea through the metaphor of imagination. He argues that freedom of speech protects the rights of both authors and readers because acts of imagination are inevitably transformative, both for producers and receivers of cultural objects. Jed Rubenfeld, "The Freedom of Imagination: Copyright's Constitutionality," *Yale Law Journal* 112 (2002): 37-38. Rebecca Tushnet points out that repetition of ideas or social scripts can be a way of expressing solidarity with others, support for a favored cause, or one's own sense of propriety as a member of a religious, political, or social group. Rebecca Tushnet, "Copyright as a Model for Free Speech Law: What Copyright Has in Common with Anti-Pornography Laws, Campaign Finance Reform, and Telecommunications Regulation," *Boston College Law Review* 42 (2001): 1, 16-17.

6. See Jack M. Balkin, "Free Speech From a Meme's Point of View" (April 4, 2003): 8, 13 (unpublished manuscript, on file with *New York University Law Review*) (explaining rapid growth of expression on Internet in terms of lowered costs of production and distribution of information).

7. See J.M. Balkin, "Media Filters, the V-Chip, and the Foundations of Broadcast Regulation," *Duke Law Journal* 45 (1996): 1131, 1145 ("In the Information Age, the informational filter, not information itself, is king."); James Boyle, "Foucault in Cyberspace: Surveillance, Sovereignty, and Hardwired Censors," *University of Cincinnati Law Review* 66 (1997): 177, 194 (noting that filtering technologies supply the State with "a different arsenal of methods with which to regulate content").

8. Lowering the costs of distribution also allows more speakers to reach across existing cultural, geographical, and disciplinary boundaries. It allows information to get past previously closed communities, it enables new communities to form based on existing interests, and it helps create new interests around which communities can form.

9. I borrow this term from C. Edwin Baker, *Media, Markets, and Democracy* (Cambridge University Press, 2002) pp. 7-14 (noting important differences between media products and typical non-information goods).

10. On The Phantom Edit, see Richard Fausset, "A Phantom Menace?," *L.A. Times* (June 1, 2002) at F1.

11. Asked about the phenomenon by an interviewer, Lucas explained, "Everybody wants to be a filmmaker. Part of what I was hoping for with making movies in the first place was to inspire people to be creative. The Phantom Edit was fine as long as they didn't start selling it. Once they started selling it, it became a piracy issue. I'm on the Artist Rights Foundation board, and the issue of non-creators of a movie going in and changing things and then selling it as something else is wrong." Gavin Smith, "The Genius of the System: George Lucas Talks to Gavin Smith About Painting by Numbers, Mind-Numbing Minutiae, and Final Cuts," *Film Comment* (July-Aug. 2002), at 31, 32.

12. James Boyle argues that a characteristic feature of the information society is that an increasing proportion of product cost goes to content creation rather than to distribution, and to message rather than medium. James Boyle, "A Politics of Intellectual Property: Environmentalism for the Net?," *Duke Law Journal* 47 (1997): 87, 93-94. That is not necessarily inconsistent with my argument that digital technologies lower costs of innovation: Both content creation and distribution costs are lowered, but distribution costs decline much more rapidly. In the meantime, digital technologies spur new forms of content creation that would have been prohibitively expensive (or impossible) in the past.

13. For a list of some of the most popular blogs, see "The Truth Laid Bear's Blogosphere Ecosystem," at http://www.truthlaidbear.com/ecosystem.php (last visited Nov. 17, 2003).

14. See http://www.televisionwithoutpity.com (last visited Oct. 27, 2003).

15. Marshall Sella, "The Remote Controllers," *New York Times*, (Oct. 20, 2002) (Magazine), at 70 (noting that "it is now standard Hollywood practice for executive producers . . . to scurry into Web groups moments after an episode is shown on the East Coast," hoping to discover what core viewers like and dislike).

16. For examples of fan fiction, see generally http://www.fanfiction.net (last visited July 10, 2003). On the clash between fan fiction and copyright law, see Rebecca Tushnet, "Legal Fictions: Copyright, Fan Fiction, and a New Common Law," *Loyola of Los Angeles Entertainment Law Journal* 17 (1997): 651; Ariana Eunjung Cha, "Harry Potter and the Copyright Lawyer," *Washington Post* (June 18, 2003) at A1; Tracy Mayor, "Taking Liberties with Harry Potter," *Boston Globe* (June 29, 2003) (Magazine), at 14. The practice predates the Internet, see Henry Jenkins, *Textual Poachers: Television Fans & Participatory Culture* (New York: Routledge, 1992) pp. 152-62, but the Internet has helped spur the formation of new communities of fan fiction writers, whose collective efforts have drawn the attention (and occasionally the ire) of television producers.

17. This is the major concern of Lawrence Lessig, *Code and Other Laws of Cyberspace* (Basic Books, 1999) [hereinafter Lessig, *Code and Other Laws of Cyberspace*], and Lawrence Lessig, *The Future of Ideas: The Fate of the Commons in a Connected World* (Vintage, 2001) [hereinafter Lessig, *The Future of Ideas*].

18. The basic conflict between centralized control of information production and distribution and routing around and glomming on that I have identified here has many different aspects. Yochai Benkler views the conflict in terms of contrasting methods of information production—a conflict between, on the one hand, an industrial model of protection that produces mass culture prepackaged for consumption, and, on the other, various models of nonproprietary and peer production. Yochai Benkler, "Through the Looking Glass: Alice and the Constitutional Foundations of the Public Domain," *Law and Contemporary Problems* 66 (2003): 173, 181 [hereinafter Benkler, "The Public Domain"]; see also Yochai Benkler, "From Consumers to Users:

Shifting the Deeper Structures of Regulation Toward Sustainable Commons and User Access,"
Federal Communications Law Journal 52 (2000): 561, 562. The same technologies that allow the
industrialization of the goods of the mind also make possible new forms of peer production and
collaboration. See J.M. Balkin, "What Is a Postmodern Constitutionalism?" *Michigan Law Review*
90 (1992):1966, 1974, 1983 (defining postmodern era as era of industrialization of products of
mind); see also Yochai Benkler, "Coase's Penguin, or, Linux and The Nature of the Firm," *Yale
Law Journal* 112 (2002): 369, 375-90 (describing rise of collaborative methods for commons-based
peer production). The struggle between these models of production, which is waged both in
politics and in law, will determine the "institutional ecology" of information production in the
next century. Benkler, "The Public Domain," supra, at 181.

19. Karl Marx, "A Contribution to the Critique of Political Economy," in *The Marx-Engels
Reader,* Robert C. Tucker ed. (W. W. Norton & Company, 1978) pp. 4-5.

20. On the emerging conflict between freedom of speech and intellectual property, see
Yochai Benkler, "Constitutional Bounds of Database Protection: The Role of Judicial Review in
the Creation and Definition of Private Rights in Information," *Berkeley Technology Law Journal* 15
(2000): 535, 587-600 (suggesting conflict between free speech rights and database protection);
Yochai Benkler, "Free as the Air to Common Use: First Amendment Constraints on Enclosure of
the Public Domain," *New York University Law Review* 74 (1999): 354, 393-401, 412-14 (arguing that
given emerging methods of production of digital information, copyright promotes neither
diversity of information nor free expression).

21. See generally Mark Lemley & Eugene Volokh, "Freedom of Speech and Injunctions in
Intellectual Property Cases," *Duke Law Journal* 48 (1998): 147.

22. For a summary of the expansion in copyright law, particularly since 1970, see Neil
Netanel, "Locating Copyright in the First Amendment Skein," *Stanford Law Review* 54 (2001): 1,
18-26.

23. Pub. L. No. 105-298, 112 Stat. 2827 (1998) (codified at 17 U.S.C. 302 (2000)).

24. Pub. L. No. 105-304, 112 Stat. 2860 (1998) (codified at 17 U.S.C. 1201 (2000)).

25. See generally Lessig, *The Future of Ideas,* supra article 17, at 180-217; Niva Elkin-Koren,
"It's All About Control: Rethinking Copyright in the New Information Landscape," in *The
Commodification of Information,* Niva Elkin-Koren & Neil W. Netanel eds. (Kluwer Law
International, 2002) p. 79.

26. Cf. *Turner Broad. v. FCC* (Turner I), 512 U.S. 622, 656 (1994) (arguing that monopoly
power and cable architecture create bottlenecks and exclude others from speaking); *Red Lion
Broad. Co. v. FCC,* 395 U.S. 367, 388-392, 392 (1969) ("There is no sanctuary in the First Amendment for unlimited private censorship operating in a medium not open to all.").

27. See 47 U.S.C. 312(a)(7) (2000) (requiring broadcasters to "allow reasonable access to or . .
. permit purchase of reasonable amounts of time" to "legally qualified candidates for Federal
elective office"); 47 U.S.C. 315(a) (2000) (establishing "equal opportunities" rule requiring
broadcasters who permit one candidate to "use" station to permit candidate's opponents to "use"
station as well); 47 U.S.C. 315(b) (2000) (requiring broadcasters to sell time at lowest unit charge
to political candidates); 47 U.S.C. 531(b) (2000) (authorizing franchise authorities to require cable
companies to set aside space for public access, educational and government channels); 47 U.S.C.
532(b)(1) (2000) (establishing "leased access" provisions which require cable operators to set aside
channel capacity for use by commercial programmers unaffiliated with cable franchise operator);
47 U.S.C. 541(a)(3) (2000) (requiring assurances in awarding cable franchises that cable access "is
not denied to any group of potential residential cable subscribers because of the income of the
residents of the local area in which such group resides"); 47 U.S.C. 335(b)(1) (2000) (requiring
direct broadcast satellite operators to set aside portion of "channel capacity, equal to not less than
4 percent nor more than 7 percent, exclusively for noncommercial programming of an
educational or informational nature"); Red Lion, 395 U.S. at 373-75 (describing fairness doctrine).

28. See, e.g., *Time Warner Entm't Co. v. FCC,* 240 F.3d 1126, 1136, 1139 (D.C. Cir. 2001) (invalidating FCC's limits on vertical and horizontal integration of cable carriers); *Comcast
Cablevision, Inc. v. Broward County,* 124 F. Supp. 2d 685, 694 (S.D. Fla. 2000) (holding that open
access requirements for broadband cable violate First Amendment rights of cable system
owners); see also *U.S. West, Inc. v. United States,* 48 F.3d 1092, 1095 (9th Cir. 1994) (striking down
ban on telephone companies also selling video content to the public), vacated as moot, 516 U.S.
1155 (1996); *Chesapeake & Potomac Tel. Co. v. United States,* 42 F.3d 181, 202 (4th Cir. 1994) (same),
vacated as moot, 516 U.S. 415 (1996). The last two cases were held moot by the Supreme Court in

light of the Telecommunications Act of 1996, Pub. L. No. 104-104, 110 Stat. 56 (codified in scattered sections of 42 U.S.C. (2000)), which repealed the statutory ban on cross-ownership.

29. See Lessig, *The Future of Ideas*, supra article 17, at 156-58 (quoting Jerome Saltzer, "Open Access is Just the Tip of the Iceberg" (Oct. 22, 1999), at http://web.mit.edu/Saltzer/www/publications/openaccess.html (last visited Oct. 20, 2003) (offering examples of gatekeeping by cable networks)).

30. See Hernan Galperin & Francois Bar, "The Regulation of Interactive Television in the United States and the European Union," *Federal Communications Law Journal* 55 (2002): 61, 62-64, 69-72 (2002) (discussing strategy of walled gardens in interactive television services); Daniel L. Rubinfeld & Hal J. Singer, "Open Access to Broadband Networks: A Case Study of the AOL/Time Warner Merger," *Berkeley Technology Law Journal* 16 (2001): 631, 656 (noting dangers of conduit discrimination as well as content discrimination).

31. Data Sheet, Cisco 6400 Service Selection Gateway, at http://www.cisco.com/warp/public/cc/pd/as/6400/prodlit/c6510 ds.htm (last visited Oct. 20, 2003); see also Jeffrey A. Chester, "Web Behind Walls," *Technology Review* (June 2001) at 94, available at http://www.democraticmedia.org/resources/articles/webbehindwalls.html (last visited Oct. 20, 2003).

32. See *Eldred v. Reno*, 239 F.3d 372, 380 (D.C. Cir. 2000), aff'd sub nom. *Eldred v. Ashcroft*, 537 U.S. 186, 222 (2003) (holding that First Amendment poses no obstacle to Congressional extension of copyright terms that shrink scope of public domain, even when extension is retroactive); *Universal City Studios, Inc. v. Reimerdes*, 111 F. Supp. 2d 294 (S.D.N.Y. 2000) (upholding constitutionality of application of Digital Millenium Copyright Act to DeCSS and enjoining linking to websites from which DeCSS might be obtained), aff'd sub nom. *Universal City Studios, Inc. v. Corley*, 273 F.3d 429 (2001); supra article 26 (citing additional cases).

33. See J.M. Balkin, "Some Realism About Pluralism: Legal Realist Approaches to the First Amendment," *Duke Law Journal* (1990): 375, 375-87 (noting "ideological drift" of free speech principle to protect propertied and corporate interests).

34. See, e.g., *U.S. West, Inc. v. FCC*, 182 F.3d 1224, 1235, 1239 (10th Cir. 1999) (invalidating, on First Amendment grounds, FCC regulations protecting privacy and sale of telephone customers' personal information). On some of the problems faced in squaring consumer privacy with a libertarian conception of freedom of speech, see Eugene Volokh, "Freedom of Speech and Information Privacy: The Troubling Implications of a Right to Stop People from Speaking About You," *Stanford Law Review* 52 (2000): 1049.

35. Balkin, supra article 33, at 384; Mark Tushnet, "An Essay on Rights," *Texas Law Review* 62 (1984): 1363, 1386-92.

36. Lessig, *The Future of Ideas*, supra article 17, at 196-202; Elkin-Koren, supra article25, at 84-85, 88-98.

37. Cf. *Truax v. Corrigan*, 257 U.S. 312, 328 (1921) (holding that attempt to ban labor injunctions violated property rights of business owner).

38. A substantial literature has developed explaining how Gilded Age ideas of freedom of contract were created out of Jacksonian and free labor ideals. See, e.g., Michael Les Benedict, "Laissez-Faire and Liberty: A Re-Evaluation of the Meaning and Origins of Laissez-Faire Constitutionalism," *Law and History Review* 3 (1985): 293; William E. Forbath, "The Ambiguities of Free Labor: Labor and the Law in the Gilded Age," *Wisconsin Law Review* (1985): 767, 798-99; Charles W. McCurdy, "The Roots of Liberty of Contract Reconsidered: Major Premises in the Law of Employment, 1867-1937," *1984 Yearbook of the Supreme Court Historical Society* (1984) p. 20. Revisions of this view have suggested that other influences were also at work, see Stephen A. Siegel, "The Revision Thickens," *Law and History Review* 20 (2002): 631, but have not undermined the basic point that corporate interests made ample use of these rhetorical resources.

39. Clinton Rossiter, *Conservatism in America*, 2d ed. (Harvard University Press, 1962) p. 128.

40. Ibid at 128-62; see Balkin, supra article 33, at 383-87.

41. See generally Arnold M. Paul, *Conservative Crisis and the Rule of Law: Attitudes of Bar and Bench, 1887-1895* (Peter Smith Publisher Inc., 1965); Benjamin R. Twiss, *Lawyers and the Constitution: How Laissez Faire Came to the Supreme Court* (New York: Russell and Russell Inc., 1962).

42. The comparison between the ideological drift of the principles of freedom of contract and freedom of speech is explored in Balkin, supra article 33, at 375-87, and J.M. Balkin, "Ideological Drift and the Struggle over Meaning," *Connecticut Law Review* 25 (1993): 869.

43. Council Directive 96/9, 1996 O.J. (L 77/20) (providing for legal protection of databases which, "by reason of the selection or arrangements of their contents, constitute the author's own intellectual creation").

44. For a discussion of recent attempts, see Dov S. Greenbaum, "The Database Debate: In Support of an Inequitable Solution," *Alabama Law Journal of Science and Technology* 13 (2003): 431, 468-78.

45. Cf. Randal C. Picker, "From Edison to the Broadcast Flag: Mechanisms of Consent and Refusal and the Propertization of Copyright," *University of Chicago Law Review* 70 (2003): 281, 293-96 (noting that digital rights management permits perfection of continuing control over use of intellectual property in digital content even after media product has been purchased).

46. Or, in Julie Cohen's memorable phrase, we are entering the era of "Lochner in Cyberspace." Julie Cohen, "Lochner in Cyberspace: The New Economic Orthodoxy of 'Rights Management,'" *Michigan Law Review* 97 (1998): 462. Paul Schwartz and William Treanor argue, by contrast, that calls for constitutional limitations on the expansion of intellectual property are the best analogy to the laissez-faire constitutional conservatism of the Gilded Age; they compare arguments for constitutional protection of the public domain to *Lochner v. New York*, 198 U.S. 45 (1905). Paul M. Schwartz & William Michael Treanor, "Eldred and Lochner: Copyright Term Extension and Intellectual Property as Constitutional Property," *Yale Law Journal* 112 (2003): 2331, 2334-35, 2394-95, 2411. They fail to consider the social and economic context in which the debate over laissez-faire conservatism occurred. In effect, Schwartz and Treanor argue that small-scale artists, software programmers, Internet end users, and consumers who seek a robust public domain are the functional equivalent of the Robber Barons and concentrated economic interests of the Gilded Age, while today's media corporations like Microsoft, Disney, and Viacom are the functional equivalent of immigrant laborers in sweatshops at the turn of the century.

Because they focus exclusively on arguments about the scope of the Copyright Clause, and pay no attention to telecommunications law, Schwartz and Treanor do not recognize that the free speech principle is the key battleground for the legal protection of capital in the information economy. Opposition to the Copyright Term Extension Act turned precisely on the fact that the political economy of the information age blurs distinctions between regulations of speech and regulations of business practices in media corporations, and that ever-expanding property rights in patent, trademark, and copyright adversely affect freedom of expression. See Brief of Jack M. Balkin et al. as Amici Curiae in Support of the Petition at 15-21, *Eldred v. Ashcroft*, 537 U.S. 186 (2003) (No. 01-618), available at 2002 WL 1041899.

Much more troubling than the Court's conclusions about the Copyright Clause in Eldred is its cavalier dismissal of the important free speech interests in limited copyright terms. See *Eldred*, 537 U.S. at 218-22. From this perspective, Eldred most closely resembles not *Lochner v. New York*, but the early twentieth-century cases *Schenck v. United States*, 249 U.S. 47 (1919), *Abrams v. United States*, 250 U.S. 616 (1919), and *Gitlow v. New York*, 268 U.S. 652 (1925), in which the Court rejected free speech claims and exercised judicial restraint. The danger is that an unrestrained legislature beholden to media interests will continually ramp up intellectual property protections at the expense of the free speech interests of others.

Schwartz and Treanor note the argument that the expansion of intellectual property arises from rent-seeking by media corporations that have corrupted the political process. Schwartz & Treanor, supra, at 2406. However, failing to recognize the First Amendment interests involved, they assume that the only issue is the adjustment of property rights between competing stakeholders. They argue that the defects of political process, even if serious, cannot justify heightened judicial review, see *United States v. Carolene Prods. Co.*, 304 U.S. 144, 152 n.4 (1938), because the theory of process protection should not apply to ordinary economic and social legislation but only to "the representation of minorities." Schwartz & Treanor, supra, at 2407. Perhaps tellingly, they omit the Carolene Products Court's argument that the theory of process protection is equally concerned with securing freedom of speech.

47. See Mark A. Graber, *Transforming Free Speech: The Ambiguous Legacy of Civil Libertarianism* (University of California Press, 1991) pp. 92-93, 122-26 (noting rise of democratic conception in Progressive period and discussing democratic elements in Zechariah Chafee, Jr.'s theory of free expression); David M. Rabban, "Free Speech in Progressive Social Thought," *Texas Law Review* 74 (1996): 951, 954-88 (discussing free speech theories of early twentieth-century progressive thinkers, including John Dewey and Herbert Croly).

48. See generally Alexander Meiklejohn, *Political Freedom: The Constitutional Powers of the People* (New York: Oxford University Press, 1960) [hereinafter Meiklejohn, *Political Freedom*];

Alexander Meiklejohn, "The First Amendment is an Absolute," *Supreme Court Review* (1961): 245 [hereinafter Meiklejohn, *First Amendment*].

49. See, e.g., Owen M. Fiss, *The Irony of Free Speech* (Harvard University Press, 1996) [hereinafter Fiss, *The Irony of Free Speech*]; Cass R. Sunstein, *Democracy and the Problem of Free Speech* (The Free Press, 1993); Owen M. Fiss, "Free Speech and Social Structure," *Iowa Law Review* 71 (1986): 1405 [hereinafter Fiss, "Free Speech and Social Structure"]; Owen M. Fiss, "Why the State?," *Harvard Law Review* 100 (1987): 781 [hereinafter Fiss, "Why the State?"]; Harry Kalven, "The New York Times Case: A Note on "The Central Meaning of the First Amendment,"" *Supreme Court Review* (1964): 191. Fiss well describes the centrality of this theory in twentieth-century legal thought: "The theory that animates this protection [of the speaker's autonomy], and that inspired Kalven, and before him Meiklejohn, and that now dominates the field, casts the underlying purpose of the first amendment in social or political terms: The purpose of free speech is not individual self-actualization, but rather the preservation of democracy, and the right of a people, as a people, to decide what kind of life it wishes to live. Autonomy is protected not because of its intrinsic value, as a Kantian might insist, but rather as a means or instrument of collective self-determination. We allow people to speak so others can vote. Speech allows people to vote intelligently and freely, aware of all the options and in possession of all the relevant information." Fiss, "Free Speech and Social Structure," supra, at 1409-10.

50. On the connections between democratic free speech theory and republicanism, see Baker, supra article 9, at 126-27, 138-43, 152-53, 170-76. On the connection to the thought of the Progressive Era, see Graber, supra article 47, at 75-121; Balkin, supra article 2, at 1947-48, 1956-58; Rabban, supra article 47.

51. Balkin, supra article 2, at 1947-48, 1956-58.

52. See, e.g., Mark S. Fowler & David L. Brenner, "A Marketplace Approach to Broadcast Regulation," *Texas Law Review* 60 (1982): 207 (arguing for repeal of most forms of broadcast regulation).

53. Meiklejohn was perhaps most overt about this, arguing that the First Amendment "has no concern about the 'needs of many men to express their opinions'" but rather is concerned with "the common needs of all the members of the body politic." Meiklejohn, *Political Freedom*, supra article 48, at 55; see also ibid at 56-57, 61 (criticizing Zechariah Chafee, Jr. for being "misled by his inclusion of an individual interest within the scope of the First Amendment," and Justice Oliver Wendell Holmes for his "excessive individualism"). Owen Fiss, likewise, has emphasized that the First Amendment's concern with autonomy is primarily instrumental: "Autonomy may be protected, but only when it enriches public debate." Fiss, "Why the State?," supra article 49, at 786.

54. Meiklejohn, *Political Freedom*, supra article 48, at 26.

55. On the social features of democracy implicit in the idea of a democratic culture, see J.M. Balkin, "The Constitution of Status," *Yale Law Journal* 106 (1997): 2313, 2314.

56. Legal scholars influenced by John Fiske have argued that intellectual property law should also serve the goals of promoting popular participation in culture, or what Fiske called "semiotic democracy." See, e.g., William W. Fisher III, "Property and Contract on the Internet," *Chicago-Kent Law Review* 73 (1998): 1203, 1217 ("In an attractive society, all persons would be able to participate in the process of meaning-making. Instead of being merely passive consumers of cultural artifacts produced by others, they would be producers, helping to shape the world of ideas and symbols in which they live."); see also Kenneth Karst, "Local Discourse and the Social Issues," *Cardozo Studies in Law and Literature* 12 (2000): 1, 27 (defining cultural democracy as "the broadest possible participation in the cultural processes that define and redefine the sort of society we shall be"). Larry Lessig's recent call for "free culture," see Lessig, *The Future of Ideas*, supra article 17, at 9-10, also has important connections to the principles of semiotic democracy and democratic culture, as does David Lange's notion of free appropriation as a right of citizenship exercised in the public domain, see David Lange, "Reimagining the Public Domain," *Law and Contemporary Problems* 66 (2003): 463, 475-83.

Important examples of this trend in intellectual property scholarship include Rosemary J. Coombe, "Authorizing the Celebrity: Publicity Rights, Postmodern Politics, and Unauthorized Genders," *Cardozo Arts and Entertainment Law Journal* 10 (1992): 365; Rosemary J. Coombe, "Objects of Property and Subjects of Politics: Intellectual Property Laws and Democratic Dialogue," *Texas Law Review* 69 (1991): 1853; Rosemary J. Coombe, "Publicity Rights and Political Aspiration: Mass Culture, Gender Identity, and Democracy," *New England Law Review* 26 (1992): 1221; Rochelle Cooper Dreyfuss, "Expressive Genericity: Trademarks as Language in the Pepsi

Generation," *Notre Dame Law Review* 65 (1990): 397; Niva Elkin-Koren, "Cyberlaw and Social Change: A Democratic Approach to Copyright Law in Cyberspace," *Cardozo Arts and Entertainment Law Journal* 14 (1996): 215, 272-73; David Lange, "At Play in the Fields of the Word: Copyright and the Construction of Authorship in the Post-Literate Millennium," *Law and Contemporary Problems* 55 (1992): 139; Jessica Litman, "The Public Domain," *Emory Law Journal* 39 (1990): 965; Madow, supra article 2; William Fisher, "Theories of Intellectual Property," at http://www.law.harvard.edu/Academic Affairs/coursepages/tfisher/iptheory.html (last visited Dec. 3, 2003).

Other scholars have sought to connect the proper scope of copyright, fair use, and the public domain to the promotion of democracy in the sense of public discussion of public issues. See Neil Weinstock Netanel, "Copyright and a Democratic Civil Society," *Yale Law Journal* 106 (1996): 283, 347-65 [hereinafter Netanel, "Copyright and a Democratic Civil Society"] (arguing that copyright promotes democracy by funding independent sectors of creativity); Neil Weinstock Netanel, "Market Hierarchy and Copyright in Our System of Free Expression," *Vanderbilt Law Review* 53 (2000): 1879. This strand of intellectual property scholarship is somewhat closer to the republican or progressivist model; it emphasizes the importance of democratic public discourse and views popular culture as valuable to the extent that it contributes to a democratic civil society. See Netanel, "Copyright and a Democratic Civil Society," supra, at 351 n310.

57. For a helpful discussion, see Robert Post, "Recuperating First Amendment Doctrine," *Stanford Law Review* 47 (1995): 1249, 1253-55. Post argues that social practices and media for the communication of ideas are central to the formation of public opinion. Robert Post, "Reconciling Theory and Doctrine in First Amendment Jurisprudence," *California Law Review* 88 (2000): 2353, 2367-69; Post, "Recuperating First Amendment Doctrine," supra, at 1275-77.

58. It was not always thus. See Post, "Recuperating First Amendment Doctrine," supra article 57, at 1252-53 (discussing *Mutual Film Corp. v. Industrial Comm.*, 236 U.S. 230, 243-45 (1915), in which Supreme Court originally held that motion pictures were not "organs of public opinion"). By 1952, the Supreme Court had come around, stating that "it cannot be doubted that motion pictures are a significant medium for the communication of ideas." *Joseph Burstyn, Inc. v. Wilson*, 343 U.S. 495, 501 (1952). The difference between the Court's statements in 1915 and 1952 reflects important changes in American society to which the Court's First Amendment doctrines eventually responded. The scope of the free speech principle always grows out of a normatively inflected recognition of sociological realities.

59. The free speech principle also applies to regulations of conduct that do not involve a generally recognized medium for the communication of ideas when the government regulates conduct because it disagrees with or desires to suppress the ideas it believes the conduct expresses. See *United States v. O'Brien*, 391 U.S. 367, 377-78 (1968) (holding that reasons for regulation of conduct must be unrelated to suppression of free expression). Thus, when government effectively treats conduct as a medium for the communication of ideas and punishes it on that basis, the free speech principle is also implicated.

60. See, e.g., *Reno v. ACLU*, 521 U.S. 844, 850 (1997) ("The Internet is 'a unique and wholly new medium of worldwide human communication.'" (quoting *ACLU v. Reno*, 929 F. Supp. 824, 844 (E.D. Pa. 1996))).

61. Meiklejohn himself argued that works of art were protected speech because they promoted knowledge, sharpened intelligence, and developed sensitivity to human values, thus helping people to make political decisions. Meiklejohn, "First Amendment," supra article 48, at 255-57. Other scholars have recognized that not all artistic expression equally promotes democratic self-government. See, e.g., Sunstein, supra article 49, at 153-59 (1993) (suggesting that nonpolitical art should be relegated to lower tier of First Amendment protection). And of course Robert Bork, who also had a democracy-based theory of the First Amendment, famously argued that art should receive no First Amendment protection if it was not political speech. Robert H. Bork, "Neutral Principles and Some First Amendment Problems," *Indiana Law Journal* 47 (1971): 26-28.

Owen Fiss believes, to the contrary, that art, particularly unorthodox art and art underappreciated by market forces, furthers the goals of collective self-determination and democratic deliberation. He argues that government programs like the National Endowment for the Arts (NEA) that subsidize art should look to art that is concerned with issues on the public agenda or that should be on the public agenda of discussion and comment. Thus, government subsidy of art should be designed to promote discussion of important public issues. Fiss, *The Irony of Free Speech*, supra article 49, at 40-45.

62. Cf. Owen M. Fiss, "The Unruly Character of Politics," *McGeorge Law Review* 29 (1997): 1, 2-7 (noting limitations of Meiklejohnian metaphor of town meeting as applied to confrontational politics).

63. On the formation of self through cultural transmission, see Jack M. Balkin, *Cultural Software: A Theory of Ideology* (Yale University Press, 1998) pp. 269-85.

64. As Julie Cohen reminds us, digital technologies tend to blur the boundaries between production and reception, speaking and reading, or even between viewing and copying. See Julie E. Cohen, "A Right to Read Anonymously: A Closer Look at "Copyright Management" in Cyberspace," *Connecticut Law Review* 28 (1996): 981, 1004-09; see also Rubenfeld, supra article 5, at 34-36 (arguing that theories of freedom of expression based in autonomy and self-expression do not sufficiently account for First Amendment right to read as well as to express one's self).

65. Memetics is an evolutionary theory that attempts to explain the development of culture through the transmission of bits of culture, or memes, which replicate themselves in human minds. The term "meme" was coined by the zoologist Richard Dawkins. See Richard Dawkins, *The Selfish Gene* (Oxford University Press, 1977) pp. 189-94. Memetic theory often tends to undermine agency and selfhood, see, e.g., Susan Blackmore, *The Meme Machine* (Oxford University Press, 1999), and thus would seem an odd choice for a theory of self-expression. But memetics can also be employed to explain concepts central to agency and selfhood like freedom, see Daniel C. Dennett, *Freedom Evolves* (Viking Books, 2003) pp. 175-92, 266, or the growth of human belief systems and human innovation, see Balkin, supra article 63, at 42-97, 173-75.

The idea of memetic democracy emphasizes the deep connections between self and agency on the one hand, and cultural evolution and the shaping of the self through cultural exchange on the other. Memetic democracy means that everyone gets to participate in the distribution and dissemination of memes, which are the building blocks of the cultural software that constitutes individuals as individuals.

66. See, e.g., Lee C. Bollinger, *Images of a Free Press* (University of Chicago Press, 1991) pp. 138-41 (contrasting burdens of education for civic life with pleasantness of entertainment); Sunstein, supra article 49, at 84-91 (decrying "low quality" programming that appeals to tastes of uneducated); Fiss, "Free Speech and Social Structure," supra article 49, at 1413 ("From the perspective of a free and open debate, the choice between *Love Boat* and *Fantasy Island* is trivial."); Fiss, "Why the State?," supra article 49, at 788 (contrasting reruns of "I Love Lucy" and MTV with "the information [members of the electorate] need to make free and intelligent choices about government policy, the structure of government, or the nature of society."). Once again, this familiar progressivist theme is already present in Meiklejohn. See Meiklejohn, *Political Freedom*, supra article 48, at 87 (attacking commercial radio for "corrupting both our morals and our intelligence"). Even Justice Louis Brandeis fell prey to this sort of cultural elitism, which pervades his famous call for protecting the right of privacy from a particular form of speech. See Samuel Warren & Louis Brandeis, "The Right to Privacy," *Harvard Law Review* 4 (1890):193, 196 (arguing that "personal gossip," "easy of comprehension [and] appealing to that weak side of human nature," "crowds the space available for matters of real interest to the community," and "destroys at once robustness of thought and delicacy of feeling").

67. In this sense the Internet simply empowers the popular appropriation and transformation of mass culture that already existed: "Much of mass culture involves programming, advertisements, architecture, and artwork produced by corporations and designed to sell products and make money. Many critiques of mass culture warn of the deleterious consequences of consumerism and mass consumption... . But a populist view [of democratic culture] also emphasizes that ordinary people are not mere passive receptors of the messages offered in advertising, television programming, and other elements of contemporary mass culture. Such assumptions are just another way of denigrating the intelligence and abilities of ordinary people. People do not uncritically absorb and assimilate the images they see on the television screen— they process, discuss, and appropriate them. People are active interpreters and rearrangers of what they find in mass culture. They use the raw materials of mass culture to articulate and express their values. Through this process, they produce and reproduce popular culture." Balkin, supra article 2, at 1948-49 (footnotes omitted).

68. The reference is to Apple's famous commercial instructing users of its iPod to "Rip, mix, and burn... . After all, it's your music." Larry Lessig uses the slogan as a metaphor for a free culture. Lessig, *The Future of Ideas*, supra article 17, at 9-11.

69. See Sunstein, supra article 49, at 87-91; see also Cass R. Sunstein, "Television and the Public Interest," *California Law Review* 88 (2000): 499, 518 (arguing that goal of television regulation is to promote deliberative democracy).

70. See Balkin, supra article 2, at 1948 ("Popular culture is neither a debilitated version of democratic culture nor a mere diversion from the sober processes of deliberation imagined by progressivism. It is not a sideshow or distraction from democratic culture but the main event. Moreover, [a] populist [approach to free expression] accepts, as progressivism does not, that popular culture—which is also democratic culture—is by nature unkempt and unruly, occasionally raucous and even vulgar. It is by turns both eloquent and mawkish, noble and embarrassing, wise and foolish, resistant to blandishments and gullible in the extreme. It is imperfect in precisely the same sense that democracy itself is imperfect.").

71. Robert Post has emphasized this limitation of the Meiklejohn model, arguing that the autonomy of public discourse, necessary for democratic self-government, is undermined by imposing managerial methods to cabin its scope and agendas. See generally Robert Post, "Managing Deliberation: The Quandary of Democratic Dialogue," *Ethics* 103 (1993): 654; Robert Post, "Meiklejohn's Mistake: Individual Autonomy and the Reform of Public Discourse," *University of Colorado Law Review* 64 (1993): 1109.

72. Meiklejohn, *Political Freedom*, supra article 48, at 24-27.

73. Ibid at 25.

74. Indeed, the standard progressivist/republican arguments for regulation of broadcast, cable, and satellite can and should be rearticulated in terms of the more populist perspective of promoting democratic culture. The key point is that the United States has adopted a hybrid system: Instead of separating the functions of editor and distributor, and treating all distribution networks as common carriers like telephone companies, it has allowed a small number of editors/speakers to own powerful distribution networks not open to all in return for accepting various public service obligations and regulations. Thus the hybrid system is based on the model of a contract or a quid pro quo.

Although the hybrid system denies the vast majority of people free access to key distribution networks, it may nevertheless have been justified in the past by its economic advantages. Arguably it offers necessary incentives for broadcasters, cable companies, and owners of satellite systems to invest in, produce, and deliver a wide variety of diverse programming for viewers and listeners that will enrich public debate and public culture. Thus, it provides considerable grist for the mill of a democratic culture.

Nevertheless, a hybrid system is hardly perfect. Heavy reliance on advertising tends to create a significant mismatch between what broadcasters deliver and what viewers want, in part because advertisers seek content that appeals to the common tastes of certain valued demographic groups (whose preferences may otherwise be quite heterogenous) rather than content that cross-cuts demographic groups or appeals to groups with comparatively little disposable income or comparatively unmanipulable consumption patterns. See Baker, supra article 9, at 13, 24-26, 88-91, 182-90. Advertisers will also tend to push for content that helps induce greater consumption instead of content that appeals to and fulfils other values that viewers might have. For example, viewers may value many kinds of content that are not strongly tied to shopping, purchasing, and consumption. They may value content that educates them or inspires them to change their lives, rethink their values, or make use of their creative powers. Finally, market forces also will, almost by definition, underproduce content that has high positive externalities (like educational content, or balanced and informative coverage of news) because the value of that content to society cannot be captured by market forces, and, all other things being equal, the greater the positive externalities, the more underproduction there will be. Ibid at 41-62, 114-18.

The hybrid model of media regulation is not constitutionally required. Rather, it is a quid pro quo or contractual arrangement, and it is constitutional to the extent that it promotes the values of a democratic culture. To be sure, regulatory quid pro quos can violate free speech rights if they impose an unconstitutional condition on free speech. However, structural regulations of the mass media that seek to counteract the limitations of mass media markets should be constitutional if there is a clear nexus between the goals of the regulation and the purposes behind the choice of a hybrid system. To the extent that structural regulations and public interest obligations of mass media compensate for the limitations of a hybrid model, they are tied to the very justifications for issuing broadcast licenses and cable franchises in the first place: They help further the goal of promoting a rich public sphere and a vibrant, participatory, and democratic culture. If government can make a sufficiently good case that the regulations will have this effect, the regulations should not be regarded as unconstitutional conditions on a media company's First Amendment rights. Likewise, public broadcasting that supplements existing markets with content that government reasonably believes to be valuable (like children's programming) should also be constitutionally permissible.

75. See supra article 68.

76. See Balkin, supra article 63, at 17-19.

77. See Madhavi Sunder, "Cultural Dissent," *Stanford Law Review* 54 (2001): 495, 498 (noting ubiquitous disputes within cultural groups about values of group and terms of membership).

78. See, e.g., Judith P. Butler, *Gender Trouble: Feminism and the Subversion of Identity* (Routledge Kegan & Paul, 1990) pp. 141-49 (noting possibilities for subversion of existing sexual roles and creation of new ones through repetition and through performance); Amy M. Adler, "What's Left?," *California Law Review* 84 (1996): 1499, 1529-31 (describing how pornography has been appropriated for feminist purposes); Judith P. Butler, "The Force of Fantasy: Feminism, Mapplethorpe, and Discursive Excess," *Differences* 2 (1990): 105, 119-20 (arguing that "discursive excess" offers opportunities for subversion and parody).

79. See Baker, supra article 9, at 41-55.

80. Purchasing media products is a kind of liberty, because it involves choice. It is also a kind of creativity, because an agreement between a willing buyer and a willing seller creates wealth. But it does not exhaust the forms of choice and creativity with which freedom of speech is concerned.

81. See Beth Simone Noveck, "Designing Deliberative Democracy in Cyberspace: The Role of the Cyber-Lawyer," *Boston University Journal of Science and Technology* 9 (2003): 1, 5, 8-10 (2003).

82. See, e.g., Lessig, *Code and Other Laws of Cyberspace*, supra article 17, at 3-8.

83. For a more general account of legal historicism, of which dynamism is a special case, see Jack M. Balkin & Sanford Levinson, "Legal Historicism and Legal Academics: The Roles of Law Professors in the Wake of *Bush v. Gore*," *Georgetown Law Journal* 90 (2001): 173, 174-75 (defining legal historicism as claim that legal conventions and forms of legal argument gradually change in response to political and social struggles that are waged through them). See also Paul Brest, Sanford Levinson, J.M. Balkin & Akhil Reed Amar, *Processes of Constitutional Decisionmaking*, 4th ed. (Aspen Publishers 2000) pp. xxxi-xxxii (articulating theory of constitutional historicism). I am using the term "dynamism" rather than historicism in order to emphasize two separate points: First, rights dynamism is internal to participants in the practice of rights discourse rather than a stance that merely studies the discourse from the outside with no particular stake in its outcome. Second, rights dynamism is forward-looking, concerned with the future of a practice whose full contours cannot be known in advance, rather than a backward-looking historicism that attempts to articulate and comprehend changes that occurred in the distant past.

Privacy, Photography, and the Press

T. ALLEN et al.

I. Introduction

Over one hundred years ago, Samuel Warren and Louis Brandeis, in perhaps "the most famous of all law review articles,"[1] called upon the courts to recognize a remedy in tort for invasions of privacy.[2] In their article, Warren and Brandeis railed against the press's pursuit of "idle gossip" and criticized the press for its "prurient taste."[3] Criticisms of the press have continued to this day,[4] and recent months have seen calls for increased protection of individual privacy from unauthorized photography.[5]

This article examines the conflict between privacy and photography[6] and argues that, although photographers should not be exempt from generally applicable laws, laws that target photography for regulation, whether facially or in practical effect, should be subject to strict judicial scrutiny. Part II of this article begins by discussing the concept of privacy and its protection under tort and criminal law. Next, Part III uses several recently proposed measures, which would expand the protection of privacy by restricting the freedom of photographers to take unauthorized photographs of people in public places, to illustrate how current First Amendment doctrine leaves photography vulnerable to oppressive governmental regulation. Part IV demonstrates the important expressive, communicative, and informative aspects of photography and argues that, because photographic expression depends on the ability to take photographs without undue governmental regulation, the courts should treat photography as an inherently expressive activity. This article concludes in Part V that, as a matter of public policy, the societal interest in protecting photographic expression, including unfettered photographic newsgathering, outweighs the interests that would be furthered by the expansion of privacy protections beyond current legal limitations.

II. The Protection of Privacy Under Existing Law

Privacy, as a philosophical or moral concept, has escaped precise definition for over a hundred years.[7] Given this difficulty, privacy may best be understood by the functions that it serves.[8] Privacy is central to dignity[9] and individuality, or personhood.[10] Privacy is also indispensable to a sense of autonomy[11] — to "a feeling that there is an area of an individual's life that is totally under his or her control, an area that is free from outside intrusion."[12] The deprivation of privacy can even endanger a person's health.[13]

Although privacy is difficult to define as a philosophical or moral concept, the legal concept of privacy has evolved over the past century to include several permutations.[14] For Warren and Brandeis, privacy meant some degree of control, recognized by tort law, over the dissemination of personal information to the public by the press.[15] Since then, this tort law conception of privacy has developed into four distinct privacy torts: intrusion upon the seclusion or solitude of another, public disclosure of private facts, publicity that places another in a false light, and appropriation of another's name or likeness for one's own advantage.[16] Notably, the courts do not consider, as a general rule, the mere taking of a person's photograph without consent to be an invasion of privacy, even if the act of taking the photograph disturbs the person being photographed.[17] However, state tort and criminal laws provide significant limitations on the methods that photographers can use to obtain photographs.

The tort of intrusion, for example, protects a person's sense of locational and psychological privacy. Section 652B of the Restatement defines the tort of intrusion as follows: "One who intentionally intrudes, physically or otherwise, upon the solitude or seclusion of another or his private affairs or concerns, is subject to liability to the other for invasion of his privacy, if the intrusion would be highly offensive to a reasonable person."[18] Thus, for example, the unauthorized taking of a person's photograph within the privacy of that person's home constitutes an actionable invasion of privacy,[19] provided that the intrusion caused the subject to suffer emotional distress.[20]

Admittedly, the tort of intrusion provides a limited degree of protection against unwanted photography. The courts consistently have upheld the rights of photographers to take unauthorized photographs of others in or from public places.[21] Dean Prosser states:

> On the public street, or in any other public place, the plaintiff has no right to be alone, and it is no invasion of his privacy to do no more than follow him about. Neither is it

such an invasion to take his photograph in such a place, since this amounts to nothing more than making a record, not differing essentially from a full written description, of a public sight which any one present would be free to see.[22]

As this passage indicates, tort law reflects the assumption that a person who leaves the confines of a private location implicitly consents to being photographed, despite the fact that individuals may have certain reasonable expectations of privacy even in public areas.[23] Indeed, there are countervailing First Amendment reasons for limiting the applicability of the tort of intrusion to nonpublic places.

In addition to the tort of intrusion, laws prohibiting harassment exist in several states.[24] Whereas the tort of intrusion generally exempts photographers from liability for taking unwanted photographs in or from public places, harassment statutes enable individuals to obtain injunctive relief from persistent press hounding, regardless of where it occurs.[25] A quarter century ago, for example, Jacqueline Kennedy Onassis obtained an injunction from a federal district court against Donald Galella,[26] a free-lance celebrity photographer and self-described "paparazzo."[27] According to Onassis, Galella had engaged in a campaign of harassment against Onassis and her family.[28] More recently, in *Wolfson v. Lewis*,[29] a couple obtained an injunction against reporters who were working on a story for the television program Inside Edition.[30] The court acknowledged that intrusion claims generally do not arise from matters occurring in public view but held that conduct amounting to persistent harassment and unreasonable surveillance could rise to the level of intrusion upon seclusion.[31] As these two examples illustrate, theories of harassment enable individuals to obtain indirect protection of even public expectations of privacy.

In addition to the aforementioned prohibitions on intrusion and harassment, a number of other laws protect individuals from overly aggressive photographers. For example, photographers cannot trespass on private property.[32] Also, assault and battery statutes prohibit photographers from engaging in or threatening unwanted physical contact with their subjects.[33] Moreover, photographers who use motor vehicles to chase their subjects risk prosecution for reckless endangerment.[34] These laws protect everyone—not just celebrities and public figures—from overly aggressive photography, and they do so without unduly restricting First Amendment freedoms.[35]

III. The Vulnerability of Photography under Existing Law

Recent events have sparked calls for limitations on unauthorized photography.[36] California's politicians, in response to celebrities' complaints about intrusive photographers, have been particularly vocal in offering these proposals. For example, Congressman Sonny Bono, who represented California's 44th Congressional District, introduced the Protection from Personal Intrusion Act.[37] The Act would add "harassment" as a new criminal offense under Title 18 of the United States Code. Unlike the harassment statutes discussed previously,[38] however, the bill is aimed specifically at aggressive photojournalists. The bill defines the term "harass" as follows:

> "Harass" means persistently physically following or chasing a victim, in circumstances where the victim has a reasonable expectation of privacy and has taken reasonable steps to insure that privacy, for the purpose of capturing by a camera or sound recording instrument of any type a visual image, sound recording, or other physical impression of the victim for profit in or affecting interstate or foreign commerce.[39]

Under the Act, liability would not hinge on whether the image or recording was actually taken or sold for profit.[40] Anyone found guilty of harassment would face imprisonment of not more than one year or a fine,[41] in addition to possible civil liability.[42]

At the state level, two California legislators have proposed restrictions on photographers' physical access to their intended subjects.[43] State Senator Tom Hayden, the ex-husband of actress Jane Fonda, has announced that he will introduce legislation creating a "safe zone" of fifty feet around all public figures—a sphere that photographers could not enter without consent.[44] Similarly, State Senator Charles Calderon, the chairman of a legislative committee on the entertainment industry, has announced that he will introduce legislation requiring photographers to stay at least fifteen feet from subjects who do not want their pictures taken.[45] In the academic realm, Professor Andrew Jay McClurg has argued that the courts ought to expand the privacy right in tort law to include a right of "public privacy."[46] McClurg would modify the

Restatement's definition of the tort of intrusion to allow recovery for certain cases of "public intrusion."[47] An examination of these proposals under existing First Amendment doctrine demonstrates the need for greater constitutional protection of photography.

As Professor Laurence Tribe explains, the Supreme Court has developed two different approaches, or "tracks," for resolving First Amendment claims.[48] Laws that target the "communicative impact" of an act—by, for example, singling out specific viewpoints or ideas for regulation—are presumptively unconstitutional.[49] Laws aimed at the "noncommunicative impact" of an act—laws that, although not targeted at specific viewpoints or ideas, have the indirect result of restricting speech—must survive ad hoc judicial balancing.[50] The Court will uphold laws aimed at the noncommunicative impact of an act, even as applied to expressive conduct, if they do not "unduly constrict the flow of information and ideas."[51]

An analysis of the aforementioned "safe zone" proposals illustrates the inability of standard First Amendment tests to protect photography fully from oppressive governmental regulation. The courts have recognized that the publication, dissemination, and display of photographs can amount to protected speech. In *Burnham v. Ianni*,[52] for example, the Eighth Circuit held that the posting of photographs by university students in a history department display case qualified as "constitutionally protected speech."[53] Moreover, the Supreme Court has stated that, as a general principle, nonverbal conduct constitutes speech if it is intended to "convey a particularized message" and if the likelihood is "great" that the message will be understood by people who observe it.[54] Under these precedents, a law that regulates the publication of certain photographic messages - or that impermissibly burdens the manner in which one publishes, displays, or disseminates photographs—would probably be an unconstitutional abridgement of speech. But although the courts have recognized that the publication, display, and dissemination of photographs can constitute speech, the courts have never held explicitly that the act of taking a photograph is itself an expressive activity. In fact, at least one court has suggested that the government could outlaw the use of cameras entirely.[55] Because current First Amendment doctrine does not treat photography as an inherently expressive activity, photography lacks adequate protection against governmental regulations, including onerous time, place, and manner restrictions such as the proposed fifty-foot "safe zones" and ban on telephoto lenses.[56]

Furthermore, although the courts will subject governmental regulations of speech to heightened scrutiny, the courts will not subject general laws, when enforced against the press, "to stricter scrutiny than would be applied to enforcement against other persons or organizations."[57] In *Cohen v. Cowles Media Co.*,[58] the Supreme Court held that the First Amendment is not a license for the press to violate otherwise valid, generally applicable laws.[59] Similarly, the lower federal[60] and state[61] courts have repeatedly rejected the argument that the First Amendment's Press Clause protects the press from criminal and civil liability.[62] Thus, for example, the courts have rejected First Amendment defenses to trespass and invasion of privacy claims.[63]

Even though the press is not immune from laws of general applicability, the Supreme Court has applied a heightened level of scrutiny to statutes that, "although directed at activity with no expressive component, impose a disproportionate burden upon those engaged in protected First Amendment activities."[64] In *Minneapolis Star & Tribune Co. v. Minnesota Commissioner of Revenue*,[65] for example, the Court struck down a special use tax on the sale of newsprint and ink because the tax had the effect of singling out publications for regulation.[66] The Court explained that differential treatment of the press, unless justified by some special characteristic of the press, is "presumptively unconstitutional."[67] As the Court clarified in *Arcara v. Cloud Books, Inc.*,[68] although "every civil and criminal remedy imposes some conceivable burden on First Amendment protected activities,"[69] courts should apply "least restrictive means scrutiny"[70] to statutes that, although regulating a nonexpressive activity, have the "inevitable effect of singling out those engaged in expressive activity."[71]

Like the tax struck down in *Minneapolis Star*, two of the proposed measures, if adopted, could have the effect of targeting the press. First, the Protection from Personal Intrusion Act would limit the crime of harassment to those attempts to capture sounds or images "for profit."[72] By defining harassment in this manner, the bill would regulate the actions of photojournalists but normally would not apply, for example, to an overly aggressive tourist seeking a photograph of his or her favorite celebrity. Second, Professor McClurg's proposal would include as one determinant of liability an inquiry into whether images were disseminated or intended for dissemination to the general public.[73] This factor would rarely, if ever, apply to nonphotojournalists. Because a court could find that these two proposals have the "inevitable effect" of singling out individuals engaged in expressive activity—reporters engaged in the publication or dissemination of photographs—these measures are constitutionally suspect. However, because the press is not immune from laws of general applicability, the press may be inhibited by generally applicable regulations of photography, such as time, place, and manner restrictions on the operation of cameras.

IV. The Inherently Expressive Nature of Photography

Although the press should not be immune from liability for the violation of generally applicable laws—such as laws against trespass and assault—the courts should subject regulations that target photography to strict judicial scrutiny. As this Part demonstrates, photographs have tremendous expressive, communicative, and informative value, and photography as a medium of expression depends on the ability of photographers to capture images without undue governmental regulation.

Photographs can communicate information in a manner that words alone cannot replicate. Vicki Goldberg, an author on the subject of photography, observes: "Photographs have a swifter and more succinct impact than words, an impact that is instantaneous, visceral, and intense."[74] Photographs "share the power of images in general, which have always played havoc with the human mind and heart."[75] Moreover, as the following two examples demonstrate, photographs have the ability to shape the national consciousness because of their expressive power.

On May 4, 1970, members of the Ohio National Guard opened fire, without warning, on a large crowd of student protesters gathered at Kent State University.[76] In an instant, eleven students were wounded, and four students lay dead.[77] John Paul Filo, a photography student who was present at the scene, photographed "a young woman kneeling in incomprehension, anguish, and finally horror over the body of a dead student."[78] Newspapers across the nation published this image on their front pages.[79] The photograph helped galvanize the stalled antiwar movement on college campuses[80] and came to "symbolize a nation's shock that its children were dying at the hands of its protectors."[81] The young woman's arrested scream "seems almost mythical, a pure image of despair far beyond words."[82]

Two years later, Huynh Cong Ut captured an image on film that, "more than any other single image[,] made America conscious of the full horror of the Vietnam war."[83] On June 8, 1972, the nightly news broadcast the photograph of several screaming Vietnamese children fleeing a napalm strike in South Vietnam. The little girl in the center of the photograph was stark naked and badly burned; she had torn off all of her clothes in a futile attempt to escape the searing effects of the napalm.[84] This photograph became "the last major icon" of the antiwar movement[85] and "probably did more to increase the public revulsion against the war than a hundred hours of televised barbarities."[86] Even the most eloquent description of this image, like the image of the screaming woman at Kent State, cannot compare to the emotive force of the image itself.[87]

Regulations that target photography directly curtail the ability of photographers to communicate their messages to others. Indeed, laws imposing time, place, or manner regulations on photography, in addition to hampering the practice of photographers' trade, can prevent photographers from capturing their intended subjects on film at all. A photographer's ability to take a picture depends upon the freedom of access to the place where the subject is located, as well as the freedom to capture an image at the right time and in the most effective manner. Photographers have advanced the notion of "the decisive moment"[88]—"the instant when action and composition resolve themselves into the most telling, most revealing arrangement."[89] As one world-renowned photographer, Henri Cartier-Bresson, explained, "in photography . . . there is one moment at which the elements in motion are in balance."[90] It is the goal of photography to "seize upon this moment and hold immobile the equilibrium of it."[91] A photographer can capture this moment simply by "moving his head a fraction of a millimeter," or "by a slight bending of the knees," or "by placing the camera closer to or farther from the subject."[92]

Moreover, this imperative—to capture "fugitive moments"[93] on film—is unique to the medium of photography. As Cartier-Bresson explained, "of all the means of expression, photography is the only one that fixes forever the precise and transitory instant."[94] Whereas writers or painters, for example, have time to reflect upon and edit their works, photographers do not—"what has gone, has gone forever."[95] A photographer therefore must compose his pictures "in very nearly the same amount of time it takes to click the shutter, at the speed of a reflex action."[96]

It is this unique link between fleeting opportunity and final product that makes regulations of photography so potentially burdensome and that necessitates heightened judicial scrutiny of such regulations. In fact, the Supreme Court historically has recognized that certain types of conduct, such as the distribution of leaflets, door-to-door political canvassing, picketing, and displaying posters and signs, are "inextricably intertwined" with speech.[97] Like these forms of political expression, photography involves expressive capacity that is inextricably intertwined with the ability to take the photographs themselves. Photography therefore should be accorded similar First Amendment protection.

V. The Societal Interest in Protecting Photography

Because privacy is crucial to the preservation of autonomy, dignity, and individuality,[98] the legal protection of privacy undoubtedly amounts to a weighty governmental interest.[99] However, the tort law conception of privacy is distinct from the quasi-constitutional right to privacy that the Supreme Court has recognized in the century since Warren and Brandeis's seminal article.[100] A person's interest in limiting the gathering and recording of his image does not amount to a right of constitutional magnitude, at least as applied against nonstate actors.[101] Such a position would be difficult to reconcile with the Court's repeated assertion that the Constitution generally shields individuals from only governmental actions.[102]

Furthermore, the governmental interest in protecting individual privacy must be reconciled with other important societal values, such as free expression.[103] Although legitimate expectations of privacy in public may weigh in favor of additional restrictions on unwanted photography, this Part argues that the important policies underlying the First Amendment's guarantees of freedom of speech and press counsel against the expansion of the right to privacy at the expense of photographic expression.

A. The Importance of Free Speech and a Free Press to Democracy

The First Amendment's protection of free expression is important both instrumentally and as an end in itself.[104] Free expression is essential to truth-seeking and to intelligent, democratic self-government,[105] as courts have acknowledged repeatedly.[106] Moreover, free expression is indispensable to self-realization.[107] Even those theorists who stress the importance of free expression to self-government and truth-seeking acknowledge that truth and democracy themselves further the goal of individual growth.[108]

A free press is also indispensable to the survival of a democratic society.[109] Freedom from restraints on newsgathering is critical to the preservation of robust political debate, which is at the center of democratic self-government. A "truly robust public debate" requires an openness to the influx of new ideas and new information, rather than "a purely formal exchange of fixed positions."[110] In fact, the dissemination of new information by the press is often the means by which the public first becomes aware that an issue is a matter of public importance.[111] Deterring the press's acquisition of information by magnifying the risk of civil or criminal liability stifles debate on matters of public importance.[112]

The Supreme Court has acknowledged that a free press is essential to the creation of an informed public capable of self-government.[113] In *New York Times Co. v. Sullivan*,[114] for example, the Court held that the "profound national commitment to the principle that debate on public issues should be uninhibited, robust, and wide-open" limited the imposition of tort liability for publication.[115] In so holding, the Court articulated "a strong vision of a common law tort liability that is tightly constrained when its application affects the public interests protected by the First Amendment."[116] The Court recognized in Sullivan that if the Constitution protected only news dissemination, and not information gathering by the press, "investigative journalism would be chilled as a result of the potential exposure to liability for criminal or tortious conduct engaged in during the newsgathering process."[117] The acquisition of news "is a logically and pragmatically necessary component of the publication of news that serves a vital constitutional function."[118]

Similarly, the protection of photographic images as speech is especially important in an era dominated by visual news media. "News is a window on the world."[119] Through the frame of news, "Americans learn of themselves and others, of their own institutions, leaders, and life styles, and those of other nations and their peoples."[120] By disseminating such information, news organizations both circulate and shape the body of public knowledge.[121] As studies have indicated, the news media play an important role in agenda-setting.[122] Increasingly, visual considerations drive the reporting of news, both on television and in print.[123]

As a general principle, therefore, the courts have been extremely reluctant to prohibit the press from investigating the truth. Although the Supreme Court has yet to extend special protection to the newsgathering process,[124] the Court's First Amendment jurisprudence reflects the principle that if free expression is to be preserved, the press must have broad latitude in the means that it employs to arrive at the truth.[125] Although the Court has rejected the argument that the First Amendment creates a special right of press access to information,[126] the Court has recognized that "without some protection for seeking out the news, freedom of the press could be eviscerated."[127] As the following paragraphs demonstrate, just as the imposition of legal restrictions on press newsgathering threatens important First Amendment interests,[128] the regulation of photography also raises the specter of governmental censorship.

B. The Importance of Protecting Photography

The proposed regulations of photography discussed above[129] illustrate the ways in which such regulations can undercut free speech and newsgathering by the press. Each of the proposed measures would burden the publication and dissemination of photographs by limiting the circumstances in which photographic images can be taken in the first place. For example, the difficulty of complying with floating "safe zones" could discourage photographers from recording the newsworthy actions of public figures.[130] Indeed, as discussed previously, onerous time, place, and manner regulations can completely prevent photographers from recording certain images.[131] Similarly, the nebulous idea of a legitimate expectation of "public privacy" could lead photographers to forgo much photography of public figures, rather than risk liability. By exposing photographers to additional potential liability for news-gathering activity, these proposals risk exerting a significant chilling effect on the public's access to important information.[132]

The advocates of the proposed measures no doubt wish to dis-courage certain unwanted newsgathering by photographers. A picture of a celebrity entering a restaurant or vacationing on a beach hardly appears to be of the same societal importance as a photo-graph of a political protest, or of a politician accepting a bribe. However, the problem with these measures is that they would also discourage the aggressive pursuit of information of legitimate concern to the public. There is simply no easy way to distinguish between legitimate newsgathering and the gathering of news that is purely sensational.[133] One-size-fits-all legislation could shield politicians and other public figures from legitimate press scrutiny. Even though legislators may have conceived the proposals as means of curbing the abuses of celebrity photographers, most of the proposals would penalize individuals regardless of the content of the information that they gathered.[134] This broad sweep is especially troubling in light of recent notable instances in which ordinary members of the public have captured newsworthy images of official misconduct.[135] It would have been troubling if these individuals had faced liability for invading the privacy of their subjects had they, for example, been within a certain distance of their subjects without consent.[136]

As a general matter, the proposed regulations of photography indicate a lack of appreciation for the press's role as a "surrogate" of the public.[137] Newsgathering is "an expensive enterprise."[138] By discouraging the acquisition of information by photographers, these proposals ignore the important "role that the press plays in informing the public about the behavior of others, in affecting the conduct of public officials and public figures, and in deterring wrongful conduct by both public officials and private individuals."[139]

Undoubtedly, there are photographers who have invaded the privacy of their subjects.[140] However, as the above discussion demonstrates, existing tort and criminal laws already protect individuals from the most intrusive invasions of privacy by predatory photographers.[141] Furthermore, the aggressive prosecution of photographers who violate existing criminal and civil laws could address abuses while still preserving First Amendment values.[142]

This article has shown that several recently proposed regulations of photography are inconsistent with fundamental First Amendment values and demonstrate the need for heightened judicial protection of photography as an inherently expressive activity. The insensitivity of a few prying photographers simply does not justify imposing rules that would curtail the press's - and derivatively, the public's - access to visual information, or rules that would make the courts the arbiters of what is legitimately in the public interest. It would be unfortunate for the United States, with its historical commitment to a strong, assertive press, to respond to recent events with such misguided, unnecessary, and constitutionally suspect legislation.

Notes

1. *Rosenbloom v. Metromedia, Inc.*, 403 U.S. 29, 80 (1971) (Marshall, J., dissenting). Samuel Warren & Louis Brandeis, "The Right to Privacy," *Harvard Law Review* 4 (1890).

2. See Warren & Brandeis, supra note 1, at 195-96.

3. Ibid. at 196.

4. See, e.g., Jeffrey B. Abramson, "Four Criticisms of Press Ethics," in *Democracy and the Mass Media*, Judith Lichtenberg ed. (Cambridge University Press, 1990) p. 229, 229-39 (discussing perceptions of reporters as greedy, hungry "jackals").

5. On August 31, 1997, Diana, Princess of Wales, and her companion, Dodi Fayed, died in a car crash in Paris while attempting to elude a group of motorbike-riding photographers. See, e.g., Craig R. Whitney, "Diana Killed in a Car Accident in Paris; In Flight from Paparazzi - Friend Dies," *New York Times* (Aug. 31, 1997) at A1. The tragedy sparked public outrage over aggressive newsgathering and prompted vigorous calls for new legal remedies in response to aggressive photojournalism. See, e.g., Howard Kurtz, "Public to Press: Just Play Fair; They're Peeved by Intrusiveness and Deception. But Are New Laws the Answer?," *Washington Post* (Sept. 15, 1997), at B4.

6. This article uses the term "photographs" to refer to all forms of visual recording, including still pictures and video film footage, and the term "photography" to refer to the taking of photographs—as opposed to the publication, display, or dissemination of photographs—by both professionals and nonprofessionals.

7. See Ken Gormley, "One Hundred Years of Privacy," *Wisconsin Law Review* (1992): 1335, 1336-39.

8. As one author argues, "privacy will remain elusive as a concept, just as liberty and freedom have remained elusive. . . . A word that represents subjective values can never be precise in meaning." Deckle McLean, *Privacy and Its Invasion* (Praeger Publishers, 1995) p. 3.

9. See, e.g., Edward J. Bloustein, "Privacy as an Aspect of Human Dignity: An Answer to Dean Prosser," *New York University Law Review* 39 (1964): 962, 970-71.

10. See, e.g., J. Braxton Craven, Jr., "Personhood: The Right to Be Let Alone," *Duke Law Journal* (1976): 699, 702-03.

11. See, e.g., Louis Henkin, "Privacy and Autonomy," *Columbia Law Review* 74 (1974): 1410, 1425; Daniel R. Ortiz, "Privacy, Autonomy, and Consent," *Harvard Journal of Law and Public Policy* (1989): 91, 92-97.

12. Stephen Goode, *The Right to Privacy* (Watts, 1983) p. 6.

13. See, e.g., Sidney M. Jourard, "Some Psychological Aspects of Privacy," *Law and Contemporary Problems* 31 (1966): 307, 310-11.

14. See Gormley, supra note 7, at 1339-42.

15. See Warren & Brandeis, supra note 1, at 195-96; see also Gormley, supra note 7, at 1343-57 (discussing "tort privacy").

16. See William L. Prosser, "Privacy," *California Law Review* 48 (1960):383, 389-407. The Restatement (Second) of Torts has adopted this four-fold division of privacy, see Restatement (Second) of Torts 652A-652E (1977) [hereinafter Restatement], as have the courts in at least 28 states, see Andrew Jay McClurg, "Bringing Privacy Law Out of the Closet: A Tort Theory of Liability for Intrusions in Public Places," *North Carolina Law Review* 73 (1995): 989, 998 & n41. Almost all of the states have recognized the invasion of privacy as a tort in some form. See ibid at 999 & n43.

17. See Phillip E. Hassman, "Annotation, Taking Unauthorized Photographs as Invasion of Privacy," *American Law Reports* 86 (1978): 374, 375. In fact, "most people do not object to having their picture taken. It is not until the picture is published . . . that they ordinarily become offended." Consequently, few cases have addressed the question whether the taking of an unauthorized picture, as opposed to the publishing of the picture, constitutes an invasion of privacy. See ibid.

18. Restatement, supra note 16, 652B.

19. See ibid. 652B cmt. b.

20. In order to create pecuniary liability for an invasion of privacy, the intrusion must be severe enough to cause the plaintiff emotional distress. See Hassman, supra note 18, at 376. As stated in *Rawls v. Conde Nast Publications, Inc.*, 446 F.2d 313 (5th Cir. 1971), the tort of invasion of

privacy "has as a principal objective the compensation of a party for the "outrage" or "mental suffering, shame, or humiliation" caused by the invasion." Ibid. at 317.

21. See, e.g., *Fogel v. Forbes, Inc.*, 500 F. Supp. 1081, 1087 (E.D. Pa. 1980); *Pemberton v. Bethlehem Steel Corp.*, 502 A.2d 1101, 1116-17 (Md. Ct. Spec. App. 1986); *Forster v. Manchester*, 189 A.2d 147, 150 (Pa. 1963).

22. Prosser, supra note 16, at 391-92; see also Restatement, supra note 16, 652B cmt. c (stating that there can be no liability for taking the photograph of a person in a public place, "since he is not then in seclusion").

23. See McClurg, supra note 16, at 1036-44.

24. See, e.g., Cal. Civ. Proc. Code 527.6 (West 1997); N.Y. Penal Law 240.26 (McKinney 1997). California defines harassment as "a knowing and willful course of conduct directed at a specific person which seriously alarms, annoys, or harasses the person, and which serves no legitimate purpose." Cal. Civ. Proc. Code 527.6(b). New York's harassment statute states that a person is guilty of harassment in the second degree when he or she possesses the "intent to harass, annoy, or alarm another person," and "follows a person in or about a public place" or "engages in a course of conduct . . . which alarms or seriously annoys" another person. N.Y. Penal Law 240.26.

25. See, e.g., Cal. Civ. Proc. Code 527.6; N.Y. Penal Law 240.26.

26. See *Galella v. Onassis*, 487 F.2d 986, 993 (2d Cir. 1973).

27. The term "paparazzo" refers to an obnoxious type of photographer. See ibid at 991. Translated literally, the term means "a kind of annoying insect." Ibid at 991-92.

28. Onassis offered evidence that Galella had "on occasion intentionally physically touched [her] and her daughter, caused fear of physical contact in his frenzied attempts to get their pictures, followed defendant and her children too closely in an automobile, [and] endangered the safety of the children while they were swimming, water skiing and horseback riding." Ibid at 994.

29. 924 F. Supp. 1413 (E.D. Pa. 1996).

30. See ibid. at 1415. The plaintiffs claimed that the reporters had invaded their privacy by engaging in aggressive newsgathering techniques, including following the plaintiffs from work, following the plaintiffs' child to school, videotaping the plaintiffs' home, and using a "shotgun mike" to record statements made by the plaintiffs within their own home. Ibid at 1415-16.

31. See ibid. at 1419-20.

32. See, e.g., Cal. Penal Code 602.5 (West Supp. 1998); N.Y. Penal Law 140.05, 140.10, 140.15 (McKinney Supp. 1998).

33. See, e.g., Cal. Penal Code 240, 242; N.Y. Penal Law 120.00, 120.05, 120.10.

34. See, e.g., N.Y. Penal Law 120.20, 120.25. In addition, most states now have criminal stalking statutes. See, e.g., Cal. Penal Code 646.9 (West 1997); N.Y. Penal Law 240.25.

35. For example, the tort of intrusion, as applied to newsgathering activity, "does not raise first amendment difficulties since its perpetration does not involve speech or other expression." Melville B. Nimmer, "The Right to Speak from Times to Time: First Amendment Theory Applied to Libel and Misapplied to Privacy," *California Law Review* 56 (1968): 935, 957.

36. See supra note 5.

37. H.R. 2448, 105th Cong. (1997).

38. See supra p. 1089.

39. H.R. 2448 2(a).

40. See ibid.

41. See ibid. In addition, the bill would impose a penalty of not less than 20 years' imprisonment and a fine if death resulted from the harassment, and a penalty of five years' imprisonment and a fine if the harassment caused bodily injury. See ibid. The bill does not allow for vicarious liability, and it exempts law enforcement activities. See ibid.

42. See ibid.

43. See, e.g., Dan Morain, "2 State Senators Back Limits on Paparazzi," *L.A. Times* (Sept. 3, 1997) at A9; Judy Peres, "Right to Privacy and Press Rights Collide in Debate over Paparazzi," *Chicago Tribune* (Sept. 9, 1997) 1, at 5.

44. Steven A. Capps, "State to Curb Photographers? Hayden to Propose 50-Foot Safe Zone for Public Figures," *Sacramento Bee* (Sept. 3, 1997), at A14. Senator Hayden has also stated that he will consider proposing a ban on telephoto lenses, which enable photographers to photograph distant locations, see Kurtz, supra note 5, and a requirement that professional photographers be

licensed, see Capps, supra. Because the test for evaluating the constitutionality of licensing programs is well settled, see, e.g., *Lakewood v. Plain Dealer Publ'g Co.*, 486 U.S. 750, 760 (1988), this article does not scrutinize Hayden's licensing proposal.

45. See Capps, supra note 44.

46. McClurg, supra note 16, at 1054.

47. Ibid at 991. McClurg would consider seven factors in assessing whether an action would be "highly offensive to a reasonable person," such as the defendant's motive, the location where the intrusion occurred, whether the defendant disseminated the images or information that he obtained during the intrusive act, and whether the images or information obtained by the defendant from the plaintiff are of legitimate public interest. Ibid. at 1058-59.

48. See Laurence H. Tribe, *American Constitutional Law*, 2d ed. (West Publishing Company, 1988) p. 791.

49. Ibid. 12-2, at 790. Defenders of such regulations have the burden of demonstrating either that the regulation falls within one of the recognized categories of unprotected speech, see, e.g., *Chaplinsky v. New Hampshire*, 315 U.S. 568, 572 (1942) (identifying certain categories of speech that do not receive First Amendment protection because they are "no essential part of any exposition of ideas"), or that the regulation furthers compelling state interests, see Tribe, supra note 48, 12-8, at 833. In the case of regulations that further compelling state interests, the Court has required a showing that the regulations are narrowly drawn to avoid unnecessarily limiting expressive conduct. See ibid.

50. Tribe, supra note 48, 12-2, at 791. This balancing approach weighs "the extent to which communicative activity is in fact inhibited [against] the values, interests, or rights served by enforcing the inhibition." Ibid 12-23, at 979.

51. Ibid. 12-2, at 792. For example, in *United States v. O'Brien*, 391 U.S. 367 (1968), the Court upheld a law regulating expressive conduct - the burning of draft cards. See ibid. at 386. In addition, the Court has upheld reasonable time, place, and manner restrictions on speech, even though they directly limit free expression. See, e.g., *Clark v. Community for Creative Non-Violence*, 468 U.S. 288, 293, 298 (1984) (stating that the O'Brien test "is little, if any, different from the standard applied to time, place, or manner restrictions").

52. 119 F.3d 668 (8th Cir. 1997).

53. Ibid. at 674.

54. *Spence v. Washington*, 418 U.S. 405, 410-11 (1974).

55. In *United States v. Gugel*, 119 F. Supp. 897 (E.D. Ky. 1954), a federal district court characterized the operation of a camera as a "lawful act" and as a "civil right" protected by the federal Constitution. Ibid. at 898. However, the court also stated that the "citizen's privilege to take pictures" could be "made specifically unlawful by statute." Ibid.

56. The proposed "safe zones," by creating spheres that photographers cannot enter without consent, would essentially regulate the "places" from which one can photograph, rather than restrict the publication, dissemination, or display of photographs once they are taken.

57. *Cohen v. Cowles Media* Co., 501 U.S. 663, 670 (1991) (holding that the press enjoys no special protection from promissory estoppel actions based on the disclosure of confidential sources).

58. 501 U.S. 663 (1991).

59. See ibid. at 670. In support of this principle, the Court pointed to a "well-established line of decisions holding that generally applicable laws do not offend the First Amendment simply because their enforcement against the press has incidental effects on its ability to gather and report the news." Ibid. at 669.

60. See, e.g., *Galella v. Onassis*, 487 F.2d 986, 995 (2d Cir. 1973); *Dietemann v. Time, Inc.*, 449 F.2d 245, 249 (9th Cir. 1971).

61. See, e.g., *Miller v. National Broad. Co.*, 232 Cal. Rptr. 668, 685 (Ct. App. 1986) (citing Dietemann, 449 F.2d at 249).

62. As the Ninth Circuit observed in *Dietemann v. Time, Inc.*, "the First Amendment has never been construed to accord newsmen immunity from torts or crimes committed during the course of newsgathering." Dietemann, 449 F.2d at 249.

63. See, e.g., *Annerino v. Dell Publ'g Co.*, 149 N.E.2d 761, 762 (Ill. App. Ct. 1958) (holding that the First Amendment is not "a license by which various press media may overstep the bounds of propriety and decency and thereby justify an invasion of the solitude of the individual"); *Anderson v. WROC-TV*, 441 N.Y.S.2d 220, 223 (Sup. Ct. 1981) (stating that "the

gathering of news . . . does not authorize, whether under the First Amendment or otherwise, the right to enter into a private home by an implied invitation arising out of a self-created custom and practice"); *Prahl v. Brosamle*, 295 N.W.2d 768, 780-81 (Wis. Ct. App. 1980) (rejecting the "constitutional privilege to trespass" claim of a reporter who followed police onto private property).

64. *Arcara v. Cloud Books, Inc.*, 478 U.S. 697, 703-04 (1986) (citing *Minneapolis Star & Tribune Co. v. Minnesota Comm'r of Revenue*, 460 U.S. 575 (1983)).

65. 460 U.S. 575 (1983).

66. See ibid. at 581-82.

67. Ibid. at 585. The Court held that "[a] tax that burdens rights protected by the First Amendment cannot stand unless the burden is necessary to achieve an overriding governmental interest." Ibid. at 582.

68. 478 U.S. 697 (1986).

69. Ibid. at 706.

70. Ibid. (internal quotation marks omitted).

71. Ibid. at 706-07. See also *Cohen v. Cowles Media Co.*, 501 U.S. 663, 670 (1991) (attaching significance to the fact that the statute at issue did not "target or single out the press").

72. H.R. 2448, 105th Cong. 2 (1997).

73. See McClurg, supra note 16, at 1059-62, 1070-78.

74. Vicki Goldberg, *The Power of Photography: How Photographs Changed Our Lives* (Abbeville Press, 1991) p. 7.

75. Ibid.

76. See ibid. at 236-37. The students were protesting the invasion of Cambodia by American ground forces. See ibid. at 236.

77. See ibid. at 237.

78. Ibid.

79. See ibid. at 237-38.

80. See ibid. at 239.

81. Ibid. at 237.

82. Ibid.; see Image 1, infra p. 1097.

83. Goldberg, supra note 74, at 244.

84. See ibid. at 241.

85. Ibid. at 243.

86. Susan Sontag, "In Plato's Cave," in *On Photography* (New York: Dell, 1977) p. 3, 18.

87. See Image in original p. 1097.

88. Henri Cartier-Bresson, *The Decisive Moment*, "Preface" (1952).

89. Vicki Goldberg, "Introduction" to Henri Cartier-Bresson, *The Decisive Moment, in Photography in Print: Writings from 1816 to the Present*, Vicki Goldberg ed. (1981) p. 384.

90. Cartier-Bresson, supra note 88, preface.

91. Ibid.

92. Ibid.

93. Ibid.

94. Ibid.

95. Ibid.

96. Ibid.

97. Tribe, supra note 48, 12-7, at 829-30.

98. See supra p. 1087.

99. The courts have acknowledged the link between privacy and dignity. See, e.g., *Briscoe v. Reader's Digest Ass'n*, 483 P.2d 34, 37 (Cal. 1971) ("Loss of control over which 'face' one puts on may result in literal loss of self-identity, and is humiliating beneath the gaze of those whose curiosity treats a human being as an object." (citations omitted)).

100. See Warren & Brandeis, supra note 1. Despite the absence of the word "privacy" in the text of the Constitution, the Court has acknowledged that the privacy essential to individual dignity and autonomy underlies the fundamental rights guaranteed by the Constitution. See, e.g., *Stanley v. Georgia*, 394 U.S. 557, 564-66 (1969); *Katz v. United States*, 389 U.S. 347, 350 & n.5 (1967); *Tehan v. United States* ex rel. Shott, 382 U.S. 406, 416 (1966). In addition, in *Griswold v. Connecticut*, 381 U.S. 479 (1965), the Court recognized a right to privacy within the "penumbras" of the First, Third, Fourth, and Fifth Amendments. See ibid. at 482, 484-86.

101. See, e.g., Tribe, supra note 48, 12-14, at 887.

102. See ibid. 18-1, at 1688 & n1. Nevertheless, the courts frequently have balanced a so-called "right" to privacy against the First Amendment's guarantee of free speech in cases involving nonstate actors. See Gormley, supra note 7, at 1374-86.

103. See supra pp. 1095-98.

104. See, e.g., Tribe, supra note 48, 12-1, at 785 (arguing that "no adequate conception of so basic an element of our fundamental law [as the First Amendment's protection of free expression] . . . can be developed in purely instrumental or 'purposive' terms").

105. See, e.g., Alexander Meiklejohn, *Free Speech and Its Relation to Self-Government* (New York: Harper, 1948) p. 88-89.

106. See, e.g., *Whitney v. California*, 274 U.S. 357, 375, 377 (1927) (Brandeis, J., concurring) (stating that freedom of speech and thought are "means indispensable to the discovery and spread of political truth" and essential to stable government and "political change").

107. See, e.g., Martin H. Redish, "The Value of Free Speech," *University of Pennsylvania Law Review* 130 (1982): 591, 593; cf. Whitney, 274 U.S. at 375 ("Those who won our independence believed that the final end of the State was to make men free to develop their faculties. . . . They valued liberty both as an end and as a means. They believed liberty to be the secret of happiness . . . .").

108. See, e.g., John Stuart Mill, *On Liberty*, John Gray ed (1859) p. 5, 38-40 (Oxford University Press, 1991).

109. See, e.g., Timothy B. Dyk, "Newsgathering, Press Access, and the First Amendment," *Stanford Law Review* 44 (1992): 927, 932 (arguing that the authors of the First Amendment "viewed freedom of the press as critically important to democratic government").

110. Paul A. LeBel, "The Constitutional Interest in Getting the News: Toward a First Amendment Protection from Tort Liability for Surreptitious Newsgathering," *William and Mary Bill of Rights Journal* 4 (1996): 1145, 1152.

111. See ibid. As the Supreme Court acknowledged in *Estes v. Texas*, 381 U.S. 532 (1965), "the free press has been a mighty catalyst in awakening public interest in governmental affairs, exposing corruption among public officers and employees and generally informing the citizenry of public events and occurrences." Ibid. at 539.

112. See LeBel, supra note 110, at 1152.

113. See, e.g., *New York Times Co. v. United States*, 403 U.S. 713, 717 (1971) (Black, J., concurring) (arguing that press access must be "protected so that [the press can] bare the secrets of government and inform the people").

114. 376 U.S. 254 (1964).

115. Ibid. at 270.

116. LeBel, supra note 110, at 1149.

117. Ibid. at 1147.

118. Ibid. at 1154.

119. Gaye Tuchman, *Making News: A Study in the Construction of Reality* (New York: The Free Press, 1978) p. 1.

120. Ibid.

121. See ibid. at 2.

122. See, e.g., Shanto Iyengar & Donald R. Kinder, *News That Matters* (University of Chicago Press, 1987) p. 4.

123. See Herbert J. Gans, *Deciding What's News: A Study of CBS Evening News, NBC Nightly News, Newsweek, and Time* (Vintage, 1979) p. 159-59 (discussing the centrality of film footage in shaping television news and news magazines).

124. See Dyk, supra note 109, at 928. See generally Robert M. O'Neil, "Tainted Sources: First Amendment Rights and Journalistic Wrongs," *William and Mary Bill of Rights Journal* 4 (1996) 1005, 1008-15 (discussing several cases that have addressed news organizations' potential liability for newsgathering practices).

125. As Justice William J. Brennan observed, broad latitude is essential "if the freedoms of expression are to have the 'breathing space' that they 'need to survive.'" *New York Times Co. v. Sullivan*, 376 U.S. 254, 271-72 (1964) (quoting *NAACP v. Button*, 371 U.S. 415, 433 (1963)); see also *Dietemann v. Time, Inc.*, 449 F.2d 245, 249 (9th Cir. 1971) ("Newsgathering is an integral part of news dissemination.").

126. See *Houchins v. KQED, Inc.*, 438 U.S. 1, 16 (1978) (plurality opinion); *Pell v. Procunier*, 417 U.S. 817, 834 (1974). For an argument that the press ought to enjoy a special constitutional right of access in newsgathering, see Dyk, cited above in note 112, at 929, 931-38.

127. *Branzburg v. Hayes*, 408 U.S. 665, 681 (1972).

128. See LeBel, supra note 109, at 1147.

129. See supra pp. 1090-91.

130. In *Schenck v. Pro-Choice Network*, 117 S. Ct. 855 (1997), the Court acknowledged the difficulty of complying with floating buffer zones and added that this difficulty created a "substantial risk" that "much more speech" would be restricted than was expressly prohibited by the injunction. Ibid. at 867. The Court also noted the probable difficulty of proving violations of the floating zones and the resulting difficulty that the courts would face in punishing violators. See ibid. at 867 n9 ("Contempt proceedings would likely focus on whether protestors who thought they were keeping pace . . . from a distance of 15 feet actually strayed to within 14 or 13 feet of the individual. . . .").

131. See supra p. 1096.

132. Cf. Jane E. Kirtley, "Vanity and Vexation: Shifting the Focus to Media Conduct," *William and Mary Bill of Rights Journal* 4 (1996): 1069, 1099-1106 (discussing CBS's decision not to broadcast an interview with a corporate whistleblower as an example of the "chilling effect" caused by a perceived threat of liability for tortious interference with contractual relations).

133. See, e.g., *Time Inc. v. Hill*, 385 U.S. 374, 388 (1967) ("The line between the informing and the entertaining is too elusive for the protection of [the free press]." (quoting *New York Times v. Sullivan*, 376 U.S. 254, 271-72 (1964)) (internal quotation marks omitted)). In any event, the Supreme Court has held that the First Amendment protects speech in general, not just political speech. See, e.g., *Zacchini v. Scripps-Howard Broad. Co.*, 433 U.S. 562, 578 (1978) ("There is no doubt that entertainment, as well as news, enjoys First Amendment protection.").

134. See supra pp. 1090-91.

135. For example, in 1991, George Holliday, an amateur cameraman, videotaped Los Angeles police officers beating Rodney King. The incident drew the public's attention to the problem of police mistreatment of racial minorities. See, e.g., "The Investigation of a Videotaped Beating; Shocking Incident Leads to Worrisome Questions About L.A. Police," *L.A. Times* (March 7, 1991) at B6.

136. Consider also the privacy interests implicated by the photographs discussed above in Part IV. The naked little girl's privacy interest in not being viewed by the public clearly conflicted with the public's interest in truly understanding the horrific events taking place in Vietnam. The photograph of the screaming woman at Kent State implicated similar privacy concerns for the dead student lying on the ground, for the student's family, and for the woman herself.

137. See LeBel, supra note 109, at 1153.

138. Ibid.

139. Ibid.

140. See, e.g., Sarah Lyall & Robin Pogrebin, "Paparazzi Relentlessly Stalked Diana: Book Reveals Manic Pursuit of Princess," *Arizona Republic* (Sept. 14, 1997) at H1 (describing a book by celebrity photographers recounting their relentless pursuit of Diana, Princess of Wales).

141. See supra pp. 1087-90.

142. In addition, one commentator advocates the re-establishment of a National News Council, through which "victims of media misconduct that was not actionable could seek formal vindication." Robert M. O'Neil, "Revive News Council to Curb Press," *National Law Journal* (September 22, 1997), at A23. Yet another alternative is the establishment of uniform ethical standards for journalists and photographers. At present, reporters in the United States "do not subscribe to a universal code of ethics or professional conduct." Kirtley, supra note 132, at 1083. The public could encourage compliance with such standards by supporting boycotts directed against publications that fail to respect those industry standards. In fact, several celebrities have urged boycotts of tabloid magazines and television programs that use footage obtained in an offensive manner. See, e.g., "More Laws Won't Stop Photographers Run Amok," *USA Today* (September 3, 1997) at 14A.

Part IV: Discussion Cases

Case #1: *Cape Publications, Inc. v. Bridges*, **Florida 1982**
A woman is kidnapped, taken to an apartment, stripped, and terrorized. The police—and the media—surround the apartment. The police eventually overcome the kidnapper and rush the woman, who clutches a dish towel in a futile attempt to conceal her nudity, to safety. A photograph of her escape, along with a biography, is published in the next day's newspaper. She sued for invasion of privacy and eventually lost the case. Is this a case where free speech should trump privacy? Do we have a right to know the personal details of the victim's life? What about the "suspected" criminal?

Case #2: *Sipple v. San Francisco Chronicle Inc.*,
On September 22, 1975, a bystander deflected a gun aimed at President Gerald Ford. Numerous media sources as well as the President declared the man a national hero. A reporter discovered that the man was a homosexual, a fact of which his family was not aware. After a motion to suppress was denied, the reluctant hero's sexuality became a national story. Should the dissemination of sensitive personal information about private citizens be legal or moral? Why/Why not?

Case #3: Photographs and the Protest against the War in Vietnam
On June 8, 1972, the nightly news broadcast the photograph of several screaming Vietnamese children fleeing a napalm strike in South Vietnam. The little girl in the center of the photograph was stark naked and badly burned; she had torn off all of her clothes in a futile attempt to escape the searing effects of the napalm. This photograph became "the last major icon" of the antiwar movement and "probably did more to increase public revulsion against the war than a hundred hours of televised barbarities." Do such considerations justify the violation of a minor's right to privacy? Should intellectual property rights allow the copyright holders of this photograph the power to re-violate the privacy rights of the victim countless times over numerous years?

PART V

Governmental and Societal Control
of Information

Carnivore, the FBI's E-mail Surveillance System: Devouring Criminals, Not Privacy

GRIFFIN S. DUNHAM

I. Introduction

"Carelessness about our security is dangerous; carelessness about our freedom is also dangerous."[1] The obvious message of this statement is to be ever-mindful of the fine line between a comfortable co-existence with the government and a pronounced separation from the government. Accordingly, decisions to support or oppose governmental action should contemplate this cautious yet responsible approach. The abstraction of the statement requires its individualized application to specific governmental action to determine whether our decision to endorse or oppose that action is prudent. One such governmental action is the FBI's implementation of Carnivore, an Internet monitoring system introduced on July 11, 2000.[2]

Carnivore was designed, and is used exclusively, to carry out court-ordered surveillance of electronic communications, e.g., e-mail.[3] Carnivore is a tangible, portable device, tantamount to a phone tap, that acts as a "sniffer," allowing the FBI to intercept and collect criminal suspects' e-mail without their knowledge or consent.[4] Carnivore is used only in limited circumstances—after FBI, Department of Justice, and judicial scrutiny—pursuant to detailed court orders prescribing and proscribing retrieval procedures.[5] The concern that Carnivore transforms George Orwell's fictitious "Big Brother" concept to reality (by allowing the FBI to engage in unfettered e-mail monitoring), however, raises the need to address the system.

Accordingly, this article addresses competing and parallel interests between the government and society to determine the legitimacy and necessity of Carnivore. The purpose of this article is twofold: first to demonstrate the need for Carnivore to enable law enforcement to keep up with criminals who utilize cyberspace to communicate criminal plans; and second to dispel privacy concerns associated with the system by allaying misconceptions and fears related to its implementation and usage.

Part II of this article addresses the catalyzing reasons for Carnivore's design and use. Part III describes the FBI's extensive and mandatory internal procedures that dictate the decision to use Carnivore to pursue a suspected criminal, and addresses the three federal statutes that can empower Carnivore's use. Part IV explains Carnivore's method of operation; i.e., how it works in each of three stages. Part V articulates the privacy concerns raised by privacy advocates, including: (1) the possibility of collecting and storing e-mail in violation of federal law; (2) Fourth Amendment infringement; and (3) a lack of FBI individual accountability by failing to employ tracking mechanisms that allow for independent oversight. Finally, this article concludes by addressing policy considerations that should shape the future for Carnivore.

II. A Background to Carnivore: Reasons for Implementation

As computer technology and usage rapidly proliferates within our society, criminals embrace this advancement by capitalizing on the opportunities and capabilities produced by that technology's increasing pervasiveness.[6] The FBI recognizes cyberspace as an efficient and increasingly popular medium for criminal activity, especially among spies, hackers, and other dangerous criminals.[7] In response to these threats against the safety of the American people, to the security of our communications infrastructure, and to the important commercial and private need for a safe, secure, and vibrant Internet, the FBI has concentrated its technological efforts and resources to fight a broad array of cyber crimes.[8] One of these efforts has been in the design and implementation of Carnivore, which the FBI hopes will increase public safety by reducing the amount of computer-assisted criminal activity. Specifically, the FBI has articulated five types of critically important crimes that Carnivore will target: terrorism, information warfare, child pornography, fraud (including white collar), and virus writing and distribution.[9]

A. Terrorism

Terrorists use information technology and the Internet to formulate plans, to raise funds, to spread propaganda, and to communicate securely.[10] Cyber terrorism—the usage of cyber tools to shut down critical national infrastructures such as energy, transportation, water, telecommunications, and other government operations, to coerce or intimidate a government or civilian population—is a very real threat with destructive potential.[11] In fact, Director of Central Intelligence, George Tenet, testifying on the worldwide threat of terrorism, stated that terrorist groups, including Hizbollah, HAMAS, the Abu Nidal organization, and Bin Laden's al Qa'ida organization are using computerized files, e-mail, and encryption to support their operations.[12] Although none of these groups have successfully employed cyber technology to infiltrate our critical infrastructures, their reliance on information technology and acquisition of computer expertise clearly indicates the knowledge, opportunity, and interest for chaotic destruction.[13]

While the danger from these organizations is currently only a potential threat, the FBI has documented acts of terrorism that were organized and conspired through e-mail and downloaded to computer systems. The FBI, using traditional law enforcement tactics, recently thwarted a terrorist group's plan to break into several National Guard Armories and steal explosives to incapacitate several power transmission sources in the southern United States.[14] FBI intelligence revealed e-mail to be a major communication method among the group in attempting to effectuate their plan.[15] Further, the FBI seized computer evidence that showed the group had downloaded information on Ricin, the third most deadly toxin in the world.[16]

B. Information Warfare

Quite possibly the single greatest cyber threat to our national security lies in "information warfare" by foreign countries and their militaries against U.S. critical infrastructures.[17] Information warfare is a product of other countries' military inferiority in comparison to U.S. forces.[18] In essence, what foreign nations lack in firepower, resources, and training, they attempt to compensate for by waging a "cyber war." This type of war attempts to exploit our "Achilles heel"—a national dependence on information technology in government, commercial, and private operations.[19]

Two Chinese military officers, cognizant of the United States' military stronghold throughout the world, recently published a book that recommended the usage of unconventional measures, including spreading computer viruses to neutralize U.S. advantages.[20] Additionally, the Russian government also recognizes that an attack on the U.S. computer infrastructure, by its catastrophic consequences, could overlap with the use of weapons of mass destruction.[21]

C. Child Pornography

Although exploitation of children is not a national security issue like terrorism and information warfare, its infiltration into our society is analogously detrimental because it reaches deep into the welfare of our communities. It is now overwhelmingly clear that computer and Internet users are using their systems to disseminate child pornography, and to arrange illegal meetings between user and child—an often violent and deadly combination.[22] As a result, the Internet has dramatically increased the access of sex offenders to the population they seek to victimize.[23] These manipulating users take on a "virtual" identity, appealing to a child's impressionable mind while maintaining the saving grace of anonymity. Once a relationship has been established, the trap has been set and the predatory Internet user now must only coerce the innocent child to take the already tempting bait.

To combat sexual predators, the FBI devised "Innocent Images," an initiative designed to capture individuals who travel between states to engage in illegal sexual activity with a child, and those who produce or distribute child pornography via the Internet.[24] The program entails FBI agents going undercover on the Internet by assuming the role of a child, arranging a meeting place with an offender, and arresting the offender(s) upon identification.[25] Capturing these offenders is extremely difficult, however, because the offenders can easily remain anonymous. They use encryption to conceal their illegal activities, which usually consist of communicating with the child and storing pornography files.[26] Innocent Images found it difficult, and sometimes impossible, to defeat the encryption.[27]

The FBI is extremely focused on and concerned with sexual predators because they possess distinct character traits. In fact, clinical studies report that a child molester will typically victimize seventy innocent children during his or her lifetime.[28] Between 1995 and 2001, the FBI investigated over 800 cases involving offenders crossing state lines to carry out an illegal sexual relationship and more than 1,850 cases involving the exchange of child pornography over the Internet.[29] All arrests pursuant to these investigations were made using traditional enforcement tactics—before the implementation of Carnivore.

D. Fraud

Internet fraud is defined as any fraudulent scheme in which one or more components of the Internet, such as Web sites, chat rooms and E-mail, plays a significant role in offering nonexistent goods or services to consumers, communicating false or fraudulent representations about the schemes to consumers, or transmitting victims' funds, access devices or other items of value to the control of the scheme's perpetrators.[30]

Understanding and using the Internet to combat Internet fraud is absolutely essential for law enforcement.[31]

The Internet provides an ideal medium to commit fraud for three reasons. First, access to the Internet essentially means access to thousands of other Internet users through chat rooms, forum discussions, and instant messaging systems. Second, as with sexual predators, fraudsters can retain complete anonymity.[32] "The crucial difference in fraud committed over the Internet is that the perpetrator can 'virtually' vanish, leaving consumers wondering who or where to turn to for help."[33] Third, fraudsters no longer face financial barriers such as mailings, hiring people to reply to the mailings, and maintaining expensive toll-free telephone services.[34]

The North American Securities Administrators Association estimates Internet-related stock fraud costs investors approximately $10 billion per year, which equals nearly $1 million per hour.[35] In just one case, on March 5, 2000, nineteen fraudsters were indicted in conjunction with a multi-million dollar insider trading scheme that used Internet Service Provider ("ISP") chat rooms as the medium to facilitate and effectuate their scheme.[36] The central "player" in the case passed inside information about clients of several other brokerage firms to two other individuals in exchange for a percentage of the profits subsequently received by acting on the information.[37] This fraudster passed information almost solely through online chats and instant messages for two and one-half years, received $170,000 in kickbacks for his services, and earned $500,000 for his partners.[38] Although the FBI captured these criminals, the traditional tactics used to arrest the individuals involved were inefficient, and keeping up with these types of criminals requires a different approach.[39]

E. Virus Writing

As computer usage increases, so does the number of computer viruses. Throughout the U.S. and other cyber-linked countries, virus writers pose an increasing risk to networks and systems.[40] In the year 2000, viruses such as the Melissa Macro Virus, the Explore.Zip worm, and the CIH (Chernobyl) Virus infiltrated systems world-wide, destroying computer programs and files.[41] Many computer viruses use e-mail as the vehicle for destruction, proliferating through the computer system when the user opens the e-mail file.

III. Carnivore Use Must Be Pursuant to Federal Statute

Before Carnivore's surgical methods are employed to pursue a suspected criminal, two safeguards fraught with substantive and procedural requirements must be satisfied: The Bureau and De-partment of Justice ("DOJ") must endorse its usage, and federal law must permit its deployment.

A. FBI and DOJ Approval

Before Carnivore is engaged, the FBI must scrutinize its appropri-ateness under the circumstances, and obtain DOJ approval.[42] FBI standard operating procedure mandates an eight-step process for determining the appropriateness of Carnivore usage. First, the FBI field agent assigned to the potential case involving Carnivore works in collaboration with the field office principal legal advisor and an attorney from the nearest U.S. Attorney's Office.[43] Together, they revise their documentation of the case's circumstances and particu-lars, and make comments and suggestions to those involved in the next level of scrutiny.[44]

After approval from field office management, the office submits the case file to the Department of Justice's Office of Enforcement Operations ("DOJOEO") in the Criminal Division, and also to FBI Headquarters.[45] Once received by Headquarters, the documents are processed and analyzed by the Legal Counsel Division and the Criminal Investigative Division.[46] Upon arrival at the Criminal Investigative Division, the case file is appropriated to the program manager in charge of the crime(s) being investigated, e.g., child pornography or terrorism.[47] This program manager thoroughly reviews the case record and file, and determines if the suspect is worthy of pursuit and if interception is appropriate.[48] The intercep-tion inquiry ends if the program manager makes a negative deter-mination.

If the program manager decides the suspect and interception is appropriate, the DOJOEO and Legal Counsel Division further refine the case findings and forward them to the Deputy Assistant Attorney General (or someone higher).[49] The Deputy Assistant Attorney General reviews the documents and decides whether to approve the case's continuation.[50] If approved, the DOJ authorizes the initial U.S. Attorney's Office to complete and file in court a final version of all documents acquired in conjunction with the investigation.[51] This file includes documents necessary to analyze the interception under federal guidelines (which will be discussed in the following section).[52] After the case is filed, the U.S. Attorney's Office applies for a court order to use Carnivore by submitting the suspect's file and the DOJ authorization to a federal judge.[53] This judge then analyzes the comprehensive record and rules and decides whether Carnivore's use would comport with federal law.[54]

B. Federal Statutory Approval

Even if Carnivore receives the requisite Bureau and DOJ endorsement, its usage must still conform to federal law. The governing federal law will be revealed in the application submitted to the federal judge, but will be either: (1) Title III of the Omnibus Crime Control and Safe Streets Act of 1968 ("Title III"); (2) the pen-trap provisions of 18 U.S.C. 3121-3124; or (3) the Foreign Intelligence Surveillance Act.[55]

1. Title III of the Omnibus Crime Control and Safe Streets Act of 1968

Title III, as amended by the Electronic Privacy Communications Act of 1986, governs all interception of electronic communications conducted by federal law enforcement investigators.[56] Before Carnivore is granted installation permission pursuant to a Title III investigation, the FBI must be pursuing a recognized Title III suspect and usage of Carnivore must comply with the procedural requirements of Title III.

a. Subject Must be a Recognized Title III Suspect

To begin the Title III Carnivore inquiry, the FBI must be pursuing a suspect believed to have committed a recognized crime under Title III.[57] Title III exhaustively enumerates these crimes, which are limited to felonies such as murder, kidnapping, child molestation, felony violations of obscenity, crimes against national security, robbery, malicious mischief, extortion, organized crime, and narcotics offenses.[58] If the suspect is not pursued for violation of an enumerated crime, Carnivore cannot be utilized.

b. Case File and Judicial Order Must Satisfy the Act's Requirements

If the subject is a statutorily recognized suspect, Title III still mandates the satisfaction of two procedural requirements before a judge can approve Carnivore's deployment. To satisfy the first requirement, the FBI, in its application for an order, must specify and particularize: (1) facts demonstrating probable cause that statutorily recognized offenses are being committed; (2) a description of the nature and location of the facilities where the communications will be intercepted; (3) a description of the communications sought to be intercepted; and (4) the identity of the suspect.[59] Finally, the FBI must indicate that normal investigative procedures have been insufficient to obtain the desired information, e.g., due to danger or technology restrictions.[60]

If the first requirement is satisfied and the federal judge grants the wiretap request, the judge's wiretap order must contain the following to satisfy the second requirement: (1) the identity of the person whose communication is to be intercepted; (2) the nature and location of the communications facilities to which interception is granted; (3) a particular description of the type of communication sought to be intercepted along with a statement of the particular alleged offense; (4) the identity, and authorizing officer, of the agency authorized to intercept the communications; (5) the authorized time period for interception,[61] which cannot exceed thirty days[62] and which should include "a statement as to whether or not the interception shall automatically terminate when the described communication has been first obtained;"[63] and (6) an order requiring the FBI to minimize the interception of communications not authorized to be intercepted under part three of the order.[64]

2. Federal Pen-Trap Statute

The Federal Pen-Trap Statute provides a less intrusive mechanism for wiretapping than its Title III counterpart, and allows law enforcement to monitor e-mail in two ways: "trap-and-trace" monitoring and "pen-register" monitoring (together, "pen-trap devices").[65] Trap-and-trace e-mail monitoring decrypts the identification of every account attempting to communicate with the suspected felon, whereas pen-register e-mail monitoring tracks all outbound communication from the suspected felon's account.[66] Unlike Title III monitoring, pen-trap devices do not inquire into the content of the communication, or substantively record communication.[67] Instead, the FBI uses the pen-trap statute to obtain destination and origination information of incoming and outgoing e-mail messages. Typically, an e-mail pen-register order will only authorize collection of the source ("FROM field"), destination ("TO field"), date, time, user account address, and duration of the message.[68]

Although a pen-trap device can only be deployed pursuant to a court order,[69] the information it can gather is inherently less intrusive than that gathered under Title III. Accordingly, the requirements to obtain a pen-trap order are less stringent than for Title III wiretap interceptions.[70] Nevertheless, the pen-trap order authorizing collection of Carnivore-monitored e-mail must specify the identity of the person with the e-mail address, the identity of the person under investigation, and the offense for which the person is under investigation.[71] Further, the FBI is precluded from inquiring and delving into the e-mail's subject line and "re" information.[72] Any law enforcement agent that uses a pen-trap device without first acquiring a court order is subject to a fine and up to a year in prison.[73]

3. The Foreign Intelligence Surveillance Act

The Foreign Intelligence Surveillance Act (FISA) allows the federal government to monitor electronic communication of foreign powers, and agents of foreign powers located in the United States, to obtain foreign intelligence information.[74] If the focus of the surveillance is not a U.S. citizen, no court order is required and only authorization from the Attorney General is necessary.[75] If the subject of surveillance is a U.S. citizen, the usage of Carnivore must be approved through a special foreign intelligence surveillance court that determines its appropriateness by using standards analogous to those used to obtain permission under Title III.[76]

IV. Method of Operation

Relative to the most technologically current computer hardware, Carnivore is considered, by experts, to be systemically unsophisticated; the computer program has been around since 1992.[77] The system configuration is comprised of: a four-to eighteen-gigabyte hard drive with 128-megabytes of RAM; a Pentium III processor; Windows NT or Windows 2000; and a two-gigabyte Jaz drive—all of which can be readily purchased through a local computer retailer.[78]

There are, however, fundamental differences between Carnivore and the typical "off-the-shelf" system. First, the Carnivore computers exclude a TCP/IP identifier, which virtually obviates the possibility of being hacked into by a network user, and include "network isolation devices," which prevent the computer from transmitting data in the unlikely event that hackers hijack Carnivore's system.[79] Secondly, the Carnivore computers are equipped with a hardware authentication device, which prevents ISP personnel or law enforcement agents from obtaining post-programming access to the contents of the computer without producing visible signs of forced entry.[80]

A. Background of Internet Communication

Unlike telephones, which work through a circuit-switching process that allocates one phone line for use between the two communicating parties, the Internet delivers messages (e-mail) via a process known as "packet switching."[81] Packet switching refers to a transmission process in which entire messages are divided into tiny packets of information before they are sent.[82] These packets consist of binary code—simply a numeric stream of many "0s" and "1s" that will eventually be reorganized into a readable message.[83] After the packets are divided, they are transmitted separately, and can follow one of thousands of different possible routes before passing through an ISP and on to its desired destination.[84] After all the packets forming the message arrive at the destination, they are recompiled into the original message.[85]

B. Carnivore's Installation and Filtering: A Process of Stages

After the FBI receives judicial approval to initiate Carnivore's setup, the physical deployment and information retrieval process begins. Specifically, the process consists of four stages: installation, filtration, segregation, and collection.

1. Stage One: Installing Carnivore

After the FBI has obtained an authorization to capture information pursuant to one of the three previously mentioned statutes, they will turn to the suspect's ISP to determine if the ISP has the technology to comply with the court order.[86] If the ISP can comply, Carnivore is not used. If the ISP cannot, the FBI engages in a cooperative effort with the ISP technicians to position Carnivore in the network where the suspect's communication packets can be isolated.[87]

2. Stage Two: Initial Filtering

Carnivore's first action is to "take a glimpse" of the ISP's traffic, which includes traffic from non-targeted individuals, and filter the packets of "0s" and "1s" at the ISP's designated speed, usually 40 mega-bits per second or much higher.[88] Carnivore filters this binary code in "real time," which means it processes at least 40 million "0s" and "1s" each second, depending on the speed of the packets.[89] This initial filtration serves to determine whether the suspect's identifying information, in accordance with the court order, is present in the binary code.[90] Carnivore essentially takes a picture each second, searching for the suspect's information. If the suspect's information is not present, every packet of information is vaporized, and not collected, stored, or saved, and Carnivore analyzes the next second's data.[91] If the suspect's information is present, Carnivore proceeds to Stage Three.[92]

3. Stage Three: Segregating the Suspect's Information

If Carnivore detects the suspect's identifying information, the packets of the suspect's communication are segregated for additional filtration and storage.[93] This filtration and storage is effectuated entirely within the Carnivore device, without known FBI or ISP technician interference.[94]

4. Stage Four: Following Collection Orders

After the Stage Two filtration and Stage Three segregation occurs, the suspect's information is filtered again to comport with the court order.[95] Carnivore checks its programming to see what it should filter and collect for processing, as determined by court order, and discards nonretrievable information.[96] For example, Carnivore determines whether the collection is for purposes of Title III, pen-trap collection, or the Foreign Intelligence Surveillance Act. Once again, this process is done entirely within Carnivore, without known FBI or ISP technician interference.[97]

V. Privacy Concerns

Since its inception, Carnivore has been scrutinized as an over-infringing device that "devours" the privacy rights of every non-targeted individual whose information passes through the system.

While activist groups and individuals have verbally denounced Carnivore and have established websites[98] to collaboratively oppose its use, the two most prominent opponents are the American Civil Liberties Union ("ACLU") and the Electronic Privacy Information Center ("EPIC"). Many of their concerns are technical in nature, rooted in Carnivore's general operation—they want to know the system's capabilities, what goes on inside the "black box," and whether the installation could expose or cause ISPs to malfunction or crash.[99]

The DOJ recognized this widespread ignorance and distrust of the system, and consequently contracted with the IIT Research Institute and the Illinois Institute of Technology Chicago-Kent School of Law ("IITRI") to address the technical concerns of the system.[100] However, the IITRI "expressly declined to address the significant legal issues surrounding the use of the Carnivore system."[101] As a result, EPIC, the ACLU, and other privacy advocates have articulated three continuing legal concerns: (1) the possibility that Carnivore conducts broad sweeps over the ISP's transmissions; (2) Carnivore's ability to transmit more than the suspect's data violates the Fourth Amendment; (3) the lack of FBI personnel accountability for Carnivore further creates a concern for over-collection through agent impropriety.[102] Until these issues have been sufficiently resolved, privacy advocates urge the FBI to suspend Carnivore deployments.[103]

A. Concern #1—Can Carnivore Spy on Every Internet User?
Many privacy advocates are concerned that Carnivore collects more data than is allowed by court order. They fear that Carnivore can read the content of all individuals' e-mails over an ISP.[104] In fact, David Sobel, General Counsel for EPIC, stated that Carnivore could easily conduct a "broad sweep" of transmission data.[105]

If so programmed, the FBI concedes that Carnivore could conceivably be able to collect and archive all unfiltered traffic from an extremely small ISP.[106] Such a notion will probably remain strictly theoretical, however, because a court order would never allow for such a broad sweeping collection, regardless of ISP size.[107] But even if a court granted such an order, there is not a realistic possibility that such a sweep would occur because of Carnivore's intrinsic storage limitations.

Carnivore does not have nearly enough power "to spy on almost everyone with an e-mail account." In order to work effectively, it must reject the majority of packets it monitors. It also monitors only the packets traversing the wire to which it is connected. Typically, this wire is a network segment handling only a subset of a particular ISP's traffic.[108]

However, withstanding intentional mis-programming, which will be discussed in Part V.C., this issue is moot because a court would never authorize such a broad sweep.

When programmed for a Title III or FISA collection, Carnivore provides the FBI with no more information than is permitted by the court order.[109] In cases involving a pen-trap order, however, Carnivore does collect "more than would be permitted by the strictest possible construction of the pen-trap statute."[110] The over-collected data is essentially useless to the FBI. Instead of only collecting the contents from the "TO" and "FROM" fields, Carnivore also replaces characters in the other fields, for example putting an "X" in the subject line.[111] Therefore, the FBI could ascertain the length of the subject line by counting the number of "Xs." Aside from these character replacements in pen-trap mode, "there was no evidence of over-collection during any of the tests."[112]

To further allay the concern of collecting more data than authorized, Carnivore has been configured to "err on the side of caution." When programmed in accordance with the court order that unequivocally prescribes the programming, Carnivore provides investigators with less information than can legally be obtained if a suspect's privacy right can be potentially infringed.[113]

B. Concern #2 — Is Carnivore Eating the Fourth Amendment?
Carnivore's purpose is to capture criminal suspects' Internet transmissions, notwithstanding the suspects' knowledge or consent. That purpose necessarily results in the clandestine acquisition of non-suspects' electronically transmitted data. Consequently, many privacy advocates question whether Carnivore comports with the Fourth Amendment when processing both the non-suspects' data as well as the suspects' information.

1. Non-Suspects' Fourth Amendment Rights

EPIC and other privacy advocates claim that much of the controversy surrounding Carnivore is derived from its ability to access and process a great deal of ISP transmissions.[114] This concept particularly concerns the organization because users not named in the court order and not targeted by the FBI have their transmissions processed through Carnivore.[115] "It is this unique aspect of Carnivore that gives rise to fundamental privacy risks,"[116] and creates a Fourth Amendment concern because the court order is a warrant for collection of the suspect's data, not the non-targeted individual's data.[117]

The central purpose of the Fourth Amendment is to protect the public's privacy and security from arbitrary governmental invasion.[118] Accordingly, law enforcement must obtain advance judicial approval of searches and seizures by obtaining a warrant.[119] While warrants are preferred, there are certain undefined, limited circumstances that allow law enforcement to conduct searches without probable cause or individualized suspicion.[120] A government action falls within these limited circumstances when the privacy interest implicated by the search is minimal, and the action serves an important governmental interest that would not be promoted if individualized suspicion of each non-targeted subject is required.[121]

Assuming non-targeted individuals have a privacy expectation in their packets of information, the standards for warrantless intrusions clearly permit Carnivore's processing. Since Carnivore is used only to pursue felons, the government obviously has an important interest in their apprehension. Non-targeted suspects have only a minimal privacy interest in their packets of information because each packet contains very little information and the intrusion - a brief, one-second processing of data—is negligible. If, however, the government opts to collect, store, and analyze a non-targeted subject's information, there is a much lower governmental interest because the non-targeted subject is not a criminal suspect, and there exists an obvious increase in the degree of intrusiveness because the packets are being analyzed. Thus, the evidence would be barred from usage by the exclusionary rule.[122] But so long as Carnivore only processes the non-targeted subject's information, the system does not violate these non-targeted subjects' Fourth Amendment rights.

2. Targeted Suspects' Fourth Amendment Rights

Privacy advocates also express concern for the suspect's Fourth Amendment rights when Carnivore is used pursuant to a pen-trap order.[123] Since pen-trap devices are less intrusive than Title III interceptions, acquiring a suspect's information does not require a showing of probable cause. Thus, advocates argue the collection of the "TO" and "FROM" fields constitutes an unjustified search and seizure of the suspect's data.[124] This argument fails, however, because the Supreme Court has determined that a suspect does not have a reasonable expectation of privacy in the information collected pursuant to a pen-trap order.[125] Even if the suspect had a reasonable expectation of privacy, the Fourth Amendment challenge would fail due to the same balancing test applied above for non-targeted subjects: the governmental interest of solving the particular crime far outweighs the minimal privacy interest the suspect has in the "TO" and "FROM" fields.

C. Concern #3—Who's Spying on the Spiers?

The purpose of Carnivore is to process ISP transmissions in strict adherence to the empowering court order, which allows gathering and storing the suspect's data, but mandates instantaneous purging of a non-suspect's data. Theoretically, this gathering and purging is effectuated after the Carnivore box is programmed in exact accordance with the court order. Since theory is not reality, privacy advocates worry that Carnivore is susceptible to programming in violation of the court order.[126] This is possible because Carnivore lacks "audit functions," which results in the absence of an individual user accountability mechanism.[127]

> Auditing is crucial in security. It is the means by which users are held accountable for their actions. There is no auditing in Carnivore. The Carnivore version 1.3.4 collection computer is always logged in as the "Administrator" rather than using individual user IDs. This Administrator log-in means that every user of the system has full control over all the resources of the system. . . . Since everyone with Administrator access has full control, there is nothing to prevent someone from using a Hex editor or other tool to [access Carnivore's advanced filter setting menu]. Therefore, it is not possible to determine who, among a group of agents

with the password, may have set or changed filter settings.[128]

This deficiency is Carnivore's most troubling attribute. Without individual user accountability, there exists no system-intrinsic disincentive for FBI agents to unlawfully program Carnivore. A simple click of a mouse (whether intentional or unintentional) changes Carnivore's configuration settings from a pen-trap collection to a full collection under Title III.[129] "There is no mechanism for detecting or minimizing the likelihood of such an unintentional setup error."[130]

The implementation of an auditing system would almost certainly reduce both intentional and unintentional violations; it may cause a potentially unintentional violator to more carefully select the proper setting, and may cause a corrupt FBI agent to abate intentions of mis-programming.

Nevertheless, until an auditing system is implemented, mis-programming can occur, resulting in collection of more data than allowed by the court order.[131] Although this excessively collected data may be subject to judicial suppression, privacy advocates could claim the mis-programming infringed on the subject's privacy right and the possibility remains of unlawfully initiating an investigation based on information learned as a result of the over-collection. It is natural to assume that privacy advocates would be unwilling to rely on the FBI's assurance that any information inadvertently gathered beyond the scope of the court order is disposed of in conformity with federal statutory and constitutional law.

Quite simply, there need to be safeguarding mechanisms in place to counteract Carnivore's systematic pitfalls. Fortunately, federal statutes and rules exist that not only protect subjects who have fallen victim to over-collection, but also deter intentional and unintentional mis-programming.

1. Title III and FISA Post-Collection Judicial Review [132]
Both Title III and FISA provide for judicial oversight when Carnivore is used. Specifically, Title III mandates the recording of the contents of the electronic communication intercepted by Carnivore.[133] Further, "immediately upon the expiration of the period of the order, . . . such recordings shall be made available to the judge issuing such order and sealed under his directions."[134]

FISA provides similar oversight language when the subject is a United States citizen, but adopts a judicially permissive, though not mandatory, review.[135] The statute provides in relevant portion:

> At or before the end of the period of time for which electronic surveillance is approved by an order . . . the judge may assess compliance with the minimization procedures by reviewing the circumstances under which information concerning United States persons was acquired, retained, or disseminated.[136]

Thus, each Title III and FISA order-issuing judge has the opportunity to compare the captured information with the court order to independently determine the legality of the obtained information, and accordingly suppress all deemed "over-collection."

2. Federal Rule of Evidence 901

Evidence must be authenticated to be admissible against a defendant at trial.[137] "[This] requirement of authentication or identification as a condition precedent to admissibility is satisfied by evidence sufficient to support a finding that the matter in question is what its proponent claims."[138] To comport with section 901, Carnivore appends to an event file for each collection in which the filter configuration is used.[139] This information makes explicit to the FBI, judge, and jury what mode controlled Carnivore's use during the collection process and what it was programmed to collect.[140] Since over-collection of the suspect's transmissions would violate the court order and the defendant's Fourth Amendment rights, the trial judge could apply the exclusionary rule to suppress illegally seized information.[141]

3. Criminal and Civil Liability; Employment Termination

Any FBI agent that engages in the illegal, unauthorized conduct of electronic surveillance commits a federal criminal offense punishable by imprisonment for up to five years, a fine, or both.[142] In addition, an individual victimized by unlawful over-collection or interception can recover damages in a civil action including punitive damages, as well as attorney's fees and other costs against the person or entity engaged in the violation.[143] Although the culpable FBI agent may not be personally liable for damages, the impending disciplinary action for causing the government liability certainly serves as a deterrent. In fact, every law enforcement agent who illegally conducts electronic surveillance is subject to immediate termination.[144]

VI. Conclusion

Internet technology has evolved exponentially over the past few years, and the future will certainly continue to realize the same growth. The accessibility to such an immense audience, coupled with a criminal's ease of anonymity, requires an approach to accommodate the growing threats made possible by the Internet.[145] Carnivore represents a permissible and responsible approach. It enables law enforcement to take one small step to level a playing field currently dominated by criminals who can routinely break the law by using an extremely evasive and criminally propitious medium.

We live in a world where criminals can remain undetected or vanish with the mere click of a mouse. Terrorists, whether foreign or U.S. citizens, are undoubtedly plotting to bomb more American structures with the intent of producing results like those witnessed on September 11th or in Oklahoma City. Pedophiles are pursuing and encroaching on innocent children every day by assuming the most clandestine identities to manipulate the child's every unsuspecting move. The governments of foreign countries are deploying intelligence teams to crack the computer codes that harbor our most important resources—such as our electrical and water supplies, gas and oil reserves, and telecommunications—to exploit our vulnerabilities and to potentially cause catastrophic and deadly results. College students are writing computer viruses solely for the thrill of destroying others' computer files. Although these hypothetical situations seem disconnected in nature, they all share a commonality—the use of electronic communication to facilitate their collusive, maniacal acts of depravity.

The government inevitably faces a "Catch 22" when deciding how to address these types of cyber criminals. If it uses investigative and surgical methods such as Carnivore, privacy advocates criticize the action as overly invasive of privacy rights. If it fails to pursue every avenue to eliminate potential threats, advocates for crime control criticize the lack of action as irresponsible policing and a failure to serve the interests of societal welfare. Unfortunately, no governmental action will ever be uniformly supported. Therefore, the government should initiate only those programs that adhere to the statement offered in this Note's first sentence—act in the interests of security while maintaining the utmost possible level of freedom. Carnivore successfully furthers this goal by increasing security while not compromising freedom.

The manner in which Carnivore collects transmissions is abstractly analogous to a law-enforcement roadblock, instituted to search for an escaped convict, that stops every vehicle (packet) traveling down a certain road (ISP). If law enforcement is not 100 percent certain the traveler is the convict (targeted suspect), the traveler is processed through the roadblock (Carnivore) and continues to the intended destination. If law enforcement is 100 percent certain, however, the traveler is detained. Privacy concerns are alleviated when considering this entire electronic "roadblock" is nondiscretionary in that decisions are made within the confines of the acutely accurate Carnivore system, and not by a human police officer, who, even if the paradigm example of objectivity, is still fraught with fallibility.

This is not to say Carnivore is perfect. Its lack of individual accountability, as well as the potential to accidentally mis-program the device, are flaws that should be remedied. As technology-based crime increases, however, so does society's need to embrace governmental action aimed at safeguarding society from this increased threat facilitated through electronic communication.

With FBI and DOJ internal policy to bureaucratically determine whether Carnivore should be used; Title III, Pen-trap, and FISA statutory prescriptions; judicial oversight coupled with federal rules to deter unlawful electronic communication interception; and continued necessary pressure from privacy advocates, Carnivore is an appropriate, prudent, and necessary law enforcement mechanism that balances the values of freedom and security that predicate and underlie this Note.

Notes

1. Adlai E. Stevenson Jr., Speech in Detroit, Michigan (October 7, 1952), in Daniel B. Baker, *Power Quotes*, 123 (1992).

2. The Carnivore FOIA Litigation, at http://www.epic.org/privacy/carnivore/ (updated Aug. 8, 2001).

3. Carnivore can also be used to record Internet sites visited by the suspect for later evaluation, but the FBI insists that usage of Carnivore is restricted to capturing e-mail transmission. See IIT Research Inst., Independent Review of the Carnivore System, Final Report ES.4-5 (2000), available at http://www.usdoj.gov/jmd/publications/carnivore<uscore>draft<uscore>1.pdf [hereinafter Review].

4. Electronic Communications Privacy Act of 2000, Digital Privacy Act of 2000 and Notice of Electronic Monitoring Act: Hearing Before the Senate Comm. on the Judiciary: Carnivore Diagnostic Tool, 106th Cong. (2000) (statement of Donald Kerr, Assistant Director, FBI Laboratory) available at http://www.fbi.gov/pressrm/congress/congress00/kerr090600.htm [hereinafter 9/6/00 Hearing].

5. Ibid.

6. Fourth Amendment Issues Raised by the FBI's "Carnivore" Program: Hearing Before the House Comm. on the Judiciary: Internet and Data Interception Capabilities Developed by the FBI, 106th Cong. (2000) (statement of Donald Kerr, Assistant Director, FBI Laboratory), available at http://www.fbi.gov/congress/congress00/kerr072400.htm [hereinafter 7/24/00 Hearing].

7. 9/6/00 Hearing, supra note 4.

8. Ibid.

9. See ibid.

10. Critical Information Infrastructure Protection: The Threat Is Real: Hearing Before the Senate Comm. on the Judiciary, 105th Cong. (1999) (statement of Michael Vatis, Director, FBI National Infrastructure Protection Center), available at http://www.fbi.gov/congress/congress99/nipc10-6.htm.

11. Cyber Attack: Improving Prevention and Prosecution: Hearing Before the Senate Comm. on the Judiciary, 106th Cong. (2000) (statement of Guadalupe Gonzalez, Special Agent In Charge, FBI Phoenix Field Division), available at http://www.fbi.gov/congress/congress00/gonza042100.htm.

12. Ibid.

13. See ibid.

14. See 7/24/00 Hearing, supra note 6, at 33.

15. Ibid.

16. Ibid.

17. See Jim Christy, "Chasing Shadows: The Human Face Behind the Cyber Threat," *Federal Communications Law Journal* 53 (2000): 185.

18. Cyber Attacks: Removing Roadblocks to Investigation and Information Sharing: Hearing Before the Subcommittee on Technology, Terrorism, and Government Information of the Senate Committee on the Judiciary, 106th Cong. (2000) (statement of Louis J. Freeh, Director, FBI), available at http://www.fbi.gov/congress/congress00/cyber032800.htm [hereinafter 3/28/00 Hearing].

19. Ibid.

20. Ibid.

21. Ibid.

22. See 7/24/00 Hearing, supra note 6.

23. Online Child Pornography, Innocent Images National Initiative, at http://www.fbi.gov/hq/cid/cac/innocent.htm (last visited Jan. 23, 2002) [hereinafter Innocent Images].

24. Preventing Child Exploitation on the Internet: Hearing Before the Subcomm. on Senate Appropriations of the Senate Comm. on the Judiciary, 105th Cong. (1998) (statement of Louis J. Freeh, Director, FBI), available at http://www.fbi.gov/congress/congress98/sac310.htm [hereinafter 3/10/98 Hearing].

25. Ibid.

26. Ibid.

27. Ibid.

28. Ibid.

29. 9/6/00 Hearing, supra note 4.

30. The Internet Fraud and Complaint Center, Bankruptcy Fraud Video, at http://www.fbi.gov/hq/cid/fc/ifcc/about/about<uscore>ifcc.htm (last visited March 2, 2001) [hereinafter IFCC].

31. Ibid.

32. Ibid.

33. Press Release, U.S. Department of Justice, Federal Bureau of Investigation, Internet Fraud Complaint Center Press Packet (May 8, 2000), at http://www.fbi.gov/pressrel/pressrel00/ifccpr.htm.

34. IFCC, supra note 30.

35. 9/6/00 Hearing, supra note 4, at 34.

36. Ibid.

37. Ibid.

38. Ibid.

39. IFCC, supra note 30.

40. 3/28/00 Hearing, supra note 18, at 27 (statement of Louis J. Freeh).

41. See ibid.

42. Donald P. Delaney et al., "Wiretap Laws and Procedures: What Happens When the U.S. Government Taps a Line," 2.1.1, at http://www.cpsr.org/cpsr/privacy/wiretap/wiretap.procedure.html (Sept. 23, 1993).

43. Ibid.

44. Ibid.

45. Ibid.

46. Ibid.

47. Ibid.

48. Delaney, supra note 42.

49. Ibid.

50. Ibid.

51. Ibid.

52. Ibid.

53. Ibid.

54. See Delaney, supra note 42.

55. Review, supra note 3, 3.1.

56. Electronic Privacy Communications Act, 18 U.S.C. 2510-2522 (2000).

57. 18 U.S.C. 2516.

58. Ibid. 2516(l).

59. 18 U.S.C. 2518(1).

60. Delaney, supra note 42.

61. 18 U.S.C. 2518(4)(a)-(e).

62. Ibid. 2518(5).

63. Ibid. 2518(4)(e).

64. Ibid. 2518(5).

65. 18 U.S.C. 3121-3124.

66. Robert Graham, "Carnivore FAQ" (Frequently Asked Questions) 3.1, at http://www.robertgraham.com/pubs/carnivore-faq.html (Oct. 6, 2001).

67. 9/6/00 Hearing, supra note 4, at 37 (statement of Donald Kerr).

68. Ibid.

69. Ibid.

70. 18 U.S.C. 3121(a). Notice that applications for the usage of pen-trap devices may be made by any federal government attorney or state investigative or law enforcement officer. Also, no special authorization is required. Ibid. 3122. In fact, any court fulfilling jurisdictional requirements is required to issue a pen-trap order if the court finds that information expected to be obtained would be relevant to an ongoing investigation. Ibid. 3123(a).

71. See ibid. 3123(b). Although the language of the statute does not explicitly state that these procedures apply to electronic communication and no case law exists to validate such an application, there have been no constitutional challenges to the FBI's usage of pen-trap devices in such a manner.

72. 9/6/00 Hearing, supra note 4, at 37 (statement of Donald Kerr).

73. 18 U.S.C. 3121(d).

74. See 50 U.S.C. 1802 (1994).

75. Ibid. 1802(a)(1).

76. See ibid. 1805(b).

77. Graham, supra note 66, 1.5.

78. Ibid.

79. Ibid.

80. Ibid.

81. Webopedia, Packet Switching, at http://www.webopedia.com/TERM/p/packet<uscore>switching.html (last modified May 1, 2001).

82. See ibid.

83. See 9/6/00 Hearing, supra note 4, at 37 (statement of Donald Kerr).

84. Marilyn McKinley Parrish, "The Internet for Church Librarians," at http://www.mph.org/plan/planspr96b.htm (April-June 1996).

85. "Digital Journey, The Human Origins of the Internet," *Systemnews*, at http://sun.systemnews.com/system-news/jobdir/submitted/2002.02/5154/5154.html (last visited March 12, 2002).

86. 9/6/00 Hearing, supra note 4, at 37

87. Ibid.

88. Ibid.

89. Ibid.

90. Ibid.

91. Ibid.

92. 9/6/00 Hearing, supra note 4, at 37.

93. Ibid.

94. Ibid.

95. Ibid.

96. Ibid.

97. Ibid.

98. See, e.g., Stop Carnivore NOW!, at http://www.stopcarnivore.org (last visited Jan. 26, 2002).

99. Mario Figueroa, "Carnivore—Diagnostic Tool or Invasion of Privacy?," at http://rr.sans.org/legal/carnivore.php (Sept. 1, 2000).

100. Review, supra note 3. The report analyzed the process assessment, system architecture, software source code, and laboratory tests. See ibid. 2-1, 2-3. However, the nature of IITRI's findings enabled them to answer questions that were not strictly technical. See ibid. 4-9.

101. E-mail from David L. Sobel, General Counsel, EPIC, to Carnivore Review Panel, U.S. Department of Justice, at http://www.epic.org/privacy/carnivore/review<uscore>comments.html (Dec. 1, 2000) [hereinafter EPIC Review].

102. See ibid.

103. Ibid.

104. "Stop Carnivore NOW!," at http://www.stopcarniovre.org/what<uscore>can<uscore>carnivore<uscore>do.htm (last visited Jan. 26, 2002).

105. See EPIC Review, supra note 101.

106. Letter from Donald Kerr, Director, FBI, to Senator Patrick J. Leahy, Senate Comm. on the Judiciary (Jan. 23, 2001), available at http://www.epic.org/privacy/carnivore/kerr<uscore>letter.html.

107. Ibid.

108. Review, supra note 3, ES.5.

109. Ibid. 4.3.1.

110. Ibid. 4.2.3.

111. Ibid.

112. Ibid.

113. Ibid. 4.3.1.

114. See EPIC Review, supra note 101.

115. Ibid.

116. Ibid.

117. See ibid.

118. *S. Dakota v. Opperman*, 428 U.S. 364, 377 (1976) (Powell, J., concurring).

119. *Terry v. Ohio*, 392 U.S. 1, 20 (1968).

120. *Chandler v. Miller*, 520 U.S. 305, 308 (1997) (citing *Treasury Employees v. Von Raab*, 489 U.S. 656, 668 (1989)).

121. *Skinner v. Ry. Labor Executives Ass'n*, 489 U.S. 602, 624 (1989).

122. *Weeks v. United States*, 232 U.S. 383 (1914).

123. Stop Carnivore NOW!, Why Carnivore is Bad for You (Reason # 1), at http://stopcarnivore.org/whyitsbad/reason1.htm (last visited Jan. 29, 2002).

124. Ibid.

125. See *Smith v. Maryland*, 442 U.S. 735, 745-46 (1979). Although this case addressed telephonic interception, the same reasoning can be applied to e-mails because essentially the same information is obtained.

126. See EPIC Review, supra note 101.

127. Review, supra note 3, 4-9.

128. Ibid. 4.2.4.

129. Ibid. 4.3.3. There is also the possibility of improperly setting Carnivore to comply with the court order. Ibid. However, this "chance of error . . . is low because of the large number of individuals involved in framing the court order and determining the feasibility of its implementation by Carnivore." Ibid.

130. Ibid.

131. Ibid.

132. As stated, the FBI receives less information when Carnivore is configured for a pen-trap collection than for a Title III or FISA collection. Therefore, mis-programming from a Title III or FISA collection to a pen-trap collection seems highly unlikely because more information is retrievable by following the court order.

133. 18 U.S.C. 2518(8)(a).

134. Ibid.

135. 50 U.S.C. 1805(e)(3).

136. Ibid.

137. Fed. R. Evid. 901.

138. Ibid.

139. 9/6/00 Hearing, supra note 4.

140. Ibid.

141. Weeks, 232 U.S. 383.

142. 50 U.S.C. 2511(4)(a).

143. Ibid. 2520.

144. 9/6/00 Hearing, supra note 4.

145. IFCC, supra note 30.

Privacy Isn't Everything: Accountability as a Personal and Social Good

ANITA ALLEN

I. Accountability Matters Too

Privacy, including private choice about personal matters, is a dominant theme in public policy in the United States. My scholarship has often emphasized the positive value of contested physical, informational, and decisional privacies.[1] Moreover, I have applauded recent federal efforts to mandate information privacy protections. The most conspicuous of these protections, Title V of the Gramm-Leach-Bliley Financial Services Modernization Act (Gramm-Leach-Bliley), the Health Insurance Portability and Accountability Act of 1996 (HIPAA), and the Children's Online Privacy Protection Act (COPPA), are far from perfect legal regimes.[2] But there is value in asking the commercial sector to modify business practices to protect data relating to the sensitive areas of personal finance, health, and family life.

The spectacle of terrorism on American soil appears to have stunned some Americans into viewing privacy as a luxury we can no longer afford, a tool of our enemies. Even after the terrible deeds of September 11, 2001, however, I remain firm in my beliefs about the importance of informational privacy. The USA PATRIOT Act and other homeland security measures enhance the power of government to intercept communications and hold individuals captive.[3] I share the worry of vocal privacy advocates and civil libertarians that new laws were hastily enacted and proposed innovations are overly broad.[4] The proposed (but abandoned) "TIPS" program threatened to turn neighbors and public servants into community spies.[5] The "Total Information Awareness" program would aggregate personal data on all Americans from diverse sources in an unprecedented effort to track a small group of people involved in terrorism.[6] In an era of increased surveillance and security, we need to reassert traditional privacy claims voiced in free and democratic societies. Intimate relations, sex, health, and personal finances still merit a privileged status.

Because privacy is under siege in the contemporary world, it is tempting to downplay the positive value of accountability for private life. Yet, although privacy is important, it is not everything. Accountability matters too. "None of your business!" in response to accountability demands is not always warranted. Privacy and accountability each in their own way render us more fit for valued forms of social participation. It is important to understand that privacy is our repose and intimate accountability our engagement and, therefore, why some accountability demands that relate to archetypical "private" and "personal" realms are legitimate. It is also important to understand the dynamics of political order that saddle some people with too much of the most onerous forms of accountability.

In this article, I will highlight personal and social goods that flow from accountability for private life. At the same time that I highlight the benefits of accountability, I will note significant risks. A series of illustrations relating to the privacy and private choices of African-Americans provides an especially useful context in which to see both the extent to which accountability for private life is a reality and the risks and benefits that flow from it. Standing in the wake of September 11, it is especially important to recognize the risks of injustice and indignity that can flow from governmental and non-government accountability mandates. By accountability mandates, I mean expectations or requirements that we (1) inform others of what we do, (2) explain ourselves to others, (3) justify our conduct to others, (4) submit to punishments or other sanctions, or (5) live routinized, transparent lives.

II. Accountability in Law and Society

Privacy is a good. But accountability is also a good. It is a fact, and it should be a value. Accountability for conduct is a pervasive feature of human association.[7] Accountability operates explicitly and implicitly in the fields of public administration and corporate governance.[8] Accountability imperatives drive the law of tort and crime. Accountability should not and cannot be total in any domain. Still, in every sector of society a degree of accountability for conduct is critical.[9] In the United States, as in other places, accountability and concerns about accountability range beyond the affairs of government and business enterprises. They range also into the territory of the personal affairs of private individuals and non-commercial enterprises.

When designating certain realms or activities "private," "personal," and the like, we imagine ourselves as citizens of a free society, each entitled to enjoy a number of states, feelings, thoughts, acts, and relationships for which we owe others no accounting. Although others have a say in what we do in our capacities as managers, employees, and motor vehicle license holders, they have no similar say in what we do as private persons. We imagine that other people are allowed to share in our private lives or not, at our discretion and on our terms, subject to a very few exceptions. We often think and talk this way, drawing a sharp divide between public and private. The political philosophies some of us hold dear pay tribute to *On Liberty*, the classic essay in which John Stuart Mill famously wrote that "the individual is not accountable to society for his actions, insofar as these concern the interests of no person but himself."[10] American jurisprudence on occasion prominently echoes Mill's sentiment. Dissenting in *Poe v. Ullman*,[11] Justice John Marshall Harlan exploited the familiar political ideal of the private home, marriage, and family to build a revolutionary constitutional case for reproductive freedom that set the stage for *Griswold v. State of Connecticut*[12] and *Roe v. Wade*.[13] Justice Harlan vigorously attacked Connecticut statutes on the ground that laws criminalizing contraception intrude "into the very heart of marital privacy" and require "husband and wife to render account before a criminal tribunal of their uses of . . . intimacy."[14]

However, accountability for the uses of intimacy is a common imperative, expectation, and deeply felt obligation in our society. As individuals, couples, families, and communities, we live lives enmeshed in webs of accountability for conduct that include accountability for intimacies relating to sex, health, child-rearing, finances, and other matters termed "private." We are accountable for nominally private conduct both to persons with whom we have personal ties and to persons with whom we do not have personal ties. We are accountable to the government, and we are accountable to non-government actors. We are accountable for plainly harmful and other-regarding conduct in our nominally private lives, for example, date rape; and we are accountable for the best candidates we have for harmless and self-regarding conduct, for example, consensual oral sex between monogamous partners in their own bedrooms. We do not simply face others' "advice, instruction, persuasion, and avoidance[,]" devices Mill approved.[15] We face social and legal demands for sanctions and other reckoning of which he disapproved. Mill's assertion that individuals are "not accountable to society" for actions that concern only themselves is debatable as a matter of ethics or political morality and as Mill himself regretted, flatly inaccurate, as a matter of fact.[16] Not only are we held accountable for what is commonly termed private life, but our accountability for some personal, arguably self-regarding, conduct extends to the extreme of criminal liability.

Accountability for and in private life is thus no mere oxymoron or confusion. Social norms of every category—religious, ethical, moral, legal, and customary—foster accountability. We are held accountable, and we hold others accountable. We feel accountable, and we feel owed accountability. As citizens and scholars we debate what is and is not private and what should and should not be private, always against the backdrop of a culture in which accountability subsists in virtually every corner of our lives.[17] Accountability for private life means that the broad areas of individual and group life regularly labeled private are not walled off. We do not label dimensions of life private because they are immune from scrutiny and judgment by official and unofficial or public and private "agents of accountability." Flourishing accountability practices and policies examine and evaluate what goes on in the personal and intimate arenas.

Legal liability for sex and sexual orientation is one of the most emotionally charged forms of accountability. Philosophers, like legal theorists, understandably focus on the implications of legal accountability because of the onerous, coercive nature of civil and criminal sanction. Legal liability for personal choices can feel particularly unjust where the individual expected to account does not share the moral, ethical, or religious outlook of the person demanding the accounting. But non-legal sanctions for conduct are potentially coercive and punitive too. It wounds the soul to suffer the social sanctions of censure and isolation.

Liability to sanction is but one form of accountability. Accountable individuals are called on to reckon with others for acts and omissions that violate norms in several other important senses. An observer would miss a stark feature of American life were he or she to allow pervasive liberal values, aspirations, and rhetoric—much of which I find congenial—to obscure the richly diverse ways in which we are constantly called upon to report, explain, justify, and otherwise answer to others for the choices we make about own lives.

In the spirit of toleration for individual differences, political liberals are skeptical of collective interference with individuals' own assessments concerning their affairs. Liberals are for leaving people alone, living and letting live. But a society cannot afford fully to leave people alone. And liberals know it. The practical reality that the non-judgmental outlook fosters mischief was captured in *Accountability*, an ironic poem crafted in ersatz African-American dialect by the troubled African-American poet Paul Laurence Dunbar.[18] The poem begins:

> Folks aint got no right to cen/suah othah folks about dey/habits;
> Him dat giv' de squir'ls de bush/tails made de bobtails fu' de/rabbits.
> . . . . We is all constructed diff'ent,/d'ain't no two of us de same;
> We cain't he'p ouah likes an' dis/likes, ef we'se bad we ain't to/blame.[19]

The words of the poem's narrator make the case against accountability, while the actions of the narrator as revealed in an unquoted final stanza illustrate the case for it. People not subject to "censuah" may lack incentives for avoiding antisocial behavior. The poem's narrator delivers a lovely philosophical argument for respecting what he characterizes as God-given human differences, but it turns out that the narrator's tribute to toleration is merely a ploy to deflect criticism for having broken the law. His words are self-serving rationalization. He is about to dine on a stolen chicken, "one o' mastah's chickens," to be exact.[20]

Accountability makes sense to committed liberals when the white man's chickens begin to disappear. Liberals recognize reasons to hold others accountable for personal matters if harm can thereby be averted. The fights are about what constitutes the relevant sorts of harm. Sex and health are considered very personal. Yet, accountability makes sense in the case of a public official whose flagrant sexual immoralities impair public duties, or a sexually active man who has concealed his AIDS from unsuspecting partners. And many liberals are prepared to recognize respects in which "personal" and "self-regarding" acts are also social and other-regarding, for example, recreational drug use, casino gambling, and third-trimester abortion. But these are modern examples. To really understand the depth of accountability for personal affairs, to really understand what counts as a chicken, we need to turn the clock back a bit.

III. Accountability to Judge and Jury

Eighty years ago a wealthy New York man, Leonard "Kip" Rhine-lander, sued to have his marriage annulled.[21] The peculiar ground for annulment was that his wife, Alice Jones Rhinelander, had deceived him as to her race. The legal proceedings and journalistic frenzy that followed led to expectations of accountability for the most intimate aspects of the young couple's lives. The courtroom drama that ensued demanded the ultimate in accountability of the information-emphatic and explanation-emphatic sorts. Mr. Rhine-lander endured opposing counsel reading aloud in court his sexually explicit love letters to his future bride. His wife's lawyers hoped to brand him in the minds of the jury as a perverted and unmanly seducer. Attorneys asked Mr. Rhinelander to explain intimacies (possibly oral sex) referred to obliquely in intimate correspondence. Alice Rhinelander was the eventual victor in the case. However, after listening to her premarital trysts with her husband detailed in court, her own lawyer insisted, with the approval of the judge in the case, that she bare her "dusky" naked breasts and legs to the jury to prove that her lover-turned-husband had to have known she was "colored" when he married her. Bizarrely, Al Jolson, the famous blackface entertainer, was dragged into court to deny an affair with Mrs. Rhinelander, solely because she once mentioned in a letter that someone she met at work called "Al Jolson" was a flirt. That a perfect stranger to the litigants was held accountable for his sex life, too, is evidence of the sweeping character of private life accountability at the time.

In the light of the Rhinelander case, blaming feminism for Anita Hill's or Monica Lewinsky's frank testimony looks like fallacious post hoc ergo propter hoc reasoning. We had accountability for private life long before Anita Hill and Betty Freidan were born. Clarence Thomas's experience in Congress might fruitfully be compared to Kip and Alice Rhinelander's.

IV. Accountability to the Media, Public, and Race

In January 2000, newspapers reported that Reverend Jesse Jackson, a married Christian minister, civil rights leader, and one-time presidential candidate, had fathered a child by a woman not his wife.[22] His lover worked for Jackson's civil rights organization.[23] Some people responded to the news with calls that Jackson be "held accountable" for his private conduct. Among them was Clarence

Page, Pulitzer Prize-winning reporter for the Chicago Tribune.[24] Claiming special ambivalence about holding others accountable for their personal lives, Mr. Page told a *Columbia Journalism Review* interviewer that he felt a special obligation to hold Jesse Jackson closely accountable, qua African-American leader.[25]

People who agreed with Page that Jackson should be held accountable could have disagreed about what forms of accountability were appropriate. When the news of a "love child" hit the stands, some people thought it would be sufficient for Reverend Jackson to confirm or deny what newspapers were reporting. They thought it would suffice for Reverend Jackson to say publicly something akin to this: "I had a sexual relationship with Ms. So-and-so, an employee of my organization, and fathered a daughter, to whom I provide this and that type of support from monies earned in this and that way."

After Reverend Jackson provided the basic facts, though, some members of the public and the media were still not satisfied. They seemed to think the Reverend owed the public, or at least his public, an explanation of the facts and circumstances of the affair:

> Although I was married at the time, and although I profess that adultery is a sin, I faltered; I had a sexual relationship with Ms. So-and-so, an unmarried employee of my organization, with whom I had enjoyed working for many years. I fathered a daughter and assumed financial responsibility for her care. I know that I have caused my wife and children pain and disappointed loyal supporters.

Others seemed to want even more from Reverend Jackson. They seemed to want an explanation that included an earnest effort at justification. The most complete explanations are both explanations that and explanations why. Justifications are explanations why. They explain, for example, why a person's conduct seemed acceptable or was acceptable under the circumstances:

> I was very lonely and feeling the emotional stress and isolation of long days and nights away from my wife, necessitated by my civil rights mission; I was overcome by Ms. So-and-so's kindness and devotion to her work; I believed I was in love with her; I ignored the call of

conscience and betrayed my faith; I am a sinner, we are all sinners, but I have asked for and received forgiveness; I am providing financial support for my daughter using only my own personal financial resources, not those of any organization.

A few people seemed to want yet more from Reverend Jackson. Beyond the information, the explanations, the justifications, they wanted his head. They wanted to bring the big guy down. They wanted him punished with moral censure, ostracization, and any criminal or civil liability appropriate for adultery and hypocrisy. They wanted accountability in the punishment-emphatic sense.

Recall that Clarence Page said, in connection with his coverage of Jesse Jackson, that as an African-American journalist he held African-American leaders to a higher standard of accountability than leaders of other races.[26] A public figure may be accountable in one sense and to one degree to the general public, but in further senses and to further degrees to members of his or her identity group.

The late Supreme Court Justice Thurgood Marshall was accountable for his personal life, not simply to the public, but also, and critically, to his African-American public. Vivian "Buster" Burey Marshall, Marshall's first wife of twenty-five years, died in 1955. That same year he married his second wife, Cecilia Suyat, who was not, in the parlance of the day, a "Negro." The victorious attorney in *Brown v. Board of Education*,[27] Marshall was one of the most influential men in the United States. Known to have had a large ego, Marshall enjoyed his stature as a voice of leadership within the NAACP. One might guess that in mid-twentieth century America, such a man could marry whomever he wanted, no questions asked. But that was far from the truth in the decade before *Loving v. Virginia*.[28] Marshall's closest advisors knew that questions would be asked about his motives for out-marriage and his intentions about continuing at the forefront of the fight for black civil rights. Marshall's second marriage threatened to be a political liability for the NAACP. His personal choice could have cost the organization money and support at a critical juncture. Showing both moral sensitivity and political savvy, NAACP leaders successfully urged Marshall to hold a press conference in which he graciously introduced his bride and affirmed his commitments to civil rights work.

More than a half-century later, accountability for out-marriage remains on the moral landscape.[29] Only about ten percent of black men marry women who are not black. Blacks are the most endogamous of the major "racial" groups in the country. Among African-Americans, those who out-marry still face a surprising degree of negative accountancy premised on feelings of betrayal. African-Americans are not the only minority group many of whose members feel accountable to the group for personal choices.

Problems of intra-group accountability exist in the world of childrearing and adoption, too. Native American women seeking to place their children for adoption are accountable to tribal authorities for adoption decisions. Although one might think that a parent's decision to place his or her child for adoption is a personal one, federal law gives Native tribes the right to veto the placement of an Indian child with a non-Indian family. Thurgood Marshall implicitly knew that accountability is an effective signaling strategy for rational, self-interested actors. If I routinize my conduct, I signal that it is safe to be my friend, lover, or partner. Having successfully evidenced the intent to cooperate, individuals can reap the benefits of appearing to be desirable partners in cooperative endeavors.[30]

V. Accountability to Government

The House of Prayer is a Christian congregation of African-Americans who take seriously the Biblical maxim that to spare the rod spoils the child.[31] In March 2001, Atlanta police seized forty-one children whose parents belonged to the church after one boy showed up at school with welts on his body.[32] He said he had been beaten with a switch at church.[33] They also arrested sixty-eight year old Reverend Arthur Allen and five House of Prayer members alleged to have encouraged or participated in child-beatings.[34] Nearly a decade earlier, in 1992, Reverend Allen had been sentenced to prison for beating a sixteen-year-old girl accused of premarital sex.[35] In trouble with the law again, Allen complained to a reporter, "We're getting persecuted. They want to dominate us with their way of life."[36]

To hold House of Prayer adults accountable to the state for their religious practices is indeed to dominate them with "our" way of life. But this is an apt example of the benevolent domination by the state that feminist legal theorists have urged for years. Tear down the doors of "private" citizens in "private" homes and "private" institutions as needed to protect the vital interests of vulnerable people. It is also the kind of domination that would not much worry a political theorist for whom freedom in pluralist societies entails or consists in non-domination. The restriction placed on the House of Prayer is not an arbitrary, whimsical power play, but an attempt at humane law by fair-minded authorities.

Child discipline is one of those components of family life that is sometimes defended by reference to privacy, as well as religious freedom. Though the sternest of libertarians can see the justice of attempting to intervene on behalf of the House of Prayer youth. I am assuming that libertarians oppose violence against children, though I admit that some libertarians may disagree with me about whether corporal punishment amounts to violence or other serious harm.

I believe one of the fathers of Libertarianism, John Stuart Mill himself, would agree with me that child beating of the sort at issue in the House of Prayer case—nonconsensual, ritualized, capable of leaving marks—constitutes harm. Preventing physical harm to children is a clear prerogative of the just, liberal state, even if what counts as physical harm is not so clear. People who harm children should be accountable for the wrong they do. Mormonism was a much-maligned religion in Mill's day, chiefly for its claim to a latter-day saint and to the virtues of polygamy. Emphasizing its remoteness in the American frontier and the voluntary nature of polygamy, Mill defended toleration of Mormonism. I do not think he would have urged similar liberty for a Christian variant closer to home that practiced child-beating.

Mill published *On Liberty* in 1859,[37] more than three decades before "privacy" and the "right of privacy" entered the American legal lexicon.[38] Yet American jurists and scholars commonly cite Mill as a champion of personal privacy. Mill was indeed a champion of personal privacy.[39] More accurately, he was a stern opponent of accountability to government and society.[40] Thought, discussion, and actions that are not harmful to others should be free.[41]

In Chapters 1 and 4 of *On Liberty*, Mill argued that moral justice requires laws and other rules, practices, and institutions that maximize aggregate long run happiness or "utility."[42] Although some people are better at judging what conduct is conducive to utility than others, when it comes to self-regarding conduct, each person is the best judge of what conduct will promote his or her own utility.[43] We have what philosophers sometimes call "privileged access" to our own emotions and needs. Therefore, as a general rule, a just government and society should only prohibit conduct that harms third parties.[44] Society should strictly limit interference with self-regarding conduct to conduct that harms others.[45] Legal paternalism and legal moralism are rejected in Mill's ideal just society. While Mill does not put it this starkly, it would seem to follow from his premises that accountability for any aspects of personal or private life that are self-regarding and not harmful to others is morally unjust. Hence, there should be limits on governmental and societal requirements that persons report what they think or do to others, explain what they think or do to others, justify what they think or do to others, submit to others' sanctions and punishments, or lead a transparent, predictable lifestyle for the sake of others.

In Chapter 2 of *On Liberty*, Mill argued that individual and social utility results from tolerance of diverse thought and discussion.[46] Humankind is not yet perfect. Until such time as it is, tolerating even unpopular thought and discussion will be conducive to aggregate, social happiness. How so? First, Mill argues, it is unwise to limit thought and discussion because what one thinks of as a dangerous falsehood may be true.[47] Humans are fallible.[48] Second, says Mill, toleration facilitates the ultimate reign of truth.[49] In addition, sacred truths tend to become moribund, unthinking dogma, unless perpetually revitalized by the challenge of dissent and falsehood.[50] We need not fear the reign of falsehood because over time truths overcome falsehoods.[51] Falsehoods being inherently less useful tend to fade away.[52] They attract few buyers in the marketplace of ideas.[53] Third, Mill concludes, there may be a kernel of truth in ideas and opinions that are largely false.[54] Those truths must not be lost to humankind.[55]

In Chapter 3 of *On Liberty*, Mill defended freedom of action.[56] Just as thought and discussion should be free, actions/conduct should be free, he urged.[57] Individuality should be tolerated in actions as well as in word and thought. [58] Yet Mill readily admitted that "no one pretends that actions should be as free as opinion."[59] Mill proposed, though, that actions should be free, subject to the obligation to refrain from harming others.[60] He urged that:

> If he refrains from molesting others in what concerns them, and merely acts according to his own inclination and judgement in things which concern

> himself, the same reasons which show that opinion
> should be free, prove also that he should be al-
> lowed, without molestation, to carry his opinions
> into practice at his own cost.[61]

To make his case for individual freedom of action, Mill asserted that "apelike imitation" of others leaves the distinctive human capacities of reason, judgment, and making life plans unexercised.[62] Human nature is like a tree, not a machine.[63] Each of us grows under the influence of nutrients into a unique shape, though we, like two maples or two oaks, belong to the same species.[64] Mill urged that human character and genius flourishes though individuality.[65] And, finally, nations flourish through a diversity of character and culture.[66]

The case Mill makes for tolerating freedom of action and thought does not offer a moral refuge for the House of Prayer, if child-beating is harmful to children. Child-rearing practices are not self-regarding in Mill's sense. Like John Locke, Mill believed the authority parents have over children is custodial and protective. Children are not parental property. The special control pregnant women have over fetuses in view of physical connectedness is not shared by the parents of fully-born children. We can also distinguish the House of Prayer incident from *Wisconsin v. Yoder*[67] and *Meyer v. Nebraska*.[68] In those cases the Supreme Court allowed religious or ethnic minorities to "harm" their children by removing them from regular public school at age thirteen and by enrolling them in private parochial school offering foreign language instruction.[69]

VI. The Good of Accountability

Accountability chills, deters, punishes, prompts, pressures, and exposes. These are evils when they amount to unjust domination or frank violation. They are not, however, always evils. Indeed, there are positive dimensions to accountability's qualification of privacy and private choice. Accountability protects, dignifies, and advantages. This was true in the House of Prayer case.

Accountability protects. That a society looks after health and safety by holding others accountable reflects the esteem in which its members are held. The forty-one Atlanta children were taken from their homes for a time because Fulton County values their well-being. At first, parents whose children were removed from their homes refused to agree to stop church-supported corporal punishment. They eventually relented. Accountability (the threat of criminal punishment, the loss of parenting privileges, and the loss of reputation in the eyes of the wider community) was protective of the children. It was also ennobling of the children's angry and befuddled parents. Accountability dignifies. The society that holds individuals to account dignifies them by presupposing intelligence, rationality, and competence for dialogic social performances of reckoning. No one expects hamsters and centipedes to give account. That is one of the reasons they get squished and locked into little cages. The fact that we expect accountability of fellow humans is a measure of the seriousness with which we regard them. A parallel point is made by moral philosophers about moral agency in general all the time. Ascribe moral rights, obligations, duties, or responsibilities as a measure of respect.

Of course, accountability can be a feature of ignoble compulsion rather than protectionism or moral dignity. Serfs and slaves are expected to answer to masters, expectations enforced with whip and chain. The threat of brutality has led subordinated peoples to signal intent to cooperate at a considerable loss to self-esteem. The accountability norms that deeply ennoble are the type that are egalitarian and reciprocal. Some African-Americans interpreted the House of Prayer intervention as secular society's unequal, non-reciprocal subordination of Black's minority culture. Reverend Allen suggested that his arrests for beating children were emblematic of the majority society's disrespect for African-American religious and cultural traditions. Yet the laws that prohibit excessive child discipline apply equally to all racial and religious groups. White, secular child abusers get arrested too in Atlanta, a Christian-dominated city with a recent history of black mayors and many black police officers.

Accountability demands that are not strictly reciprocal and egalitarian are potentially ennobling, if they flow from the requirements of care and caretaking rather than from political domination. Accountability is a demand of love and nurture. The intense accountability for intimacies demanded by long-term lovers is missed when Alzheimer's, Huntington's, or senile dementia sets in. Intense accountability is part of the parent-child relationship, too. Parents need and want accountability of their children. One of the saddest things about having a child who is mentally disabled is missing out on the experience of teaching the arts of description, explanation, justification, censure, and seeing those lessons consistently put to work. A remote, autistic son speaks not at all; when manic, a bipolar daughter does not provide coherent reasons and explanations for conduct.

Physical discipline is a common expectation of good parenting in most African-American families, communities, and churches, notwithstanding the opposition to corporal punishment in the wider society. It is not just the tiny House of Prayer that tells black parents to beat black children. The House of Prayer parents who subscribed to church beatings believed that physical discipline teaches accountability. They believed corporal punishment molds children into respectful youth and law-abiding citizens. Some forms of accountability proffered in the name of love and care are ill-conceived. African-Americans must understand that harsh corporal punishment, though customary and Biblical, is not a cause of good citizenship in a modern society. Children who are spanked, whipped, or beaten by well-intentioned parents may be more likely to turn into violent adults. There is absolutely no evidence that the factors that lead black youth to crime include parents withholding the switch. Black church practices do evolve and change. In the meantime, black children remain accountable to black parents, who remain accountable to grandparents, neighbors, and churches for the choices they make concerning discipline.

Accountability norms are ties that bind. If you imagine lines drawn between each one of us and the people to whom we are accountable for personal matters, the resulting picture is a dense network of such lines—a web of accountability. The web of accountability relationships is both flexible and sticky. The web is sticky in the sense that socially determined and reinforced expectations impel us. Expectations impel us, for example, to tell our mothers certain things, to explain certain things to our friends, and to justify much to our employers. The web is flexible in the sense that we have a good deal of freedom to stretch and mold the connections to suit individual taste. Not all accountability imperatives result from contract or choice. Still, it is oftentimes possible to avoid reporting, explaining, justifying, and so on, because we live in a society that permits a degree of "exit," economists' compact term for voluntary separation and self-isolation. It is not costless to escape societal accountability imperatives—the cost is sometimes loneliness—but we can often do it. We can work ourselves loose. We do not have to tell our mothers everything. We can compartmentalize our friends and get new jobs. We stick, but the good news about life in the United States is that we are not generally stuck.

To be sure, some people feel more stuck than others. Just how stuck we are and feel is an empirical question. Faced with evidence of a great many people unable to express a core identity and associated preferences because of punitive accountability norms, I would abandon my belief that "we are not generally stuck." In liberal societies, political freedom limits accountability to the state. The extensiveness of political freedom in the United States underlies my observation that "we are not generally stuck." But in any society, including the most liberal, the combined force of account-ability to state, community, kin, and friend will qualify both freedom and privacy.

Some cautionary points follow from the web of accountability relationships one observes in the United States. First, in the name of public health, safety, security, and morals, punitive legal account-ability for certain forms of ordinary personal conduct have flour-ished in modern liberal societies. It has not been so long that birth control bans, interracial marriage prohibitions, and sodomy stric-tures were pervasive in American law. We still live with criminal sodomy and adultery bans. Liberalism has never meant the end of accountability to the state for what a great many people consider their personal lives. A perpetual danger is that the ambition to protect will result in simple intolerance and oppression. A perpetual regret is that, in addition to affronts to privacy and freedom, affronts to culture and identity will be costs of accountability to the state for personal matters. Ethno-racial and sexual orientation minorities pay such costs everyday; sometimes for better, as in the case of the House of Prayer's disciplinary violence, sometimes for worse, as in the case of legal intolerance of gays and lesbians.

Second, although in liberal societies the government steps back from extremes of intervention, extremes of accountability are not limited to legal norms or totalitarian regimes. Unofficial, normative accountability in liberal democratic societies can be constraining in many of the same ways that official accountability to the state is constraining. A liberal society—or segments of a liberal society—may be a moralistic or clannish one, for example, in which people are bound to admit, confess, forbear, etcetera, because of their creeds and affiliations. Accountability is a device of group identity and solidarity employed by many familial, religious, and racial groups to positive effect. But suffocating, harsh, non-governmental accountability can make a person wretched.

Finally, I use the term "the New Accountability" to stand for the observed intensification of accountability experienced in the United States in the past decades. The New Accountability is a product of Americans' extensive social, economic, and political freedoms, and our ambivalence about forms of privacy that secret truths useful to others. The fact that people in liberal societies are not generally subjected to state punishment for their beliefs or "self-regarding" conduct may itself heighten accountability expectations. Indeed, contemporary Americans are expected to exteriorize internal and intimate worlds in ways they would not if there were a price to pay. In societies in which sexually active unmarried women are stoned, no one would think to design a television program in which women are asked to talk about their sex lives.

The New Accountability means a demand for bare private facts and then, inevitably, more. For with the revelation of bare private facts comes the call for detail. State that you have AIDS and expect people to want to know how and why you contracted it. They will want to know what medications you are taking and your prognosis. They will want to know if you have a partner and your partner's AIDS status. It feels good sometimes to speak intimate truth to strangers. It feels good to know that others take a compassionate interest in the details of your life. So we talk. But we are not always socially free to stop talking. The New Accountability means strangers may have no compunction about demanding more than you wish to tell and putting facts about you to uses that offend and hurt you. The freedom and openness of our conduct means just that many more people know of it and perhaps witness it. Just that many more curious, interested, nosey, inquiring people exploit accountability-entitling ties. The links they find may be as attenuated as membership in the public claiming a right to know what is at all interesting, educational, informative, newsworthy, or governmental. As the New Accountability demonstrates, substantial accountability for personal life is a product of excessively tolerant and intolerant societies.

Notes

1. I discuss privacy sympathetically in a number of articles and three books. My books are: *Uneasy Access: Privacy for Women in a Free Society* (University Press of America, 1988) and Richard

C. Turkington & Anita L. Allen, *Privacy Law*, 2d ed. (West pub., 2002). My survey articles include: "Constitutional Privacy," in *A Companion To Philosophy Of Law And Legal Theory*, Dennis Patterson ed. (Blackwell Publishers, 1996) p. 139; "Genetic Privacy: Emerging Concepts and Values," in *Genetic Secrets*, Mark Rothstein ed. (Yale University Press, 1997) p. 31; "Privacy," in *A Companion To Feminist Philosophy*, Iris Marion Young & Alison M. Jaggar eds. (Blackwell Pub., 1998) p. 456; "Privacy as a Practical Value," in *Oxford Handbook Of Practical Ethics*, Hugh LaFollett ed. (Oxford University Press, 2003) p. 485; "The Jurispolitics of Privacy," in *Reconstructing Political Theory*, Uma Narayan & Mary Lyndon Shanley eds. (Pennsylvania State University Press, 1996) p. 68; and "The Public Right to Know," in *The Encyclopedia Of Ethical Issues In Politics And The Media*, Ruth Chadwick ed. (Academic Press, 2000) p. 251.

2. The Gramm-Leach-Bliley Act, Pub. L. No. 106-102, 113 Stat. 1338 (1999) (codified in scattered sections of 12 U.S.C. and elsewhere), requires financial institutions to protect the security and confidentiality of customers' nonpublic personal information. The Health Insurance Portability and Accountability Act of 1996, Pub. L. No. 104-191, 110 Stat. 1936 (1996), sets standards for security of confidentiality of health information and medical records. The Children's Online Privacy Protection Act of 1998, Pub. L. No. 105-277, 112 Stat 2681-728 (1998) (codified at 15 U.S.C. § 6501 (2000)) (COPPA), requires commercial Web sites to refrain from collecting personal data from children under thirteen without parental consent. I assess COPPA in Anita L. Allen, "Minor Distractions: Children, Privacy, and E-Commerce," *Houston Law Review* 38 (2001): 751.

3. Uniting and Strengthening America by Providing Appropriate Tools Required to Intercept and Obstruct Terrorism Act of 2001 (USA PATRIOT Act), Pub. L. No. 107-56, 115 Stat. 272 (2001).

4. See the ACLU, Electronic Privacy Information Center, civil liberties group, and privacy advocacy group positions at http://www.aclu.org/Privacy/PrivacyMain.cfm (last visited April 13, 2003), http://www.epic.org/privacy/terrorism (last updated Nov. 12, 2002), http://www.libertydefense.com/privacy.html (last visited Apr. 13, 2003), and http://www.privacyrights.org (last modified Mar. 31, 2003), respectively.

5. *See* http://whitehouse.gov/news/releases/2002/01/20020130-8.html (last visited Apr. 13, 2003).

6. *See* Jim Garamone, "Boards to Oversee Total Information Awareness Program," *American Forces Press Service* (February 7, 2003), available at http://www.dod.mil/news/Feb2003/n02072003_200302074.html. See also ACLU and EPIC positions at http://aclu.org/Privacy/Privacy.cfm?ID=11323&c=130&Type=s (Mar. 23, 2003), and http://www.epic.org/privacy/profiling (last updated Feb. 3, 2003), respectively.

7. Richard McKeon, "The Ethics of International Influence," *Ethics* (1960): 120, 187-203.

8. *See, e.g., Accountability In Urban Society: Public Agencies Under Fire*, Scott Greer, Roland D. Hedlund, & James L. Gibson eds. (Sage Pub., 1978); Peter French, *Collective And Corporate Responsibility* (Columbia University Press, 1984); Robert B. Wagner, *Accountability In Education* (Taylor & Francis Books Ltd., 1989).

9. Accountability "is an essential and undismissable desideratum for orderly social interaction" without which "it is impossible to conceive of a society resembling an organized interlocking of individual actions, or for that matter maintaining sociality and intersubjectivity." G.R. Semin & A.S.R. Manstead, "The Accountability of Conduct: A Social Psychological Analysis," *European Monographs In Social Psychology* (Taylor & Francis Books Ltd.,1983) p. 32, 32-185.

10. John Stuart Mill, *On Liberty* (Oxford University Press, 1948) p. 115. In the second paragraph of Chapter V of *On Liberty*, Mill lays out the maxim I quote that "the individual is not accountable to society for his actions, in so far as these concern the interests of no person but himself."

11. 367 U.S. 497 (1961).

12. 381 U.S. 479 (1965).

13. 410 U.S. 113 (1973).

14. *Poe*, 367 U.S. at 553 (Harlan, J., dissenting). Quoting the Justice in full: "In sum, even though the State has determined that the use of contraceptives is as iniquitous as any act of extra-marital sexual immorality, the intrusion of the whole machinery of the criminal law into the very heart of marital privacy, requiring husband and wife to render account before a criminal tribunal of their uses of that intimacy, is surely a very different thing indeed from

punishing those who establish intimacies which the law has always forbidden and which can have no claim to social protection." Ibid. Harlan was not prepared in this case to extend the realm of non-accountability to traditionally prohibited acts including adultery or homosexuality. Ibid.

15. Mill, *supra* note 10, at 115.

16. Ibid.

17. While some tolerant individuals try to avoid the most overtly moralistic accountability discourses and practices, it is nonetheless fair to say that: "In our private lives we wade in a constant stream of accountability initiatives. People hold their children, parents, partners, friends, neighbors, colleagues, and fellow citizens accountable for any kind of presumptive misbehavior--for political incorrectness, insubordination, disorderliness, bad memory, drinking and smoking, sexual misconduct, sinful behavior, lack of courtesy, strategic errors, factual ignorance, whatever. Because there are lots of rules that guide our private lives, there are lots of opportunities for private agents of accountability to step in to monitor and enforce compliance." Andreas Schedler, "Conceptualizing Accountability," *The Self-Restraining State*, Andreas Scheduler, Larry Diamond, & Marc F. Plattner eds. (Lynne Rienner Publishers, 1999) p. 2.

18. Paul Laurence Dunbar, "Accountability," *The Complete Poems of Paul Laurence Dunbar* (Dodd Mead, 1895) p. 5-6.

19. Ibid. at 5. The narrator makes a case for both toleration and divine intent:
When you come to think about it,/how it's all planned out it's/splendid.

Nuthin's done er evah happens,/'dout hit's somefin' dat's in/tended; Don't keer whut you does, you has/to, an' hit sholy beats de/dickens,--/Viney go put on de kittle, I got/one o' mastah's chickens. Ibid. at 6.

20. Ibid. A rational slaveholder who wanted to reduce the likelihood of losing food to rational underfed unpaid labor would have to increase surveillance or increase the penalty of detection.

21. *See generally* Earl Lewis & Heidi Ardizzone, *Love On Trial: An American Scandal In Black And White* (W. W. Norton & Company, 2001).

22. Lauren Janis, "Q&A—Clarence Page on Jesse Jackson," available at http://www.cjr.org/year/01/2/qanda.asp. Page stated: "We will always be aggressive in looking for accountability of public figures. I was one of the first reporters to report on the questions surrounding Jackson's operation Push for Excellence and their expenditures of federal funds back in 1980. Jackson doesn't like accountability. But that hasn't stopped us. When it gets into private life, I know I am less aggressive in pursuing those stories. . . . . When it comes to the private life of any official, you approach it with ambivalence. But my philosophy is, when in doubt, let it out. Our impulse should be in favor of releasing information to the public, not suppressing it. . . . . As an African-American who has been covering the Reverend Jackson and other civil rights figures for over thirty years, I particularly feel that it is my responsibility to be as aggressive as possible. . . . I am very concerned about leadership in general and about the quality of black leadership. And he is the most widely known and respected black leader. I feel obliged to be more aggressive because I feel a special responsibility to African-Americans and others in Jesse Jackson's constituency to hold him accountable. Like a sort of consumer advocate." Ibid.

23. Ibid.

24. Ibid.

25. Ibid. at 9-10.

26. Janis, *supra* note 22, at 9.

27. 349 U.S. 294 (1955).

28. 388 U.S. 1, 12 (1967).

29. Randall Kennedy, *Interracial Intimacies: Sex, Marriage, Identity, and Adoption* (Pantheon, 2003).

30. Eric A. Posner, *Law and Social Norms* (Harvard University Press, 2000) p. 5.

31. *Proverbs* 23:13-14.

32. Amanda Ripley, "Whippings in the Pulpit: A Congregation Loses 41 of its Children to the State After a Boy Tells the Police What Happened at Church," *Time* (April 2, 2001), at 47.

33. Ibid.

34. Ibid.

35. Ibid.

36. Ibid.

37. Mill, *supra* note 10.

38. Samuel D. Warren & Louis D. Brandeis, "The Right to Privacy," *Harvard Law Review* 4 (1890): 193.

39. Mill, *supra* note 10, *passim*.

40. Ibid.

41. Ibid.

42. Ibid. at 5-21, 92-114.

43. Ibid. at 93-94.

44. Mill, *supra* note 10, at 92-93.

45. Ibid.

46. Ibid. at 22-68.

47. Ibid. at 65.

48. Ibid.

49. Mill, *supra* note 10, at 65.

50. Ibid.

51. Ibid. at 22-68.

52. Ibid.

53. Ibid.

54. Mill, *supra* note 10, at 65.

55. Ibid.

56. Ibid. at 69-91.

57. Ibid.

58. Ibid.

59. Mill, *supra* note 10, at 69.

60. Ibid.

61. Ibid. at 69-70.

62. Ibid. at 69-91.

63. Ibid.

64. Mill, *supra* note 10, at 69-91.

65. Ibid.

66. Ibid.

67. 406 U.S. 205 (1972).

68. 262 U.S. 390 (1923).

69. *Yoder*, 406 U.S. at 213-36; *Meyer*, 262 U.S. at 399-403.

National Security at What Price?
A Look into Civil Liberty Concerns in the Information Age under the USA Patriot Act

JACOB R. LILLY

Introduction

Throughout history, each time a severe national security threat was recognized by the United States, the legal system was called upon to answer one important question: To what extent may a democratic society violate the very rights it was founded upon in order to ensure the survival of that society? In answering this question, the government and the courts have applied various tests that should theoretically standardize this evaluation and effectively preserve some minimum level of personal rights while maintaining the necessary protections for society as a whole.

Five examples from the history of this balancing act stand out. In the American Civil War, it was the executive, not the judiciary, which established the tests, resulting in little regard given to individual rights and in widespread constitutional violations. In both the Japanese-American internment cases and the McCarthy era, there were even greater violations. Here the courts mandated the constitutional tests. These tests, however, did little more than legally justify any action the government thought necessary. The anti-terrorism efforts of the 1990s and 2000s, the Foreign Intelligence Surveillance Act (FISA)[1] and the Uniting and Strengthening America by Providing Appropriate Tools Required to Intercept and Obstruct Terrorism Act (USA PATRIOT Act),[2] extended such constitutional violations into the sphere of electronic surveillance. Additionally, the acts themselves provided their own constitutional tests based upon the earlier framework created by the courts. The egregious civil liberty violations in these examples prove the inability of previous constitutional tests to curb those violations and the necessity of a more effective test that still allows the government the necessary tools to protect the United States from external enemies.

This article not only examines the historical issues that present themselves in this context but also looks at new complexities found in the information age and terrorism's unique challenge of asymmetrical warfare.[3] By taking an in-depth look at the infringement of civil liberties during these historical moments of grave national security concerns and analyzing the USA PATRIOT Act's "electronic information" effects, this article hopes to develop a framework in which to address both civil liberty and security concerns in the modern information age. In doing so, this article proposes a "one step lower" test that could be applied to current and future security scenarios.

This article will therefore examine (1) the history of civil rights in times of threats to the security of the country, culminating in the USA PATRIOT Act, (2) specific civil rights concerns within the electronic information spheres of the USA PATRIOT Act, and (3) a proposed new constitutional test that would more effectively balance the interests of individual rights and national security. The application of the "one step lower" test will provide the courts with a flexible standard to safely balance personal rights with the need to defend the United States for the limited duration of a national security crisis.

I. Civil Rights Infringements for National Security Reasons

The history of infringements upon civil rights in times of crises in national security provides a useful insight into the evolution of these infringements and a backdrop upon which the USA PATRIOT Act can be evaluated. In fact, an examination of problems in the USA PATRIOT Act without understanding the historical context of civil rights violations in the United States would provide an unrealistic assessment of the problems at hand and would prove of little use in attempting to prepare for future crises. In order to properly evaluate the context of the personal rights dilemma, we will briefly examine a number of representative examples, including the American Civil War, the internment of Japanese-Americans during World War II, McCarthyism during the Cold War, FISA, the antiterrorism legislation of the 1990s, and the events leading to the adoption of the USA PATRIOT Act. Additionally, this section includes a primer on electronic surveillance in the United States.

A. The American Civil War[4]

While certainly not the first civil rights intrusion in the name of national security,[5] the American Civil War provides perhaps the most egregious early infraction of those rights. At the outbreak of the Civil War, President Abraham Lincoln declared a state of national emergency and suspended all rights in certain key border states.[6] In addition to using federal troops to intimidate state legislators and influence their decisions,[7] Lincoln imprisoned 13,000 civilians and suspended the writ of habeas corpus so that no inquiry could be made into the validity of their detainment.[8] Included in this number were civilians arrested for "discouraging volunteer enlistments."[9] Lincoln had federal troops occupy, by force, large portions of the Maryland countryside, arrested a mayor and nineteen members of the Maryland state legislature, and refused to honor a writ of habeas corpus issued by Chief Justice Taney for a prominent Baltimore citizen who had been "arrested by the military on a charge of aiding the enemy."[10] In Missouri, Lincoln armed 10,000 civilians and used them to disperse gatherings of southern sympathizers.[11] The legislature of Missouri, which was pro-Union, met under the protection of the military, while the governor was effectively discouraged from continuing with the duties of his office.[12] President Lincoln's successful flouting of the Constitution, while no doubt necessary to save the Union, established a dangerous precedent.[13]

President Lincoln's assumption of wartime powers and temporary termination of certain individual constitutional rights was effectively evaluated only by the executive branch.[14] Lincoln's actions demonstrate a belief that only the president could appropriately balance the rights of the individual with the nation's will to survive the threat to its liberty. Lincoln believed that the proper constitutional test was whether the president should "risk[ ] losing the Union that gave life to the Constitution because that charter denied him the necessary authority to preserve the Union."[15] This administrative test of power would become the model for future generations of American presidents during times of domestic crisis.[16]

B. Internment of Japanese-Americans During World War II[17]

During World War II, the United States arrested and incarcerated 110,000 people of Japanese descent.[18] The detentions started the evening of December 7, 1941, and continued for over a year.[19] Initially, the Departments of Justice and the Army favored an exclusion policy that would keep Japanese-Americans from sensitive areas only, but three months after Pearl Harbor, the Western Defense Command (WDC)[20] switched to a policy of internment.[21] WDC justified its actions with the belief that many Japanese-

Americans sympathized with Japan and would commit acts of sabotage to support a possible invasion.[22] The fact that two-thirds of the Japanese-American population had American citizenship did not have any real effect on the decision to intern or the subsequent court decisions upholding that internment as constitutional.[23] Conditions in the camps got so bad that, in addition to living behind barbed-wire fences, these citizens had to live in horse stalls.[24] Furthermore, no specific threat was required; placement in the camps could be justified by race alone.[25]

A succession of cases challenged the internment as a violation of the president's war powers and as a violation of the "equal protection of the laws as guaranteed by the Fifth Amendment,"[26] culminating in *Korematsu v. United States*.[27] The Supreme Court was called upon to confront the very question presented in this Note: To what extent may a democratic society violate the very rights it was founded upon in order to ensure the survival of that society?[28] First, the Court heard *Hirabayishi v. United States*,[29] in which the constitutionality of a curfew targeted entirely at one ethnic group was considered permissible under the theory that "the challenged orders were defense measures for the avowed purpose of safeguarding the military area in question, at a time of threatened air raids and invasion by the Japanese forces."[30] Then in *Korematsu*, the Supreme Court, despite articulating the requirements for strict scrutiny for the first time, held that the internment was constitutional.[31] The Court accepted the military's findings that no means were available that could separate those who would probably commit sabotage and other disloyal acts from innocent civilians.[32] Furthermore, the Court noted, "hardships are part of war."[33] In arriving at its conclusion, the Court decided that the proper test in evaluating civil liberty violations during times of crises was to place great deference on the president's war powers and that the Fifth Amendment must be subservient to those powers.[34] The same year that the Supreme Court decided *Korematsu*, it also ruled in Ex Parte *Mitsuye Endo*[35] that the continued detention of "concededly loyal" Japanese-Americans was unwarranted,[36] without specifically overruling *Korematsu*.[37] However, the court based its decision on the fact that Congressional authorization of the detainment of Japanese-Americans was only with regard to an initial period of evacuation and the fact that Congress later took corrective action regarding the detainment.[38] Even while finding the detainments unconstitutional, *Mitsuye Endo* still granted great deference to the military and focused its discussion of wartime powers on deference to the president and Congress.[39]

C. The Cold War—McCarthyism[40]

After Allied success in World War II, the United States and the Soviet Union quickly reverted to their former antagonisms.[41] As the United States increasingly confronted this new enemy, it found itself involved in a new war, a "cold war."[42] In response, Congress conducted the House Un-American Activities Committee hearings[43] and passed such legislation as the anticommunist oath provisions of the Taft-Hartley Act of 1947[44] and the McCarran Act of 1950.[45] This legislation sought to criminalize communism, membership in a communist organization, and expressions of sympathy towards communist positions.[46] The Supreme Court then agreed to review anticommunist legislation in *Dennis v. United States*.[47] The Court articulated a balancing test that "in each case [courts] must ask whether the gravity of the 'evil,' discounted by its improbability, justifies such invasion of free speech as is necessary to avoid the danger."[48] In order to evaluate the potential invasion of free speech, the court adopted the "clear and present danger" test first articulated in *Schenk v. United States*[49] and held that mere membership in the Communist Party was sufficient to justify government action.[50] Significantly, *Dennis* recognized the elimination of a continuing peril, in this case the overall threat of communist expansion, as a legitimate national security goal.[51] The "clear and present danger" test, while still maintaining deference to the war powers of the president, was the first real attempt at balancing the interests of national security and personal liberty. However, this new test could not prevent the continued violation of the constitutional rights of many American communists during the Cold War.[52]

D. FISA (1978)

The Foreign Intelligence Surveillance Act of 1978[53] provided the next major infringement of civil rights in the interest of national security. FISA was designed to enhance U.S. intelligence capabilities overseas during the Cold War and, as a protection, restrict those activities within the United States.[54] FISA's civil rights concerns focused on foreign nationals within U.S. territory and specifically required that a FISA warrant be used to obtain "foreign intelligence information."[55] However, the FBI and CIA recently revealed that they had used these measures to conduct electronic surveillance of

Martin Luther King, Jr., and other members of the civil rights movement.[56]

FISA powers were granted to the executive branch on the theory that the FBI was not investigating crimes at all[57] but was investigating activities of foreign intelligence agencies and, thus, the lower threshold[58] for obtaining wiretap warrants was acceptable.[59] Under this theory, FISA expanded the definitions of intercept orders, pen-traps,[60] search warrants, and subpoenas.[61] FISA did so by authorizing the Attorney General to conduct intercept orders for up to a year before informing the Foreign Intelligence Surveillance Court,[62] discussed infra, and did not obligate any reporting of the orders if the intercepts were completed within the one year framework.[63]

FISA imposed several limits upon the government. First, both FISA and Executive Order 12,333[64] permitted surveillance against an American citizen within U.S. borders to be undertaken only after the Foreign Intelligence Surveillance Court[65] issued a written order.[66] Additionally, the surveillance could not be undertaken if the information sought could have been obtained by less intrusive means.[67] The court was supposed to hold warrant applications to a standard of probable cause and only apply the warrants to those considered agents of a foreign power.[68] However, Executive Order 12,333 2.3 allowed for information to be collected and disseminated if the information was needed to "protect the safety of any persons or organizations, including those who are targets, victims or hostages of international terrorist organizations."[69] Any information obtained about U.S. citizens who were not targets of an investigation could not be retained or disseminated by those intelligence agencies.[70] The procedures for collection, retention, and dissemination of civilian information by intelligence agencies are further codified by the classified regulations issued by those agencies.[71] Despite these precautions, between 1996 and 2000, all 4,275 FISA warrants applied for were granted.[72]

E. Basic Elements of Electronic Surveillance in the United States

In the U.S. legal system, four basic methods of electronic surveillance exist.[73] These methods are (1) warrants authorizing the interception of communications, (2) search warrants authorizing the search of physical premises, (3) trap-and-trace devices[74] and pen-traps,[75] and (4) subpoenas requiring the production of tangible records, such as printed e-mails or telephone logs.[76] When the surveillance is conducted for domestic reasons, these categories require a sliding scale of proof in order to be activated.[77] Interception orders and search warrants must meet the Fourth Amendment's probable cause standard.[78] Court orders for certain documents, such as ISP[79] e-mail logs, require a lower standard. The government merely has to show reasonable grounds for believing that the information being sought is relevant and material.[80] Pentrap surveillance uses an even lower standard in requiring only a sworn government declaration as to the relevance of the information being sought.[81] Each of these standards applies only when the surveillance conducted is of a domestic nature.[82]

Domestic surveillance within the United States and abroad is carried out by a variety of federal agencies. The Federal Bureau of Investigation (FBI) is the primary federal agency responsible for domestic activities,[83] with the National Security Agency (NSA)[84] and the Central Intelligence Agency (CIA)[85] forbidden by U.S. law from monitoring domestic activities and able only to operate outside the United States.[86] All three agencies are responsible for overseas surveillance, assisted by the Departments of State, Treasury, and Justice.[87]

F. The War Against Terrorism—The 1996 Antiterrorism Act

The 1996 Antiterrorism Act (AEDPA)[88] arose out of a February 1995 White House proposal to combat what was perceived as a growing threat from international terrorist groups.[89] The act included the establishment of a special court that could use secret evidence to deport non-citizens accused of association with terrorist groups,[90] empowered the executive branch to criminalize fundraising for groups designated as terrorists,[91] re-enforced the McCarran Act,[92] created the new federal crime of terrorism,[93] created further exceptions to posse comitatus law,[94] expanded the use of pre-trial detention,[95] and loosened the rules governing federal wiretaps.[96] The AEDPA was enacted as a delayed response to the terrorist attacks on the World Trade Center in 1993 and in Oklahoma City in 1995.[97]

The AEDPA contained provisions that strike at the very heart of civil rights, in its finding of guilt by association. Civil rights groups complained about four central provisions of the act: (1) the definition of terrorism, (2) the criminalization of support for certain groups, (3) the ideological exclusions in immigration law, and (4) the alien terrorist removal procedures.[98] Under the act, the designation of a terrorist organization was made by the Secretary of State[99] and was defined as "any . . . organization 'engaged in terrorist activity' that threatens the 'security of the United States.'"[100] The definition of national security included economic interests of the United States, and the definition of terrorism included almost any act of force.[101] The consequences of being so designated by the Secretary of State made all members of that group ineligible for visas[102] and criminalized the donation of money or other resources to such a group.[103] Civil liberties groups objected to these designations because some groups so designated also conducted substantial humanitarian activities.[104] The primary objection to this clause did not revolve around the restrictions on donations (which can be justified in order to prevent resources from landing in the hands of terrorists) but the wide range of investigative powers granted to the FBI in the name of enforcing these measures.[105] Even more fervent objections arose to the renewed use of ideological exclusions in the immigration process.[106] Under this reborn policy, guilt by association with any group or advocacy of any idea deemed contrary to national security interests met the standard.[107] Previous law had forbidden only people who were reasonably believed to have engaged in terrorist or criminal activity.[108] Further provisions that drew objections included the alien removal procedures, which allowed for the use of secret evidence that did not have to be disclosed in a public court.[109] The AEDPA effectively lowered FISA's previous constitutional protections and was specifically tailored to create legislatively enacted standards of review in place of constitutional tests. This continued the switch from reliance on presidential authority to reliance on legislative mandates during times of crisis in civil liberties.

G. The USA PATRIOT Act

On September 11, 2001, terrorists hijacked American Airlines flights 11 and 77 and United Airlines flights 93 and 175 and, in a horrible act of terrorism, crashed them into the World Trade Center and the Pentagon and brought another plane down in Pennsylvania.[110] President George W. Bush and members of Congress quickly called for new legislation to ensure that such a disaster could never happen again, and law enforcement was given the tools necessary to combat terrorists.[111] The resulting legislation, the USA PATRIOT Act,[112] was intended to close the loopholes in American security that allowed the terrorists to remain undetected while conducting their operation.[113] The bill was passed on October 26, 2001, and signed into law by President Bush.[114]

II. Civil Liberty Concerns within the USA PATRIOT Act

Within the USA PATRIOT Act, concerns over possible electronic civil rights intrusions can be classified into four basic categories: (1) intercepting Web activities, (2) expanding Internet Service Provider privileges, (3) using the Fourth Amendment's "sneak and peek" provisions in new ways,[115] and (4) lowering wiretap standards. Recognizing the inherent danger of the USA PATRIOT Act, Congress placed limiting sunset provisions upon its most worrisome elements.[116] The USA PATRIOT Act, like the legislation previously discussed, jeopardizes personal rights by replacing constitutional tests with legislative directives. In the electronic arena, the four areas examined here provide the clearest example of this effect.

A. Intercepting Web Activity—Pen Registers and "Trap and Trace"

Pen registers and "trap and trace" devices present a unique problem to civil liberties law. A pen register is defined by the USA PATRIOT Act as "a device or process which records or decodes dialing, routing, addressing, or signaling information transmitted by an instrument or facility from which a wire or electronic communication is transmitted."[117] Originally, pen registry law was written only for telephones and governed the real-time interception of all numbers dialed from a particular telephone.[118] As such, the law then referred only to numbers dialed, telephone lines, and originating numbers. Before the USA PATRIOT Act, the use of a device to monitor the transmission of those phone numbers required a court order, but the court was granted no discretion because it was required to approve all applications for such an order that the government certified were likely to obtain information relevant to a current criminal investigation.[119]

A "trap and trace" device has been defined as "a device or process which captures the incoming electronic or other impulses which identify the originating number or other dialing, routing, addressing, and signaling information relevant to identifying the source of a wire or electronic communication."[120] "Trap and trace" devices can be used to determine the number of origin for a telephone call.[121]

The effect of pen registers on personal rights is that pen registers can capture a great deal more information than merely a telephone number.[122] Not requiring probable cause for these devices rested on judicial reasoning that neither the "trap and trace" nor the pen register devices could, prior to the USA PATRIOT Act, capture the substantive material of the communication in question.[123] The USA PATRIOT Act's expansion of and consolidation of the definitions of pen registers and "trap and trace" devices endanger the original distinction upon which the lower level of scrutiny was justified. The expanded definition would now seem to cover Web surfing, e-mail messages, electronic fax distributions, and any other electronic form of communication.[124] The FBI justifies these definitional expansions by interpreting Web traffic as substantially similar to telephone conversations.[125] Despite the substantial differences, including the vast amount of information available from an e-mail routing protocol that cannot be gleaned from listening to a phone conversation, this issue has never been litigated and remains unresolved.

B. Expanded ISP Privilege Granting

The USA PATRIOT Act expands existing laws concerning Internet Service Providers in three key areas. First, the act allows ISPs to voluntarily surrender large amounts of non-content related data to the government without user permission.[126] Second, a simple subpoena is now all that is necessary to acquire IP addresses,[127] duration and session times, and payment sources.[128] Third, the USA PATRIOT Act authorizes the government to intercept any communication from a "computer trespasser" if the owner or operator of the protected computer in question authorizes it to do so.[129] The key definition at stake is what constitutes a protected computer, and it has been broadly defined in the bill to include one "which is used in interstate or foreign commerce or communication."[130]

In addition to allowing broad discretion and authorization for both the ISPs and computer owner and operators, the USA PATRIOT Act removes most judicial oversight of this particular task.[131] In situations that do not result in prosecution, the computer users whose activities are targeted are likely never to discover the monitoring, and therefore they would be effectively unable to challenge the provision in court.[132] Furthermore, law enforcement could unduly pressure owners and operators of computers to obtain permission for the interception and to circumvent the safeguards built into the PATRIOT Act.[133]

C. Sneak and Peek Searches Under the Fourth Amendment

The USA PATRIOT Act expands delayed notice of search and seizure by increasing the number of possible exceptions under which authorities may secretly search premises for physical evidence without notifying the owner.[134] Rule 41(d) of the Federal Rules of Criminal Procedure requires officers to leave a receipt for all items seized in a search.[135] However, the FISA and wiretap provisions under Title 18 both allow for delayed notice of intelligence operations and communication interception.[136] The Second Circuit in *U.S. v. Villegas* allowed covert searches in which no physical evidence was removed, but the court cautioned that certain procedural safeguards were needed in order to prevent the abuse of such powers.[137] The court suggested that one such safeguard could be a showing of reasonable necessity for the delayed notice.[138] Contrary to the Second Circuit, the Ninth Circuit held that a delayed notice could not extend beyond a seven-day period except upon a strong showing of necessity.[139] However, the court did allow for a good-faith exception.[140] The USA PATRIOT Act expands the use of these "sneak and peek" seizures.[141]

D. Lower Wiretap Standards

Wiretaps have traditionally been reserved for very specific crimes, and wiretap law has historically lagged behind the advent of new technological means of communication. More properly titled "law enforcement intercept orders,"[142] the USA PATRIOT Act adds terrorism and computer abuses as defined in the Computer Fraud and Abuse Act (CFAA)[143] to the list of acceptable intercepts.[144] While few would see a problem in adding terrorism to this list or in expanding intercepts to cover voice mail, the CFAA presents a more complicated danger in that the law may be broken by merely violating security classifications[145] or by violating the Atomic Energy Act of 1954.[146]

Traditionally, Title III of the Crime Control and Safe Streets Act of 1968[147] governs electronic surveillance in criminal investigations.[148] With the exception of minimal emergency situations, Title III imposes the normal probable cause requirement upon law enforcement, requires a warrant in most situations, and enforces the doctrine through judicial oversight and the inadmissibility of the evidence in court.[149] Under Title III, broad investigative power, including the use of roving wiretaps,[150] can be granted once the probable cause element is satisfied.[151] Furthermore, the standard for intercepting the numbers called from a particular phone is the substantially lesser standard of merely having the government certify that the information is "relevant to an ongoing investigation."[152]

Initially, the USA PATRIOT Act contained provisions that lowered wiretap standards even further. The Bush administration's proposal included an allowance for the use of wiretap information obtained by foreign governments in a manner that would previously have been deemed illegal when used against U.S. citizens in trials inside the United States.[153] However, this proposal was later dropped at the insistence of members of Congress who were worried about the act's constitutionality.[154]

E. Effect of Sunset Provisions—Are They Adequate Safeguards?

The USA PATRIOT Act provides a similar solution to many of the civil rights concerns that previous incursions into these rights had relied on. The act provides that a number of the more suspect or dangerous provisions will expire after a standard period of no less than four years.[155] Included in these provisions are the wiretap authorities,[156] pen registry interception,[157] foreign intelligence information,[158] and roving surveillance.[159] Most notably, not included in the act's sunset provisions are the immunity for compliance with FISA wiretap provisions,[160] the authorization to sneak and peek,[161] the overriding of certain privacy provisions in the Cable Act,[162] single jurisdiction search warrants in cases of terrorism,[163] and the expansion of the Electronic Communications Privacy Act[164] to include e-mail routing information.[165] None of the measures adopted requires a reporting requirement either to Congress or the courts, making congressional determinations of renewal problematic at best.[166]

Sunset provisions allow for the termination of suspect laws but do nothing to solve the violations that occur while those laws run their course. Should one of the provisions of the USA PATRIOT Act be interpreted in a manner that seriously violates personal privacy rights, a sunset provision would provide little comfort to those whom the provision was used against. In order to safely use sunset provisions, the issue at hand must be significantly close to being constitutional that the amount of damage done to a person or group of people is minimal in comparison to the national security gained. This is not to say that a great deal of damage done to a small number of persons or groups would be acceptable if it served the greater societal good but, rather, that the damage to each individual would be of small enough magnitude that the intrusion into whichever right is in question would not result in significant harm.

III. The Future Balance of Civil Rights and National Security in a Technology Environment

A. Why Is a New Standard Necessary?
A new constitutional test is necessary because previous tests and standards have failed to adequately protect individual rights during crises in national security, the USA PATRIOT Act and the electronic age present increased challenges and previously unseen circumstances, and existing constitutional tests cannot properly meet these new challenges and circumstances.

The historical examples provided in Part I are but a small sampling of the numerous and repeated infractions of civil rights in times of national security.[167] These examples reveal an ever-changing and inadequate standard that failed to stop some of the more shameful incidents in the history of the United States. Neither President Lincoln's balancing, McCarthyism, nor the Supreme Court's justification for the internment of Japanese-Americans effectively protected individual or even group liberties.

FISA and the anti-terrorism legislation of the 1990s reveal more recent attempts by Congress and various presidential administrations to curb not only the civil liberties of certain individuals and groups but also the ability of the courts to review and redress constitutional violations that might have already occurred. The obvious historical failure to protect individual rights, along with the dubious value to national security of some of these actions,[168] reveal a need for a new constitutional test that will better protect individual rights in times of crisis.

The USA PATRIOT Act—and the information age it was enacted in—present new challenges that courts, applying the current legal tests, are ill-prepared to handle. Our electronic age presents a dizzying array of new technology and new methods of carrying out surveillance, searches, and seizures, with little direction about how to constitutionally evaluate these new methods.[169] FISA, the AEDPA, and the USA PATRIOT Act recognize this problem and attempt to use legislation to define constitutionality, including standards of scrutiny, without explicitly doing so.[170] While congressional mandate may seem the logical way to accomplish a task the courts seem unable to handle, this legislation hinders the basic watchdog function of the courts.[171] The judicial branch cannot abandon its oversight duties in the midst of ever-changing technology and threats to national security but must develop constitutional tests that can effectively balance the competing interests of national security and individual rights.

Such is the case because current legal regimes are not enough, by themselves, to effectively balance the interests in question. This country has a duty to protect its citizens from external threats and to protect individual liberties guaranteed in the Constitution and its Bill of Rights. In recognition of the fact that these duties have come into conflict repeatedly throughout the history of the United States, there are three options. One, the United States could abandon all constitutional guarantees during wartime and only follow the dictates of national security. Given the implausibility of this option, alternatively the United States could enforce all constitutional rights regardless of the peril to the country. This approach would allow for the continued application of all current constitutional tests and a relatively straightforward legal analysis. However, the historical situations previously mentioned show that there are at least some circumstances in which the interests of national security and the interest in protecting all individual liberties conflict.[172] Applying current constitutional tests, regardless of the peril to the country, would deny the government the tools necessary to defend the country in the moments of greatest need.[173] Given these conflicting interests, the best solution would be a new balancing test that could adequately protect individual rights while still allowing the government certain leeway in times of crisis.

B. EFF's and EPIC's Proposed New Constitutional Standards

As Justice Burger once stated for the Court, "It is 'obvious and unarguable' that no government interest is more compelling than the security of the Nation."[174] Given that national security and civil rights will frequently be in conflict, the Electronic Freedom Foundation (EFF) and Electronic Privacy Information Center (EPIC) have developed criteria for evaluating national security legislation. While these criteria are not legal standards, they are useful in evaluating the effectiveness of the legal standards meant to protect individual rights.

EFF advocates consideration of six factors when evaluating the civil rights implications of electronic media security legislation.[175]

Those elements are as follows: (1) carefully limiting all investigations into bona fide terrorist groups to means with appropriate oversight, (2) granting the courts the power to punish any abusers of these new laws, including governmental organizations, (3) enabling courts to exclude evidence obtained in contravention of the safeguards built into national security legislation, (4) defining vague terms in the legislation in favor of civil liberties, (5) requiring certification by the attorney general that a wiretap applies to ISPs and others served with roving wiretaps, and (6) creating congressional accountability for all organizations, so that the sunset provisions may be properly evaluated.[176] While not the entire EFF wish list for national security legislation, this list shows a clear attempt to recognize the USA PATRIOT Act (and future legislation of a similar nature) as temporary and required only so long as the problem exists.

EPIC takes a different approach to arrive at similar conclusions.[177] EPIC's five-point plan for the USA PATRIOT Act involves the following: (1) advocating that law enforcement already possesses broad authority under the AEDPA, (2) instituting a requirement of "clear and convincing need" for each provision, (3) narrowly tailoring national security statutes to avoid infringing upon the rights of millions of legal users of the Internet and other electronic media, (4) preserving to the greatest extent possible the distinction between domestic criminal surveillance and foreign intelligence gathering, and (5) limiting the expanded investigative powers to terrorist activities by not allowing those powers to be used in common criminal investigations or in cases where the nature of the activity is unknown.[178] EPIC's standards revolve around the conviction that the government should be required to show a clear need for any violations of civil rights and to ensure as little intrusion as necessary into the lives of U.S. citizens by separating the various apparati that conduct foreign and domestic surveillance work.[179] In requiring this separation, EPIC hopes that institutional specializations, mission orientations, and internal cultures will develop along different lines for the agencies tasked with surveillance.[180]

C. The Proposed Test—"One Step Lower"
In light of the factors proposed by EFF and EPIC and of the infringements in civil liberties noted above, the appropriate test to apply to future legislation during times of national security crisis is

the "one step lower" test. The "one step lower" test consists of three parts. First, the court must apply an intermediate scrutiny-like analysis of the legislation in question. Then the court must determine the appropriate standard of review absent any crisis in national security. Finally, the court must apply the next lowest test, in order from most restrictive to least restrictive upon government action, than the test that would normally be applied absent a national security crisis. For example, if during a time of impending attack by another country, the United States passed a law that would normally be considered content-based, the courts would, after deeming national security an important governmental interest, apply the intermediate test articulated above. If the overall legislation passed that test, and the court determined that the legislation in question would under normal circumstances be reviewed using a strict scrutiny standard, the court would then apply the "one step lower" test and apply the next lower level of review, in this case, intermediate scrutiny.

In order to apply this test, the originating piece of legislation first must undergo analysis similar to the intermediate scrutiny articulated by the Supreme Court for First Amendment questions. If legislation were challenged, courts would have to decide whether to apply the "one step lower" test or the more traditional constitutional analysis. The most obvious identifying marker of proper evaluation would be whether the government raises national security as a justification for the constitutionality of the bill when it is challenged. Once the government raises national security as a justification, the law must undergo an intermediate analysis to determine whether the law in question is substantially related to an important government interest. As every court will no doubt recognize national security as an important governmental purpose, the court's evaluation will center on whether the specific action taken is substantially related to the government's interest in protecting the country. Additionally, the narrowly tailored requirements of intermediate scrutiny will ensure at least some limitations on the scope of any national security legislation.

Once the decision to apply the "one step lower" test is made, the legislation would then be analyzed and classified under either the First Amendment or the Fourth Amendment. The primary concern of this Note, and arguably the USA PATRIOT Act as well, is with Fourth Amendment search and seizure principles. However, the "one step lower" test can be applied to either the First or Fourth

Amendments. As such, an order of magnitude must be established for the different tests applied by the Supreme Court. Under First Amendment analysis, the order follows logical succession. A court that would normally apply strict scrutiny would now apply intermediate scrutiny. Likewise, if the court decided to use the "one step lower" test, a rational basis test would be used when normally intermediate scrutiny would apply. The Fourth Amendment presents more of a challenge in determining the order of the tests, but once an agreed-upon order is established, the tests would be easy to apply. Under the Fourth Amendment, the order of tests, ranging from most restrictive to least restrictive might be: warrant based on probable cause always required;[181] probable cause plus exigent circumstances without a warrant;[182] probable cause only, with no warrant necessary;[183] Terry-level stops for a limited duration with the corresponding reasonable suspicion standard;[184] and "special government need" searches along the lines of current "administrative-code inspections"[185] and border searches.[186] It is important to note that special government-need searches, with their limited standard of review, cannot be used then as a justification to apply the lowest possible standard and thus circumvent this test.

The rankings of the different tests are this author's own and are meant to illustrate how the proposed test could work. However, the "one step lower" test could apply the rankings of the test in any order that a later court would decide. The only element necessary is that a court, preferably the Supreme Court, would establish a ranking of the tests involved so as to simplify and standardize lower courts' application of them.

Any legislation that had the "one step lower" test applied to it would be required to have constitutional safeguards built in. This safeguard would be a sunset provision for all the measures to which the test would be applied. The sunset provision would provide that any measure controversial and constitutionally questionable enough to have to avail itself of the "one step lower" test would expire at the termination of hostilities or after a period of two years, whichever is lesser. This termination period is necessary due both to the indeterminate nature of modern warfare and the continual threat of terrorism. Sunset provisions ensure that measures that are constitutionally questionable but justified in the name of immediate necessity do not become permanent law and that they instead expire at the end of the crises to the security of the nation. Furthermore, the two-year standard requires that ongoing crises and terrorist threats cannot be used to grant a carte blanche for lowered standards of review for extended periods of time.

The proper remedial sanction for Fourth Amendment violations would follow the traditional exclusionary rule[187] and "fruit of the poisonous tree"[188] doctrines. Evidence obtained in violation of the standards of the "one step lower" test would be excluded from use in court, and any evidence derived from it would also be excluded. This would deter police from breaking the lowered standards of review in place during a national security crisis.

Additionally, a defendant would have available the affirmative defense that the evidence used against him was obtained by the use of a national security exception even though the defendant was not connected in any way to an organization or situation that would pose a danger to the country. The defendant would be required to prove by a "preponderance of the evidence" that the investigator was or should have been aware that the defendant was not involved in activities threatening national security. If the investigating officer should have been aware of the lack of national security implications, the normal higher standard of review would apply. This provision prevents the "one step lower" test from being used as a tool during times of crisis in national security to investigate and prosecute non-terrorists. By placing the burden of proof on the defendant, the provision would give the government the benefit of the doubt in the application of these new laws, while still protecting against flagrant abuses of the expanded governmental powers granted under the "one step lower" test.

D. Why the "One Step Lower" Test Would Work

The "one step lower" test would work better than previous tests because it replaces an eclectic range of tests with one simple, relatively easy to apply test yet builds upon existing constitutional law standards, such as intermediate scrutiny and the various Fourth Amendment standards. Furthermore, the proposed test provides better protection for individual rights during times of crisis in national security.

Despite the relatively complicated constitutional area to which the "one step lower" test would be applied, the test remains relatively simple to apply. As such, it replaces the myriad case law, statutes, and executive standards that have been propagated in times of war with a single standard. It is a standard that can be applied regardless of the circumstances. Furthermore, the standard is broad enough to evolve with ever-changing technologies and threats. The "one step lower" test is designed to be both general enough and flexible enough to apply to the USA PATRIOT Act, other constitutional crises during times of national security threats, and further into the future, until such time as a better balancing of interests can be achieved.

Additionally, the "one step lower" test is easily adaptable because it is composed of existing tests. Parties will not need to litigate over the meaning of the new test. All that is necessary is for the court to apply the traditional intermediate scrutiny test to determine if the conduct in question meets the narrowly tailored prong and reasonably relates to a legitimate government interest. Then the court selects the next less restrictive test and applies that test, again with its historic development, to the incident in question. While the problem of analogizing to previous circumstances and events remains, the court is not required to create or define new legal standards. The proposed test would only require the application of already existing standards to new problems and would thus serve the interests of judicial economy.

Finally, and most importantly, the "one step lower" test best protects individual rights during times of crisis by ensuring that minimum standards are met even during the darkest of times. The "one step lower" test balances individual rights against the country's right to survival by acknowledging the national security interest and correspondingly applying a test that is lower than what would be applied in a normal situation. However, the real strength of the proposed test is that it only allows for a reduction in constitutional protections by an order of one and prevents the government from using reasons of national security as a rug under which to sweep drastic changes. The protections built into the "one step lower" test ensure that the actions taken are necessary for the emergency in question, narrowly tailored to meet that objective, expire after an appropriate amount of time, and still afford at least a basic minimum of constitutional rights no matter how dire the situation. By doing so, the "one step lower" test most effectively preserves some core constitutional rights while allowing for latitude in governmental action during the crises that most require extreme defensive measures.

Conclusion

On September 20, 2001, President George W. Bush declared, "we're in a fight for our principles, and our first responsibility is to live by them."[189] History shows, however, that when we are fighting for our principles, we have frequently failed to live by them. Previous constitutional tests applied during times of crisis have resulted in large-scale constitutional infringements and deprivations. Moreover, the USA PATRIOT Act and terrorism in the electronic age provide ever developing challenges in a legal setting that has difficulty keeping up. This Note's proposed test would provide a clearer, more effective safeguard for those principles in this new and changing world and would provide the necessary balance between protecting individual rights and the society that shelters them.

Notes

1. Foreign Intelligence Surveillance Act of 1978, Pub. L. No. 95-511, 92 Stat. 1783 (1978) (codified as amended at 50 U.S.C. 1801-63 (2000)).

2. Uniting and Strengthening America by Providing Appropriate Tools Required to Intercept and Obstruct Terrorism Act of 2001, Pub. L. No. 107-56, 115 Stat. 272 (2001).

3. Asymmetrical warfare is warfare between two opponents who use different combat techniques. Guerrilla warfare, in which one side fights using traditional tactics and the other uses hit-and-run tactics with little regard for the conventions of warfare, is an example of asymmetrical warfare. See Ian O. Lesser et al., *Countering the New Terrorism* (Rand Corp., 1999) p. 94-96.

4. For a detailed discussion of President Lincoln's actions during the imposed state of emergency, see James M. McPherson, *Ordeal by Fire: The Civil War and Reconstruction*, 3d ed. (McGraw-Hill Pub., 2001); Stephen B. Oates, *With Malice Toward None: The Life of Abraham Lincoln* (Prennial, 1977); Bruce Catton, *This Hallowed Ground: The Story of the Union Side of the Civil War* (Garden City, NY: Doubleday, 1956).

5. Intrusion into protected civil rights in the name of national security has been a fact as long as the United States has existed under the Constitution. Perhaps the most infamous of these early incidents were the Alien and Sedition Acts under President John Adams and the Federalists, who used the threat of outside interference in American politics as a pretext for silencing Thomas Jefferson and the emerging Democratic-Republican Party. For a discussion, see *Encyclopedia of American History*, Richard B. Morris ed. (New York: Harper, 1965) p. 129-30.

6. These states were Maryland, Kentucky, Missouri, and Tennessee. Catton, supra note 5, at 27-41.

7. McPherson, supra note 5, at 166-67.

8. See Debora K. Kristensen, "Finding the Right Balance: American Civil Liberties in Time of War," *The Advocate* (December, 2001) at 20; Catton, supra note 5, at 28.

9. 147 Cong. Rec. S11,020 (daily ed. Oct. 25, 2001) (statement of Sen. Feingold), available at www.senate.gov/feingold/releases/01/10/102501at.html.

10. Charles Warren, *The Supreme Court in United States History* (Beard Books, 1922) p. 90-91. See Catton, supra note 5, at 28; Ex parte Merryman, 17 F. Cas. 144 (C.C.D. Md. 1861) (No. 9,487).

11. See Catton, supra note 4, at 31-35.

12. Ibid.

13. President Lincoln's violations of civil liberties were not the first in American history. The Alien and Sedition Acts, Andrew Jackson's unlawful detention of reporter Louis Louailler, and military actions during "Dorr's Rebellion" in 1842 all violated personal civil liberties in the

name of national security. See Kristensen, supra note 8, at 20. The Civil War, however, provides a clear and comprehensive example of those violations and the first real attempt to balance individual rights with national security.

14. See ibid. at 21.

15. Ibid.

16. See ibid.

17. See generally Jacobus tenBroek et al., *Prejudice, War and the Constitution* (University of California Press, 1968); *Eugene V. Rostow*, "The Japanese American Cases—A Disaster," *Yale Law Journal* 54 (1945): 489.

18. See 147 Cong. Rec. S11,020 (daily ed. Oct. 25, 2001) (statement of Sen. Feingold).

19. See tenBroek, supra note 17, at 101.

20. WDC was the military command for the western states charged with overseeing their defense from possible Japanese land and sea attacks. Ibid at 100, 352 n.2 (citing U.S. Army, *The Army Almanac* 601 (1951)).

21. tenBroek, supra note 17, at 120.

22. tenBroek, supra note 17, at 110.

23. See tenBroek, supra note 17, at 311.

24. See William Manchester, *The Glory and the Dream: A Narrative History of America* (Little Brown & Co., 1974) p. 300-01 (describing the conditions of the internment camps).

25. See *Korematsu v. United States*, 323 U.S. 214, 217-19 (1944).

26. Ibid. at 235 (Murphy, J., dissenting).

27. Ibid.

28. See ibid. at 228-29.

29. 320 U.S. 81 (1943).

30. Ibid. at 94-95.

31. *Korematsu*, 323 U.S. at 216-20 (interpreting the equal protection element of the Fifth Amendment to require strict scrutiny of governmental actions based on racial classification).

32. Ibid. at 218-19.

33. Ibid. at 219.

34. Ibid. at 217-18. The dissent argued for a new test to determine the validity of a deprivation of constitutional rights, based on "whether the deprivation is reasonably related to a public danger that is so 'immediate, imminent, and impending' as not to admit of delay and not to permit the intervention of ordinary constitutional processes to alleviate the danger." Ibid at 234 (Murphy, J., dissenting). See also Micah Herzig, "Note, Is Korematsu Good Law in the Face of Terrorism? Procedural Due Process in the Security Versus Liberty Debate," *Georgetown Immigration Law Journal* 16 (2002): 685, 687-88.

35. 323 U.S. 283 (1944).

36. Ibid. at 302.

37. See ibid. at 300-02.

38. See ibid.

39. See ibid. at 294-305. Some authors contend that *Korematsu* still applies in the post-September 11, 2001, era. See, e.g., Herzig, supra note 35, at 690.

40. For a discussion of anticommunist activities within the United States from 1900 to 1950, see William M. Wiecek, "The Legal Foundations of Domestic Anticommunism: The Background of *Dennis v. United States 2001*," *Supreme Court Review* (2002): 375.

41. Ibid. at 406-23.

42. See ibid.

43. Ibid. at 398-99.

44. Taft-Hartley Act of 1947, Pub. L. No. 80-101, 61 Stat. 136 (1947).

45. Internal Security (McCarran) Act of 1950, Pub. L. No. 81-831, 64 Stat. 987 (1950).

46. See Wiecek, supra note 40, at 423-28.

47. 341 U.S. 494 (1951).

48. Ibid. at 510 (quoting *United States v. Dennis*, 183 F.2d 201, 212 (2d Cir. 1950)).

49. 249 U.S. 47, 52 (1919).

50. See *Dennis*, 341 U.S. at 510-11.

51. Ibid. See also Steven A. Osher, "Privacy, Computers, and the PATRIOT Act: The Fourth Amendment Isn't Dead, But No One Will Insure It," *Florida Law Review* 54 (2002): 521.

52. See Wiecek, supra note 40, at 429-34.

53. Foreign Intelligence Surveillance Act of 1978, Pub. L. No. 95-511, 92 Stat. 1783 (1978) (codified as amended at 50 U.S.C. 1801 (2000)).

54. See 50 U.S.C. 1802; Osher, supra note 51, at 532; Electronic Frontier Foundation, EFF Analysis of the Provisions of the USA PATRIOT Act, at http://www.eff.org/Privacy/Surveillance/Terrorism militias/20011031 eff usa patriot analysis.html (Oct. 31, 2001) [hereinafter EFF Analysis]. The Electronic Frontier Foundation (EFF) is a non-profit group whose purpose is to advocate for the protection of individual digital privacy protections. More information on the EFF is available at http://www.eff.org.

55. S. Rep. No. 95-604, at 1; see ibid. at 1-19 (1978).

56. See EFF Analysis, supra note 54, at Executive Summary 3(b).

57. See 147 Cong. Rec. S11,020 (daily ed. Oct. 25, 2001) (statement of Sen. Feingold).

58. The threshold established is lower than probable cause. Ibid

59. See ibid.

60. Pen-trap devices intercept in real time all numbers dialed from a telephone. See EFF Analysis, supra note 54, at I.A.

61. See ibid.

62. Pub. L. No. 107-56, 115 Stat. 283 (2001).

63. See EFF Analysis, supra note 54, at I.A.

64. Exec. Order No. 12,333, 3 C.F.R. 200 (1982), reprinted in 50 U.S.C. 401 (2000).

65. FISA, 50 U.S.C. 1803 (1994).

66. See Exec. Order No. 12,333; Nat'l Sec. Agency, Legal Standards for the Intelligence Community in Conducting Electronic Surveillance, at http://www.fas.org/irp/nsa/standards.html (Feb. 2000) [hereinafter NSA Legal Standards].

67. See NSA Legal Standards, supra note 66.

68. See ibid.

69. Exec. Order No. 12,333.

70. See NSA Legal Standards, supra note 66.

71. See ibid at app. A (CIA Headquarters Regulation 7-1, Law and Policy Governing the Conduct of Intelligence Activities) (accompanying classified report only); app. B (Department of Defense Directive 5240.1-R, DoD Activities that May Affect U.S. Persons), available at http://cryptome.org/dod5240-1-r.htm) (last visited Mar. 9, 2003); app. C (U.S. Signals Intelligence Directive 18), available at http://cryptome.org/nsa-ussid18.htm) (last visited Mar. 9, 2003).

72. See Susan Herman, "The USA PATRIOT Act and the U.S. Department of Justice: Losing Our Balances?," at http://jurist.law.pitt.edu/forum/forumnew40.htm (Dec. 3, 2001).

73. See EFF Analysis, supra note 54, at I.A.

74. In a conventional telephone, trap and trace devices can identify the number and routing information of an incoming telephone call. 18 U.S.C. 3127(4) (2002).

75. See supra note 60.

76. See EFF Analysis, supra note 54, at I.A.

77. See ibid.

78. See ibid; U.S. Const. amend. IV; Katz v. United States, 389 U.S. 347 (1967).

79. ISP stands for Internet Service Provider, which facilitates the link between an Internet user and access to the data paths of the Internet. See 17 U.S.C. 512 (2002).

80. See ibid.

81. See ibid.

82. For a discussion of the standards for foreign surveillance, see discussion supra Part I.D.

83. Exec. Order No. 12,333 1.14, 3 C.F.R. 200 (1982), reprinted in 50 U.S.C. 401.

84. Ibid. 1.12(b).

85. Ibid. 2.4.

86. 50 U.S.C. 403-3(d)(1) (2000) ("The Agency shall have no police, subpoena, or law enforcement powers or internal security functions.").

87. See generally Exec. Order No. 12,333 (providing for the effective division of responsibilities in intelligence gathering and the protection of civil rights).

88. Antiterrorism and Effective Death Penalty Act of 1996, Pub. L. No. 104-132, 110 Stat. 1214 (1996).

89. See James X. Dempsey & David Cole, Terrorism & the Constitution: Sacrificing Civil Liberties in the Name of National Security (New Press, 1999).

90. See AEDPA 401.

91. See ibid. 303.

92. See Internal Security (McCarran) Act of 1950, Pub. L. No. 81-831, 64 Stat. 987 (1950).

93. This provision was later dropped before the bill was made law. Dempsey & Cole, supra note 90, at 106, 196 n.2.

94. The law governs the use of military force in police functions. See 18 U.S.C. 1385 (2002); Roger Blake Hohnsbeen, "Fourth Amendment and Posse Comitatus Act Restrictions on Military Involvement in Civil Law Enforcement," *George Washington Law Review* 54 (1986): 404.

95. This provision was also later dropped. Dempsey & Cole, supra note 89, at 106, 196 n.2.

96. This provision was authorized in the Intelligence Authorization Act for fiscal year 1999. Pub. L. 105-272, 112 Stat. 2396, 2413 604 (amending 18 U.S.C. 2518(11)(b)); see Dempsey & Cole, supra note 89, at 142-43.

97. See Dempsey & Cole, supra note 89, at 105-16.

98. Ibid. at 117-26.

99. See AEDPA 302, 110 Stat. at 1248-50.

100. Ibid.

101. Ibid. 302.

102. Ibid. 411.

103. See Ibid. 303.

104. See Dempsey & Cole, supra note 89, at 121-22.

105. Ibid.

106. Ibid at 123-26.

107. Ibid.

108. Immigration Act of 1990, Pub. L. 101-649, 104 Stat. 4978 (1990).

109. Dempsey & Cole, supra note 89, at 126. See AEDPA 401-43.

110. See Jennifer C. Evans, "Hijacking Civil Liberties: The USA PATRIOT Act of 2001," *Loyola University of Chicago Law Journal* 33 (2002): 933, 934.

111. See Ibid. at 934, 963-68.

112. USA PATRIOT Act, Pub. L. No. 107-56, 115 Stat. 272 (2001).

113. See EFF Analysis, supra note 54, at II; Evans, supra note 110, at 967-70.

114. Evans, supra note 110, at 967.

115. "Sneak and peeks" are searches conducted under a proper warrant but in which the usual notification of the owner of the property is delayed for a period of days. See ibid. at 973 & nn262-68.

116. See 147 Cong. Rec. S10990, S10991 (daily ed. Oct 25, 2001) (statement of Sen. Leahy).

117. 18 U.S.C. 3127(3) (2001). See also Electronic Privacy Information Center, Analysis of Provisions of the Proposed Anti-Terrorism Act of 2001, at www.epic.org/privacy/terrorism/ata analysis.html (Sept. 24, 2001) [hereinafter EPIC Analysis]. Electronic Privacy Information Center (EPIC) is a public-interest research center focusing on emerging civil liberty issues, the First Amendment, and privacy concerns. More information on EPIC is available at http://www.epic.org.

118. See ibid.

119. See ibid.

120. 18 U.S.C. 3127(4) (1994).

121. Ibid.

122. See EPIC Analysis, supra note 117.

123. See *Smith v. Maryland*, 442 U.S. 735, 741 (1979).

124. See EPIC Analysis, supra note 117.

125. See ibid.

126. EFF Analysis, supra note 54, at Executive Summary 1.c.

127. IP addresses are temporarily assigned addresses that identify the computer user. They are assigned by the ISP provider.

128. EFF Analysis, supra note 54, at Executive Summary 1.c.

129. EPIC Analysis, supra note 117.

130. 18 U.S.C. 1030(e)(2)(B) (2000).

131. See EPIC Analysis, supra note 117.

132. See ibid.

133. See Peter Murphy, "An Examination of the United States Department of Justice's Attempt to Conduct Warrantless Monitoring of Computer Networks Through the Consent

Exception to the Wiretap Act," *Connecticut Law Review* 34 (2002): 1317, 1321-30; Sharon H. Rackow, "How the USA PATRIOT Act Will Permit Governmental Infringement upon the Privacy of Americans in the Name of "Intelligence" Investigations," *University of Pennsylvania Law Review* 150 (2002): 1651, 1674-80.

134. See Marcia Coyle, "New Search Law Likely to Provoke Fourth Amendment Challenge," *Sierra Times* (October 30, 2001) at http://www.sierratimes.com/archive/files/oct/30/armc103001.htm.

135. Fed. R. Crim. P. 41(d).

136. See Coyle, supra note 134.

137. *United States v. Villegas*, 899 F.2d 1324, 1336-37 (2d Cir. 1990).

138. Ibid.

139. *United States v. Freitas*, 800 F.2d 1451 (9th Cir. 1986).

140. Ibid at 1456-57.

141. 18 U.S.C. 3103(a) (2002).

142. This terminology is used because many intercepted communications no longer travel over wires. Changes in means of communication have created an overlap between the wiretap category and seizure of other means of communication. Cindy Cohn, "EFF Analysis of the Provisions of the USA PATRIOT Act—That Relate to Online Activities," at http://www.eff.org/Privacy/Surveillance/Terrorism/20011031_eff_usa_patriot_analysis.php.

143 USA PATRIOT Act 1030.

144. See EFF Analysis, supra note 54, at II.A.

145. USA PATRIOT Act 1030(a)(1). This is one possible interpretation of the term "protected computer" and the author's evaluation of the statute. The concern is that someone who knowingly accesses a computer that she does not have a high enough security clearance for, even though she has a lower security clearance, could be liable under this statute.

146. Pub. L. No. 83-703, 60 Stat. 755 (1954). See also EFF Analysis, supra note 54.

147. 18 U.S.C. 2510-22 (1994).

148. Herman, supra note 72; Rackow, supra note 133, at 1657-58.

149. Herman, supra note 72; see Rackow, supra note 133, at 1659.

150. Roving wiretaps have the constitutional problem of failing to satisfy the particularity requirement of the Fourth Amendment for the place to be searched. See Herman, supra note 72.

151. Ibid.

152. Ibid.

153. See 147 Cong. Rec. S11,020 (daily ed. Oct. 25, 2001) (statement of Sen. Feingold), available at www.senate.gov/feingold/releases/01/10/102501at.html.

154. Ibid. at S11,021.

155. 18 U.S.C. 2510 (2002); EFF Analysis, supra note 54, at IV.

156. 18 U.S.C. 2516 (West 2000 & Supp. 2002).

157. USA PATRIOT Act 214, 50 U.S.C. 1842 (West Supp. 2002).

158. Ibid 218, 50 U.S.C. 1822 (West Supp. 2002).

159. USA PATRIOT Act 206, 50 U.S.C. 1805 (West 1991 & Supp. 2002).

160. Ibid. 225.

161. USA PATRIOT Act 213, 18 U.S.C. 3103a (West 2000 & Supp. 2002).

162. USA PATRIOT Act 211, 47 U.S.C. 551 (West 2001 & Supp. 2002).

163. USA PATRIOT Act 219, Fed R. Crim. P. 41(a) (West 1976 & Supp. 2002).

164. Pub. L. No. 99-508, 100 Stat. 1848 (1986); 18 U.S.C. 5210 (West 2000 & Supp. 2002).

165. USA PATRIOT Act 210, 18 U.S.C. 2703 (West 2000 & Supp. 2002).

166. See Electronic Frontier Foundation, "USAPA Sunset Provisions Could Leave Congress in the Dark" (December 17, 2001), at http://www.eff.org/sc/20011212 eff usapa analysis.html (last visited Oct. 16, 2002) [hereinafter EFF Sunset Provisions].

167. For additional examples, see Kristensen, supra note 8, at 20-21.

168. See supra Part I.C.

169. See, e.g., Jeffrey Yeates, "CALEA and RIPA: The U.S. and the U.K. Responses to Wiretapping in an Increasingly Wireless World," *Albany Law Journal of Science and Technology* 12 (2001): 125, 126-27 (2001).

170. See discussion supra Parts I.D., I.F., I.G.

171. For example, FISA created a special court outside of the normal chain of review. While this may seem to be an attempt to preserve constitutional rights, the court has considerable

power, little constitutional oversight, and an extremely low standard of review. See supra notes 5-76 and accompanying text.

172. See discussion supra Part I.A. There seems, for example, to be little dispute about the effectiveness of President Lincoln's actions in preserving the United States. See Kristensen, supra note 8, at 21.

173. See *Terminiello v. City of Chicago*, 337 U.S. 1, 37 (1949) (Jackson, J., dissenting) (declaring that the Constitution is not a "suicide pact").

174. *Haig v. Agee*, 453 U.S. 280, 307 (1981).

175. See EFF Analysis, supra note 54, at Executive Summary, Future Actions.

176. See ibid.

177. See EPIC Analysis, supra note 117.

178. See ibid.

179. See ibid.

180. See ibid.

181. See *Katz v. United States*, 389 U.S. 347, 354 (1967) (holding that a search that implicates a person's constitutionally protected reasonable expectation of privacy generally requires a warrant based upon probable cause).

182. See *Minnesota v. Olson*, 495 U.S. 91, 100 (1990) (holding that warrantless entry of a home, outside of hot pursuit of a fleeing suspect, is permissible if police have probable cause to believe evidence will be destroyed, the suspect will escape, or harm will come to police or other individuals).

183. See ibid. at 100-01.

184. See *Terry v. Ohio*, 392 U.S. 1, 20 (1968) (holding that a reasonable suspicion governed a short, minimal search on the street that lasted for only a few minutes and only briefly seized the suspects).

185. See *Camara v. Municipal Court*, 387 U.S. 523, 538-39 (1967) (holding that in administrative searches, such as one conducted by a housing inspector, probable cause means "reasonable suspicion").

186. See *United States v. Ramsey*, 431 U.S. 606, 619 (1977) (holding that a person may be stopped without any individualized suspicion and searched at an international border or an equivalent entry point to the United States).

187. See *Mapp v. Ohio*, 367 U.S. 643, 655-60 (1961) (holding that the exclusionary doctrine keeps evidence that was unconstitutionally obtained by police from being used at trial against a defendant).

188. See *Nardone v. United States*, 308 U.S. 338, 341 (1939) (holding that the "fruit of the poisonous tree" doctrine requires that any evidence obtained as a direct result of police violation of a defendant's constitutional rights must also be inadmissible).

189. President George W. Bush, Presidential Response Concerning the Events of September 11, 2001, 2001 U.S.C.C.A.N. D37, cited in Lori Sachs, September 11, 2001: "The Constitution During Crises: A New Perspective," *Fordham Urb. L.J.* 29 (2002): 1715, 1716.

Part V: Discussion Cases

Case #1: Encryption and National Security

In 1992 Phil Zimmerman developed a program called PGP that offered users near unbreakable encryption. The National Security Administration (NSA) questioned him and noted that use and distribution of encryption tools was unlawful under an Arms Regulation law—cryptographic tools are listed as national security threats along with tanks, biological weapons, and nuclear warheads. The National Security Administration's position was that the widespread use of encryption software will allow criminals a sanctuary to exchange information necessary for the completion of illegal activities. On the other hand, strong encryption seems necessary for online transactions and electronic privacy. Should the government prohibit the use of strong encryption? Is this a case where individual privacy and financial effectiveness should be sacrificed for national security?

Case #2: Wearing an Anti-Disclosure Suit

Suppose that Fred creates and wears an anti-disclosure suit that shields him in public spaces entirely. All that his fellows know is that someone is present—they do not know if Fred is old or young, male or female, tall or short, etc. In simply wearing his anti-disclosure suit Fred does nothing wrong. Does this necessarily worsen anyone? In this example to discover much about Fred would require violating his property rights or liberty rights. Alas, the suit and what it shields is his to control. Should wearing an anti-disclosure suits be prohibited? How about masks or disguises?

Case #3: Racial Profiling and Terrorism

Soon after the attack on Pearl Harbor and the entry of the United States into WWII, President Franklin D. Roosevelt signed Executive Order 9066 which ordered the round-up and placement of 120,000 Japanese Americans into internment camps in California, Idaho, Utah, Arizona, Wyoming, Colorado, and Arkansas. The reason given for incarcerating 120,000 U.S. citizens of Japanese descent was that these individuals—because of their cultural and religious ties to Japan—were national security threats. Post 9-11, similar reasons have been given for the profiling and detainment of Muslim Americans. Is such profiling and detainment morally and legally justified?

Selected Bibliography

Agre, P. E., and M. Rotenberg. "Technology and Privacy: The New Landscape." *Journal of the American Society for Information Science* 50.7 (1999): 631–33.

Alderman, Ellen, and C. Kennedy. *The Right to Privacy.* New York: Knopf Press, 1995.

Alfino, M. "Information Ethics in the Workplace: Misplacing Privacy." *Journal of Information Ethics* 10 (2001): 5–8.

Allen, Anita L. *Uneasy Access: Privacy for Women in a Free Society.* Lanham, MD: Rowman and Littlefield, 1988.

——. "Women and Their Privacy: What Is at Stake?" In *Beyond Domination*, edited by Carol C. Gould. Ottawa: Rowman and Allanheld, 1984. 233–49.

Beauchamp, Tom L. "The Right to Privacy and the Right to Die." *Social Philosophy and Policy* 17 (2000): 276–92.

Becker, Lawrence C. *Property Rights: Philosophic Foundations.* London: Routledge and Kegan Paul, 1977.

——. "Deserving to Own Intellectual Property." *Chicago-Kent Law Review* 68 (1993): 609–29.

Benko, Robert P. *Protecting Intellectual Property Rights.* Washington, D.C.: American Enterprise Institute for Public Policy Research, 1987.

Boonin, Leonard G. "The University, Scientific Research, and the Ownership of Knowledge." In *Owning Scientific and Technical Information*, edited by V. Weil and J. Snapper. New Brunswick and London: Rutgers University Press, 1989.

Bovard, James. *Terrorism and Tyranny: Trampling Freedom, Justice, and Peace to Rid the War of Evil.* New York: Palgrave Macmillan, 2003.

Boyle, James. *Shamans, Software, and Spleens.* Cambridge MA: Harvard University Press, 1996.

Branscomb, Anne W. *Who Owns Information.* New York: Basic Books, 1994.

Brin, David. *The Transparent Society: Will Technology Force Us to Choose Between Privacy and Freedom?* Reading, MA: Perseus Publishing, 1999.

Bugbee, Bruce. *Genesis of American Patent and Copyright Law.* Washington, D.C.: Public Affairs Press, 1967.

Cate, Fred H. *Privacy in the Information Age.* Washington, D.C.:
Brookings Institution Press., 1997.

Child, James W. "The Moral Foundations of Intangible Property." In
Intellectual Property: Moral, Legal, and International Dilemmas,
edited by A. Moore. Lanham, MD: Rowman and Littlefield,
1997.

Davis, Michael. "Patents, Natural Rights, and Property." *Owning
Scientific and Technical Information,* edited by V. Weil and J.
Snapper. New Brunswick and London: Rutgers University
Press, 1989.

DeCew, Judith Wagner. *In Pursuit of Privacy: Law, Ethics, and the Rise
of Technology.* Ithaca, NY: Cornell University Press, 1997.

— —. "In Pursuit of Privacy: Law, Ethics and the Rise of Technology." *Journal of Government Information* 25 (1998): 307–8.

— —. "Alternatives for Protecting Privacy while Respecting Patient
Care and Public Health Needs." *Ethics and Information Technology* 1 (1999): 249–55.

— —. "The Priority of Privacy for Medical Information." *Social
Philosophy and Policy* 17 (2000): 213–34.

Denning, Dorothy. "To Tap or Not to Tap." *Communications of the
ACM* (March 1993). Reprinted in M. Erman, M. Williams, and
M. Shauf, *Computers, Ethics, and Society* (New York: Oxford Uni-
versity Press, 1997), 247–63.

Diffie, Whitfield, and S. Landau. *Privacy on the Line: The Politics of
Wiretapping and Encryption.* Cambridge, MA: MIT Press, 1998.

Etzioni, Amitai. *The Limits of Privacy.* New York: Basic Books, 1999.

Forester, Tom. and P. Morrison. *Computer Ethics: Cautionary Tales
and Ethical Dilemmas in Computing.* 2d Edition. Cambridge, MA:
MIT Press, 1990.

Frey, R. G. "Privacy, Control, and Talk of Rights." *Social Philosophy
and Policy* 17 (2000): 45–67.

Friedman, David. "A World of Strong Privacy: Promises and Perils
of Encryption." *Social Philosophy and Policy* 13 (1996): 212–28.

— —. "Privacy and Technology." *Social Philosophy and Policy* 17
(2000): 186–212.

Garfinkel, S. "Database Nation: The Death of Privacy in the Twenty-
first Century." *Telecommunications Policy* 24 (2000): 625–28.

Gordon, Wendy J. "Property Right in Self Expression: Equality and
Individualism in the Natural Law of Intellectual Property." *Yale
Law Journal* 102 (1993): 1533–1609.

— —. "Assertive Modesty: An Economics of Intangibles." *Columbia Law Review* 94 (1994): 2579–93.

Greenawalt, Kent. "Privacy and Its Legal Protections." *Hastings Center Studies* 2 (1974): 45–68.

Hardin, Russell. "Valuing Intellectual Property." *Chicago-Kent Law Review* 68 (1993): 659–74.

Hauptman, Robert, ed. "Ethics and the dissemination of information." *Library Trends* 40 (1991): 199–372.

Horowitz, Irving Louis. *Communicating Ideas*. New York: Oxford University Press, 1986.

— —. "Networking America: The Cultural Context of Privacy v. Publicity." *Knowledge, Technology, and Policy* 12 (2000): 85–90.

— —. "National Consequences of International Terrorism." *Society* 39.2 (2002): 6–10.

Inness, Julie C. *Privacy, Intimacy, and Isolation*. New York: Oxford University Press, 1992.

Johnson, Deborah, and J. Snapper. *Ethical Issues in the Use of Computers*. Belmont, CA: Wadsworth Press, 1985.

Johnson, Deborah, J. Snapper, and Helen Nissenbaum. *Computers, Ethics, and Social Values*. Englewood Cliffs, NJ: Prentice Hall, 1995.

Johnson, Jeffery L. "A Theory of the Nature and Value of Privacy." *Public Affairs Quarterly* 6 (1992): 271–88.

— —. "Constitutional Privacy." *Law and Philosophy* 13 (1994): 161–93.

Kuflik, Arthur. "The Moral Foundations of Intellectual Property Rights." In *Owning Scientific and Technical Information*, edited by V. Weil and J. Snapper. New Brunswick and London: Rutgers University Press, 1989.

Lessig, Lawrence. *The Future of Ideas: The Fate of the Commons in a Connected World*. New York: Random House, 2002.

— —. *Free Culture: How Big Media Uses Technology and the Law to Lock Down Culture and Control Creativity*. New York: Penguin Books, 2004.

Levy, Steven. *Hackers: Heroes of the Computer Revolution*. New York: Dell Publishing Co., 1984.

Machlup, F. *Production and Distribution of Knowledge in the United States*. Princeton: Princeton University Press, 1962.

Machlup, F., and Penrose. "The Patent Controversy in the Nineteenth Century." *Journal of Economic History* 10 (1950): 1–29.

Mangan, Mark and J. Wallace. *Sex, Laws, and CyberSpace: Freedom and Censorship on the Frontiers of the Online Revolution*. New York: Holt and Company, 1997.

McMullin, E. "Openness and Secrecy in Science: Some Notes on Early History." *Science, Technology, and Human Values* 10 (1985): 14–23.

Meiners, Roger, and Robert Staaf. "Patents, Copyrights, and Trademarks: Property or Monopoly." *Harvard Journal of Law and Public Policy* 13 (Summer 1990): 911–48.

Moore, Adam D. "Owning Genetic Information and Gene Enhancement Techniques: Why Privacy and Property May Undermine Social Control of the Human Genome." *Bioethics* 14 (Spring 2000).

— —. "Privacy and the Encryption Debate." *Knowledge, Technology, and Policy* 12 (Winter 2000).

— —. "Intellectual Property, Innovation, and Social Progress: The Case Against Incentives Based Arguments." *The Hamline Law Review* 26 (2003).

— —. "Intellectual Property: Theory, Privilege, and Pragmatism." *The Canadian Journal of Law and Jurisprudence* 16 (July 2003).

— —. "Privacy: Its Meaning and Value." *American Philosophical Quarterly* 40 (July 2003).

Moore, Adam D., ed. *Intellectual Property: Moral, Legal, and International Dilemmas*. Lanham, MD: Rowman & Littlefield, 1997.

— —. *Intellectual Property and Information Control: Philosophic Foundations and Contemporary Issues*. New Brunswick, NJ: Transaction Publishing, 2001, 2004.

Nelkin, Dorothy. *Science as Intellectual Property*. New York: Macmillan, 1984.

— —. "Ironies in the Public Response to Information Technology." *National Forum* 74 (1994): 7–10.

Nelkin, Dorothy, and L. Andrews. "DNA Identification and Surveillance Creep." *Sociology of Health and Illness* 21 (1999): 689–706.

Nimmer, M. "Does Copyright Abridge the First Amendment Guarantees of Free Speech and Press?" *UCLA Law Review* 17 (1970).

Nissenbaum, Helen. "Protecting Privacy in an Information Age: The Problem of Privacy in Public." *Law and Philosophy*, 17 (1998): 559–96.

— —. "Toward an Approach to Privacy in Public: Challenges of Information Technology." *Ethics and Behavior* 7 (1997): 207–19.

Parent, W. A. "Privacy, Morality, and the Law." *Philosophy and Public Affairs* 12 (1983): 269–88.

Paul, Ellen Frankel, F. Miller Jr., and J. Paul, eds. *The Right to Privacy*. Cambridge: Cambridge University Press, 2000.

Pennock, J. R., and J. W. Chapman, eds. *Privacy*. Nomos XIII. New York: Atherton Press, 1971.

Plant, A. *The Economic Theory Concerning Patents for Inventions*. 1934.

Pool, Ithiel de Sola. *Technologies of Freedom*. Cambridge, MA: Harvard University Press, 1983.

Posner, Richard A. *Economic Analysis of Law*. Boston: Little, Brown and Co., 1972.

— —. "The Right of Privacy." *Georgia Law Review* 12 (Spring 1978): 393–422.

— —. "Privacy, Secrecy, and Reputation." *Buffalo Law Review* 28 (Winter 1979): 1–56.

Posner, Richard A., and Landes. "An Economic Analysis of Copyright Law." *Journal of Legal Studies* 17 (June 1989).

Rachels, James. "Why Privacy Is Important." *Philosophy and Public Affairs* 4 (Summer 1975): 323–33.

Reiman, Jeffrey H. "Privacy, Intimacy, and Personhood." *Philosophy and Public Affairs* 6 (Fall 1976): 26–44

Rosen, J. *The Unwanted Gaze: The Destruction of Privacy in America*. Random House, 2000.

Samuelson, P. "Creating a New Kind of Intellectual Property: Applying the Lessons of the Chip Law to Computer Programs." *Minnesota Law Review* 70 (1985): 471–531.

— —. "Why the Look and Feel of Software User Interfaces Should Not Be Protected by Copyright Law." *Communications of the ACM* 32 (1989): 563–72.

Sanford, Bruce W. *Libel and Privacy*. Englewood Cliffs, N.J., 1996.

Schoeman, Ferdinand D, ed. *Philosophical Dimensions of Privacy: An Anthology*. Cambridge: Cambridge University Press, 1984.

— —. *Privacy and Social Freedom*. Cambridge: Cambridge University Press, 1992.

Spinello, Richard A. *Ethical Aspects of Information Technology*. Englewood Cliffs, NJ: Prentice Hall, 1995.

— —. *Case Studies in Information and Computer Ethics*. Englewood Cliffs, NJ: Prentice Hall, 1997.

Spinello, Richard A., and H. Travani. *Intellectual Property Rights in a Networked World: Theory and Practice.* Hershey, PA: Information Science Pub., 2004.

Spooner, Lysander. *The Law of Intellectual Property.* Weston, MA: M & S Press, 1971 (originally published in 1855).

Sykes, Charles. *The End of Privacy: The Attack on Personal Rights at Home, at Work, On-Line, and in Court.* New York: St. Martin's Press, 2000.

Tavani, Herman. "Informational Privacy, Data Mining, and the Internet." *Ethics and Information Technology* 1 (1999): 137–45.

— —. "Data Mining, and the Challenge for Normative Privacy." *Ethics and Information Technology* 1 (1999): 265–73.

— —. "Privacy Enhancing Technologies As a Panacea for Online Privacy Concerns: Some Ethical Considerations." *Journal of Information Ethics* 9 (Fall 2000):26–36.

Tavani, Herman, and F. S. Grodzinsky. "Cyberstalking, Personal Privacy, and Moral Responsibility." *Ethics and Information Technology* 4 (2002): 123–32.

Thomson, Judith Jarvis. "The Right to Privacy." *Philosophy and Public Affairs* 4 (Summer 1975): 295–314.

Waldron, Jeremy. "From Authors to Copiers: Individual Rights and Social Values in Intellectual Property." *Chicago-Kent Law Review* 68 (1993): 841–87.

Westin, Alan F. *Privacy and Freedom.* New York: Atheneum, 1967.

Winter, Sidney G. "Patents in Complex Contexts: Incentives and Effetiveness." In *Owning Scientific and Technical Information,* edited by V. Weil and J. Snapper. New Brunswick and London: Rutgers University Press, 1989.

Index

About the Editor

Adam D. Moore (Ph.D., The Ohio State University) is an assistant professor in the Philosophy Department and Information School at the University of Washington. He specializes in philosophy of law, applied ethics, information policy, and political philosophy. Professor Moore is the author of *Intellectual Property and Information Control* (Transaction Pub., 2001, 2004) and editor of *Intellectual Property: Moral, Legal, and International Dilemmas* (Rowman & Littlefield, 1997). His articles have appeared in many journals, including *American Philosophical Quarterly, Bioethics, The Journal of Value Inquiry, Business Ethics Quarterly, The Hamline Law Review, The Canadian Journal of Law and Jurisprudence*, and *Knowledge, Technology, and Policy*.